Charles Swanlund: for C.A.S. Jr., G.S., K.L.S., and K.L.S. with love and gratitude

Kirk Bane: for M.B., J.B., and P.W.B. with affection and appreciation

"It is admitted by all, that cultivated mind is the guardian genius of Democracy, and while guided and controlled by virtue, the noblest attribute of man. It is the only dictator that freemen acknowledge, and the only security which freemen desire."

President Mirabeau B. Lamar, First Message to Congress, December 21, 1838

Contents

INTRODUCTION AND ACKNOWLEDGMENTS

A Lone Star Reader had its genesis in the late spring of 2009 at a popular downtown Bryan Tex-Mex café. One afternoon, over plates of savory enchiladas, we began to discuss our favorite Texas history scholars, which articles we admired, what books we valued. And then we hit upon an idea: Why not assemble, for students and general readers alike, a state history anthology?

A Lone Star Reader is the result. In its pages, readers will find the work of leading academics and lay historians. They will encounter a wide variety of writing styles and a broad range of views. But every selection, we believe, is approachable, engaging, informative, and representative of the best in Texas scholarship. We hope our readers agree.

We wish to thank, first and foremost, our families, whose love and support made this endeavor possible. *A Lone Star Reader* is dedicated to them. We are also grateful to the following individuals for their assistance on this project: Stephanie Ramirez and Amanda Smith at Kendall/Hunt; Blanche Brick, Brandon Franke, Eric Miller, and other Social Science colleagues at Blinn College-Bryan; Tai Kreidler, Executive Director of the West Texas Historical Association; Bill O'Neal at Panola College; Donna Anstey at Yale University Press; Peggy Gough at the University of Texas Press; Linda Salitros at Texas A&M University Press; Joanna Conrad and Judith Keeling at Texas Tech University Press; D. Clayton Brown at Texas Christian University; and Suzanne Campbell at Angelo State University. A special tip of the (ten-gallon) hat goes to Ty Cashion at Sam Houston State University and Steve Hardin at McMurry University for opening doors, providing counsel, and offering encouragement, and to Gary Cartwright and Scott Sosebee, Executive Director of the East Texas Historical Association, for their extreme generosity. Finally, we offer gratitude to a special company of professors, mentors, and confidants who helped shepherd us down the long, and sometimes winding, academic road: Robert Money and James Moody at Lake Superior State University; Robert Shadle and Nick Pappas at Sam Houston State University; Ben Procter (writing teacher par excellence), Kenneth Stevens, James T. Chambers, Frank Reuter, and the late Donald Worcester at Texas Christian University; Jon P. Alston, Victor Treat, and the late John Canup at Texas A&M University; Paul H. Carlson at Texas Tech University; Jeff Mitchell at Arkansas Tech University; Ray Wheeler at the University of Cincinnati; and Tom Britten at the University of Texas-Brownsville.

About the Editors

Charles Swanlund holds a B.S. from Lake Superior State University and an M.A. from Sam Houston State University. He teaches Texas history at Blinn College in Bryan.

Kirk Bane holds a B.A. and M.A. from Texas A&M University and a Ph.D. from Texas Christian University. He teaches Texas history at Blinn College in Bryan.

Enslaved

ANDRÉS RESÉNDEZ

ANDRÉS RESÉNDEZ IS PROFESSOR OF HISTORY AT THE UNIVERSITY OF CALIFORNIA—DAVIS. HE IS THE AUTHOR OF *CHANGING NATIONAL IDENTITIES AT THE FRONTIER: TEXAS AND NEW MEXICO, 1800–1850*, *A TEXAS PATRIOT ON TRIAL IN MEXICO: JOSE ANTONIO NAVARRO AND THE TEXAN SANTA FE EXPEDITION*, AND *A LAND SO STRANGE: THE EPIC JOURNEY OF CABEZA DE VACA*.

ALVAR NUNEZ CABEZA DE VACA BEGAN HIS INCREDIBLE ODYSSEY IN TEXAS WHEN HE WASHED ASHORE NEAR GALVESTON IN NOVEMBER 1528. IN THIS SELECTION, DR. RESENDEZ RECOUNTS THE TRIALS OF CABEZA DE VACA AND HIS THREE COMPANIONS—FELLOW SPANIARDS ALONSO DEL CASTILLO AND ANDRES DORANTES AND ESTEBANICO, AN AFRICAN—DURING THEIR TIME AS SLAVES OF THE COASTAL INDIANS.

★ ★

After being hurled onto the beach, Cabeza de Vaca and his emaciated crew spent some time regaining their strength. They built fires and roasted some of their remaining corn. A man named Lope de Oviedo, who was evidently healthier and stronger than the others, climbed up a tree to survey the land. "He discovered that we were on an island," Cabeza de Vaca writes, "and he saw that the land was rutted in the way that it usually is where cattle roam, and it seemed to him for this reason that it must be land inhabited by Christians, and thus he reported it to us." The news must have been electrifying.

The men had reached an elongated island which was only 1.5 miles wide but 15 miles long. It must have been either Galveston Island or, more likely, the island immediately to the south.

Cabeza de Vaca ordered Lope de Oviedo to explore further without straying too far. He found a trail and followed it for a little over 1 mile to a small Indian village. As the huts were abandoned, the Spaniard took a pot and filled it with mullet and started to make his way back to the beach. A small dog followed him. Once on the trail, he also noticed three Indians with bows and arrows behind him. They called out to him. The castaway managed to rejoin his group before being overtaken, and the three natives prudently stopped at a distance. But within half an hour, 100 Indian men, all fully armed, had surrounded the Spaniards. Cabeza de Vaca makes only one dry but telling observation: "Whether or not they were of great stature, our fear made them seem like giants."

Resistance was completely out of the question. Of the forty men in Cabeza de Vaca's contingent, not six would have been able to stand. The famished outsiders would either die on the spot or reach a compromise with the native islanders. The two Spanish leaders, Cabeza de Vaca and the Royal Inspector Alonso de Solis, decided to approach the indigenous fighters and call out to them. The Indians came forward. The two royal officials gave out bells and beads, and the Indians gave the two strangers arrows in return, which is a sign of friendship. And through gestures the Indians made the castaways understand that they would be back the next morning with food. The Spaniards must have spent a night filled with foreboding. The idea of making preparations to resist an attack must have crossed their minds.

The next day at sunrise, the Indians returned. As promised, they brought with them fish and some curious roots unknown to the foreigners—quite likely cattail roots—that were about the size of chestnuts and that the Indians dug out from under water with great difficulty. In the afternoon the natives brought some more food. They had grown so confident that this time they came accompanied by women and children. The stranded men, so strikingly different, must have been for the Indians fascinating to observe. The natives kept visiting the castaways' camp for some days, always delivering fish and roots.

As the Spaniards regained some strength, they thought about resuming their journey to Pánuco. They dug the raft out of the sand and dragged it to the edge of the water. The weakened but resourceful men must have gathered some water and probably saved some of the roots that they had been given. When everything seemed ready, the men removed their clothes so as to keep them dry, and then waded into the cold water to push the raft off from the shore. After they leapt aboard and had traveled some distance, a huge wave hit them, and, as Cabeza de Vaca explains, "Since we went naked and the cold was very great, we dropped the oars from our hands." The raft drifted just a little longer before another large wave overturned it. The Royal Inspector Alonso de Solís and two other men clung to the barge so tenaciously that they became trapped underwater and drowned. All of the other men were plunged into the cold and tempestuous ocean; they were half-drowned and shivering when they made it back to the beach.

The Spaniards lost all their remaining possessions in that failed attempt to leave the island. They had been shedding baggage throughout Florida and the Gulf Coast, and now the process was complete. The castaways now faced the New World quite literally naked. "It was November," writes Cabeza de Vaca, "and the cold was very great; and we were so thin that with little difficulty our bones could be counted, and we appeared like the very image of death."

At the time of the Florida expedition, North America was colder than it is today. From the 1300s thru the 1800s, the world experienced a prolonged period of cooling, and the evidence suggests that the years from 1527 to 1529 were especially harsh. Cabeza de Vaca had complained about the cold in the middle of the Florida summer; the winter must have been daunting indeed.

Already hypothermic from their spell in the water, the men returned to their camp, where mercifully they found some last embers to rekindle a fire. They spent the next few hours huddled and commiserating: "And thus we were beseeching our Lord for mercy and the pardon of our sins, shedding many tears, each one having pity not only for himself but for all the others whom they saw in the same state." As their situation became more desperate, the stranded men sought strength and consolation in their religious beliefs.

When the Indians returned at sunset to bring food as usual, they were shocked to see the Christians so changed. They withdrew immediately, and Cabeza de Vaca had to run after them to try to explain what had happened. Gradually, the natives came to understand the disaster that had befallen their guests. They also saw the bodies of two of the drowned Europeans. At last, they sat down among the castaways. "And with the great grief and pity they felt on seeing us in such a state," Cabeza de Vaca writes, "they all began to weep loudly and so sincerely that they could be heard a great distance away." The weeping lasted for more than half an hour. "And truly," the Royal Treasurer marvels, "to see that these men, so lacking in reason and so crude in the manner of brutes, grieved so much for us, increased in me and in others of our company even more the magnitude of our suffering and the estimation of our misfortune."

Once the weeping ended, Cabeza de Vaca resolutely asked the islanders to take them to their homes. There was no alternative that he could see, as the stranded men would otherwise die of exposure and hunger. And the Indians seemed willing to oblige. But even in these desperate circumstances, there were some expeditioners who opposed the plan, especially those who had been to Mexico and had seen or heard about Aztec practices of human sacrifice and ritual cannibalism. "We should not even speak of it"—they had objected—"because if they took us to their houses, they would sacrifice us to their idols."

The Indians went away to make some preparations. They returned that night, having kindled four or five great bonfires between the coast and their hamlet. They feared that without such a precaution some of the foreigners might fall unconscious and die from exposure during the short journey from the beach to the village. When everything was ready, the Indians started carrying the castaways, taking them to the first fire, "and when they saw that we had regained some strength and warmth, they carried us to the next one, so rapidly that they almost did not let our feet touch the ground." Not all the Spaniards consented to go with the islanders. At least five men chose to stay by the beach on their own, a decision they would soon come to regret.

When Cabeza de Vaca and his companions arrived at the village, they saw that the Indians had prepared a large house with many fires inside. The dancing began barely an hour after the outsiders had arrived, and the celebration lasted all night long. "For us there was neither rejoicing nor sleep"—Cabeza de Vaca recalled—"as we were awaiting the moment when they would sacrifice us." But the men survived through the night, and the next morning the Indians gave them more food and continued to treat them kindly, allaying their fears.

The Indians' generosity was astonishing. They had taken food to the Europeans twice a day for some time and had gone to great lengths to transport them to their camp and give them shelter. Potentially they would have to sustain this helpless crew through the winter. For a small community of not more than a few dozen families, feeding forty additional adults would constitute a significant drain on their food supplies.

That same day Cabeza de Vaca spotted a native man carrying some European objects that had not come from his raft. The Royal Treasurer anxiously asked the native where he had procured the items. Amazingly, he responded to Cabeza de Vaca through signs that he had received these objects from other men like himself, and that this second group was farther away but also on the island.

This revelation must have caused great commotion among the stranded men. Cabeza de Vaca immediately sent two of his men to look for these other Europeans, but the scouting party did not have to travel far. The other group of castaways was already on its way to the village, having been alerted about Cabeza de Vaca's crew by other Indians who lived on that side of the island. They turned out to be the contingent under the command of Captains Andrés Dorantes and Alonso del Castillo, which must have also included Estebanico. "Upon encountering us," Cabeza de Vaca recalls, "they received a great fright to see us in the condition we were in."

The reunion must have seemed to all like a miracle. They had last seen each other at the crossing of the Mississippi River and had faced so many dangers in the intervening weeks that each group must have assumed that the other had perished.

Tantalizingly, the members of the Dorantes-Castillo party were still in possession of their raft. At least some of the men would have a chance of going forward to Pánuco. The eighty men set to work immediately. They decided that the strongest among them would continue; the rest would remain on the island to recover and perhaps would attempt to reach Spanish-controlled territory by land in the spring.

But the raft was unable to support the castaways' hopes. When they launched it a few days after their reunion, it immediately broke apart and sank to the bottom. The men were now without crafts or provisions. Moreover, winter was looming and many of the men were naked, so swimming across rivers and bays was impossible. Pánuco would have to wait until the spring.

But even without the raft, the castaways decided to send an advance party to the south. Four men would make a last-ditch effort to reach Pánuco over the winter. They must have been given clothing and provisions. Perhaps a small raft was built for them. These four men were among the strongest survivors and were all good swimmers. Unfortunately, even they were unable to reach Christian lands; all four died in the attempt.

After this disaster, the remaining Spaniards, emaciated and destitute as they were, must have come to count themselves as fortunate. At least they had washed up among friendly Indians.

The survivors of the Pánfilo de Narváez expedition were the first outsiders to have lived in the immense territories north of Mexico and to come in contact with many peoples across North America. It was an experience that neither the Spaniards nor their Amerindian hosts would forget.

At contact, both groups appeared strikingly different. The contrasts were so patent that many Europeans openly discussed whether the natives were human at all and vice versa. Two large contingents of the human species had reestablished contact after a very long time. The peoples of the New World were descended from a small group of men and women who had crossed the Bering Strait some 12,000 years ago and migrated to America, the last great land mass of the world that had remained unpopulated. Shortly after this migration episode, both worlds lost touch once again.

Over the millennia, these true pioneers of the New World explored the entire continent and multiplied until reaching some 60 or 70 million by the fifteenth century (comparable to Europe's population at the time). They built monumental ceremonial centers, established impressive trading networks, and waged war on one another. It was a world unto itself, unconnected to and unconcerned with the rest of the planet. Recent DNA evidence confirms that all Native American lineages can ultimately be traced back to Asia, but that for thousands of years they evolved completely independently from all other humans. It was not until 1492, when Columbus reached the Caribbean, that these two huge fragments of the human family were finally reunited.

Despite their long separation, the Old and the New World had undergone remarkably parallel developments. The peoples of both worlds had domesticated plants and animals; organized themselves in chiefdoms, principalities, monarchies, and empires; and developed forms of writing and mathematics. Most early European explorers were initially drawn to the stark differences between themselves and the natives they encountered. Cabeza de Vaca and his men, unlike other explorers, had the luxury of direct and patient observation. Moreover, their lives depended on the commonalities.

The island where the two rafts had landed harbored two small indigenous groups: the Capoques and the Hans. The sheer appearance of these two groups was daunting. They were tall, not infrequently reaching 6 feet, easily towering over the Spaniards. The natives went about completely naked, and their physique was robust and flexible. They were fond of piercing one nipple, sometimes both, and inserting through the holes large reeds that could be as thick as two fingers and two and a half palms in length. They also pierced their lower lip, inserting yet another reed, although this one *only* half a finger in thickness. Only the women covered part of their bodies, making garments out of a tree fiber, while the maidens wore deerskins.

Cabeza de Vaca and his crew lived with one of the two bands, though he fails to mention which one. The Dorantes-Castillo contingent resided with the other. It appears that the two groups of survivors were allowed to visit each other freely at first, for relations between

Capoques and Hans were cordial. Even though they spoke mutually unintelligible languages, the two bands had no qualms about sharing their commodious island. Each group must have numbered perhaps 400 or 500 individuals.

Nothing could have prepared the castaways for the lifestyle they would have to adopt to survive. The Capoques and Hans were fully nomadic peoples. They led a roving life, seldom spending more than a few weeks in any given site. They had but few possessions and lived in simple, semicircular tents that were easily constructed and that provided only minimal protection from the elements. Their simple dwellings, however, belied their extraordinarily sophisticated use of their environment. Their knowledge of the coastal flora and fauna was simply unmatched. They were expert foragers. The Capoques and Hans moved in seasonal, deliberate patterns meant to take advantage of specific food items in a range that was not confined to their island but also extended into the flat, low-lying coastal prairie on the mainland. Their hunting skills were formidable as well. In Cabeza de Vaca's estimation, their hearing and eyesight were so sharp and attuned to even the slightest movement so as to rank among the best in the world.

When the two rafts made landfall in November, the Capoques and Hans must have just arrived at the island to spend the winter there. They typically subsisted on fish and roots, which were plentiful at first, but the natives knew well that things would deteriorate steadily, reaching a low point in February when the starchy tubers begin to sprout and are no longer edible.

The winter of 1528–1529 was extraordinarily harsh. The cold and a series of great storms prevented the Indians from wading into the water to dig up the roots. Fishing became extremely difficult and generally yielded nothing. The houses may have been portable, but they afforded little protection against the inclement weather. Many castaways were unable to survive. "In a short time, of us eighty men who arrived there from both ends [of the island], only fifteen remained alive." With these few words, Cabeza de Vaca glosses over what must have been two months of unabated horror. Men must have been dying almost daily.

The miserable winter conditions may have seemed apocalyptic to the last survivors, but the natives understood this hungry spell as part of an annual cycle. As winter eased into spring, and the roots began to sprout and were no longer edible, the Capoques and Hans began making preparations to go to the mainland in search of the one food item that was available all year round: oysters. Ordinarily they subsisted on these mollusks for three or four months of the year and, as some of the survivors pointedly observed, "in fact eat nothing else." Around April the Indians also combed the shore, "eating blackberries the entire month, during which time they do not cease to perform their *areitos* [feasts] and celebrations." In the summer it was time to hunt deer and bison, though without overlooking other food sources, including spiders, lizards, snakes, and rats. In the fall the Capoques and the Hans went back to their island to catch fish and harvest the aquatic roots, recommencing the yearly cycle.

Living on the coast of Texas was not easy. The survivors of two rafts of the Narváez expedition had tried to spend the winter on their own and wound up cannibalizing each other. Yet for centuries, these coastal natives had survived and even thrived in the same environment. Even though other indigenous groups both to the south and to the north cultivated corn, the Capoques and Hans and their descendants relied solely on the bounty of the land.

What had begun as a guest-host relationship between the natives and the Spaniards eventually degenerated into a relationship between masters and slaves. The transition was gradual but unmistakable. No doubt, the castaways did not take long to outlive their initial welcome. The Capoques and Hans had been extraordinarily generous to the marooned explorers, but with the onset of winter, the strangers must have been expected to pull their own weight. The Indians were surely shocked at how useless the foreigners were. The castaways must have been laughably incapable of hunting with bows and arrows, and their fishing skills could not have been much better, as their knowledge of local traps, weirs, and edible fish was minimal. Since the strangers could not be entrusted with manly occupations, they were given women's work. They had to dig for roots, carry firewood, and fetch water.

One incident in particular strained their relationship. Not all of the Spaniards had taken up residence with the Indians. Five raftsmen had chosen to spend the winter by the beach; their fear of being sacrificed and eaten by the natives must have been overpowering. It had been a grave mistake. And the very thing that they dreaded the most—cannibalism—came to pass, albeit not in the way that they had expected it. Finding themselves without any food and in great necessity, they ate one another. And as Cabeza de Vaca notes with disarming logic, "Only one remained because he was alone and had no one to eat him."

When the Indians learned what had happened, they became very upset. "The scandal among them was such that they would have killed the men had they seen them at the start; and all of us would have been in grave danger." Ironically, in later centuries Europeans accused the native peoples of coastal Texas of cannibalism. Little did they know that in the sixteenth century the Europeans themselves had been the cannibals, and the Indians the ones appalled by such behavior.

The castaways' situation became even more precarious when the native islanders began dying from an "illness of the bowels," perhaps dysentery spread by the decomposing bodies of the Europeans. About *half* of all the Indians on the island died. It was an astonishing calamity and a terrible foreboding of the demographic disaster that would soon engulf the entire continent due to the introduction of new pathogens to the New World. Perhaps with good reason, the strangers were held responsible. "And taking this to be very true," Cabeza de Vaca writes, "the Indians agreed among themselves to kill those of us who remained."

As the natives prepared to carry out their intentions, the Indian man who had come to own Cabeza de Vaca intervened. He forcefully defended the castaways by reasoning that if they had the power to cause illness among the natives, then they surely would have prevented the deaths of so many of their own kind. This Indian man, who must have been sufficiently influential to hold slaves and go against general opinion, noted that none of the foreigners did any harm or ill and concluded that the best thing to do was to let them be. Somehow his point of view carried the day, and the lives of the strangers were spared.

The men would remain on the island as slaves to the natives. Life became so harsh for the survivors that they took the habit of calling the island *Malhado*, the "Isle of Ill fate." For the next six years or so the castaways' lives revolved around unceasing work. Their chores were deceptively trivial: carrying wood, digging for roots, or fetching water. There was nothing insidious or cruel about these activities, but they were constant as well as physically challenging and often painful. The heavy stumps chafed directly against their bare backs, and the bearers' feet were hurt from walking over summer-hot sand and amidst fierce spiny plants. Cabeza de Vaca's fingers bled constantly from digging roots; and he was forced to venture completely naked through thickets of cattails and other plants.

By this time, the survivors were entirely at the mercy of their masters. The native children mocked the Christians almost daily. According to Cabeza de Vaca, "Any child would give them a good hair pulling, and for them this was great fun, the greatest pleasure in the world." That was merely juvenile humor; the adults did not hesitate to use violence to obtain compliance. The captives reported being beaten with sticks, slapped in the face, and having their thick beards jerked out. A minor omission, delay, or infraction could bring about severe punishment, even death. Cabeza de Vaca recounts how three Christians were killed "only for daring to go from one house to another . . . and another three who remained alive expected to meet the same end." The castaways' daily anxiety over being punished or killed must have taken a dramatic toll. None of them could depend on staying alive from one day to the next. One Spaniard who had committed no infraction at all was killed simply because one Indian woman had a dream "of I don't know what nonsense," the castaways recall, "because in those parts they believe in dreams and kill their own children because of dreams."

Undoubtedly, the castaways had become slaves. Yet it is also important to note that societies like the Capoques and Hans were not "slaving societies," in the sense that they did not actively procure and exploit slave labor. They certainly possessed slaves, which were a byproduct of their continuous warfare with neighboring groups or came about when wandering strangers like the castaways "joined" these bands to escape starvation. However, this system was a far cry from that employed by more centralized and hierarchical societies like Portugal and Spain, for instance, or other indigenous societies in the American continent. For the coastal peoples of Texas, slaves were decidedly marginal to their survival and well-being. For one thing, a slave may have represented one more pair of arms but also an additional mouth to feed. Rather than systematically procuring and exploiting slaves, they were tolerated like stray dogs and permitted to stay as long as they made themselves useful. Indeed, as the castaways would discover, some of the natives of Texas flatly refused to take them, even as slaves. But once the castaways had gained admittance, their lives depended entirely on the will of their masters. This peculiar context did not lessen the sufferings of Cabeza de Vaca and his companions. But it helps us understand why the castaways were enslaved only gradually, why they had to seek out unwilling masters who often abused them, and why during their six-year stay along the Texas coast they were able to flee from one indigenous clan to another.

The once-mighty conquistadors had endured a precipitous fall. Life as an abused slave must have been indescribably bitter for the likes of Cabeza de Vaca and Captains Dorantes and Castillo. Castillo could have enjoyed the life of a judge or a municipal officer, had he only chosen to stay in Europe. What foolish impulse had compelled him to join the Narváez expedition and forsake a lifetime of comfort and happiness? Captain Dorantes may have been more of a man of action, perhaps more accepting of reversals of fortune and violence. After all, he already bore a scar on his face from military action. But surely he never imagined spending his last days on earth enslaved by a bizarre, naked people halfway around the world.

And what to say of the Royal Treasurer? Generations of Cabeza de Vacas had worked to further the imperial aims of Spain. His grandfather had been the famous captain who had conquered Gran Canaria. With the history of his ancestors in mind, Álvar Núñez Cabeza de Vaca must have also dreamed of great acts of conquest and bravery when the Florida expedition got underway. Yet his ambitions had been shattered in the whirlwind of a hurricane, a colossal navigational mistake, a difficult march through Florida, a harrowing raft passage, and a sordid enslavement. Surely this nobleman suffered greatly as he tried to reconcile himself to spending the balance of his life digging for roots until his fingers bled and stoically withstanding beatings at the hands of natives who would never understand what he was meant to be.

The man best able to cope psychologically with the adverse conditions was in all likelihood the African Estebanico. He was no stranger to the life of bondage, as he had already once been captured, taken away from his homeland, and sold in Europe. His sufferings certainly increased in the New World as the expedition foundered, but his social standing had changed but little. He had been Dorantes's slave; but now his master had himself become enslaved, an odd twist of fate that probably gave Estebanico a certain unspeakable satisfaction. Although it is possible that his subordination to Dorantes and the other Spaniards persisted in some fashion, the fact that the white Europeans were also enslaved must have reduced the disparities. Indians, not Spaniards, exercised the ultimate authority now, a fact that must have complicated immensely Dorantes's ability to enforce his authority over the African. With the passing of time, Estebanico became just another slave largely undistinguishable from his former masters.

Estebanico's sheer survival is miraculous. All the other castaways were elite Spaniards who were likely to outlast Africans, simply because they were better nourished and their bodies had been less exposed to the ravages of punishing physical labor. Moreover, Europeans in commanding positions were able to use their authority in ways that shielded them from danger and maximized their chances of survival. And yet, Estebanico managed to outlive dozens of Spaniards who could have reasonably expected to be among the last men standing. By all accounts, he was the ultimate survivor. He had experienced the life of bondage on three different continents and had been forced to face incredible perils and adventures. Against astonishing odds, he had survived through it all.

The last remaining castaways endured as slaves on the coast of Texas for six years. By the spring of 1529, after that first brutal winter, only eighteen or so castaways remained alive. They became dispersed among the Capoques and Hans as they followed their respective masters.

Cabeza de Vaca's experience was especially trying because all of the European and African castaways hosted by his particular band of Indians (we don't know which of the two) died over the winter. By the spring he was the only remaining castaway within this band. In the spring Cabeza the Vaca's masters took him to the mainland. The Royal Treasurer's sense of loneliness and abandonment was compounded by a severe and prolonged illness that came to afflict him at this time.

It was also a time of despair. During his lengthy convalescence, Cabeza de Vaca learned that the majority of the castaways, still living on the island of Malhado with the other band, had agreed to resume their quest to Pánuco. This sizable contingent of twelve men—which included Dorantes, Castillo, and Estebanico—crossed to the mainland, not far from where Cabeza de Vaca was struggling to regain his health, and started journeying south.

The Royal Treasurer knew about his companions' intentions through his indigenous masters. Dorantes and Castillo even tried to contact Cabeza de Vaca, but were unable to see him. In any case, he could not travel. His companions' departure must have been a crushing blow for the Royal Treasurer.

Cabeza de Vaca had little choice but to entrust himself to the mercy of God. His religious convictions constituted his last refuge. In the summer or fall of 1529, his captors took him back to Malhado. There the Royal Treasurer found out that not all the explorers had left for Pánuco, but that two very frail castaways had stayed behind at the island. Like Cabeza de Vaca, these two men had been unable to follow the Dorantes-Castillo contingent. There must have been a great deal of comfort in this news. These two men were Lope de Oviedo, the tree climber who had first explored Malhado, and another Spaniards by the name of Jerónimo de Alaniz.

Cabeza de Vaca remained with the same band of Indians for more than a year, traveling between Malhado and the mainland. But they treated the Royal Treasurer harshly and forced him to do a great deal of work. Cabeza de Vaca resolved to flee the island and join another band that lived in a forest on the mainland. These Indians were called the Charrucos. He must have come in contact with them during his travels with the native islanders.

Thus began a new phase in Cabeza de Vaca's life. The Charrucos were at war with other groups surrounding them. They needed a neutral broker able to trade even in the midst of hostilities, and an outsider like Cabeza de Vaca was the perfect conduit. With the encouragement of the Charrucos, the former Royal Treasurer became an itinerant merchant carving for himself an extraordinary role among the Indians of the region. We can only imagine Cabeza de Vaca's trepidation as he ventured into new lands wholly exposed and carrying valuable wares, but the Charrucos urged him to go from one place to another to procure the things that they needed. Thus, for two years the resourceful castaway plied the trade.

Cabeza de Vaca started his remarkable trading journeys by collecting among the Charrucos objects that were coveted by the peoples of the interior. Such coastal items included pieces of sea snail shells and the hearts of the animals themselves. He also took "sea beads"—a decidedly poetic if somewhat vague description that may refer to pearls—as well as a certain kind of shell that was used in the interior to cut a fruit that resembled a bean. (The natives used this fruit in their curing ceremonies and it was therefore greatly prized.) Armed with these goods, Cabeza de Vaca then ventured through the interior for weeks at a time, covering great distances of 120 miles or more. He must have been fed along the way and allowed to wander through the territories of various peoples, apparently without conflict.

In exchange for his coastal goods, Cabeza de Vaca received hides, which were always in great demand among the Charrucos. He also brought back red ocher, "with which they smear themselves and dye their faces and hair," as well as flints, glue, and hard canes to make arrows. "And this occupation served me well"—Cabeza de Vaca explains—"because practicing it, I had the freedom to go wherever I wanted, and I was not constrained in any way nor enslaved, and wherever I went they treated me well and gave me food out of want for my wares, and most importantly because doing that, I was able to seek out the ways by which I would go forward."

Only the two fellow castaways who had remained on Malhado prevented Cabeza de Vaca from attempting to set out toward Pánuco. Jerónimo de Alaniz died some time later. But Lope de Oviedo endured on the island. Thus every year Cabeza de Vaca made his way across the bay to visit Lope de Oviedo and talk him into escaping together. Cabeza de Vaca's visits to Malhado are remarkable, for it means that his former masters no longer sought retribution for his escape, but perhaps were now more interested in gaining access to the Royal Treasurer's wares.

Despite Cabeza de Vaca's efforts to convince him, Lope de Oviedo was reluctant to leave the island, and kept postponing the date of their escape. He preferred to cling to his life in Malhado, however precarious and tormented, rather than risk death in unknown lands and amongst even more violent and unpredictable peoples.

After three years, however, Cabeza de Vaca finally prevailed. In the spring or summer of 1532, the two survivors made their escape toward Pánuco. Lope de Oviedo did not know how to swim, so Cabeza de Vaca had to help him get across the bay to the mainland. They must have followed the same route that the Dorantes-Castillo party had taken years earlier, painstakingly moving through a region of four rivers until they fell in with a group of Indians known as the Quevenes. These Indians conveyed startling information to the two fugitives. The Quevenes first said that farther south there were three other Christians who were still alive. Cabeza de Vaca and Lope de Oviedo then asked about all the others, and the Quevenes responded that they had all died of cold and hunger. More ominously, the Quevenes said that the Christians were treated badly in that area and remarked that some neighboring Indians had even killed three Christians for their own amusement. By way of demonstration, the Quevenes proceeded to take Lope de Oviedo and hit him with a stick and slap him, "and I did not lack my share," Cabeza de Vaca writes, "and they threw mud balls at us, and each day placed arrows aimed at our hearts, saying that they wanted to kill us as they had killed our other companions."

Lope de Oviedo, hard to convince in the first place, became discouraged and decided to return to the island. The Royal Treasurer tried to reassure his companion, talking to him for a long time. But he could not prevent Lope de Oviedo from going back to Malhado. His fate is unknown.

The Royal Treasurer proceeded alone with the Quevenes; there would be no turning back for him. They took Cabeza de Vaca to a lush, twisting river where various groups had gathered to eat nuts. When Cabeza de Vaca approached a dwelling where the Indians had taken him, Andrés Dorantes came out. The captain was greatly astonished to see a fellow Spaniard whom he had given up for dead so long ago. "We gave many thanks to God upon finding ourselves reunited," Cabeza de Vaca recalls, "and this day was one of the days of greatest pleasure that we have had in our lives." It was the fall of 1532; the two Spaniards had not seen each other for three and a half years.

Cabeza de Vaca and Dorantes then went together to see Castillo and Estebanico, who were also encamped at what they called the "river of nuts." All four must have been able to spend some time talking and sharing their remarkable stories of endurance. Only then did Cabeza de Vaca learn of what had happened to these fellow castaways.

After that first disastrous winter of 1528–1529, Dorantes and Castillo had led most of the survivors out of the island of Malhado in the spring. The first step had been to persuade the people of Malhado to get them across to the mainland on canoes, as many of the castaways could not swim. Somehow these men were still in possession of some objects salvaged from their raft that they used as trade goods and gifts. To get to the mainland, the outsiders had to part with a valuable cloak of sable skins that they had pilfered during the raft voyage. The cloak was deemed to be "the finest to be found anywhere in the world," its scent was said to resemble that of "ambergris and musk, and it was so strong that it could be detected at a great distance." The natives must have been sufficiently impressed, for they consented to letting this group of survivors go and even agreed to transport them to the other shore.

Once on the mainland, the members of the Dorantes-Castillo party had occasion to demonstrate their dogged tenacity. For weeks they walked along the shore, heading south. The terrain could hardly be more difficult: in fact, no other portion of the coast between the Mississippi River and the Rio de las Palmas is more intricately crisscrossed by water than the section they were now trying to traverse south of present-day Galveston Bay. They had to negotiate no fewer than four large rivers and at least three straits or bays. In each instance they were forced either to build makeshift rafts, repair abandoned canoes, or beg for the assistance from local Indians.

The passage took a heavy toll. Some of the men drowned along the way, while others were killed by Indians. The party dwindled from twelve to ten to six and at last to only three: Dorantes, Castillo, and Estebanico. These three survivors were forced to "join" the local Indians to save themselves from starvation. They were enslaved and reduced to following their respective masters, thus becoming separated. Still they somehow were able to keep sporadic contact with one another, and even at times to work side by side.

The reunion of these three castaways with Cabeza de Vaca in the fall of 1532 was momentous. It was a time of renewed hope and enlarged possibilities. The four men broached the subject of escape. "I told [them]"—Cabeza de Vaca recalls—"that my purpose was to go to the land of Christians and that on this path and pursuit I was embarked." Dorantes responded that he too had been urging his two companions to flee for years, but that neither Castillo nor Estebanico had wanted to go. These last two men were at a crushing disadvantage: they did not know how to swim. The costal environment amounted to the most extravagant prison that God could have devised for them.

Now there might be a way out. The miraculous reunion had changed the castaways' possibilities of escape in one crucial respect: there were now two swimmers to help the nonswimmers. All four were hardy survivors well acquainted with the Indians and with the coastal environment. They hatched a plan. After a long hiatus, the foursome would resume their quest to regain Christian lands.

La Salle's Grand Dream

James E. Bruseth and Toni S. Turner

James E. Bruseth is Director of the Archaeology Division at the Texas Historical Commission. In 1996–1997, Dr. Bruseth headed the excavation of La Salle's lost ship, *La Belle*. Freelance writer and fundraiser Toni S. Turner assisted in the vessel's recovery.

In 1685, valiant French explorer Robert Cavelier, Sieur de La Salle, planted a small colony, Fort St. Louis, on Garcitas Creek, several miles upstream from Lavaca Bay. His endeavor, however, was doomed to fail. In this selection, Bruseth and Turner discuss La Salle's ambitious vision of founding a French base on the Gulf of Mexico.

★ ★

In the name of the most high, powerful, invincible, and victorious Prince, Louis the Great, by the grace of God, King of France and Navarre, fourteenth of the name, I, this ninth day of April one thousand six hundred and eighty-two, do now take, in the name of His Majesty and of his successors to the crown, possession of this country of

Louisiana, its seas, harbors, ports, bays, adjacent straits, and all nations, peoples, provinces, cities, towns, villages, mines, minerals, fisheries, streams, and rivers.

—Robert Cavelier, Sieur de La Salle, April, 1682

Less than four years before *La Belle* was lost on the Texas coast, La Salle, in a vast marshland with no one to hear him but a small band of followers and some curious local Indians, had claimed possession of one-third of the North American continent for France. After a long and arduous journey, he had finally discovered where the mouth of the Mississippi River emptied into the Gulf of Mexico.

The French claim in the New World now extended from the upper reaches of Canada to the shores of the Gulf of Mexico, encompassing savannas, forests, deserts, and plains. The land was watered by innumerable rivers, streams, and creeks and populated by thousands of American Indians who knew nothing of this moment or its implications.

A DRIVEN MAN

Scion of a wealthy family of merchants, La Salle was born in 1643, baptized a short time later, and grew up in Rouen, a major port on the River Seine in Normandy. Early in his life, La Salle joined the Jesuit priesthood, as did many French boys from well-to-do families. Entering the monastery meant La Salle must relinquish his share of the family's fortune, for he was expected to make the church paramount. Trained in the Jesuit Order, he became a teacher.

La Salle's quiet and introspective temperament, however, did not suit the vocation of teaching unruly schoolboys. He appealed to his Father Superior to be sent to a mission in China, where he could experience the excitement of remote parts of the world. His request was denied. Undaunted, he then petitioned to go to Portugal to teach mathematics; this request was also refused. With this rejection and after twelve years as a Jesuit, La Salle submitted his resignation.

La Salle then decided to travel to New France, or today's eastern Canada, to join his elder brother, the Abbé Cavelier, a priest of St. Sulspice in Montreal. In the spring of 1666, at the age of 23, La Salle thus made his first journey to the New World. Despite its unforgiving climate, the colony of New France was a bustling place, though its remoteness often weakened the rule of law. Opportunities for entrepreneurs were abundant. European powers had long sought a water passage through the New World to China and the East Indies for trade. The St. Lawrence River, leading to the Great Lakes and beyond, seemed a likely route. There was even talk of a great river that might traverse the continent and discharge into the Gulf of California.

The young La Salle was intrigued by the wealth and prestige that awaited the explorer who might discover such a route across North America. The conditions would be harsh, to be sure: there would be hostile Indians, severe winters, and uncertain food supplies. Nevertheless, he began to devise a plan—and met considerable opposition. The Jesuits, who had built a series of missions in the Upper Great Lakes, controlled the region through their religious emissaries and profited from the fur trade with the Indians, although they could not admit that profit was a motive in their endeavors. La Salle appeared to be a threat to the Jesuits' monopoly over trade.

The merchants of New France were even more alarmed at his intentions. Discovery of a new water route through the continent might interrupt the trade in furs and hides that flowed through Montreal and Quebec. The merchants did not wish to see their rewarding enterprise disrupted by this brash young Norman with grandiose ideas. These two groups, Jesuits and merchants, were to become the "enemies" about whom La Salle lamented many times during moments of despair: "I am utterly tired of this business; for I see that it is not enough to put property and life in constant peril, but it requires more pains to answer envy and distraction than to overcome the difficulties inseparable from my undertaking."

North American rivers and lakes were the seventeenth-century equivalent of modern highways, and knowledge of their locations could be turned into great monetary gain. Louis Joliet and Father Marquette, who had discovered the Mississippi River in 1673, were the first to understand the relationship of that river to the Great Lakes. They observed that the Mississippi, flowing southward, probably emptied into the Gulf of Mexico, rather than the Gulf of California. However, Joliet and Marquette never reached the Mississippi's mouth.

La Salle, who by this time had already begun searching for a transcontinental water route, received news of the Joliet-Marquette expedition with great interest. He formulated a plan to chart this potential watercourse through North America. If the Mississippi flowed into the Gulf of Mexico, it might be possible to establish a warm-water port at the mouth of the river. Furs and hides could be transported downstream, allowing the riches of Canada and the Great Lakes to be transported to France year-round. Traders could avoid the cold climate of eastern Canada and the icebound streams and lakes that made commerce impossible in winter. Moreover, France could control the land along the Mississippi, creating a vast empire that would keep the English and Dutch in the east and the Spanish in Mexico.

The realization of this grand dream would require a new series of forts along the river and substantial financial backing. La Salle had previously secured private funding to establish forts at various points along Lakes Michigan, Erie, and Ontario. But he was a poor manager, and each time a series of mishaps had eliminated the profits he promised his backers. Adding to his difficulties, his Jesuit detractors constantly undermined his credibility in Montreal and Quebec.

There was another problem: La Salle's own personality. He often lapsed into a mysterious sickness, described as a "moral malady." He probably suffered from periods of depression and might today be diagnosed as manic-depressive. This chronic debilitation fed La Salle's arrogant and demanding nature, which in turn created a recurring inability to inspire and direct his men amid the challenges of exploring the wilderness. His failings were so severe that during a trip along the Ohio River in 1679 one of his servants tried to kill him by mixing hemlock into his salad. La Salle was sick for more than forty days. From that time on, he carried an antidote with him to protect against poisonings.

Though in 1682 he had traveled down the Mississippi River and found its mouth, La Salle knew his plan would be met with skepticism in France. His only choice was to present his case to the king himself. He traveled back to France in 1683 and petitioned Louis XIV to establish a colony where the Mississippi River met the Gulf of Mexico. In an effort to foil his plan, La Salle's enemies had written to France that he was unfit for future explorations in the

New World. La Salle tried to get support from merchants in Rochefort and La Rochelle, but his reputation for leading failed enterprises in New France preceded him. Finally, he headed to Paris to enlist the support of two abbés, Claude Bernou and Eusèbe Renaudot, who enjoyed the favor of the French court. They agreed to lobby on La Salle's behalf.

Spain had declared war on France the preceding October, and tensions between the two countries could not have been higher. La Salle was counseled that an expedition through the Gulf of Mexico would attract more royal support than a return to the Mississippi River mouth by way of New France and the St. Lawrence River. The French king was angry with Spanish opposition to foreign ships traveling in the Gulf of Mexico. French vessels violating this zone were captured and their crews imprisoned. La Salle's effort would be a bold statement against Spain's efforts to control the gulf.

Thus, from the point of view of the French monarch, the timing was just right for such a mission, but it was even more propitious when one considered Spain's current role in the New World. Spain had ignored Nueva Vizcaya, what is now northern Mexico, since the early explorations of Pineda, Cabeza de Vaca, and De Soto had failed to find gold, silver, or other wealth there. Spain had also lost control of the seas with England's defeat of the Spanish Armada in 1588 and had difficulty monitoring significant portions of its territorial claims. This was especially true of territories north of today's Mexico between Florida and New Mexico.

It was against this backdrop of international incident and intrigue that La Salle presented his plan to the king in 1683. He proposed a three-pronged approach. First, he would establish a fort at the mouth of the Mississippi River to maintain the French claim to Louisiana. Second, he would establish trade with thousands of Indians and convert them to Christianity. Finally, he would establish a permanent colony, a base from which the future invasion of Spain's Nueva Vizcaya could be launched.

For the French Crown, the colony was a critical part of La Salle's plan. While Spain had been shipping gold, silver, and other treasures from the New World, France had been forced to content itself with beaver pelts from its Canadian colonies. Louis saw his opportunity to capture some of Spanish King Charles II's wealth.

Several variations on La Salle's proposal were discussed, some involving the use of French buccaneers to help invade Nueva Vizcaya and seize control of the silver mines. The king finally granted La Salle the authority to "command . . . all the lands of North America that may hereafter be submitted to our [French] rule, from Fort St. Louis on the Illinois River to Nueva Vizcaya." Louis also gave La Salle substantial support for the expedition, including two ships rather than the one he had originally requested. Specifically, La Salle was granted the naval gunship *Le Joly* and a *barque longue* (light frigate) christened *La Belle*. As it turned out, these two ships did not possess enough cargo space for such a venture, and La Salle was forced to lease two other vessels, the frigate *l'Aimable* from La Rochelle ship owner Jean Massiot and a small ketch, *Le Saint-François*, from François Duprat, also of La Rochelle. The king's grant included full crews, a hundred soldiers, and funds to hire carpenters, masons, coopers, and other skilled workers to establish his colony. The expedition included about three hundred persons in all.

Some supplies, such as goods to trade with the Indians, were not provided by the king, which meant that La Salle and his men had to buy them. The explorer had persuaded twenty thousand Shawnee, Illinois, and Miami Indians to settle around Fort St. Louis des Illinois, which he had established in 1682. La Salle's plan was that these Indians would hunt and trap in the northern Great Plains and Great Lakes and bring the furs and hides to the fort for trade, where he would ship them down the Mississippi River to the settlement he envisioned on the Gulf of Mexico, and then onward to France. From the warm gulf port, France could import goods year-round, a distinct advantage over the ports of Montreal and Quebec, where the St. Lawrence River was iced over half the year. The medium of exchange that would drive all this would be the glass beads, brass pins, finger rings, iron knives, and hatchets they purchased to trade to the Indians.

DESTINATION: A NEW WORLD

La Salle set sail from La Rochelle, France, on July 24, 1684, to fulfill his dream of a colony at the mouth of the Mississippi River—and to enrich himself.

On January 1, 1685, after a long and difficult journey across the ocean, La Salle's expedition sighted land along the Gulf Coast, somewhere in today's Louisiana west of the Mississippi. By this time, only three vessels remained: *Le Joly*, *l'Aimable*, and *La Belle*. The *Saint-François* had been captured by Spanish privateers off the western coast of Hispaniola as the ship traveled from Port de Paix to Petit Goäve.

La Salle had been warned about strong easterly currents that carried ships towards the Bahamian Channel. Upon sighting land, he concluded that they had not made enough westward progress and were in fact east of the Mississippi. He decided to travel west, following the Gulf Coast as closely as possible.

For the next two and a half weeks the ships continued to sail westward, turning toward the southwest as they progressed. La Salle remained certain that the Mississippi lay in this direction. Measurements of latitude were taken daily to help chart their progress, but longitude—a time-dependent measurement—could not be accurately calculated until the eighteenth century. Consequently, there was no accurate method to determine exactly how far west they were traveling—a problem La Salle recognized. In addition, an astrolabe La Salle suspected to be faulty had hampered measurements of latitude during his 1682 journey down the Mississippi River, so those earlier calculations were erroneous as well. To complicate the situation further, some period maps showed the Mississippi flowing into the Gulf of Mexico through what is now central Texas. Despite these problems, La Salle believed the Mississippi River lay farther to the west, and he instructed Captain Beaujeu to continue sailing in this direction.

Finally, they noticed that they were moving more southwest than west, and suspected they might have passed the Mississippi. La Salle and Beaujeu quarreled about their location, but La Salle remained resolute that they were near one of the western branches of the great river. The relationship between the two men had deteriorated to the point that they were communicating only through official letters couriered back and forth; their deep mutual antipathy may be seen in a letter La Salle wrote when Beaujeu wished to return to France rather than assist in landing the colonists:

> ***[Y]our longboat does not give me time to reply to your letter with so much consideration as you have devoted to writing it, though the way in which you vent your spleen in the letter suggests that you wrote it rather more hastily than its length would require.***
>
> ***It is no fault of mine, Monsieur, if you have not already provided for the safety of His Majesty's ship; but I know on what grounds you ask me for pilots to take it into this river which I never intended that it should enter, and more than I wished to stop it at this shore. You may take it where you think fit.***

On January 17, 1685, La Salle determined it was time to land his men, explore the coast, find the river, and locate a place to establish the colony. He was probably near Cedar Bayou and the western end of today's Matagorda Island in Texas. After several days of surveying the surrounding countryside, the expedition's chronicler Henri Joutel noted, "The country did not seem very favorable to me. It was flat and sandy but did nevertheless produce grass. There were several salt pools. We hardly saw any wild fowl except some cranes and Canadian geese which were not expecting us."

Early in February, La Salle ordered Joutel to disembark with 120 to 130 men and march up the coast to find a large river that he was convinced would be the west branch of the Mississippi. Joutel complained that the men had little or no military experience: "Truthfully, although we had 120 to 130 men with us, 30 good men would have been better and would have done more and perforce eaten less, to which end they were without rival . . . these were all men who had been taken by force or deceit. In a way, it was almost like Noah's Ark where they were all sorts of animals. We likewise had men of different nationalities. The soldiers had been recruited by the lower ranking officers of the navy, who received a half pistole [five francs] for each man, by whatever means possible."

The party eventually encountered what they thought was a large river, which was actually Pass Cavallo, today's name for the entrance into Matagorda Bay. The three vessels arrived shortly afterward, and La Salle came ashore to inspect the terrain. He found a location on the western side of Pass Cavallo suitable for establishing a temporary camp, called the Grand Camp, and ordered *La Belle* and *l'Aimable* to come through the pass. On February 16, the ship's pilots made a sounding and determined that the two vessels could enter. They marked the entrance with buoys to guide the two ships away from hazardous sandy shoals.

La Belle came through the pass without difficulty about two in the afternoon and anchored inside Matagorda Bay. La Salle ordered that cargo be unloaded from *l'Aimable*, the expedition's main supply ship, which was five times larger than *La Belle*, so that she could also enter the pass. Eight iron cannons were removed from the ship and taken ashore to the temporary camp. On February 19 *l'Aimable*'s Captain Aigron was satisfied that adequate cargo had been unloaded, although much remained on board. According to Joutel, "On the 20th, La Salle ordered the captain to approach the bar, adding that when the sea was high, he should signal to him to be towed. La Salle also ordered the pilot of *La Belle* to help the captain of the *Aimable* with what he had to do as that ship had already entered. But the captain sent the pilot back, telling him that he was capable of bringing the ship in without him."

When the water level was sufficiently high, La Salle signaled for the ship to enter the pass. At about the same time, he was told that local Karankawa Indians had taken some of his men hostage. La Salle was now compelled to go search for them. He traveled about a league and a half (about three miles) until he found the Indian village, but before entering it he could see *l'Aimable*'s sails, indicating that she was beginning to enter the pass. She appeared to do so incorrectly, however, running too close to the shoals. La Salle was greatly concerned, but he was powerless to influence the situation. Soon a cannon was fired, indicating distress aboard the ship. Next *l'Aimable*'s sails were furled, confirming his fear that a disaster had occurred. La Salle met with the Indians, retrieved his men, and returned to assess the damage to his supply ship.

L'Aimable was grounded hard against a sandbank. Upon questioning the captain and crew, La Salle grew suspicious that the captain, Aigron, had intentionally run the ship aground. Aigron was unhappy with La Salle's efforts to find the Mississippi, believing that the explorer had missed the river and was taking the expedition into uncharted areas that would result in failure of the colony. La Salle concluded that Aigron had deliberately steered the ship past the buoys marking the safe entry and directly onto a sandbank. Once the ship was stuck, the captain could have thrown out an anchor and freed the vessel. Witnesses stated that, instead, the captain ordered the ship to sail forward until she was firmly grounded on the shallow sandy bottom. There was now no hope of saving the ship.

According to Joutel, "we learned how the captain had disgraced himself. The incident made one conclude that the mischief must have been by design or premediated act. Four buoys had been placed and one only had to steer by them. Moreover, a sailor was in the topmast for seeing better. Although the sailor continually called out 'to luff sail,' the ill-intentioned captain called out to the contrary and gave the command to bear down until he saw he was on the sandbanks."

L'Aimable, a large private merchant vessel, contained much of the planned colony's provisions. La Salle prepared to unload as much cargo as possible, but the ship was far from shore and he had only small longboats. The crew could remove cargo when the waters were calm. But *l'Aimable* broke apart one night during a period of heavy seas, and in the morning the buoyant cargo was found floating in the water.

In early March *Le Joly*'s captain, Beaujeu, decided to return to France. He had orders only to accompany La Salle to the New World and unload his ship's cargo. Once this had been accomplished, his job was done. Beaujeu was impatient to leave the wild country and the arrogant explorer with whom he often quarreled, and a number of the colonists decided to join him. La Salle asked Beaujeu to ensure that supplies would be sent back to assist his colony. On March 14, *Le Joly* departed with 120 of the original 300 colonists, leaving La Salle with a diminished number of men and greatly compromised provisions for building a settlement. La Salle's request for more supplies was delivered to officials in France, but it was never honored.

With only *La Belle* and 180 colonists, La Salle began to seek a more permanent location for his fort. He sought a safe site where he could leave many of the colonists while he searched overland for the Mississippi. When he found the river, he would build his second and final settlement. La Salle and a few men left the temporary camp near Pass Cavallo in late March, 1685, and began searching along the western side of Matagorda Bay for a more suitable site for a fort. He found a creek that he called "the River of the Bison" (now known as Garcitas Creek) flowing into the north-western part of today's Lavaca Bay. On a high, flat rise on the western side of the creek, about four miles upriver from the bay, he began construction of the temporary settlement, Fort St. Louis, where he would begin colonizing the Gulf Coast.

Provisions from *l'Aimable* and *Le Joly*, together with cargo from *La Belle*, were moved to a supply depot about midway between the pass and the Grand Camp. From the depot they were transported by canoe upriver to the fort. Wood suitable for buildings was not readily available, so La Salle commanded his men to travel a league inland and bring back trees of suitable size. This proved difficult work, and several men died from the exertion. Finally La Salle resorted to salvaging timbers from *l'Aimable* to build the fort.

A two-story structure similar to buildings La Salle had constructed in Canada was erected. It was divided into four rooms: one for La Salle, another for the priests, a third for the officers of the expedition, and a fourth, the upper story, for supplies. Smaller structures were erected to house other members of the expedition. *L'Aimable*'s eight cannons would help fight off Karankawa Indian attacks.

With the settlement established, La Salle again concentrated on finding the Mississippi. Now realizing that the river almost certainly had to be toward the east, he organized an exploration party. He left supplies for the colony on *La Belle*, along with all of his personal possessions and those of his men. He instructed her captain to proceed as far up the bay as possible, where he should lay anchor and wait for La Salle's return. The exploration party, meanwhile, would travel along the shore and head east to find the Mississippi.

La Salle expected to be gone about ten days; instead he was absent for more than two frustrating months. The Indians he encountered along the way knew nothing of the great river. In fact, these native peoples did not even speak the languages he had heard along the Mississippi on his earlier travels. La Salle traded for horses and food with the Caddo Indians and returned to Fort St. Louis, where he was devastated to discover that his sole remaining ship had been lost in a storm.

Le Belle had contained all the remaining supplies to build his final New World colony. With his grand dream of a French settlement on the Gulf of Mexico in great jeopardy, La Salle's only recourse now was to go overland to his settlement at Fort St. Louis des Illinois and up to Canada to get supplies—a journey of twelve hundred miles.

MURDER ON THE TRAIL

On January 12, 1687, La Salle and sixteen men departed the small settlement on Garcitas Creek to obtain supplies from Canada. It was to be the explorer's last expedition.

Remaining at Fort St. Louis were twenty men, women, and children—a meager fragment of the more than 180 who had stayed to help build the settlement. Disease and Indian attacks had taken the rest. The survivors would be stranded on Garcitas Creek for two years, waiting in vain for La Salle's return with the desperately needed provisions. In late 1688 or early 1689, the Karankawas would launch a final attack on the vulnerable outpost, killing almost all the remaining colonists and kidnapping several children.

In March, 1687, La Salle and his overland party reached a spot near today's Navasota, Texas, where they crossed the River of the Canoes and camped. During La Salle's previous trip, he had buried food supplies at a crossing a short distance downstream. He gave orders for some of his men to go and recover the stores because hunting was lean this time of the year. The men found the food, but it was spoiled. Luckily, La Salle's trusted Shawnee Indian hunter, Nika, shot two buffalo while returning to their leader. The men stopped to smoke the meat and sent word to La Salle.

As the men prepared to eat the portions that could not be smoked, La Salle's nephew, Colin Morenger, instructed them that he would control the remaining food and would decide who would eat what portion. For the dispirited men who had endured countless hardships and depredations, this was the final insult, and they plotted to kill Morenger. Revenge was planned by five men: Duhaut, Liotot (the expedition surgeon), Hiems, Tessier, and L'Archevêque. Later that night, they murdered Morenger, Nika, and La Salle's servant, Saget.

The murderers had accomplished their immediate plan, but they knew that La Salle, still at the other camp and waiting for the buffalo meat, would exact punishment. The five planned yet another murder: the assassination of Robert Cavelier, Sieur de la Salle. They knew that La Salle would soon come looking for them, and they waited in ambush.

Within a few days, a gunshot warned the men that La Salle was nearby. Duhaut and L'Archevêque crossed the river on a trail that La Salle would follow and waited in the bushes. As the explorer approached, L'Archevêque stepped into view. La Salle asked where Morenger was, and L'Archevêque replied that he had drifted away. Before La Salle could respond, Duhaut, who was hidden from view, fired a musket shot into the explorer's head, killing him.

At the age of 43, after twenty years of conquering and colonizing the wilderness of North America, the great explorer lay dead. La Salle's killers took his possessions, even his clothing, and left his body "to the discretion of the wolves and other wild animals."

Introduction: Reversed Colonialism

Pekka Hämäläinen

Pekka Hämäläinen, Associate Professor of History at the University of California—Santa Barbara, is author of *The Comanche Empire*. His current project, *The Shapes of Power: Frontiers, Borderlands, and Empires of North America, 1600–1900*, is under contract with Yale University Press.

From approximately 1750 to 1850, Comanches—as warriors, traders, and diplomats—dominated the American Southwest. Known as the "Lords of the South Plains," these formidable Indians "manipulated and exploited the colonial outposts in New Mexico, Texas, Louisiana, and northern Mexico." The Spaniards, French, Mexicans, and Anglo-Americans, Dr. Hämäläinen asserts, "were all restrained and overshadowed" by Comanche hegemony. In short, *The Comanche Empire* chronicles "the familiar tale of expansion, resistance, conquest, and loss, but with a reversal of usual historical roles: It is a story in which Indians expand, dictate, and prosper, and European colonists resist, retreat, and struggle to survive." In this selection, Hämäläinen discusses recent scholarship and proposes his cogent arguments.

★ ★

This book is about an American empire that, according to conventional histories, did not exist. It tells the familiar tale of expansion, resistance, conquest, and loss, but with a reversal of usual historical roles: it is a story in which Indians expand, dictate, and prosper, and European colonists resist, retreat, and struggle to survive.

At the dawn of the eighteenth century, the Comanches were a small tribe of hunter-gatherers living in the rugged canyonlands on the far northern frontier of the Spanish kingdom of New Mexico. They were newcomers to the region, having fled the political unrest and internal disputes in their old homelands on the central Great Plains, and they were struggling to rebuild their lives in a foreign land whose absorption into the Spanish world seemed imminent. It was here, at the advancing edge of the world's largest empire, that the Comanches launched an explosive expansion. They purchased and plundered horses from New Mexico, reinvented themselves as mounted fighters, and reenvisioned their place in the world. They forced their way onto the southern plains, shoved aside the Apaches and other residing nations, and over the course of three generations carved out a vast territory that was larger than the entire European-controlled area north of the Río Grande at the time. They became "Lords of the South Plains," ferocious horse-riding warriors who forestalled Euro-American intrusions into the American Southwest well into the late nineteenth century.

The Comanches are usually portrayed in the existing literature as a formidable equestrian power that erected a daunting barrier of violence to colonial expansion. Along with the Iroquois and Lakotas, they have been embedded in collective American memory as one of the few Native societies able to pose a significant challenge to the Euro-American conquest of North America. But the idea of a Comanche barrier leaves out at least half of the story. For in the mid-eighteenth century Comanches reinvented themselves once more, this time as a hegemonic people who grew increasingly powerful and prosperous at the expense of the surrounding societies, Indian and Euro-American alike. Gradually, a momentous shift took shape. In the Southwest, European imperialism not only stalled in the face of indigenous resistance; it was eclipsed by indigenous imperialism.

That overturn of power relations was more than a historical glitch, a momentary rupture in the process of European colonization of indigenous America. For a century, roughly from 1750 to 1850, the Comanches were the dominant people in the Southwest, and they manipulated and exploited the colonial outposts in New Mexico, Texas, Louisiana, and northern Mexico to increase their safety, prosperity, and power. They extracted resources and labor from their Euro-American and Indian neighbors through thievery and tribute and incorporated foreign ethnicities into their ranks as adopted kinspeople, slaves, workers, dependents, and vassals. The Comanche empire was powered by violence, but, like most viable empires, it was first and foremost an economic construction. At its core was an extensive commercial network that allowed Comanches to control nearby border markets and long-distance trade, swing surrounding groups into their political orbit, and spread their language and culture across the midcontinent. And as always, long-term foreign political dominance rested on dynamic internal development. To cope with the opportunities and challenges of their rapid expansion, Comanches created a centralized multilevel political system, a flourishing market economy, and a graded social organization that was flexible enough to sustain and survive the burdens of their external ambitions.

The Comanches, then, were an interregional power with imperial presence, and their politics divided the history of the Southwest and northern Mexico into two sharply contrasting trajectories. While Comanches reached unparalleled heights of political and economic influence, material wealth, and internal stability, the Spanish colonies, the subsequent Mexican provinces, and many indigenous agricultural societies suffered from a number of disruptions typical to peripheral regions in colonial worlds. Without fully recognizing it, the Spaniards, French, Mexicans, and Anglo-Americans were all restrained and overshadowed in the continent's center by an indigenous empire. That empire—its rise, anatomy, costs, and fall—is the subject of this book.

Great American Indian powers have captivated scholarly imagination since Hernán Cortés fought his way into Tenochtitlán and Francisco Pizarro marched into Cuzco. Over the years, historians and archaeologists have uncovered several imperialistic or quasi-imperialistic Native American polities that dominated other indigenous societies. The Aztecs, Incas, and other empire-builders in the precontact Americas come easily to mind, but one might, with a little more effort, also think of the Powhatans in early seventeenth-century Tidewater Virginia, Haudenosaunee—the Iroquois confederacy—in the seventeenth-century Northeast, or the Lakotas on the nineteenth-century northern plains.

This book belongs to that genre while also stepping outside of it. Comanches, it shows, fought and subjugated other Native societies, but more important to their ascendancy was their ability to reduce Euro-American colonial regimes to building blocks of their own dominant position. Comanches achieved something quite exceptional: they built an imperial organization that subdued, exploited, marginalized, co-opted, and profoundly transformed near and distant colonial outposts, thereby reversing the conventional imperial trajectory in vast segments of North and Central America.

Comanches, moreover, did that during the eighteenth and early nineteenth centuries, the high tide of imperial contestation when colonial powers jostled for preeminence across North America. The colonial Southwest was a setting for several dynamic and diverging imperial projects that converged and clashed in unexpected ways. As Spanish, French, British, and U.S. empires vied with one another over land, commerce, and raw materials, Comanches continued to expand their realm, profoundly frustrating European fantasies of superiority. The result was a colonial history that defies conventional wisdom. A longstanding notion has it that the course and contours of early American history were determined by the shifts in Euro-American power dynamics and the reactions of metropolitan headquarters in Madrid, London, Versailles, Mexico City, and Washington to those shifts. The Southwest, however, is a striking exception. Metropolitan visions mattered there, but they often mattered less than the policies and designs of Comanches, whose dominance eventually reached hemispheric dimensions, extending from the heart of North America deep into Mexico. Indeed, Comanche ascendancy is the missing component in the sweeping historical sequence that led to New Spain's failure to colonize the interior of North America, the erosion of Spanish imperial authority in the Southwest, and the precipitous decay of Mexican power in the north. Ultimately, the rise of the Comanche empire helps explain why Mexico's Far North is today the American Southwest.

Yet for all their strength and potential for expansion, Comanches never attempted to build a European-style imperial system. A creation of itinerant nomadic bands, the Comanche empire was not a rigid structure held together by a single central authority, nor was it an entity that could be displayed on a map as a solid block with clear-cut borders. Unlike Euro-American imperial powers, Comanches did not seek to establish large-scale settlement colonies, and their vision of power was not direct rule over multiple subject peoples. They did not publicize their might with ostentatious art and architecture, and they left behind no imperial ruins to remind us of the extent of their power. Preferring informal rule over formal institutions for both cultural and strategic reasons, Comanches nevertheless created a deeply hierarchical and integrated inter-societal order that was unmistakably imperial in shape, scope, and substance. The numerous Comanche bands and divisions formed an internally fluid but externally coherent coalition that accomplished through a creative blending of violence, diplomacy, extortion, trade, and kinship politics what more rigidly structured empires have achieved through direct political control: they imposed their will upon neighboring polities, harnessed the economic potential of other societies for their own use, and persuaded their rivals to adopt and accept their customs and norms.

To understand the particular nature of Comanche imperialism, it is necessary to understand how Comanche ascendancy intertwined with other imperial expansions—New Spain's tenacious if erratic northward thrust from central Mexico, New France's endeavor to absorb the interior grasslands into its commercial realm, and the United States' quest for a transcontinental empire. Comanches, to simplify a complex multistage process, developed aggressive power policies in reaction to Euro-American invasions that had threatened their safety and autonomy from the moment they had entered the southern plains. Indeed, the fact that Comanche territory, Comanchería, was encircled throughout its existence by Euro-American settler colonies makes the Comanches an unlikely candidate for achieving regional primacy. But as the Comanches grew in numbers and power, that geopolitical layout became the very foundation of their dominance. Their overwhelming military force, so evident in their terror-inspiring mounted guerrilla attacks, would have allowed them to destroy many New Mexico and Texas settlements and drive most of the colonists out of their borders. Yet they never adopted such a policy of expulsion, preferring instead to have their borders lined with formally autonomous but economically subservient and dependent outposts that served as economic access points into the vast resources of the Spanish empire.

The Comanches, then, were an imperial power with a difference: their aim was not to conquer and colonize, but to coexist, control, and exploit. Whereas more traditional imperial powers ruled by making things rigid and predictable, Comanches ruled by keeping them fluid and malleable. This informal, almost ambiguous nature of Comanches' politics not only makes their empire difficult to define; it sometimes makes it difficult to see. New Mexico and Texas existed side by side with Comanchería throughout the colonial era, and though often suffering under Comanche pressure, the twin colonies endured, allowing Spain to claim sweeping imperial command over the Southwest. Yet when examined closely, Spain's uncompromised imperial presence in the Southwest becomes a fiction that existed only in Spanish minds and on European maps, for Comanches controlled a large portion of those material things that could be controlled in New Mexico and Texas. The idea of land as a form of private, revenue-producing property was absent in Comanche culture, and livestock and slaves in a sense took the place of landed private property. This basic observation has enormous repercussions on how we should see the relationship between the Comanches and colonists. When Comanches subjected Texas and New Mexico to systematic raiding of horses, mules, and captives, draining wide sectors of those productive resources, they in effect turned the colonies into imperial possessions. That Spanish Texas and New Mexico remained unconquered by Comanches is not a historical fact; it is a matter of perspective.

In this book I examine the Comanche power complex as part of an emerging transatlantic web that had not yet consolidated into an encompassing world economy. Seen from this angle, the eighteenth- and early nineteenth-century Southwest and Mexican North emerge as a small-scale world-system that existed outside the controlling grip of Europe's overseas empires. Comanchería was its political and economic nucleus, a regional core surrounded by more or less peripheral societies and territories whose fortunes were linked to the Comanches through complex webs of cooperation, coercion, extortion, and dependence. The world-system approach to history has often been criticized for being overly strict and mechanistic, which it is. I have used its spatial language and metaphors selectively but also advisedly, fully aware that they convey a certain kind of rigidity and permanence. Viewed against the backdrop of constantly shifting frontiers of North America, the intersocietal space the Comanches occupied and eventually dominated was marked by unusually hard, enduring, and distinctive power hierarchies.

This Comanche-centric world was by no means self-contained; it was anchored from its inception to the broader colonial world through the strong administrative and economic networks among New Mexico, Texas, northern Mexican provinces, and Mexico City. But these institutional linkages often had less impact on the colonies' internal development than Comanche policies did; the troubled and convoluted history of New Mexico, Texas, Coahuila, and Nueva Vizcaya may have had as much to do with the Comanches as with the ebbs and flows of New Spain's imperial fortunes. In fact, the systemic connections between Comanchería and northern New Spain gave the Comanches a modicum of exploitative power over the Spanish empire as a whole. When New Mexico was founded at the turn of the sixteenth and seventeenth centuries, it was expected to fuel Spain's imperial veins with raw materials and laborers, but by the eighteenth century the colony was leaking so much wealth into Comanchería that it could survive only by continuous financial backing from Mexico City. Texas functioned through much of the late eighteenth and early nineteenth centuries as a money-draining, often tributary defensive province against Comanche expansion. By subsidizing its far northern frontier, then, the Spanish empire in effect drained itself to feed and fend off an indigenous empire.

Although I focus on a particular place in time in this book, my arguments engage in the broader debates about colonialism, frontiers, and borderlands in the Americas. Over the past three decades, historians have conceived entirely new ways of thinking about Native Americans, Euro-Americans, and their tangled histories. Moving beyond conventional top-down narratives that depict Indians as bit players in imperial struggles or tragic victims of colonial expansion, today's scholarship portrays them as full-fledged historical actors who played a formative role in the making of early America. Rather than a seamless, preordained sequence, the colonization of the Americas is now seen as a dialectic process that created new worlds for all involved. Indigenous societies did not simply vanish in the face of Euro-American onslaught. Many adjusted and endured, rebuilding new economies and identities from the fragments of the old ones. Indians fought and resisted, but they also cooperated and coexisted with the newcomers, creating new hybrid worlds that were neither wholly Indian nor European. By foregrounding indigenous peoples and their intentions in the story of early America, recent scholarship has reinvigorated a field that only a generation ago was suffocating under its parochial and mythologizing tenets.

Significant as this revisionist turn has been, it is not complete. Too often the alterations have been cosmetic rather than corrective. Historians have sanitized vocabularies and updated textbooks to illuminate the subtleties of colonial encounters, but the broad outlines of the story have largely remained intact. Outside a cadre of Native and early American specialists, the understanding of Indian—Euro-American relations is still limited by what Vine Deloria, Jr., called "the 'cameo' theory of history": indigenous peoples make dramatic entrances, stay briefly on the stage, and then fade out as the main saga of European expansion resumes, barely affected by the interruption. With too few exceptions, revisionist historians have limited themselves to retelling the story of colonial conquest from the Indian side of the frontier. They have probed how Native peoples countered and coped with colonial expansion and have largely overlooked the other side of the dynamic—the impact of Indian policies on colonial societies. Such an approach reinforces the view of European powers as the principal driving force of history and tends to reduce indigenous actions to mere strategies of subversion and survival. To recover the full dimension of Indian agency in early American history, we must once again reevaluate the intersections among Native peoples, colonial powers, frontiers, and borderlands. We have to turn the telescope around and create models that allow us to look at Native policies toward colonial powers as more than defensive strategies of resistance and containment.

This book offers new insights into that effort, and it does so by questioning some of the most basic assumptions about indigenous peoples, colonialism, and historical change. Instead of perceiving Native policies toward colonial powers simply as strategies of survival, it assumes that Indians, too, could wage war, exchange goods, make treaties, and absorb peoples in order to expand, extort, manipulate, and dominate. Instead of reading Indian dispossession back in time to structure the narrative of early America, it embraces the multiple possibilities and contingency of historical change. At its most fundamental level, it promotes a less linear reading of Indian-white relations in North America. After the initial contacts, when Indians usually held the upper hand over the invaders, the fate of indigenous cultures was not necessarily an irreversible slide toward dispossession, depopulation, and cultural declension. As the history of the Comanches illustrates, almost diametrically opposite trajectories were possible. Before their final defeat in the canyonlands of the Texas Panhandle in 1875, Comanches had experienced an astounding ascendancy from the margins of the colonial world into imperial prominence as a dominant people who thrived and expanded in the midst of Euro-American colonies for over a century.

The history of Indian–Euro-colonial relations, as we today understand them, is inseparable from the history of the frontier, which forms another theoretical thread of this study. Over the past fifteen years or so, the frontier has made a forceful reentry into the very center of North American historiography. Recast as a zone of cultural interpenetration, the frontier is finding new relevance among historians who not so long ago had rejected Frederick Jackson Turner's frontier thesis as an ethnocentric and narcissistic rendition of the European takeover of North America. Instead of Turner's binary dividing line between civilization and savagery—or as seedbed of American virtues—historians have reenvisioned the frontier as a socially charged space where Indians and invaders competed for resources and land but also shared skills, foods, fashions, customs, languages, and beliefs. Indian-white frontiers, new work has revealed, were messy, eclectic contact points where all protagonists are transformed—regardless of whether the power dynamics between them are evenly or unevenly balanced. This has brought the frontier closer to its rival concept, the borderland, which Herbert Eugene Bolton, the pioneering historian of Spanish North America, coined to challenge Turner's constricted Anglo-centric vision. Skepticism toward the nation-state as the main unit of historical analysis, a hemispheric vision, an appreciation of cultural and political mutability, and an emphasis on indigenous agency are the traditional strengths of borderlands history; today they are the strengths of frontier studies as well.

This book makes use of several insights of new frontier-borderland studies. On a macrolevel, it shows how Comanches moved goods, ideas, and people across ecological, ethnic, and political boundaries, creating transnational (or transimperial) networks of violence and exchange that defied the more rigid spatial arrangements Euro-American powers hoped to implement in the Southwest. On a microlevel, it shows how Comanches forged intimate small-scale, face-to-face markets with Euro-Americans, creating nascent versions of what Daniel Usner has called "frontier exchange economies," self-sufficient trade systems that mostly existed outside of the burgeoning transatlantic economy. It describes how Comanches forced the colonizers to modify their aggressive ways and at the same time recalibrated some of their own practices to adjust to the Euro-American presence, engaging in the kind of process of mediation, mutual invention, and cultural production Richard White has called "the middle ground." Geopolitically, Comanches' Southwest would seem to fit into Jeremy Adelman's and Stephen Aron's recent redefinition of a borderland: it was a place where interimperial rivalries enhanced Native peoples' strategic options by permitting them to play off colonial powers against one another.

And yet the new frontier-borderland studies can explain the world I am describing only partially. The Southwest depicted in this book is a violent and traumatic place where Natives and newcomers saw one another more as strangers and adversaries than as co-creators of a common world; it was only incidentally a place where frontier exchange economies or middle grounds could flourish. When Comanches and Euro-Americans met to discuss such contentious and conceptually slippery matters as war, peace, reciprocity, loyalty, and justice, they sometimes relied on creative and expedient misunderstandings that were so fundamental for the creation of middle grounds, but more often than not, they understood each other all too well and generally did not like what they saw. Euro-Americans deemed Comanches needy, pushy, oversensitive, and obstinate in their pagan beliefs, and in turn appeared greedy, arrogant, bigoted, and grotesquely boorish to Comanche sensibilities. In the end, most attempts at meaningful cross-cultural mediation crumbled against the insolence of Euro-Americans and the impatience of Comanches. Negotiating from a position of growing physical and political power, Comanches adopted an increasingly assertive stance toward colonial powers. Their foreign policy became less a matter of accommodating Euro-American expectations than rejecting, reforming, or simply ignoring them.

Viewed broadly, the Southwest under the Comanche regime becomes a case study of alternative frontier history. From a Comanche point of view, in fact, there were no frontiers. Where contemporary Euro-Americans (as well as later historians) saw or imagined solid imperial demarcations, Comanches saw multiple opportunities for commerce, gift exchanges, pillaging, slave raiding, ransoming, adoption, tribute extracting, and alliance making. By refusing to accept the Western notion of sovereign, undivided colonial realms, they shredded Euro-American frontiers into their component parts—colonial towns, presidios, missions, ranches, haciendas, Native villages—and dealt with each isolated unit separately, often pitting their interests against one another. In the colonial Southwest, it was Comanches, not Euro-Americans, who mastered the policies of divide and rule.

Similarly, Comanches' assertive and aggressive policies toward Euro-Americans were only secondarily a borderland product. Comanches certainly benefited from their location between competing colonial regimes, but they had little in common with the Indians found in most borderland histories. Rather than marginalized people balancing between rival colonial regimes to enact minor alleviations in imperial policies, Comanches were key players who often forced the would-be colonizers to compete for *their* military support and goodwill and navigate *their* initiatives and intentions. In character and logic, the eighteenth- and early nineteenth-century Southwest was unequivocally a Comanche creation, an indigenous world where intercolonial rivalries were often mere surface disturbances on the deeper, stronger undercurrent of Comanche imperialism.

In popular imagination, the American Southwest before the United States takeover in 1848 is a study in imperial failure. The overstretched and stiflingly bureaucratic Spanish empire, with its North American headquarters in Mexico City, had spread its resources too thinly across the Western Hemisphere to affix its northernmost provinces firmly into its imperial structure. The French, while more resourceful than their myopic Spanish rivals, were too erratic and too preoccupied with Old World power politics, the British colonies, and Canadian fur trade to do anything imperially impressive with Louisiana or the western interior. The fledgling Mexican Republic was so fragile and fractious that it lost both New Mexico and Texas in less than three decades. Reduced to a caricature, the Southwest of the mainstream view appears a medley of politically weak and isolated Native tribes, exhausted empires, and dysfunctional republics, a fragmented world ripe to be absorbed by Anglo Americans who alone possessed the imagination, drive, and means to subjugate and control vast regions. If weighed against such a background of imperial indifference and political impotence, Comanches' accomplishments would seem to diminish in significance: their ascendancy intersected with exceptional Euro-American vulnerability, and they became a dominant power by default.

I start with a different premise—far from an imperial backwater, the Southwest was a dynamic world of vibrant societies, and Comanches had to suppress and absorb vigorous imperial projects to achieve dominance—and draw on a string of pathbreaking studies that have given the history of the early Southwest a new look. Dismantling the long-standing stereotype of reactionary and unimaginative Spanish colonists, David Weber has demonstrated how high-ranking authorities in central Mexico and local officials in New Mexico, Texas, and Louisiana constantly and creatively modified the empire's frontier policies to extend Spanish claims and power into the heart of North America. That same political and strategic dynamism, Weber has further shown, defined the Mexican Southwest, although the infant republic lacked the resources and expansionist ambitions of the Spanish empire. Ross Frank has demonstrated that Bourbonera New Mexico was more tightly integrated into New Spain's imperial centers and consequently more dynamic and prosperous than has been assumed, and Andrés Reséndez has revealed a robust Mexican nation-building project in the north after 1821. Ned Blackhawk has drawn attention to the Spaniards' enormous capacity to employ—and endure—violence in advancing their imperial interests. In revisiting the history of the Comanches, ethnohistorians like Morris Foster and Thomas Kavanagh have dispelled the stereotype of a simple hunting society by uncovering elaborate political systems, social institutions, trade networks, and pastoral herding economies. Together, these and other new studies have demolished the old image of the Southwest as a world of innately passive peoples, frozen in time and disconnected from the main currents of American history.

Historians have also begun to create new syntheses that illustrate how this rediscovered human ambition, energy, and ingenuity shaped the evolution of cross-cultural relations in the Southwest. Gary Clayton Anderson has examined the region as a contested and culturally elastic meeting ground where many Native groups resisted conquest through ethnogenesis, by constantly reshaping their economies, societies, and identities. In a seminal study, James Brooks has recast the region as an ethnic mosaic connected by an intercultural exchange network that revolved around "kinship slavery" and blended indigenous and colonial traditions of servitude, violence, male honor, and retribution into a distinctive borderlands cultural economy. With such insights, the Southwest is now emerging as a vigorous world of enduring social subversion where Natives and newcomers remained roughly equal in power and where familiar dichotomies of Indians and Europeans, or masters and victims, often became meaningless.

I also take a broad long-term look at intercultural relationships in the Southwest but draw a distinctive, two-pronged conclusion. I show how Comanches cooperated and compromised with other peoples but also argue that their relations with the Spaniards, Mexicans, Wichitas, and others remained grounded in conflict and exploitation. Comanchería's borders were sites of mutualistic trade and cultural fusion, but they were also sites of extortion, systematic violence, coerced exchange, political manipulation, and hardening racial attitudes. The key difference between the existing studies and this book centers on the question of power and its distribution. According to Brooks's landmark *Captives and Cousins*, for example, the intricate patterns of raiding, exchange, and captive-seizure knitted disparate peoples into intimate webs of interdependence, equalized wealth distinctions among groups, and worked against the emergence of asymmetrical power relations. The Southwest he—and others—portrays was a place of nondominant frontiers where neither colonists nor Natives possessed the power to rule over the other. My argument, in a sense, is more traditional: such actions as raiding, enslaving, ethnic absorption, and even exchange generally benefit some groups more than they do others. In the Southwest, moreover, that process toward inequality was a cumulative one. Once the Comanches secured their territorial control over the southern plains in the mid-eighteenth century, they entered into a spiral of growing power and influence that stemmed from their ability to extract political and material benefits from the urban-based societies in New Mexico, Texas, and the Great Plains.

The conspicuous differences between earlier studies and this book rise from different conceptual framing and scaling. Recent works on Indian—Euro-American relations in the Southwest—as in North America in general—share a particular focus: they look at events through a local lens, stressing individual and small-group agency over the larger structural forces. Suffused with subaltern interpretations, they tend to focus on the fringe peoples living on the frontiers' edges and trace how they engaged in cross-cultural dialogue and came together to form new hybrid communities, gradually shading into one another. Occupied with the local, the specific, and the particular, they are less concerned with the broader political, economic, and cultural struggles. Hierarchies of power, privilege, and wealth, while not ignored, are relegated to the background of the central story of cross-cultural cooperation and assimilation.

In this book, in contrast, I examine the inhabitants of the Southwest in larger aggregates. While recognizing that ethnic and cultural boundaries were often porous, I look at those peoples as they identified and understood themselves: as distinct groups of Apaches, Comanches, Spaniards, French, Mexicans, and Anglo-Americans. With this shift in frame and focus, local arrangements may become somewhat blurred and lose some of their primacy, but the broader panorama opens a clearer view to the governing macroscale dynamics. It shows that the American Southwest, for all its wide-ranging cultural mixing, remained a polarized world where disparate ethnic groups clashed and competed bitterly with one another, where inequities of wealth and opportunity remained a tangible fact of life, and where resources, people, and power gravitated toward Comanchería.

Besides adjusting the analytical scale, the reconstruction of Comanche power has entailed a basic visual reorientation. Instead of looking at events from colonial frontiers inward—a traditional approach that inevitably ties explanations to contemporary Western biases—this book looks at developments from Comanchería outward. Viewed from this angle, Comanche actions take on new shape and meaning. Acts that previously seemed arbitrary or impulsive fall into coherent patterns with their own internal logic and purpose. A foreign policy that previously appeared an opportunistic search for microlevel openings on white-controlled imperial frontiers now emerges as planned, synchronized, and domineering. We see how Comanches did not merely frequent colonial markets; they fashioned an imposing trading empire that mantled much of the Southwest and the Great Plains. They did not merely respond to political initiatives dictated from abroad, but actively sought and stipulated treaties. Far from being situational opportunists, they fused exchange, organized pilfering, and targeted destruction into a complex economy of violence, which allowed them to simultaneously enforce favorable trade agreements, create artificial demand for their exports, extort tribute payments from colonial outposts, and fuel a massive trade network with stolen horses, captives, and other marketable commodities. Seen from Mexico City, the far north often seemed chaotic and unsettling; seen from Comanchería, it appears nuanced, orderly, and reassuring.

Understanding Comanches' rise to power requires more than unearthing previously veiled patterns and structures: it also requires describing events and developments on Comanche terms. To capture the fundamental nature of the Comanche empire, we need to uncover meanings behind words, motives behind actions, strategies behind policies, and, eventually, the cultural order that drove it all. This, however, is a daunting task because the available sources do not readily lend themselves to deep cultural analysis. Euro-American colonial records, the documentary spine of this book, address virtually every aspect of Comanche political economy from warfare, exchange, and diplomacy to material production, slavery, and social relations, but although the records are rich in depiction and detail, the picture they yield is nevertheless the one-dimensional view of an outsider. Government reports, captivity narratives, travelers' journals, and traders' accounts tell us a great deal about Comanche actions but rarely shed light on the cultural motives behind those actions. Few contemporary observers possessed the analytical tools to understand the subtleties between Native and non-Native cultural logic, and even fewer possessed the ability—or the inclination—to write down what they learned. The available sources are thus almost invariably infected with gaps, accidental misreadings, and intentional misconstructions, leaving historians to work with material that is fragmentary at best and outright erroneous at worst.

In my endeavor to recover Comanche motives and meanings from the flawed evidence, I have employed an array of historical and ethnohistorical methods. I have prioritized accounts that recount, even in a mutated form, Comanche voice—while keeping in mind that that voice is recorded through a cultural colander and that it belongs often to privileged headmen, seldom to the poor and deprived, and virtually never to women and the young. I have cross-checked Spanish, French, Mexican, and Anglo-American documents against one another to create more stereoscopic and, arguably, more accurate portrayals of Comanche intentions and objectives. Throughout the writing process, I have compared historical documents to ethnographic data, processing Euro-American-produced materials through an ethnohistorical filter. This has involved a cautious use of "upstreaming" whereby one works back from more recent and more complete ethnological observations to decipher practices and behaviors of earlier periods. Even more reluctantly, I have sometimes relied on "side-streaming," deducing interpretations about Comanche cultural values from generalized models of Native societies of the Great Plains and other regions.

This kind of methodological layering and rotation of viewpoints helps outline the broad contours of Comanche cultural order, but the resulting picture is still only an approximate one. Regardless of their origin, all colonial records are marred with similar deep-seated biases, while upstreaming runs the risk of presentism, tainting analysis with a sense of static timelessness; it assumes that Native peoples and their traditions have somehow been immune to modernity and have somehow remained unchanged through centuries of dispossession, population loss, and cultural genocide. Side-streaming threatens to submerge unique Comanche traits under crude blanket definitions of Indians in general and Plains Indians in particular. Shortcomings like these can produce what historian Frederick Hoxie has called "cookbook ethnohistory": complex cultures are collapsed into shorthand recipes, human behavior is reduced to a culturally or genetically determined reflex, and individual impulses become irrelevant. As an antidote against this kind of trivialization, Hoxie urges historians to describe societies in their own, inherently asymmetrical terms and create less linear stories that leave room for the surprising and the puzzling.

Taking a cue from Hoxie, I have embraced rather than downplayed the contradictory aspects of Comanche behavior. The Comanches depicted in this book were empire-builders who did not possess a grand imperial strategy and conquerors who saw themselves more as guardians than governors of the land and its bounties. They were warriors who often favored barter over battle and traders who did not hesitate to rely on lethal violence to protect their interests. They were shrewd diplomats who at times eschewed formal political institutions and peacemakers who tortured enemies to demonstrate military and cultural supremacy. They were racially color-blind people who saw in almost every stranger a potential kinsperson, but they nevertheless built the largest slave economy in the colonial Southwest. Their war chiefs insulted, intimidated, and demeaned colonial agents with shockingly brutal words and gestures, but their peace leaders spoke eloquently of forgiveness, pity, and regret, using elaborate metaphors and ritual language to persuade their Euro-American counterparts. Above all, the Comanches were not a monolith obeying an unyielding cultural code but rather an assemblage of individuals with different and sometimes conflicting personalities, interests, and ambitions. They shared certain core values and objectives, but they also disagreed and quarreled over the methods, goals, and costs of their policies. The Comanche society, in short, was a complex one in which several standards of conduct coexisted simultaneously.

Historian Bruce Trigger has explained Native American behavior from a slightly different angle than Hoxie by focusing on the underlying mental processes of learning, judging, and reasoning. Assuming a middle course in the long, drawn-out debates over cross-cultural variations in human motivations, Trigger argues that while traditional cultural beliefs continued to shape Native American responses to European contact and colonialism, in the long run more universal pragmatic assessments and calculations came to play a dominant role. This kind of cognitive reorganization, Trigger maintains, occurred at all levels of behavior but was most visible in those areas that relate more directly to Indians' material well-being—technology and power. For Trigger, the outcome of colonial contact was not a makeover of Native Americans into "universal economic men," nor was it an unyielding persistence of otherness.

Following Trigger, I pay particular attention to the changes that occurred over time in the underlying principles of Comanche behavior. The introduction of horses, guns, and other Old World technology arguably prompted Comanches to view their place and possibilities in the world in a different light, while close political and commercial interactions with colonial powers exposed them to the logic and laws of European diplomacy and the market. Comanches may have initially perceived European goods through the mold of their idiosyncratic traditions, but that did not prevent them from grasping the tremendous military and material advantages of horses, firearms, and metal—or from employing those advantages against Euro-Americans themselves. Similarly, like many other indigenous peoples, Comanches may have at first viewed the mounted, gun-using newcomers as all-powerful otherworldly beings, yet within years they learned to manipulate the Spaniards' all-too-human weaknesses to their own advantage. Within a generation or so after the first contact, Comanches had learned to distinguish between the motives and methods of the different colonial powers and to exploit those differences to advance their own political and economic agendas. Grounded in utilitarian calculations of self-interest, such behavior was rational in the sense most contemporary Euro-Americans and later historians would have understood the term.

And yet the yawning gulf separating Comanche and Euro-American cultural and mental worlds never disappeared—far from it. Regardless of their universal features, the actions and policies of Comanches remained embedded in a system of reality that was distinctly non-Western in nature. To the limited extent that it is possible to unveil the intentions that went into the actions of eighteenth- or early nineteenth-century Indians, it seems plain that the rationale of Comanche behavior remained worlds apart from that of Euro-Americans.

On the face of it, Comanche actions fell into unambiguous categories—trading, raiding, enslaving, and so forth—that were easily recognizable and understandable to contemporary Euro-Americans and modern historians alike. But the similarities are only skin deep; a more focused look reveals how Comanche actions time and again transcended familiar categories and defied easy labeling. Unlike Euro-Americans, Comanches did not separate trade from larger social relations but instead understood it as a form of sharing between relatives, either real or fictive. They considered theft a legitimate way of rectifying short-term imbalances in resource distribution rather than an antagonistic act that automatically canceled out future peaceful interactions. They killed, waged war, and dispossessed other societies, not necessarily to conquer, but to extract vengeance and to appease the spirits of their slain kin through dead enemy bodies. Capturing people from other ethnic groups did not necessarily signify a passage from freedom into slavery but a move from one kinship network to another. Even gift giving, the leitmotif of American Indian diplomacy, contained what appears at least on the surface a striking contradiction. Like most American Indians, Comanches considered gift exchanges a prerequisite for peaceful relations, yet they demanded one-sided gift distributions from Euro-American colonists, readily relying on violence if denied.

Like many other imperial powers, then, Comanches employed aggressive power politics without necessarily considering their actions as such. They built a hierarchical intersocietal system with policies that were often geared toward securing gifts, conciliation, reciprocal services, and new relatives from peoples whom they may have considered as much kin and allies as strangers and enemies. Indeed, the fact that Comanches did things differently may well have been one of their greatest political assets. Their ability to move nimbly from raiding to trading, from diplomacy to violence, and from enslaving to adoption not only left their colonial rivals confused; it often left them helpless. Western insistence upon uniformity in principle and action, a disposition that manifested itself most clearly in centralized state bureaucracies, rendered their policies slow and heavy-handed in comparison to Comanches' strategic fluidity. Euro-Americans compartmentalized foreign relations into distinct, often mutually exclusive categories and found it exceedingly difficult to deal with peoples who refused to recognize such categories. Unable to dissect, classify, and comprehend the Comanches and their actions, colonial agents were also unable to contain them.

Herein lay the ultimate paradox. While initially Comanches adjusted their traditions, behaviors, and even beliefs to accommodate the arrival of Europeans and their technologies, they later turned the tables on Europe's colonial expansion by simply refusing to change. By preserving the essentials of their traditional ways—and by expecting others to conform to their cultural order—they forced the colonists to adjust to a world that was foreign, uncontrollable, and, increasingly, unlivable.

The chapters that follow tell two intertwined stories. The first story examines cross-cultural relations on the southern plains, in the Southwest, and in northern Mexico from the perspective of Comanches, exploring how this nation rose to dominance and how it constantly reinvented itself to sustain external expansion. The other story looks at events from the standpoint of the Spaniards, Mexicans, Apaches, and others who variously competed and cooperated with the Comanches but ultimately faced marginalization and dispossession in the Comanche-controlled world. These two stories are woven into a single narrative thread, which in turn is embedded within the broader framework of Europe's overseas expansion. This contextual approach shows how local, regional, and global forces intersected to shape Comanche expansion and how Comanches both suffered and benefited from fluctuations and contingencies in the emerging transatlantic world. Comanche expansion lasted for a century and a half, but it was not a linear, uninterrupted process. There were surges, lulls, retreats, and regroupings, and the Comanche power complex went through repeated mutations, many of them epochs unto themselves. The chapters that follow are organized around those shifts and cycles, which both reflect and challenge the more traditional historical turning points in American history.

New Light on Felipe de Rábago y Terán

DONALD E. CHIPMAN AND LUIS LÓPEZ ELIZONDO

DONALD E. CHIPMAN IS EMERITUS PROFESSOR OF HISTORY AT THE UNIVERSITY OF NORTH TEXAS IN DENTON. HIS BOOKS INCLUDE *MOCTEZUMA'S CHILDREN: AZTEC ROYALTY UNDER SPANISH RULE, 1520–1700*, *SPANISH TEXAS, 1519–1821*, AND *NOTABLE MEN AND WOMEN OF SPANISH TEXAS*. INDEPENDENT SCHOLAR LUIS LÓPEZ ELIZONDO LIVES IN MEXICO.

IN THIS SELECTION, CHIPMAN AND ELIZONDO PROVIDE FRESH INFORMATION ON INFAMOUS SPANISH PRESIDIO OFFICER FELIPE DE RÁBAGO Y TERÁN.

★ ★

Felipe de Rábago y Terán commanded two presidios in Texas in the middle decades of the eighteenth century. His first captaincy was at San Francisco Xavier de Gigedo near the present-day town of Rockdale, where he assumed authority in early December 1751; his second was at San Luis de las Amarillas just outside modern-day Menard, where he arrived on September 30, 1760. During the nine-year interval between these postings, Rábago became the most notorious of all presidio commanders in Spanish colonial Texas. Indeed, for nearly eight of those years, following his possible involvement at San Xavier in the murder of a Franciscan priest

"New Light on Felipe de Rábago y Terán" by Donald E. Chipman and Luis López Elizondo from *Southwestern Historical Quarterly* Vol. CXI, No. 2, October, 2007. Used with permission of the Texas State Historical Association. The full version of this article with notes available in *Southwestern Historical Quarterly* III (October 2007): 161–181.

and a tailor from San Antonio, he was either under house arrest at Presidio Santa Rosa María del Sacramento in Coahuila or incarcerated in the public jail of the adjoining town. The circumstances that prompted the release and reassignment of a person of such questionable reputation to the largest military garrison in Texas are little short of remarkable.

The full story of Rábago, however, has not been told because historians, including the primary author of this article, who have written about Rábago have not had the benefit of documentation that has recently surfaced. Luis López Elizondo, an independent researcher and historian in Múzquiz, Coahuila, and Jerome Farrell, a British citizen and seven-times-removed nephew of Rábago, both have uncovered and generously shared new material relative to the captain's tainted career in Texas. The fresh evidence provided by these two researchers and Robert S. Weddle, the author of a recent book, makes this article possible.

Seldom do historians get the opportunity to set the record straight by correcting their own words in print. That we are occasionally able to do so reminds us that history is an ever changing discipline that must be revised in the light of new evidence, from which flows new conclusions.

During the late 1740s, Franciscan priests of the missionary college of Querétaro spearheaded efforts to found religious outposts some 130 miles northeast of San Antonio on the San Gabriel River. By July 1749, three missions collectively known as San Xavier sought to address the spiritual needs of Tonkawas, Akokisas, Bidais, Deadoses, and Cocos. Lacking, however, was a military garrison to provide protection against marauding Lipan Apaches. This lack of security encouraged desertions on the part of the neophytes and hampered religious proselytization by the friars.

To remedy the situation, on March 11, 1751, the viceroy of New Spain formally appointed Felipe de Rábago y Terán as captain of a not yet established presidio on the San Gabriel River. It is worth noting that Rábago's command had previously been approved at the court of Ferdinand VI on March 6, 1750. Don Felipe's specific orders included the recruitment of a maximum of fifty soldiers, as well as a number of civilian settlers to support the missionary enterprise.

Why Rábago? This is a question that has not been adequately addressed until now, but it will hardly surprise anyone to learn that family connections figured importantly in his appointment. Don Felipe was born on May 12, 1722, in the small mountain village of Tresabuela in Cantabrian province, northern Spain. He was the sixth and youngest offspring of Felipe de Rábago y Terán and Lorenza Roiz Fernández. Those familiar with modern Spanish surname conventions might surmise that this child would be named Felipe de Rábago (y) Roiz. Instead, he was given the exact surname of his father. While a bit unusual, it was far from rare in earlier times when surname usage varied considerably among brothers and sisters.

Capt. Felipe de Rábago, to distinguish him from his father with the same surname, benefited from a long line of ancestors associated with the town of Tresabuela. The senior Rábago and his father were both aldermen in the area's city council. Both are also listed as "hidalgo" in local census returns—meaning they were members of the lowest rung of Spanish nobility.

Don Felipe's grandfather and great grandfather were likewise *vecinos* (citizens) of Tresabuela. More important, a branch of the family in Tresabuela included the famous Jesuit priest Francisco de Rábago y Noriega who became the confessor of King Ferdinand VI (1746–1759). In the mid-1700s fray Francisco, probably a distant cousin of don Felipe, wielded considerable political influence at the Spanish court.

Captain Rábago also had family connections in Mexico City. His eldest brother, José de Rábago, was a knight of Santiago and chief accountant of the Royal Mint. The captain, himself, had acquired substantial wealth in trade between Mexico City and Zacatecas. A combination of family connections and personal wealth made Rábago a seemingly ideal appointment as commander of a presidio in a poor, distant province on the northern frontier of New Spain. However, family background and money did not guarantee character, which was singularly lacking in the young captain. As for judgment, during his first command in Texas, Governor Jacinto de Barrios y Jáuregui (1751–1759) cryptically remarked of Rábago that he possessed less of it than money.

Since Rábago was especially enjoined to cooperate with the Franciscan priests in Christianizing and Hispanicizing Indians at the mission sites on the San Gabriel River, his performance to that end would be extraordinarily lax. En route to his command, he made extended stopovers in Monclova and San Antonio. At those locales he made it clear that he had already developed an intense dislike for mission padres.

In accord with his instruction to enlist as many as fifty soldiers and a few settlers for his command, Rábago recruited Juan José Ceballos, a tailor in San Antonio. Soon after, the young captain began intimate relations with Ceballos's wife, a liaison that continued on the march to the missions. At the Cíbolo River, the cuckolded husband protested the captain's conduct and found himself in chains, charged with threatening the commander of the expedition.

On reaching the San Xavier missions, Rábago stated that his instructions from the viceroy required one of the missionaries there to serve as chaplain of the new garrison. Appointed in that capacity by his religious superior in San Antonio was fray Miguel Pinilla of Mission Nuestra Señora de la Candelaria. Pinilla then sought to end the illicit affair between Rábago and Ceballos's wife by asking the former to send the woman back to San Antonio. Instead of complying with the chaplain's request, Rábago apparently blamed the maltreated husband for forcing the issue. He had Ceballos shackled against the wall of his cell, placed a cot before him, and ravished the man's wife in his presence.

By late December 1751, Rábago had selected a site for Presidio San Xavier de Gigedo and had begun construction of the garrison. During Christmas Eve festivities, he learned that Ceballos had broken free of his fetters and fled to Mission Candelaria where he sought refuge in its chapel. On the following day, Rábago rode his horse into the chapel, apprehended the unfortunate Ceballos, returned him to confinement, and cuffed him about for good measure.

Fray Pinilla was outraged, pointing out that on Christmas—one of the most scared days of the Christian calendar—Rábago had brazenly violated an ecclesiastical sanctuary. The chaplain demanded that Ceballos be returned to the mission and that Rábago apologize for his actions. On December 27, Rábago returned the unfortunate settler but offered no apology. From that day forward, Pinilla and Rábago would be locked in a contest of wills. And it would not end well.

Both men complained about each other in letters written to officials in Béxar. Captain Rábago asked that fray Pinilla be removed as chaplain. The request was denied by his superior. Fray Pinilla joined fellow priests at San Xavier in drafting a litany of complaints about unsympathetic governors and troublesome civilians in Texas who had repeatedly undermined their efforts and those of their former co-religionists to save the souls of Indian neophytes. They nevertheless charged that all "impostures," "craftiness," and "machinations" of past administrators and settlers had been "outdone by the malice of this man [Rábago]."

With their captain as role model, soldiers at the presidio, most of whom were separated from their families, began intimate relations with Indian women at the three missions. In the words of historian fray Juan Agustín Morfi, "the neophytes saw themselves deprived of their wives and daughters by the soldiers, oppressed by excessive labor, insulted every moment of the day, and denied the right to voice their misfortune."

Some of the more Christianized Indian women sought expiation of their carnal sins in the confessional, and as a result evidence mounted of gross misconduct by soldiers at the presidio. On February 19, 1752, an astonished Rábago and his entire command found themselves excommunicated by decree of fray Miguel Pinilla. This initially served only to worsen animosities between the chaplain and the presidials. The latter reacted by tearing up the decree and burning it. But on reflection, the soldiers soon worried about the fate of their souls. One by one they begged forgiveness, and by March 1, 1752, all had received sacramental penance, granted by fray José Ganzábal.

When first apprised of the situation at San Xavier, authorities in Mexico City expressed serious concerns over the ban. The military adviser to the viceroy voiced sympathy for poor ignorant soldiers stationed 430 leagues from the capital. He thought their irreverence did not deserve "the ultimate knife and penalty of the church." The viceroy's legal adviser opined that if the mission Indians learned the severity of the penalty, which carried the certainty of Spaniards burning in their version of hell, they would think "the captain crazy and might kill him."

This incident of excommunication passed, but it left bitter resentments in its wake, especially with Rábago and the soldiers. Then in late spring 1752, perhaps the most infamous, certainly the most controversial, double murder in Texas colonial history occurred at one of the San Xavier missions. The victims were fray José Ganzábal and the luckless tailor Juan José Ceballos. It appears that the prime target, chaplain Miguel Pinilla, escaped death because of where he was seated at a table during the men's evening meal and darkness that perhaps spoiled the aim of assassins.

At just before nine o'clock on the night of May 11, 1752, Ceballos and the two priests sat down for supper at Mission Nuestra Señora de la Candelaria. The former Béxar tailor had been granted permanent refuge at the mission after Rábago returned him there on the previous December 27.

And it will be remembered that both priests had been involved with the excommunication of the captain and soldiers of the presidio. The night was warm, and the door of a small cell had been opened to catch a cooling breeze. A single candle lighted the interior of the cubicle. Ceballos was seated with his back to the portal; to his right sat fray Ganzábal; while opposite Ceballos and farthest from the door was fray Pinilla.

The quiet of the evening was shattered by the blast of a Spanish musket, its charge penetrating Ceballos's chest cavity and killing him instantly. Fray Ganzábal grabbed the candle, rushed to the door of the cell, and peered into the darkness. At that very instant a Coco Indian arrow struck the padre in the left armpit and penetrated his heart. As the mortally wounded priest sank to the floor, the candle blew out, pitching the cubicle into darkness. A second shot fired from a musket failed to find fray Pinilla, its intended victim.

There followed almost eight years of charges and countercharges. The extensive legal record, as presented by the prosecution and defense, is filled with contradictory testimony and evidence. The documentation also contains some of the more arcane Spanish one is likely to encounter in reading eighteenth-century materials. Deriving accurate translations of the proceedings has been greatly facilitated by Luis López Elizondo.

Given the circumstances that surround the murders at Mission Candelaria, the question of the complicity of Captain Rábago, charged as he was to provide security for the mission outposts, quickly arose. His illicit relations with Ceballos's wife and his rough handling of her husband, as well as his heated disputes with fray Pinilla, provided ample motive for his involvement in foul play. However, he was not one of the assassins. On the fateful night of the murders and at the precise moment of their occurrence, Rábago had an ironclad alibi. Roused from bed at the presidio on hearing the loud reports of firearms, the captain gathered a few men, mounted a horse, and dashed off to Mission Candelaria. There he discovered the bodies of Ceballos and Ganzábal.

On May 15 Rábago sent an account of the murders to the viceroy. Recognizing that he might well be held responsible if soldiers under his command were the perpetrators, the captain placed full complicity on the Coco Indians. In doing so, he stressed the intractable nature of these natives and their refusal to accept conversion to "our holy faith." The presidio captain, in a self-serving manner, insisted that only the clatter of his horse's hooves and his prompt response had kept the Cocos from killing all of the priests and their neophytes. The darkness of night, however, had prevented him from immediately pursuing the evildoers. He next contended that these very Indians, who belonged to a nation infamous for the commission of murder and robbery, had many years ago been responsible for the death of Capt. Domingo Ramón at La Bahía del Espirítu Santo. Lastly, Rábago begged permission from the viceroy to wage a war of extermination against the Cocos. The request was denied, but the possible involvement of these Indians in the slaying of Ceballos and Ganzábal is highly questionable.

Ten days before the assassinations, the Coco Indians had deserted Mission Candelaria en masse. On May 1 two Cocos entered the presidio armed with bows and arrows. Rábago ordered the Indians seized, disarmed, and beaten. Fearing further reprisals, the Indians fled to the countryside on that very night. Rábago claimed that he sent out soldiers to track the Indians and return them to the mission, but the troopers failed to find any of them.

Prior to their exodus, the Cocos also had good reasons to dislike Juan José Ceballos. The Candelaria resident came upon a member of the nation who without authorization had killed a cow at the mission and was in the process of skinning it. Ceballos castigated the Indian and tried to seize the meat for proper distribution and apportionment. The Coco then engaged in a heated dispute with the tailor and called on fellow Indians to assist him in resisting the seizure. A crowd soon gathered around Ceballos, setting off a melee of shouting, shoving, and protesting natives. To defend himself, Ceballos struck one of the Indians a strong blow with the handle of his knife. Far from settling the matter, this blow led to still more Indians descending on the lone Spaniard. To control them, Ceballos fired his musket, and the ball struck the thigh of a Coco chieftain. This temporarily quieted the Indians, and the dispute passed without further violence. Nevertheless, this incident added fuel to reports of misbehavior among the Cocos, and it increased their dislike for the missionaries and their permanent resident, Ceballos.

Other suspects in the double murder were five soldiers at the presidio and their Indian ally, Andrés—a young Hispanicized Indian of the Sayopín nation. Andrés and his Christianized wife, Luisa, had been joined in marriage by fray José Ganzábal at Mission Candelaria. The young bride, however, soon caught the lustful eye of Martín Gutiérrez, a soldier at the presidio. With the concurrence of Andrés, Gutiérrez arranged for sexual favors from Luisa in exchange for a horse loaned to her husband for "three moons."

It seems that this unholy arrangement was revealed to fray Ganzábal in the confessional. Whether the priest broke the seal of penitential secrecy is uncertain, but it is likely that fray Ganzábal strongly rebuked Luisa for her infidelity. She in turn probably informed her husband and Gutiérrez that Ganzábal was aware of their arrangement. What is absolutely certain, as revealed in the inquest to the murders, is that Gutiérrez became a prime suspect in the double slayings of May 11, 1752.

The only alleged eyewitness account of the murders came from the Sayopín Indian Andrés, employed at Mission Candelaria as a ditchdigger. He placed the blame on Martín Gutiérrez, Tomás Yruegas, Joseph Miguel de Sosa, Manuel Carrillo, Juan José Sánchez (alias Marín), and eventually himself. While hunting turkeys on the afternoon of May 11, Andrés encountered the five presidials along Brushy Creek, a source of water for the missions and the garrison. Two of the men were armed with muskets; the other two, with bows and arrows. The bows and arrows appear to have been the very weapons that had been seized by Captain Rábago at the presidio on May 1.

When Andrés came upon the soldiers, they lay in ambush, hoping to kill fray Pinilla as he walked to his favorite fishing hole. Their plans changed when the padre failed to appear. The men then decided to wait until nightfall. Under the cover of darkness, they would have a good opportunity to kill the two priests and Ceballos at Mission Candelaria. The soldiers then invited Andrés, who had far greater familiarity with bow and arrow, as well as his own reasons to dislike fray Ganzábal, to join them, and he agreed to do so.

The soldiers, disguised as Indians under skins of buffalo and deer, approached the mission at dusk. Andrés and four Spaniards remained hidden in a small creek bottom, while Gutiérrez crept forward as scout. Through the open door of a small room, he observed that the three men had just sat down to eat. Gutiérrez then returned to his companions and informed them that the time for action was at hand. According to Andrés, Gutiérrez fired the fatal ball into the back of Ceballos; and as fray Ganzábal rushed to the door of the cubicle and peered into the night, the Indian himself let fly the arrow that pierced the padre's heart. Fearful of disclosure if they took time to seek out fray Pinilla, the assassins may have fired the second shot into the air or into the darkened cell. Andrés, soon mounted on horseback and accompanied by his wife, set out immediately for San Antonio; the soldiers returned to the presidio.

Although Rábago persisted in his claims that the Coco Indians were the actual assassins, there are good reasons to question his assertion. First, it is generally accepted that the Cocos had little or no experience with Spanish firearms, nor did they have access to them. If that was indeed the case, how did they acquire Spanish muskets, how did they learn to load these weapons, and how did they learn to fire at least one of them with accuracy? Second, by Rábago's own admission, his soldiers could not find any of the Coco Indians after they had fled the mission ten days prior to the murders. Finally, there is the eyewitness account of the Indian Andrés who would soon confess that he had shot the arrow that pierced fray Ganzábal's heart.

It took Andrés and his wife Luisa several days to reach Béxar. Shortly after their arrival, they were summoned to testify in an investigation into the double murders, conducted by Captain Toribio de Urrutia. Initially, Andrés claimed that he and Luisa had left Mission Candelaria two days prior to the slayings. Luisa, in her deposition, identified herself with the aid of a translator as a member of the Orejona (Orejón) nation and supported her husband's testimony. According to her, she and Andrés shared food and drank chocolate with the two priests, leaving them in good health (*sano*) before setting out on foot for San Antonio. Later, the couple came upon other Indians who had caught two horses. Andrés bargained for one of the mounts, which they then rode to Béxar.

Unfamiliar with Spanish legal proceedings, Andrés apparently entrapped himself by giving precise testimony relating to the murders, including the names of five Spanish co-assassins. He also related that Ceballos had been shot with a musket and that Ganzábal had been felled by an arrow. When asked how he knew this, since he claimed to have departed Mission Candelaria two days prior to the murders, Andrés then confessed that he had killed the priest.

There was no admission of guilt by the accused soldiers, and certainly none from Capt. Felipe de Rábago. Nonetheless, Spanish officials initially concluded that overwhelming circumstantial evidence pointed to their complicity. The six of them were removed from the San Xavier presidio and in late 1752 sent off to house arrest at Presidio Santa Rosa María del Sacramento in Coahuila, or in some cases to incarceration in cells at the nearby town. Remarkably, Rábago, although under a legal cloud, received orders to take control (*posesión*) of the Sacramento presidio. And, he managed to gain custody of Andrés and Luisa, who remained under his control for the better part of eight years!

A successor of Felipe de Rábago as captain of the San Xavier presidio was Pedro de Rábago y Terán, then governor of Coahuila and captain of Presidio Santa Rosa in Monclova. Historians have consistently labeled this man as don Felipe's uncle—no doubt because of the similarity of their names, and because don Pedro was a considerably older man. The relationship between the two men is now affirmed to have been nephew/uncle, but as commonly believed don Felipe's father did not have a brother named Pedro.

Shortly after Felipe de Rábago and the five accused soldier-assassins began their confinement in Coahuila, deteriorating conditions at the San Xavier missions doomed the entire enterprise. The ranks of the six Franciscans assigned to the area had temporarily shrunk to just one—murder and a death from natural causes reduced their number to four; of those remaining, three were summoned to San Antonio to report on the deaths of Ganzábal and Ceballos. Although three priests were soon dispatched to San Xavier to bolster the mission undertaking there, lack of rainfall in 1753 caused the San Gabriel River to recede into stagnant pools. Both soldiers and padres sought permission from the viceroy to relocate the missions and the presidio to a more favorable location, but two years of petitions failed to garner official sanction to abandon the site.

In late summer 1755, the padres and captain of the presidio acted on their own and moved all operations at San Xavier to the banks of the San Marcos River. That venture quickly failed, in large part because of an epidemic that struck the two relocated missions. It is generally believed that this contagion also claimed the life of Pedro de Rábago. Instead, there is reliable evidence that he died at his post in Monclova in March 1756.

Following the death of Pedro de Rábago, all remaining assets on the San Marcos River were moved south to the Guadalupe in that same year. At this locale, two missions and a presidio enjoyed a brief existence. They, however, were so close to San Antonio's five missions and its presidio that their continuation made little sense. Presidio San Xavier de Gigedo ceased to exist when its soldiers and equipment were moved to Béxar. Within two years all remnants of this garrison were relocated to a new presidio with a different name on the San Saba River. These events would figure tangentially in the eventual return of Felipe de Rábago y Terán to the Texas scene. The remaining missions on the Guadalupe River would also help Rábago gain his freedom but not for another three years.

Near the end of the San Xavier enterprise, in 1754 fray Alonso Giraldo de Terreros founded the first Franciscan mission for Eastern Apache Indians to the west of Presidio San Juan Bautista. Less than a year later, the Apache neophytes rebelled, burned the mission, and fled en masse. Undaunted, the Franciscans insisted that the mission had failed because it was located too far south from the center of Apachería.

Dovetailing with the Franciscans' continuing desire to establish another mission for the Apaches were reports of mineral wealth near the Pedernales, Llano, and San Saba Rivers, northwest of San Antonio. Three reconnaissance expeditions to the region in the mid-1750s served only to confirm the existence of an enormous mound of hematite. The last of these explorations in 1756, however, brought back information gleaned from Apaches who alleged that a mountain of silver lay just a few days' journey to the north.

So, a combination of religious zeal and the lure of wealth served as a powerful magnet that motivated Spaniards to move a mission on the Guadalupe River to a site about four miles east of modern-day Menard. This second Franciscan mission for the Apaches would end in tragedy and death on March 16, 1758. Mounted enemies of the Apaches, including hundreds of Taovayas (Wichitas), Comanches, Bidais, Tejas, and Tonkawas, descended on Mission Santa Cruz de San Sabá, killing two priests and eight civilians and soldiers, as well as burning all buildings to the ground. Nevertheless, the destruction of this mission and the Spanish punitive expedition to the Red River that followed in 1759 also served to free Felipe de Rábago y Terán.

Just how the Red River campaign of Diego Ortiz Parrilla and its aftermath helped resurrect the career of Felipe de Rábago has never been clearly understood until now. Thanks to a new book by Robert S. Weddle, with translations by Carol Lipscomb, the interconnectedness of these events becomes crystal clear. While in Spain in 1979, Bob Weddle, arguably the dean of Texas colonial historians, found a diary of the Ortiz Parrilla expedition in a Madrid library. Weddle photocopied the holographic account, brought it to Texas, and filed it away in his personal library for two decades. But he did not dismiss it from his thoughts. While editing entries and planning others for the *New Handbook of Texas* with Chipman, he mentioned the diary. It so happened that Carol Lipscomb, a doctoral student in history at the University of North Texas, had begun a dissertation topic that addressed the relationship of Comanche Indians with Spaniards during the colonial, Mexican, and revolutionary periods of Texas history. Weddle, when apprised of her work, generously loaned the photocopied diary to Lipscomb, who translated it into English and used it as a primary source in her dissertation. This subsequently led to a major collaborative effort by the two, resulting in a 2007 publication.

In *After the Massacre*, the author points out that among Texas historians it is a well-accepted article of faith that the 1759 Red River campaign of Col. Diego Ortiz Parrilla ended in a complete rout of Spanish troops and the abandonment of several pieces of artillery. The origins of those conclusions, as Weddle persuasively argues, may be initially traced to the writings of Antonio Bonilla in 1772 and their continuation in the later works of fray Juan Agustín Morfi, Hubert H. Bancroft, William E. Dunn, and Lesley Byrd Simpson.

The campaign diary of Juan Ángel de Oyarzún casts a very different light on the actual events of the 1759 Red River campaign. Weddle questions whether the battle can even be judged a Spanish defeat at all. Rather, it probably moved the Taovayas and other Wichita groups to begin peace initiatives with the Spaniards. True, Spanish losses were significant, but the Indians suffered greater ones. And finally, there is no evidence of the Indians immediately celebrating victory—rather, there followed weeping and wailing for their killed and injured. How, then, has the historical record been distorted for so long?

Weddle carefully traces the origins of what he labels the "bad press" given the Ortiz Parrilla campaign to none other than the malicious and slanderous undertakings of Felipe de Rábago y Terán! Bitter over his nearly eight years of confinement in Coahuila, seething over his former garrison being incorporated into that of San Sabá, and determined to use any means possible to obtain his freedom, Rábago was apparently undeterred by a single scruple. He had to destroy Ortiz Parrilla's reputation to resurrect his own. His first priority, however, was to get out of jail;

his second was to travel to Mexico City and gain an audience with the viceroy; his third was to clear himself and those accused with him of complicity in the San Xavier murders; and his fourth was to use his considerable personal wealth and possibly family influence to be restored to command in Texas—this time as Ortiz Parrilla's successor at the San Sabá presidio.

Ortiz Parrilla's difficulties with the Red River campaign of 1759 had begun when he tried to recruit soldiers for the venture. Initially, Ortiz Parrilla asked for aid from presidios in northern Mexico in 1758, but it was denied because those garrisons feared for their own safety. However, a brazen attack by Indians of the north on the San Sabá horse herd on March 30, 1759, resulting in the death of nineteen soldier-herdsmen and the loss of nearly 700 horses and pack mules, brought extreme pressure from Mexico City on garrison commanders in northern New Spain. This forced them reluctantly to give up members of their troop. With aid from some of these presidios, including Santa Rosa María del Sacramento in Coahuila, Ortiz Parrilla finally assembled a force of more than five hundred men. These included presidials, militiamen, Indian auxiliaries from Mexico, mission Indians, and Apaches.

After the pitched battle on the Red River, Ortiz Parrilla and his troop returned to San Sabá on October 25, 1759. Within days the commander summoned his officers and sought to persuade them to launch a new campaign against all Indians who were friendly toward or allied with the Taovayas and other Wichitas. For a variety of reasons, including approaching winter weather and the scarcity of forage for the horses, the officers demurred. Disappointed, Ortiz Parrilla appointed an officer in charge at San Sabá and led the bulk of his recruits to San Antonio where they were disbanded.

On reaching Béxar, Ortiz Parrilla must have been exasperated by rumors that had surfaced about the performance of his command during the recent campaign. As Weddle points out, a good bit of the problem may initially be attributed to the commander's own doing. Two days after the battle, Ortiz Parrilla sent Indian runners to San Antonio with a report of it. The resulting garbled account of the engagement and its aftermath, which was put in writing by fray Mariano de los Dolores and forwarded to Presidio San Juan Bautista, greatly exaggerated the extent of the colonel's losses. Specifically, it was reported that a bloody battle had been fought in a deep wood, and resumed later on a plain, which resulted in "the impossibility of counting the dead because so many men had fled." The friar concluded by writing, "The evident danger consists of losing this province."

The Oyarzún diary confirms that soldiers from Santa Rosa María del Sacramento were recruited for the Red River campaign and discharged at San Antonio to return there. With them came a sense that both San Sabá and San Antonio were threatened by Indians stirred to anger by the Red River campaign. Regardless of how this information reached Felipe de Rábago, whether from Presidio San Juan Bautista or from the returning presidials, he used the somewhat panicky aftermath of the Ortiz Parrilla expedition to gain his freedom.

Rábago took action to that end in late 1759. Posted in his behalf by Gabriel Gutiérrez de Terán, likely a relative, was a 4,000 peso bond (*fianza*). This permitted Rábago to leave confinement and travel to Mexico City for an audience with the viceroy. In his deposition, Rábago complained of the grave afflictions and illnesses that he had suffered while incarcerated. He especially lashed out at the proceedings, which had asserted his complicity in the homicides at Mission Candelaria—when in fact the Coco Indians had been the actual perpetrators.

Rábago also alleged unfairness in the 1752 inquests into the homicides, especially the inquest conducted in San Antonio by Capt. Toribio Urrutia. He contended that ample evidence of his own innocence had been ignored, because his Franciscan enemies had pressured Urrutia into accepting suborned testimony against him and the five soldiers. The incarcerated captain was particularly outraged over the badgering of Andrés, which resulted in his perjuring himself by confessing that he had killed fray Ganzábal. As mentioned earlier, Andrés had remained in close proximity with Rábago for some eight years, and it just so happened that prior to don Felipe's deposition, the Sayopín Indian had conveniently recanted his confession.

In placing the blame for the homicides on the Coco Indians, Rábago obviously had the distinct advantage of there being no Indians present to defend themselves. He then sought to prove that Andrés and the five soldier-suspects could not possibly be the actual perpetrators. All had alibis that placed them either in the company of other Spaniards at the time of the homicides, or they were verified to have been some distance away from the crime scene at around 9 P.M. on May 11, 1752—making it impossible for them to have been culpable. Accordingly, in the same proceeding that allowed Rábago to leave confinement and travel to Mexico City, he set forth a strong argument for dismissal of all charges against the other suspects. That he was completely successful may stretch the credulity of readers, but in freeing himself and the others, Rábago would later tarnish the reputation of Diego Ortiz Parrilla, a competent military commander and presidio captain.

There is little doubt that Ortiz Parrilla saw his Red River campaign as a success, accomplished against tremendous odds. However, panic had ensued at Béxar, based in large part on the misconstrued message carried there by Indian runners. Priests in San Antonio asked that additional soldiers be immediately assigned to San Antonio de Béxar to protect against a feared attack by "the barbarous enemy nations of the North . . . recently offended and castigated by our arms."

Ortiz Parrilla sought to defend his performance in the Red River campaign by sending lengthy reports to the viceroy in Mexico City. In them he accurately described the situation in Texas. Its presidios had soldiers of poor quality, its security was threatened by increasing foreign influence on the northern tribes from the French and English, and its settlers faced new dangers from the Indians' access to firearms. He also asked that he be retained as commander of Presidio San Luis de las Amarillas, arguing that he was best able to deal with the dire circumstances that faced the province. It was not to be. While Ortiz Parrilla relied on letters and reports to Mexico City, Felipe de Rábago gained the ear of the viceroy.

On June 7, 1760, Interim Viceroy Francisco Caxigal de la Vega handed down a definitive sentence in response to Felipe de Rabago's deposition of the previous year. Three of the accused—Felipe de Rábago, Tomás Yruegas, and the Indian Andrés—received a most welcome verdict of innocence.

In response to recommendations made by the *fiscal* (legal adviser to the viceroy), "to the end of establishing the veracity and certitude of the depositions made by the Indian Andrés and his wife," the viceroy concluded it was not possible "that the said Indian could have been implicated in the deaths." After encountering the soldiers along Las Ánimas Creek on the very day of the murders, Andrés and his wife "then slept that same night farther on at the place called Garrapatas [ticks]." Therefore, this "makes null and void the charges" against him.

As to the confession of Andrés, supported by his wife's testimony, that he had fired the arrow that killed fray José de Ganzábal, the viceroy unleashed a torrent of invective against those who had interrogated them. "The fervor [*pasión*] with which the judges proceeded, pressuring the accused by extraordinary means into making a confession, grilling them with accusatory questions, and committing the grave offense of trying to pressure the witnesses in changing their testimonies to suit themselves—the truth of which is made manifest in the judicial charges instituted . . . , which have resulted in plenary charges." The viceroy concluded by stating categorically "that the true perpetrators had been Coco Indians."

The viceroy next addressed the alleged complicity of Felipe de Rábago: "[Since] Captain don Felipe de Rábago had been accused by circumstantial evidence and without plenary proof in the charges, this ought not to have resulted in either capital or corporal punishment of him." Continuing, the viceroy stated: "One does not find fundamental reasons why the said captain should not be exonerated of guilt, which has the effect of releasing him from incarceration, under the surety provided by don Gabriel Gutiérrez de Terán."

Finally, the viceroy summarily dismissed charges against the accused soldiers, stating:

> When one has considered all of the evidence that has mounted against the esteemed accused, as it manifests itself, not only were they not complicitous, but also that they could not have committed [the murders] at the mission Candelaria at that hour and time in which the deaths occurred, given the distance [from the mission] that they found themselves and in which they remained at the time, there can be no doubt that justice requires definitive absolution of crimes, with the conclusion that no further charges of the aforementioned homicides be made against Captain Rábago, Sergeant Sosa, Yruegas, and the Indian Andrés.

That Felipe de Rábago emerged with a clean slate from this legal proceeding, there can be no doubt. Viceroy Caxigal de la Vega ordered that he be released from prison and "rightfully absolved of all offenses, charges, damages, and loss of reputation as used against him." Furthermore, he was to "be restored to the employee of his majesty and transferred to the Río de San Sabá where command of his company shall be handed over to him."

Reinstating Felipe de Rábago to his "former" command was an exercise in tortuous reasoning on the part of the viceroy and his advisers, since Presidio San Xavier de Gigedo had ceased to exist some time ago. As mentioned, all remnants of it had been incorporated into the garrison on the San Saba River. Appointing Rábago to command at San Luis de las Amarillas meant removing its captain, Diego Ortiz Parrilla. When the colonel learned of Caxigal de la Vega's verdict, he was in Mexico City; and he immediately sought an audience with the viceroy.

Because he had expected to remain in command at San Sabá, Ortiz Parrilla failed to take along his personal belongings when he set out for the capital. Unfortunately, he would never again see those possessions. But this was minor compared to the potential loss of his reputation and blow to his pride. Refusing to beg, he informed Viceroy Caxigal that he lamented "the conditions to which this resolution reduced me." Caxigal was sympathetic, and he told Ortiz Parrilla that he would order Rábago to do what was right in the matter.

In compliance with the viceroy's orders, Rábago paid a visit to Ortiz Parrilla's residence on the following day. The newly appointed captain offered to look after Ortiz Parrilla's personal effects at San Sabá as though they were his own, but it was an empty promise. In the words of Robert S. Weddle: "The seasoned military commander . . . succumbed to the blandishments of an inveterate con man. As for Rábago, he soon would be on the frontier, out of the viceroy's reach, as well as Ortiz Parrilla's."

Felipe de Rábago was not content with his restored reputation and appointment as commander of the largest military garrison in Texas. He not only failed to look after Ortiz Parrilla's personal effects, as he had promised to do, but launched a "smear campaign" aimed at destroying the reputation of his predecessor in command. Weddle offers convincing arguments of Rábago's success in the latter. He also points to Antonio de Bonilla's historical summary of the Texas province to 1772 as the first to articulate this impression, as well as present a distorted view of the Red River campaign.

Rábago arrived at the San Sabá presidio in late September 1760 and completed two troop inspections before the end of the following month. Assembled before him was a total force of ninety-seven men. Two of his senior officers were absent in San Antonio, but the remaining troopers were all well equipped with arms and tack. Most of the soldiers also had multiple mounts, likewise reflecting well on Ortiz Parrilla's former command. This was in stark contrast to a similar inspection conducted six years into Rábago's captaincy. At that time, the San Sabá commander recorded ninety-nine presidials. His commissioned and noncommissioned officers numbered sixteen. The remaining eighty-three soldiers ranged from those with five years and several months of experience to ten with none. Their ages varied from fifty-eight to twenty-one. Rábago noted that most of his troopers lacked food, clothing, and arms.

Overall, Rábago's second command in Texas drew heated opposition from the friars in the province, who continued to hold him responsible for the death of one of their own at San Xavier—never mind that the official verdict of the viceroy had affirmed the former captain's innocence. Nonetheless, Rábago's apparent enthusiasm for promoting missions for the Lipan Apaches left the friars somewhat puzzled. One of his harshest critics, Fray Juan Agustín Morfi, opined that his actions were perhaps an attempt "to eradicate the perverse memory of his conduct, or . . . because he wished to make amends to religion for the damages he had occasioned as a result of his previous scandals."

On reflection, Morfi probably gave too much credit to Rábago. His weakening of the San Sabá presidio by drawing off troops to guard two satellite missions for Lipan Apaches, which he founded without authorization on the upper Nueces River in present-day Real County, underscores his bad judgment. He chose to believe that the Lipans were sincere in their quest for Christianization, when ample evidence suggested otherwise. The Apaches were almost exclusively interested in using the Spanish to protect them from their powerful and hated enemies, the Comanches and Taovayas. However perfidious the Apaches were in using this approach, it was not at all different from the Spaniards who were skilled in playing off one Indian group against another—a constant from the conquest of Mexico to the end of the Spanish colonial era in the Americas.

In the first five years of Felipe de Rábago's command at San Sabá, he spent more than twelve thousand pesos of his own money on provisions, clothing, and livestock for the presidio and the two missions to the south. But even the stone walls of Presidio San Luis de Amarillas, constructed by Rábago, came under siege by Comanches and Taovayas for as long as two months, and "the continuous state of warfare went on for years."

Rábago's pleas for assistance from Mexico City fell on deaf ears, especially after the 1763 Peace of Paris when he could no longer play on fears of the French. When the Marqués de Rubí carried out his tour of inspection at San Sabá in August 1767, he noted that the largest military garrison in Texas had been reduced to a "beggarly existence." He issued a devastating assessment of the presidio by likening its effectiveness against Indian attacks to that of a ship "anchored in mid-Atlantic . . . [to prevent] foreign trade with America."

Following the Rubí inspection, attacks on San Sabá began anew. Although the Indians were never able to force their way beyond the stone walls of the presidio, they destroyed spring crops in 1768, perhaps contributing to an outbreak of scurvy and a growing mutinous attitude among the presidials.

Without authorization, Rábago left his command and traveled toward Mexico City. Until recently, it has been widely believed that he never reached his destination. But reports of his probable death at San Luis Potosí have proved erroneous. Again, thanks to new documentation provided by Jerome Farrell, something of an amazing paragraph, if not chapter, in the life of Felipe de Rábago has come to light.

In 1768 Rábago became a knight in the Order of Santiago. As mentioned, his brother as head of the Royal Mint in Mexico City had previously been knighted in the same order. It also suggests that his relative in Spain, who was the royal confessor to King Ferdinand VI, might have exerted some influence in don Felipe's acceptance into knighthood. It was required procedure for all prospective members of Spain's military orders to submit proof of their worthiness to the title of Caballero. Rábago's Prueba de Caballero contains his place and date of birth, as well as information on his immediate and extended family.

Finally, because of his familial interest in Felipe de Rábago, Jerome Farrell has unearthed the will of Francisco Fernández de Rábago, a nephew of don Felipe, drawn up in Madrid in September 1801. In it Fernández de Rábago stated that his uncle died in Mexico City in 1770. This will also contains a tantalizing suggestion that Felipe de Rábago left a last testament, perhaps filed away somewhere in a Mexico City archive. Specifically, there is mention of a *mayorazgo* (entailed estate) set up in Cádiz, close to the church of San Agustín, which remained in the Rábago families for generations. The entailed estate was ordered founded (*mandó fundar*) by don Felipe de Rábago y Terán. Farrell has confirmed that Rábago, who apparently did not marry and never seemed short of money, sent fifty thousand pesos to his sister, María, in Spain, which she used to establish the Cádiz *mayorazgo*.

What then is the new light cast on the life and career of Felipe de Rábago y Terán in this article? Thanks to the research of Jerome Farrell, Luis López Elizondo, and Robert Weddle, buttressed by Carol Lipscomb's translations, we have a better understanding of how such a dissolute person twice received appointment as a presidio commander in Texas in the middle decades of the 1700s. Rábago's personal wealth and the likelihood of family influence in both Spain and Mexico helped secure his first posting at San Francisco Xavier de Gigedo on the San Gabriel River. Following the double murders committed at a San Xavier mission in May 1752, circumstantial evidence of Rábago's possible complicity in them led to his removal of command in Texas and extended confinement in Coahuila. But even under a legal cloud for the better part of eight years, during much of that time, Rábago enjoyed the title of captain of the presidio where he was technically under house arrest. Again, this suggests family connections that ameliorated the circumstances of his sentence. And while not previously mentioned, in 1759 when Rábago was able to post bond that would permit him to travel to Mexico City, his incarceration in a public jail may well have resulted from another illicit affair with the wife of a soldier—this time at Santa Rosa María del Sacramento.

The definitive sentence of the viceroy in Mexico City regarding the murders at San Xavier is a remarkable indictment of the officials who had conducted the inquest at Béxar in 1752. This, too, suggests that Rábago had capital with Spanish officials. His reassignment to his "former command" of a presidio that no longer existed is likewise a curious legal conundrum.

The contributions of Weddle and Lipscomb's book explain how an initially garbled account of the Red River campaign of Ortiz Parrilla served as a springboard for Rábago's release from jail and his reassignment in Texas. They then document how Rábago cleverly damaged the reputation of his predecessor at San Sabá to his own advantage, as well as how that deliberate smear campaign distorted the actual events of 1759. It is unfortunate that Rábago's vindictiveness then entered the mainstream of historical writing on the subject where it has remained for far too long. Finally, it is noteworthy that Rábago left his post at San Sabá without permission in 1768 and yet managed to receive appointment as a caballero of the Order of Santiago in that same year.

That said, there is nothing in this new information that suggests a more favorable valedictory on the life and career of Felipe de Rábago—indeed, this new research serves only to further besmirch the man. If he had redeeming qualities, they have failed to emerge from available evidence.

Los Tejanos:

Mexican Texans in the Revolution

PAUL D. LACK

PAUL D. LACK IS EXECUTIVE VICE PRESIDENT FOR ACADEMIC AFFAIRS AND DEAN AT STEVENSON UNIVERSITY IN MARYLAND. PRIOR TO ACCEPTING THIS POSITION, HE TAUGHT HISTORY AT MCMURRY UNIVERSITY IN ABILENE, TEXAS. DR. LACK AUTHORED THE PIONEERING STUDY, *THE TEXAS REVOLUTIONARY EXPERIENCE: A POLITICAL AND SOCIAL HISTORY, 1835–1836.*

IN 1835, MORE THAN 4,000 TEJANOS LIVED IN TEXAS. THEY RESIDED CHIEFLY IN FOUR SETTLEMENTS: NACOGDOCHES, VICTORIA, BEXAR, AND GOLIAD. THE TEXAS REVOLUTION OF 1835–1836 DIVIDED MEXICAN TEXANS AND BROUGHT THEM SUBSTANTIAL HARDSHIP. SOME TEJANOS REMAINED NEUTRAL WHILE OTHERS SUPPORTED MEXICO. MANY TEJANOS, HOWEVER, ACTIVELY AIDED THE TEXIAN CAUSE, INCLUDING SUCH MEN AS JUAN SEGUÍN, VICTOR LOUPY, AND PLÁCIDO BENAVIDES. IN THIS SELECTION, DR. LACK EXAMINES THE TEJANO ROLE IN THE TEXAS REVOLUTION.

★ ★

The experience of Tejanos in the Texas Revolution, while distinctive from that of any other group, was not characterized by uniformity. Numbering over 4,000 on the eve of the conflict, the Texas Mexican population resided mostly in four communities. Except in Nacogdoches, with a Tejano population of over 600, they found themselves engulfed by the war. The approximately 450 De León colonists from in and around Victoria felt the effects less severely at first than did the 1,600 in the Béxar area and the 1,350 in the Goliad region, where the people suffered from living in the war zone. Essentially, the Tejano experience centered around problems of military occupation, with the victorious side changing four times in less than a year. Almost any behavior, even that designed to protect themselves from the ravages of war, made the Tejanos seem like traitors from the perspective of one army, if not both, which in any case ravaged the people's food and other resources.

From October, 1835, until the end of March, 1836, the war took place in the Tejano homeland. The conflict not only ended the physical distance between Anglo and Mexican Texans but threw the two peoples together in an atmosphere of extreme tension. Initially, though they had not themselves begun the hostilities, Tejanos volunteered for the Texas side in substantial numbers, but enthusiasm for the war soon declined, and for significant reasons. The bitter experiences of living in occupied territory caused disillusionment. Political factors also led to growing doubts, as the cause changed from federalism within the Mexican nation, which many Tejanos supported, to independence, which left them in a minority status. These influences evolved in different ways, depending on circumstances unique to each community.

Tejanos serving in the Texas cause came mostly from the town of San Antonio de Béxar in the fall of 1835. Names and numbers of volunteers cannot be determined with precision because of the absence of muster rolls for them for this period, but several sources indicate substantial recruitment early in the war. Years later San Antonio citizens claimed that 160 Tejanos had participated in the siege, service for which, as local resident Sam J. Smith wrote in 1874, "they got no pay or credit." Juan Seguín, who commanded one of the native companies, identified the origins and numbers of the Tejano recruits of 1835: his company of thirty-seven men had entered at Salado Creek in October; Salvador Flores and Manuel Leal together raised forty-one volunteers from area ranches; fourteen (mostly Bexareños) deserted from Cos's forces in the city. Plácido Benavides brought a company of twenty-eight from Victoria, and an additional Tejano detachment of about twenty from the forces at Goliad later arrived along with a similar number of isolated enlistments from there.

From a variety of other sources, most especially bounty and donation grant records, the names of ninety-one Tejanos who served in the fall of 1835 have been ascertained. Biographical information on these men reveals the following profile: most were young, the average age being 27.5 (25 when measured by the median figure), about four to six years younger, in fact, than the Anglo volunteers of this period. Nevertheless, a majority of them had already married. Native-born Texans (85 percent) naturally dominated the ranks, and the few who had come north to settle from Mexico had done so seven to fifteen years earlier. The place of residence of these volunteers becomes even more difficult to establish; however, Bexareños clearly outnumbered any other group. Only fifteen of those who saw service in 1835 can be identified as from outside of the Béxar municipality, and the census records suggest that town residents were twice as numerous as those from the ranches. As Seguín recalled, his company was the largest, and it "was made up of men from this city [San Antonio]."

Bexareño soldiers made contributions commensurate with their numbers. From his initial meeting with General Austin at Camp Salado on October 22, Captain Seguín energetically executed a number of varied responsibilities. Recruitment continued up to the storming of the city on December 5, but the unit became active from its inception. As the commander in chief wrote on November 24, the company of "native Mexicans . . . was very efficient in the cause." On the fourteenth of that month Austin dispatched a unit under Salvador Flores on an "important" mission away from the scene of the siege. Primarily sent to scout for centralist reinforcements south of the Nueces River, its orders also involved capturing horses and burning the grasslands to inhibit enemy movement. The Tejanos seemed especially adept in this kind of service, no doubt because of their knowledge of the countryside. Austin praised them for capturing expresses directed to the centralist forces in Béxar, but he also made it clear that "Cap. Seguín and his men were at all times ready and willing to go on any service they were ordered. They uniformly acquited themselves to their credit as patriots and soldiers."

This service included participation in battle. Seguín's men saw action with Bowie at missions San José and Concepción in November, and Tejanos answered the call for volunteers to storm the city on December 5. Antonio Cruz, of the Béxar company, so distinguished himself in the fighting at the Veramendi house as to attract commendation by no less of an anti-Mexican than Travis. Nonsoldiers also got into the action as the conflict came literally into their homes. Among these María Jesusa de García stood out, because, in the words of an act subsequently passed by the Texas Congress, she "was wounded and permanently disabled in rendering extraordinary services to the army of Texas at San Antonio." García had attempted to carry water to the Texans on December 5 in spite of the heavy Mexican barrage. These acts of individual valor gained particular recognition, but one veteran of the campaign extended the plaudits to the community as a whole. "Our army owe[s] many thanks to the brave inhabitants" of the city, he wrote on Christmas day, for they "ranked themselves on the side of liberty, and fought bravely with the Texan forces. Were all the Mexicans such ardent lovers of liberty, as the citizens of San Antonio, we should not now be left to fight our battles alone."

That a sizable force of Bexareños turned out for the Texas cause came as no great surprise to the leaders of the rebellion, for the city had acquired a reputation of opposition to the military-centralist party. The more remarkable feature of the high level of volunteering was that those from town found sufficient opportunity to participate despite a form of martial law imposed by General Cos. On October 15, a full week before the Texas army arrived at Salado Creek near the town, he ordered Political Chief Angel Navatro to devise and administer a passport system. Essentially, this edict forbid anyone from leaving without a pass from either Cos or Navarro. The civil authority complied, periodically supplying a list of persons who had been given exit permits, but the commander expressed dissatisfaction with enforcement. The system had been in place but a few days when local resident Zeferino Ruiz boldly left town with no pass and even more brazenly returned with a note from one of the rebel leaders. According to further correspondence from Cos, only "a few inhabitants among this population have heeded the policy"; therefore, he informed Navarro, beginning November 18 and "without exception" anyone caught violating the passport rule would be sentenced to forced labor. This level of noncompliance occurred in the face of a strong night patrol, staffed by both infantry and cavalry.

The Texas forces expected to benefit from the enemy's problems in controlling the town population. Before the army had even arrived one observer predicted that the number of Cos's troops required "to keep down the citizens" would be a significant advantage. In fact, several residents managed to leave town to join the Texas cause. Austin indicated that these included both "deserters" from the Mexican army and "inhabitants who have connected with us." Movement between Béxar and the rebel lines seems to have occurred almost constantly. Macedonio Arocha, one of the recruits, recalled later that he went back and forth at night from town to Seguín's company several times, to visit his family and to obtain extra provisions. Friendly Bexareños even helped the Texas artillery overcome its ammunition shortage by returning used cannon balls. Perhaps most importantly, the people of the city provided information on the centralist army and through intermediaties like rancher José María Solmas sent out confidential communications.

Those who left the town brought complaints about the military rule of General Cos. According to reports made to Bowie and Fannin at Espada mission on October 22, "a large number of the citizens of Bexar and of this place, are now *laying out*, to prevent being forced to perform the most servile duties." Erasmo Seguín "and others of the most respectable citizens" were reputedly to be made "to sweep the public square, and in case [Cos] whiped [*sic*] us, to make their Ladies, grind tortias for his soldiers." The general eventually forced the elder Seguín to walk to his son's ranch, leaving behind the remainder of the family to endure the Texas barrage for the rest of the siege. Cos also impressed mules and drivers and perhaps other property, and he reportedly razed houses on the outskirts of town to provide a more favorable field of fire in case of a rebel assault.

Hearing these reports, the Texas leaders came to expect more support from the Bexareños. Following a month of loosely conducted siege warfare, Austin issued a "Proclamation to the Inhabitants of Bexar" that amounted to an invitation for them somehow to make peace. This document enumerated an eight-point set of terms, half of which concerned capitulation and withdrawal, matters more appropriately directed to Cos or his superiors. Remaining provisions promised fair representation for Béxar and a kind of amnesty: "No Citizen will be persecuted nor molested in any way in either their persons or property on account of their political opinions." Finally, Austin indicated that all who sought the protection of his plan should present themselves to the army of Texas. After this pronouncement the besieging forces increasingly considered the remaining residents to be enemies and suspected those who moved back and forth between the town and the Texan lines as potential spies rather than useful informants. Naturally, this changing opinion led to increased tensions between Béxar civilians and the Texans.

Relations also worsened because of the army's growing demands for supplies. Actually, from the date of their arrival in October the Texas forces had but a meager commissary and little cash with which to make purchases. Even officers who attempted to respect private property had difficulty in establishing ownership of the corn, beans, and beef they needed; further they could not always determine the genuine needs of the local population, some of whom they suspected of intending to withhold from the Texans in order to sell to the centralists in town.

As late as November 16 Austin had to explain to Antonio de la Garza why he would not be permitted to transport his maize and beans to the plaza while it remained in enemy hands. The commander assured his correspondent that war's end would bring restoration of civil authority and payment for properties confiscated from patriotic citizens (not enemies).

Soon after their arrival in the neighborhood it became obvious that, lacking the money with which to make purchases, the Texans would resort to impressment. Responding to queries regarding dealings with the recalcitrant *mayordomo* of Espada mission, Austin ordered Bowie and Fannin to use persuasion, give certificates of credit, and keep an accurate accounting: "In the event this arrangement will not satisfy him there is no resource left but to follow the Law of necessity, and take what you want." However oppressive this policy might have been in these matters Austin showed more patience and restraint than did most other members of the army. One of the first assignments given Seguín was contracting with area ranch owners for corn and beans to be paid for in bank bills or on public credit. On November 17 Austin ordered Quartermaster Patrick C. Jack to organize a food-gathering expedition. This officer received authority to take charge of all wagons and oxen, employ loyal teamsters, and oversee the harvesting of the grain. Austin also attempted to prevent soldiers from killing beef and to exempt certain fields from being ravaged by the army.

Despite these efforts, the Texas commander obviously knew that much property had been taken without attention to any form of payment. A week after his resignation Austin reminded the provisional government of its responsibility "to ascertain the amount of property thus [by compulsion] made use of, and to provide for a Just compensation." Nevertheless, over four years later Josefa Jiménez still had not settled the account for the corn "that during the storming of Bexar was taken from her by the volunteer army of Texas," as her claim read. These contributions burdened both poor and affluent. In 1840 a congressional resolution awarded Erasmo Seguín $3,004 for the oxen, mules, corn, beans, beef, and other supplies he had furnished in 1835.

Had it not been for the moderating presence of Austin the impact of the war on the Tejano population of Béxar might well have been far worse. Many other officers like Fannin favored a more concerted scorched earth policy. On November 5 the general wrote his thoughts on military strategy to the Consultation. While he agreed basically that circumstances of war had undercut the middle ground, Austin opposed "laying waste the country round Bexar. I think [that] too hard on the inhabitants who are our friends." For some time this issue was a source of internal disaffection in the Texas army, but the general continued to order his subordinates to discriminate between friend and foe in raiding area ranches.

These divisions on treatment of civilians still existed among the soldiers as they stormed the city and battled house-to-house between December 5 and 10. Consequently, one unit shot a boy who tried to escape from a captured dwelling and arrested three women and a priest. Another company stormed a stone house and shot inside until it heard the "screams of women & children" and then paroled the men who laid down their arms, allowing all of them to flee to an area away from the fighting. In making peace General Edward Burleson agreed to restore private property "to its proper owners," to protect the citizens of Béxar "in their persons," and not to molest civilian or soldier "on account of his political opinions hitherto expresed."

The question of the war's impact on civilian life in Béxar had not greatly distracted either of the armies as they pursued the laws of necessity and confiscated, consumed, or destroyed property. The people of Béxar endured a battle that literally reached into their homes. The Texas tactics of turning houses into strongholds involved forced entries, tearing holes out of walls and ceilings, and reinforcing doors and windows with dirt and furniture. These methods left the city marked by heaps of ruins. Further, the siege created shortages for civilians trapped in the town; even those in farming areas controlled by Texans found that the army used up staples at an alarming rate. At the time of arrival in the outskirts of Béxar no less qualified an observer than West Point-trained Fannin described the provisions as virtually inexhaustible. Yet, less than a month later he reported to Austin, "We have nearly consumed all the corn &c near here." These shortages translated into privation for Tejano civilians. Their sacrifices of liberty and property were substantial if only because the armies were large and more stationary than at any other time in the war.

The people of the Goliad area also experienced the traumas of military rule in the fall of 1835. The size and character of the occupation differed from that of Béxar in that the Texans triumphed there very early in the war, on October 9, and held the post with a garrison that seldom exceeded one hundred men. However, commander Dimitt asserted absolute control over both resources and the civil authorities, resulting in a form of domination at least equal to that suffered by the Bexareños. By late in the year, as Texas forces gathered in and around Goliad for a projected assault against Matamoros, the Tejanos of this region had to endure the pressure of a large, hostile army in their midst. In early spring, 1836, centralist troops arrived and added the hardships of battle to the sufferings of the people.

Not all these problems could have been predicted. The entire region acquired a reputation for lukewarmness toward the Texas cause; yet, Tejanos from both Victoria and Goliad volunteered initially in support of the rebellion. When Texans from Matagorda arrived at the de León colony on their way to conquer the Mexican fortress, Alcalde Juan Antonio Padilla, who considered it "disgraceful to live under the military yoke," joined the expedition. He brought into the ranks other prominent Victorians, including the empresario's son Silvestre de León and son-in-law Plácido Benavides. Austin described Padilla as "a true friend to Texas and to Liberty." Miguel Galán, from Goliad, volunteered on October 10, the day after the fort capitulated, to be joined soon by Paulino de la Garza, Agustín Bernal, and some of the men who had been serving in the Mexican garrison. Controversy soon developed, as Col. Benjamin Fort Smith wrote to his friend Austin, over what to do with "the Mexican Volunteers." "We know Not as yet how far they may be relied upon," he opined. Dimitt resolved the issue by sending Padilla "with a Small detachment of creole troops" under Benavides to Béxar for Austin to deal with personally. This company of about thirty men remained for the duration of the siege and participated with distinction in some of the fiercest fighting in December.

What Dimitt apparently intended, and clearly achieved, amounted to a purging of Mexicans from his force. Although rancher Miguel Aldrete remained affiliated with this unit, even signing the controversial declaration of December 22, and men like Tomás Amador served the Texans as a messenger, Anglo and Irish colonists dominated the Goliad command for the remainder of 1835. Lacking the potentially moderating influence of "native" troops, the Texans became an army of occupation pitted against the people of the region. Perhaps the commander did not believe that he needed a Tejano perspective because, as one veteran later wrote, Dimitt "had a Mexican wife and was, for all practical purposes, a Mexican." Undoubtedly, the people of Goliad would not have concurred in this conclusion.

Even though a sizable body of centralist supplies fell into Texas hands with the capitulation of the fort, Dimitt immediately began to impress the property of local citizens. On October 10 he seized "into the public service" $120 worth of beef belonging to C. [J.] E. Vasquez. A few days later Domingo Falcón and A. Volors forcibly surrendered some of their cattle to the Texas army, and other residents of the vicinity furnished twenty horses for the use of the soldiers. Through the month of November the people continued to make more forced contributions—animals, corn, wagon wheels, a rifle, a string of ponies, even a crowbar—nothing seemed to escape the army's clutches. Dimitt's grasp reached one hundred miles north to the ranch of Erasmo Seguín, who lost five hundred dollars worth of mules to impressment.

The garrison's most insatiable need seemed not to be food but transportation. In order to move Irish colonists out of the war zone and send provisions to Béxar. Dimitt seized both carts and teamsters. On November 13 Alcalde Galán enumerated the sufferings of the Goliad residents in a letter to Austin: "[The soldiers are] breaking into houses, ravaging the corn without the consent of property owners, killing cows randomnly without making an effort to know who they belong to, impressing servants without the consent of their masters, and then letting them loose without supervision . . . [or] paying them for their labor." The commander also made the people work on fortifying the plaza and perform other forms of manual labor.

The citizens of Goliad responded in several ways. As Dimitt himself explained, "immediately after the place was taken," they began to seek refuge in the countryside. Some fled from the section altogether. On October 25 he continued to affect surprise at this reaction, claiming "I have done, and have said, every thing which I could do, or say, to pacify and inspire them with confidence." Dimitt attributed the people's conduct to awe of the military display earlier made by the centralists. Other observers assigned responsibility to the policies of the Texas military in general and its local leader in particular. John J. Linn complained to Austin of the many "acts of tireney" of Dimitt, "a great enimey of the Mexicans." All but twenty had left town; "the people are afraid to come [back] as they do not want to be made hewers of wood and Drawers of water."

Having left their homes in search of security, in early November the Tejanos sought to rectify their situation through politics. Many enthusiastically welcomed the arrival of Governor Viesca, who came with an armed guard on November 11 in his flight from the centralists; as a legally constituted federalist leader, he must have seemed a potential deliverer. But Dimitt's refusal to receive the governor "in an official capacity" incited what the Texas officer called "insubordination, . . . discontent, and . . . a spirit of opposition, both in and out of the fort." Tejanos held a public meeting on the twelfth and protested military usurpation of democratically elected civil authority. All but one of the thirty-two who signed this document were Tejanos, but they gained some support among soldiers.

Dimitt promptly declared martial law. His order proclaimed: "All persons manifesting an opposition dangerous to the cause espoused by the People of Texas—All who oppose, or threaten to oppose, the observance of order, of discipline, and subordination, or who endeavour to excite discontent wither in the Fortress, or within the Town, will be regarded as public enemies, arrested as such, and dealt with accordingly." Specifically, no one could arrive or leave without reporting and obtaining a passport. This policy brought on an additional set of protests, mostly directed to Austin and seeking replacement of the Goliad commander. Thomas G. Western, who had as the post's adjutant opposed Dimitt on the Viesca matter, explained that the inhabitants had not only "flown to the country for Security . . . [but also] prepared hiding places to which to escape at the very sound of the name Dimitt." The alcalde catalogued the various infringements on popular liberry and pointed out the irony of these being committed in the name of the liberal cause. Austin promptly ordered Dimitt's ouster and informed Galán that the replacement would respect civil authority; however, the Goliad garrison kept Dimitt in power. A public meeting at Texana renewed the Tejanos' request for protection by the provisional government, but by then their fate more than ever rested with the increasingly powerful and antagonistic Texas army. Many area Tejanos continued to hide.

These inherited tensions, combined with newer aggravations, poisoned Tejano-military relations during that period. Considerable underground support existed for the centralists, and the U.S. volunteers and other troops who swelled in numbers between December and February held militantly anti-Mexican attitudes. Fannin reported from the fort in February that "no aid need be expected from Mexicans." Recruits from the United States likewise expressed skepticism about Tejano trustworthiness. As one wrote, the citizens of La Bahía "professed to be hearty in the cause of the revolution" but actually fled from town in order to hedge their fate. This perceived vacillation, which the people attributed to a desire to escape the unruly behavior of the Texas troops, led the soldier to doubt both words and deeds of support. He did admit that "the absconded citizens of Goliad . . . received us kindly, and treated us with hospitality, professed the warmest hospitality to our cause, and denied having any communication with the Mexican army."

Residents of this region provided several kinds of service to Texas. Juan A. Zambrano went to Matamoros as a spy for Austin and fell prisoner to Urrea. Plácido Benavides, shortly after leading a company in the storming of Béxar, likewise set out on an intelligence-gathering mission to centralist-held territory near the Rio Grande. In early February he returned with news of an impending invasion, information that Fannin ignored, to his later grief. Other Tejanos made less spectacular contributions. Miguel Benítez, also a veteran of the siege, along with other drivers carried ammunition and other stores from the coast. Victor Loupy probably filled as many roles as any Texan in the Revolution. He volunteered for the army at Goliad on October 9 and subsequently acted as soldier, interpreter, and contractor, supplying Fannin's troops with more than four hundred head of cattle. The centralists captured and imprisoned him; after the Revolution a Texas secretary of war endorsed Loupy's application for back pay with a commendation for his "long and meritorious service."

One mercantile enterprise involving Tejanos from this region resulted in a substantial loss of property. José María Carbajal and his brother-in-law Fernando de León, of Victoria, chartered the *Hannah Elizabeth* in November to carry arms and other goods from New Orleans to the Texas forces. The vessel and proprietors fell prey to a centralist ship operating near the coast in December; their goods ended up in the hands of a group of Matagordans who had commissioned a coastal raider that recaptured the *Hannah*. Despite their vigorous protest, the Victorianos received none of the proceeds from the auction of the salvaged supplies. Nevertheless, Acting Governor Robinson appointed de León as aide-de-camp to organize the militia of Victoria, "believing that you are willing to serve your country in any way that you can be useful."

The Tejano masses lost their property in the conflict not through business dealings but by the continuing impressment policies of the Texas army. Once again in early 1836 as in the previous year the most sought-after of their possessions were draft animals. To some extent earlier and then especially during the attempted retreat in March, A. C. Horton and other press gangs rounded up every yoke of oxen, team of mules, or stray horse they could find. Leg-weary infantrymen also attempted spur-of-the-moment appropriations from Tejano corrals, but they sometimes found the mounts too wild to be handled.

Most of the people of La Bahía stayed in their rural sanctuaries. Troops new to the town found little but "empty streets," as one wrote. "All of the inhabitants had kept indoors, and only a few aged Mexicans deigned to look at us from the small air-holes which form the windows of their cabins." For Tejanos even flight to ranches no longer provided protection from the more numerous and disorderly recruits who conducted frequent forays in search of provisions and enemies.

When hostilities came to this region in February and March, more Tejanos fought on for the invaders than for Fannin. The wonder is that any sided with Texas at all, given the state of military-civilian relations. About ten Mexican Texans saw action in the Nueces River area, of whom two were killed and the others captured. As the action came closer to Refugio, Tejano participation on the side of the Revolution dwindled, although Mariano Carbajal and one other perished at Goliad. Either from simple charity or in support of the Texas cause, several Tejanas aided the few soldiers who had managed to escape the fate of Fannin and his men. These acts of mercy included tips about the locations of Urrea's soldiers as well as provisions of food and clothing.

Whether they welcomed the invasion or opposed it, the coming of the war into their homeland devastated the lives of many Tejanos. Some who considered themselves noncombatants died in the guerrilla-like fighting around Refugio from March 11–13. They also lost equipment, horses, cattle, and other property; especially devastated were those who resided in the town, which rebel forces under William Ward burned on March 13. That same fate befell La Bahía, as Fannin set it ablaze just before beginning his tardy retreat. Santa Anna later used the fact that the Texas brand of warfare had "reduced [the Tejanos] to the most dreadful situation" to justify the vengeful treatment of Urrea's captives. At Victoria, which of all the Mexican-dominated communities of this area had shown the greatest loyalty to the Texas cause, the authorities had reserved twenty yoke of oxen to assist civilian evacuation in case of a centralist victory. Fannin impressed these at the last minute, depriving the people of the means of flight. Ironically, the Texas army later used their failures to evacuate as evidence of Tory sentiment.

However harsh his policies toward the enemy, Urrea promised not "'to molest the inhabitants of the country who remained at their homes and took no part in the war.'" Yet, according to an official who carried this message, "'the general would depend on the citizens for much subsistence.'" This included a measure of cooperation as well as material support. Urrea forced the principal leaders of Victoria to report and perform certain duties. Fernando de León had to turn over hidden contraband goods. His brother-in-law Manuel Escalera served under compulsion as a courier for Urrea.

In this period between December and April, 1836, the community of Béxar had as before lent more voluntary support to the Texas cause than had the areas to the south. Still, many of the problems experienced by Goliad also characterized the situation in the departmental capital. In the fall hostilities had been more intense and thus destruction greater in Béxar, and the people continued to supply an army of occupation after the surrender of Cos. For the entire period from December to April this community continued to feel in innumerable ways the burden of war.

Like other Texans, a majority of the Tejano soldiers returned to civilian life as soon after the December 5 victory over the centralists as possible, and most of those who served in 1835 did not join the army again in the spring of 1836. Instead, Anglo and Tejano veterans alike looked first to the care of their families in the belief that those who had not yet gone to war should do so. Though few at the time saw this retirement as anything but natural, some critics subsequently cited it as evidence of a lack of patriotic zeal. A substantial number of Bexareños in fact remained militarily active, albeit in a somewhat irregular fashion. Captain Seguín led a body of cavalry which tracked the movement of Cos's forces to scout their threatened return from south of the Rio Grande. Company commander Salvador Flores and a few others risked themselves in "spy" work north of that river to detect centralist troop movement, but throughout most of early 1836 the military authorities did not actually seek Tejano participation.

During the month of December Tejanos of the town and the surrounding area still lived under military rule, as General Ed Burleson's successor, Francis W. Johnson, made no attempt to reestablish civil authority. The masses of people, though "greatly impoverished" in Neill's words, had to share their provisions with the military. Much of the burden of feeding the army of occupation still rested on area farmers. One such group living near San José mission resisted impressment of six wagon loads of corn with such "pitiful pleas" that the press gang leader consulted his superiors about returning the grain. Eventually, he decided that the farmers had been deceitful in claiming that this "was their only food until the next harvest" because they had actually intended to sell part of their holdings in town. The profit motive and dislike of Americans, not "dread of famine kept them from sharing their surplus with us." It seems not to have occurred to him that the impressed corn comprised the people's only asset in acquiring other goods from town because most of the farmers received certificates of credit, not negotiable currency, for the commodities taken by Seguín, Johnson, and other officers in December and January.

By contrast to what he considered the grim behavior of the rural people. Herman Ehrenberg perceived a more light-hearted spirit in town. Residents who had fled during the siege returned soon after the peace of December 11 so that "bustle and animation again filled the streets, where Texans and Mexicans walked about their business without fear or resentment." Most of the native people seemed content to pursue their traditional pleasures and welcomed as "guests" the American volunteers who made up the bulk of the local garrison. Without the displays of protest that had occurred at the mission, merchants like Francisco A. Ruiz and José A. Navarro sold on credit a variety of supplies ranging from beef, corn, and other food to horses, mules, and cooking utensils. Nevertheless, the burden of having supplied armies since October had exhausted the area economy by January. Neill reported that even the ubiquitous cattle had come into short supply, and he received authorization to employ vaqueros at twenty dollars per month to drive in beef from the range. This promise of employment on credit hardly improved the economy. According to the acting governor, "the unfortunate inhabitants [were] reduced by the war, from opulence and ease, to penury and want."

This material suffering did not lead to overwhelming disaffection by the people, as seen by a consensus of the military leaders stationed in Béxar. Only Travis seemed to fear Tejano treachery. In contrast, Neill wrote emphatically to Houston on January 14, "I can say to you with Confidence, that we can rely on great aid from the citizens of this town, in case of an attack." He cited the voluntary contribution of supplies by Gaspar Flores and Luciano Navarro as evidence of this genuine support. Within the next two weeks Bowie and G. B. Jameson confirmed Neill's assessment, with the latter giving praise to Seguín and others of "the most wealthy and influential citizens." This account also noted the problem of "loose [military] discipline" that led to soldier-civilian tensions.

Neill had restored civil authority when he became head of the post at the end of 1835, but disorder associated with the struggle to succeed him threatened to undo the amicable relations he had created. The elevation of Bowie over Travis in this contest in February, as the latter wrote, made "everything topsy turvey." Bowie began interfering with private property, preventing citizens from carting their goods to the country, and in effect he abrogated civil government by releasing prisoners from jail. This act brought on conflict. Judge Seguín angrily resigned in protest, and Bowie retaliated by calling an armed parade of the Alamo troops, all of whom acted in what the post adjutant described as "a rumultously and disorderly manner," attributable to the drunkenness of the Texas forces.

Part of these tensions grew out of the awareness of many Bexareños of the impending centralist invasion and their reaction to this threat. As the above episode revealed, a large number of citizens had been fleeing the town since mid-January. Knowledge of centralist plans did not indicate treason; rather, the local population simply took seriously the reports of those who had been dispatched to the Laredo area to gather intelligence. The Texas commanders also had access to this information but refused to retreat from the Alamo fortress.

When Santa Anna's men began arriving on February 22, they found the town reduced in population but not entirely abandoned. Some of the people stayed at home in support of the invading force, but more often they had hopes of maintaining an undeclared neutrality. In part this waning of support for Texas may have been the result of the growing tensions between civilians and the Texas army; however, the most significant influence on local Tejano behavior was the failure of the military to prevent the centralist reoccupation. Like many Anglo colonists, Bexareños who supported the cause often chose to provide for the welfare of their families first before joining or reenrolling in the service. In fact, when the ranks of the Alamo defenders are defined to include all those who served under Neill in early February as well as Travis and Bowie later in the month, the number of Tejanos becomes nineteen rather than the three cited by Travis. Mostly from Béxar, this Tejano contingent of defenders ranked next to Gonzales in number of recruits and represented nearly twenty percent of the Texans who served in the army at San Antonio in the first two months of 1836. Many of the Bexareños received discharges from commander Neill and left to help evacuate their families, or like Seguín became messengers in one of the many last-ditch efforts to bring reinforcements to the fortress. Some, as historian Walter Lord suggests, may also have chosen to retire from what obviously had become a losing cause. The list of those who braved the assault in the Alamo should also include four or five Bexareñas and nine dependent children who had accompanied their husband-father-protectors into the fort.

Generally, Santa Anna seemed determined to demonstrate restraint in his relations with the local population. A few Béxar homeowners had to quarter Mexican officers, and the Mexican president eventually confiscated and auctioned property belonging to "colonists" in the town, but his army apparently paid for more commodities than did the impressment-prone Texans, who once again had herded local cattle and seized corn and other property in their hasty flight into the fortress. Townspeople had considerable freedom of movement, some even managing to wander into and out of the fort after the siege had begun. In battle, too, most of the destruction of local property emanated from the Texans—Travis's men burned many houses in La Villita in an attempt to reduce the cover of the attackers.

The day after the final assault the victorious general ordered Bexareños to return home where they would be protected in their domestic life. Actually, they did not easily or quickly resume normal routines. Alcalde Francisco Antonio Ruiz led a delegation of citizens forced to identify corpses, cart off Mexican bodies for burial, and prepare the funeral pyre for the defenders. Other leaders, including political chief Ramón Músquiz, established hospitals and attended the wounded before and after the battle. For the next two months civilians and soldiers suffered from scarcity of food and high prices. Nevertheless, the people endured these sufferings and still managed to display courtesy and kindheartedness, according to an American physician stationed there in April and May.

A large number of Béxar residents fled before the invading force came onto the scene. Having placed their families in some rural sanctuary or on the road to the east and presumed safety, many of the men rallied to one of the military units forming in the vicinity of the Colorado River. Seguín, after failing to stir movement from Fannin, went to the neighborhood of Gonzales and organized some of these recruits into a company. Houston used this command as a rear guard during the long retreat and proposed similar duty for it at San Jacinto. At the insistence of its leader and men like Antonio Menchaca the Tejano company engaged in the battle as part of the left wing of the Texas army and behaved with suitable gallantry. Most estimates give the number in this unit at twenty-two to twenty-four (Seguín's recollection placed the figure at forty-six, including those who served in the rear baggage detail); adding those from Nacogdoches and other parts of Texas, thirty-two Tejanos can be identified by name as having served at this decisive battle. Most of them were young, averaging but twenty-five years in age, and 60 percent were single, characteristics that reflected the fact that family men had been diverted from service by the need to provide for their dependents. Thirteen others besides Seguín had also served in the Béxar siege of the previous fall. Far more Bexareños had turned out for the Texas cause in the spring of 1836 than served in the battle of San Jacinto. Among those who gathered at Gonzales in early March, General Houston sent a company of twenty-five to forty under the command of Salvador Flores to defend families that had remained on their farms. Another body of about thirty soldiers escorted civilians from Béxar to Nacogdoches.

Whichever destination they decided on, the fleeing civilians confronted substantial risks. Siege veteran Agustín Bernal took his family forty miles from town to the ranch of Tía Calvilla on the San Antonio River. He "was obliged to remain at that place," as he recalled years later, "to protect his wife and young child against the Indians and some parties of Mexican outlaws." Some of the women and children set off to the east with neither protectors not adequate equipment. The Tejana wife of Erastus (Deaf) Smith loaded her two sets of twins and personal possessions in a bulky cart but had no draft animals. She borrowed a team from her fellow refugees on her one-leg-at-a-time journey. The more affluent Seguín family attempted to save three thousand sheep and a herd of cattle by driving them past the Colorado River, in the common but mistaken notion that Texas forces would stop Santa Anna's advance at that point. Slowed by their possessions and by the snarl of other families on the miserable roads, most of the Seguín animals fell to the pursuing division of General Joaquín Ramírez y Sesma. The family members managed to get away to San Augustine and then to Nacogdoches, but without their assets they had to sell personal property, including even clothing, just to avoid starving. Illness as well as poverty beset the Seguíns during their brief stay in east Texas.

Their experience may have been particularly unpleasant because they entered an isolated and suspect Tejano community in Nacogdoches, where the Revolution engaged the Hispanic people politically—invariably in opposition—but not militarily and had less impact socially than elsewhere. Leaders of the Texas cause had attempted at the outset "to try and Rase the Maxacans" as a group, in the words of George A. Nixon, but repeatedly failed. Tejano militiamen did agree to serve as a home guard unit; however, this same official later wrote, "they Seeme Not to under Stand the Busi[-]ness." This ruse of feigned ignorance allowed the masses to stay at home, but individuals made contributions to the war effort. In early November the Nacogdoches vigilance committee head informed Thomas J. Rusk that "the most wealthy" of the Tejanos have "furnished horses and money for the equipment" of a company of U.S. volunteers that came through town on the way to Béxar. These contributors included Miguel Cortines, "one of the few Mexicans whose energies have been used in our cause," Rusk later wrote. The supplies included a horse and four rifles valued at $210. In December Bernard Pantallion provided nearly one thousand eight hundred pounds of beef and pork to another of these companies, and others gave horses or worked as cooks, couriers, or servants.

Although the Tejanos of east Texas refused to form into a single body and march to the front as a unit, individually they did join the army, Anglo-American criticisms notwithstanding. Most of this volunteering occurred in fall of 1835, before the cause had become independence, when at least six "natives" from the region served in the siege of Béxar. Squite Cruse enlisted at Jasper on October 14; the remainder were from Nacogdoches. They came from a variety of personal circumstances, some of them being young and single, while Esteban Mora, forty-eight years old, had a wife and four children living at home. Juan José Ybarbo, another married man in his forties, received an honorable discharge that testified also to his bravery and his financial contributions to the Texas forces. Casimiro García fell prisoner to General Cos during the siege while serving in Rusk's company.

Despite these examples of individual participation, the Tejanos as a whole remained a separate community in Nacogdoches. When newcomer William F. Gray arrived there in early February, he observed that "there is no social intercourse between them [Anglo Americans] and the Mexicans." The latter impressed him as "a quiet, orderly, and cheerful people, . . . unthrifty and unambitious," though some seemed atypically "intelligent and respectable." His own experience indicated a less than absolute segregation, in that Anglos frequented the Tejano gambling houses, but a high degree of separation clearly characterized both political and social behavior.

Anglo-Tejano tensions continued well beyond the battle of San Jacinto. In June military authorities still considered the issue of drafting Nacogdoches Tejanos, and the local vigilance group discussed using force to make them join the revolutionary cause. At the end of the month Houston wrote to the head of that committee urging him "not to adopt any harsh measures towards the Mexicans in the neighborhood of Nacogdoches. Treat them kindly and pass them as tho' there was no difficulty or differences of opinion. *By no means* treat them with *violence*." Though the General's advice apparently forestalled an immediate conflict, his argument rested on a flimsy public relations reasoning: "The world would damn our cause if we shed blood at home" before defeating the invader decisively. Thus, the future boded ill for the Tejanos as a group, and individually they began to suffer loss of liberty even during the summer of 1836. Local Mexicans found themselves detained illegally by private citizens, and the courts sentenced a Tejano to a whipping and a term of forced labor for a six-dollar fraud case.

Residents of the other Tejano communities continued to face the problems of living in occupied Texas during the entire summer of 1836. Though centralist armies retreated to the Rio Grande in May, all of the west remained an insecure area for several months. Many Tories evacuated southward with the army as it left Béxar on May 25. "The remaining citizens," as a U.S. soldier-physician there reported in his journal, "seem to be much relieved at the departure of the troops, with which they have been oppressed for three months. Some of them broke out into transports that made them out quite ludicrously. . . . Navarro was seen capering about the streets like a boy in perfect ecstasy of glee. He said that now he should recover his health; that nothing but the impure air occasioned by the residence of the Mexican troops had made him sick." Unfortunately, this celebration proved to be premature both for Navarro, who died two weeks later, and for the community as a whole, which continued to experience the difficulties of wartime occupation. Worries about reinvasion kept refugees in east Texas or in their rural hideaways, leaving the town depopulated. Some of the people of the municipality faced dire enough conditions that they set out to plunder the retreating army of Vicente Filisola as it retreated beyond the Nueces. Seguín arrived in Béxar in early June with such a small company that he felt insecure from a potential attack by Tories and from marauding Indians who threatened to rob, murder, and otherwise ravage the entire area.

These various forces of disorder meant that the Bexareños would live under military rule for the remainder of the year, and army measures were often harsh. Initially, at least, the commander operated from a vision of restraint. Rusk specifically ordered Col. James Smith, head of a force dispatched to relieve Seguín at Béxar on June 8, that "you will be careful on going to San Antonio to prevent any unnecessary interruption to the citizens there. Such conduct as entering their homes and taking their property you will certainly forbid [as] improper" in that the people who remained in town had demonstrated friendship toward the Texas cause. Unfortunately, according to reports that reached Mexico that summer, the soldiers did exactly what the General had forbidden. Perhaps in response to this treatment, several townspeople joined those who had earlier given themselves over to centralist protection. This resumed flight renewed army fears of Toryism. Further, some of the people evidently drove their cattle southward with them, thus exacerbating fears of a reinvasion force being fed by Texas beef. Army-civilian relations had become a vicious cycle.

When Seguín departed the town on June 21, he ordered the people of the region to herd their animals eastward, out of potential enemy use, as evidence of loyalty to Texas. Their subsequent conduct failed to satisfy the military leaders. A month later Rusk wrote, "I wish in a few days to give Bejar a shake." This general's earlier goal of a civilian-army accord had largely vanished by August. Residents protested about their treatment, but Rusk could only express "eternal regret . . . that the distress of War should fall upon families of women and children." He promised that "in no case will they be injured by our Troops." His letter to Miguel Arciniega held out little hope for relief: "Bejar being the frontier however must be for some time the Theatre of War and as such will be exposed to many hardships & inconvenience." At the end of August he ordered Col. Francisco Ruiz to visit the town and use his knowledge to ferret our disloyal persons. To the friends of Texas the general offered scant relief: personal protection and promises to pay for the articles they furnished to the army. Property that the military claimed to be public would be repossessed from private hands; those who drove off their cattle toward the Rio Grande would be treated as enemies. Even in the early fall a harsh regimen continued to dominate the community. On September 17 Seguín received orders to recruit a full brigade and a militia force to replace the small regular company previously stationed in the town. His instructions allowed use of military justice to preserve order "provided that sever[e] punishment does not extend to loss of life or limb."

Refugees hiding in the east fared hardly better than the Bexareños remaining closer to home. Seguín and Antonio Menchaca did not gain leave to retrieve their families from Nacogdoches until mid-July. The effects of a fever epidemic still lingered a month later when they set out for home on what proved a traumatic journey. For much of the time only Menchaca felt well enough either to lead the wagon train or attend to the sick. They arrived home to find the town still largely deserted and, "to crown their misfortunes," as Seguín recalled years later, "their fields laid waste, and their cattle destroyed or dispersed." His own ranch had been "despoiled" either "by the retreating enemy, [or] had been wasted by our own army; ruin and misery met me on my return."

The devastation may have seemed like a sudden transformation to the refugees, but it had in fact begun months earlier and affected all property owners whether they stayed home or fled. Seguín should not have been much surprised, for he had issued receipts for goods offered to or impressed by the army from other affluent Tejanos like the Navarros and José Antonio de la Garza. Life and property continued to be in danger as late as mid-October 1836 when a raiding party from Mexico entered San Antonio in search of plunder and perhaps revenge. Seguín, then a Colonel, still offered the local population little in the way of security other than the lame advice of driving their cattle out of the war zone. Those who clung to their homes in contravention of this policy were even regarded as "pretended friends" of Texas by the leading newspaper of the Republic.

In the communities of Victoria, Goliad, and Refugio, the people experienced problems similar to those of the Bexareños but made worse by several factors. When the centralists troops arrived in the spring of 1836, most of the Mexican residents had stayed at home and made their peace with the new order. Since Urrea sought to win support from the local population and left but a small force of occupation behind as he marched east, the inhabitants lived under a relatively light-handed rule through the late spring. In contrast to the situation in Béxar, few of the natives celebrated the retreat of the centralist army in the second half of May. The withdrawal occurred in two phases, first by the division under Filisola, followed closely by that of Urrea.

These generals agreed that the retreat left the people in desperate position but launched into a protracted debate about who should be held responsible. Urrea blamed Filisola for ordering the evacuation and leaving the locals behind in a state of such depravity that no army could possibly subsist there, much less offer protection. Filisola claimed that he had attempted to prepare Goliad as a base for operations, a policy that Urrea had undermined by spreading panic as he passed through on the road to Matamoros. Further, the latter general allegedly had impressed so many draft animals and carts that the people had no means of fulfilling his advice to accompany the centralist army in retreat. However vigorously they debated the matter of blame, the two leaders agreed that many Tejanos had fled with the Mexican army and that those who stayed behind had been left defenseless to cope with a mean-spirited, vengeful Texas force. Neither general bothered to record popular responses, but one other officer did. The people, he wrote in his diary, expressed surprise at being compelled to abandon their property and retreat with the army: "The residents of Goliad, who had suffered much, became quite angry with us and insulted us, saying that we were fleeing as cowards from a handful of adventurers."

Many of the area Tejanos remained on their homelands, either because they lacked the means to flee, chose to resist, or felt themselves safe because they had never voluntarily supported the centralist cause. However, their previous loyalties counted for little in the summer of 1836. The doomsayers had been right; the Texas army arrived on the scene in a vindictive mood, already disposed to hate Mexicans. Their attitude worsened with the discovery of the grisly remains of the victims of the Goliad massacre.

Poor discipline added to the indiscriminate nature of army policies, as did the weakness of the commissary, which forced commanders to rely on local provisions. Limited in power at first by its small numbers, the army soon grew from four hundred to two thousand. An advanced unit under Col. Sidney Sherman camped near Victoria on May 23, looking for provisions and spies among the citizens, thus setting the tone for subsequent army policies. Rusk arrived there before the end of the month and extended the military influence to Goliad and San Patricio by sending out companies to forage for more supplies and probe for traitors. The commander of one such expedition reported on May 30 that he had found few arms and no documentary evidence to implicate the inhabitants of the ranches he had raided. Nevertheless, he impressed horses and intended to arrest enough family heads to serve as "examples" but not so many as to leave the women entirely defenseless.

His and other groups of soldiers continued these forays in the next few days, reaching all the way to the Nueces River. On June 2 Captains H. Teal and H. W. Karnes reported an adverse response to these activities. Some "Mexicans citizens . . . stated that they was at there Ranch and some of our scouts came up and took them prisoner with some others and robed of there guns and there horses," threatening to remove them to Victoria. The officers protested these attacks for undermining support among the inhabitants, who had responded by fleeing with their cattle. The "rascooly" civilians had used army outrages to convince many of the "old settlers" that "they wood all be killed and they think that you are after them as hard as you can march."

Many of these arrests, insults, and property confiscations resulted from the excesses of soldiers acting outside of army control. Several observers shared this conclusion. John J. Linn's account of the outrages against area Tejanos attributed them to soldiers, especially new recruits from the United States, who operated from a "creed [of] the total extermination of the Mexican race and the appropriation of their property to the individual use of the exterminators." He praised the commander for attempting to control these attacks against civilians and for offering "asylum" to Fernando de León. This head of the Victoria family that had lent so much support to the Texas cause suffered a bushwhacking while at army headquarters. A veteran of this period concurred in absolving Rusk of blame for these disgraceful attacks against the persons and property of the De Leones; he attributed the outrages to adventurers who excused their plundering by false allegations of their victims' unfriendliness. Yet, this account made it clear that the general had failed either to obtain a return of stolen goods or to control the band of army outlaws.

Further, army leaders also seized civilian property in large quantities. Wealthier ranchers and merchants turned over not only cattle but also wagons, mules, oxen, rum, salt, and tobacco. The quartermaster, other officers, and even the commander himself issued some receipts for these goods, but much of what they took went undocumented and thus uncompensated.

María Antonio de la Garza, of Victoria, surrendered around sixty head of cattle to the Texas army and received no certificate of impressment for over a year. Luckily, she managed to gain Rusk's endorsement of her claim, with an inscription that revealed much about the process. She had, in fact, "placed her cattle at the disposition of the army and many of them were used," wrote the general, "what number or quality I am unable to say."

Rusk's policy may have been haphazard at first, but it soon became purposeful: throughout the western frontier the people would be removed and their land despoiled of its most valuable property, cattle. This strategy would provision the Texas army, deny support to a threatened enemy reinvasion, and remedy the irritant of civilian-military conflict. Tejanos, who comprised virtually all the people of this broad region, would suffer loss of their possessions, livelihood, and liberty so that the Revolution might be furthered. The Tory behavior of the area hardly served to excuse this oppressive policy, since a majority of that persuasion had already fled with the centralist forces or in response to attacks by the army of occupation in early summer. Most who remained and suffered from this forced evacuation had been loyal to the Texas Revolution. As in Béxar, Rusk's strategy was not implemented in a coherent fashion, but the army did compel substantial numbers to leave their homes.

On June 19 Rusk informed the secretary of war of the issuance of orders "to all the Families Mexicans and all to fall back at once and clear the Country." He offered residents of the entire region between the Guadalupe and Nueces rivers a grim choice—to flee either to Mexico or to a part of Texas out of the war zone, driving out their herds or surrendering them to the control of the army. In actuality, the Tejanos could not protect their properties because they lacked means or opportunity to remove possessions and must leave lands and homes to the mercy of the military. Feigning ignorance of the policy did not provide an effective shield. "Some of the Mexican families," in Rusk's words, "are pretending that they have no orders to remove," but he handled this ploy by reiterating his policy and sending cavalty units to enforce it. He paid particular attention to forcing the evacuation of the leading family of Victoria, the De Leones, by boarding them under guard onto vessels routed to New Orleans. The ranks of evacuees included Benavides, whose revolutionary service had most recently included fighting against Urrea, and José María Carbajal, also a staunch and early supporter of the federalist cause. The army loaded about eighty members of this extended family on the *Durango* at Matagorda Bay on June 26, bringing a large measure of success to Rusk's orders to "dispose of the Families."

He intended to make a complete evacuation of all the Tejano-dominated areas, but enforcement became less rigorous away from Victoria. Carlos de la Garza gave no response to the soldiers who brought the removal orders to his ranch near Refugio and thus led his people into successful resistance. This act capped his thorough and consistent opposition to the Texas cause. In spite of this glaring exception, Rusk's otherwise ruthless policy allowed him to police the region more successfully for the remainder of the summer. Into the fall Texas authorities continued to issue orders to drive the livestock belonging to unfriendly citizens out of the valleys of the San Antonio and Nueces rivers.

The ravages of the war and immediate postwar period left a permanent mark on the entire area. For years the De Leones remained in exile in Louisiana while their Anglo neighbors or newcomers to the area piled up legal claims to Tejano property. Exparriates Benavides and Carbajal never resettled in Texas; others in the family came back only after much of the land had been taken over by others and the cattle had been long-since lost. Poverty dogged this once-powerful clan both during and after their exile. The population centers of the region also underwent transformation. Victoria became what one historian has described as "a wild Anglo-American town, dominated by an army and many newcomers that distrusted and hated the Mexicans." Goliad and Refugio were largely destroyed during the fighting of the spring of 1836. Some of the Tejano residents were killed in the war, and many more became exiles south of the Rio Grande or exiles from their native land under the unrelenting pressure of the Texas army of occupation. Though exceptional ones like Carlos de la Garza remained to keep the Tejano heritage alive, the area as a whole suffered large-scale depopulation.

Many Tejanos attempted to save their birthrights and perform their patriotic duties by volunteering for military service in the summer of 1836. Near the end of the year the *Telegraph and Texas Register* reported that "Col. Seguín, the untiring friend of Texas," commanded a force of about eighty "Americans" in the regular army and two hundred "Mexican citizen volunteers." Not nearly that number received the bounty grants due for service for the period May to December, 1836. Of those who did, about 40 percent had participated in earlier campaigns and tended to be young (in the mid-twenties, on the average) and single (62 percent). Virtually all of these veterans had followed Seguín into the army from the Béxar municipality. The Tejanos who joined for the first time in this period possessed as a group much less uniformity. Though the largest number volunteered in the Company "B" Cavalry of Bexareños led by Seguín's lieutenant, Manuel Flores, many served in one of the other units, usually some kind of mounted rangers, formed at various times and places in the summer and fall of 1836. Next to Béxar, Nacogdoches yielded the largest number; the region from Victoria to San Patricio, at that time being largely depopulated by Rusk, produced scarcely any soldiers. In personal characteristics these first-time volunteers showed more variety—they were older by an average of five years, some being in their fifties, and were more likely to be married than were the earlier Tejano recruits. These attributes suggest a powerful and broad compulsion to demonstrate loyalty to Texas during this time of growing ethnic tensions.

Service of various kinds may have helped to advance the cause of the Tejanos individually or even as a community, as in the case of Béxar, but as a whole Texas policy toward citizens of Mexican descent had become capricious by the summer of 1836. Their problems steammed mostly from living in a year-long war zone where they suffered from military policies of harsh material exploitation and ruthless denial of liberty. Well before the end of summer sweeping anti-Mexican prejudice had largely triumphed over restraint. Army-enforced deportations and property confiscations had become indiscriminate under General Rusk, with the burden falling as heavily on the patriotic Bexareños and Victorianos as on the defiant Tories of Refugio. For Tejanos the Revolution established a tradition of trouble and portended a future of overwhelming governmental discrimination and societal prejudice.

Determined Valor and Desperate Courage

Stephen L. Hardin

Stephen L. Hardin is Professor of History at McMurry University in Abilene. His books include *Texian Iliad: A Military History of the Texas Revolution* and *Texian Macabre: The Melancholy Tale of a Hanging in Early Houston.* He served as history consultant for the 2004 film, *The Alamo.*

The battle of the Alamo will never be forgotten. In this selection, Dr. Hardin discusses the resolute Texian defense of the old Spanish mission, which fell to Santa Anna's forces on the morning of March 6, 1836.

★ ★

Alamo defenders watched their adversaries pour into Béxar in what seemed an unending stream. So that the rebels would not misunderstand their intent, Mexicans hoisted the red flag of no quarter atop San Fernando Church. Then in accordance with established procedures of siege warfare, they offered the garrison an opportunity to surrender and made their requirements known: "The Mexican army cannot come to terms under any conditions with rebellious foreigners to whom there is no other recourse left, if they wish to save their lives, than to place themselves immediately at the disposal of the Supreme Government from whom alone they may expect clemency after some considerations are taken up." Travis informed the enemy courier that a response would be forthcoming. And it was—a single shot hurled from the eighteen-pounder. There could be no mistaking the meaning of such a succinct reply.

With the formalities out of the way, the Mexican cannoneers set about reducing the adobe walls. Once they had knocked down the walls, the garrison would have to surrender in the face of overwhelming odds. Although Jameson had once referred to the works as "Fortress Alamo," he had clearly done so in jest. "The Alamo never was built by a military people for a fortress," he had explained to Houston, "tho' it is strong, there is not a redoubt that will command the whole line of the fort, all is in the plain wall and intended to take advantage with a few pieces of artillery."

Jameson had detected a major drawback; all was, indeed, "in the plain wall." Unfortunately, the advent of heavy cannon had rendered the curtain wall obsolete four centuries earlier, necessitating a complete transformation of defensive positions and siege craft. The most important developments in both were the work of French engineer Marquis Sébastien Le Prestre de Vauban. By the nineteenth century, it was accepted that one would storm a fortress only if no other option were available. Rather, a careful siege with sufficiently powerful artillery placed in prepared trenches would eventually breach a wall, whereupon the garrison would surrender, defeat being a foregone conclusion.

By the standards of its day, the Alamo was certainly no fortress. It lacked mutually supporting strong points—demilunes, bastions, hornworks, ravelines, sally ports, and the like. There were simply no strong points from which its defenders could oppose an assault. Nor was it logistically self-sustaining; the defenders could not hope to outlast the besiegers. Although the fort contained a good water well, the food supply might have lasted four weeks at most. It did not even command a significant terrain feature, such as a vital pass or port. A perceptive Texian, Dr. J. H. Barnard, identified the chief disadvantage of both La Bahía and the Alamo: "Situated in an open prairie country, they controlled no passes, nor obstructed any route that could check or impede the march of an enemy army. They simply defended what ground they stood upon, and what their guns could reach, and no more, and were from fifty to seventy miles distant from any settlers upon which they could rely for supplies and succor."

Of course, the Spanish priests and presidial troopers who had constructed Mission San Antonio de Valero in 1718 never intended it to function as a fortress. The adobe walls were more than sufficient to stop the arrows of the hostile Indians and to keep friendly neophytes from escaping. The abandoned mission had served as the barracks for the dragoons of the Flying Company of San José y Santiago del Alamo de Parras, who gave it the unit's name. For convenience, locals shortened the post's name to the Alamo. Presidial troopers rested easily behind those thick walls; the Comanches did not have artillery.

But Santa Anna did. The chances are remote that any Texian inside the Alamo, including the lawyer-turned-engineer Green Jameson, was aware of Vauban's system of fortification. They were not, however, blind to the obvious. Travis and Bowie were firm in their determination to defend the Alamo, but both understood it would be only a matter of days before the enemy artillery breached the walls; they were well aware that their survival depended on the speed with which Texians rallied to their aid. They made that clear on the first day of the siege when the co-commanders wrote Fannin in Goliad: "We have but little Provisions, but enough to serve us till you and your men arrive. We deem it unnecessary to repeat to a brave officer, who knows his duty, that we call on him for assistance." Despite all the hyperbole about preferring to "die in these ditches" and "victory or death," Bowie and Travis were not suicidal. They simply could not imagine that fellow Texians, once aware of their perilous position, would not rush to their aid.

Neither could Santa Anna. He was more concerned about Texian reinforcements coming to break the siege than the meager force bottled up inside the fort. He did not intend to be caught in Béxar as Cós had been. When he heard rumors that two hundred men from Goliad were on the march to relieve the Alamo, Santa Anna ordered General Ramírez y Sesma to intercept them with his cavalry. In addition to sending Ramírez y Sesma's horsemen, he also dispatched the Jiménez infantry battalion out in search of the enemy.

Mexican officers never seemed to worry about the Alamo itself; when its food was exhausted, its fall was certain. His Excellency dismissed the post as an "irregular fortification hardly worthy of the name." Never missing a chance to criticize Santa Anna, de la Peña described the Alamo as "an irregular fortification without flank fires which a wise general would have taken with insignificant losses." Filisola agreed: "By merely placing twenty artillery pieces properly, that poor wall could not have withstood one hour of cannon fire without being reduced to rubble.

Perhaps, but the Mexicans did not have twenty pieces of artillery. They had brought fewer than ten light fieldpieces. Artillerymen customarily relied upon heavy siege guns to reduce enemy fortifications; such weapons were on the way but could not arrive until March 7 or 8. Lacking heavy ordnance, the gunners had to place their smaller cannon closer to the walls, but venturing within two hundred yards of the fort in daylight was an invitation to the deadly Texian riflemen. Working after dark, therefore, the Mexicans began digging a series of entrenchments that grew nearer to the old walls each night.

Inside the Alamo, Bowie's health continued to decline. On the second day of the siege, he collapsed completely. The malady must have been a form of respiratory ailment, for it was variously described as "hasty consumption" and "typhoid pneumonia." (Contrary to persistent legend, Bowie did *not* fall from a gun platform.) Whatever his affliction, Bowie could no longer function as commander, so he instructed his volunteers to obey Travis.

Now in full command, Travis prepared to meet the enemy. If the Mexicans made a frontal assault with infantry, the defenders could inflict heavy losses with rifles and artillery. Anglo-Celtic frontiersmen reared on stories of the victory of Jackson's riflemen over British regulars at New Orleans were naturally drawn to the thick walls around the Alamo. The high adobe ramparts would be as impenetrable as the cotton bales that had shielded their forebears a generation before. Far from being bent on self-sacrifice, Travis and the garrison remained in the fort because they were convinced that they could hold it until reinforcements arrived.

Texian rifles continued to take their toll on the enemy. Atop walls that were in some places twelve feet high, defenders could easily hit unwary Mexicans at two hundred yards. The Mexicans' Brown Bess muskets, on the other hand, were ineffective at ranges of more than seventy yards. The "mountaineers" and "hunters," for whom Tornell had expressed such contempt, soon proved their worth as marksmen, dropping men at ranges the Mexicans thought impossible.

Travis wisely placed Crockett and a unit of skilled riflemen at what seemed the weakest link in the fort's defensive perimeter, the low picket barricade between the chapel and the south wall. The Mexicans soon had reason to avoid the area opposite Crockett's post.

Crockett and his riflemen could kill at long range, but in the event of an enemy assault, the defenders greatest assets would be their cannon. Neill had scrounged some twenty-one pieces of ordnance, but Jameson had not mounted all of them by the time the siege began. Sutherland recalled that "not more than about twenty were put to use during the siege." That figure was confirmed by a number of Mexican reports. In a diagram of the fort, Sánchez-Navarro depicted tubes lying on the ground, supporting Sutherland's testimony that the defenders had not mounted all their artillery.

Best estimates are that Jameson had judiciously mounted nineteen pieces at various points. He placed the eighteen-pounder on the south-west corner to cover the town. Travis commanded a battery of nine-pounders on the north wall. In the chapel, three twelve-pounders covered the area east of the fort. One of the guns was a gunade, a stubby, short-range naval gun of the period. No one has ever determined why a ship's gunade had been taken to a post 150 miles from the nearest coast, but Jameson did not stop to question Providence and reportedly mounted the seagoing ordnance on the west wall.

Despite its fortunate supply of artillery, the garrison nevertheless faced some serious disadvantages. The fort was much too large for so few men to defend. The main plaza contained almost three acres, making the defensive perimeter almost a quarter of a mile long. The small number of Texians could not possibly defend a perimeter that large; it was a case of too much space and too few riflemen. It was also a matter of too few cannoneers for all the cannon. Prevailing doctrine allotted a six-man crew to each piece of ordnance. Travis began the siege with about 150 men; if he had followed that rule and manned all available cannon, 114 of his men would have been assigned as gunners. Travis, of course, did no such thing. Fewer men could fire a cannon if necessary, just not so quickly. In fact, it is unlikely that more than three gunners manned any piece of Alamo artillery. Even at that, rifles along the 440-yard perimeter were spread pitifully thin.

Both riflemen and gunners were vulnerable to enemy counterfire. The Alamo, built as a mission, did not have firing ports. Jameson seemed to have constructed makeshift catwalks, but when the Mexicans approached within the seventy-yard range of their muskets, the defender's upper bodies were exposed. Those men who fired from atop the small rooms along the west wall were even more exposed. Most of the cannon were positioned to fire not through the breastworks but over them. The men had constructed gun emplacements by piling dirt against the inside of the walls, but this arrangement left artillery and artillerymen silhouetted against the sky. Colonel Juan Almonte recorded that on the second day of the siege, Mexican artillery fire dismounted two pieces of Alamo ordnance, including the prized eighteen-pounder. Texians soon had the guns back in operation, but the incident revealed their precarious position.

Once the Mexicans had their artillery in place, they maintained an almost constant fire upon the Alamo. On February 24, in his famous letter addressed to the "People of Texas & all Americans in the world," Travis reported, "I have sustained a continual Bombardment & cannonade for 24 hours & have not lost a man." Although the Texians were lucky not to have suffered any casualties, that happy consequence likely stemmed from the fact that the enemy was directing most of its fire against the wall. Almonte recorded that during the night of February 25 the Mexicans erected two more batteries. Prudence demanded they work at night; that day "in random firing the [Texians] wounded 4 of the Cazadores de Matamoros battalion, and 2 of the battalion of Jimenes, and killed one corporal and a soldier of the battalion of Matamoros."

At first Travis had matched the enemy shot for shot, but by day four he realized how much powder and ball that policy was consuming. The defenders needed to conserve ammunition in the event of an assault. Crockett's men were the exception. Their long rifles wasted less powder with better results. The deadly rifles rarely missed their marks. The remainder of the garrison, frustrated by a growing feeling of impotence, could only sit and endure.

Exhausted defenders grew steadily weaker. Travis did not have enough men to rotate sentries, so each of them slept at his post. Conditions worsened as a blue norther swept through, dropping the temperature to thirty-nine degrees. A party of defenders sallied out of the fort to forage for firewood but were repulsed by Mexican skirmishers equipped with the Baker rifle that could kill at 170 yards. Texians accorded these enemy riflemen more respect than they did the line infantry with smoothbore muskets and so scurried back to the safety of the fort.

Both Suzanna Dickenson, wife of Artillery Captain Almeron Dickenson, and Colonel Travis noted Crockett's efforts to bolster the flagging morale of the garrison. Mrs. Dickenson recalled that he often cheered the troops with his fiddle. Travis reported in a letter to Houston that "the Hon. David Crockett was seen at all points, animating the men to their duty." Even the stricken Bowie had his cot brought out in the open, where he attempted to encourage the men from his sickbed. Despite all efforts, the strain began to tell. Arkansas artilleryman Henry Warnell bitterly expressed their anxieties: "I'd much rather be out on that open prairie. . . . I don't like to be penned up like this." But in more thoughtful moments, others realized that without cover they could not last an hour against vastly superior Mexican numbers. By the seventh day, the men could see through the desperate attempts to boost their spirits. Only reinforcements could do that.

At least a few were on their way. On February 24 Travis had dispatched Captain Albert Martin to the settlements with his "Victory or Death" letter. The courier rode all night and most of the next day to reach his hometown of Gonzales, some seventy miles away. To his commander's plea for assistance, he added one of his own: "Since the above was written I heard a very heavy Canonade during the whole day [and] think there must have been an attack made upon the alamo[.] We were short of Ammunition when I left[.] Hurry on all the men you can in haste[.]" Alamo messengers John W. Smith and Dr. John Sutherland had reached the town earlier, and Martin's arrival heightened the sense of urgency. The proud men of Gonzales had been the first to shoulder their rifles against centralist oppression; how could they refuse now when fellow Texians needed their help.

The Gonzales Ranging Company of Mounted Volunteers boasted a grandiose title but only twenty-two effectives. With news of the fighting, a few others joined up. The company was a frontier porpourri: New York hatter George Kimball; nineteen-year-old newlywed Johnnie Kellogg; and Béxar carpenter John W. Smith, eager to rejoin his Alamo comrades. The oldest, at forty-one, was Isaac Millsaps; the youngest, William P. King, was only sixteen. By the time of their departure on February 27, their ranks had increased to twenty-five, and another eight joined on the march. Travis had made it clear that a "thousand or more" Mexicans surrounded the fort; fully aware of the disparity of numbers these thirty-two men gamely rode on. Numbers did not always decide a fight; in October, eighteen Gonzales men had held off a hundred Mexican dragoons until their neighbors arrived. Now the fighting men of Gonzales were riding to repay their debt.

The Gonzales volunteers reached the outskirts of Béxar on the night of February 29. They had been fortunate; Santa Anna was expecting Fannin's relief force to come from La Bahía and had therefore detailed Ramírez y Sesma to patrol the Béxar-Goliad road to the southeast. Approaching from the northeast, the Gonzales contingent encountered little opposition. They could see the clusters of Mexican campfires and hear the calls of the sentries. Stealthily making their way through the brush, the men felt their way toward the walls looming ahead in the darkness. Just before three o'clock, they were nearing the fort when a skittish Alamo sentry fired, wounding one of the Gonzales men in the foot. The rest called out to stop shooting. The defenders eagerly swung open the gates to welcome the long-awaited reinforcements. Their spirits must have fallen when they saw how few there were.

March 1 was, nevertheless, a day of celebration inside the Alamo. Travis, of course, had hoped for many more than thirty-two men, but the Gonzales contingent had at least shown that a determined force could make it through the Mexican cordon, and surely more were on the way. The irrepressible Crockett played his fiddle, and Scotsman John McGregor joined in on the bagpipes. In honor of the new arrivals, Travis even allowed the gunners two precious shots to let Santa Anna know that they had not forgotten him. Knowing ammunition was in short supply, the men sighted carefully. The first ball crashed into the town's Military Plaza; the next tore through the roof of an adjoining house. The gunners had no way of knowing it, but the building served as Santa Anna's head-quarters. That shot might have produced propitious results had His Excellency been there to receive it.

March 2 saw a return to siege routine. The Mexicans continued their cannonading, and the defenders observed that the enemy artillery edged even closer to the walls. Travis could not imagine why Fannin and his four hundred men had not arrived. It had been nine days since he and Bowie had summoned him, plenty of time for the ninety-five-mile journey.

The next day, Travis poured out his feelings in a letter to the Independence Convention meeting at Washington-on-the-Brazos:

> ***Col. Fannin is said to be on the march to this place with reinforcements, but I fear it is not true, as I have repeatedly sent to him for aid without receiving any. . . . I look to the colonies alone for aid; unless it arrives soon, I shall have to fight the enemy on his own terms. I will, however, do the best I can under the circumstances; and I feel confident that the determined valor and desperate courage, heretofore exhibited by my men, will not fail them in the last struggle; and although they may be sacrificed to the vengeance of a Gothic enemy, the victory will cost the enemy dear, that it will be worse for him than defeat.***

Travis had begun to accept the fall of the Alamo as a distinct likelihood, but he was not a man with a death wish. He never stopped calling on Texians to rally to his aid. "I hope your honorable body will hasten on reinforcements, ammunition, and provisions to our aid as soon as possible. We have provisions for twenty days for the men we have. Our supply of ammunition is limited." In his letters to the Convention, Travis continued to stress the vital importance of Béxar, which he described as the "great and decisive ground." Better to fight Santa Anna on the frontier, he argued, than "to suffer a war of devastation to rage in our settlements."

Travis also wrote his close friend Jesse Grimes, revealing more of his true feelings. Now as always, he asserted, the men of the Alamo were staunch supporters of Texas Independence:

> ***Let the Convention go on and make a declaration of independence, and we will then understand, and the world will understand, what we are fighting for. If independence is not declared, I shall lay down my arms, and so will the men under my command. But under the flag of independence, we are ready to peril our lives a hundred times a day, and to drive away the monster who is fighting under a blood-red flag, threatening to murder all prisoners and make Texas a waste desert. . . . If my countrymen do not rally to my relief, I am determined to perish in the defense of this place, and my bones shall reproach my country for her neglect.***

Travis's fiery words were in vain. On March 3, courier James Butler Bonham arrived from Goliad with the grim news that Fannin would not be coming. He had received the messages from Travis and Bowie calling for his assistance and on February 28 had actually begun the march to Béxar. But Fannin had never been personally committed to the relief of the Alamo, and when an ox cart broke down less than a mile from Goliad, his resolve evaporated. Accepting the advice of a council of his officers, he called off the expedition and led his men back to La Bahía.

That same evening, Fannin explained his decision in a letter to Acting Governor James W. Robinson. Some have criticized Fannin's failure to relieve the Alamo, but from a strategic standpoint his reasons were valid: "It is now obvious that the Enemy have entered Texas at two points, for the purpose of attacking Béxar & this place—The first has been attacked and we may expect the enemy here momentarily—Both places are importent—and at this time particularly so."

He added that his supplies were running short: "We have not in the garrison supplies of Bread Stuff for a single day and as yet but little Beef and should our Supplies be cut off our situation will be, to say the least—disagreeable." He expressed sympathy for the valiant "volunteers now shut in Béxar" but concluded that permitting his command to be cut off with them would ill-serve the interests of Texas. Abandoning Goliad would leave the eastern door open to Urrea's advance. Travis and his men would have to manage without Fannin's help.

By day eleven of the siege, the constant battering by Mexican artillery had weakened the walls. Santa Anna had established a battery within "musket shot" of the north wall. At that range, he did not need siege guns; each round shot hammered the crumbling adobe until a portion of the wall collapsed. Jameson directed work parties throughout the night, buttressing the wall with odd pieces of timber. The chief engineer realized that these were only stop-gap measures. In the event of a determined attack, the north wall could not hold.

On March 5, day twelve of the siege, Santa Anna called a meeting of his officers to discuss the possibility of an assault. Most of the officers present were amazed that the question was even being considered. The walls were already crumbling, and in two or three days the siege guns would arrive. Many argued that, surrounded by such a superior force, the defenders were no real threat. No Texian relief column had been sighted, so there was no reason for haste. They needed only to wait until the garrison's provisions ran out, when Travis would have no choice but to yield. Lieutenant Colonel de la Peña recorded that the majority of officers "were of the opinion that victory over a handful of men concentrated in the Alamo did not call for a great sacrifice."

Despite these reasonable objections, Santa Anna stubbornly insisted on attacking. He cited morale as a factor, claiming that "an assault would infuse our soldiers with that enthusiasm of the first triumph that would make them superior in the future to those of the enemy." General Ramírez y Sesma—no doubt still fancying himself as Murat—eagerly agreed with His Excellency. Oddly, so did Colonel Almonte, who normally demonstrated better judgment. It became obvious that Santa Anna had already decided; the meeting had merely been a matter of form. De la Peña recalled that most of the officers were horrified at Santa Anna's decision but "chose silence, knowing that he would not tolerate opposition."

Inside the Alamo, Travis had also assembled his men for a conclave. According to legend, he drew a line in the dust with his saber, inviting all who were resolved to stay and die with him to cross. Evidence does not support the tale, but apparently Travis did gather the men for a conference. Mrs. Dickenson remembered that he "asked the command that if any desired to escape, now was the time to let it be known, and to step out of ranks." Shortly thereafter Frenchman Louis Rose is said to have escaped, which may mean that Travis told each man to decide for himself whether to stay or go.

Reliable Mexican accounts, however, suggest a different story. According to them, a *bexareña* left the fort after the meeting. She told Santa Anna that morale was low and that defenses were crumbling. De la Peña recounted:

> ***Travis's resistance was on the verge of being overcome; for several days his followers had been urging him to surrender, giving the lack of food and the scarcity of munitions***

as reasons, but he had quieted their restlessness with hope of quick relief, something not difficult for them to believe since they had seen some reinforcements arrive. Nevertheless, they had pressed him so hard that on the 5th he promised them that if no help arrived on that day they would surrender the next day or would try to escape under the cover of darkness; these facts were given to us by a lady from Bejar, a Negro who was the only male who escaped, and several women who were inside and were rescued by Colonels Morales and Minion.

General Filisola also recalled that the garrison had considered the possibility of surrender:

On that same evening [March 5] about nightfall it was reported that Travis Barnet [William Barret Travis], commander of the enemy garrison, through the intermediary of a woman, proposed to the general in chief that they would surrender arms and fort with everybody in it with the only condition of saving his life and that of all his comrades in arms. However, the answer had come back that they should surrender unconditionally, without guarantees, not even for life itself, since there should be no guarantees for traitors. With this reply it is clear that all were determined to lose their existence, selling it as dearly as possible.

The prospects of an honorable surrender seemed to have alarmed Santa Anna. De la Peña speculated that the general was determined to precipitate an assault before the garrison could yield. A capitulation would not create a favorable "sensation"; the president-general "would have regretted taking the Alamo without clamor and without bloodshed, for some believe that without these there is no glory." There was no need for concern. There would be clamor and bloodshed aplenty.

The Mexican army would assault in Bonaparte's column formation. The self-proclaimed Napoleon of the West intended to hurl his troops toward the Alamo like irresistible missiles, terrify the rebels with overwhelming mass, and win a glorious victory to add to his laurels. Santa Anna organized his force into five units; four columns would attack from every point of the compass, while he personally commanded the reserves. The lancers would form a cordon around the fort "to prevent the possibility of escape."

The attack orders of March 5 set the onslaught for five o'clock the next morning. The Mexican artillery fell silent later that afternoon. Officers told soldiers to get plenty of rest, for they would be called to arms at midnight to take their positions. The general hoped that weary rebels would also take advantage of the lull to get some sleep. He intended to surprise the garrison. If the Mexicans approached the fort silently, they could be over the walls before the bleary-eyed defenders reached their stations.

The men of the Alamo welcomed the silence, ominous though it was. For twelve days, they had endured an almost constant bombardment. Travis posted a few men in listening posts outside the fort and dispatched sixteen-year-old Jim Allen with his last request for assistance. Then, succumbing to lack of sleep, he turned the watch over to Adjutant John Baugh and collapsed on his cot. All was quiet inside the fort as the stroke of midnight heralded the beginning of day thirteen of the siege: March 6, 1836.

At that same moment, the Mexican camp came alive, contrasting sharply with the stillness of the Alamo. Sergeants tapped their sleeping men awake with the wooden staffs that were the symbols of their rank; when that failed, the toe of their boots roused groggy recruits. Sappers distributed ladders and crowbars; noncoms saw that all shako straps were firmly fastened; officers made sure that all men were wearing shoes or sandals—proper footgear would be crucial when scaling walls. And, of course, weapons were inspected. The general's order had been specific: "The arms, principally the bayonets, should be in perfect order."

By 5:00 A.M. all was in readiness. The morning was chilly and many of the troops had been shivering in place for hours. Column commanders informed His Excellency that the men were becoming restless. Finally at 5:30, Santa Anna gave the word to move out.

All went smoothly as the Mexicans moved silently through the early morning moonlight. A massed column provided an excellent target, but it was a necessary formation for controlling recruits who were boxed in by steadier veterans. Cós, commanding the lead column, marched toward the northwest corner. Colonel Francisco Duque, at the head of the second column, angled from the northwest toward the patched breach in the north wall. Colonel José María Romero came in behind the fort from the east. Colonel Juan Morales led his column toward the low parapet by the chapel, supposedly the fort's soft spot. Lines of light infantry skirmishers fanned out several yards in advance of the columns; armed with Baker rifles, it was their assignment to pick off any defenders who showed their heads. They caught the snoozing Texian sentinels outside the walls; an efficient bayonet thrust, a blade drawn across the throat, and they died quickly—but more critical, silently. Unopposed and undetected, the columns approached inexorably nearer to the walls.

Bathed in bright moonlight that cast eerie, unearthly shadows across the landscape, the Alamo loomed ahead. The tension finally became unbearable. A soldier deep within one of the columns shouted, "Viva Santa Anna!" "Viva la Republica!" another countered. Soon hundreds of voices filled the air. Santa Anna was incensed by these "imprudent huzzas," for he knew the noise would alert the slumbering rebels.

It did. John Baugh heard the clamor and then saw the columns, already within musket range of the walls. The adjutant raced across the plaza, adding his voice to the cacophony from outside. "Colonel Travis! The Mexicans are coming." Joe, Travis's slave, slept in the same room with his master, and each staggered from his cot, grabbed his weapons, and rushed to the north wall battery. Travis shouted as he ran: "Come on, boys, the Mexicans are upon us and we'll give them Hell!" He must have wondered why the sentries outside the walls had not sounded the alarm. When he reached the battery and saw how far the enemy had advanced, he knew the answer.

Texian gunners had loaded their cannon. Lacking proper canister shot, they had crammed their ordnance with chopped-up horseshoes, links of chain, nails, bits of door hinges—every piece of jagged scrap metal they could scavenge. Packing that lethal load, the artillery doubled as giant shotguns. In that light and at that range, they could not miss their massed targets.

A gust of metal fragments swept the columns like a "terrible shower." The close-packed bodies of the soldiers soaked up the force of the scatter shot. Rusty shards slammed home, slowed as they plowed through the ranks, and finally stopped, lodged in flesh.

Then came round shot. Nine-pound iron balls probed further into the mass, gouging great swaths of destruction. Far worse than the roar of cannon was the sickening thud of iron striking flesh. The attackers were frightfully exposed; de la Peña watched in horror as "a single cannon volley did away with half the company of chasseurs from Toluca." Huddled together as they were in tight formation, even those untouched by enemy fire were splattered with blood and bits of flesh torn from their less fortunate friends. Bashing bodies, round shot paid multiple dividends; flying bone fragments proved as lethal as grapeshot. Those trapped inside the column could see little, but they heard the bedlam—the anguished screams of mangled comrades.

But Texians were also suffering losses. Rebel riflemen had to reveal themselves in order to fire on the attackers; the accurate Baker rifles swept the parapets, and at this range even Brown Bess could kill. The fort was lit from within by gunfire. Outlined against the light, the men atop the walls "could not remain for a single second without being killed." Travis was among the first to fall. He had just emptied both barrels of his shotgun into a column when a slug smacked into his forehead, sending him tumbling down the earthen ramp. With his master down and dying, Joe took refuge within one of the rooms along the west wall.

The Mexicans, shattered by grape and round shot, took scant notice of Texian casualties. Facing this deadly welter of fire, some demoralized recruits faltered, but the officers and noncoms stood firm. Sergeants beat the men back into ranks with their thick staffs, the officers with the flat of their swords. The men could not retreat far, for at their rear were the lancers Santa Anna had posted to prevent the escape of his own troops as well as the Texians.

The Mexican assault troops were taking heavy casualties, but ragged formations regrouped and drove forward. Viewing the debacle, Santa Anna committed the reserves, but stayed out of rifle range himself. Once more, the brave Mexican infantry charged into the maelstrom.

The devastating fire savaged Mexican ranks. Ordered columns were ripped asunder, but still they came. Unit integrity broke down as the columns of Cós and Duque swirled together at the base of the north wall. Advancing from the east, Romero's formation was swept by artillery fire from atop the chapel. To avoid effects of the deadly grapeshot, the column performed a right oblique toward the north wall, where it ran into the intermingled mob of Duque and Cós. Morales's attack against the palisade faltered as well. Contrary to expectations, that portion of the perimeter was anything but weak. In the face of direct fire from a cannon and Crockett's riflemen, the column angled to the left toward the southwest corner and the eighteen-pounder.

Once the surviving Mexicans reached the base of the wall, their problem became one of climbing over. They concentrated their main effort on the north wall and Jameson's makeshift repairs. Travis's nine-pounders, however, had taken a heavy toll. "The few poor ladders that we were bringing had not arrived," a Mexican officer reported, "because their bearers had either perished on the way or escaped." Yet the rough-hewn repairs to the north wall had left numerous gaps and toeholds. Realizing the time had come to conquer or die, the Mexicans began hoisting each other over the jerry-built barricade.

Desperation and sheer mass finally supplanted careful planning. General Juan Amador began the difficult twelve-foot climb over the north wall, challenging his soldiers to follow. The general and his men grappled up and over the parapet and dropped into the plaza below. Amador and his men inside the Alamo located the north wall postern and swung it open. Their comrades flooded through, penetrating the Alamo's defensive perimeter. From that moment, the outcome of the assault was never in doubt.

The Texians abandoned the north wall. As they fell back, Alamo gunners turned their cannon toward the wave of Mexicans rushing through the postern. Combined rifle and artillery fire ripped into the uniformed soldiers pinned against the inside of the wall. But now, when rapid fire was essential, rifles were a disadvantage; the long grooved barrels that rendered them so accurate also made them slow to load. When the fort's guns were swung northward to counter the enemy pouring through the postern, the Morales column, which had taken refuge behind some nearby stone huts, rallied and charged up and over the south wall. The cannoneers were slain before they had time to spike their gun. Seeing the enemy on the front and rear walls, outflanked Texians in the courtyard fell back to the final defensive line inside the long barracks. At the same time, Crockett's riflemen withdrew into the chapel.

Jameson had prepared well. The barracks doors facing the courtyard were buttressed by semicircular parapets of dirt secured with cowhides. From windows and loopholes, the defenders shot down Mexicans in the plaza. But in their haste to fall back to the long barracks, the crews on the northwest battery had failed to spike their guns. Mexicans loaded the captured cannon, swung them around, and systematically blasted each door. Realizing the utter hopelessness of their situation, a few of the rebels tried to surrender. De la Peña remembered their pathetic attempts: "Some . . . desperately cried, 'Mercy, valiant Mexicans,' others poked the points of their bayonets through a hole or a door with a white cloth, the symbol of ceasefire, and some even used their socks." There was a brief lull as Mexicans advanced, but as they entered the quarters they were ruthlessly gunned down by other Texians who "had no thought of surrendering."

Angry Mexicans charged through the shattered openings to finish the work begun by the captured cannon. In the darkened rooms of the long barracks, the adversaries grappled with Bowie knife and bayonet. Having seen their men shot down after flags of truce had been raised, the *soldados* took no prisoners, slaughtering even the wounded. A few Texians sought to escape by bounding over the east wall and running for cover, but the lancers made short work of them. The butchering was repeated in the rooms along the south wall; even the delirious Bowie, too weak to rise from his sickbed, found no mercy. But then, neither would he have asked for it.

The chapel was the last to fall. The Mexicans swung the eighteen-pounder, blew down the sandbags guarding the main entrance, and pushed through by the dozens. Bonham and

Dickenson fell beside their cannon on the battery at the rear of the church. Crockett and six of his men fought on until they were literally overwhelmed. This was no longer war; it was wanton slaughter; and General Manuel Fernández Castrillón ordered his soldiers to spare these helpless men.

Even after all the defenders had been killed or captured, dazed Mexicans continued to shoot at shadows. As a cat scurried among the ruins, a superstitious *soldado* shouted: "It is not a cat, but an American!" The feline was immediately killed. One can easily appreciate this wanton blood lust; these men had seen friends mangled by artillery, riddled by rifles, gutted by Bowie knives. Having survived the slaughter themselves, they were taking no chances.

Upon being informed that the Alamo had fallen, Santa Anna ventured into the fort. As he was surveying the carnage, General Castrillón brought forward Crockett and the others. The chivalrous Castrillón attempted to intercede on behalf of the defenseless prisoners, but Santa Anna answered with a "gesture of indignation" and ordered their immediate execution. De la Peña reported that several officers were outraged at the murder of helpless men and refused to enforce the command. But "in order to flatter their commander," nearby staff officers who had not taken part in the assault fell upon Crockett and the others with their swords and hacked them to pieces. De la Peña recorded that "these unfortunates died without complaining and without humiliating themselves before their torturers."

How true to pattern. Crockett's motto—or at least the one attributed to him—had been, "Be sure you're right, then go ahead." Once in Congress, his colleagues had urged him to support President Andrew Jackson's Indian bill. To do otherwise, they assured him, was political suicide. He replied in genuine Crockett style: "I told them I believed it was a wicked, unjust measure, and that I should go against it, let the cost to myself be what it might; . . . that I would sooner be honestly and politically d______nd, than hypocritically immortalized. . . . I voted against this Indian bill, and my conscience yet tells me that I gave a good honest vote, and one that I believe will not make me ashamed in the day of judgement."

He was, of course, soundly walloped in the next election, but satisfied that he had taken the honorable course, Crockett stubbornly ignored the consequences. Most of those who had fallen alongside him readily understood that brand of righteous bullheadedness. To remain loyal to their upbringing and the legacy of their rebel forebears, resistance to Santa Anna could be their only recourse. Behind the walls of the Alamo, they cast their final vote against centralism, a system they believed "wicked" and "unjust." March 6 was judgment day for them all; like Crockett, none had reason to be ashamed.

Dreadful Havoc

Stephen L. Moore

Military historian Stephen L. Moore is the author of *Savage Frontier: Rangers, Riflemen, and Indian Wars in Texas* (four volumes), *Last Stand of the Texas Cherokees: Chief Bowles and the 1839 Cherokee War in Texas*, and *Eighteen Minutes: The Battle of San Jacinto and the Texas Independence Campaign*.

Fought on April 21, 1836, San Jacinto was the final land battle in the brief but bloody Texas Revolution. Drawing heavily on the personal correspondence of those who participated in the engagement, Moore describes that decisive day in Texas history.

★ ★

The announcement of the decision to fight acted like electricity.

—Private George B. Erath, Company C, First Regiment

Private James Winters noted that General Houston "passed around among the men gathered at the campfires and asked us if we wanted to fight. We replied with a shout that we were most

"Dreadful Havoc" from *Eighteen Minutes: The Battle of San Jancinto and the Texas Independence Campaign* by Stephen L. Moore, 2004. Reprinted by permission.

anxious to do so. Then Houston replied, 'Very well, get your dinners and I will lead you into the fight, and if you whip them, every one of you shall be a captain.'"

Deaf Smith's party had long since departed on its mission to destroy Vince's Bridge. The noon hour had passed silently in the Texas camp. Men waited anxiously taking a late lunch near the campfires. Captain Juan Seguin was joined during his afternoon meal by Colonel Tom Rusk, the Secretary of War.

> *When he had done eating, he asked me if the Mexicans were not in the habit of taking a siesta at that hour. I answered in the affirmative, adding, moreover, that in such cases they kept under arms their main and advanced guards, and a line of sentinels. General Rusk observed that he thought so; however, the moment seemed to him favorable to attack the enemy, and he further said: "Do you feel like fighting?" I answered that I was always ready and willing to fight, upon which the General rose, saying: "Well, let us go!"*

By 3:00 p.m. it was clear to Sam Houston that the enemy was not ready to attack, but instead was fortifying himself. The noon meeting of Texas officers had decided not to attack immediately, but to instead await the enemy's first move.

Company H's Captain Stevenson wrote on April 23 that "Gen. Houston, seeing that they did not intend bringing on the attack, and fearing that they would receive reinforcements, determined to attack them on their own ground."

Some of the officers present would later claim that they helped influence General Houston's eventual decision to call for an attack. According to Colonel Robert Coleman, it was Colonel Wharton, the adjutant general, who advised Houston that the majority of the officers were for fighting immediately, even though four key officers had voted to delay.

Colonel Mirabeau Lamar, who had been one of those most inspired to lead a fight against the enemy soon after joining the army the previous week, was pushing his opinion again. After the noon war council, Lamar claims to have sought out Houston and again expressed his desire to start the battle. According to Lamar, Houston replied that he had always been ready to fight but now his officers were opposed to fighting. "And so are the men," Houston added.

Lamar was shocked at this response. Although four key officers had voted against fighting immediately at the noon council, he knew that the strong majority of troops were all for fighting as soon as possible. Lamar was quick to pass on this news.

> *Soon after this, I saw Col. John A. Wharton, and repeated to him what Gen. Houston had said. Wharton inquired, "Do you think he will fight?" My reply was: "He says he will."*
>
> *Taking leave of me, the Colonel repaired immediately to Gen. Houston, and asked him if he would order a battle provided the army was ready to make the attack. Houston said he would. This I got from Wharton, immediately after his leaving Houston. In a short time there was a general rejoicing through the camp; and Wharton was dashing from point to point, ordering a general parade, and* marshaling the troops for battle.

Sam Houston later flatly denied speaking with Mirabeau Lamar. He claims that he and Lamar, in fact, had no further conversations whatsoever on April 21 after Lamar had turned down the general's offered command of the artillery.

"PARADE YOUR COMPANIES"

Colonel Edward Burleson decided to take a consensus of his First Regiment captains. Burleson, originally a member of Captain Billingsley's Mina company, sent Private George Erath out to round up his regiment's company commanders.

This second officer council occurred around 3:00 p.m. according to Captain Robert Calder. Burleson rode along the line of encampment of his regiment and ordered Captains Calder, Wood, Roman, Billingsley, Baker, Stevenson, Heard, and Fisher to meet him at a pecan tree several hundred yards away. Also present were "some of the lieutenants of the regiment," plus Private Erath and Orderly Sergeant Russell Craft of Billingsley's company.

Captain Calder later wrote of the gathering of Burleson's key officers.

> ***They followed on, and assembled accordingly, when our Colonel told us he wished to take our vote upon the best time for attacking the enemy—whether immediately or at four o'clock the next morning. All the captains but Moseley Baker and myself voted for immediate attack; Baker and myself for four o'clock in the morning. Upon which we were ordered to parade our companies for immediate action.***

Captain Heard later claimed that he also voted to wait until morning to attack. He felt that "it was so late in the evening that the wounded would suffer by being out in the night."

Unbeknownst to Heard and Calder, Colonel Sidney Sherman's Second Regiment had also gathered to discuss the time of the attack. They had been called together by Lieutenant Colonel Joe Bennett. "Houston sent me through the camp to see the captains and men and ascertain their feelings about fighting that afternoon," he recalled.

Bennett and Colonel Sherman—surrounded by Captains Arnold, Logan, Seguin, Murphree, Ware, McIntire, Gillaspie, Bryant, Kimbro, and Wyly—found an equally strong desire to attack among their commanders. Colonel Burleson mounted and rode to share his regiment's sentiment with Sherman. Burleson soon returned and announced, "Captains, parade your companies. The other regiment had decided to fight immediately. I don't want mine to be a minute behind."

Lieutenant Colonel Bennett reported to General Houston, telling him "the men were ready to fight. Houston then ordered the troops to be paraded."

"Joy was depicted on the countenance of every man, and there was a rejoicing throughout the camp," wrote Colonel Coleman. "I have never seen sober men animated to the same degree." George Erath wrote, "The announcement of the decision to fight acted like electricity."

Thus at 3:30 p.m. on April 21, 1836, the Texian troops paraded for battle. Sam Houston's official report:

> ***At half-past three o'clock in the evening, I ordered the officers of the Texan army to parade their respective commands, having in the meantime ordered the bridge on the only road communicating with the Brazos, distance eight miles from our encampment, to be destroyed, thus cutting off all possibility of escape.***
>
> ***Our troops paraded with alacrity and spirit, and were anxious for the contest. Their conscious disparity in numbers seemed only to increase their enthusiasm and confidence, and heightened their anxiety for the conflict. Our situation afforded me an opportunity of making the arrangements preparatory to the attack without exposing our designs to the enemy.***

Texas drummers George Brown and Dick, the former slave, called the men to parade with a gentle tapping. Private John W. Hassell of Captain Calder's company wrote that "the drum beat general parade, which was cheering [to] every man."

Within half an hour, Houston's men were fanned out in four divisions directly in front of the mossy hardwood grove in which they had spent the night. Houston estimated that he had 783 men present, although records would later show that approximately 930 Texans were on hand on the afternoon of April 21.

The fate of Texas now rested upon the shoulders of these men. General Houston began his final inspection of the troops, moving from the extreme right wing toward the left. He was mounted on a fine grayish-colored stallion named Saracen.

According to Private Jesse Walling of the Nacogdoches Volunteers, Houston had exchanged his own pony for the gray stallion, which belonged to Private Dexter Watson of Captain Kimbro's San Augustine company. "Sam exchanged horses to get one of a different color, and mounted Dexter Watson's fine gray, and Watson rode the bay pony," wrote Walling.

Sometimes described as white, Saracen was remembered by San Jacinto veterans to be gray in color. "Sam Houston's horse that [he] was on going into battle was a dapple gray," wrote Private James Hill. Sergeant Moses Austin was equally sure that the horse was "gray upon which he went into battle." Finally, Captain James Gillaspie recalled going into battle with Sam Houston "riding a gray horse."

To the extreme right was Colonel Lamar, saddled up with sixty-two other cavalrymen under Captains Karnes and Smith. Private John Ferrell noted that Deaf Smith "wore a Mexican sombrero and rode a Spanish pony" this day.

Next were Lieutenant Colonel Henry Millard's ninety-two regulars under Captains Andrew Briscoe and Amasa Turner. Marching near the regulars was the six-piece Texas band of Dick, George Brown, and fifers John Beebe, Martin Flores, Luke Bust, and Frederick Lemsky. To the left and slightly ahead of these divisions were the thirty-two men of the artillery corps with the two six-pounder Twin Sisters cannon. They were under command of Colonel Hockley, Captain Isaac Moreland and First Lieutenant William Stilwell.

Colonel Hockley, Inspector General for the Army, had been placed in acting command of the artillery forces due to the injury of Lieutenant Colonel James Neill in the previous day's skirmish.

To the left of the artillery, and forming the center of all forces, was Colonel Burleson's First Regiment, eight companies and 386 men strong. Finally, Colonel Sherman's Second Regiment, ten companies and 330 men strong, formed the left wing of the Texas Army. Colonel Wharton, the adjutant general, joined Sherman to help lead the Second Regiment.

The surgeons were momentarily perplexed with how to act during the fight. According to General Houston, "there was no particular assignment of the surgeons made at the battle of San Jacinto." Doctors Booker, Fitzhue, Davidson and Labadie consulted each other on whether they should stay back from the fight or march along. Their surgeon general, Dr. Alexander Ewing, had not given them any direction. The doctors all agreed to fight with their weapons "as circumstances might direct," shook hands all around and marched with their respective divisions. Fitzhue took the center, Davidson the right, and Labadie took to the left with Colonel Sherman's Second Regiment, where his former company under Captain Logan was marching.

Riding past the troops from right to left, General Houston stopped in front of Colonel Burleson's division to listen to company commanders giving motivational speeches.

Captain Moseley Baker, the former editor who now commanded the largest company at San Jacinto, reminded his men that "Travis, Crockett, Bowie and their companions" held out bravely against forces "twenty times their number." Baker told his men he was confident in their ability but "if there be one who is not fully satisfied, he is at liberty to remain at camp, for I do not wish my company disgraced by a single act of cowardice."

Baker's speech at San Jacinto was later written out from memory by Private John Menefee. He later recalled his captain saying:

> ***Remember, you are fighting an enemy who gives no quarter, and regards neither age nor sex. Recollect that your homes are destroyed; imagine your wives and daughters trudging mud and water, and your children crying for bread, and then remember that the author of all this woe is within a short distance of us; that the arch fiend is now within our grasp; and that the time has come at last for us to avenge the blood of our fallen heroes and to teach the haughty dictator that Texas can not be conquered and that they can and will be free.***
>
> ***Then nerve yourselves for the battle, knowing that our cause is just and we are in the hands of an Allwise Creator, and as you strike the murderous blows, let our watchwords be "Remember Goliad"; "Remember the Alamo."***

Baker reportedly also told his men to offer no quarter to the enemy. A token of this measure was displayed in the form of a red handkerchief. A vote was taken on whether the no quarter rule should be followed and only one man, Private John Money, voted against it. "A red handkerchief was therefore hoisted for a flag," wrote Corporal Isaac Hill.

Just behind Baker's company was that of Captain Calder. He felt that Baker's speech was a very moving appeal to the men's patriotism. "Not being an orator myself," wrote Calder,

"I requested my company to avail themselves of Captain Baker's sentiments, and so make the effect double."

General Houston also moved along the Second Regiment's lines. Captain James Gillaspie of Company F recalled that "Gen. Houston passed down in front of the regiment and spoke to every captain belonging to it." At Captain David Murphree's Columbia company, Goliad Massacre survivor Charles Shain said that Houston told them "that such as could not stand the bayonet, must stay behind."

Shain and the other massacre survivors needed no pep talk to find motivation to avenge the loss of their comrades. In addition to the Goliad Massacre survivors, there were two Texans present at San Jacinto who had been in the Alamo shortly before its fall: Captain Juan Seguin and Antonio Cruz, who had been late messengers from the fortress.

General Houston stopped in front of Captain Arnold's Second Regiment company and had a conference with Tom Rusk, deciding that the Secretary of War should stay with Sherman's regiment at the start of the attack. After the battle was joined, Rusk would then ride across the field to report to Houston how the Second Regiment was doing.

Peering across the mile-wide prairie from atop trees, the Texans could see no activity in the Mexican campground. Even stranger, no sentries were noted along the camp's perimeter. Was Santa Anna cleverly and quietly waiting to pounce once they marched forward?

With but one way to find out, Sam Houston trotted Saracen before his paraded companies about 4:00 p.m. and ordered, "Trail arms! Forward!"

Unbelievably, General Houston had finally given the order that hundreds thought might never come. Farmers, lawyers, teachers, politicians, doctors, merchants, rangers, soldiers of fortune, traders, old men and young boys moved out from their mossy thicket onto the plains of San Jacinto.

Sergeant Swearingen of Captain Turner's company wrote that "the infantry was ordered to trail arms and advance until within 50 yards of the enemy before we fired." The order "trail arms" meant for the soldiers to carry their rifle or musket in the right arm, extending downward so that the muzzle was tilted forward and the butt was near the ground.

James Tarlton, of Baker's "no quarter" company, was impressed with the undaunted spirit of the Texans as they finally marched across the field. He had brought volunteers from Kentucky six months before, only to just miss out on the battle for San Antonio. Tarlton was now encouraged by this "handful of raw, undisciplined volunteers, just taken from their ploughs and thrown together with rifles without bayonets, no two perhaps of the same calibre."

Colonel Rusk felt that "all the divisions advanced in good order and high spirits." Rusk noted old Jimmy Curtis, the former ranger, carrying two guns. At fifty-seven years of age, Curtis was the third oldest Texan on the battlefield at San Jacinto. "I asked him what was his reason for carrying more than one gun," remembered Rusk.

"Damn the Mexicans!" Curtis exclaimed. He had recently lost his son-in-law and another relative at the Alamo and planned to kill two Mexicans in return "or be killed myself."

The tall coastal grass on the plains of San Jacinto afforded the Texans the opportunity to move forward without being seen. Private Edward Miles of the First Regiment's Company A recalled that the prairie before him was "covered with high serge grass." They were also aided by a slight ridge in the middle of the field which, coupled, with the high grass, helped disguise the progress as the Texian army advanced over the mile-wide prairie.

Sam Houston had no idea of the other elements that were working in his favor on April 21. Santa Anna's troops since midday had allowed a laxness to take hold that would do them no favor.

After General Cos' four hundred reinforcement troops had arrived mid-morning, Santa Anna maintained an escort force of thirty-two selected infantrymen on horseback, mounted on officers' horses. These men were to protect Santa Anna's personal escort force and to watch for and protect Colonel Garcia's expected supply train that was approaching from Harrisburg with another one hundred men.

Captain Miguel Aguirre, commanding this special guard force, was sent by General Cos during the noon hour to make an inquiry of Santa Anna. Cos requested that "his troops be allowed to eat and to feed and water the horses since that had not been done since the day before."

General Santa Anna agreed. "The compassionate tone with which they made these requests caused me to agree," he later wrote. He cautioned Captain Aguirre, however, that their needs should be satisfied quickly and that Aguirre should return at once and occupy the guard position that he held command over.

As events turned out, Aguirre failed to return to his position. Santa Anna decided to satisfy some of his own needs as well.

> ***Since I was worn out from having spent the morning on horseback and had not slept the night before, I lay down in the shade of some trees while the troops were preparing their meals. I had them call General Don Manuel Fernández Castrillón, who was acting as major general, and told him to guard the camp and to advise me of the least movement on the part of the enemy. I likewise charged him to awaken me as soon as the troops had finished eating because it was necessary to act decisively as soon as possible.***

SHERMAN'S SECOND REGIMENT DRAWS FIRST BLOOD

Spyglasses had shown no movement whatsoever in the Mexican camp as the Texan troops pushed forward across the San Jacinto battleground on April 21, 1836. The artillery company hauled the Twin Sisters up the rising slope toward Santa Anna's camp as the wall of Texans, hundreds of yards wide, advanced on the Mexicans. The cannoneers pulled the two heavy cannon with leather straps through the tall prairie grass toward a slight rise in the center of the field.

The Texans certainly moved out silently. An early account by Dr. Labadie states that "the music struck up a lively air as we bid good-by to our camp." This is highly unlikely. Although the Texian band marched with the regulars, most battle participants later related that their music was not started until after the first shots had been fired.

Forward across the battleground marched the volunteer regiment under Colonel Burleson and the regulars under Lieutenant Colonel Millard, while on the extreme right of the Texans rode Colonel Lamar's cavalry. On the extreme left of the advancing Texas forces was Colonel Sherman's infantry regiment.

Sherman's men moved quickly and silently through the mossy live oaks and tall grasses of the little thicket which ran along the edge of the marsh. They advanced with good cover toward the Mexican camp, with almost no chance of being spotted until they were within the last one hundred yards. The tree cover and the slight rise in the ground toward Santa Anna's forces disguised their movements well. All sources, including General Houston's official report, agree that Sherman's Second Regiment on the left wing reached the Mexican camp first.

Sherman's flankers encountered a division of Mexican soldiers in the woods near camp and opened fire. The surprised *soldados* fired shots at the advancing Texans, but quickly fell back to their own campground for protection.

"Captain Arnold's company was the first in the regiment in the charge upon the enemy in battle," wrote Private Philip Martin. "I was the fifth or sixth man from Col. Sherman." Martin's fellow infantryman Stephen Sparks agrees that Hayden Arnold's First Company was first to fire on April 21.

> ***My captain's company was the front of the regiment, and we marched in double file. We were ordered not to fire until we could see the whites of the enemies' eyes. When we got within 300 yards of the ditch we were ordered to charge, and we charged in double file. There was only one man in front of me who fired before I did, and so I got the credit for firing the second gun on our side. We had out-traveled the first regiment, and had driven [Colonel Juan] Almonte about 200 yards before the first regiment got near Santa Anna's breastworks.***

Private Alfonso Steele of Captain Gillaspie's Sixth Company wrote that Sherman's men were ordered to fire "when we got up within sixty or seventy yards."

Marching across the battlefield with Edward Burleson's First Regiment, Captain William Heard witnessed the start of action near a heavy point of woods near the Mexican camp.

> ***There was a sharp fire took place at that point. In a few moments I looked in that direction and saw the Mexicans running along the edge of the woods, and Sherman and his men after them. This greatly encouraged me and those near where I was. We shouted at the top of our voices: "Yonder they go, boys, and Sherman after them!" This happened when our regiment was some distance from the enemy, and before we had fired a single shot. Sherman and his men pursued them in hot haste, and they crossed the breast-work where it joined the timber. This circumstance had more to do in gaining the victory than any move that took place on that day.***

Another First Regiment company commander, Robert Calder, agreed. He wrote that Sherman's Second Regiment "had the honor of breaking the right wing of the enemy before we attacked his centre."

For many of Sherman's men, their first shot was the only volley they had time to fire. The fighting quickly became hand to hand as the Second Regiment swarmed over the right end of the Mexican breastworks. This end of the Mexican camp was occupied by the regiments of General Cos and Colonel Almonte.

The Mexicans began firing back on the Texans, but they had clearly been caught off guard. Colonel Sherman was given credit for being the first to shout "Remember the Alamo! Remember Goliad!" He would not be the last to hurl these inspirational phrases on April 21.

Colonel Rusk also noted that, "There was a general cry which pervaded the ranks—'Remember the Alamo! Remember La Bahia!' These words electrified all." He felt that the "unerring aim and irresistible energy of the Texan army could not be withstood."

Further behind Captain Arnold's First Company was the nineteenman Fourth Company of Captain William Ware. The surprise certainly came before Ware's men reached the enemy lines, for Private James Winters states that "before we got in sight of the Mexicans, they began firing at us." After the Second Regiment was fully engaged, Winters recalled that "Rusk started out with us, but turned and went with the artillery."

First Sergeant Edward Thomas Branch, charging with Captain William Logan's Third Company, felt that "no officer stood higher" than Colonel Sidney Sherman as he led the Second Regiment against Santa Anna's campground. He wrote to his commander that "I distinctly recollect seeing you in the timber in the midst of your regiment." Branch's first lieutenant, Frank Hardin, was equally inspired by Sherman's conduct "in the heat of the action." While stopping to reload his gun, Hardin encountered Sherman hurrying to direct the fire of his regiment.

Satisfied with the progress of Sidney Sherman's men in completely surprising the enemy, Secretary of War Rusk moved across the field with his young aide, Dr. Junius William Mottley, riding alongside him. As previously arranged, he intended to report to General Houston on the progress of Colonel Sherman's regiment. As Rusk passed Colonel Hockley's artillery, he noted that the Mexican army had opened fire with its cannon on the Texas cavalry.

As they neared Houston, Mottley was knocked from his horse by a copper-ball rifle shot through the stomach, which would later prove fatal. Rusk wrote that shortly thereafter Mottley's "spirit took its flight to join the immortal Milam and others in a better world."

Unable to help the young doctor, Rusk rode swiftly to Sam Houston. As he approached, the Texas general's horse was hit by a volley of shots. Passing about forty yards from the Mexican lines and in front of the Golden Standard, Houston's borrowed horse suddenly buckled, its gray coat splattered crimson red as five shots found their mark in the animal's chest. It is likely that the horse was hit with grape shot from the Mexican cannon. Houston said that Saracen died almost instantly, "having been pierced with five balls."

As Houston's noble stallion silently collapsed, he literally slid off and landed on his feet. From the First Regiment's Company A, Private Achelle Marre caught a riderless horse for the general and Houston mounted its saddle. The horse was small and Houston's long legs dangled below the stirrups.

Riding his second horse of the battle, Sam Houston pushed forward. With the Mexican army being routed on one side and the main camp fully alerted, the remainder of the Texian forces rushed into the conflict.

Colonel George Hockley, leading the artillery, put it well: "A general conflict now ensued."

BURLESON'S FIRST REGIMENT ENGAGES

While Sherman's men were quick to stir up the enemy by sweeping through the woods, he also alerted the enemy as to the others moving directly toward the Mexican camp.

Colonel Lamar's cavalry was in advance of the infantrymen and his horses were fired upon by the Golden Standard, the Mexican cannon. The Mexican riflemen quickly joined in and began to fire upon Colonel Burleson's First Regiment. Joseph Lawrence had joined Lamar's cavalry for the day from Captain Stevenson's company to help offset losses from the previous day. Approaching the Mexican camp, Lawrence felt that the shooting suddenly became intense.

> ***As we advanced they did not see us until we were within a hundred yards of them. Then they fired a terrific volley of small shot at us. But fortunately they shot over our heads. It seemed at one time that if one had held his hat two feet above his head, it would have caught twenty bullets or more.***

Burleson's men had been ordered to fire when within fifty yards of Santa Anna's camp, but they suddenly found the battlefield erupting into gunfire earlier than expected. Flashes of fire and smoke erupted among the breastworks of packsaddles up ahead in the Mexican camp.

Deaf Smith, having seen to the destruction of Vince's Bridge, raced back to the Texas troops just as they were marching across the San Jacinto battlefield. His horse filthy and foaming from hard riding, Smith raced to Houston and announced that the bridge at Vince's had been cut. The general later wrote that Smith said "Vince Bridge was cut down, and set on fire." Houston then sent Smith to spread the word among the advancing lines that there would be no reinforcements. Houston himself "dashed in front of Burleson's regiment, and announced the fact to the army."

Sergeant Swearingen of Company B relates:

> ***Our riflemen having nearly 100 yards left to go than we had [planned] commenced the action with small arms before we did with our muskets. The musketry and riflemen kept advancing as they fired. When within about 20 steps of the enemy's line we were ordered to charge with bayonets. As soon as we were ordered to the charge and brought our guns to the proper position, the enemy gave way, except about 60 men around the cannon and protected by breastwork of corn sacks, salt, barrels of meal, and boxes of canister shot. They fell by the bayonet and swam in one mangled heap from that time until they reached the bayou.***

Captain Calder, leading Company K over the slight rise in the prairie, estimated that Burleson's regiment came under fire "before we were within three hundred yards of them.

In the meantime our fire was reserved until we were within sixty yards of their line." Calder wrote that the Texans had moved forward "in regular order and almost perfect silence," indicating that there was no music played until the battle began.

Private Sion Bostick of Captain Baker's Company D recalled, "We moved down a slope slowly, but when we started up a long sloping ridge, we all went in double-quick. Every one of us was yelling: 'Remember the Alamo! Remember Fannin!'"

Burleson's regiment escaped harm from the first volleys fired at them from the Mexican camp. "They overshot us with their muskets," wrote Private Alfred Kelso of Captain Heard's Company F. Private Samuel Hardaway, who had escaped being captured with Fannin in March and had since joined Captain Baker's Company D, agreed that "they seemed to shoot above us." Ed Miles of Captain Wood's Company A felt that "the enemy's shots passed over us like hail."

Reserving their fire, the Texans began descending the slight slope toward the camp and then began to take a few casualties from the enemy's fire. Santa Anna's *soldados* had adjusted their aim and began to hit some of the advancing Texans.

Private Ed Blakey of Billingsley's Company C was mortally wounded as he crested the slight rise. George Erath, running alongside him, picked up Blakey's gun and shot back, throwing down his own. His own gun had become choked while reloading after his first shot.

Another man of Billingsley's company was shot down while advancing on the Mexican breastworks. Private Thomas Mays, a thirty-four-year-old originally from Tennessee, recalled:

> ***When in about 250 or 300 yards distant from the breastworks I was cut down by a musket ball, which entered my left thigh (the ball is still in [me]). While on the ground wounded, R. M. Cravens, who had just fired off his gun, stopped near by to reload it, when I requested him to remain with me. He did so, and we laid down with our heads towards the battle, with our guns to protect us.***

Once Burleson's First Regiment came under fire, the silence they had maintained instantly converted to a cacophony of simultaneous shouting and shooting. Shouts of "Remember the Alamo" rang out down the lines as the firing began. Captain Calder noted an almost immediate "confusion and panic in the ranks of the enemy."

As the general battle commenced, the Texas field musicians began to play. There were four fifers—Frederick Lemsky, John Beebe, Martin Flores and Luke Bust. The little band also had two drummers, George Brown and Dick, the former slave. They had remained silent during the march across the field until the firing commenced. They opened with "Will You Come to the Bower?" once the shooting erupted.

Some accounts have that the Texas musicians began playing as the army marched forward. Private John Menefee later claimed that the troops "marched upon the enemy with the stillness of death. No fife, no drum, no voice was heard, until at 200 yards," he wrote. Captain Calder's account agrees that the Texians initially advanced in "almost perfect silence."

Menefee's assertion that no music was played until the Texans were close to the Mexican camp is generally accepted by historians. Certainly no element of surprise could have been achieved by six musicians playing drums and flutes! Once the first shots were fired, the musicians then had reason to burst into inspiring tune.

Private John Hassell wrote in June 1836 that Colonel Burleson "ordered Yankee Doodle played" as he commanded his men to move forward at double-quick pace. Private Walter Lane of the cavalry would later insist that the band played an old folk song called "The Girl I Left Behind." While both of these tunes may have been played at some point, the song most commonly accepted as that played during the march into battle at San Jacinto is Thomas Moore's "Will You Come to the Bower?"

The fact that this particular song did not have more military use for the soldiers to step to is indicative of the ragtag little Texas band. The members were from three different companies and certainly this little corps had not practiced much together. "Will You Come to the Bower?" was a popular tune of the time that each man likely knew well enough to play.

According to Colonel Coleman, the Twin Sisters were first fired "when we had approached within two hundred yards." Gunner John Ferrell agreed that "we unlimbered at about 2 hundred yards from the Mexican breastworks." At the same moment, General Houston rode to the center of Colonel Burleson's regiment and cried out loudly, "To the charge! To the charge!" The Texas foot soldiers immediately "set forward in double quick time, and in one minute the action became general."

The roar of the Twin Sisters was inspiring to many of the foot soldiers. "Every man sprang forward with renewed energy," recalled John Swisher. The artillerymen worked rapidly, and the Twin Sisters kept up a steady firing. Swisher felt that "the thunder of their roar is very potent in scaring the wits out of the enemy, and is worth ten bands of martial music in inspiring the troops."

Swisher noted that the First Regiment came under fire while still a considerable distance from the enemy camp. He felt that the Mexican army fired "incessantly" and fought valiantly around their cannon. "During the charge the air seemed to be full of hissing bullets," he wrote. Bullets struck the ground around the feet of the charging men, while others whistled past their ears.

First Lieutenant John Borden of Captain Baker's Company D found some of his men holding their fire until the distance narrowed. During the early firing, Captain Baker was one of the first Texans to be wounded on April 21. Sergeant Moses Bryan later stated, "I had three holes shot in the skirts of my frock coat—the coat flew out as we advanced in a trot. And I heard bullets whistling as they overshot us."

When Captain Baker went down, Lieutenant Borden assumed acting command as he found the battle erupting about him.

> ***In a very short time, perhaps a minute, the firing became general; smoke from the cannon and small arms rendered it almost impossible to see the shape or size of our enemy. But on we pushed, pell-mell, helter-skelter.***

Burleson's regiment would within minutes begin mixing with that of Sidney Sherman's as the Texans rushed upon the Mexican campground.

Captain Juan Seguin's Tejano company fought valiantly. Sam Houston would later write to Seguin's father of "his brave and gallant bearing in the battle of San Jacinto, with that of his men." Commanding "the only Mexican company who fought in the cause of Texas at the Battle of San Jacinto," Seguin also earned Houston's "warmest regard and esteem."

As his company approached camp, they were ordered to fire a volley into Santa Anna's men. Having been ordered to keep low while approaching, Seguin's men lay low and quickly reloaded. Corporal Ambrosio Rodriguez remembered hearing First Sergeant Manuel Flores hollering at his companymen to "Get up! Santa Anna's men are running."

As he led his twenty-four-man unit into battle, Seguin noticed Private Juan López, the teenage orphan boy who had joined his company at the Buffalo Bayou crossing two days prior. López was "entering boldly the fight, brandishing on one hand an old rusty sword, holding on the other a gun stick at the top of which was fastened a red kind of rag." Captain Seguin ordered López to throw down the pole and take the rifle of Private Manuel Tarin, "who declared himself sick and unable to fight." In the boy's Republic pension application, Seguin would later write that young López "fought as bravely as any man in the Army and recd. a slight flesh wound in the left knee."

During the battle near the Mexican camp, one Mexican officer called out for mercy. According to Colonel Rusk, the officer called out to Tony Menchaca of Captain Seguin's company, calling him "a brother Mexican." The enemy soldier pleaded with the Tejano to save his life.

"No, damn you, I'm no Mexican," replied Menchaca. "I'm an American. Shoot him!" Another soldier fired and killed the Mexican officer.

SANTA ANNA'S FORCES OVERRUN

The activities of General Santa Anna at the moment of the Texian assault upon his campground have long been debated among historians. Accounts of Mexican veterans admit that the conditions were very relaxed and that many men were resting from the previous days' long marches.

General Santa Anna had retired to his own tent to rest. One of the more controversial stories to later circulate was that El Presidente was entertaining young Emily D. West, the indentured servant captured at Morgan's Point three days before. Santa Anna had been without female companionship for more than two weeks. He had taken a "bride" in a mock marriage, performed by a Mexican officer impersonating a priest, in San Antonio before the final assault on the Alamo. The attractive seventeen-year-old rode with the Mexican command on the San Jacinto campaign until April 2. High waters on the Guadalupe River would not allow her heavy carriage to cross, and she was sent back to Mexico City in her carriage, which reportedly included a trunk full of silver.

Santa Anna's men had captured several of Colonel Morgan's indentured servants on April 19 at New Washington, including Emily West. As chaos befell the Mexican army, some believe that the Mexican commander-in-chief was being distracted by Emily West. Her generally accepted description of being a mulatto girl led some to later believe that she was the inspiration for the song "The Yellow Rose of Texas." Sam Houston reportedly knew of the Miss Emily story, although many historians dismiss the whole event as a grandiose piece of Texas folklore.

Colonel Delgado and the other Mexican officers were caught completely off guard as the Texans raced forward. In his diary, he recorded the state of affairs as Houston's men closed in on their camp.

> ***At this fatal moment the bugler on our right signaled the advance of the enemy upon that wing. His Excellency and staff were asleep; the greater number of the men were also sleeping; of the rest, some were eating, others were scattered in the woods in search of boughs to prepare shelter. Our line was composed of musket stacks. Our cavalry was riding bare-back to and from water.***

Colonel Castrillón had just shaved and bathed himself when the commotion erupted. Moments earlier, he had been engaged in conversation with other members of Santa Anna's staff. Santa Anna claimed that Castrillón had carelessly neglected to visit the guard lines a single time while Santa Anna and Cos' men were resting. "Following his example the other leaders and officers did the same thing, and thus part of the troops were asleep, and those who were awake were completely relaxed," wrote General Vicente Filisola.

Santa Anna's personal secretary, Ramón Caro, felt that the president unfairly pushed blame on Castrillón. He felt that the commander-in-chief was equally liable for vigilance against an enemy "who on the day before makes a false attack to feel our strength."

Santa Anna later wrote that he was "sleeping soundly" when he was awakened by the firing. He immediately became aware that his forces were under attack and that "there was unexplained disorder. The enemy had surprised our advance posts." General Santa Anna immediately attempted to organize a defensive force against the Texans.

He organized an attack column under Colonel Manuel Céspedes which consisted of the Guerrero permanent battalion and detachments from Toluca and Guadalajara. Céspedes, joined with a column under Lieutenant Colonel Santiago Luelmo, marched forward to contain the main fire of the Texans. The Mexican cannon was commanded by Lieutenant Ignacio Arenal, who kept up a continual fire against the Texans during the early moments of the battle.

"I SHOT OLD BETSY SIX TIMES"

During the early minutes of the battle of San Jacinto, the surprised Mexican soldiers managed to put up strong resistance. Their makeshift breastworks offered something of a haven for their riflemen. "Their breastworks were composed of baggage, saddle bags, and brush, in all about four or five feet high," remembered James Winters of Sherman's regiment. "There was a gap eight or ten feet wide through which they fired the cannon."

Once Colonel Sherman's Second Regiment began sweeping into the Mexican camp, these breastworks offered no protection. Few men had bayonets on their rifles, so their firearms became warclubs once the opportunity to reload was lost. The Texans used their muskets and rifles to bash the enemy and many of their guns were broken off at the breech.

Private Michael J. Brake of Captain Logan's company snapped his shotgun in half during the battle. Captain Hayden Arnold's expensive London Younger gun, which he valued at $35, was shot nearly off at the breech. During the continued action, his gun was entirely broken and discarded on the battlefield.

Private Jesse Davis had a close call while fighting with Captain Murphree's Columbia company. Early in the battle, his gun began acting up. Davis took a seat on a fallen log to repair it amidst the fighting and confusion. Hearing a comrade shout to him, he looked up in time to see a Mexican officer advancing on him with a drawn sword. Davis whirled, grasping the barrel of his rifle, and struck the officer a terrific blow on the side of the head. As his victim crumpled, Davis collected the Mexican's sword and moved on into battle, discarding his own broken gun.

The cavalry companies of Captains William Smith and Henry Karnes raced into the Mexican camp to join the hand-to-hand fighting. "In a second we were into them with guns, pistols and bowie knives," wrote Private Walter Lane. "In a short time, they were running like turkeys, whipped and discomfited."

Deaf Smith was as valiant on the battlefield as he had proven as a spy throughout the Texas Revolution. As the Texas infantry advanced across the field, he had galloped ahead and directly up to the breastworks. Secretary of War Rusk happened to catch a view of old Deaf in action at the Mexican lines.

> ***Just as he reached it, his horse stumbled and fell, throwing him over his head among the enemy. Having dropped his sword in the fall, he jumped up, drew one of his belt pistols, presented it at the head of a Mexican, who was attempting to bayonet him, and the percussion-cap exploded without the pistol's going off. Upon which, Smith threw the pistol at the head of the Mexican, staggered him back, seized his gun, took it from him, and defended himself with it, until the infantry got up to his relief.***

Private James H. Nash, a fellow scout of Captain Karnes' company, came to Smith's rescue. Spurring his own horse, he ran down the Mexican officer and allowed Smith to finish off the soldier with the Mexican's own saber.

Rusk noted a number of brave acts of individuals on April 21. One of these was John Robbins, who had given up his horse on April 20 to one of Sherman's volunteers. His horse was killed in the action, and Robbins was forced to fight on foot this day. To further add to his situation, he lost his gun in the heat of battle near the breastworks. Charging through camp, he was seized by a Mexican soldier who had lost his gun also. Colonel Rusk noted the two "stout men" fall to the ground in hand-to-hand combat. "Robbins managed, whilst contending on the earth, to get out a Bowie-knife, which he had in his belt, and quickly ended the contest, by cutting the Mexican's throat."

During the close-quarters duel, Private William Sadler, the former ranger captain who had joined the Nacogdoches Volunteers, was attacked by a Mexican soldier wielding a straight-bladed dagger. In the ensuing wrestle, Sadler won possession of the dirk, which would remain a prized possession of his for many years.

Although some Texans had been shot down while advancing over the center of the battlefield, the larger number of casualties occurred in front of and inside the Mexican campground. Advancing under heavy fire, Colonel Burleson's First Regiment took twice as many casualties as Sherman's Second Regiment, which had advanced under better cover.

Albert Gallatin, first sergeant of Captain Ware's Company B, wrote the *Texas Almanac* in 1872 to confirm that his company fought with Colonel Sherman and that "I was wounded in that battle." From Ware's little nineteen-man company, four men were killed or wounded as they charged the Mexican breastworks.

Second Lieutenant George A. Lamb was shot down and killed while charging with Ware's company. A twenty-one-year-old who had come to Texas in 1834 as an orphan from South Carolina, he was later honored as the namesake of Lamb County, Texas. Second Sergeant William Carvin Winters was shot in the knee and fell. Private George Washington Robinson was also seriously wounded and fell near the enemy's breastworks. Despite losing nearly a quarter of his men in the first moments of battle, Captain Ware's other men fought bravely ahead.

First Sergeant Thomas Patton Fowle of Captain Smith's company was mortally wounded while leading his cavalrymen in the charge against the Mexican encampment. A Boston native who was a scholar of the French, Spanish and Italian languages, young Fowle died on the San Jacinto battlefield.

Private John Hassell of Burleson's regiment considered San Jacinto "an open field fight" in which revenge was the "prevailing feeling or sentiment." He wrote to his father on June 21 with his actions during the battle.

> ***Our cannons, our muskets, our rifles and pistols played, it appeared to me, the most delightful tune I have ever heard since the world commenced. I had [a] first rate rifle and about this time I was using her, sir, with all my might. She run about forty [inches] to the ground and shot first rate.***
>
> ***I took notice to some of the big yellow bellies and when Betsy would bore a hole in them, the claret would gush out large as a cornstalk. One big fellow, I remember, who I shot in the neck and it appeared that it had near cut his head off. I shot old Betsy six times and a holster pistol one time. In the seven shots I know that I killed four.***

Mitchell Putman of Captain Heard's company was wounded in the right arm near the body by an escopeta ball, which caused a partial paralysis of his arm. Another of Heard's men, Leroy Wilkinson, was severely wounded and would die within two weeks from the effects of his wounds.

Captain Stevenson's Company H moved steadily toward the Mexican campground. Private James Hill recalled the enemy's breastworks "beginning at [a] point of timber and extending out a considerable distance in the prairie." Stacked with "brush, blankets, sacks of corn, flour, camp equipage, aparajos [packsaddles]" and other packing, Hill found the enemy's breastworks to be "bulletproof."

Two of Stevenson's men were shot down as the company approached the breastworks. Second Sergeant Ashley Stephens was shot through the calf in each leg, although no bones were broken. Unable to walk, he would lie bleeding on the battlefield for many hours. Private John Tom was also hit in a leg, the force shattering the leg below the knee and leaving his foot dangling.

George Washington Lonis, a member of Captain David Murphree's company, was severely wounded in the chest. Known as "Washington," Lonis fired on the enemy many times before falling. According to Dr. James Phelps, he saw Lonis fall and went to his aid with three other members of Murphree's company. George Wright, James Hayr and Claiborne Rector picked up a blanket from the abandoned baggage of the fleeing Mexican army. These four placed Lonis aboard the blanket and carried him back to the rear of the action, where Dr. Phelps could tend to him.

As they laid him over on his side, Lonis came to long enough to announce, "I fired my gun thirteen times, and I saw twelve of the yellow bellies fall."

Dr. Phelps found that Lonis had been shot through the right lung straight through front to back. Every breath was a bloody, gurgling respiration which Phelps could hear. Although seriously wounded, Lonis would survive and he and his wife settled in Guadalupe County, Texas.

Another of the Murphree company to be hit was twenty-year-old Private Elbridge Gerry Rector. "I was in the battle of San Jacinto and was wounded in the arm and side," wrote Rector in 1902. "The wound in the side is hurting me at this writing." Private Elijah Votaw of Captain Gillaspie's unit "was wounded by a canister shot in the breast."

Benjamin Brigham, the young soldier of ill health who had finally gotten a good night's sleep, was severely wounded early in the battle. Advancing across the field behind the Twin Sisters, he threw up his arms and cried out to his captain as he fell face forward. His messmate Francis Cooke, who had taken Brigham's guard detail so that he could finally rest before battle, later learned of the loss of his buddy.

> ***Brigham was my friend and my comrade. We ate together, slept together, fought together. We were two boys about nineteen years of age, fighting for the same cause. I would have done anything for him, and I weep for him today, as I wept for him sixty-five years ago when I looked for him after the battle and found he was no more.***

Brigham's captain, Robert Calder, considered him a "noble young comrade" who "although a boy in years, his solid sense and judgement would have done credit to most men at maturity of years."

The discipline of the Texans quickly broke down as they raced into the Mexican camp. Every man discharged his firearm as rapidly as possible, then furiously reloaded his gun and fired again. Reloading the muskets required men to stop and work on their weapons. With gun loaded and charged, each man then ran ahead and sought out his next victim. They did not wait for orders to fire again. Nor did many wait for the regiment of companymen to fire in unison.

Private Alfonso Steele had only gotten off his second round by the time he noted some of the Mexicans in camp fleeing ahead of him. He stopped in the timber to reload again and then ran on ahead of some of Captain Gillaspie's company. He raised his gun to shoot another Mexican, but Steele was shot through the body before he could fire.

As he fell, David Rusk of Captain Arnold's Nacogdoches Volunteers called for some men to stay and help him. "No, take them on," implored Steele.

> ***One of our own men in passing asked me if he could take my pistol, but by this time I was bleeding at the nose and mouth so I couldn't speak; so he just stooped down and got it and went on. After laying there awhile I managed to get to a sitting posture and drink some water I had in a gourd. This stopped the blood from coming from my nose and mouth.***

TWIN SISTERS AGAINST THE GOLDEN STANDARD

The Second Regiment routed the newly arrived troops under General Cos, most of whom had been lying down asleep before the shooting began. Some of these inexperienced men rushed into battle without even their guns. While General Cos' reinforcements proved to be outclassed, the *soldados* manning Santa Anna's Golden Standard cannon proved to be fierce fighters. From the center of the battlefield the Twin Sisters fired away, steadily pounding the Mexican forces. The Golden Standard only fired three rounds before a shot from the Twin Sisters hit the Mexican cannon's water bucket, wounding or scaring off most of the gunners.

John M. Wade, a former company commander during the Bexar siege, was working one of the Twin Sisters with Ben McCullough and John Ferrell. It was their gun that carried away the water bucket of the Mexican long-nine and did other damage.

Gunner Ben McCullough later wrote:

> ***At the battle of San Jacinto, I was in command of one piece of artillery. The fire of it opened upon the enemy, about two hundred yards distant. We advanced after each discharge, keeping it in advance of the breastworks, at which time I had aimed the gun, but was delayed in firing for a moment by General Houston, who passed across some thirty paces in front of the gun, and was nearly that distance in advance of every man in that part of the field.***

When Burleson's First Regiment and Millard's regulars had advanced within about one hundred yards of the Mexican breastworks, the Texan artillery corps was slightly in advance of the infantrymen. At this moment, a division of Mexican soldiers under Colonel Manuel Céspedes charged upon Hockley's artillery.

To First Sergeant Lyman Rounds of Captain Briscoe's regulars it seemed that his men were unfairly exposed during the march across the field.

> ***Although an admirer of Genl. Houston, I think he made a rather unmilitary movement in making the attack. He formed in double file, marched at a right angle on the enemy's left until within musket range, filed to right by flank, so that our Co. (A) had to march the entire length of the Mexicans' line under fire, before we could face to the front and return their fire.***

Despite the exposure to his company, Rounds and every member of Colonel Millard's regulars escaped injury on April 21. Every other division of Texans, in fact, suffered casualties except for the regulars!

At the height of the fight, General Manuel Fernando Castrillón, Colonel Juan Almonte and Lieutenant Colonel Pedro Delgado shouted encouragement to their men to fight.

General Castrillón, commanding the Mexican artillery, turned his cannon's attention from Lamar's cavalry in order to assist the charge of Colonel Céspedes and Lieutenant Colonel Santiago Luelmo upon the Texan artillery. The Golden Standard was turned in the direction of Burleson's regiment and quickly readied to fire. The soldier preparing to light the fuse, however, was shot down by a Texas infantryman.

"The First Regiment, at that instant, with the most deafening yell I ever heard, charged upon the breast-work," wrote Colonel Rusk. The Twin Sisters barked angrily at the same moment that Burleson's screaming soldiers charged forward.

"We rushed forward with great impetuosity," wrote Captain Stevenson after the battle, "jumped the enemy's breastworks, the Alamo being our war cry." He added, "Our rifles created dreadful havoc among them, and they gave way in every direction."

The two advancing Mexican columns under Céspedes and Luelmo were crushed and forced to turn tail. Luelmo fell dead and Céspedes, seriously wounded, joined the retreat. The flight of Colonel Céspedes caused some of those manning the Golden Standard to panic as well. Twenty-five-year-old Lieutenant Ignacio Arenal, however, fought bravely until the end with the cannon crew.

General Castrillón stood on, stoically extorting his comrades to fight on. Colonel Rusk noted that Castrillón was "standing on the ammunition boxes, behind the piece, exposed from head to foot." Castrillón tried in vain to sustain his men at the cannon. "When he found that to be impossible, he folded up his arms, stood and looked sullenly, and without moving, upon our troops, who were advancing upon him, until they arrived at or near the breast-work."

According to one of the Mexican eyewitnesses, First Sergeant Francisco Becerra, Castrillón was determined to die fighting. "When it was discovered the army of Gen. Santa Anna was defeated," he recalled, "several of the officers and non-commissioned officers of the command went to General Castrillón and begged him to leave the field." According to Becerra, Castrillón felt that it "was a matter of no consequence should they all be killed, but it was a great loss to Mexico should he fall."

Walter Lane of Captain Karnes' company considered Castrillón "an old Castillian gentleman" who proudly accepted his own fate in the face of superior numbers. Lane claims that Colonel Rusk even implored the Texans not to kill Castrillon, "and knocked up some of their guns; but others ran round and riddled him with balls."

Tom Rusk, in examining the proud artillery general's body after the battle, "found that several rifle-balls had passed directly through his body." Of European Spanish descent, Castrillon was considered by Secretary of War Rusk "to be quite a gentlemanly, honourable man."

Colonel Hockley, designated to lead Captain Moreland's artillery on April 21, found plenty to be proud of. One man cited for conspicuous bravery among Hockley's unit was Private Montgomery Baxter. The rammer and sponger of No. 2 cannon of the Twin Sisters, Baxter had joined the company at the Brazos when it was organized upon the arrival of the cannon. He was cited by fellow companyman Thomas Green as having "acted very gallantly in the battle of San Jacinto." Green further stated that "due to the excessive fatigue of that day," Baxter became sick at the army's campground and died of fever at Harrisburg about a week after the battle.

Colonel Hockley wrote that his men kept up "a hot fire" and proudly noted that their first shot "caused their loud shooting to cease."

The Texans quickly captured the Mexican artillery piece. Captain William Wood certified that Private Achelle Marre, who had come to Texas in January with Sherman's men, was "among the few who took the cannon the Golden Standard" at San Jacinto.

Marre was reportedly assisted in this capture by Private John Bunton, one of the ten signers of the Texas Declaration of Independence present at San Jacinto. Bunton used his rifle to club one of the officers at the cannon while Marre drew a Mexican saber and cut down two more of the Golden Standard's gunners.

Colonel Burleson's First Regiment and Colonel Millard's two companies of regulars "charged upon and mounted the breastwork of the enemy, and drove them from their cannon," wrote Rusk. "The cavalry, under Colonel Lamar, at the same time fell on them with great fury and great slaughter."

The Mexican camp was quickly in disarray. "In ten minutes after the firing of the first gun," wrote Colonel Rusk, "we were charging through the camp, and driving them before us." The enemy took to flight, "officers and all," both on horseback and on foot, with Texans in hot pursuit.

Others estimated that it took slightly longer to break the Mexican resistance. Private Charles Shain of Captain Murphree's company wrote that "Our whole army was across the breast work in fifteen or twenty minutes after the battle commenced. The Mexicans were then running in all directions." General Sam Houston's official report states that it was "about eighteen minutes from the time of close action" until his army had succeeded in completely unnerving their opponents.

The confusion was so complete that Santa Anna himself was seen not to stick around, recalls Captain Calder.

> ***They were immediately thrown, by the charge of Sherman on their right and our attack on their left and centre, into the wildest confusion. Santa Anna and a portion of his staff, with his cavalry, broke from the field at the first discharge, escaping around our right wing. A ridge was between my position and the ground they passed over, but I saw their heads and a portion of their persons, as they were flying from the camp.***

A "PANIC STRICKEN HERD": FLIGHT OF SANTA ANNA

Santa Anna's secretary, Ramon Caro, was disgusted with the "lightning rapidity" in which the Texans had been able to overrun their superior Mexican force. "It is too much to admit that even the cavalry had unsaddled their horses and turned them loose to graze, while the enemy was in sight," he wrote.

Santa Anna, having rushed from his tent, found that even his best attempts to organize a strong stand were lost in the madness. Colonel Delgado claimed to have seen "His Excellency running about in the utmost excitement, wringing his hands and unable to give an order." Delgado noted General Castrillón on the ground, saw that Colonel Antonio Treviño was killed and that Colonel Marcial Aguirre was "severely injured." He tried to rally some of the fleeing dragoons as they raced for the trees beyond camp, "but all efforts were in vain." Delgado felt that "the evil was beyond remedy; they were a bewildered and panic stricken herd."

"With all hope lost and every man for himself," wrote Santa Anna, "my desperation was as great as my danger." A servant of Colonel Juan Bringas, Santa Anna's aide-de-camp, offered the general a horse and urged him to save himself. Reportedly remarking, "The battle is lost," Santa Anna accepted the stallion, leaving his own fine saddle and horse behind in the rush of excitement.

Santa Anna looked about for his personal escort and found only two soldiers from it who were saddling up. These men said that their fellow officers and men were already on the run. Santa Anna then tried to take the road toward Thompson's Pass, where he had last left the division under General Filisola.

Secretary Caro saw Santa Anna "coming already in flight" and he immediately followed El Presidente on horseback. "Thank God we were not among the last who fled," he wrote, "for of those, very few survived to tell the tale."

THE HALT CONTROVERSY

Sherman's and Burleson's regiments, together with Hockley's artillery, Millard's regulars and Lamar's cavalry, all came together in busting up the Mexican camp with a deadly fury. "Where our two regiments got together, and the Mexicans rallied," wrote Stephen Sparks, "about ten acres of ground was literally covered with their dead bodies."

James Tarlton of Baker's company wrote the next day that "I was enabled to be the third man" who entered the Mexican breastworks. "The destruction of human life was speedy and immense," wrote Private Samuel Hardaway of Baker's company shortly after the battle.

Soon after Dr. Mottley had been shot down, Major General Houston was also painfully wounded on the San Jacinto battlefield, although most did not realize this fact until after the battle. Riding his second horse of the day, he was stoically riding up and down the battle lines shouting, "Fire away! God damn you, fire!"

Private William Taylor, riding into combat with Captain William Smith's cavalry company, felt that Houston was highly visible during the peak of the battle.

> ***General Houston placed himself at the head of the First Regiment in front of the enemy's breastwork. The cavalry to which I belonged were on the right of it. During the engagement, General Houston was at least thirty paces in front of the interior line, animating his men to the charge at the top of his shrill voice, that was as distinct and as familiar to all as distant thunder.***

During the battle, "I met not officers of my staff," recalled Houston, "and spoke to no one of them, from the time the charge was ordered."

Houston was moving across the battlefield and was near Millard's regulars when he was struck. Colonel Rusk later wrote that "Major General Houston acted with great gallantry, encouraging his men to the attack, and heroically charged, in front of the infantry, within a few yards of the enemy, receiving at the same time a wound in his leg."

According to Robert Coleman, the general was wounded after riding "from the 1st regiment to the extreme right of Millard's command." In view of Rusk and the regulars, Houston's second horse was suddenly hit by several shots near the breastworks. As his horse collapsed, he felt a sharp pain in his left ankle as a musket ball struck home. Houston's son, Andrew Jackson Houston, later wrote that "The Texan General was twice dismounted by the enemy's fire. His first horse was killed, having been shot 5 times."

The fact that Houston lost two horses in the opening minutes of the battle of San Jacinto was reported by several participants. Captain Stevenson of the First Regiment wrote in a letter two days after the battle that "Gen. Houston had two horses killed under him, and was shot through the leg." James Winters in 1901 would relate that Houston "had two horses killed from under him, and was on his third one before he passed the Mexicans' works." Dr. Labadie, in speaking with Houston late on April 21, said that Houston told him, "I have had two horses shot under me."

General Houston was hit in the left leg by what was called a copper ball, although it was most likely made of brass. "His second [horse] was shot at the same time that the General's left ankle was shattered by a copper ball from an escopeta," wrote his son. It is interesting to note that most historians have listed Houston as having been shot in the right leg. In 1853, Houston wrote to his wife that "I still suffer slightly in my left leg, from the same cause, that I complained of at home, the San Jacinto wound."

The confusion over which leg Houston was wounded in is the likely result of artist interpretation. The battle accounts of those present do not list which leg Houston was wounded in. For his famous 1886 San Jacinto painting, William Huddle chose to show the Texas general with a bandaged right leg.

Although never confirmed, there were at least a few rumors that Houston was shot by one of his own men. Ellis Benson, fighting with the artillery, agreed that Houston was shot while charging on his horse between the two opposing lines and in front of Texas troops. According to Benson, he was shot in the ankle that was facing the Texan lines.

Colonel Mirabeau Lamar, the poet from Georgia who now commanded the cavalry, also later asserted that Houston could have been shot by one of his own men. In his private papers, he drew a comparison between Houston and the poem *Iliad.*

> ***With dread that he might defraud the eager band of victory at San Jacinto it was said that an excellent marksman of Captain William S. Fisher's company in the early part of the action thought it safest to temporarily depose Achilles [Houston] by a touch on the heel.***

Houston stumbled and nearly fell before a comrade caught him and helped him to stand on his one good leg. Adjutant Nicholas Lynch soon arrived and, "with the assistance of others, placed the General upon his fine roan charger." Because of how quickly he mounted his third horse of the day and resumed leading his men, few soldiers were even aware that their general had been shot.

In addition to being shot, Houston was also accused after the battle by a number of men of trying to call a halt to the battle. Various versions of this event have been offered by battlefield participants. Several witnesses declared that Houston ordered his forces to halt midway in the battle but that his superior, Secretary of War Thomas Rusk, countermanded the order.

In support of this claim is an account by Dr. Nicholas Labadie, who observed Colonel Rusk riding in full gallop toward the left rear of the forces when Houston ordered the halt. Colonel Coleman wrote that as "the soldiers were storming the enemy's works," and forcing the Mexican soldiers to retreat, Houston had just crossed a ravine some distance from the Mexican campground. "Houston approached and ordered a halt." According to Coleman, Houston felt that "glory enough has been gained this day, and blood enough has been shed."

Captain Heard, leading the First Regiment's Company F, wrote in 1859 that Houston ordered a halt after the Mexican army had been driven from its camp "to a boggy drain." Heard supported Coleman's belief that Houston called out that enough blood had been shed.

The boggy area behind the main Mexican campground was a small bayou feeding into Peggy's Lake. In this soggy muck, numerous horses and mules had bogged down. From this area, General Houston reportedly issued his halt command.

Labadie says Colonel Rusk immediately countermanded this direct order, shouting at the top of his voice, "If we stop we are cut to pieces. Don't stop—go ahead—give them hell!"

Captain Billingsley and Captain Baker both agreed that Rusk implored the men to fight on, in spite of Houston's call to halt. "Well and truly did they respond to his encouraging voice," wrote Billingsley. "The hour, so long delayed, had at length come for vengeance."

Colonel John Wharton reportedly rode up to the general and implored him to continue the fight, as Sidney Sherman's regiment was still hotly engaged in driving the enemy.

Colonel Sidney Sherman wrote a letter to *The Galveston Weekly News* of June 23, 1855, which stated that even Colonel Wharton's influence "did not avail at the time Houston called a halt, for Rusk did, in violation of Houston's positive orders, take the responsibility of ordering the troops to advance." Sherman felt that this halt "would have sacrificed my regiment, as it was then engaged in the timber on the enemy's right." Although Wharton urged the continued advance just as strenuously as Rusk, Sherman felt that the Secretary of War was the only person that could

> ***with any propriety assume the command. On his doing so, Houston called upon men to bear witness that the responsibility would not fall upon him, and then he left the field. The battle was won, and the Commander-in-Chief has had no use for the witnesses he called upon.***

Other participants would later claim that the "halt" order was merely directed at a small portion of the army. Captain Amasa Turner had managed to reorganize a portion of his company after passing through the enemy's breastworks. "In the course of two hundred yards they all got into line, and we joined in the rout, in something like order in my company." During the pursuit beyond the Mexican campground, Turner claimed that Lieutenant Colonel Henry Millard rode up, ordering his company to halt.

As quickly as Turner had halted his company, Colonel Wharton rode up asking, "Regulars, why have you stopped?" Millard spoke to Wharton, and then Millard gave orders for Captain Turner's regulars to march back to the battleground and place a guard around the Mexican camp. Captain Isaac Moreland had reported to Houston that some men were looting and vandalizing the property in the Mexican camp. According to Turner's account, General Houston had hollered at these men to "halt," and had then dispatched Millard to bring a company to act as guardians over the Mexican loot.

Captain Turner therefore felt that Houston had not "ever ordered a halt of the army, or even wished or expected to halt it, but that he articulated the word 'halt,' surrounded by his staff and aides, I have no doubt."

General Houston's own defense of the "halt" controversy agrees with the above events. After the right wing of the enemy had broken and the Mexican camp had been overrun, Houston found his infantry in confusion. He later wrote:

> ***The Commander-in-Chief cast his eyes to the right and perceived that the Infantry, 200 strong under Col. Millard, was in some confusion. He galloped to the Colonel and asked the cause. He replied, "my horse was wounded," which was correct.***
>
> ***The General faced to the left, and led the Infantry to meet a solid column of the enemy numbering about 500 men, and advancing on the Infantry in good order. When within about thirty yards the General ordered the Infantry (or Regulars) to halt and fire. This fire of the Infantry literally mowed down the enemy and if any survived they fled.***

Houston's detailed explanation of this controversy says that he did indeed try to organize men who were pursuing some 240 of Colonel Juan Almonte's men across a ravine beyond the Mexican campground. This bog was some "five to six hundred yards" beyond the battlefield along "the route of the refugees." At the bottom of the ravine was a quagmire in which horses and mules had become stuck. Houston, in his own words, "ordered them to halt and form, and not to advance upon the enemy in disorder." He also ordered Deaf Smith to announce to the fleeing Mexicans that they would be treated as prisoners of war if they would surrender. He then gave further orders to Colonel Rusk to "receive their surrender."

It is at this point of the battle that Rusk would have been close enough to Houston to hear that he ordered a halt, which Houston admittedly did in order to organize these troops near the boggy ditch. Houston next ordered one of the regular companies under Captain Turner to stop its pursuit of the enemy and return to camp to guard the spoils of war from looters. "This order was obeyed, and Capt. Turner's company remained on the field during the night," wrote Houston. "Gen. Houston remained at the ravine until the return of Gen. Rusk, and the[y] return[ed] together over the field of battle to the Texas Camp."

The whole "halt" controversy, therefore, was likely later stirred up by Colonel Coleman's hatred and spread by other political opponents of Sam Houston who chose to agree with Coleman's version. Houston was trying to stop one company and get it under control versus the entire army.

Captain Robert Calder later wrote that if Houston indeed did call a halt, it very well may have been aimed more at organizing the companies before charging again. "I very much doubt if any captain could, at short notice, have formed any five of his men together," wrote Calder. "Under these circumstances, it might appear that such an order was proper."

Lieutenant John Borden, leading Company D of the First Regiment after Captain Baker had been wounded, was not even sure who called for a halt. "Supposing it came from head-quarters, in the absence of my captain," Borden wrote, "I endeavored, as the second in command, to rally the members of our company."

He quickly found this to be impossible. Every man was "fighting and charging Mexicans" on his own accord. "No respect was paid to the order to halt—at least, so little that it had no direct bearing upon the movements either of the enemy or our own men."

Sam Houston would deny to his death that he had ever given a direct order to halt. Rusk later wrote that he only recalled Houston order some men that had become entangled in a bog to halt and reform. Whatever events actually transpired in the heat of battle would not seriously affect the rising popularity of Sam Houston in Texas.

The "halt" controversy did not have any significant effect on the fighting psyche of the troops on the San Jacinto battlefield. Most, in fact, never heard of such an order being called until long after the conflict had ended. Even if an order had been heard over the crack of gunfire and cannon reports, it is doubtful that many would have heeded the call to stop.

The Texans' zeal for revenge, aimed against the Mexican army that had massacred and executed hundreds of Texas soldiers at the Alamo and Goliad, drove them like a pack of hounds frenzied by the action of the hunt. Even after the contest was decided, these men continued to drive their fleeing opponents to an impenetrable area beyond the Mexican campground, and there a general massacre ensued.

Home, 1836

GREGG CANTRELL

GREGG CANTRELL HOLDS THE ERMA AND RALPH LOWE CHAIR IN TEXAS HISTORY AT TEXAS CHRISTIAN UNIVERSITY IN FORT WORTH. IN ADDITION TO HIS LANDMARK BIOGRAPHY, *STEPHEN F. AUSTIN: EMPRESARIO OF TEXAS*, DR. CANTRELL IS COAUTHOR OF *THE HISTORY OF TEXAS* AND COEDITOR OF *LONE STAR PASTS: MEMORY AND HISTORY IN TEXAS*.

STEPHEN F. AUSTIN ARRIVED IN TEXAS IN 1821. HIS SCRUPULOUS DEALINGS WITH THE MEXICAN GOVERNMENT AND ANGLO COLONISTS ALIKE EARNED HIM A REPUTATION AS AN HONORABLE MAN. THE RAUCOUS POLITICS OF THE REVOLUTIONARY PERIOD, HOWEVER, DIMINISHED AUSTIN'S STANDING IN THE EYES OF MANY TEXIANS, AND HE LOST THE 1836 PRESIDENTIAL ELECTION TO THE HERO OF SAN JACINTO, SAM HOUSTON. IN THIS SELECTION, CANTRELL DISCUSSES THE FINAL YEAR OF THE FATHER OF TEXAS, WHO DIED OF PNEUMONIA IN DECEMBER 1836.

★ ★

Austin arrived at the mouth of the Brazos on June 27, seasick as usual. With his head literally still swimming from his voyage on the Gulf, he immediately leaped into motion to bring the disorganized affairs of Texas into some semblance of order. Not surprisingly, he believed that his countrymen were blundering in their handling of the current situation. Most Texans seemed to think that the danger from Mexico was past and that the war was over for good. Austin wrote to Mirabeau B. Lamar, who was commanding the army while Sam Houston received treatment in Louisiana for his battle wound. "No treaty made with Santa Anna will be respected" by the Mexican government, he warned prophetically. Volunteers en route from the United States would turn back when they heard that the war was over. "In Gods name no more armistices or treaties with prisoners," he urged Lamar. "Our course now appears to be a plain one. The country must rally *en masse* and meet the enemy. . . . I shall try and be with you in the army as soon as I can, as a private soldier. Every man in Texas must shoulder his arms."

Austin did not march off to join the army right away, of course. He spent the next two weeks on the lower Brazos, conferring with his old friend David G. Burnet, who had been elected provisional president by the March convention, and the other civil and military leaders of the new Republic. Austin was devising a plan to end the war permanently and guarantee the safety of Texas. The scheme required the cooperation of two generals-turned-presidents, Antonio López de Santa Anna and Andrew Jackson. The idea was to get Santa Anna to write to Jackson with a request that Old Hickory mediate a permanent cessation of hostilities between Texas and Mexico, to be backed up by the U.S. military, after which Santa Anna would be returned to Mexico.

The Mexican president was being held twelve miles up the river near the village of Columbia, where the provisional government had established its temporary capital. Col. Juan Almonte, who had often visited Austin in his Mexico City prison cell in 1834, and another of Santa Anna's staff officers, Col. Gabriel Nuñez Ortega, were also housed in the small cabin owned by William Jack. The government had moved them to this isolated location after repeated death threats from revenge-hungry Texans. On the afternoon of July 1, Austin arrived there and was ushered in to meet with Santa Anna. The two-room Texas cabin contrasted sharply with the National Palace in Mexico City, scene of their last meeting. If Austin took any noticeable satisfaction from their reversal of fortunes, there is no record of it. Perhaps he reminded himself that it was Santa Anna who had let him out of prison in Mexico City. In any case, this was no time for reproaches. Austin got down to business and carefully explained the situation to the captive president. After a long discussion, Santa Anna agreed to Austin's plan. Austin returned each of the next three days, finally leaving for Velasco with Santa Anna's letter to Jackson in hand.

Ultimately, Jackson could not agree to Austin's plan, because the United States had already recognized the new regime in Mexico City, which had repudiated Santa Anna. But it was clear from Austin's actions since returning to Texas that he intended to resume the central role in Texas affairs that he believed was rightfully his. He was, in essence, already acting as chief diplomatic strategist for the provisional government. Austin explained his position in a letter to U.S. Army Gen. Edmund P. Gaines, to whom he had written urging American military intervention on Texas's behalf. "I make these suggestions as a citizen of Texas," he stated. "I hold no office, but can go into the Cabinet whenever it may be necessary." Indeed, one observer unfriendly to Austin described him as "being defacto the head or ruler of the present cabinet." The next few weeks, though, revealed that Texas's needs—as Austin perceived them—would not allow him to continue as a mere citizen or even as a cabinet member. The increasingly unpopular Burnet called for the election of a permanent government in September. It was impossible for Austin to stand by and watch others take control of his beloved Texas at such a critical time.

On July 20, Austin traveled back down the Brazos to Velasco to meet with Archer and Wharton, who had just returned from the United States. For two days the reunited commissioners worked to produce a formal report of their mission, along with a detailed account of their receipts and expenditures on the trip. Naturally the talk turned to politics and the upcoming elections. In a brief memorandum of the visit, Austin left a two-sentence account of what transpired: "Archer and Wharton at this time requested that I would be a candidate for the Presidency of Texas. B Hardiman [Bailey Hardeman], S. Rhoads Fisher and many others also requested it."

It is unlikely that Austin needed much persuasion. He had consistently demonstrated his belief that he knew best how to guide the affairs of Texas, and his actions since returning from the United States reinforce the conclusion that he had no intention of returning to private life at this critical time. On August 4 he announced his candidacy:

> ***I have been nominated by many persons, whose opinions I am bound to respect, as a candidate for the office of President of Texas, at the September elections.***
>
> ***Influenced by the governing principle which has regulated my actions since I came to Texas, fifteen years ago, which is to serve the country in any capacity in which the people might think proper to employ me, I shall not decline the highly responsible and difficult one now proposed, should the majority of my fellow citizens elect me.***
>
> ***My labors and exertions to settle this country and promote its welfare are well known. My object has been the general good, and the permanent liberty and prosperity of Texas. In the pursuit of this object I can say with a clear conscience that I have been honest and sincere in my intentions, and shall continue to be so, whether I am acting as a private citizen or as a public officer.***

He concluded his announcement by stating his position in favor of immediate annexation of Texas by the United States.

Austin retired to Peach Point for a few days of rest. His health had been poor since his return to Texas. As soon as he announced his candidacy, defamatory rumors about him began to circulate. The most persistent one was that he had been involved with Sam Williams and the others in the now infamous Monclova Speculations. "This is utterly false," he wrote to Thomas Rusk on August 9. "I never have been, am not, and never will be interested in those speculations, directly nor indirectly, and no one in Texas is more opposed to them than I am." He disclaimed full knowledge of the Speculations until very recently, "and I do not know that I understand it all yet," he declared, "for these events all took place in my absence." By this point he probably understood more than he admitted, but it was certainly true that he had disapproved of the transactions from the beginning and that he had no personal interest in them. In their two brief meetings since 1834, Williams seems to have made a point of not discussing the affair, and Austin, valuing their long friendship, appears not to have asked.

The other damaging rumor was that Austin had saved Santa Anna. "That man was saved by Gen. Sam. Houston . . . [and] by the Cabinet of Texas subsequently," he correctly pointed out. "I think he merited death, and that the country ought not to have been compromised to save him." In the latter statement Austin was speaking disingenuously, or from a lack of full understanding of the events following the Battle of San Jacinto. Houston's shrewd handling of Santa Anna after the battle had resulted in the removal of all remaining Mexican troops from Texas. Austin claimed that this "saved the balance of the Mexican Army" to invade another day, but Houston, who was in a better position to know the capabilities of his own army in the chaotic aftermath of the battle, understood that having those Mexican troops out of Texas was far safer than continuing the campaign in hopes of another improbable victory. As a candidate, Austin simply could not go on record as favoring the sparing of Santa Anna. He rationalized his own subsequent dealings with the Mexican leader on the grounds that "my object was to try to get the intervention of the U.S. and to have Texas annexed to the U.S." Persuading Santa Anna to write Jackson with the mediation proposal did no harm, and might have done much good, he emphasized.

Opposing Austin in the race was Henry Smith, who sought vindication for his controversial—and nearly disastrous—course as governor during the revolution. Smith no doubt believed that he could count on the support of former War Party men like himself, in opposition to the Peace Party candidate, Austin. But Austin had good reason to believe that he himself could be elected. With Wharton and Archer—themselves both old War Party men—endorsing him, and with the support of his own colonists and friends, surely he could defeat Smith, whose ego and tactlessness had almost cost Texas the war.

Austin soon found it difficult to contain the rumors and accusations that his opponents were spreading. The charges that he had been involved in the Monclova Speculations and had saved Santa Anna were at least legitimate political issues—had they been true. But now the opposition stooped even lower, criticizing him for leaving the country during the war "to eat fine dinners, drink wine, etc.," while others bore the brunt of battle.

Part of Austin's problem was the perception of him as the "government" candidate, due to his long standing as a political leader, his friendship with the unpopular Burnet, and his active role in current public affairs. One foe, army officer Henry Millard, succeeded in combining this perception with all the other accusations into one remarkably scurrilous charge—that the "primary object" of the provisional government "is now to Elevate Stephen F. Austin to the presidency and no stone will be left unturned by them to effect their object that they may again come into power under his patronage. Genl. Austin is with them hand and glove and their ostensible object in my opinion is to throw us back under the Mexican Dynasty by the release of Santa Anna who will confirm their power in Texas with all their fra[u]dulent claims of 1300 Leagues and powers to perpetuate their authority."

From his position as editor of the pro-Austin *Telegraph*, Gail Borden watched with dismay as the empresario's political capital plummeted. The future milk entrepreneur wrote Austin on August 15, saying that even some of Austin's "*old* devoted friends" would not vote for him unless they could be convinced he had taken no part in the Monclova Speculations. Still resting at Peach

Point, the candidate had done little to counter the charges. At Borden's urging he published a letter emphatically denying involvement in the Speculations and defending his actions as commissioner to the United States. He also answered the charge that he had opposed independence, justifying his pragmatic course during the fall of 1835 as a well-intentioned attempt "to keep the seat of war beyond the limits of Texas, until the country was better prepared, and by that means save the families from the devastations of invasions which they have suffered." In doing so, he argued, he was merely adhering to an "idea which was entertained by many" at the time and sustaining the Consultation, which adopted the same policy.

The accusations hurt, but Austin still felt confident enough in his election to offer the secretary of state's office to William S. Archer, provided, as Austin noted, "that the *sovereigns* elect me." Archer, an influential U.S. congressman from Virginia and kinsman of Branch Archer, would help Austin achieve his primary platform promise—securing the annexation of Texas by the United States.

Austin's hopes were shattered on August 20, when, with less than two weeks remaining before the election, Sam Houston entered the race. Like Austin, Houston acted the reluctant candidate, claiming to have been spontaneously nominated by various groups throughout Texas. He explained in his announcement that "the crisis requires it or I would not have yielded."

No record survives of the empresario's reaction to this news. After Austin's death, his relatives claimed betrayal on Houston's part, saying that Houston reneged on an earlier promise never to oppose Austin for any public office in Texas. The only firsthand account of this promise comes from Houston himself years later. Writing to Austin's nephew Guy Bryan in 1852, Houston told of a "free friendly and confidential interview" that the two men had on the eve of Austin's departure for Mexico City in 1833. "I assured him if he succeeded in obtaining a State Government, that I would never oppose him, for any Civil office in the state, but render him my cordial support thereafter," Houston recalled. He claimed that he made this promise so that Austin would not worry about Houston engaging in "intrigue against him" in his absence. Austin of course did not succeed in getting statehood for Texas during his Mexico trip, so if Houston's version is correct, the promise was moot in 1836. Nevertheless, in his 1852 account Houston still provided a reasonable justification for his decision to run. With Austin representing the Peace Party and Smith the War Party, he explained, "I was firmly impressed with the belief, that if either of the Gentlemen should be elected, it would be next to an impossibility to organize and sustain a Government. . . . Not being identified with either of the Parties, I believed, I would be enabled to consolidate the influence of both, by harmonizing them so as to form and sustain an administration." He offered a similar explanation to Emily Perry in 1844, who dismissed it as a "lame excuse."

Broken promise or not, Austin now realized that he stood little chance of election. He still knew his fellow Texans better than anyone did, and he accurately predicted what would happen: Houston would carry East Texas, the Red River settlements, and most of the army vote. Most discouraging, though, was his realization that he could not even count on his own colonists. "Many of the old settlers who are too blind to see or understand their interest will vote for him," he told James Perry, suggesting that he clearly considered himself a superior choice for president.

Three days later Austin's predictions proved accurate. The Hero of San Jacinto won in a landslide with 5,119 votes to Austin's 587. Perhaps most humiliating was the fact that Henry Smith polled 743 votes, even though he had withdrawn from the election and thrown his support to Houston. James Morgan, one of Austin's old settlers, echoed the disappointment of the empresario's supporters: "The first general election of Texas is now all over and a majority of the candidates have the sad news by now. Austin knew long ago that he would be turned down by the people he had tried so hard to serve. Republics are proverbial[l]y ungrateful and we feel certain that Austin anticipated just about the kind of political deal that was handed to him." Another friend, Edmund Andrews, sought to console the defeated candidate in a colorful analogy with which Austin undoubtedly would have agreed. "The body Politic is unlike Every other machine that Ever Existed," Andrews theorized, "other machines may be thrown out of order by some accident but this is only right by accident."

The impact of the defeat on Austin can be gauged only indirectly. He certainly tried to take it in stride. In his pre-election letter to Perry predicting the outcome, he seemed to express some relief that he would "have a good prospect of some rest this year, and time to regulate my private affairs, which need regulating very much." To his credit, his correspondence reveals no record of lingering bitterness; apart from a passing remark about the "blindness" of the colonists who voted for Houston, he had no negative words about the victor. Indeed, the week Houston was inaugurated Austin told James Perry, "I think that matters will go on well and smoothly in both the Executive and Legislative departments. There evidently is a disposition to harmonise in all persons."

Despite his apparent indifference to the outcome, the election must have wounded Austin deeply. It could not have been easy to accept such overwhelming rejection by his people in favor of a relative newcomer whose principal contribution to Texas (at least in Austin's estimation) had been one lucky military victory. Yet Austin had virtually predicted his own fate long before the Texans rose in revolt against Mexico. The words he wrote to Mary Holley in 1831 now proved singularly prophetic:

> ***A successful military chieftain is hailed with admiration and applause, and monuments perpetuate his fame. But the bloodless pioneer of the wilderness, like the corn and cotten he causes to spring where it never grew before, attracts no notice. He is either cried down as a speculator, or his works are too unostentatious to be worthy of attention. No slaughtered thousands or smoking cities attest his devotion to the cause of human happiness, and he is regarded by the mass of the world as a humble instrument to pave the way for others.***

The final days of the presidential race coincided with Austin's worst attack of fever since the death of his brother. He had ridden out to the army's headquarters at Victoria, probably to electioneer among the troops. The fever struck while he was there, and he made it back to Peach Point only with great difficulty. For the rest of September he languished in bed at his sister's house. By the first of October he was "just able to sit up," and on the twelfth he reported that he was "now barely able to crawl about a little." His illness interfered with his plans for picking up the pieces of his long-neglected and highly complicated private business affairs. He had no house of his own; San Felipe had been put to the torch during the Revolution. The land office had been closed during the war, and many settlers still awaited titles. He had hundreds of outstanding accounts to collect. Austin asked Perry to build him a two- or three-room cabin at Peach Point to house himself, the clerks he would need to employ in finishing up the land business, and visiting settlers. Furnishings would have to be sent from New Orleans.

By late October he was still weak but recuperating enough to make plans for attending Houston's inaugural ball. "I have been solicited to go into the new cabinet as Secretary of State—or to go to the U.S. as minister," he reported on the twenty-fifth, three days after the inauguration. "I have declined." The "solicitation" appears not to have been a formal invitation from Houston to join the cabinet; probably it was some sort of preliminary inquiry aimed at discovering Austin's current state of mind. In fact, he expressed interest in the diplomatic mission to Washington, but leaving Texas at this point was out of the question. "I have all the land office business to close," he told Perry. "Who can I trust it with in my absence? If S. M. Williams failed me while I was in prison in the city of Mexico, who can I hope will not fail me now? Besides all this my health is gone, and I must have rest to nurse my constitution and try and restore my strength."

The Williams situation tormented him. The more Austin had learned of the Monclova Speculations, the more he held Williams responsible for their baleful consequences. Although the empresario had criticized the Speculations since he first heard of them in Mexico City, the presidential race forced him to condemn his old friend's actions much more publicly than he had done before. The condemnations were not just for political purposes, either; Austin truly resented Williams for jeopardizing Austin's reputation, as well as the security of Texas itself in 1835. The controversial actions of the Monclova legislature, after all, had helped to set in motion the events that propelled Santa Anna and his army into Texas in the first place.

Williams remained in the United States during the presidential campaign. There he learned that Austin was speaking out against him in Texas. "I am informed that you charge me with a want of regard for your standing and character," he wrote to Austin. The denunciations by Austin "hurt and crushed . . . my spirit," he declared. Convinced that he had done nothing wrong, he prayed Austin to tell him "of what it is you complain in me." Williams could only believe that disloyal friends had turned Austin against him. "And be assured," he told his longtime mentor, "great as is my affliction under your censure—greater is my esteem for you; and no matter what may be the exertions of my enemies; no matter what you may believe necessary as your course toward me—and no matter what I may suffer—I will disappoint their hearts expectation; for long long ago have I sworn eternal friendship—long ago have I sworn, come what will, come *what* may never to forget the confidence which once existed between us, and all the machinations of hell shall not change my purpose nor my determination." As much as Austin's criticism stung him, the proud Williams would not admit wrongdoing. In that regard, as in so many others, the two men were much alike.

It was a month before Austin received the letter and two more weeks before he was well enough to answer. "I read your letter with such feelings as a drowning man would seize a plank," the empresario wrote.

> ***Sam Williams you were wound around and rooted in my affections more than any man ever was or ever can be again. I wished and hoped to see or hear something that***

would convince me I was wrong or had too seriously viewed your acts etc since I left in 1833. [Y]ou were to have closed the land business pending of the old colonies and attended to the last one. [N]othing was done or next to nothing, and I still have all that cursed trouble on my hands besides the censure and Gabble of discontent. . . . [Y]ou also must have known that all the odium of those things, would be cast on me by the envious and slanderous owing to our long friendship and relations. The fact is Williams that all those Monclova matters, I mean the speculations, and precipitating the country into war, were morally wrong, they have some very criminal and dreadfull features. I am too much debilitated to say more. [Y]ou say your motives were good. In the name of God convince me of that.

Three more weeks passed. Though he still had heard nothing from Williams, Austin could no longer stand the thought of a permanent estrangement between them. It was his forty-third birthday, and he was depressed, lonely, and ill. He urged Williams to return to Texas and "to stop all that kind of wildness both in talking, acts and business—harm enough has been done already by it—do no more. [Y]ou have greatly vexed and worried and distressed me. So much so that my brain has been greatly fevered. . . . [Y]ou have done wrong and have greatly injured, your friends, yourself, and your country—but that is past—let it be a lesson to you for the future." Austin recommended that Williams forget about public affairs and focus his considerable talents on business. As for the Monclova Speculations, Austin stated, "I am trying to banish even the recollection of it from my mind, and when I fully recover my health, hope shall be able to do so. In [the] future I never mean to speak of it or allude to it, if I can avoid it." Austin apparently still believed that Williams had cost him the presidency and—much more important—his standing as the leader of the Texans. But he had "cursed" the Monclova affair "in so many forms and shapes," he added, "that my anger is becoming almost exhausted and will, I sincerely hope, finally wear away." The final words to his letter reveal both the lingering hurt and the continuing bond that the empresario felt for his old protégé: "Williams you have wounded me very deeply, but you are so deeply rooted in my affections, that with all your faults, you are at heart too much like a wild and heedless brother to be entirely banished. Come home."

Sam Houston won the presidency in a landslide, but along the way he had created some bitter opponents, many of them Austin's friends and supporters. They charged him with cowardice during the long retreat across Texas following the fall of the Alamo. They blamed him for the burning of San Felipe. They said his officers forced him against his wishes to turn and fight at San Jacinto. They pointed to his failed marriage and his drinking as evidence of moral depravity. To Austin's credit, he never indulged in any of this mudslinging, even in private correspondence. His intelligence and astuteness as a judge of character somehow enabled him to see that the new president—so different in background, style, and temperament from himself—would not be the loose cannon aboard the ship of state that many supposed. Ultimately Austin probably could see some of the validity in Houston's justification for entering the race; the heroic general *could* be a unifying factor in these critical first days of the new republic.

"I have *full confidence* that all will go right," Austin told James Perry, "and that by next March we shall belong to the U.S." He and the new president agreed on the main issue of the day—the desirability of annexation—and even on lesser matters, such as what to do with the still-captive Santa Anna. As Houston began forming his cabinet, Austin again voiced his approval, saying that "the administration of Genl. Houston has entered upon its duties under the most favorable auspices, and the utmost harmony, and union prevails in all the departments and also in the community at large."

On October 28, 1836, Houston wrote to inform Austin of his confirmation as secretary of state by the Texas senate. Houston either ignored Austin's earlier, informal refusal of the offer or—more likely—he knew not to take it seriously. In any case, Houston presented the appointment to Austin as a fait accompli, putting a certain amount of pressure on him to accept. Austin's relatives subsequently claimed that the empresario agreed to serve reluctantly, but Houston recalled it differently in 1852, saying that Austin "readily accepted" the appointment. Houston's version appears closest to the truth, for Austin accepted the offer on October 31, only three days after Houston offered the already-confirmed position. Allowing time for Houston's letter to travel down the river from Columbia to Peach Point, Austin could not have agonized for long. He did, however, accept the office conditionally. "Your Excellency is fully aware of the debilitated state of my constitution and health, and also of the labors which devolve upon me in the land department," he reminded Houston. "I however accept of the appointment and am ready to enter upon the duties of the office, with the understanding that I be allowed the privilege of retiring should my health and situation require it."

Houston kept his promise to form a government in which all former factions would be represented. To counterbalance Austin, he appointed Henry Smith treasury secretary. Wharton received the important post of minister to the United States. The war department portfolio went to Houston's own trusted lieutenant, Thomas J. Rusk, while Austin's old friend and supporter Samuel Rhoads Fisher became navy secretary. In the September election Texans had voted almost unanimously in favor of seeking immediate annexation by the United States. As Austin remarked a week after assuming office, "public opinion has settled down upon one all absorbing point, which is *annexation to the United States without delay*."

Austin's task was to set the diplomatic wheels in motion. It was not a particularly burdensome duty. He drafted formal instructions for Wharton to take with him to Washington. Arrangements were completed for Santa Anna's release; in accordance with the wishes of both Austin and Houston, the Mexican leader would be quietly escorted out of Texas and accompanied to Washington, where he would meet with Andrew Jackson before being sent home. Once back in Mexico, his presence would surely prove divisive enough to divert attention from Texas. Other items on the secretary of state's agenda included efforts to arrange an exchange of prisoners from the recent war, and the drafting of a proclamation against the African slave trade.

Attending to his private business affairs probably occupied more of Austin's time and energy during November and December than did his official duties. He described the state of those affairs in a letter to an old family friend from Missouri:

> ***I have no house, not a roof in all Texas, that I can call my own. The only one I had was burnt at San Felipe during the late invasion of the enemy. I make my home where the business of the country calls me. . . . I have no farm, no cotton plantation, no income, no money, no comforts. I have spent the prime of my life and worn out my constitution***

> *in trying to colonize this country. Many persons boast of their 300 and 400 leagues acquired by speculation without personal labor or the sacrifice of years or even days. I shall be content to save twenty leagues or about nineteen [ninety] thousand acres,* acquired very hard and very dear indeed. *All my wealth is prospective and contingent upon the events of the future.*

The events of the past three years had changed Austin's personal financial outlook, both for the better and the worse. In the short term things were worse. The expenses of his long ordeal in Mexico, the mission to the United States, and the call of public service in Texas had resulted in new debts that could be paid only by selling land at depressed wartime prices. However, he still had massive landholdings, and with Texas now free from Mexico, there would be no limits on the amount of land an individual could own. (Mexican law would have required him to sell all but eleven leagues, or about forty-five thousand acres, after twelve years.) He knew that taxes would be high in the new republic, and he would have to sacrifice much land in order to hold onto the remainder. One thing had not changed since 1821: Stephen F. Austin's financial future was still closely tied to that of Texas itself. The key to that future now lay with annexation. If Texas could enter the Union, the U.S. Army would assume the burden of national defense; all trade barriers between Texas and the United States would be removed; and most important of all, prospective land buyers would pour into the new state, knowing that their property would be secure.

Complicating Austin's business affairs was the situation of his sister's family. He was very concerned about Emily. Her health had not been good for some time, and the war had created much hardship for her and her family. Back in June, just as Austin was returning from the United States, she had made plans to sail for New Orleans to escape the expected reinvasion by Mexico and to make arrangements for placing her younger children in school. But Austin, acutely aware of how it would look if his own family fled at that time, apparently insisted that she "stay at home and abide the fate of Texas." Now he sold enough land to raise $3,000 for her to make the trip. "I would sell all I have at any sacrifice rather than she should continue in the unhappy and fretful state she has been in ever since I returned home," he told Perry. "She must spend next Summer in the U.S. It will restore her health and spirits, and correct the fretful habit which sickness and hardships have produced." Austin would not consider letting Perry sacrifice his own land for the purpose. He also purchased a twenty-seven-year-old slave, a mule, and a pony and sent them to Perry for use at Peach Point until such time as he could retire from public life and begin farming for himself. In spite of all that had happened, he still clung to his old fantasy of a quiet life on the farm.

Columbia, Texas, was a raw little village wholly inadequate to serve as the capital of the new republic. Austin found lodging at the home of George B. McKinstry, an Irishman who had come to Texas in 1829 by way of Georgia. He and Austin had not gotten along particularly well in past years, because McKinstry had been a War Party activist and close ally of the Whartons in prerevolutionary days. McKinstry's house was little more than a shack on the outskirts of town. He rented Austin a "shed room" on the house's north side, which served as both bedroom and office for the secretary of state. The room had no fireplace or stove. Between official visits from congressmen and colonists concerned with land matters, he found few opportunities for quiet or privacy.

In late December a bitter norther blew into Texas. Austin caught a severe cold. It would not have been a cause for concern in a healthy person, but he had not been healthy for months. Moses Austin Bryan was again serving as his uncle's secretary, and he grew concerned. Henry Austin arrived, as did George Hammeken, who had been such a good friend to Austin in Mexico City. Branch Archer, who had a medical degree from the University of Pennsylvania, monitored his condition and administered opium. By Christmas Day Austin's condition had improved. At Henry's suggestion, the men shaved him, changed his linen, and carried him from his bed in the cold north room into the main room of house and made him a pallet in front of the fireplace. The weather had moderated, but later another strong norther blew in. At Austin's request, he was carried back to his bed in the other room.

His conditioned worsened. The cold settled into his lungs and turned into pneumonia. Two more doctors were called in on the twenty-sixth, and after some disagreement they agreed to administer an emetic, or vomiting agent, in hopes of clearing his lungs. The remedy seemed to work, but it left the patient very weak. He returned to the pallet before the fire, where he passed a sleepless night. Several times during the night he managed to leave the pallet and sit down at a small table, with his head resting in his hands, a position which allowed for better breathing. But he was too weak to sit upright long, and soon he had to lie down again.

At daybreak on the twenty-seventh James Perry arrived, and Moses Austin Bryan showed him to Austin's bedside. The empresario was lucid, but the doctors were on the verge of giving up. At nine o'clock one of the doctors applied a blister to Austin's chest, which somehow seemed to offer some relief. "Now, I will go to sleep." Austin whispered. For the next two hours he drifted in and out of consciousness, occasionally waking enough to ask for a little tea. Around eleven-thirty he woke, as if from a dream, and in a faint voice said. "The independence of Texas is recognized! Don't you see it in the papers? Doctor Archer told me so!" He then slipped back into unconsciousness. Thirty minutes later he died.

Of Myths and a Republic

JOE B. FRANTZ

DISTINGUISHED TEXAS HISTORIAN JOE B. FRANTZ (1917–1993) TAUGHT FOR ALMOST FORTY YEARS AT THE UNIVERSITY OF TEXAS IN AUSTIN. HIS NUMEROUS PUBLICATIONS INCLUDE *GAIL BORDEN: DAIRYMAN TO A NATION*, *THE AMERICAN COWBOY: THE MYTH AND THE REALITY*, *6,000 MILES OF FENCE: LIFE ON THE XIT RANCH OF TEXAS*, *THE DRISKILL HOTEL*, AND *TEXAS: A BICENTENNIAL HISTORY*. DR. FRANTZ ALSO DIRECTED THE LBJ ORAL HISTORY PROJECT.

AFTER AN EVENTFUL DECADE AS AN INDEPENDENT NATION, TEXAS BECAME THE TWENTY-EIGHTH STATE IN THE UNION. AT HIS FAREWELL SPEECH ON FEBRUARY 19, 1846, PRESIDENT ANSON JONES DECLARED: "THE FINAL ACT IN THIS GREAT DRAMA IS NOW PERFORMED. THE REPUBLIC OF TEXAS IS NO MORE." IN THIS SELECTION, DR. FRANTZ DISCUSSES THE DRAMATIC DAYS OF THE TEXAS REPUBLIC. ALONG THE WAY, HE OFFERS ASTUTE OBSERVATIONS ON TEXAS NATIONALISM AND LONE STAR PRIDE.

★ ★

Undoubtedly one source of the traditional Texas image—or caricature—of roughness and political instability was the attitude of John Quincy Adams. In his latter-day congressional period, he carried on an effective campaign of opposition to its admission to the Union. Adams saw the admission of Texas as part of the southern plot to extend slave territory, and he had a strong bias against admission of any western territory anywhere. President James K. Polk's war against Mexico merely confirmed New Englanders' suspicion that Adams was correct.

Whatever the reasons for the myth and the almost universal dislike (and Lord knows Texas produces plenty of loud-mouthed politicians and spoiled rich who fuel the myth), the Texas myth is the cross that Texans bear. They naturally leave the state in a defensive posture, knowing that at the best they are likely to be treated as intellectual colonials and at worst as bizarre creatures. Walter Prescott Webb, a native Texan recognized as one of the most influential historians of the twentieth century, once observed that "Texans should learn silence." And J. Frank Dobie, another native, said, "Texans are the only 'race of people' known to anthropologists who do not depend on breeding for propagation." Unfortunately Texans multiply over drinks, and by imagination.

Dobie himself brings home the point. A short, square-built man with a face carved from the old rock, he was steeped in classical literature, wrote with tender feeling about men and animals, and could build a sentence and a paragraph with as much craft as anyone in the nonfiction field. He published a score of books, none of which have gone out of print a decade after his death. His interest was man and his relationship with his environment, and he studied mustangs and coyotes for clues to universal behavior. And yet when he died, no less careful a newspaper than the *New York Times* started its lead as follows: "J. Frank Dobie, nationally known Texas humorist. . . . " No one who knew Dobie would have called him a humorist to his face, but the *New York Times*, not a frivolous newspaper, could not see him as a Texan without also seeing him as a humorist—someone to be taken not quite seriously.

Without further belaboring the Texas myth, I should add that I believe its real genesis lies in the Texas Revolution, in which a group of upstart Anglos defeated a sometimes brilliant general leading an army of a nation whose roots are a century older than those of the United States and which in 1835–1836 was at least the equivalent of the United States in size and in strength. The fact that Texas persisted as an independent republic for ten years and itself showed some intimations of empire-building cemented the myth. The War against Mexico, fought to a great extent *over* Texas, merely sealed the mythical package. The facts that the Walker model of the Colt revolver was introduced in this war, that the Texas Rangers performed splendidly albeit without much discipline and with an utter lack of respect for regular army leadership, and that Texas provided a staging area for the invasion of Mexico tied the ribbons on the mythical package. Naturally Texans—native or newly arrived—have overglorified their period of independence and have created their own myth of a free and wild heritage.

Myth or not, some facts remain. On hearing that Texas had won its independence at San Jacinto, most Texans in the United States as well as most Anglos in Texas undoubtedly felt that Texas would immediately be annexed into the Union. But they didn't reckon with anti-Texas prejudice in the States on the one hand and with the confidence of Sam Houston in Texas on the other. At the same time Andrew Jackson did not feel that good politics permitted him to annex Texas, and his successor, Martin Van Buren, preferred to leave events as Jackson would have ordained them.

By this time Texans had a taste of independence. They began to see themselves as Spain and Mexico had intended them to be—effective buffers between the two major nations of North America. If they could whip Mexico in Texas, why could they also not whip Mexico in New Mexico, California, Coahuila, Chihuahua, Sonora, and who knew where else? They began to dream of an empire stretching to the Pacific. Likewise, they began to suspect they had their own Manifest Destiny, with the result that they were not going to supplicate before the altar of the United States. Prejudice and pride proved difficult to reconcile, and Sam Houston, the most remarkable Texan personality of the nineteenth century, was the type of man who could exploit such a situation for high stakes.

If in late spring of 1836 any Texans were arrogant, they simply did not understand the predicament into which they had projected themselves. True, they deserved to enjoy some elation over having defeated Santa Anna and having in effect run the Mexican army out of Texas. But they had no assurance that they could hold Texas against reinvasion by a determined Mexican army. They had no political parties, no viable government, no taxing authority, and no money. All they had accomplished was to defeat the Mexicans at San Jacinto.

Ten days after the Alamo had fallen, an *ad interim* government had been established under the presidency of forty-eight-year-old David G. Burnet. He had lived in Texas continuously since 1826 as a sometime empresario, had been a judge and a member of the conventions of 1833 and 1836. Conservative, sensitive, full of bombast and born to be unpopular, Bumet would have encountered insuperable problems under the best of circumstances. As president during eight months of chaotic transition, he lost his support and became extremely disenchanted. Once other Texans even tried to arrest him, but he refused to resign or to accept the resignation of his cabinet, thereby probably preventing a military takeover.

On the other hand, Lorenzo de Zavala, his vice-president, from a village in Yucatan, was an ardent liberal. During the Mexican revolution the Spanish imprisoned him at the castle of San Juan de Ulloa, where he studied medicine and English. Representing Yucatan in the Spanish Cortes in Madrid when he learned that Mexico had declared independence, he returned home to be a member of the Mexican legislature. He became governor of the state of Mexico in 1827 but fled because of persecution by the army. After another overturn he became national secretary of the treasury as well as governor of the state of Mexico, and then in 1829 he received an empresario contract to introduce 500 families into Texas. In 1832 he returned as governor of the state of Mexico, then became a member of the Mexican Chamber of Deputies in 1833 and minister to France under Santa Anna.

Like the Texans, Zavala in Paris decided that Santa Anna had no intention of observing the Constitution of 1824 and resolved to resist as a Texan. He built a home on Buffalo Bayou outside future Houston, moved in his family, and was at Washington-on-the-Brazos to sign the Texas Declaration of Independence. He remained as vice-president from March 17 until the following October 17. Less than a month later he was dead.

Zavala's presence further emphasizes that in great part the Texas revolution was a fight of liberals against tyranny, rather than Anglos against Mexicans. Although Zavala could foresee a long and assured role in the Mexican upper political hierarchy, nonetheless away off in the security of Paris he felt that Santa Anna was sabotaging the spirit of freedom and left for Texas to help restore that freedom. In a sense he is chicano *numero uno* in Texas.

In Texas Sam Houston was no undiluted hero, and citizens of the new Republic tended to factionalize according to the degree of favor or disfavor certain groups felt toward Old Sam. Pro- and anti-Andrew Jackson sentiment also infected many Texans, and Houston was still considered by many as the protégé of the president. In fact, Jackson supposedly was grooming Houston for the presidency when the latter walked out on his bride and on the Tennessee governor's office to disappear among the Indians along the western border of Arkansas, take an Indian wife, and drink a barrel or so of whiskey a day to forget whatever it was that had caused his walk-out in the first place.

But then Houston had sobered up, except for occasional aberrations, and had shown up in Texas, where he brought a fine reputation as a governor of a state and a frontier fighter. Without any previous recommendations he would have been an impressive man in any company; here he rose to commander-in-chief of the Texas forces. But as he had retreated steadily before Santa Anna, many soldiers and civilians alike had decided he was cowardly. When his Fabian tactics brought total victory in an 18-minute battle at San Jacinto, many others hailed Houston as a genius. His detractors regarded him as lucky.

Running for president against Houston were Henry Smith, notable primarily for having married three sisters in succession, and Stephen F. Austin, a reluctant candidate urged on by the anti-Houston element. But Austin was like many another prime candidate on the North American scene—when his opportunity arose, he had already passed his time. As seen, he had opposed independence at the outset of the trouble. He had also opposed placing Santa Anna before a firing squad. When the returns came in, Houston received approximately 80 percent of a total vote of nearly 6,000. His vice-president was Mirabeau B. Lamar, a man of letters whom we will meet again. In the same election on the first Monday in September 1836, the voters approved the new constitution, the only constitution accepted without acrimony in the history of Texas. Also placed before the voters was a referendum on annexation to the United States. Only ninety-one persons disapproved.

Under the constitution the President served three years, except for the first term, and could not succeed himself. Houston served from October 22, 1836 to December 10, 1838, Lamar until 1841, Houston again until 1844, and Anson Jones until the Texas flag was replaced by the United States flag on February 19, 1846.

The transition from colony to constitutional republic was accomplished quickly and with a minimum of disorganization. The progress of Texas in this experience proved a much smoother process than that of the earlier thirteen colonies into the United States. But in fairness to the United States, its problem was exacerbated by having to meld thirteen colonies into some sort of union, whereas Texas was a single entity to begin with.

Challenges were manifold. Texas wanted to be recognized by other nations of the world. It needed to become self-supporting. It had to be able to defend itself against the United States from the east and Mexico from the south (which has given Texans an historic sympathy for the plight of

Germany, caught between Russia and France). The problem of peace with the Indians would remain for nearly another half-century. And the question of boundaries would help bring on the war against Mexico, as well as delay affiliation of the Republic with the United States. Also on hand were the expansionist elements from the United States, who had helped provoke the Texas war for independence and who asked regularly why San Jacinto should mark the end of territorial aggrandizement. They wanted to expand into other Mexican areas, to create a real empire that would compete with both the United States and Mexico on more or less even terms. And everyone wanted land.

Land was available and was given away prodigally. Since the Republic had no money, it paid its overdue soldiers in land scrip. Banks were outlawed, reflecting the Jacksonian bias against the speculative wildcat banks that helped bring on the Panic of 1837 back in the States. Since apparently people can no more live without banks than they can live without sin, some banking function was necessary—in fact, had been necessary since the whole revolution had begun. Just as the Continental Congress had its Robert Morris and the Union would produce its Jay Cooke, so the Texas Revolution and subsequent Republic witnessed the rise of the mercantile firm of McKinney and Williams to underwrite the Texas Revolution.

Thomas F. McKinney was a horse raiser and a man of action, while his partner, Samuel May Williams, from Rhode Island, had picked up experience and contacts in most of the Atlantic and Gulf ports, as well as in Latin America. As secretary and sometime partner to Stephen F. Austin, he also knew almost everyone among the older Anglo-Texan inhabitants. The firm operated in the little seaport town of Quintana and later in Galveston. When the upstart government of Texas could neither raise funds nor obtain credit, merchants in New Orleans and Mobile, as well as in such farther away places as Charleston, Baltimore, and Providence, advanced guns and powder, cloth for uniforms, and all the other sinews of war to the account of McKinney and Williams, which in turn forwarded these elements to whatever Texas government existed at the time. The result was that McKinney and Williams underwrote a good portion of the Revolution and their faith in turn led other merchants to help the struggling government. Without them, the Revolution possibly could not have been pulled off successfully, Texas would not have gained its independence at this time, and the Texas myth would be interesting but hardly overwhelming.

Penurious—or cheap—the Congress of the Republic of Texas and later the legislature of the State of Texas postponed paying the partnership for its efforts. After the original partners moved on to their graves, their heirs tried periodically to collect until the 1940s, when the Supreme Court of Texas ruled that the payment could be made to heirs only by passage of an amendment to the state constitution. At this point the heirs gave up, knowing full well that the Texas voting citizenry would never approve paying a debt more than a century old to people who hadn't even been born when the debt was incurred.

Patriotism was not a total loss to McKinney and Williams, however. They were given a banking privilege under a Republic of Texas constitution that permitted no banking. They could issue bills, but just couldn't call it a bank. Later, when Texas became a state, the state constitution also forbade banking, but again McKinney and Williams were permitted to continue their banking function. When Texas became a state in the Confederacy, its Confederate state constitution forbade banking, but McKinney and Williams continued their banking, even though Williams was dead and the partnership had really ceased to be active after 1853. Significantly, when bills issued by the Republic of Texas were being discounted 50 to 60 percent in the New Orleans mart and often in Texas, McKinney and Williams's bills were being discounted only 10 to 20 percent. In short, faith in the financial stability of these two men ranked much higher than faith in the Republic of Texas even though their treatment at the hands of successive Texas governments was shoddy, to say the least.

At the outset of independence Sam Houston, using his finely honed sensitivity and ignoring his personal preferences, chose a cabinet which he thought would work best for his country's interests. Among its members he named Austin as his secretary of state and Henry Smith as secretary of the treasury. Partially as a result of overwork and exposure in the service of Texas, Austin died about two months after taking office, only forty-one years old. He is often referred to as the Father of Texas, and the state is dotted with proud people who mistakenly say that they were descended from this bachelor.

So now Texas faced the joys of nationhood for a decade. Without regard to finances, its Congress established a standing army of 3,587 troops, in addition to a battalion of 280 mounted riflemen to protect the frontier. The Congress also authorized the President to accept 40,000 volunteers, an unrealistic figure that could only have been intended to be read in Mexico. Since Texas had no money, Houston's concern was reducing or eliminating an army payroll rather than enlarging it. Furthermore, the army was made up largely of latecomers who felt no more loyalty to Texas than they had to Mexico. These adventurers, invaluable though their services may have been, had refused to accept Lamar when the previous president, David G. Burnet, had named him their commander. Burnet had then made the worst possible choice for replacement, Felix Huston, a man of few qualifications who had left Natchez owing $40,000 while raising an army to assist Texas (after Texas had already won its freedom). Houston replaced Huston with Albert Sidney Johnston, a West Point graduate from Kentucky who became one of the more admirable Texan military leaders for the next quarter of a century. Huston challenged Johnston to a duel, wounded his replacement so critically that he could not take command, and remained on for a time.

But Sam Houston was wily, and while General Huston was busily trying to obtain the support of Congress for an invasion of Mexico, President Houston furloughed all but 600 of his troops. Soon the remainder were turned out, leaving Texas with only local militia and Rangers.

The worry that Mexico might invade remained uppermost in the minds of the Texians, as they then called themselves. Little basis existed for this anxiety, though Mexico never recognized the independence of Texas and still claimed the region. Nothing much happened during Houston's first term except that the president invited more acrimony by giving Santa Anna his freedom, providing that the deposed dictator go to Washington to persuade President Jackson to annex Texas. Although Houston knew that Santa Anna was not the right man for a forlorn mission, for Santa Anna no longer held either Mexico or Texas, he sent the Mexican general with an escort just to get him off his hands and out of Texas, where he was a nuisance. When Santa Anna arrived in Washington, Jackson sent him back to Vera Cruz aboard a United States frigate.

When Mirabeau Buonaparte Lamar succeeded Houston, he was much more straightforward in his foreign relations than his predecessor. He tried to effect an understanding with his former overlords, to the extent of sending Secretary of State Barnard E. Bee to Mexico in May 1839 to offer the Mexican government up to $5,000,000 to recognize Texas's independence and a Rio Grande boundary. Bee never proceeded beyond Vera Cruz. Where Texas would obtain the $5,000,000 is uncertain; but in view of later developments the sum, if paid, would have represented a bit of a coup for Mexico, who eventually lost Texas and received nothing in return. Lamar then sent another agent, James Treat, who did make it to Mexico City and hung around for ten months while the Mexicans encouraged him just enough to keep him from returning home.

The story of Texas-Mexican relations is too complicated to detail here. In the midst of Treat's mission a Republic of the Rio Grande was established formally in. January 1840 as an antidote against the centralism of Mexico, backed by the states of Coahuila, Nuevo León, and Tamaulipas. Although Texas informally favored the new republic, it was so eager to obtain Mexican recognition of its own independence that it would not give official or forthright aid. When Antonio Canales of Camargo, one of the Rio Grande leaders, asked President Lamar for assistance, he was ignored. But because he thought that Texans were aiding the republic, President Bustamante of Mexico requested that the war against Texas be resumed. Lamar issued a proclamation admonishing all citizens of Texas "to abstain from all attempts to invade the territory of Mexico." When the Republic of the Rio Grande finally faltered in November 1840, Texas lost interest in the movement and undoubtedly congratulated itself on its forbearance.

On Treat's eventual return to Texas, Lamar recommended a declaration of war to force Mexico to recognize Texas. Congress refused. Lamar then sent one more mission, but the Mexicans refused to receive it. The president allied Texas with the Mexican state of Yucatan, in revolt against the central government, but the Yucatan revolution came to naught and did nothing for Texas. What next?

In his eagerness to fix the Rio Grande as a boundary Lamar attempted to push the Texas dream toward the Pacific. His first object was the string of settlements along the upper Rio Grande, of which the most notable is Santa Fe. This time a careful Congress vetoed his idea, but Lamar raised and equipped his own caravan. The party of 270 set out from Austin on June 21, 1841, and included among its three commissioners one Mexican, José Antonio Navarro, a signer of the Texas Declaration of Independence, a Mason, sometime legislator and congressman, and father of four future Confederate sons, who would lose almost four years of his life to the expedition. The purpose: take Santa Fe and establish the authority of Texas in New Mexico.

Whether the expedition was as visionary then as it seems now is debatable. Lamar had no Gallup Poll to tell him how the New Mexicans felt, but reports indicated that the hold of the Mexican government there was shaky. New Mexico, Lamar was eager to believe, was ripe for new leadership. For the economic determinists the Santa Fe expedition strikes another positive blow. Broke and not getting any better off financially with any alacrity, Texas was desperate for trade. In the United States a Santa Fe Trail had proved a two-way commercial highway from Missouri to New Mexico since 1821, when Mexico had abrogated the Spanish policy of exclusiveness in trade.

Something akin to a road across the plains had been worked out, and mule- and ox-drawn wagons made the trip regularly, sometimes with military escort but not necessarily. The trail would continue to be important until the coming of the railroad in 1880, and its promise of enduring significance was not lost on the Texans. But how to divert this trade to Texas?

Although priorities get mixed, hope of empire seems to have outweighed even economics. On April 14, 1840, Lamar sent a letter to Santa Fe which was bold and undoubtedly ill-advised. He told the New Mexicans that their self-interest lay in joining the Republic of Texas, and that Texans would soon arrive to work out union. It seemed to him like such a good idea that the offer could hardly be refused. And so on June 19, 1841, the officially designated Santa Fe Pioneers set out. When commissioners, merchants, teamsters, and even journalists were added to the soldiers, the group totaled 321. Twenty-one ox-drawn wagons carried merchandise worth $200,000, plus the logistics for five companies of infantry and one of artillery.

When the first traders from Franklin, or Independence, Missouri, had reached Santa Fe, life for the visitors in the Mexican outposts had been one long fiesta, Texans thought that they too would be received as heroes, but instead Governor Manuel Armijo of New Mexico had called out his militia to resist what he looked on as an invasion. The Mexicans used a member of the Santa Fe expedition, Captain William G. Lewis, convincing him to persuade his fellow travelers in the advance party to lay down their arms. When the main force drew as close as Tucumcari on October 5, Lewis again persuaded the Texans that the Mexicans would treat them right if they would just put their fate in the hands of their hosts. Without firing a shot, the Mexicans took the entire expedition. Actually the Mexicans were getting secondhand goods, for the Texans had already been so done in by the desert plains that even capture seemed like succor.

Unfortunately the Mexicans looked on the Texans as something between prisoners of war and rebellious Mexican citizens. The visitors were subjected to a long, often brutal march to Mexico City, where they were imprisoned. When the United States got in the act, the Mexicans finally decided that discretion called for release of the prisoners. Those who made it home told harrowing tales.

Texas had no credit of good will with Mexico, and the Santa Fe expedition more than overdrew the account. In Mexico Santa Anna was once again in charge of the government, and early in 1842, he invaded the new republic. But the Mexicans ran out of steam quickly and retired to the far side of the Rio Grande. About all they accomplished was to fan anti-Mexican sentiment in Texas, to resurrect Texan vigilance against invasion from the south, and to scare the Texans witless.

Even Sam Houston panicked, declared a public emergency, and ordered the archives removed from Austin to Houston. Whether Houston was alarmed or opportunistic remains debatable. He had always preferred the town named for him, ostensibly because of its convenience to the sea but more likely because of his pride in name. The fact that in 1841 one Austin citizen was scalped at the town's nearby spa, Barton Springs; that a party of Comanches, led by a chief in war dress, marched near the French minister's house; and that in this raid a white boy was killed and a Negro boy captured, lends some credence to Houston's desire to remove the capital back toward the coast. Furthermore, like recent presidents he was deluded by having received three-fourths of the vote for president on his re-election bid. Just when he thought he had a mandate, Congress undercut him. With more than a thousand Mexican troops at San Antonio, Austinites fled, leaving only about two dozen families in the town.

Thus Houston gave the order for the archives to be removed, justifying his action on grounds that loss of the national archives would profoundly injure the country. Austinites were outraged. The move was opposed not only from a prestige standpoint but because property owners feared a sharp decline in real estate prices. And Austinites would sooner fight Sam Houston than Mexicans. At Bastrop, thirty miles to the east of Austin on the Houston road, a patrol was established to detain all wagons carrying government records. Houston had to back down.

The Mexicans gave him a second opportunity with an invasion in September, when General Adrian Woll again took San Antonio, this time for nine days. Houston asked Congress to permit the archives to be removed. If the Texans couldn't keep the Mexicans from taking San Antonio twice in one year, what hopes did they have in case a determined bid was made by Mexico to move another seventy miles farther to the Texas capital? Nevertheless Congress turned Houston down again.

Houston then ordered two military men to remove the archives secretly under pretense of saving them from an incipient Indian invasion. Accordingly twenty men and three wagons under the command of Colonel Thomas I. Smith loaded the wagons with papers from the Land Office. They headed north out of Austin and bedded down at Kinney's Fort. It was December 30, with a blue norther barreling in and rain falling as though poured from buckets, and nobody would get out on a night like this just to save an archive. But twenty men from Austin did, and no sentries had been posted. Colonel Smith treated his pursuers with discretion and agreed to return the archives on New Year's Eve, 1842. For one of the few times in his life, Sam Houston had lost permanently.

With the archive war over, the country could give more time to Mexican threats. But the invaders disappeared almost with settlement of the archives question. Texans had been all for chasing into Mexico that summer, but Houston had refused to be rushed into a war that he thought was unnecessary. By November 750 men led by General Alexander Somervell were ready to invade on their own. On December 8 they recaptured Laredo from the Mexicans; that seemed to satisfy the blood-thirst of many of them, who promptly returned home. Somervell took his men down the Rio Grande on a ten-day march and then turned them inland towards Gonzales. At this juncture a number of the men refused to go home and insisted on an invasion.

Under Colonel W. S. Fisher about 300 men began a march to Mier, a *pueblito* on the Mexican side of the Rio Grande. There the Texans ran into more resistance than they could handle and were forced to surrender. Marched deep into Mexico, they escaped once but were recaptured and drew black beans to determine which of their number should compose the one-tenth to be shot. Ironically, after months of confinement, the survivors were released by no less than Santa Anna.

Despite losing at Santa Fe, the Texans made a second try in that direction. In the spring of 1843 Colonel Jacob Snively gathered 180 men in North Texas for a raid on the Santa Fe Trail where it crossed the Panhandle area of Texas between Missouri and Santa Fe. But an escort of United States troops captured the Snively expedition, so that once again Texas pride was dented.

Although all of this coming and going proved abortive for both Texans and Mexicans, the expeditions had real value. They kept Texas advertised in the States, with the result that Texas never quite retreated from the public's mind.

With Houston and Jackson resisting efforts toward annexation on either side of the Sabine and Red rivers, the issue still would not die. The United States had recognized Texas almost at once, and Jackson's last official act before leaving office in March 1837 had been to name a chargé d'affaires to the Republic of Texas. Beginning in the following August and continuing into 1838, annexation remained an ever present issue in Washington. During the morning of every session of Congress from June 16 to July 7, 1838, John Quincy Adams made a speech opposing the annexation of Texas. When Congress adjourned without acting, the Texans, represented in Washington by Anson Jones, announced the "formal and absolute withdrawal" of the offer by Texas to be annexed.

For the nonce the issue died. Revived in 1842 and again in 1843, annexation could not be pushed through. Meanwhile Texas was hanging on as an independent nation and beginning to demonstrate some coziness with the British. Fear of British influence impacted on Washington, and on October 16, 1843, the United States open negotiations for annexation by treaty. The treaty progressed as far as being signed by two Texans and by John C. Calhoun, representing the United States. Within two months the Senate of the United States had rejected the treaty. A national election was imminent, and neither slaveholding nor free-soil senators wanted to lay their careers on the line on the Texas issue. The fate of Texas would be decided at the polls.

The leading Democratic candidate in the States was Martin van Buren, who had conducted an adequate administration following Andrew Jackson. When Van Buren refused to endorse the annexation of Texas, James K. Polk, another Jackson protégé who had succeeded Sam Houston as governor of Tennessee, received the nomination as an all-out supporter of Texas. Running against Polk was Henry Clay, the old Whig. In principle Clay approved the annexation of Texas, but for practical considerations he preferred to go slow.

In those days the election was held in November as now, but the president continued in office until the following March. Accordingly President John Tyler, reading the vote if not the polls, interpreted Polk's election as meaning that a majority wanted immediate annexation. A month after the election he placed the question before Congress. Probably wisely, the proannexation forces had decided that they could never summon the two-thirds majority necessary to receive Texas by treaty. A joint resolution would require only a simple majority and could probably pass. They guessed correctly: on February 28, 1845, Congress passed a joint resolution providing for annexation.

Under terms of the joint resolution Texas could become a state if its people approved and if it left its boundary adjustments to the United States; if Texas would cede its public property, except for its public lands (which would be used in part to pay its debts), to the United States; and if Texas would prohibit slavery in any state created north of parallel 36°30′. Texas would also be permitted to divide itself into five states if it chose.

If Texans did not accept the offer before January 1, 1846, the whole process would begin again. Congress also authorized Tyler to withhold the proposal if he chose. Tyler didn't choose, and he named Andrew Jackson Donelson as his agent to submit the offer to Texas. When shortly Tyler left the Presidency and Polk replaced him, the only change in policy was Polk's urgency to complete annexation.

Once again Texas was on the throne. Both England and France were paying court, trying to persuade the Texans that their destiny lay in continued independence. Mexico too became tractable, preferring an independent Texas to having the United States crowding its border. The British chargé in Texas, Captain Charles Elliot, persuaded President Anson Jones to keep Texas uncommitted until he could obtain from Mexico a treaty guaranteeing Texas independence if Texas in turn would agree never to unite with the United States. But this was at the official level. Among Anglo Texas citizens the urge to return to the womb was growing, and Jones called a convention to meet on United States Independence Day, July 4. When Congress met, Jones had two propositions ready—the proposal of annexation and the treaty of peace with Mexico, which Elliot had somehow managed to put through Mexican official circles in an incredibly short time. Unanimously the Texas Congress accepted the offer of annexation to the United States, approved the president's proclamation calling for election of delegates to a constitutional convention for the State of Texas, and then went home. In two months the convention for annexation drew up a state constitution, a record short time which couldn't begin to be duplicated in Texas (or probably any other state) nowadays. In October the voters approved the terms of annexation and the state constitution. The constitution was accepted by Congress, and on December 29, 1845, President Polk signed the act that made Texas the twenty-eighth state in the United States of America. Texas had easily beaten the deadline of the United States Congress.

On February 19, 1846, Texans gathered in front of the state capitol to watch the Texas flag taken down and the stars and stripes of the United States run up in its stead. President Jones announced his withdrawal as president in favor of J. Pinckney Henderson as governor and wound up his farewell speech with these words:

"The final act in this great drama is now performed. The Republic of Texas is no more.

Nowadays most public places in Texas have two flagpoles, one for the flag of the United States and one for the Lone Star flag of Texas. Without consulting the law on the subject, most Texans intuitively believe that the Texas flag should not fly below the flag of the United States or any other banner, but alongside it as an equal.

In the more than a century since that historic day, both Texans and other North Americans have often debated whether anyone gained from associating Texas with the Union. Texas pride and Texas nationalism have been trying qualities to live alongside, while with some justification Texans have frequently felt that the United States held an animus toward them. At best the marriage has been uneasy, always threatening to come apart except that neither party had anywhere else to retreat. The advantages of staying together outweigh the advantages of separateness.

With the right to subdivide into five states, Texas has frequently considered whether it might wield more national power by having ten United States senators. But the temptation invariably founders on the practical belief that the five-state delegation might lose its unity. And besides, emotional issues exist—which state would inherit the Alamo, and which would have to accept the often hapless Houston Astros of the National Baseball League? East Texas, the "countriest" portion of the state, would have to claim Van Cliburn, the concert pianist, while Central Texas, with ever so much more sophisticated tastes, would enjoy Willie Nelson, the country-western Hall of Famer. In short, division would bring no end of problems.

Texas has produced its share of great men, both early and late, and none greater than Sam Houston. Still, probably no one articulated the nationalism of Texas better than Mirabeau B. Lamar, its first vice-president and second president, but more than that: an eminently civilized man who wrote poetry, fathered Texas education, and generally belonged to the type of citizen who uplifts. He remains the supreme albeit sometimes misguided philosopher of the state. In his inaugural he talked about "the wealth, talent, and enterprise" of Texas and promised to promote the "true basis of all national strength and glory."

"[Under] the most trying circumstances, from the dawn of the revolution up to the present period [Texas] has maintained a dignity, sobriety, and harmony which might stand as an example for older and longer established governments," he told his listeners, adding that Texans possessed a larger share of the world's blessings "than almost any other people on the Globe." He averred that his eyes were "exclusively directed to the glory of the nation," which harbored no evils that patriotism would not remove. For the future he recommended that Texans look "with a single eye to her glory and greatness and sacrifice all narrow-minded selfishness upon the hallowed altar of patriotism.

Lamar opposed annexation, saying that "however strong be my attachment to the parent land, the land of my adoption must claim my highest allegiance and affection." Annexation promised nothing positive for Texas but would only demonstrate "that we had riven the chains of Mexican despotism only to fetter our country with indissoluble bonds, and that a young Republic just rising into high distinction among the nations of the earth had been swallowed up and lost, like a proud bark in a devouring vortex." As only one of twenty-eight states, the sovereign Republic of Texas would be "reduced to the level of an unfelt fraction of a giant power," would become a tributary vassal "pouring her abundant treasures into the lap of another people than her own," and as "the cornucopia of the world" would give the United States far greater wealth than it would be able to extract as a state.

Lamar pointed out the frequent insults to the national pride of Texas. Official circles in the United States often looked on Texans as a "band of desperadoes" and heaped a "species of national indignities which a proud and spirited people may not bear, and which a patriot, jealous of his Country's as his own honor, should feel bound to resent.

> ***And shall we blindly & madly precipitate ourselves into the deadly and destroying embraces of such a baleful people. . . . We have been told by them distinctly that they will not receive us as brethren—that our country is but the home of the wicked and the***

> ***worthless, where vice is pestilential and virtue laughed to scorn; and like the spaniel that licks the hand that assails him, we continue knocking for admission at the door from which we are abruptly ordered with indignity and insult.***

These are just words, but they are words that, reiterated, drive home points. Constant repetition reinforced the natural pride which any underdog feels in winning against a favored opponent. Texans had plenty to celebrate in settling a frontier area, in achieving independence, and in making their independent nation work. They had heroes, particularly Sam Houston, who in his way could be as eloquent as Lamar but without Lamar's excess. But under Lamar Texas pride was elevated to a national characteristic, a way of life.

A Great Captain and a New Weapon

CHARLES M. ROBINSON, III

CHARLES M. ROBINSON, III, IS PROFESSOR OF HISTORY AT SOUTH TEXAS COLLEGE IN MCALLEN. A PROLIFIC AUTHOR, HIS BOOKS INCLUDE *GENERAL CROOK AND THE WESTERN FRONTIER*, *BAD HAND: A BIOGRAPHY OF GENERAL RANALD S. MACKENZIE*, *A GOOD YEAR TO DIE: THE STORY OF THE GREAT SIOUX WAR*, *SATANTA: THE LIFE AND DEATH OF A WAR CHIEF*, AND *THE MEN WHO WEAR THE STAR: THE STORY OF THE TEXAS RANGERS*.

IN THIS SELECTION, ROBINSON DISCUSSES THE TEXAS RANGERS DURING THE CAPTAIN JACK HAYS ERA. REPUBLIC OF TEXAS PRESIDENT SAM HOUSTON LAUDED THE FEARLESS INDIAN FIGHTER. "THE FRONTIER OF OUR COUNTRY WOULD HAVE BEEN DEFENCELESS BUT FOR HIS GALLANTRY AND VIGILANCE," HOUSTON ASSERTED. ROBINSON ALSO RECOUNTS THE IMPORTANCE OF THE NEW COLT'S REVOLVER, A WEAPON FAVORED BY CAPTAIN HAYS.

★ ★

Jack Hays was only one of several outstanding Ranger captains during the Republic, but he is the most famous because he was the type of frontiersman who inspires legends. Barely an adult when he rose to command, he nevertheless won the admiration of Sam Houston himself, who observed, "The frontier of our country would have been defenceless but for his gallantry and vigilance united With fine capacity." Indeed, he was so widely known by reputation that people were surprised when they saw him for the first time. Pioneer John W. Lockhart, who met Hays in a hotel lobby in Washington-on-the-Brazos, said:

> *I thought that my eyes had deceived me. Could that* **Small, Boyish Looking Youngster,** ***not a particle of beard on his face, homely palefaced young man, be the veritable Jack Hays, the celebrated Indian fighter, the man whose name was sung with praise by all Texians? It could not be, I thought, but I soon found out that it was the veritable "Captain Jack."***

John Coffee Hays had the right credentials to achieve greatness in Texas. Like Sam Houston, he was a Tennessean, born on his family's plantation near Nashville on January 28, 1817. His father, Harmon Hays, was related to Andrew Jackson's wife, Rachel, and named his son for longtime family friend and Jackson protégé Col. John Coffee. The areas's social life centered around the Hermitage, which the Jacksons had built on land purchased from Harmon Hays. Here Jack and his brothers met the great men of the frontier and nation, including the up-and-coming Houston, who numbered Harmon among his friends.

Harmon Hays died when Jack was fifteen years old, and he was placed with a well-meaning uncle who urged him to try for West Point. Not liking the prospect of military regimentation, he left his uncle's home and worked his way westward over the next four years. He arrived in Texas shortly after the Battle of San Jacinto and, finding the new republic's rough-and-tumble army suited him better than the spit and polish of the American military, promptly enlisted as a scout and surveyor. After a stint in the army, he joined a Ranger company commanded by Henry Karnes, distinguishing himself in fights against Indians and Mexicans and developing a reputation for cool, daring leadership.

Besides being an outstanding leader, Hays more than any other individual is responsible for arming the Rangers with another great Texas legend—the Colt's revolver.

Hays achieved his reputation as a leader in the 1840s, a decade unusually rife with bloodshed, for the Texans were beset by both Comanches and Mexicans. Despite several peace treaties, Comanche raids had stepped up during the second half of the 1830s, and the number of captive women and children had grown.

Hostilities opened with a seemingly innocuous event. On January 9, 1840, three Comanches brought a Mexican captive to San Antonio, saying they had been delegated to negotiate a peace. Their message was passed on to Secretary of War Albert Sidney Johnston (later a noted Confederate general), who instructed Lt. Col. William S. Fisher of the First Infantry to meet with the Indians in San Antonio. If the Comanches brought their white captives, it would be considered a pledge of good faith, and they could depart unmolested after the treaty conference. If, however, they did not bring the captives, the chiefs would be detained as hostages.

The Comanches returned on March 19. The party consisted of sixty-five men, women, and children, but only one captive, fifteen-year-old Matilda Lockhart, who had been taken two years earlier. She obviously had been tortured during much of her captivity; her nose was almost completely burned off, her hair had been singed to the scalp, and she was covered with fresh bruises and sores.

Twelve of the main chiefs were escorted into the "Council House," as the old Spanish government house was sometimes known, while the other Indians passed the time in the courtyard. A quick conversation with Matilda Lockhart determined the other white prisoners were held at the main Comanche camp and would be brought in one or two at a time in hopes of large and continuous ransom payments.

Assembling his troops around the building, Colonel Fisher told the chiefs they would remain as hostages while the Comanche women, children, and warriors returned to their camp for the captives. Troops were brought into the room, and the chiefs drew knives and strung their bows. Fisher told the soldiers to fire if the Indians did not surrender calmly. At that moment, one chief stabbed a sentry and was shot. The others attacked the troops, who opened fire. Within moments all twelve chiefs were dead.

Hearing the commotion, the warriors and soldiers outside began fighting. Some Comanches headed toward the nearby San Antonio River, while others barricaded themselves into outbuildings around the Council House. When the shooting stopped, thirty chiefs and warriors, three women, and two children were dead, and twenty-seven women and children and two old men were prisoners. Among the Texans, seven soldiers and bystanders were killed and eight wounded.

During the weeks following the Council House Fight, an uneasy truce prevailed while the two sides negotiated and exchanged prisoners. The death of the twelve chiefs left the Comanches temporarily demoralized, and it took them time to recover. By early summer, however, they had retreated into the hills west of Austin and San Antonio and begun planning a revenge raid. They were encouraged by Gen. Valentín Canalizo, the Mexican commandant in Matamoros, near the mouth of the Rio Grande. As word of the Mexican involvement filtered north into Texas, Dr. Branch Archer, who succeeded Johnston as secretary of war, called up volunteer units against a potential raid. But when the weeks passed and nothing happened, the volunteers were mustered out and allowed to return home.

The Great Comanche Raid of August 1840 took the Texans completely by surprise. Mexican agents in Texas had kept in touch with the Indians and apparently convinced them to delay until the volunteers disbanded. On August 4, a war party consisting of about six hundred Comanches and Kiowas moved out of the hills and descended onto a relatively uninhabited area of the coastal plains. By the afternoon of August 6, they were spotted on the outskirts of Victoria, where the citizens prepared a defense. Avoiding the town itself, the Indians spent that day and the next in the immediate vicinity, stealing horses, burning and killing, and taking some women and children prisoner.

From Victoria, the raiders rode on to the small coastal settlement of Linnville. They struck that town on the morning of August 8, taking the citizens completely by surprise. Most fled in boats to the steamer *Mustang*, anchored in the bay. Those who didn't make it were captured or killed. The refugees on the steamer spent the rest of the day watching as the Indians burned and plundered the town. When they finally retreated, they carried several hundred horses and mules loaded with plunder taken from warehouses at the port.

Even before the sack of Linnville, the Texans were gathering their forces. Early reports of Indian movement had prompted two ad hoc Ranger units, under Capts. Adam Zumwalt and Ben McCulloch, to head out in pursuit. The two units came together on the morning of August 7. By noon they were joined by the old Indian-fighting Ranger John Tumlinson with sixty-five men from Victoria and Cuero, who, unaware of the raiding around Victoria, were returning from a scouting expedition.

As word of the attack on the towns spread, more soldiers, Rangers, and militia assembled, and Maj. Gen. Felix Huston assumed command. Guided by Tonkawa scouts under their veteran Chief Placido, the Texans moved inland and on August 12 intercepted the returning Comanches at Plum Creek, about twenty-seven miles southeast of Austin. Huston sent Ranger Robert Hall ahead with five men to reconnoiter. The Indians were strung out along the prairie, and to Hall the column "looked to be seven miles long." Skirting the column to the Comanche rear, the Texans could see warriors decked out in the plunder of Linnville.

> ***Many of them put on cloth coats and buttoned them behind. Most of them had on stolen shoes and hats. They spread the calico over their horses, and tied hundreds of yards of ribbon in their horses' manes and to their tails.***

By the condition of their fighting equipment and tribal regalia. Hall surmised they had been preparing for the raid for a long time.

At that moment, an officer and a private inexplicably blundered into the Indian line and were surrounded. The officer managed to break free and escape, but the private was killed in sight of the Rangers. Hall told his men to keep back a safe distance and fire whenever they had a target. The men obeyed, and they skirmished for about two miles until they got back to the main body of Texans, and the battle opened in earnest.

The cautious General Huston ordered the Texans to dismount, form into line, and open fire, but the bullets glanced off the tough rawhide of the Comanche shields. Seeing this, veteran fighters waited until the Indians wheeled about on their ponies, then shot them as they turned. As their losses mounted, the Comanches began pulling back out of range. Pressed by Ben McCulloch and Edward Burleson, Huston ordered a charge.

The sudden Texas assault startled the Comanches, but some fought back. A load of buckshot hit Ranger Nelson Lee near his elbow. He dropped his reins and his uncontrolled horse carried him straight into the Indians. Other members of his company rode after him and rescued him.

Hall took a bullet in his thigh. "It made a terrible wound and the blood ran until it sloshed out of my boots." He fell off his horse, but managed to stagger to his feet just as an Indian rode up. Hall raised his rifle, but the Indian threw up his hands and shouted, "Tonkaway!"—identifying himself as one of old Placido's scouts.

The Comanches were routed, and the Texans chased them until their horses gave out. In the confusion, the Comanches left behind their plunder and captives. Some of the captives were recovered alive, but several had been killed when the Comanches realized they were defeated. One woman was seriously wounded but saved from death because her steel corset had deflected her captor's arrow. A considerable amount of Mexican equipment was found, indicating the Comanches had been supplied from that quarter.

Two months later, on October 14, an ad hoc Ranger company under Capt. John Moore with Lipan scouts attacked a large Comanche camp on the upper Colorado River. The Indians were completely routed, bringing public demand for more campaigns. These were the last major expeditions for the time being, however. The Republic was completely penniless.

Jack Hays was in the Battle of Plum Creek, although not a key participant; the day really belonged to veteran Rangers Ben McCulloch and Ed Burleson. Nevertheless, Hays had already earned a solid reputation with a military expedition against Laredo under Col. Eurastus "Deaf" Smith in 1837, returned on two separate occasions in 1839 with Ranger expeditions of his own, and was in several Indian fights with Henry Karnes's Rangers. His prestige was such that when the Texas Congress reorganized the frontier defense forces in January 1841, the twenty-three-year-old Hays was appointed to command one of three new Ranger companies. Records of these units are sketchy, but apparently Hays and the other two captains. John Price and Antonio Pérez, were responsible for enlisting the men.

Nelson Lee, who had recovered sufficiently from his buckshot wound to join Hays's company, recalled:

> ***He was a slim, slight, smooth-faced boy . . . and looking younger than he was in fact. In his manners he was unassuming in the extreme, a stripling of few words, whose quiet demeanor stretched quite to the verge of modesty. Nevertheless, it was this youngster whom the tall, huge-framed brawny-armed campaigners hailed unanimously as their chief and leader when they assembled together in their uncouth garb in the grand plaza of Bexar [San Antonio] . . . for young as he was, he had already exhibited abundant evidence that, though a lamb in peace, he was a lion in war. . . .***

Hays's calculated aggressiveness inspired frontiersmen to say an enemy fled "as if Jack Hays, himself, were after them."

Yet to say he was a daring youth amid grizzled pioneers does injustice to his men. The frontier drew people from all walks of life, and Hays's Rangers were no exception. One of the company, Benjamin Highsmith, remembered many of them as "men of education and refinement. Around the campfire at night it was not uncommon to hear men quoting from the most popular poets and authors, and talking learnedly on ancient and modern history."

In addition to Highsmith, who had carried messages out of the Alamo for Travis, Hays's Rangers at various times included such men as Samuel Walker, who, while not an intellectual, would help design the first purely military Colt's revolver; Ben McCulloch; P. H. Bell, a future governor of Texas; and Creed Taylor, around whom would one day center the most vicious blood feud in Texas history. As Rangers, however, they were young men looking for excitement.

"Discipline is almost wholly lacking," a visiting German naturalist observed, "but this lack is made up for by the unconditional devotion to the leader, who by example leads all in the privations and hardships they usually endure. No one is punished. The coward or incompetent must face the disgrace of dismissal. A uniform is not prescribed and everyone dresses to suit his taste and needs."

Creed Taylor remembered that before one fight, "[w]e dismounted and tightened up our saddle girths belts and etc, and while doing this I was struck with the spirit of dare-devil levity that seemed to have siezed every man."

When the new company organized, Hays's salary was set at $75 a month, later raised to $150. The men were listed at $30 a month, although at first no one was paid because the Republic was in the process of stabilizing its badly inflated currency. It was not a terribly critical problem, however, because the militia acts that governed the Rangers initially allowed only fifteen men. They furnished their own arms, horses, and equipment. The government supplied ammunition and, officially at least, provisions. In reality, the Rangers in the field were cut off from supply and so lived by hunting or on provisions seized from Mexican trains. As a long arm, most carried single-shot muzzle-loading Jaeger rifles across the pommels of their saddles. Hays and a handful of others carried Col. Samuel Colt's revolver.

Colt was not the first to invent a multishot revolving firearm, and he undoubtedly was inspired after seeing British attempts. Nevertheless, the Colt handgun, patented on February 25, 1836, was the first practical revolver, and by the end of that year, Colt was producing revolving pistols and rifles in his newly established factory in Paterson, New Jersey. The handguns included a pocket model in .28 caliber, and two .31-caliber belt models. The No. 5 (actually the fourth model produced) was a holster pistol in .36 caliber. Colt's Patent No. 5 had a total production of a thousand, many of which went to Texas, and for that reason it is known as the Texas Paterson.

By almost any later standard, the Texas Paterson was a crude, clumsy weapon. It was a cap-and-ball arm, with the five chambers in the cylinder charged from the front, the powder and ball being loaded separately. Each chamber had a nipple in the rear for a percussion cap that, when struck by the hammer, flashed directly into the chamber and ignited the powder charge. Once the chambers were loaded, they were sealed with grease, so that the powder blast from one would not ignite the others and cause the cylinder to explode in the hand of the user. The trigger normally folded into the frame and popped out when the gun was cocked; there was no trigger guard. The single-action mechanism required the hammer to be pulled back manually in order to turn the cylinder and cock the gun.

Yet for all its faults, the Texas Paterson was revolutionary. It fired five times before it was empty, compared to other contemporary handguns that had to be reloaded after each shot. And it was wonderfully uncomplicated, with only three basic components—frame, cylinder, and barrel. When it was empty, one simply removed the barrel, charged the chambers in the cylinder simultaneously from a five-spout powder flask, inserted the bullets, sealed the chambers, capped each nipple, replaced the barrel, and resumed firing. Paterson boxed sets often included an extra cylinder, doubling the amount of firepower before reloading. For its time, it was a brutally efficient weapon, and on the frontier, it could be used with devastating effect. J. W. Wilbarger, who was familiar with the arm, later wrote, "With these improved fire arms in their hands, then unknown to the Indians and Mexicans . . . one ranger was a fair match for five or six Mexicans or Indians."

Oddly enough, the advantages of the Colt's Patent Revolver were not immediately evident in Texas. The War of Independence had left the country penniless and enormously in debt. Given Houston's peace policy and his aversion to a standing army, such weapons as remained after the war were deemed sufficient for the Republic's needs. But President Lamar's decision to take the offensive against the Indians and maintain a state of preparedness against Mexico required new arms purchases from abroad.

In the spring of 1839, Lamar received a visit from an old friend, John Fuller, owner of a successful Washington, D.C., hotel. Before embarking on his trip, Fuller had obtained several samples of the company's products, including the No. 5 pistol. Upon arriving in Texas, Fuller demonstrated the arms to Col. George W. Hockley of Texas's Bureau of Ordnance. A conservative officer who preferred the old-fashioned single-shot flintlock pistols and muskets, Hockley was unimpressed. The expanding Texas Navy, however, was delighted with the Colt's revolver, and on April 29, 1839, Navy captain Edward Moore, on a procuring mission to the United States, was instructed to negotiate purchase of 180 of these handguns for use by naval boarding and landing parties. According to Moore, "The Colt's pistols used by the Texas Rangers before annexation were all supplied from the Navy, after they had been in constant use by that arm of the service for upwards of four years. . . ."

Thus Colt's Texas Paterson revolver, ancestor of the gun that became synonymous with the American West, originally went west as navy surplus!

Jack Hays apparently obtained his first Colt's revolver in 1839, not long after it appeared in Texas. He may have purchased it through David K. Torrey, a prominent Waco trader, who wrote him from New York about Colt's "beautiful pattern of belt pistol." At the time, Colt's revolvers were almost unknown outside government circles, scarce, and very expensive for private citizens on the frontier, so several years would pass before they became commonplace among either citizens or Rangers.

With or without Colt's revolvers, the Rangers still had to contend with Indians. The Comanches had begun to recover from the shock of Plum Creek and were moving back down toward the settlements. By the summer of 1841, they once again were raiding ranches and driving off cattle in the vicinity of San Antonio. On June 24, Hays led an expedition that struck a trail that led northwest to Uvalde Canyon. The command consisted of Hays's own company, now made up of sixteen Texans, and a company of twenty *tejano* Rangers under a captain identified as "Flores" but who probably was Antonio Pérez.

About two miles from the entrance to the canyon, they encountered a raiding party of ten Indians bound for San Antonio. The Rangers charged, pushing the Indians into a thicket. The Comanches gave ground grudgingly, forcing the Rangers to fight the distance. The thicket was too dense for a charge, so Hays had it surrounded while he and two others slipped in. Fighting broke out, and a fourth Ranger joined. Eight of the Indians were killed, and a wounded warrior and woman were captured. A Ranger named Miller was slightly wounded.

Hays reckoned that the main Comanche camp was within striking range, but when he followed the trail he realized it was farther than he had thought. His horses were becoming jaded, so he returned to San Antonio.

Still determined to find the main camp, Hays took a company of fifty Rangers and ten Lipan scouts under the war chief Flacco and headed back toward Uvalde Canyon. The Comanches, meanwhile, had retreated westward, deep into the Hill Country, "where the white men had never before made a track."

As the Rangers and Lipans neared the camp, they ran into a Comanche hunting party, which turned about and rushed back to alert the others. Taking twenty-five of his best riders on fast horses, Hays chased them eight miles, catching the main band as the women were packing to flee. About a hundred warriors rode out to block the Rangers and lead them away from the camp, and a running fight ensued for about ninety minutes. Hays's exhausted horses finally forced him to abandon the chase. Several Rangers were wounded. Hays could not determine Indian losses, because they recovered their dead and wounded.

The search for the Comanche camp had taken the Rangers so far west of the line of settlement that they were completely out of provisions. On their return trip, they slaughtered and ate their worn-out horses. Nevertheless, the expedition had carried the Texans into an area the Comanches had previously believed secure, and they abandoned their depredations around San Antonio.

Part of Hays's success in these early expeditions was attributable to his skill as a tracker who could find an enemy trail that was almost invisible. John W. Lockhart observed:

> ***In the dry and rocky portions of West Texas a squad of fifteen or twenty Indians could go through the country without leaving much sign, consequently a trailer was considered a very effective man. This faculty Captain Hays had to a very marked degree, it almost amounted to instinct with him; he could ride along at a good pace and see the signs where other men could see nothing, hence his great tact in overhauling and finishing Indians. It is said that often he would dismount and observe the small pebbles, and by noticing the slightest displacement made by the horses, could, in a moment, tell in what direction they had gone.***

In the field, Hays would halt his men a couple of hours before sunset, preferably near fresh water. Some were sent to hunt game for supper, while others tended the horses and built fires. After dark, when they had finished eating, they mounted up and rode until they found a secluded spot for camp. The object was to get far away from their cooking fire, whose telltale curl of smoke could be seen for miles. Two hours before dawn, they were in the saddle again. "Thus we passed day after day, and night after night, scouring in all directions the wide plains of Texas," Nelson Lee wrote.

Given the historical record of Hays's daring and audacity, it is not surprising that he inspired legend as well. The most famous story concerns a single-handed stand against a band of Comanches atop Enchanted Rock near Fredericksburg, some seventy miles west of Austin. The story first appeared in Samuel C. Reid's *The Scouting Expeditions of McCulloch's Texas*

Rangers, published in Philadelphia in 1847. It was among the Hays exploits that Reid picked up around Ranger camps during the Mexican War.

According to Reid, the incident occurred about 1841 or 1842, when Hays and his men were attacked by Indians near the base of the "hill." Separated from his men, Hays retreated "to the top of the hill. Reaching the 'Enchanted Rock,' he there intrenched himself, and determined to sell his life dearly, for he had scarcely a gleam of hope left to escape."

For almost an hour, he held them off by bluff, the mere act of raising his rifle enough to keep the Indians under cover. Finally, they grew bolder, and started to rush his position. Hays discharged his rifle, "and then seizing his five-shooter, he felled them on all sides." After three more hours, his men finally made their way through the horde of warriors and rescued their leader.

> *"This," said the Texian, who told us the story, "was one of* **'Jack's'** *most narrow escapes, and he considers it one of the* **tightest little places** *that he ever was in. The Indians who had believed for a long time that he bore a charmed life, were then more than ever convinced of the fact."*

Reid himself obviously never saw Enchanted Rock, because he described it as "forming the apex of a high, round hill, very rugged and difficult of ascent. In the center there is a hollow, in the shape of a bowel, and sufficiently large to allow a small party of men to lie in it, thus forming a small fort, the projecting and elevated sides serving as a protection." In fact, Enchanted Rock is the hill itself, a giant granite dome, formed by a volcanic upheaval about a billion years ago, and one of the oldest geological features of North America. Eons of rain and wear have pitted the top with shallow depressions ranging from a few inches to hundreds of feet across, but scarcely deep enough to protect a man against attackers. But the slopes of the rock are broken by rifts and caves that could shelter a man in a fight. Thus, like many legends, the Enchanted Rock Fight probably was based on an actual event that was embroidered in Ranger camps over the passage of time. Whatever the case, it illustrates the nerve and imagination that made Hays the great captain of the 1840s.

While Hays and his men dealt with Indians, the government struggled to keep afloat. Lamar's term expired, and on December 13, 1841, Sam Houston resumed the presidency with the finances in shambles. Nine days later, Dr. Anson Jones, the brilliant, Machiavellian secretary of state, bluntly told the cabinet, "The country is *absolutely* without present means of any kind: her resources are large, though *prospective*, but her credit is utterly prostrate." The government's entire annual revenue, he continued, would not be sufficient to pay even the interest on the national debt.

To reduce the pressure on the administration, Jones proposed a virtual shutdown of the country's military, and a corresponding overhaul of priorities.

> *Our policy, as regards Mexico, should be to act strictly on the* **defensive.** *So soon as she finds we are willing to let her alone,* **she will let us alone.**
>
> *The navy should be put in ordinary; and no troops kept in commission, except a few Rangers on the frontiers.*

The Indians should be conciliated by every means in our power. It is much cheaper and more humane to purchase *their friendship than to* fight *them. A small sum will be sufficient for the former; the latter would require millions.*

By a steady, uniform, firm, undeviating adherence to this policy for two or three years, Texas may and will recover from her present utter prostration. It is the stern law of necessity which requires it, and she must yield to it, or perish!

Jones concluded with a direct attack against the national preoccupation with adventure, stating bluntly that Texas "cannot afford to raise another crop of 'Heroes.'"

Houston proposed drastic cuts in the national budget. The navy, cruising the Bay of Campeche to support insurgents in Yucatán, was to be brought home and laid up. New peace emissaries would be sent to the Indians. Government departments would be consolidated, and many positions established under Lamar would be eliminated. Inflated paper money would be recalled, and replaced with a strictly controlled currency.

The president believed if the Texas Congress adopted his recommendations he might "yet save the country." Nevertheless he was uneasy about troubles on the Indian frontier, and the Mexican attitude plainly worried him. The Santa Fe Expedition had infuriated Mexico, as did the Texas Navy's presence in the Bay of Campeche. More than anything else, however, the Mexicans were enraged because some of the "cowboy" gangs of the Nueces Strip had joined an ill-fated effort by rebel leader Antonio Canales to establish an independent republic of Mexican states along the Rio Grande. Despite Jones's wait-and-see position, on December 29 Houston wrote his wife, "Our chance . . . for invasion by Mexico is greater than it has been since 1836."

Houston's fears were realized. In March 1842, the Mexican general Rafael Vásquez invaded Texas and occupied San Antonio. The city was largely deserted, because Rangers had shadowed the invading force and the citizens were more or less prepared for evacuation. After two days of plundering, Vásquez freed three of Hays's Rangers whom he had captured and started back for Mexico.

Throughout the spring and summer, fear mounted over the prospect that Vásquez's incursion was only a prelude. By August, the Texans in San Antonio were unable to obtain ammunition locally, because it had all been sold to Mexicans. Ranger William A. A. Wallace, called "Big Foot" because his feet were outsized even for his six-foot-two-inch, 240-pound frame, told Hays he had seen "at least a dozen strange Mexicans in town . . . who did not live there." Because Wallace knew virtually every *tejano*, this was ominous.

Hays sent Wallace and another Ranger to Austin to obtain ammunition. Upon arriving, they found the capital in an uproar over an Indian raid and were pressed into service to hunt down the marauders. When they finally headed back to San Antonio, they encountered a couple of Hays's men, who told them the city was occupied by a large Mexican expeditionary force under Gen. Adrian Woll.

Woll's invasion caught San Antonio completely off-guard. Hays and most of the Rangers were on a scouting expedition, and those who had remained in town barely escaped the Mexican cavalry. The Mexicans found the district court in session, and judge and attorneys were among the prisoners marched in chains back to Mexico. Besides the immediate blow to the legal system in San Antonio, the threat of a repeated invasion canceled courts in at least four other western counties over the next several months. Austin was only sixty miles to the north, and Houston, who despised Lamar's artificial capital almost as much as he despised Lamar himself, used the invasion as an excuse to relocate the government to Washington-on-the-Brazos. It remained there for over two years until returning permanently to Austin.

Woll held San Antonio until September 20, when he started back toward Mexico. In November a force of 750 Rangers and militia under Gen. Alexander Somervell marched toward Laredo on a retaliatory raid. They occupied the town on December 8, then continued down the Rio Grande, and on December 19, the force was ordered to return to Gonzales. A retaliatory blow—however minor—had been struck in Laredo, and as Jones had warned, Texas could not afford more heroes.

Hays and many of the other ranking Rangers joined Somervell in obeying the order. But some three hundred men, including prominent Rangers Big Foot Wallace and Samuel Walker, refused. Organizing themselves into a separate command under Col. William Fisher, they started toward Mier, southwest of the Rio Grande, about ten miles from the present city of Roma, Texas. The ensuing debacle, known to history as the Mier Expedition, was an act of sheer mutiny not involving Rangers in any sort of legitimate capacity. However, the roster included former and future Rangers, and the fate of the expedition had a far-reaching impact on Texan-Mexican relations. For those reasons, some discussion is in order.

The three hundred Texans seized Mier, but soon found themselves surrounded and vastly outnumbered by Mexican regular troops. After a desperate battle on the town square, the survivors surrendered and were marched south into the Mexican interior. At Hacienda Salado, south of Saltillo, they overpowered their guards and escaped. Some died in the wastes of northern Mexico, and others simply disappeared. A scant handful, including Ranger Nelson Lee, managed to reach Texas and safety. The remainder, unfamiliar with the country, were rounded up and returned to Salado, where Santa Anna ordered them decimated by firing squad. There being 176 prisoners, a jar was filled with 159 white beans and seventeen black beans. A white bean meant life; a black one death.

The drawing was in alphabetical order, and when it reached *W*, Big Foot Wallace found only a few beans left on the bottom of the jar. His hand, which was as outsized as his feet, barely fit in the neck, and he had to feel around for a bean with two fingers. It was white. When he gave it to the Mexican officer supervising the drawing, the latter grasped his hand and called the other officers to come look at its size. Wallace would remember the man because of that incident.

The men who had drawn the black beans were shot immediately after the lottery, and an eighteenth man, Capt. Ewen Cameron, was later shot near Mexico City on special orders of Santa Anna because Cameron had led the initial break at Hacienda Salado. The remainder, including Wallace and Sam Walker, joined Woll's prisoners from San Antonio in the grim fortress of Perote on the road between Mexico City and Veracruz.

While the San Antonio and Mier prisoners sat in Perote, waiting repatriation and nursing their hatred toward Mexico and all things Mexican, life at home returned to normal. Texans are a resilient people, and Houston, eager to reestablish some semblance of peace, confined his efforts against Mexico to diplomacy. As early as September 14, 1842, with Woll in San Antonio, the president had written Jack Hays:

> ***The situation of our frontier is very unhappy in its influence upon the prosperity of individuals, as well as upon the general interests, settlement and growth of our country. To remedy existing evils is a matter of primary importance to our situation. You are so situated [in San Antonio] that you can determine what course will be proper and safe to pursue. I have thought that advantage might result to us if trade were opened to San Antonio and to such other points as would be safe. In 1838 we had friendly relations and commerce with Mexico, so far as the frontiers were concerned, and had it not been for the cow boys and Canales and his gang, we would never have had any further troubles. . . .***

Hays himself appears to have been willing enough to comply. He realized that his Rangers were primarily scouts and mounted riflemen, more adept at fighting Indians and keeping an eye on Mexican movements than provoking an open conflict with Mexico. Most of his efforts continued around his Indian expeditions.

Between these expeditions the Rangers passed their time amusing themselves with the social and sporting life of San Antonio. Their profession was dangerous, and about half of all Rangers were killed every year. The life expectancy of the average Ranger upon joining the service was two years. and they intended to make the most of their leisure time. Cockfighting was a major event in San Antonio on Sundays. After church everyone, including the priest, joined in the sport. Most nights, the *tejanos* held dances and the Rangers attended. Hays himself "was sometimes seen whirling around with some fair señorita."

Economics still plagued Texas, and eventually the Ranger companies authorized under the 1841 defense acts were disbanded. Houston, however, was certain the Texas Congress would authorize a new peacekeeping force, and when Hays called on him in January 1844, the president suggested he arm his men from the Texas Navy's supply of Colt's revolvers. From his own experience, Hays knew the value of the weapon. After getting an order from the secretary of war, he went to the naval depot at Galveston, where he drew the revolvers, extra cylinders and bullet molds, and other accessories. The Colt's revolver's time had come.

As anticipated, the Texas Congress approved a new defense act, designating Hays by name to command a Ranger company of forty privates and one lieutenant. They were to be enlisted for four months, although this could be extended by presidential order in an emergency. And, thanks to Houston's foresight, they were armed with revolvers. As a frontier weapon, the Colt's had its baptism of fire on June 8, 1844, after reports arrived in San Antonio of Indian depredations along the Guadalupe River northwest of the city. Hays, who was now a major, took fifteen of his new Rangers, including Sam Walker, who had returned to Texas following his release from Perote. They hunted for the Indians as far as the Pedernales River west of Austin and, finding nothing, were returning home when they discovered the Comanches had crossed their trail and were following them.

A small group of warriors taunted the Rangers, retreating when the Texans started toward them. Surmising this was a decoy party trying to lead him into a trap, Hays ordered his men to take cover in a stand of timber. As the Rangers neared the woods, however, the main band of Comanches emerged from the trees. Hays estimated "some sixty-five or seventy warriors . . . led by two especially brave and daring chiefs."

The Rangers charged, and after a vicious hand-to-hand fight, the Indians slowly began falling back. One of the chiefs, however, started exhorting the warriors, raising himself up in his saddle and gesturing to hit the Rangers one more time.

"Any man who has a load, kill that chief," Hays ordered.

"I'll do it," Richard Addison (Ad) Gillespie answered, and, taking careful aim with his long rifle, he shot the chief out of his saddle.

The Indians charged a second time. The Rangers used their revolvers, "two cylinders and both loaded," one survivor recalled.

"The repeating pistols, the 'five shooters' made great havoc among [the Indians]," Indian Superintendent Thomas Western reported to Houston, "some 30 or more were the killed and wounded, finally they fell back carrying off their dead and wounded and encamped in sight, where they remained, the belligerent camps in sight of each other. . . . "

Sam Walker was badly wounded—at first the Rangers feared mortally—and Gillespie was severely injured. Hays was afraid to move them, so he sent one of his men into San Antonio for help. The Indians were too badly battered to travel far, and the two camps glared at each other across the prairie until Ben McCulloch arrived with twelve more men. The Indians departed, and the Rangers remained in place until Walker and Gillespie were well enough to be moved.

Walker recovered from his wounds and drew a sketch of the fight showing a small band of pistol-packing Rangers chasing a horde of Indians. He sent the sketch to Sam Colt, who had artist W. L. Ormsby engrave it on the cylinders of the heavy .44-caliber six-shooters introduced in 1847. Ormsby's imaginative interpretation erroneously depicts the Rangers as uniformed soldiers, but this does not detract from the cold, functional beauty of the weapon.

Family, Religion, and Music:

"The Strength to Endure"

RANDOLPH B. CAMPBELL

RANDOLPH B. CAMPBELL IS PROFESSOR OF HISTORY AT THE UNIVERSITY OF NORTH TEXAS IN DENTON. HIS STUDIES INCLUDE *GONE TO TEXAS: A HISTORY OF THE LONE STAR STATE*, *SAM HOUSTON AND THE AMERICAN SOUTHWEST*, *GRASS-ROOTS RECONSTRUCTION IN TEXAS, 1865–1880*, AND *AN EMPIRE FOR SLAVERY: THE PECULIAR INSTITUTION IN TEXAS, 1821–1865*.

ON THE EVE OF CIVIL WAR, THE STATE'S SLAVE POPULATION APPROACHED 200,000. DENIED THEIR FREEDOM, BLACK TEXANS FACED LIVES OF "HARSHNESS AND HOPELESSNESS." DR. CAMPBELL ARGUES, HOWEVER, THAT THREE IMPORTANT FACTORS—FAMILY TIES, RELIGIOUS FAITH, AND SONG—HELPED "SLAVES SURVIVE THE PSYCHOLOGICAL ASSAULT OF BONDAGE." ☙

★ ★

His wife having been sold, and facing punishment himself, a slave who belonged to Irving Jones in Anderson County committed suicide. He "stood it as long as he could," said the bondsman who told the story. Slave suicides were not at all common, however. Bondsmen, although most faced a lifetime of manual labor with at best adequate material conditions

"Family, Religion, and Music: The Strength to Endure" by Randolph B. Campbell from *An Empire for Slavery: The Peculiar Institution in Texas, 1821–1865*, 1989, pp. 153–176. Reprinted by permission of Louisiana State University Press.

while subject to punishment largely at the whim of their masters, very seldom took their own lives. Their instinctive will to live was threatened by the harshness and hopelessness of bondage, but at the same time it was encouraged by several institutions that mitigated the psychological conditions of servitude. What aspects of Texas slaves' lives contributed to the mental and emotional strength to endure, and what behavioral adjustments did bondsmen make in order to survive? These questions serve as a focus for the next two chapters.

Sizes of slaveholdings affected the psychological as well as physical conditions of servitude. Approximately one-third of Texas bondsmen belonged to small holders, whereas the great majority were on farms and plantations having at least ten slaves. Those who lived in smaller holdings, especially the few who resided in towns, benefited mentally and emotionally from having greater control over their own working and living conditions than did their plantation counterparts. Some may have had an advantage also in that closer daily contact with their masters led to greater recognition of their humanity. At the same time, these bondsmen, particularly those on small farms, were likely to spend most of their time under the close supervision of their owners with only a few other people who shared their situation. The presence of as many or more whites than blacks probably served as an oppressive reminder of their inferior status as slaves while reducing their opportunity to share the support that bondsmen could give each other. These slaves endured, but only the plantation majority had an opportunity to demonstrate the truth of an old adage about strength in numbers. They were in a better position to create families, worship according to their own religious ideas, and have their own music.

Slave families had no legal existence in Texas. A treatise on the state's laws affecting married women, written in 1901, concluded that "since there can be no valid marriage between persons who are incapable of assenting to any contract, it follows that slaves could not marry, even with the consent of their master, so as to constitute them husband and wife. . . . Contubernism was their matrimony; a permitted cohabitation not partaking of the nature of lawful marriage, which they could not contract." Since slave marriages had no standing under the law, it followed that fathers and mothers had no legally protected relationship with their children. The state supreme court demonstrated this in 1849 when it ruled that a district court jury had erred in assessing the value of a woman and her child together in determining the damages due for the theft of the two bondsmen. The two had to be assessed separately, the court said, since they were distinct pieces of property. Obviously, slaveowners had no legal compulsion to create or respect family ties of any sort.

A few masters went to the extremes possible under these circumstances and forced their slaves to reproduce without regard to any family relationships. Women were put with men, Annie Row remembered, like "the cows and the bull" and bred for "bigger niggers." Other former slaves spoke of "breeding," "traveling," or "stud" Negroes who in some cases went from one plantation to another to sire slave children. Fannie Brown said that although she had children before 1865, "I never did have no special husband before the war. I marries after the war." Children who were simply "bred" as animal-like property could be treated as such as they grew older. "We mostly were like cattle and hogs are today," said Jane Cotten.

Some owners, unwilling to "breed" their slaves but determined to insure reproduction, forced "marriages" between their men and women. Seventeen-year-old Rose Williams, for example, did not understand what was expected when her master told her to move from her parents' cabin and live with one of his male bondsmen. She fought back at first and drove the man from her bed and the cabin. Finally, however, after remonstrances and threats from her owner, she gave in. The circumstances of this "marriage" marked her for life. When asked by a WPA interviewer if she had married after slavery, she replied: "Married? Never! No sir! One experience enough for this nigger. After what I'se do for the master, I never want any truck with any man." Other former slaves indicated that Williams' "marriage" was not an isolated case. Betty Powers, for example, fairly snorted when her WPA interviewer inquired about slave marriages. "Did we'uns have weddings?" she said. "White man, you know better than that. Them times colored folks am just put together. The master say, 'Jim and Nancy you go live together,' and when that order give it better be done."

Most masters, however, did not interfere in the sexual lives of their slaves to the point of "breeding" or forcing "marriages." Instead, they permitted the formation of families and the bearing and rearing of children within a family setting. In some cases, a woman and her children were referred to as a "family." In 1860, for example, when Reuben Hornsby, Jr., of Austin bought a woman and her seven children, the bill of sale described his purchase as "a family of eight Negroes." A Johnson County bill of sale referred to "a certain family of Negroes, Viz Emily aged about twenty-six years and her four children." Such records suggest that the female-headed black family at least existed during slavery. Generally, however, the word *family*, as it was used by slaveholders and slaves alike, meant the nuclear social unit—a man, his wife, and their children.

Texas bondsmen themselves provided extensive evidence concerning the existence of nuclear families. In a sample of 181 slave narratives, 60 percent remembered living with both parents on the same home place and another 9 percent recalled that their fathers lived nearby on a neighboring farm or plantation. Inventories from probate records also provide numerous examples of nuclear families existing among bondsmen. Jared E. Groce's Austin County estate, for example, had sixty slaves when it was inventoried in February, 1840. Kinship ties were specified for forty-four bondsmen, while sixteen were not identified with a particular family. Most of the families consisted of a man, his wife, and their children, and others, while not "complete" in this way, gave evidence of long-term kinship ties. One, for example, was made up of an "old woman" (age fifty-eight), two of her sons aged twenty-eight and eighteen, and a six-year-old granddaughter. Another was headed by a fifty-two-year-old blacksmith who had five children aged sixteen to three but no wife. The Joseph Mims estate in Brazoria County had seventy-two slaves in January, 1845. Fifty-nine of these lived in twelve family units, only one of which was headed by a female. John Millican of Brazos County owned sixty-seven slaves at the time of his death in 1859. Ten were not identified with particular families, but the others lived in twelve families, eight headed by husbands with wives, three by women, and one by a man with no wife. William Ward of Brazoria County had eighty-two slaves in 1864, and only two did not belong to one of the nineteen families on his plantation. Eighteen of these families were headed by men. Abram Sheppard of Matagorda County owned only ten slaves in 1856, but eight of them belonged to one family headed by a fifty-year-old man. In Cass County in 1849, eight of W. M. Freeman's thirteen bondsmen belonged to one family. Two of the other five slaves were a sixty-year-old woman and her sixteen-year-old son, but they were not designated a "family" in the inventory. In short, the evidence from slaves and slaveholders alike strongly suggests that the majority of bondsmen in Texas lived at least part of their lives within a traditional family setting.

Masters had good reasons for permitting and even encouraging their slaves to live in families. Treating bondsmen with humanity and having them reproduce within a secure family setting, regardless of what the law allowed, was more socially acceptable than "breeding" or forced "marriages." Moreover, owners recognized how determined slaves were to have families and how important family ties were to the mental and emotional state of their bondsmen. Masters could see that the family led both to children and to ties and obligations that made their bondsmen more controllable in servitude. Considerations of humanity aside, few would deliberately deny an institution that served their own purposes so well. Masters were advised that "marital rights and conjugal ties ought to be scrupulously respected." Nevertheless, there was noticeable variation in what they were willing to do to permit and preserve slave families.

When a man and woman on the same place wished to marry, they had to get their owner's permission. This was generally no problem, but the wedding ceremonies that followed varied markedly from one master to another. Some couples, once they had permission, simply moved into a cabin together, whereas others had elaborate wedding ceremonies with ministers presiding. The most common celebration was a "broomstick wedding" in which the bride and groom literally jumped over a broomstick together. According to one legend, the first one over would "rule" the family. In any case, such weddings essentially amounted to, as one former slave said in disgust, "no ceremony, no license, no nothing, just marrying."

A good many families began when men and women from neighboring farms made matches and asked their respective masters for permission to marry. For example, J. W. Devereux's diary for January 25, 1846, noted a marriage between one of his females and Sam Loftus "by consent of all parties. Sam brought a consent and good recommendation from his master." Henry Lewis who lived in Jefferson County described such a match from the slave's point of view: "My first wife named Rachel and she lived on Double Bayou. She belong to the Mayes place. First time I see her I was riding the range seeing about cattle. I was living on Master Bob's place in Jefferson County and I have to get a pass to go to see her. I tell Master Bob I want to get married and he say, 'all right.' Then I have to go and ask Mr. Mayes and he say, 'all right.' Us had a big wedding." When slaves on different farms and plantations married, they generally had to remain apart during the week and be together only on weekends and special holidays such as Christmas week. Such arrangements were far from ideal for the bondsmen, and they were not good business for the owner of the husband either, in that children born to such unions generally belonged to the owner of the mother. It was not uncommon, however, for one slave or the other, usually the man, to be bought or traded so that the couple could live together. For example, Hattie Cole, George Sells, Martha Spence Bruton, and Gill Ruffin all remembered their fathers being bought from other masters in order to unite them with their wives and children. At times, women were sold for similar reasons. When, for example, George Scott prepared to buy a slave named Liddy from

Thomas B. Huling in 1860, the latter wrote his mother, "I have no objections to sell her as she has her husband belonging to Scott."

Slave families tended to be large, since, after all, children were valuable, and reproduction was encouraged. Women often had their first child while in their late teens and then had another every two years until they were in their forties. Even with the very high infant mortality of that age, many women had four or five living children by the time they reached the age of thirty, and some had spectacularly large families. For example, in 1859, a forty-five-year-old Brazos County woman named China had children aged twenty-eight, twenty-four, twenty-two, twenty, eighteen, sixteen, fourteen, twelve, ten, eight, seven, six, four, and an infant. Of course, white families also tended to be large during this era.

Slave families, regardless of how they were created or their size, played a vital role in providing the mental and emotional strength necessary to endure bondage. Family ties gave slaves love, individual identity, and a sense of personal worth—all from relationships with people like themselves, not from their masters or from others of a clearly superior status. "If you love me like I love you," a Harrison County slave woman wrote her husband in 1862 while he served his master in the Confederate army, "no knife can cut our love into [*sic*]." Judge John Scott wrote to Ashbel Smith about what happened as he prepared to ride his circuit in 1839 and take a hired slave with him as a body servant. "I agreed with Dr. Anderson for his man Thornton," he wrote, "but the rascal runaway, & will not go with me, alleging that he wishes to sleep with his dear wife, etc." One of Smith's own slaves also objected to leaving home even briefly. "Albert got home, safely, on Monday night," M. S. Tunnell informed Smith. "He takes the separation from his family to heart considerably. He said he would rather be set up and shot, then the trouble would be soon over." Clearly the relationships between these men and women were vital parts of their everyday lives.

Slave husbands and wives apparently wanted to divide responsibilities as much as possible along the lines that were traditional in mid-nineteenth-century families. Men, for example, hunted and fished when they could in order to provide additional food. Women kept their homes and took care of the children.

Slave children received love, support, and discipline from their parents. Delia Barclay, for example, remembered how weekend visits from her father who lived on a nearby plantation were a special part of her life. On one occasion, she became so excited at his arrival that she ran across the porch, caught her toe in a crack between the planks, and nearly pulled it off. Martha Spence Bruton told her WPA interviewer that after her mother died her father had to be "mammy and pappy." On Sunday morning, she said, "He'd get out of bed and make a big fire and say 'Jiminy cripes! you children stay in bed and I'll make the biscuits.'" Mollie Dawson described the way children who misbehaved got a good spanking. All most parents had to do, she said, "was to look out the corner of the eye at the kids and they got good right now." Mandy Morrow recalled what happened when she decided to sneak off to the barn and try smoking a pipe. Her mother missed her because things were too quiet and found her in the barn. "She pulled me out of there. Now, white man, there am plenty of fire put on my rear and I see lots of smoke." Finally, the experience of Hannah Mullins at the time of emancipation showed the meaning of her family. She had been living at her master's house as a playmate for his children, but at freedom "my pappy comes after me and we'uns all live together in the cabin instead of me living in the master's house with the kids."

Families were one focal point for survival for many slaves, and yet, paradoxically, families also could bring almost unbearable pain. Husbands generally could not protect their wives from whippings or from sexual abuse by white men. Wives at times saw their husbands beaten and humiliated by overseers and masters. Children had to see their parents unable to protect each other or themselves. Jacob Branch, for example, remembered how awful it was to see his mother whipped. "Many's the time I edges up," he said, "and tries to take some of them licks off my mama." The greatest pain from family relationships, however, came from the fact that they were always subject to disruption by the actions of slaveowners.

Some owners showed notable concern that the family ties of their bondsmen not be disrupted. These masters not only kept husbands, wives, and children together while they lived, they also wrote wills directing that family ties be respected in the settling of their estates. John J. Webster of Harrison County, for example, wrote: "It is my further will that my Negroes be so distributed as to allot the families by families in the partition, that members of the same family may remain together." Dr. E. Stevens of Brazoria County directed his executors to sell all his property for cash but added the proviso that "the slaves shall be sold in families." Richard Carter of Brazos County left all his slaves to his wife. At her death, one large family (a man, his wife, and their eight children) plus four "orphan" Negroes would become the property of his daughter. The other slaves were to be sold, provided that another large family of eight "shall all be sold together to a purchaser, so that they may not be seperated." Samuel McGowen of Polk County bequeathed all his sixtyfour slaves in family units, adding a special instruction that two of the families "shall choose for themselves whichever of my children they may like to live with (the one chosen paying the other a fair consideration)." These masters, and the many others who gave similar directions concerning at least some of their bondsmen, obviously appreciated the strength and importance of the slave family.

Estate administrators and the guardians of minors with slave property also expressed concern at times for the preservation of families. One guardian in Colorado County asked the probate court's approval for hiring to herself the seven slaves belonging to her wards because "it would be painful to separate Negroes united by ties of blood." Rebecca Hagerty proposed to buy part of a Cass County plantation as a place to work the slaves under her care as guardian of Anna Hawkins. This was best, she told the court, because the bondsmen "consist of famillies, say, men, women, and children all of which are unsuitable to hire out." Other guardians and administrators went ahead and hired out slaves but kept families together in the process. For example, the administrator of William A. Nail's Colorado County estate sought and obtained the court's permission to hire out a family together for 1856. David G. Mills, as administrator of Sterling McNeel's huge Brazoria County plantation, hired out six families in 1857. Several large families belonging to William Routt's estate in Washington County were hired out for 1858, although the administrator reported that John, his wife, and their five children were "not hired no one wanting them."

While some owners and estate managers made notable efforts to keep slave families together, others went only so far as was not terribly inconvenient. The will of Dr. John L. Graves is a good example. His wish was that "in making a division the Negroes shall be so divided as to avoid as far as practicable consistently with a just apportionment the separation of the persons constituting a family." Amelia Swanson of Harrison County directed that her slaves' families be kept together as much as possible. The administrator of Susan A. S. Gardner's estate in Colorado County petitioned to hire out two families of slaves for 1857. He kept one family together but hired three members of the second to one hirer and two to another.

Thus, many Texas slaves belonged to masters or came under the control of estate managers who made at least some effort to preserve families; many others, however, were the property of owners who showed absolutely no concern for family ties. In some cases, relationships among husbands, wives, and children were disrupted by the move to Texas from older southern states. For example, Ben Chambers of Jasper County remembered how the move to Texas from Alabama had disrupted his family. He and his mother belonged to Lazarus Goolsby who migrated, while his father's master remained behind. Chambers never saw his father again. John Bates told a similar story: "My mother belonged to Harry Hogan and my father belonged to Mock Bateman . . . I don't know much about him [father] because we moved to Limestone County Texas while I was small leaving my pappy in Arkansas. I never saw him no more." Eli Davison's owner decided in 1858 to leave his own wife in Dunbar, Virginia (now West Virginia), take a few slaves, including young Eli, and begin anew in Texas. Davison was permanently separated from his mother and father. Some young slaves were not even fortunate enough to come to Texas with one of their parents or their original owner. Instead, they were bought elsewhere and brought to the Lone Star state by a new master. Sarah Perkins and her brother, for example, traveled from Tennessee after being sold to Charlie Jones. The boy died en route and was buried beside the road; Sarah was so sickly that she was given away in San Antonio. Ashbel Smith bought three slaves, aged ten, twelve, and seventeen, in 1838 in New Orleans and shipped them to Galveston. Smith's bill of sale and shipping manifest provide no evidence, of course, on the family relations of these young bondsmen, but it is obvious that they were purchased and brought to Texas without their fathers or mothers.

Slave families that survived migration or were formed in Texas also were subject to disruption at any time. Contemporary observers, newspaper advertisements, and former slaves all provide evidence that masters could and did sell bondsmen without regard to age or family ties. Nicholas Doran P. Maillard described an auction during 1840 in Fort Bend County in which a family of four was sold to three different purchasers—the father to one, the wife and an infant to another, and a boy to a third. The Clarksville *Northern Standard* carried an advertisement in 1857 offering a thirteen-year-old girl for sale or barter for a boy or cattle. Lizzie Atkins remembered having two brothers and a sister sold from her family when she was six or seven years old. James Brown described slave families being broken up on the auction block, and Josie Brown saw "children too little to walk split from their mammys and sold right on the block in Woodville."

Perhaps the ultimate example of selling a young slave occurred in Austin County during May, 1859, when James Strawther, who was in severe financial difficulty, sold a six-week-old female for $75. Strawther warranted the infant a slave for life, but did "not warrant her soundness in any manner." The purchaser was Strawther's sister, who soon became the administrator of his estate and a partial heir of his property, so perhaps the infant was never separated from her mother. Nevertheless, the transaction reveals that there was no limit on the age at which slaves could be, and were, sold.

Slave children sometimes were given away as well as sold. Sarah G. Burleson of Hays County, for example, gave her daughter-in-law, Louisa, "a certain negro boy named Phillip of copper complexion and about six years of age." The boy's mother had already been given to one of Burleson's sons (not Louisa's husband). Minerva Bratcher at age six was part of the "dowry" accompanying one of her master's daughters who married in the mid-1850s. The 1862 will of David Barton of Burnet County directed that a girl named Caroline be given to the yet-unborn child being carried by his wife.

Slave families were broken up by migration, sales, and gifts. However, the death of a master created an even greater likelihood of disruption. In many cases, immediately after an owner died, his farm or plantation came under the management of an administrator who then hired out the bondsmen belonging to the estate and in the process often broke up slave families, sometimes year after year. For example, William Steen's De Witt County estate included four nuclear families when it was inventoried in January, 1847. The estate's administrator immediately hired out its slaves for the remainder of that year and in the process disrupted all four families. In Rusk County, six slaves belonging to one estate, including a forty-year-old man, a thirty-year-old woman, and her three children aged fourteen, twelve, and six, were each hired to different renters each year from 1859 to 1862. The boy was separated from his mother and served four different masters before he reached the age of ten.

Hiring out constituted a temporary disruption, but final estate settlements, some of which took place soon after a slaveholder's death and others not until after years of administration, often resulted in the permanent breakup of slave families. Although some slaveowners in their wills sought to protect families, many others made no such provision or even directed the separation of husbands, wives, and children. William C. Sparks of Bell County, for example, left his ten slaves to his six children "share and share alike." Robert O. Reeves of Grayson County and Thomas H. Snow of Polk County also wrote wills that left slave families at the mercy of an equitable division of their estates. Lewis M. H. Washington of Travis County left one slave couple to his wife, but his will also directed that a woman named Charlotte be sold and that each of his four stepchildren be given one of Charlotte's five children. The fifth child went to Washington's wife. Ephraim D. Moore's will bequeathed one slave to each of his seven children. Any slaves born before the will took effect, Moore wrote, will be "kept by them that may have their mother." In similar fashion, John Robbins divided six slaves among his five heirs. The youngest bondsman involved was only four. Isaac Vandorn of Matagorda County wanted his wife to keep all his slaves together during her lifetime. At her death, however, each of his three children was to pick one slave, and the others were to be divided equally. Clearly, these wills permitted or necessitated the disruption of families.

In cases where slaveowners died intestate, settlements partitioning estates according to state laws on the subject often broke up slave families. William Steen's estate again provides a good example. When this estate was partitioned into eight "lots" of approximately equal value in April, 1848, all four families were disrupted in some way. For example, Armystead, a thirty-four-year-old blacksmith, saw his wife Aggey and three children combined with another man to create Lot #3, while he was placed in Lot #6 with a fifteen-year-old girl. Peter W. Gautier, Sr., of Brazoria County had fifteen slaves who comprised six families when his estate was inventoried and partitioned in 1848. In the partition, four of the families were kept intact but two were disrupted. Sancho and Lucy, who were both thirty-three, had their nine-year-old son placed with another family. The Polk County estate of Nicholas M. Callahan had such extensive debts that seven slaves including a twenty-two-year old woman and her four children aged six, four, two, and one, were sold in 1849. The same man bought Letty and her youngest child, but the other three children went to three different purchasers. Probate records provide case after case of this sort, but the point is obvious—estate settlements constituted a major threat to slave families in Texas.

The breakup of a slave family was heart-rending. When eight-year-old Charlie Sandles was traded to a new master, he cried for a week. Tempe Elgin's master moved from Arkansas to Texas, taking her mother and sister, and leaving behind her father who belonged to a different master. The man ran away and followed them for sixty miles, urging his wife to run away and live with him. She, however, would not leave her children, so he gave up. His family never saw him again. Albert Henderson, drawing an analogy from his rural background, said that slaves when sold from each other "bawled" like cattle that had lost their calves. James Brown remembered seeing "them cry like they at the funeral when they am parted, they has to drag them away."

Many slaves demonstrated a willingness to sacrifice virtually everything else in their lives in order to preserve their families. Millie Ann Smith described how she was brought to Texas with her mother and two sisters. Her father, who belonged to a different master, ran away, followed his wife and children to Texas, and begged their owner into buying him so that he could be with his family. Wash Ingram of Panola County told a similar story. His family lived in Virginia, he said, and his father ran away but remained in the neighborhood. Then his mother died, and he and the other children were sold to Jim Ingram from Texas. His father followed the children all the way to Louisiana before catching up with them and becoming Ingram's slave also in order to be with his family. Walter Rimm told his WPA interviewer a story that, he said, "makes the impression on me all my life." At a slave auction on his master's place, a man from "outside" put a fifteen-year-old girl on the block. Suddenly, there was a scream from an older woman who had features very similar to the girl: "Ise will cut my throat if my daughter am sold." The owner talked to the woman, failed to calm her, and took the girl off the auction block. Her threat had preserved a family relationship, at least for the time.

When slave families were disrupted, fathers, mothers, and children did the best they could to stay in contact and visit each other. The Christmas holidays were an especially likely time for families to be reunited, although many were able to get together more often. Charlie Sandles, for example, visited his parents from Saturday night until sundown on Sunday. Mollie Dawson's father lived on a neighboring plantation, and at times she left her home to visit him at his. One of Preston R. Rose's slaves went to California with him during the early 1850s, and somehow managed to obtain freedom and stay in the new El Dorado. In May, 1851, he wrote Rose, saying "I cannot come home this season, but would like much to have my family with me, if any arrangement could be made. Please let me know how much money it will be necessary for me to send you for their freedom." W. Steinert, a German visitor to Texas in 1849, traveled from New Braunfels to Austin by a stagecoach that included a slave woman and child among its passengers. To his surprise, when the stage reached Austin a Negro woman ran up and almost literally pulled the child from the coach, crying, "My baby, my little baby." Steinert then found that "the very happy woman was the mother of the child. The christian whites had torn mother and daughter apart by a sale. On the other hand they were humane enough to permit the visit."

Some efforts to renew family ties after long periods of disruption were truly heroic. Mary Armstrong's mother was sold from her home in Missouri to Texas before the Civil War. Upon being manumitted in 1863, Armstrong decided to go to Texas in search of her mother. She was almost returned to slavery in Austin, saving herself only with her manumission papers, before finally locating her mother in Wharton County after the war. Louisa Picquet was born in South Carolina, the child of a mulatto slave named Elizabeth Ramsey and her master. Eventually a man from Texas bought the mother, and Louisa was sold to a man in New Orleans and became his concubine. Upon his death, she was manumitted and given enough money to move to Cincinnati, where she married a mulatto named Henry Picquet. Louisa then continued a search for her mother that had begun almost as soon as they were separated. Finally, a friend who traveled to Texas told her of a Mr. Horton who fit the description of the man who had bought her mother. This was Albert C. Horton, a former lieutenant governor and acting governor of Texas and one of the state's largest slaveholders. She began a correspondence with her mother and with Horton in 1858 or 1859, seeking to buy her mother's freedom. Horton asked $1,000; Picquet convinced him to take $900 and raised the money through severe personal economies and a public request for funds. A note in the Cincinnati *Daily Gazette* of October 15, 1860, thanked everyone who had contributed to purchasing the freedom of Elizabeth Ramsey and invited them to call at the Picquets' home to be thanked personally by mother and daughter.

Following the Civil War, the Freedmen's Bureau in Texas received numerous inquiries from blacks in other states concerning family members. A letter of July 20, 1866, from Topeka, Kansas, for example, contained a request from David Barber for "information concerning his wife Sophia Howard, who with her 6 children were sent to Collin Co., Texas in 1861." Charles White of Elizabeth City, North Carolina, wrote in June, 1867, asking that the bureau "procure and return to him his wife and two children John Westley & Florence who before the war were sent to Victoria, Tex." These men were attempting to restore families that had been disrupted for more than five years.

No more eloquent testimony to the vital importance of the slave family can be imagined than the determination of the bondsmen themselves to form and preserve bonds between husbands/fathers, wives/mothers, and children. A few may have sought to escape the heartbreak of family disruptions by avoiding such ties. William Byrd told of slaves who tried not to let children know who their parents were, and Lu Lee said women sometimes forced themselves to miscarry by taking calomel and turpentine. But this was not typical. "Nobody can tell me now," wrote Steinert after witnessing the joyous reunion of a mother and her child in Austin, "that the Negroes do not have fatherly and motherly love in their hearts." The bonds of love and support between the men, women, and children who created slave families, in spite of the fact that a majority of those families probably faced disruption at some time, provided much of the emotional strength necessary to endure servitude.

Religion appears to have been second only to the family in helping slaves survive the psychological assault of bondage. Its role, however, depended on how spiritual instruction was given and how slaves heard and received the various articles of faith and religious precepts. Religion could be highly supportive of slavery when it taught that men had to obey their temporal masters in the same manner that they served their spiritual ruler. Bondsmen were instructed to be loyal, virtuous, and industrious, with the idea that, as one traveler put it, "a good christian is not a bad servant." On the other hand, Christianity could be subversive of slavery when it taught that all men, black and white, stood on an equal footing before God and were equally capable of attaining eternal salvation. Most Texans, while they certainly did not mean to undermine their Peculiar Institution, did not deny this most fundamental Christian assumption. At least, then, religion offered many slaves the promise, as Mary Gaffney put it, of an eternity "where they would not be any more slaves." At best, there was the hope for deliverance as the Bible told of people delivered from bondage and sin. Many years later, Ellen Ford remembered how her family had prayed for freedom and insisted that "emancipation wouldn't have come if it hadn't been for the prayers of my mother and grandmother."

Slaveholders probably had fewer reasons to encourage or even permit religious instruction and worship among their bondsmen than they had for allowing slave families. Religion was not generally as vital to the slaves' emotional well-being, and it involved nothing of such practical value as procreation. Under these circumstances, some masters did their best to prohibit all religious activities. They did not allow their bondsmen to attend church or even to worship on their own. According to Sarah Ashley, who belonged to Mose Davis near Coldspring, "there wasn't any meetings allowed in the quarters. The boss man even whip them when they have the prayer meeting." "Sometimes," she added, "us run off at night and go to . . . camp meetings, but I was plumb growed before I ever went to church." John Bates's Uncle Ben read the Bible and told the others on his place that some day they would be free. Their master heard and said, "Hell, no, you will never be free, you ain't got sense enough to make the living if you was free." He said the Bible had put bad ideas in people's heads and took it away from Ben. Bates remembered, however, that his uncle got another Bible and "he keeps this one hid all the time." In 1857, Ashbel Smith's overseer refused the slaves permission to attend services on Sunday, which they, as was their practice in all such disputes, protested to their master.

Preventing religious activity was thus virtually impossible. Most masters, therefore, did not attempt to prohibit worship, and some actively encouraged it. Their purposes ranged from the cynical view that Christian virtues made better slaves to the sincere conviction that the souls of all, black as well as white, should be saved. Wes Brady complained that he heard only about obeying and not stealing. There was "nary a word about having a soul to save." But Albert C. Horton, a Baptist deacon and one of the largest slaveholders in Texas, took a genuine interest in the spiritual welfare of his bondsmen. He built a church, employed a minister, and personally read the Bible and prayed with his servants. Most slaveholders probably had mixed motives. As one Harrison County minister said of the slaveholders in his area, "all seem to understand, that while the Gospel qualifies their servants for immortality and eternal life, at the same time it makes them better servants here—better to their earthly masters—more obedient, industrious, trusty, and faithful."

Bondsmen on some places simply held local services that created as little bother as possible. Charlotte Beverly said that her master sometimes allowed one of the slaves who was "a sort a preacher" to speak to the others. However, he had to preach with a tub over his head, because if he got too "happy" and loud someone would come from the big house and end the "disturbance."

It was common, however, for slaves to belong to organized churches and attend regularly scheduled services. Most Texan slaveholders who attended church belonged to one of the "standard" Protestant denominations—Methodist, Baptist, Presbyterian, Episcopal, Cumberland Presbyterian, and Disciples of Christ (Christian church)—and all these churches baptized slaves. The Methodist church, the largest denomination in antebellum Texas, claimed 1,000 blacks by the mid-1840s and reported nearly 7,500 Negro members and probationers in 1860. Complete membership statistics for the Baptist church, the second largest in the state in 1860, are not available, but clearly thousands of slaves belonged to it, too. In 1861, for example, the Colorado, Austin, Little River, and Grand Cane Baptist associations, which represented fewer than half of such associations in Texas, reported 1,087 Negro members. The other denominations were far smaller, but they, too, baptized slaves. Caleb Ives, the Episcopal minister who organized Christ Church at Matagorda in 1839, accepted "colored" members, and when Texas became a separate diocese in 1859, its first bishop, Alexander Gregg, ministered as regularly to slaves as to whites. The Cumberland Presbyterians accepted Negroes as full members of their local congregations. The Colorado Presbytery, for example, reported 256 white and 44 black communicants in 1860. The Disciples of Christ's pioneer "Old Liberty" Church in Collin County was founded by 16 whites and 5 slaves. In short, only a minority of Texas' slaves actually belonged to organized churches. But thousands had been baptized, many others doubtless attended services, and a good many more worshipped on their home places. Certainly most had access to some form of religion.

Some of the slaves attended worship services with their masters, sitting in pews especially designated for them. Far more common, however, were special meetings for black church members on Sunday afternoon or night. In some cases, the Methodists and Baptists permitted even more separate worship through the formation of all-black congregations. By 1860, for example, the Methodist church had thirty-seven "missions" to the slaves with a total membership of 2,585 bondsmen. The Colorado Baptist Association at its 1854 meeting permitted the "Colored Church on J. H. Jones' plantation, Matagorda County" to join as a separate congregation. The next year, however, the Union Baptist Association rejected a similar request by the "Africa Church at Anderson" on the grounds that "the establishment of independent Churches among our colored population would be inconsistent with their condition as servants, and with the interests of their masters." Separate worship services were acceptable, the association said, "but always to be aided in this work by the presence and counsel of some judicious white members."

The matter of separate slave congregations raised a more fundamental question—who was to minister to the bondsmen? Obviously, the slaveholders intended that white preachers provide religious instruction, but, as slavery matured in Texas, black ministers were not uncommon. In Washington County during the 1840s, a slave named John Mark preached so well to white and black alike that, when his owner moved, local planters bought and deeded him to three ministers in trust for the Methodist church. In 1853, the Texas Conference of the Methodist Episcopal Church, South, elected John Mark "to deacon's orders as a local preacher." The Trinity Presbytery of the Cumberland Presbyterian church in 1848 authorized a man called "Brother Henry," the property of William Roberts, to preach, to baptize other blacks, and to "administer the sacraments of the supplies" to them. Slaves in the Indian Creek community of Jasper County built the Dixie Baptist Church in 1853 with the aid of Joshua Seale. One of Seale's slaves, Richard, was the church's founding minister. Bondsmen in the area reportedly "flocked into the wooden church every Sunday and dared not think of missing." Some black preachers, of course, ministered without the formal approval of any denomination. Some were recognized locally and preached on their own places and adjoining plantations, while others repeated and interpreted what they heard from white ministers. In any case, extensive evidence from church records and from the slaves themselves indicates that many and probably most had the opportunity to hear a religious message presented by a fellow slave. Indeed, black ministers were numerous enough by 1860 that the Texas Conference of the Methodist Church received a recommendation from its committee on African missions to withdraw approval from meetings "conducted by colored men" and stop "licensing or renewing the licenses of colored men to preach."

What did bondsmen hear when they attended worship services? White ministers, as noted above, generally told the slaves to be loyal, honest, and industrious in order to attain ultimate salvation. Blacks who led worship services often had their words carefully monitored by slave-owners or other white supervisors. Nancy Jackson and Simpson Campbell, for example, both remembered how their ministers were instructed to preach obedience to earthly masters. Josie Brown said that the slaves on her place had to hold their church meeting "in the yard, so the white folks could see the kind of religion expounded." Those who preached "wrong" views were likely to have short careers. Sarah Ford told about a preacher named "Uncle Lew" who said that the Lord had created all men equal. "Uncle Jake," the black driver, told the master, and "Uncle Lew" found himself a field hand again the next day. And yet, in spite of all efforts to insure that slaves heard only the "right" religious message, those who worshipped were well aware of the other implications of a belief in God and Jesus. Even without an "Uncle Lew" to tell them, they understood that all men stood equally before their creator. This meant, at the very least, the promise of salvation for all, and, at best, it was a promise of redemption. Religious faith helped many thousands of slaves to endure.

In Texas, as elsewhere across the South, slaves' music contributed significantly to their adjustment to servitude. Music was an acceptable form of expression that served the needs of blacks in a variety of ways. Slaves sang to set a pace for their work and to express their emotions. As Vinnie Brunson told a WPA interviewer, "the Negro used to sing to nearly everything he did. It was the way he expressed his feelings and it made him relieved, if he was happy, it made him happy, if he was sad, it made him feel better, and so he naturally sings his feelings." Slaves also used music as a deceptive form of communication. Richard Carruthers of Bastrop County remembered how, as a youth with the job of managing livestock, he watched for the overseer, Tom Hill, and used a song to warn his fellow bondsmen in the cotton field. When Carruthers sang "Hold up, hold up, American spirit," the field hands knew that they were about to receive a visit from "Devil Hill." In a similar vein, when one of Rosina Hoard's owner's sons tried to teach some of the slaves the ABCs, lookouts stood ready to give a musical warning if the master approached. Above all, slave music contained protests against bondage and expressions of the dream of freedom. One song protested:

Master sleeps in the feather bed,
Nigger sleeps on the floor
When we all get to Heaven,
They'll be no slaves no more!

"We hummed our religious songs in the field while we was working," Millie Ann Smith of Rusk County said. "It was our way of praying for freedom, but the white folks didn't know it." Slave music was thus a means of expression, communication, and protest. Bondsmen often said a great deal more through song than their masters knew or cared to recognize, and in the process they exercised one more means of withstanding the psychological pressure of slavery.

Many Texas slaves had some opportunity for education in reading and writing because the Lone Star state had no laws intended to prevent slave literacy. Some owners deliberately sought to prevent any education of slaves because it would lead to running away and other expressions of discontent. Even in some of these cases, however, members of the white family, usually children, ignored the objections of the master and mistress and tried to teach young slaves to read. Susan Merritt, for example, remembered being hit with a whip when her mistress caught her being taught to read by one of the family's daughters. Many owners, however, had no objections if their slaves were taught, and others sought deliberately to give a minimal education and take advantage of it. Andrew Goodman's master, for example, urged his bondsmen to learn all they could, and Robert Prout attended a Sunday morning "school" taught by his owner. W. L. Sloan of Harrison County educated some of his slaves to the point that they could keep records on cotton picking and other plantation work. Others had similar opportunities, although not all cared to learn. Liza Jones, for example, said that she cried to go out and play when one of her master's daughters tried to teach her to read and write. Such reluctance may have been nothing more than the expression of a child's desire to play rather than work, but it may also have been an indication that formal education was relatively unimportant to slaves. It seems that literacy did not confer any special status, unless combined with preaching, and had no particular mental or emotional benefits. No doubt informal education—the knowledge of what it meant to be a slave and how to get along in the system—was more important than formal learning.

This type of education, however, was provided by families and other slaves in the quarters and cannot be documented.

Texas slaves, as they endured bondage, generally gained mental and emotional strength from their families, religion, and music. Still, however, they had to adjust their attitudes and day-to-day behavior to the pressures of bondage. How Texas blacks behaved as they faced the widespread harshness and essential hopelessness of slavery constitutes another vital aspect of the psychological conditions of servitude.

Living in Confederate Texas

Ralph A. Wooster

Ralph A. Wooster, dean of Texas Civil War historians, is Distinguished Professor Emeritus of History at Lamar University in Beaumont. His studies include *The Secession Conventions of the South, Lone Star Generals in Gray, Texas and Texans in the Civil War,* and *Civil War Texas: A History and a Guide.*

In the following selection, Wooster examines life in Confederate Texas. He addresses such topics as the shortage of basic goods, the influx of refugees from neighboring areas, the challenges faced by the cotton trade during wartime, conscription, the relationship between state officials and Confederate authorities, and Texas Unionism. Wooster also considers the role of women and slaves in Civil War Texas.

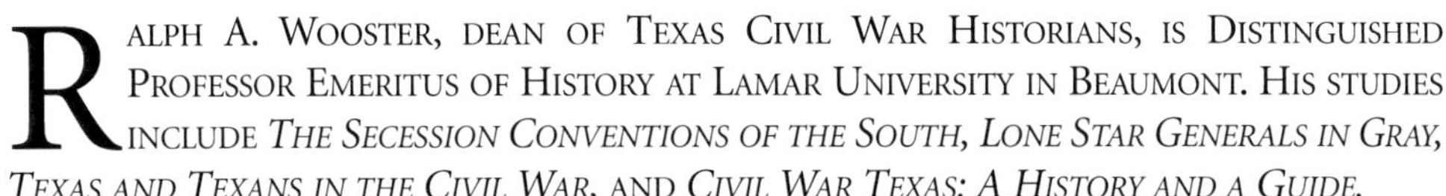

★ ★

By the end of 1863 the vast majority of adult white male Texans, ninety thousand according to Gov. Francis Lubbock, were serving in Confederate or state military forces, some far away from the state. Those men, women, and children who remained at home faced new challenges as they adjusted to the impact of war.

A frontier state, Texas suffered less than the other Confederate states. The major battles of the war were fought in Virginia, Tennessee, and Georgia, where physical devastation was immense. Although Galveston was occupied briefly, Brownsville, Indianola, and South Texas were under federal control in the winter of 1863–64, and El Paso was occupied by federal troops following Sibley's retreat in 1862, most of those living in Texas did not have direct contact with the enemy. Even so, there were changes in lifestyles. The blockade of the Southern coastline cut off many imports from Europe and other parts of the world. Too, the great variety of goods purchased from Northern manufacturers were no longer available. As a result, there were shortages of many items, especially coffee, medicine, clothing, shoes, and farm implements.

Some Texans were using substitutes to replace imported coffee as early as the fall of 1861. A Confederate soldier, David Kennard, stationed at Virginia Point across from Galveston Island, wrote to his parents on November 28, 1861, explaining that he had learned how to make potato coffee. Young Kennard apparently found the substitute fairly satisfactory. Not everyone was so agreeable. The British visitor Lt. Col. Arthur Fremantle noted that "the loss of coffee affects the Confederates even more than their loss of spirits; and they exercise their ingenuity in devising substitutes, most of which are not generally very successful." While traveling through East Texas, Fremantle was served a mixture called Confederate coffee, made of rye, meal, Indian corn, and sweet potatoes. Eliza McHatton Ripley, a refugee from Louisiana in Texas, observed that peanuts, sweet potatoes, rye, beans, peas, and cornmeal were used as coffee substitutes, all of which she called "wretched imitations, though gulped down, when chilly and tired, for lack of anything better."

In her travels in Texas, Mrs. McHatton-Ripley noted that "all household and family goods were scarce." "A needle dropped or mislaid was searched after for hours; if one was broken its irreparable loss was lamented," she observed. Amelia Barr, the Englishwoman who later became one of America's most prolific authors, lived in Austin with her family during the war. In her memoirs she recalled that because of the shortage of pins and needles "some were compelled to use mesquite thorns for pins."

Some newspapers suspended publication because of the shortage of paper, while others reduced their issues to smaller size. Shortages of salt occurred after federal armies overran Saltville, Virginia, and Avery Island, Louisiana, two major sources of commercial salt for the Confederacy. Salt became so scarce that some Texans dug up the floors of smokehouses and leached the dirt to recover the salt drippings. Bark, herbs, and berries were used for dyes, willow bark and red pepper were mixed as a substitute for quinine, and backs of wallpaper served as writing paper. Occasionally there were shortages of specific food items, but apparently these were not so serious as those leading to bread riots in Richmond, Mobile, and Atlanta.

The shortage of commodities was exasperated by the large number of refugees who came to Texas from Arkansas and Louisiana to escape invading Union armies. East Texas, especially the towns of Tyler, Rusk, Marshall, and Corsicana, was particularly affected by this onrush of refugees. The city of Houston also received refugees from Galveston as a result of that city's federal occupation. Many of the refugees found life in Texas to be harsh. They complained of heat, dust, wind, insects, reptiles, and boorish neighbors. Young Kate Stone of Brokenburn plantation in northern Louisiana believed she had discovered "the dark corner of the Confederacy" in East Texas. Most refugees adjusted to conditions in the Lone Star State, however. Even Stone, who complained constantly about poor accommodations and unsanitary conditions, later admitted that the last twelve months she spent in Confederate Texas "was the happiest year" of her life.

Trade through Mexico allowed Texans to obtain some of the goods that in normal times came through Gulf ports. In exchange for cotton, Texans received military supplies, medicines, dry goods, ironware, liquors, and coffee. By the end of the first year of the war, wagon trains moved across South Texas carrying thousands of bales of cotton from Texas, Arkansas, and Louisiana plantations and farms. Almost overnight Matamoros, the Mexican town across the Rio Grande from Brownsville, became a thriving metropolis with cotton buyers, speculators, agents, and merchants from all over the world eager to obtain cotton. From Matamoros cotton was taken in river steamers down the Rio Grande to Bagdad, a small town on the coast, for transshipment to oceangoing vessels. By the time of the Union occupation of Brownsville more than 150,000 bales of cotton had passed through Matamoros. When Brownsville was captured, the Texans moved the trade upriver to Laredo and then down the Mexican side of the Rio Grande. By the end of the war 320,000 bales of cotton had been shipped across the Rio Grande.

Some goods continued to be brought into Texas through the Union naval blockade by fast steamers or sailing schooners. Galveston was the favorite port for blockade runners but Sabine Pass, Velasco, Matagorda, Indianola, and Corpus Christi were ports of call for those bold enough to run the blockade. Most of the Texas trade went through Havana, Cuba. Fast, light vessels made the dash across the Gulf. Once in Cuba, cotton was transferred to larger, neutral flagships heading for Europe, or in some cases a seaport in the United States. Returning vessels brought war materials or consumer goods to Havana; these were then transferred to blockade runners heading for Texas. The exact number of such attempts is unknown but most historians believe blockade runners came in and out of Texas ports well over a thousand times. The majority of these runs were successful. Historian Tuffly Ellis estimates blockade runners were captured in only 10 to 15 percent of their voyages in and out of Texas ports.

Control of the cotton trade became an issue of dispute between Edmund Kirby Smith, the Confederate commander of the Trans-Mississippi Department, and Pendleton Murrah, who succeeded Francis Lubbock as governor in 1863. Smith created a Cotton Bureau through which his department attempted to purchase and resell Texas cotton, the profits of which would be used for purchasing military supplies. Texas planters protested what they considered to be unfair costs for transporting their cotton to bureau depots. Too, they resented the threat of impressment if they did not cooperate with the bureau. Under Governor Murrah's leadership, the Texas legislature created its own cotton plan, which gave Texas planters protection from Confederate impressment. General Smith complained that the Texas plan hurt his efforts to provide arms and ammunition for his troops. For a brief time an impasse prevailed, but Murrah finally agreed to appeal to Texas planters to deliver their cotton to Smith's bureau for sale.

A more serious disagreement between Confederate authorities and Texas officials occurred over conscription. State leaders argued that individuals enrolled in the militia were not subject to

Confederate conscription laws, a position with which General Magruder and Elkanah Greer, head of the Conscript Bureau of the Trans-Mississippi Department, strongly disagreed. The issue came to a head with the passage of two new militia acts by the Texas legislature in December 1863. One measure, which created what came to be called the Frontier Organization, declared that adult white males residing in frontier counties were to be organized into militia companies for border defense. Another act provided that able-bodied men living elsewhere in Texas would be retained in the state militia. Generals Smith and Magruder argued that these laws conflicted with Confederate laws which had superiority over state statutes. After some quarreling between officials, Murrah agreed to a compromise whereby the state would retain militiamen already under arms but these men would be subject to Confederate authority in an emergency. On the issue of conscripts who resided in frontier counties, however, Murrah refused to budge. He insisted that these individuals serve in the Frontier Organization. The matter was referred to Richmond for resolution, but the war ended before the matter was resolved.

Although Murrah disagreed with Confederate officials over matters such as conscription, impressment, and the cotton trade, Texas leaders generally were cooperative with both Kirby Smith and Richmond authorities. Murrah's predecessors as governor, Edward Clark and Francis Lubbock, worked closely with Confederate officials in recruiting, organizing, and equipping military units from Texas for Confederate service. Clark, who became governor when Houston refused to take the Confederate oath of loyalty, served as chief executive for less than a year. Lubbock, who narrowly defeated Clark in the autumn elections of 1861, was a staunch supporter of the Davis administration and worked tirelessly to improve state-national relations. In the summer of 1862 he issued an invitation to the governors of Arkansas, Missouri, and Louisiana to meet with him at Marshall, Texas, to discuss issues of mutual concern to the Trans-Mississippi states. A second conference was held at Marshall in August 1863, this time at the request of departmental commander Kirby Smith. Lubbock believed that both conferences led to improved relations and greater cooperation between state and Confederate officials.

Lubbock and Murrah had to deal with those Texans who remained loyal to the Union and did not support the Confederacy. Some Texans opposed secession and the Confederacy at the outset but later came to accept the Confederacy. James W. Throckmorton of Collin County was perhaps the best known of this group. Throckmorton, leader of the eight delegates in the Secession Convention who voted against disunion, served as a regimental commander in the Confederate Army and was later a brigadier general in state service. Ben H. Epperson, a lawyer and businessman from Red River County, was a Unionist who urged Sam Houston to resist secession, but once the war was underway contributed money to raise and equip Confederate troops. Galveston lawyer William Pitt Ballinger opposed secession but helped to acquire artillery for the defense of the island and was later appointed receiver of confiscated enemy property. Wealthy slaveholder and Unionist William C. Young of Cooke County raised a regiment of Confederate cavalry, which he led in occupying federal posts in Indian Territory.

The majority of Texas Unionists did not become supporters of the Confederacy like Throckmorton, Epperson, Ballinger, and Young. Some, like Elisha M. Pease and David G. Burnet, attempted to be neutral or to remain silent while the war went on. Others found neutrality or silence more difficult. Attorney George W. Paschal, a friend and associate of former governors Pease and Houston, tried to accept the decision of his fellow Texans regarding secession, but spoke out against conscription, impressment, and other measures he considered unconstitutional, leading to his arrest and imprisonment by local authorities. Similarly, Texas Unionists George Whitmore, an East Texas state representative, and Dr. Richard Peebles, one of the founders of Hempstead, were arrested for their opposition to the Confederacy.

Sam Houston accepted the will of the people on the issue of secession but continued to criticize actions of the government he believed to be illegal or undemocratic. When his oldest son, Sam Houston Jr., joined the Bayland Guards of the Second Texas Infantry, the old hero of San Jacinto often visited the drills and claimed to be a private in the company. Houston followed the news of the war closely, criticizing fellow Texan Albert Sidney Johnston (who had been an ally of Houston's old rival Mirabeau B. Lamar) for his failures in Kentucky and Tennessee and congratulating John B. Magruder for "driving from our soil a ruthless enemy." Houston remained a critic of Confederate President Jefferson Davis, with whom he had served in the United States Senate. In one of his last letters written before his death in July 1863, Houston declared that Davis "deserves to be shot" for the appointment of incompetent generals like Henry H. Sibley.

Some Texas Unionists fled from the state to avoid conflict. James P. Newcomb, editor of the *Alamo Express*, left for Mexico after a mob wrecked his office. Noah Smithwick, pioneer blacksmith and veteran of the Texas Revolution, went to California where he lived for the next thirty-eight years. Unionist Swen Magnus Swenson, Swedish merchant, banker, planter, and rancher, remained in Texas for two years after secession, but fled the state in fear for his life in the autumn of 1863. He spent the rest of the war in Mexico and New Orleans. A close friend, federal judge Thomas DuVal of Austin, also lived the latter part of the war in New Orleans. Melinda Rankin, Northern-born missionary and teacher, was another Unionist who left the state. She returned to Brownsville during the federal occupation but departed when the Union Army pulled out. Wealthy merchant, cotton broker, and railroad developer William Marsh Rice transferred his business to Matamoros, where he continued his business ventures. He moved to New York City after the war but retained commercial interests in Texas.

Slightly over two thousand Texans, including forty-seven African Americans and 958 Mexican Americans, served in the Union Army. Edmund Jackson Davis, a native of Florida who had lived in Texas since 1848, became leader of this group. A successful attorney and judge in South Texas, Davis opposed secession but declared he accepted the decision of the people on this issue. Like Sam Houston, however, Davis refused to take the oath of allegiance to the Confederacy. After a year of controversy with local Confederates he left for Mexico. From there he journeyed to Washington, where he received a colonel's commission and authorization to raise a regiment of cavalry. He returned to New Orleans, where he recruited Texans who had left their home rather than serve the Confederacy. His regiment, the First Texas Cavalry (Union), served briefly in campaigns in the Louisiana bayou country in 1863 and came to Texas with the Union Army that occupied Brownsville in November 1863.

John L. Haynes, veteran of the Mexican War and state representative from Starr County, followed Edmund J. Davis to Mexico in March 1862. A native of Virginia, Haynes had lived in South Texas for over a decade. During that time he prospered as a merchant and married

Angelica Wells, a granddaughter of Martin Van Buren. He was very sympathetic to Mexican Texans and rejected the strong anti-Tejano attitude of Anglo leaders. He traveled with Davis to New Orleans and Washington and helped organize the First Texas Cavalry (Union). When a second regiment of Unionist cavalry was formed at Brownsville in December 1863, Haynes became its commander. Over half of the recruits of Haynes's regiment were Mexican Americans, the majority born in Mexico. Many of these Tejanos and Mexicanos joined the Union Army as a means to strike back at their old oppressors in Confederate Texas. In the spring of 1864 the First and Second Texas Cavalry (Union) formed a cavalry brigade, commanded by Davis, who was later promoted to the rank of brigadier general.

Andrew Jackson Hamilton was another Texan who became a brigadier general in Union service. An Austin lawyer, state representative, and political ally of Sam Houston, Jack Hamilton was elected to the United States Congress as an Independent Democrat in 1858. He opposed secession and worked with Southern and Northern moderates who attempted unsuccessfully to find a compromise to the sectional controversy. In the spring of 1862 he and several fellow Unionists fled to Mexico. From there he traveled to Washington, where he met with President Lincoln. Hamilton was appointed brigadier general of volunteers and military governor of Texas. Along with Edmund J. Davis he returned to Texas with Bank's army in late 1863. When the Union Army withdrew from South Texas in 1864 Hamilton went to New Orleans, where he remained until the war ended.

The extent of Unionist feeling in Texas is difficult to measure. The historian Claude Elliott estimated that one-third of the Texas population actively or passively supported the federal cause. He believed that another third of Texans remained neutral and only one-third actively supported the Confederacy. Elliott's estimate of Unionist strength is reasonable, but he probably understated the degree of support for the Confederacy in his calculations.

Unionist support within the state was strongest in the German counties of Central Texas and in the North Texas counties along the Red River. While many German voters supported secession, others opposed disunion and resisted serving in the Confederate Army. In the Texas hill country, Germans organized a Union Loyal League, ostensibly to provide frontier protection. Confederate authorities considered the League subversive. In April 1862, Gen. Hamilton P. Bee, then commanding the Texas western subdistrict, declared martial law, a measure later extended to the entire state by Gen. Paul O. Hébert. Confederate officials sent Capt. James Duff and a detachment of Texas Partisan Rangers into the Fredericksburg area to enforce Confederate conscription laws and to disband military companies organized by the Union League.

Most of the Unionist military companies were disbanded, but sixty-one men led by Fritz Tegener attempted to leave the state and join the Union Army. They left the Kerrville area in early August heading for the Rio Grande. They were overtaken near the Nueces River on August 10 by a detachment of Partisan Rangers commanded by Lt. C. D. McRae. The larger and better equipped Ranger force made a surprise attack on the Unionists early that morning, killing thirty Germans and wounding eighteen others. The wounded Unionists were later executed by the Confederates. In his report of the so-called battle of the Nueces, McRae defended this action, writing that the Unionists "offered the most determined resistance and fought with desperation, asking no quarter whatever; hence, I have no prisoners to report . . ."

Unionist sentiment was also prevalent in several northeast Texas counties. Some of the Unionists in the region formed a secret Peace Party opposed to military conscription and supportive of the Union. Local authorities were convinced that these dissenters were planning some type of insurrection. In October 1862, mass arrests of suspected Unionists occurred in Gainesville, the seat of Cooke County and suspected center of insurrectionist activity. A citizens' jury convicted and executed forty-two of those arrested in what came to be called "the great Gainesville hanging." In the next several weeks other suspected Unionists were hanged in neighboring Grayson, Wise, and Denton Counties.

As the war continued, the number of those Texans avoiding military service grew. Some of these were dedicated Unionists opposed to the Confederacy; others were individuals who had served in the army but deserted for personal reasons. In the course of the war over four thousand Texans were listed as deserters. Nearly three-fourths of these lived in the woods and brush country of the northern subdistrict of Texas. Brig. Gen. Henry E. McCulloch, commander of the district, attempted to convince them to come in and give themselves up, but with little success. He eventually turned to Col. James Bourland, commander of the Border Regiment, a tough-minded, disciplinarian known as the "Hangman of Texas," for assistance. Bourland was thorough but oftentimes ruthless in his pursuit of deserters. Stories circulated throughout the region that Bourland and his men frequently murdered suspected Unionists and deserters while holding them as prisoners.

Although there was opposition to the war, the majority of white Texans supported the Confederacy and the war effort. Estimates of the number of Texans serving in the military vary, but it appears that four out of every five white adult males of military age were in Confederate or state military units at one time or another. This left a major responsibility for managing homes, farms, and plantations to the women. For some, such as Sarah Devereux of Rusk County and Rebecca Hagerty of Harrison County, this was not a new experience as they had supervised plantations before the war. For others, such as Lizzie Neblett of Grimes County and Mary America Connor of Cass County, this was a new undertaking, as they took over responsibilities for husbands in the army.

Some Texas women entered professions, such as teaching, formerly reserved for men. Many performed volunteer work in hospitals and sick wards, formed aid societies to make sheets, pillowcases, and bandages, or assisted servicemen and their families to find food, clothing, and shelter. A few women served in the army disguised as men. Some, such as Sophia Butts Porter of Grayson County, provided Confederate authorities with information concerning enemy troop movements. Sally Scull, a legendary figure in South Texas, freighted cotton in wagons to the Rio Grande, where she exchanged the cotton for guns and ammunition for the Confederacy. Kate Dorman and Sarah Vosburg of Sabine Pass brought food and drink to Dick Dowling and his men at Fort Griffin during the Union attack.

Many Texas women who managed farms and plantations during the war had the responsibility of directing the work of African-American slaves. Texas had a slave population of 182,000 in 1860. This was increased by more than thirty thousand slaves "refugeed" by Arkansas, Louisiana, and Mississippi planters fleeing from federal forces that occupied these states. Although Confederate conscription laws exempted individuals supervising twenty or more slaves, few Texas planters took advantage of the law to escape military service, thus plantations and farms were operated by Texas women and older men during the war.

Most Texas slaves continued to labor as faithfully as before the war and caused little trouble for those supervising them. Historian Randolph Campbell points out that "slaves in Texas generally knew what the war meant, but they did relatively little to hinder the Confederate military effort or contribute to Union victory." No major slave rebellions occurred during the war and the number of those running away did not increase dramatically. This was due in part to a sense of loyalty some slaves felt toward white families and in part because there was little opportunity to do otherwise. When emancipation did come at the end of the war Texas slaves greeted the event with joy.

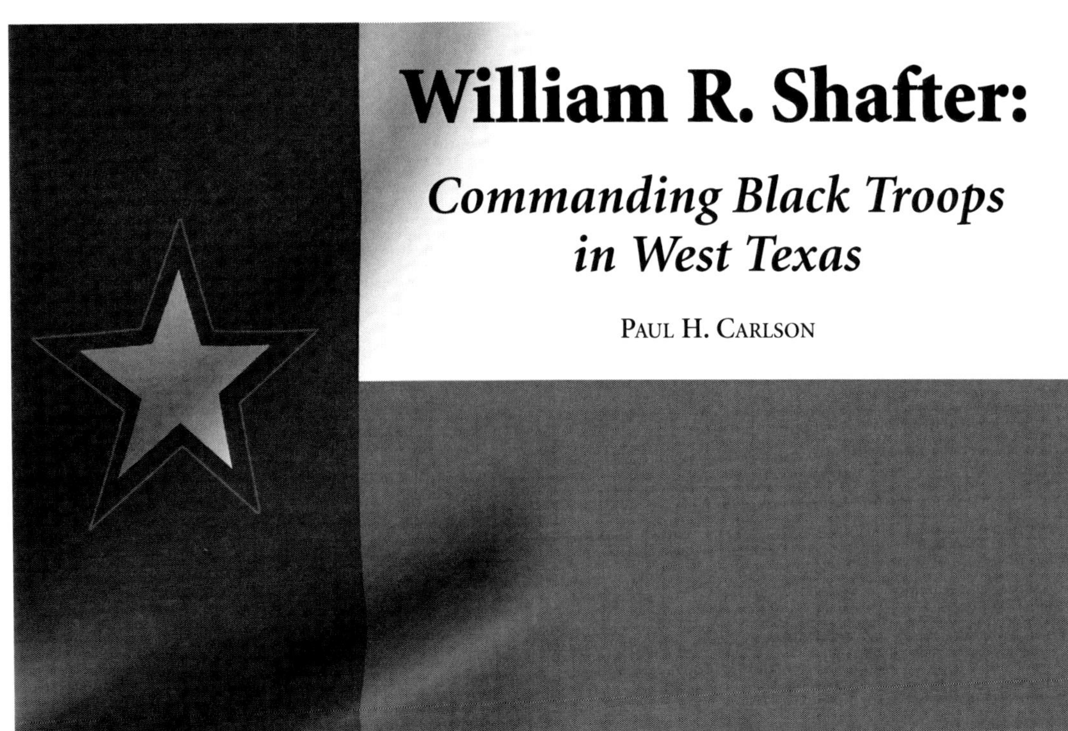

William R. Shafter:

Commanding Black Troops in West Texas

PAUL H. CARLSON

PAUL H. CARLSON TAUGHT HISTORY FOR MANY YEARS AT TEXAS TECH UNIVERSITY. HIS STUDIES INCLUDE *THE BUFFALO SOLDIER TRAGEDY OF 1877, THE PLAINS INDIANS, DEEP TIME AND THE TEXAS HIGH PLAINS: HISTORY AND GEOLOGY, THE COWBOY WAY: AN EXPLORATION OF HISTORY AND CULTURE,* AND *AMARILLO: THE STORY OF A WESTERN TOWN.*

AFRICAN AMERICAN TROOPS, KNOWN AS BUFFALO SOLDIERS, SERVED BRAVELY ON THE TEXAS FRONTIER. IN THIS SELECTION, DR. CARLSON DISCUSSES THE CAREER OF LIEUTENANT COLONEL WILLIAM R. SHAFTER AND EXAMINES THE WHITE OFFICER'S RELATIONSHIP WITH HIS BLACK COMMAND.

★ ★

From the West Texas Plains in the mid-1870s Captain Theodore Baldwin complained to his wife, "I do not think you would like to scout with Colonel Shafter." The note was understated indeed. A martinet of force and persistence, Lieutenant Colonel William R. Shafter of the Twenty-Fourth United States Infantry Regiment always drove vigorously the black troops of his command. Many young officers, such as Captain Baldwin, grumbled about his dogged determination.

Typical of Shafter's drive was an episode in 1875. Upon leaving Casas Amarillas Lake, near present Littlefield on the Llano Estacado, in a southwesterly direction, Shafter had hoped to find sufficient water for his men and horses in the large circular depressions characteristic of the High Plains. During the first two days he was successful, but having found no water by the expiration of the third day, he concluded that he must either strike for the Pecos or turn back. Characteristically, the resolute officer ordered his African American command to make for the Pecos some eighty miles distant. During the following two days and one night of marching, the troops suffered desperately from heat dust, and thirst. On the last night out, many of the officers, having lost all hope of reaching the river, wrote messages to be taken home by those fortunate enough to survive. Worn men were tied in their saddles; others at gun point were forced to keep up. Shafter cajoled, wheedled, and drove his men. After great hardship and privation, everyone safely, but exhaustively, reached the river. In such aggressive style, for more than a decade, Shafter directed black troops.

His black infantry in West Texas, however, was not the first that Shafter had led. During the Civil War he had enjoyed command of a volunteer unit and afterward in Louisiana with the colorful Ranald Mackenzie had organized and trained one of the regular army's first all-black regiments. In 1867 with his troops he had been ordered to the lower Rio Grande and the following year moved to West Texas at Fort Clark.

As a subaltern to Ranald Mackenzie, Shafter at first had few field assignments. But with each opportunity to command he relentlessly pursued horse thieves, cattle rustlers, desperadoes, or Indian raiders who were ravaging the West Texas frontier. As one result he quickly became recognized as the most energetic man of his rank in the Department of Texas. As another he was soon considered a rough, insensitive commander of black troops who, to achieve a sense of discipline, did not hesitate to exert extraordinary and ruthless power. In 1870 his reputation followed him to Fort Concho, at present San Angelo.

Here, the post surgeon was amazed at the energy and restlessness with which Shafter attacked his garrison chores. In his report for January 1870, the surgeon wrote that Shafter "has displayed an abundance of energy, devoting the first days of arrival to thoroughly policing the post . . . [and] seeing a large corral . . . in the process of construction." In the weeks that followed Shafter continued to push his African American command in construction activities. The next month, the surgeon reported that "work upon the guard house and corral is progressing with unprecedented rapidity."

Vigorous and efficient in his post command, Shafter likewise was energetic in the field. In mid-August, after being ordered to Fort McKavett, he planned to scour thoroughly the lower Pecos River. Taking 6 officers and 128 enlisted men of the Ninth Cavalry and Twenty-Fourth Infantry, he marched southwestward to the river, reaching it at a point about twenty miles below present Sheffield.

Here, Shafter temporarily divided his command. Leaving most of it in camp at the Pecos, he and Captain Edward M. Heyl, Ninth Cavalry, with fifteen men crossed to the west bank of the river, climbed up onto the table lands, and marched due south for twenty miles, keeping all the time within four miles of the river. Using his field glasses to examine each ravine, Shafter discovered no indications of Indians. There, he left the river and rode southwestward for six or seven miles to Painted Rock Arroyo, only ten miles from the Rio Grande. Again finding no signs of Indians, with his patrol he returned to the rendezvous camp.

For nearly a month afterward the command scouted in the vicinity of the lower Pecos. The hard-driving Shafter ordered his men to check every ravine. It was monotonous, exhausting work. No Indians were seen, neither were there trails nor other indications of Indians having passed through the country recently. Nevertheless, Shafter doggedly pushed his men to the task. The persistence brought some luck: eight Indian ponies, which Shafter estimated had been near the Pecos for six months, were caught.

In mid-September, unable to locate either Indians or recent signs of them, Shafter finally directed his tired troops back toward Fort McKavett. While returning, his scouts located several abandoned Indian villages, about thirty-five miles west of the headwaters of the North and South Llano rivers. One had contained possibly as many as 150 Indians. Nearby they discovered a large, permanent body of water about two hundred yards long and deep enough to swim horses. For years the army had heard reports of the water pond, but its location had been known only to the red men. Consequently the pond was a favorite and secure place for Indians who committed depredations in the country near the headwaters of the Nueces.

The Pecos River campaign proved significant. Having marched nearly five hundred miles, the scout showed that no Indians were lurking in the vicinity of the Pecos and the headwaters of the Llano rivers. Eight horses had been captured. A strategic and favorite Indian camping place had been located, and no longer would the Indians be able to use the water hole as a safe rendezvous. Moreover, in the psychological warfare that figured vitally in Indian fighting, the expedition demonstrated to the Plains warriors that bluecoat troopers could campaign successfully in an area that Indians previously had thought inaccessible to the army.

Twice the following year Shafter led black soldiers into such supposedly impenetrable lands. In June 1871 with a command totaling eighty-six officers and enlisted men, he turned a routine pursuit of Comanche horse thieves into a major exploration of the Monahans Sand Hills and across the Llano Estacado. He destroyed an abandoned Indian village, two dozen buffalo robes, skins, and a large supply of provisions. He captured twenty horses and mules. He discovered that Comanches and Lipan and Mescalero Apaches, longtime enemies, had concluded a peace in the Sand Hills and that Comancheros used the area as a place of barter.

A month later Shafter penetrated another Indian sanctuary. This time he drove his black command from Fort Davis on an exhausting five-hundred-mile scout into the torrid Big Bend region of the Rio Grande. Here with his troops he explored the country, crossing and recrossing trails, noting important water holes, and marking the sites of old Indian camps. At San Vincente he discovered an important Apache crossing on the river. He reported abandoned Indian encampments twenty-five miles southwest of Pena Blanca. The grass along his line of march was excellent, but the only wood he found was very large cottonwood trees along the streams. Where he struck the Rio Grande, there was no timber.

Although it had killed no Indians, the expedition had found abundant evidence that Apaches used the Big Bend as a sanctuary. Perhaps more important, Shafter added considerably to the geographical knowledge of the Chihuahuan deserts and Big Bend mountains. Indeed, the information he gained about their nature and resources enabled the army later to maneuver more confidently in the region. In addition, it smoothed the way for later settlement.

No sooner had Shafter returned to Fort Davis than an Apache chief, who frequented the Big Bend and who had gone to Presidio to negotiate with the Mexican authorities for release of some children captives of his band, sent word from Presidio del Norte that he wished to surrender. Shafter sent Lieutenant Isaiah H. McDonald to receive the surrender. But perhaps because the Mexican residents there, who gained their living largely by supplying United States Army posts, did not welcome complete harmony between Indians and Americans, the *alcalde* of Presidio warned the chief that his departure would prejudice release of the children. Whatever the reason, McDonald returned to Fort Davis empty-handed. Shafter agreed with his lieutenant that "the local authorities at Del Norte do not want [the Apache] to make or keep peace with the United States."

Meanwhile, at Fort Davis Shafter was active. He supervised the repair of buildings, the construction of corrals, and the remodeling of the hospital. In addition, whenever necessary, he protected his black troops against racial injustice and discrimination. In one incident he took the stage coach lines to task. The infantry in the West was often assigned to guard stage lines. At the end of such a tour of duty men usually returned to the post on an inbound stage. Unfortunately, Shafter's black troops at least once were kept off the stage and forced to walk back to the barracks. Indeed, the El Paso Mail Lines station keeper at Leon Hole refused to provide food and shelter for the station guards. The tempestuous Shafter became incensed and immediately warned the stage company officers against further discrimination toward his men. When the black guards were put off the stage, he wrote, they were obliged to walk to Fort Stockton and along the way to obtain their rations "by their wits." He demanded that his troops should "be fed by the company or allowed facilities at the stations for cooking their own rations." He would "be glad to furnish mail escorts as long as they are wanted," he concluded, "but they must be properly treated." Apparently his letter got results for the records show no further complaint against the stage company.

In another incident Shafter challenged civilian authorities. When the volatile sheriff of Presidio County injudiciously entered Fort Davis to arrest a black soldier for public drunkenness, Shafter, aware that the bluecoat would be summarily prosecuted, would not allow the officer to remove the trooper. Although such belligerency represented a serious breach of military discipline, Shafter refused to subject his troops to what he regarded as legal hazing.

The consequences proved critical. Although the trooper was never arrested, Shafter was immediately removed from Fort Davis. Later, the incident may have been included as evidence to deny him an early graduation to the rank of colonel. Much later, in 1887, after he had obtained the colonelcy, the incident apparently was offered as one excuse to block his promotion to the rank of brigadier general.

Although temporarily rebuked, Shafter was not forgotten. Since the Department of Texas needed durable, effective officers, in the summer and fall of 1872 with his crack command of black troops he teamed for three months with Ranald Mackenzie on the Llano Estacado. While Mackenzie with one force scouted the Palo Duro and crossed the High Plains to Fort Sumner and beyond, Shafter with another examined the Caprock escarpment along the Salt Fork (Main Fork) of the Brazos. His black command made certain that there were no Indians lurking at the foot of the Staked Plains, although it found abundant evidence of old Indian camps near all the springs it visited. In addition, the command located water and fuel supplies and for future operations in the vicinity of present-day Slaton and Lubbock made a map of the country scouted.

The following year Shafter with his black troops aided Mackenzie again. This time he helped during preparations for the celebrated raid into Mexico against the Kickapoos. Although he did not cross into Mexico with Mackenzie, Shafter performed valuable service for the expedition. He provided important information on the Mexican population, the location of villages, and the whereabouts of Mexican troops. Mackenzie stated that he was under great obligation to Shafter for his cordial cooperation and active support throughout the 1873 expedition.

In 1875, after a lengthy stint in New York to study infantry equipment, Shafter led a huge command of African American troops for six months on the Staked Plains of West Texas and Eastern New Mexico. The Llano Estacado campaign, as it was called, proved grueling. At one stretch during the wearisome expedition Shafter in ten days marched his men nearly three hundred miles. Since they were seldom in camp for more than one night, the men, in addition to marching thirty miles a day, had to pack their tents and other field equipment each morning and unpack it again each night. The subsequent wear and tear on both men and animals prompted one officer to complain that "our horses will go to the devil very fast at the rate Col. Shafter charges the whole command."

The comment could not have been more pointed. In the field Shafter demonstrated an unsurpassed ability to get the utmost out of his soldiers. During the agonizing 1875 expedition, in which his command covered over 2,500 miles of the High Plains, many of Shafter's men returned from the first crossing of the Plains without shirts or shoes, most were missing some article of clothing, and all were exhausted. Nevertheless, only two weeks later, Shafter started back across the Plains again, and hardly had he completed the second crossing when a third was commenced. The Llano Estacado campaign was as successful as it was difficult. It swept the Plains clear of Indians, destroyed completely the dreary myth of the Plains as the dreaded Sahara of North America, and paved the way for settlement, which quickly followed.

Even more arduous and successful was Shafter's 1876 expedition to the mouth of the Pecos River. Three times during the strenuous, five-months-long campaign, Shafter marched his well-disciplined black troops across the rugged Coahuila deserts of Mexico. In each instance the troops rode in over 100 degree heat, and on one occasion they went sixty-five miles through the parching desert without water. During the summer his men twice engaged and defeated Indians. Two large camps of hostiles were completely destroyed, another in the Carmen Mountains was discovered and its location noted, 137 horses and mules and much stolen stock was recovered, and an estimated eighteen Indians were killed or captured.

Shortly after the close of the Pecos River expedition, Shafter became commander of the District of the Nueces. Embracing the upper Rio Grande border area from Laredo to old Fort Leaton, the region was a natural haunt and even a highway for roving bands of Lipan and Mescalero Apaches who slipped across the Rio Grande to prey upon the abundant cattle and horse herds along the upper reaches of the Nueces. Any luckless cowboy or traveler who got in their way, the Indians killed. One raid in 1878 resulted in the death of eighteen citizens, including some women and children.

Protecting the Rio Grande frontier was no easy task. Not only was the topography of the territory on both sides of the river barren and waterless, but Mexican troops resented the presence of American soldiers south of the border. As a result, relations between the United States and Mexico were strained, and Mexican leaders protested each American violation of their country's soil. Moreover, by criticizing the border crossings, Democratic leaders in Washington hoped to embarrass the Rutherford B. Hayes administration. Consequently, Lieutenant Colonel Shafter needed to act with astute diplomatic good will and with the consummate skill demanded of desert campaigning.

Shafter was not timid in his new task. The audacious commander kept his bluecoats in the field. Small patrols suffered through December's cold, scouting relentlessly each trail and vigilantly watching for evidence of raiding parties from Mexico. The perseverance paid dividends. In January 1877, after some marauders were seen, Shafter from his headquarters at Fort Clark quickly dispatched Lieutenant John L. Bullis of his regiment and Captain Alexander B. Keyes, Tenth Cavalry, and over one hundred officers and men some 125 miles deep into the Santa Rosa Mountains of Mexico. The Bullis-Keyes raid recovered much stolen stock and led to the return of several horses and mules.

Additional border crossings followed. In March Shafter waded the Rio Grande with a large detachment of black troops, but too late to rescue from jail two men, who had guided his troops the year previous, sentenced to die as traitors. In July Bullis splashed across the river but with little luck in striking Indians or recovering stolen stock. In the fall, as raiding increased, Shafter twice directed well-armed expeditions to pursue hostile Indians to their sanctuaries in Mexico.

Indeed, Shafter took personal command of the first expedition. The raid into Mexico began near the end of September after black scouts reported to Bullis, scouting along the Rio Grande near the mouth of Las Moras Creek, that marauders had entered Texas. Bullis immediately sent word by courier to Shafter at Fort Clark. In turn the district commander ordered the scrappy lieutenant with his force of ninety men to cross the river on the twenty-eighth and wait for Shafter who, with about three hundred troops of the Eighth and Tenth cavalries, was on his way to join him. When he rode into camp about 2:00 p.m. the same day, Shafter ordered Bullis to start after dark for the Indian village near Saragosa. He promised to protect Bullis's rear in the event that there were wounded soldiers who might slow the retreating command.

Both officers were well aware that a Mexican force of some two hundred soldiers, as well as dozens of thieves and desperadoes in the vicinity, would be watching for a favorable opportunity to strike the exhausted invaders.

About 11:00 p.m. Bullis started. Alternating his pace between a trot and a gallop during the long night ride, he reached Saragosa, about forty miles distant, at sunrise. Marching up Perdido Creek, he caught by surprise at about 8:00 a.m. the Lipans and Mescaleros who fled for safety upon sighting the charging American troops. Bullis's scouts and troops chased the terrified Indians for four or five miles, capturing before reining to a halt four women, one boy, twelve horses, and two mules. After burning the small village and destroying the camp equipage, Bullis, turning his troops due north toward the head of the San Diego River where he was to meet Shafter, marched at a fast walk or trot until he reached the appointed rendezvous about 9:00 p.m. His troops, who had been in their saddles continuously for twenty-two hours, rolled from the horses in exhaustion. The support troops were nowhere in sight.

Meanwhile, Shafter had waited until morning before starting for the rendezvous. After moving slowly up the San Diego River, he encamped a few miles from its head. On the following morning, September 30, a little after sunrise, he spied Bullis, who had had an apprehensive, but undisturbed, night's rest, moving northeastward toward the Rio Grande and not far behind a column of approximately ninety Mexican troops from Saragosa under Colonel Innocente Rodriguez. Immediately, he broke camp and joined his trusty subordinate.

The combined command, nearly four hundred troops, continued toward the river at a brisk walk all day and late into the night. Colonel Rodriguez cautiously followed about a mile behind for a distance of ten miles, but then suddenly disappeared when Shafter began to maneuver his troops in preparation for battle. No engagement took place, nor were any shots fired, and, when Shafter again headed for the Rio Grande, some of the officers grumbled about running from "a handful of Mexicans." After wading the river at Lasora Crossing near San Felipe about midnight, Shafter rested his command for two days before returning to Fort Clark, where he arrived on October 4.

The raid brought unfavorable reaction in the capitals of both countries. In Mexico City, the newspapers, exaggerating its significance, indicated that the American troops had flagrantly violated international law. They also boasted of how a small Mexican force of only ninety troops had easily repelled an American force four times its number. In Washington, the raid became an important factor that influenced the decision of Congress to investigate the Texas border troubles.

The Congressional investigations revealed the need for additional troops in the District of the Nueces. Accordingly, in February 1878, when Colonel Ranald Mackenzie arrived with his Fourth Cavalry, Shafter was relieved of his command. Still assigned to the district, however, he once again found himself closely teamed with his former colonel.

With adequate troops to end the depredations, Shafter and Mackenzie wasted little time in bringing peace to the border. In April and May they planned and organized a major raid to destroy in Mexico hostile Indian lairs, and in June, with the army's approval, they carried it out.

Twice during the bold assault there were confrontations, but not clashes, with Mexican troops who turned away after first challenging the Americans. Perhaps embarrassed that his troops had backed down in the face of the hated gringos, Porfirio Dfaz, President of Mexico, took steps to cooperate with the United States in haulting depredations north of the Rio Grande. Consequently, no further border crossings were necessary and by the end of 1878 tension along the river had relaxed demonstrably.

Early the following year Shafter left Texas. In March his long-awaited promotion to colonel came through, and he was transferred to the First Infantry Regiment stationed in Dakota. He returned to Texas in late 1880 to pursue followers of Victorio, the marauding Apache. Later he moved to Arizona to help pacify Apache renegades. In 1891, following the Wounded Knee incident, he participated in the Siouan Campaign, and in 1898, during the Spanish-American War, he led the American Expeditionary force to Cuba.

The techniques of command vary, of course, with the personality of the commander. While some men prefer to lead by suggestion or example or other methods, Shafter chose to drive his subordinates by bombast and by threats, and he believed that profanity was the most convincing medium of communication. Although his mannerisms achieved spectacular results, they did not win affection among his men. Good-humored, even jolly, in his intimate personal relationships, he was likely to give short, blunt answers to his subalterns, he would never allow his orders to be challenged, and he always demanded the same dogged determination from his men that he himself gave to field maneuvers.

Clearly, as a commander of black troops in West Texas, the volatile Shafter was tough and aggressive. Energetic, resourceful, and courageous, he possessed initiative, looked out for the welfare of his men and animals, and was utterly unafraid of responsibility. When he thought that they were not being treated properly, he vociferously defended his African American soldiers, and he always spoke highly of their ability. Most officers learned to like him and his men, although he rarely enjoyed their affection, always remembered him as a zealous and forceful commander.

Conquered

DAVID LA VERE

DAVID LA VERE IS PROFESSOR OF HISTORY AT THE UNIVERSITY OF NORTH CAROLINA—WILMINGTON. AN AUTHORITY IN NATIVE AMERICAN HISTORY, HIS STUDIES INCLUDE *LIFE AMONG THE TEXAS INDIANS: THE WPA NARRATIVES*, *THE CADDO CHIEFDOMS: CADDO ECONOMICS AND POLITICS, 800 AD-1835*, AND *THE TEXAS INDIANS.*

IN THIS SELECTION, DR. LA VERE PROVIDES AN OVERVIEW OF NATIVE AMERICANS IN THE LONE STAR STATE FROM THE CIVIL WAR UNTIL JANUARY, 1881, WHEN THE FINAL INDIAN BATTLE IN TEXAS OCCURRED. NOW CONQUERED, INDIANS FOUND THEMSELVES CONFINED ON RESERVATIONS, FORCED TO SUBMIT TO THE WHITE MAN'S CULTURE. LA VERE RECOUNTS IMPORTANT EVENTS LIKE THE RED RIVER WAR OF 1874–1875, AND DISCUSSES SUCH NATIVE AMERICAN LEADERS AS SATANTA, VICTORIO, AND QUANAH PARKER.

★ ★

The Indians of the now-defunct Brazos and Clear Fork reserves barely had time to get settled in southwestern Indian Territory before the Civil War thundered to life. The withdrawal of U.S. troops from forts in Texas and Indian Territory left the line of white settlement unprotected. Frightened settlers, who earlier had demanded the extermination of the Reserve Indians, now

"Conquered" reprinted from *The Texas Indians* by David La Vere, 2004 by permission of Texas A&M University Press.

begged them to ally with Texas and serve as a buffer against both Comanches and Union forces. By late 1861 Texas and Confederate diplomats were fanning out to Indian villages and soon the Indians found themselves just as divided as the United States. Among the Five Civilized Tribes, the Choctaws and Chickasaws, closest to Texas and with many of their leaders slave owners as well, sided almost wholly with the South. The Cherokees, Creeks, and Seminoles split and engaged in their own bloody civil war, with some factions remaining loyal to the Union and others to the Confederacy. Many of the wealthier proConfederate Indians moved their families, livestock, and slaves to North Texas, which they hoped would be out of reach of Union raiding parties. Down in Texas, a few Alabama-Coushattas served briefly with the 24th Texas Cavalry but by late 1862 had left the service and returned to their homes in East Texas.

The former Brazos Reserve Indians, now on the Wichita Reservation in Indian Territory, also split. Some Caddo and Wichita bands went to Union-held Kansas. Others moved farther west, willing to brave the plains, the Comanches, and the Kiowas to get away from the war. A large faction stayed put and sided with the South, especially when their Indian agent, Matthew Leeper, accepted a commission in the Confederate Army. The turmoil of the war years provided an opportunity for old enemies to even old scores. On October 23, 1862, a large band of Indians attacked the Confederate-allied Wichita Agency. They burned the agency headquarters, killed some Confederate officials, but concentrated mainly on the Tonkawas, killing Chief Placido and about a hundred of his people. The Wichitas, Caddos and other Indians at the agency scattered. No one could say exactly what instigated the Tonkawa Massacre, as it has come to be called. Some said it was an attack by pro-Confederate Wichitas, Comanches, Shawnees, and Delawares on the pro-Union Tonkawas. The Wichitas and Comanches blamed the Shawnees and Delawares, saying they were taking revenge for Tonkawa cannibalism. Others said it was a Union attack on the Wichita Reservation and the Tonkawas just happened to be in the way. Whatever the reason for the attack, the few surviving Tonkawas fled back to Texas, settling around Fort Belknap, not far from their old reserve at Clear Fork. There they served as scouts for Confederate Texas forces. Only years after the Civil War, would the government step in and provide a reservation for the Tonkawas in the northern part of Indian Territory, well away from their old Texas Indian neighbors.

In Texas, the Civil War brought more raids and violence. Comanches, Kiowas, Kiowa-Apaches, Kickapoos, and others, their supplies of manufactured goods severely curtailed by the war, stepped up their raids into Texas in hopes of replenishing their supplies. For Texans, this could not have come at a worst time as there were fewer people to give chase. Federal troops had been withdrawn to Union territory, while the Confederacy stripped Texas of many of its fighting men, leaving fewer Ranger companies, most of these undermanned. With raids on the increase, the line of settlement halted its westward march and even backtracked about a 150 miles. Nevertheless, Ranger companies, such as those led by Sul Ross, attacked as they always had. Ross's company had attacked a Comanche camp in December, 1860, and come away with Cynthia Ann Parker, who had been taken by the Comanches in 1836. By this time, Cynthia Ann had become a Comanche. She spoke no English, had a Comanche husband and family, and was the mother of the soon-to-be-famous Comanche chief Quanah Parker. So for the second time in her life, she was stolen away from her family. Brokenhearted, she did not live long after.

MEXICAN KICKAPOOS AND SEMINOLES

While Comanches, Kiowas, and Kiowa-Apaches struck from the north, Kickapoos out of Mexico raided across South Texas. Kickapoos were immigrant Indians, a band of which had settled in East Texas in the early nineteenth century. After the Kickapoo War of October, 1838, most Texas Kickapoos moved beyond the line of settlement or to Indian Territory. However, a small band of about eighty immigrated to northern Mexico and settled around the town of Morelos in the State of Coahuila. Mexico warmly welcomed these Kickapoos and soon the men were serving as scouts and auxiliaries for the Mexican army in their pursuit of Comanches, Kiowas, and Apaches.

In 1849 the number of Mexican Kickapoos increased with the arrival of Seminole chief Coacoochee and his band. Coacoochee, better known as Wild Cat, had fought the United States during the Seminole Wars. Forced to move to Indian Territory, he wanted as little to do with Americans as possible and so determined to move to Mexico. Many Kickapoos agreed with Wild Cat's assessment of Americans and about 250 Seminoles, Kickapoos, and African Americans decided to join him. The next year, Wild Cat was again recruiting in Indian Territory and convinced another 250 or so to immigrate to Mexico. About half the Kickapoos returned to Indian Territory the next year, however most Mexican Kickapoos and Seminoles were again serving as auxiliaries, turning back raiding parties that crossed into that part of Mexico. Though most Seminoles would eventually return to Indian Territory, the remaining Mexican Kickapoos became so successful in battling Indian raiders that Comanche and Kiowa attacks in Coahuila dropped off considerably. During the 1850s, while Mexican Kickapoos battled Indians south of the Rio Grande, Kickapoos in Indian Territory joined with their Comanche and Kiowa trade partners and heavily raided Texas settlements along the upper Colorado and Brazos Rivers and as far west as the Pecos. In 1858 even the El Paso mail route was threatened and several California-bound immigrant trains in West Texas were attacked.

Several incidents during the Civil War served to increase Kickapoo raids. As the Civil War divided the Kickapoos and other peoples of Indian Territory, a band of about six hundred Kickapoos under Chief Machemanet decided to immigrate to Mexico in December, 1862. Wanting to avoid Texas settlements, Machemanet's village swung wide into West Texas, but in Tom Green County near present-day Knickerbocker, a Confederate patrol spied the Indian horse herd, shot down three Kickapoo peace emissaries, and attacked the immigrants. The Kickapoos held their ground, retook their horses, and sent the patrol reeling, with sixteen cavalrymen shot out of their saddles. The Kickapoos resumed their journey and joined their kinspeople in Mexico. Word of Machemanet's village's prosperity soon reached the remaining Kickapoos in Kansas and Indian Territory, and in September, 1864, seven hundred Kickapoos under Chiefs Pecan, Papequah, and Nokoaht began their own migration to Mexico. As before, they swung wide to avoid Texas settlements. However, on January 8, 1865, while camping on Dove Creek near present-day Mertzon, they were attacked by a detachment of Confederate scouts and militia. Once again, the well-armed Kickapoos held fast and aimed a devastating fire on the charging Confederates. In an all-day fight, the Texas Confederates had twenty-six men killed, sixty wounded, and sixty-six horses killed. The survivors barely managed to escape during the night, while the victorious Kickapoos, losing a total of fifteen warriors, continued their move into Mexico. Once there and settled, the Kickapoos determined to take revenge on Texas for twice attacking peaceful migration parties.

During the next two decades, the Mexican Kickapoos certainly took their retribution. Over the years, as the Mexican Kickapoos battled Comanche, Kiowa, and Apache raiding parties, a benefit had been the horses, mules, and goods they acquired in battle. These items found ready markets in Mexico and brought prosperity to the Kickapoos. After the Civil War, as raiders struck less frequently into northern Mexico, the Kickapoos were deprived of these commodities. While supplies dwindled, the demand remained; so to acquire the ever-wanted horses and goods, the Kickapoos began raiding ranches and farms on the Texas side of the Rio Grande. A great semicircle, curving from Laredo in the south up to San Antonio and then west to Terrell County, became the Mexico Kickapoos' area of operations. Atacosa County, just south of San Antonio, became a favorite raiding ground. South Texans demanded protection, claiming the Kickapoos were much worse than the Comanches and Kiowas North Texans faced. A government commission investigating the Kickapoo raids in 1872 calculated that between 1865 and 1872, Kickapoo raiders had taken five hundred thousand head of cattle and fourteen thousand horses, most making their way to markets in Mexico. No count was given of the number of women and children taken captive nor the number of ranches burned and men killed.

Finally, in 1873, the government ordered Colonel Ranald S. Mackenzie and the U.S. Fourth Cavalry to deal with the problem. Mackenzie and his four hundred men rode into Mexico without Mexican permission and on May 18, while the Kickapoo warriors were away hunting, attacked their village at Remolina. Though the women, children, and old men fought back as best they could, the Fourth burned the village and supplies and killed an untold number of Indians. They also took forty women and children captives, who were quickly herded up to Fort Gibson, in the northeastern part of Indian Territory.

Mackenzie's raid had the desired effect, rapidly pushing along the Kickapoo removal plan the government had sought. Authorities believed the best way to stop Kickapoo raids was to get them to return to the United States and take a reservation in Indian Territory. Several approaches had been made but each had been rebuffed. With some of their villages destroyed, the realization that the United States would cross into Mexico if need be, and the knowledge that forty of their kinspeople were being held in Indian Territory, many Kickapoos agreed to return to the United States. In August, 1873, 317 Mexican Kickapoos moved back to Indian Territory, reaching Fort Sill in late December. The next year they were assigned a reservation in the central part of Indian Territory, just east of present-day Oklahoma City. In 1875 another 114 Kickapoos returned from Mexico, leaving about 100 Kickapoos along the Mexico-Texas border. Many of their descendants still live in Mexico, but a few crossed the Rio Grande and settled around Eagle Pass, where they became the Texas Band of Kickapoo Indians and remain there to this day. While Mexican and Texas bands of Kickapoos sporadically raided into Texas over the next few years, counterattacks by U.S. cavalry had the desired effect, and by 1880 the Kickapoos had ceased being a threat to Texas.

RAIDS AND RESERVATIONS

The Civil War provided opportunities for Kickapoo raids into Texas, and it did the same for the Comanches, Kiowas, and Kiowa-Apaches, who seemed to grow ever more powerful. By 1864 they threatened the Santa Fe Trail, the supply route to Union-held New Mexico. To protect the trail, on November 25, 1864, Union colonel Kit Carson and his New Mexico Volunteers attacked a series of Comanche, Kiowa, and Kiowa-Apache camps near Adobe Walls. These were the ruins of an old Bent–St. Vrain trading post built in 1840 on the Canadian River in the Texas Panhandle. Though Carson's men managed to destroy one Indian camp, unexpectedly strong resistance from the Indians forced the troops to retreat to New Mexico, barely getting away with their lives. Though the battle secured the trail, it did not deter Comanche and Kiowa raids on Texas farms and ranches.

Four days after Kit Carson's attack, not far to the northwest at Sand Creek in southeastern Colorado, the Colorado militia attacked Chief Black Kettle's peaceful Cheyenne village, killing and scalping well over a hundred Indian men, women, and children. The Sand Creek Massacre shocked both the eastern establishment and Washington officials. When the Civil War ended five months later, Congress turned its attention to the Plains Indians and determined to bring about what they hoped would be a lasting peace. In October, 1865, government representatives met with various Comanche, Kiowa, Kiowa-Apache, Cheyenne, and Arapaho chiefs in Kansas. After several days of negotiations, feasts, exchange of presents, and the restoration of captives, they hammered out the Treaty of the Little Arkansas River. Essentially, the treaty provided for the Comanches and Kiowas to receive virtually all the Texas Panhandle and western Oklahoma as a reservation. Even better, they could hunt outside the reservation boundaries, south of the Arkansas River until the buffalo were gone and the area settled. They would also receive between ten and fifteen dollars per person annually for the next forty years. In return, the Indians were to allow the government to build forts along the Sante Fe Trail and refrain from raiding U.S. citizens and Indians people friendly to them.

While certainly Indian-friendly, the treaty was dead on arrival in Washington. Texans protested bitterly and would have none of it. Similarly, cost-conscious senators severely amended it, making renegotiation virtually impossible. Many individual Kiowas and Comanches also opposed the treaty, refusing to be fenced in or fenced out of lands they had long called home. In the end the treaty was not ratified and raids continued into Texas, with Texans complaining that between May, 1865, and July, 1867, Indians had killed sixty-two people, wounded forty-two, and taken another forty captive.

Help for Texans was not long in coming. With the Civil War over, the U.S. Army now reoccupied Texas forts. Immediately after the war, the United States sent more than fifty thousand troops to Texas, most stationed on the Texas-Mexico border to prevent any spillover from the French invasion of Mexico. Others served on Reconstruction occupation duty. By 1867 their numbers had been reduced to three thousand but with a good number of these now stationed farther west in forts guarding the line of settlement. Texas now hosted the 17th Infantry, 19th (Black) Infantry, 38th (Black) Infantry, 114th (Black) Infantry, 117th (Black) Infantry, 6th Cavalry, and 4th Cavalry. Later would come the famous 9th and 10th (Black) Cavalry. None of these units remained congregated at any one place. They were divided into company-size units, usually of about ninety to one hundred men, and distributed among various forts. For example, the 4th Cavalry was headquartered at Camp Sheridan in San Antonio, where its headquarters and B, C, D, F, L, and M companies remained. But Company A was stationed at Fredericksburg; Company G, at Clinton; Company H, at La Grange; Companies E and P, at Fort Brown; and Company K, at Fort Inge. In time, other units would come and go, but as always, they gave chase whenever raids were made.

Most of these encounters were small unit actions, such as running battles or brief skirmishes, rarely involving more than a score or two of men on either side. And though cavalry troopers and Texas Rangers often served together, there was little love between them. As one soldier believed, the Rangers were far superior to the army in the field but their tendency to "kill every Indian on sight without pardon" made them less civilized than U.S. troops, who "endeavored to kill as few as possible and to capture alive if possible."

As before, the army turned to the reservation Indians for help. Tonkawas from around Fort Griffin, along with Caddos, Wichitas, and Delawares from the Wichita Reservation in southwestern Indian Territory served as scouts and auxiliaries for the Rangers and cavalry. In December, 1866, Toshaway and a few other Penetaka Comanche chiefs, as well as Caddo chiefs George Washington, Tinah, and Jim Pockmark all agreed to serve as scouts. The number and variety of Indian scouts serving with the army grew considerably. By late 1874 one cavalry officer reported his detachment of scouts included Wichitas, Tawakonis, Wacos, Kichais, Caddos, Delawares, Shawnees, Pawnees, Arapahos, and Comanches.

The continued raids, the good example of the Indians of the Wichita Reservation, and the failure of the Little Arkansas treaty made Congress redouble its efforts to get a workable treaty with the Southern Plains Indians. In October, 1867, government negotiators met with various Comanche, Kiowa, Kiowa-Apache, Cheyenne, and Arapaho chiefs at Medicine Lodge Creek in southern Kansas. By this time, many more chiefs were open to the reservation idea. Buffalo on the Southern Plains were fast disappearing, a crippling blow to people for whom it was the staff of life. The attacks and potential attacks by Rangers and cavalry often meant life had to be lived on the run. Hunger, warfare, disease, as well as the steady westward migration by non-Indians made many chiefs realize that times were changing and their people now had to walk a different road. They advocated peace, if at all possible. Twenty Comanche and Kiowa chiefs signed the Treaty of Medicine Lodge Creek, which stipulated peace between their people and the United States. The Indians gave up all claims to lands in Texas and accepted a much smaller reservation between the Red and Washita Rivers in the southwestern part of Indian Territory. They agreed to adopt "civilization" by sending their children to school and becoming farmers. The United States pledged to build the schools and provide teachers, blacksmiths, carpenters, instructors, clothing, farming implements, and even agricultural instruction. The Comanches, Kiowas, and Kiowa-Apaches still had the right to hunt on lands south of the Arkansas River as long as the buffalo ranged there. Their reservation lands were guaranteed to them, none of which could be taken without approval of three-fourths of the adult male population. In return, the Indians were to receive annual clothing distributions as well as twenty-five thousand dollars a year for thirty years, sometimes in cash, sometimes in goods. To ensure the peace, just over a year later in 1868 the government built Fort Sill almost dead center in the new Comanche-Kiowa reservation.

Just to the north, the former Texas Reserve Indians on the Wichita and Affiliated Bands' reservation set an example of acculturation. With the end of the Civil War, scattered bands of Taovayas, Tawakonis, Wacos, Kichais, Nadacos, Hainais, Cadodachos, and Delawares returned to their reservation and settled down to farming. The Penetaka Comanches of the old Clear Fork Reserve settled nearby. Now able to live in peace, their lands guaranteed and their persons protected, the Wichitas and Affiliated Bands, as they were collectively called, seemed to prosper, growing large crops of corn and melons, raising small herds of cattle and pigs, even building a sawmill. Young men might divide their time between hunting, farming, and scouting for the government. "Progressive" chiefs, such as Guadeloupe and George Washington of the Cadodachos, José Mariá of the Nadacos, Black Beaver of the Delawares, Toshaway and Esahabbe of the Penetaka Comanches, along with Tawakoni Dave and Tawakoni Jim, urged their people to settle down, send their children to school, and peacefully walk this white man's road. On the reservation, a curious melding of cultures began taking place. Through proximity and intermarriage, the many different bands began to form into one. Where there had been Taovayas, Tawakonis, Yscanis, and Kichais, soon there were only Wichitas. Similarly, the Cadodachos, Nadacos, and Hainais became collectively known as the Caddos. While the Indians themselves still recognized traditional bands and lineages, most non-Indians in Texas and Indian Territory now just saw Wichitas, Caddos, Delawares, Comanches, Kiowas, and Apaches. Adding to this melting pot, Wichitas, Delawares, and Caddos sometimes intermarried, as did some whites who settled nearby.

PEACE POLICY AND THE RED RIVER WAR

Of course, not all Comanches, Kiowas, and Kiowa-Apaches wanted to settle down to farming as the Wichitas and Caddos did. Nor did they accept their "progressive" chiefs' willingness to live on a reservation. Many chiefs and warriors, particularly younger men, refused to give up the culture and lands they valued. They determined to resist at all costs. The Kwahadi Comanches absolutely refused to settle on the reservation, while other bands might drift on and off at will. Most men still saw raiding as the road to individual status and power. Fueling their fire were failures and missteps by the U.S. government. Despite all its promises of clothes, blankets, and food, government indifference, bureaucratic foul-ups, corrupt contractors, and a primitive transportation system meant that supplies often came late and were usually short and substandard. Food supplies were inadequate, and though the Indians could leave the reservation to hunt for food, the buffalo were quickly disappearing. Already starvation stalked the Comanches and Kiowas. Discontent with the treaty increased as many Indians believed the government only fulfilled those treaty stipulations that worked to its favor. Some chiefs who had signed the treaty, such as the Kiowas Satank and Satanta, now turned against it. By the early 1870s Comanches, Kiowas, even Cheyennes, in search of food, goods, status, and revenge, rode into North Texas, hitting cattle herds, stagecoaches, wagon trains, isolated ranches and farms, and virtually anybody who crossed their path.

President Ulysses S. Grant's "peace policy" did nothing to stop the raids. Looking for scapegoats for the United States' disastrous Indian policy, eastern churchmen pointed to corrupt, spoils-system Indian agents, accusing them of cheating the Indians of their due and so causing much of the conflict. When Grant became president in 1869 he began appointing churchmen and missionaries as Indian agents, which everyone hoped would bring about peace, hence the term "peace policy." The Comanche-Kiowa reservations came under the authority of Quaker missionary Lawrie Tatum. Tatum was honest and his heart was in the right place, but he was naive when it came to Indians. Kiowa chiefs Satank, Satanta, and Big Tree, who had grown up in the rough-and-tumble world of Kiowa politics, easily manipulated Tatum and played to his sensibilities. Comanche and Kiowa raiders found they could strike into Texas and then take refuge back on the reservation in time to receive their share of allotment goods, boasting of their exploits and unpunished by Tatum who wanted to believe the best of everyone. Each successful raid emboldened the young men. They even raided the Fort Sill horse corral as well as that of the agency itself. Army officers fumed over Tatum's reluctance to arrest and punish them. Texans complained loudly, demanding the government do something about the raids stemming from Tatum's slipshod reservation. As one Texan wrote, "Give us Phil Sheridan and send Philanthropy to the devil."

Then, in mid-May, 1871, the Kiowas overplayed their hand. Satanta, old Satank, Big Tree, and more than a hundred other Kiowas rode down into North Texas and set up an ambush on Salt Creek Prairie, along the Fort Richardson road not too far from Jacksboro. A small wagon train appeared that was escorted by a few cavalrymen, but as the Kiowas prepared to attack, the shaman Mamanti urged them to let it go as another, far better wagon train would soon appear. The Kiowas allowed the wagon train to pass. They did not realize that in the train was General William Tecumseh Sherman, general in chief of the United States, who was personally investigating the validity of Texas' complaints. Not long after, as Mamanti predicted, a second train of ten freight wagons loaded with supplies clopped by and the Kiowas attacked. Of the twelve teamsters, five escaped; seven were killed, some tortured to death, all mutilated. The wagons were plundered and burned, and the Kiowa raiding party made off with all the supplies they could carry, as well as forty-one government mules.

Word of the wagon train attack quickly spread. Sherman, now at Fort Sill, was determined to capture the raiders. The Kiowa raiding party returned to the reservation to receive their ration allotments, and when Tatum asked Satanta about the attack, the chief readily admitted it. He had lost three men, so was willing to call it even. Still, he boasted to Tatum, "If any other Indian claims the honor of leading that party he will be lying to you. I led it myself." Tatum now had to forget his Quaker sensitivities. With Satanta's boast as proof, he determined to arrest the leaders of the raiding party. Tatum, Sherman, and Colonel Benjamin Grierson stood on Grierson's porch at Fort Sill; troopers were concealed around the quadrangle and inside the house. When Satanta, Satank, and several other chiefs arrived to "size up" Sherman, the troopers sprang the trap. For a tense moment it was touch and go, but the chiefs surrendered without a shot being fired. Satanta, Satank, and Big Tree were arrested and sent to Texas to stand trial. En route to prison, Satank was killed while trying to escape. But his death seems more like suicide, with the old man not willing to be imprisoned. In Texas, Satanta and Big Tree were tried and sentenced to death. However, public opinion suggested that keeping them in prison might be a better way to end the raids. The idea seemed valid, so Satanta and Big Tree were imprisoned at the Texas State Penitentiary at Huntsville. And it did seem to diminish Kiowa raiding into Texas. Nevertheless, many people, particularly the Five Civilized Tribes in Indian Territory, called for clemency and begged Texas to eventually release the two chiefs.

While the imprisonment of Satanta and Big Tree may have caused the Kiowas to think twice about raiding into Texas, it made little impact on the Comanches and their strikes continued. Then, on September 29,1872, up in the Texas Panhandle, Colonel Ranald Mackenzie and his Fourth Cavalry attacked a large village of more than 260 lodges of combined Kwahadis, Kotsotekas, Yamparikas, Noconis, and Penetakas. The Fourth Cavalry killed twenty-four Comanches, burned the village and its utensils, and took 124 women and children captives. These were taken to Fort Sill, essentially hostages to ensure the good behavior of the Comanches. They remained prisoners until June, 1873. During this time, Comanches raids slackened considerably. The women and children were later returned to their families and a few raids took place. Without the woman and children in custody, the government tried to tie Comanche behavior to the impending release of Satanta and Big Tree. It demanded that at least five Comanche raiders be turned over for punishment or the Kiowa chiefs would not be released. The Comanches refused and in October, 1873, its bluff called, the government finally released Satanta and Big Tree as it had promised, despite demands from Texans and Sherman himself to keep the two in prison.

The spring of 1874 saw tensions at near breaking points across the Southern Plains. Texans had no illusions about the freeing of Satanta and Big Tree and prepared for more raids. The Comanches and Kiowas were angry. Angry at their chiefs' imprisonment and the short rations; angry about American horse thieves out of Kansas who stole Indian ponies and peddlers selling cheap whiskey to the Indians on credit, often getting them so deeply in debt that they had to forfeit what little cash they received from their annuities. But what really enraged them were the buffalo hunters. In the late 1860s American buffalo hunters armed with high-powered rifles began invading the Great Plains. By 1870 they had wiped out the buffalo on the Central Plains, taking only the hide, maybe the tongue, and leaving the rest to rot. Now they cast greedy eyes toward the few remaining buffalo south of the Arkansas River. By 1874 buffalo were almost impossible for Comanche and Kiowa hunters to find. With government rations often late or short, the reservation Indians began to starve. Ignoring Indian complaints, the government did nothing to stop the buffalo hunters, in fact, some officers encouraged them, realizing that killing off the Plains Indians' main source of food was the best way to defeat them. With the government turning a blind eye, by the summer of 1874, a number of hunters had banded together and were killing off the buffalo in the heart of the Comanche and Kiowa hunting grounds in the Texas Panhandle.

Now many Comanches, Kiowas, and Southern Cheyennes had had enough. On June 27, 1874, about three hundred Comanche and Cheyenne warriors attacked a band of buffalo hunters at Adobe Walls, the site of Kit Carson's fight ten years earlier. And so began the Red River War, the last desperate fight of the Southern Plains Indians to remain free. Not all Comanches, Kiowas, or Southern Cheyennes wanted war or joined it. A good many chiefs and their followers had long recognized that their way of life was changing and so had grudgingly accepted the white man's road. War, they understood, would be a disaster and could not be won. Still, fiery young chiefs, such as Quanah Parker of the Noconi Comanches, who led the attack on the buffalo hunters, and Isatai, a young shaman who urged the war, were determined to try. From the first, the Indians experienced mixed results. The hunters, with their high-powered rifles, held off the Indians for several days, suffering only a few losses, and killing at least fifteen warriors, maybe many more. Nevertheless, the hunters quickly abandoned the area once the Indians withdrew. On July 12, a large party of Kiowas successfully ambushed a troop of Texas Rangers at Lost Valley, west of Jacksboro and not far from where the wagon train had been ambushed three years earlier.

The attacks drove a stake through the heart of President Grant's "peace policy." Those Indians siding with the war factions left the reservation to try to live on the Southern Plains as they once had. Given the okay by Washington, army troops out of Fort Sill marched onto the reservations where they made lists of "friendly" and "hostile" Indians. The friendlies, consisting of a majority of Kiowas, as well as all the Penetaka Comanches and about half the Yamparikas and Noconis, were rounded up and placed on Cache Creek within the reservation boundary. As it always had with Indian peoples, family came first and hostiles were able to take advantage of the confusion. They often slipped in to the friendly area for food and rest. At the same time, hostiles posing as friendlies sometimes left the camp and made raids of their own.

By late August several hostile factions of Comanches and Kiowas, many of whom had participated in the Adobe Walls or Lost Valley fights, settled around the Wichita Agency at Anadarko, using the peaceful Wichitas, Caddos, and Delawares as protection. On August 22, when the army demanded the Comanches and Kiowas give up their weapons, a battle broke out at the Wichita Agency. Over the next two days, a fierce firefight raged. About seven non-Indians were killed; the Comanches and Kiowas lost around fourteen. The agency store was looted, and many of the farms of the peaceful Indians were burned, including that belonging to Delaware chief Black Beaver. Starting a grassfire to cover their retreat, the Comanches and Kiowas made their way to the safety of the breaks of the Red River.

The army was already on the offensive, putting more than five thousand men into the field. Columns out of Kansas, Indian Territory, Texas, and New Mexico all converged on the Texas Panhandle. Once again, the Wichitas, Caddos, Delawares, and Penetaka Comanches served as scouts and auxiliaries. Though parties of Comanche, Kiowa, and Cheyenne warriors raided ranches and small wagon trains when they could, they soon found themselves on the run, constantly hounded by army detachments and the Indian scouts. On August 30 cavalry under the command of General Nelson Miles defeated a large camp of Cheyennes at the Battle of the Cap Rock on Prairie Town Fork of the Red River. To escape, the Indians burned their lodges, abandoned their camp utensils, and scattered into the scorching Llano Estacado. A month later, on the night of September 28, Colonel Ranald S. Mackenzie's Fourth Cavalry, along with Tonkawa and Seminole scouts, surprised and destroyed a large camp of Comanches, Kiowas, and Cheyennes inside Palo Duro Canyon, just south of present-day Amarillo. Though the Indians only lost three men killed, they were totally routed. Mackenzie captured more than 1,400 Indian horses and the entire camp of tepees and utensils. Understanding the importance of both to the Indians, Mackenzie kept 350 of the horses and mules for his own men and methodically killed the remaining thousand-plus animals. He then destroyed the entire village and its contents.

For the Indians, the loss of so many horses and tepees, as well as winter food and clothing, proved a crushing defeat. Even the elements turned against them. The horrendous 100-plus-degree heat and drought of the summer now gave way to incessant rains and autumn chill. Constantly harried by the army in what has come to be called the "wrinkled hand chase," many cold, wet, hungry, shelterless hostiles opted for reservation life. Slowly, bands of defeated Comanches, Kiowas, and Cheyennes made their way back toward Fort Sill. Blue northers and blizzards of December sent back more until only a few bands remained at war. On February 25, 1875, the last 250 Kiowa holdouts, led by Lone Wolf, surrendered. Finally, on June 2, the last Comanche warriors under Quanah Parker came in, bringing an end not only to the Red River War, but also to the free life the Southern Plains Indians had always known. Seventy-four Comanche, Kiowa, and Cheyenne warriors, some of them not involved in the war at all, were imprisoned for three years at Fort Marion, Florida. Satanta was sent back to the Texas State Penitentiary in Huntsville. Despondent, he committed suicide in March, 1878, by jumping from an upper-story window. Now all Texas Indians were on reservations.

APACHE INCURSIONS INTO WEST TEXAS

By the 1870s the Lipan Apaches, whose heyday in Texas had been in the seventeenth century, and the Kiowa-Apaches, who had migrated south with the Kiowas in the late eighteenth century, had largely disappeared from Texas. The Lipans had been pushed ever farther south by the Comanches, and by the 1870s, the Lipans, as a recognized division, had ceased to exist. What few remaining Lipans there were had either integrated with other more numerous Apache bands in New Mexico and Arizona or become hispanized peasants living in northern Mexico. During the latter part of the nineteenth century, when Texans mentioned the name "Apache," most were thinking of the Kiowa-Apaches. The Kiowa-Apaches had been defeated along with the Kiowas and Comanches during the Red River War of 1874–75 and took their place on the reservation around Fort Sill. On the reservation, the Kiowa-Apaches dropped the term "Kiowa" and became known just as the "Apaches," or more specifically, the Apache Tribe of Oklahoma.

Then, in 1881, the very last Indian raids ever made into Texas took place. They came from the Chiricahua Apaches, a band not previously known for venturing into Texas. The Chiricahuas mainly confined their activities to the mountains of southern Arizona, southern New Mexico, and northern Mexico. During the 1870s, as the U.S. government tried to concentrate the many different and often antagonistic divisions of Apaches onto the San Carlos Reservation in Arizona, some Chiricahua leaders, such as Naiche, Geronimo, and Victorio, resisted. Geronimo and Naiche never made it to Texas, at least as warriors, but Victorio and his band of Chiricahuas put a scare in West Texans.

In 1877 the government tried to move Victorio and his band of Chiricahuas and Mescaleros away from Ojo Caliente in central New Mexico to the huge San Carlos Reservation in Arizona. Victorio refused, pointing out that he and his people had been living at Ojo Caliente peacefully for the past decade. When the government insisted, Victorio, an excellent tactician, began raiding into Mexico, New Mexico, and West Texas, mainly in the area between Fort Davis and El Paso. The government ordered two African American cavalry units, the Ninth Cavalry and Tenth Cavalry, to give chase. The Tenth recruited Tigua Indian scouts to lead them. In early 1880 the Tenth Cavalry, which had been moved from Fort Concho to Fort Davis, went after Victorio and found itself being led on a fifteen-hundred–mile wild-goose chase. They returned to Fort Davis in May without ever catching a whiff of Victorio. Sent back on the Apache's trail, the Tenth Cavalry caught up with Victorio's band. On June 11 Tigua scouts and the Tenth Cavalry "buffalo soldiers" slugged it out with the Apaches just west of Valentine. Twenty Apaches and four Tiguas were killed. In August, at Rattlesnake Springs in the Guadeloupe Mountains, the army and Apaches met again in a three-hour battle. Once again, Victorio and his band managed to slip away and headed toward Mexico. In September a detachment of Texas Rangers joined the chase and illegally entered Mexico during their hunt. They also had no luck in catching up with Victorio. As one writer calculated, during fourteen months of raiding in Mexico, New Mexico, and Texas, Victorio's band, "seldom more than seventy-five strong, had taken the lives of more than one thousand whites and Mexicans while eluding three American cavalry regiments, two American infantry regiments, a huge number of Mexican troops, and a contingent of Texas Rangers."

However, Victorio's luck was quickly running out. In October, 1880, he and his people took refuge in a mountainous area of northern Mexico called Tres Castillos. On October 15 a detachment of Chihuahua State Militia managed to surround the band and in an all-day battle defeated the Apaches, killing Victorio and all his warriors. The women and children were taken captive and held in Chihuahua City for the next several years. However, though Victorio was dead, some of his band who had not been at Tres Castillos were roaming far West Texas. In January, 1881, at the Sierra Diablo Mountains of West Texas, the last Indian battle in Texas took place. Tigua Scouts fighting alongside Texas Rangers caught up with the last Apaches and routed them. With this, the Indian wars in Texas came to an end, as did the freedom of any and all Indians who had once called Texas home.

RESERVATION LIFE

By 1881 only two small recognized Indian "tribes" remained in Texas: the Alabama-Coushattas, with their tiny reservation in Polk County of East Texas, and the Tiguas near El Paso. In the late 1860s Texas tried to get the federal government to take over administration of the Alabama-Coushattas but nothing came of it and for the next several decades the state virtually ignored the small group of Indians. As for the Tiguas, though Texas had granted them about thirty-six acres of land in 1854, through actions by the Texas legislature and unscrupulous whites, they lost virtually every inch of it. Finally in 1871 the Incorporation Act restored about twenty acres to the Tiguas. The remainder of the nineteenth century saw the Tiguas ignored by the state and federal governments and left to their own devices. None of the other Texas Indians, such as the Comanches, Kiowas, Apaches, Caddos, and Wichitas, lived in Texas anymore. They were on reservations in southwestern Indian Territory.

Defeated and virtually prisoners on their reservations, these Texas Indians in Indian Territory relied on government allotments of cattle, flour, and clothing, though some did try to plant crops and raise cattle. Many Comanches and Kiowas shrewdly learned how to make do on the white man's road. The Kiowa-Comanche reservation contained huge expanses of lush grasslands, excellent for fattening cattle. The Comanches, under the leadership of Quanah Parker, and the Kiowas to a lesser extent, now began leasing their lands to Texas cattlemen for cash payments called "grass money." By 1885 Texas cattlemen were running 75,000 head of cattle on the Kiowa-Comanche reservation, using 1.5 million acres and paying only six cents an acre per year. Though less than market value, grass money did provide about $55,000 a year for the Kiowas, Comanches, and Apaches. Twice a year the cattlemen distributed the grass money. In the summer of 1885 the companies paid each Indian on the Kiowa-Comanche reservation $9.50, all in silver dimes. Many government officials disliked the idea of the Indians leasing their lands, rather than farming them, so in 1890 the United States declared the cattle leases null and void and ordered the cattle off the reservation. Making matters worse, whites living near the reservation often targeted its resources. For example, white settlers often slipped onto the reservation and stole Indian timber to be used as fence posts, housing, and firewood. As one settler recalled, a local missionary had been caught stealing wood by a Kiowa. "White man talk heap Jesus on Sunday," the Kiowa commented, "and steal Kiowa's wood on Monday." It got so bad that an Indian police force had to be created to keep white thieves out of the reservations.

During the twenty-five-odd years of the reservation experience in Indian Territory, the Indians not only had to adjust to farming and ranching but also got "heap Jesus." By the late 1870s Roman Catholic, Presbyterian, Methodist, and Baptist missions had been founded in Anadarko, Oklahoma, and around Fort Sill, where they experienced varying degrees of success. Although many Indians might have gone to church on Sunday, most still attended their traditional ceremonies and dances, at least when they could, as reservation agents normally banned these as "uncivilized." Quanah Parker, who became the main spokesman for the Comanche people, and a few Caddo chiefs founded the Native American Church, which blended traditional Indian beliefs, peyote use, and Christianity. While agents, white churchmen, and even some "progressive" Indians condemned the "peyote road" as mere drug use and a throwback to tribal days, the adherents advocated a peaceful, harmonious, industrious life, and their ceremonies were always quiet and dignified. The church spread rapidly and soon had adherents across Indian America. In 1944 the Native American Church received a charter, with its stated purpose to "promote morality, sobriety, industry, charity and right living." The Native American Church still exists and many American Indian people across the United States are quite active in it. Other religious movements, such as the 1890 Ghost Dance, touched reservation Indians in Indian Territory, but this passed peacefully without causing the bloodshed it brought to the Lakotas at the Battle of Wounded Knee in that year.

Along with religion, the United States also forced American-style education on the Indians. Schools, such as the Riverside Indian School at Anadarko, taught Indian girls and boys domestic and mechanical arts. Besides English, basic reading, writing, and arithmetic, the girls were taught how to sew, cook, and clean. Boys learned how to be farmers or carpenters. Little effort was made to prepare the students for the modern industrial world nor were they given courses that would lead them to universities. Many children were sent to boarding schools far away from their families, such as Rainy Mountain Boarding School near Gotebo, Oklahoma; Chilocco Indian School in northern Oklahoma; Haskell Institute in Lawrence, Kansas; or the most famous of all, Carlisle Indian School in Carlisle, Pennsylvania. At these schools, boys had their hair cut; their old "Indian" clothes were burned; and they were prohibited from speaking their native tongue.

While the government and the churches actively tried to erase traditional Indian culture, the Comanches, Kiowas, Apaches, Wichitas, Caddos, and others also found themselves changing by virtue of the ever-increasing number of Americans around them. White and black storekeepers, teachers, preachers, government officials, cowboys, and ranch hands lived on or around the reservations and came into contact with the Indians in a variety of ways. Many non-Indian men married Indian woman, "squaw men" as they were called. Some of these were loving husbands and from the union came children who lived with a foot in both the Indian and American worlds. Other "squaw men" were opportunists who hoped to get their hands on as much Indian land and resources as they could. Claiming they were now a member of the "tribe," they demanded every benefit they could, but then turned to the U.S. government when tribal governments attempted to control their activities. Indian culture changed rapidly. As Indian women came into contact with white women, dress styles and cooking methods changed. Although some people remained committed to the past, others learned how to walk the white man's road.

Still, by the mid-1880s many government officials and philanthropists believed the Indians were not "civilizing" fast enough. Seeing only reservation poverty and not the community it contained, these "friends of the Indians" felt that communal reservation land was hampering Indian "progress." The key to Indian "civilization" and prosperity, they believed, was to break up the reservations, give each Indian family its own plot of land, teach them to become small farmers, and force them to swim in the ocean of profits and losses. This approach ignored several realities. The Caddos and Wichitas had been successful farmers for hundreds of years and had their own ideas of farming. The Comanches and Kiowas never possessed any form of agriculture nor had any desire to learn how to plow a field. Cattle leasing was rather profitable and more conducive to reservation geography than farming. And finally, small farms in America were on their way out, being replaced by agribusiness, and the United States was fast becoming urban and industrialized. But as Merrill Gates, a "friend of the Indian," saw it: "To bring [the Indian] out of savagery into citizenship we must make the Indian more intelligently selfish before we can make him unselfishly intelligent. We need to awaken in him wants. In his dull savagery he must be touched by the wings of the divine angel of discontent. Then he begins to look forward, to reach out. . . . Discontent . . . is needed to get the Indian out of the blanket and into trousers,—and trousers with a pocket in them, and with a pocket that aches to be filled with dollars!"

So despite almost unanimous protests by the Indians, the U.S. government passed the Dawes Severalty Act of 1887, which would give 160 acres of land to each head of an Indian family and lesser amounts to unmarried or orphaned Indians. Excess land would be sold off by the government, with the proceeds going into Indian accounts to pay for their education and the purchase of stock and farming implements. Most whites, especially land-hungry settlers, small ranchers, railroad companies, and oil companies strongly supported the Dawes Act. Only the big cattle companies of Texas protested, and not because the Dawes Act was bad for the Indians but because they would lose their cattle leases.

Gates said of the Dawes Act, it would be "a mighty pulverizing engine for breaking up the tribal mass." It was. The Dawes Act finally caught up with the Comanches, Kiowas, Apaches, Wichitas, Caddos, and Tonkawas in the 1890s as the Jerome Commission began negotiating the reservation allotment process. In June, 1891, the commission managed to get the Wichitas, Caddos, and Delawares to accept $715,000 for their 574,000-acre reservation, about $1.25 per acre. Congress approved the plan in 1895 and shortly thereafter the reservation was broken up and the Indians began receiving their individual plots of land. In October of that same year, the commission pressured the Tonkawas to give up their 90,000-acre reservation for $30,600 and take individual allotments. In October, 1892, after much arm-twisting, the commission managed to get the Kiowas, Comanches, and Apaches to sell their several-million-acre reservation for $2 million. Congress ratified the agreement in 1900 and the allotment process began soon after. The Tonkawa reservation was thrown open to white settlement first, in September, 1893. A few years later, on August 6, 1901, the surplus land on the Kiowa-Comanche-Apache and the Wichita and Affiliate Bands reservations were sold off to white buyers.

The negotiation and ratification process was not without controversy. According to the 1867 Medicine Lodge Creek Treaty, the government could not take any of the Kiowa-Comanche-Apache reservation without approval of three-fourths of its adult male Indian population. There were grave doubts as to whether three-fourths of the reservation Indians actually approved the Jerome Commission agreement in 1892, but the government ignored these concerns. Showing a shrewd understanding of American society, Kiowa chief Lone Wolf field suit on this point to prevent the allotment from taking place. *Lone Wolf v. Hitchcock* wound its way through the court system and in 1903, the U.S. Supreme Court rejected Lone Wolf's arguments, ruling that Congress could make any law it wanted for the Indians and was not bound by previous treaties. If Indians had any doubt that they were conquered, the ruling in *Lone Wolf v. Hitchcock* put those doubts to rest. Before allotment, many reservation Indians had prospered as ranchers by running their cattle on the communal lands. They now found themselves in bad shape, their allotment too small for ranching and the land too poor for small-scale farming. Within just a few years, many Comanches, Caddos, Kiowas, Wichitas, and Apaches had lost their allotments to whites and sunk even deeper into poverty.

Tiguas around El Paso had their own land problems during the last half of the nineteenth century. In 1871 the State of Texas, with the urging of unscrupulous Anglo land speculators, incorporated the Tigua's town of Ysleta. On paper, the new city was the largest in the state at the time—thirty-six square miles. Suddenly, the Tiguas found their property heavily taxed, and when they could not pay it was confiscated and sold to Anglos. Much of their land had been taken from them by 1874 when the incorporation was declared illegal. Just as bad, in 1877 the Tiguas were barred from using the salt beds near the Guadalupe Mountains that had attracted the Jumanos in years past. For centuries the Tiguas, as well as the Jumanos and

Pueblos, had gotten their salt from these dry lakebeds. They were considered communal property. Local speculators at El Paso, including Judge Charles Howard, tried to gain control of the salt beds and prohibited the Indians from using them. This began the El Paso Salt War in which the Tiguas and nearby Hispanic settlers rose up and attacked the Anglos, killing five, including Judge Howard. Troops had to be sent in to stop the violence. In the end, the Tiguas still lost access to the salt beds.

By the turn of the twentieth century the Indians of Texas, both those living in and out of the state, had been defeated. It had not taken long, just under 400 years from the time Cabeza de Vaca washed ashore at Galveston; about 180 since Spain established a firm presence in Texas; only 64 years since the Texas Revolution; and a mere 35 since the end of the Civil War. Despite a valiant defense, people who had once fearlessly roamed the Southern Plains and whose lands had stretched from the piney woods of western Louisiana to the Rocky Mountains of New Mexico found themselves confined to tiny reservations or land allotments. Nor were they free to live their lives as they wanted. Traditional religious ceremonies were banned. Certain types of clothing were too. They could not do with their allotment as they saw fit and were even told how they must slaughter cattle. Government officials forcibly interfered in the lives, politics, and religion of these Indians to a degree that other Americans would never have tolerated. Even the education provided for them was second-rate and did not prepare them for the modern, industrialized twentieth century.

A Wild Time in the Old Town Tonight, 1875–1879

TY CASHION

TY CASHION IS PROFESSOR OF HISTORY AT SAM HOUSTON STATE UNIVERSITY IN HUNTSVILLE. HIS BOOKS INCLUDE *PIGSKIN PULPIT: A SOCIAL HISTORY OF TEXAS HIGH SCHOOL FOOTBALL COACHES*, *THE HUMAN TRADITION IN TEXAS*, AND *A TEXAS FRONTIER: THE CLEAR FORK COUNTRY AND FORT GRIFFIN, 1849–1887*, A REVISIONIST HISTORY OF OLD NORTHWEST TEXAS.

IN THIS SELECTION, CASHION VIVIDLY DESCRIBES LIFE AT FORT GRIFFIN, A ROUGH AND ROWDY SETTLEMENT OF SALOONS, DANCE HALLS, BROTHELS, AND GAMING ESTABLISHMENTS. SOLDIERS, BUFFALO HUNTERS, AND COWBOYS POPULATED THE NORTHWEST TEXAS OUTPOST, AND LAWLESS ACTS WERE COMMON. STILL, DR. CASHION POINTS OUT, "GRATUITOUS KILLINGS WERE RARE AND VIOLENCE WAS NEVER TAKEN LIGHTLY" BY LOCAL AUTHORITIES.

★ ★

One summer day in 1877, Charles Bain's stage delivered the *Jacksboro Frontier Echo* to Fort Griffin. Between the headlines and the local news, the paper dedicated an entire page to a devastating railway strike that had left much of Pittsburgh "in ashes." Pennsylvania militiamen, on hand to preserve the peace, instead provoked a riot by turning their rifles and Gatling guns on an unsuspecting crowd of factory workers and curious spectators who had gathered at a railroad roundhouse. Later that day and throughout the night several thousand civilians responded by attacking the troops with any kind of weapon they could find. The mob pillaged the city and destroyed buildings, railroad cars, and other property. A month later the *Echo* reported that "forty persons killed and two-thousand six-hundred cars destroyed are among the fruits of the late strike at Pittsburgh."

About the same time as the riot, news coming out of Northwest Texas created the impression that keeping order was beyond the ability of civil authorities at Fort Griffin as well. In December 1876 the *Fort Worth Democrat* reported that vigilantes in Shackelford County had just hanged almost a dozen horse thieves, adding: "Their bodies will make good food for the vultures." And only a month earlier the *Frontier Echo* vividly recounted the brutal slayings of two freighters by a pair of outlaws who had hired their team. After departing the village, the murderers marched the drivers into the brush; one of them shot his man point-blank in the head, the other pistol-whipped his victim to death. The *Dallas Daily Herald* covered an equally violent incident. This time it was a gunfight inside a Griffin saloon, where the sheriff and county attorney left one reckless cowboy dead and another wounded. Two bystanders had also been killed—one "with his brain oozing from the hole in his forehead."

While the strikers at Pittsburgh erupted as one body protesting their intolerable conditions, Griffinites acted as individuals, seemingly resorting to violence in the normal course of their affairs. Compared with other frontier communities, Fort Griffin was a bloody boomtown, but the sensational reports emanating from the little outpost did not always paint an accurate picture. Such incidents were infrequent but widely reported, giving the impression of lawlessness out of proportion to daily life. Travelers, in fact, frequently expressed surprise at finding Fort Griffin so peaceable. Editor Robson wrote tongue-in-cheek that a number of itinerant prospectors thought they would "see nearly every citizen a walking arsenal"; they also expected to "hear of at least one man being killed here regularly each day in the week and several killed on Sunday." Wildness was nevertheless ever present in the whiskey houses and brothels lining Griffin Avenue, and the volatile environment indeed invited occasional violence.

Griffin's "heyday" began about 1875, shortly after D. M. Dowell reopened the Flat to settlement. The socially deprived enlisted men welcomed the development, and despite the efforts of everyone concerned with maintaining military discipline, the army had little success keeping the soldiers away from the rough-and-tumble little town. The fort's medical officer noted that "the habits of the men might be materially improved by the removal of a number of lewd women living in the vicinity of the post." He also complained that recently a soldier had been wounded by a "pistol ball" in one of Griffin's "drunken haunts." Inspector General N. H. Davis resigned himself to accepting the "nuisance under the bluff," remarking that "this kind of evil . . . will follow the troops to any locality they may go."

Colonel Buell did not surrender so easily; in February 1875 he ordered his men to stay out of the Flat. The enlisted men openly flouted him, however, and several of them even erected shacks in the village. To the colonel's consternation, the situation further degenerated. In October a dispute over sectional differences resulted in a bloody row between drunken soldiers and civilians. When the troops threatened to burn the settlement, the townsmen vowed they would march on the fort. A few weeks later the colonel removed one of the worst offenders, a man named Krause, even though he held a legal lease for what Buell described as a "grog shop and gambling hole." Ill feelings lingered, and in January an infantryman on sentinel duty fired a round into the Flat, mortally wounding a civilian.

When the first session of the district court met in recently organized Shackelford County during June 1875, Judge J. P. Osterhout dealt severely with lawbreakers. In thirty-seven cases during the five-day session he found a dozen men guilty of gambling and selling liquor illegally, and although the fines ranged from only $10 to $15, some of the accused faced multiple counts. Many of the same men who sold illegal spirits were also pandering prostitutes, a more serious crime that cost the guilty parties between $100 and $150. In many instances attorneys for the defendants got cases discharged or transferred to the more lenient county court. The signal was nevertheless unmistakable: the legal community would hold miscreants accountable for their actions. Many petty delinquents such as those listed on the court docket as Banjo Bob, Curley, Smokey Joe, and Frenchy skipped town rather than face Judge Osterhout. Among them was Doc Holliday, whose single crime at Fort Griffin resulted in a gambling and liquor charge.

Osterhout also presided over more serious cases. He issued warrants for two suspected murderers who fled Fort Griffin before Sheriff Henry Jacobs could apprehend them. Several men facing assault charges also eluded the court. W. L. Browning was not as lucky. He was convicted of trying to murder an acquaintance, John Jackson. According to the testimony of Jackson's sister, the two men were sharing a watermelon outside a picket residence when they suddenly began arguing. As Browning pulled a gun, Jackson hit his arm with a shovel and then bolted indoors to get a shotgun. The defendant also ran to the house and began shooting through a crack in the wall, firing so close to the witness that she suffered powder burns. Browning, by then outgunned, retreated across the river. The Court of Appeals in Austin upheld Osterhout's verdict after the defendant contested the decision of the local jury.

Despite its earnest efforts, the court could not stem the proliferation of vice and violence at Fort Griffin. As the activity in saloons, gambling dens, dance halls, variety theaters, and brothels grew with the great bison hunt and cattle trail traffic, increasingly prosperous merchants and businessmen convinced officers of the court to wink at the "victimless" crimes. A more tolerant climate indeed existed when citizens in Northwest Texas elected J. R. Fleming to the district court bench in 1876. A resident of the frontier town of Comanche, eighty miles southeast of Fort Griffin, he understood loose social conditions. Judge Fleming concentrated on controlling violence and let the justices of the peace work with local people to set community standards. During two terms that year he issued a lone indictment for "selling liquor without a license" and a single charge against one "Swayback Mag" for prostitution. Even into the 1880s visitors who remained within the wide latitude of acceptable behavior at the Flat could enjoy a spree without running afoul of the law. "Old Griffin had its night life," remarked one-time resident "Jet" Kenan; "everything went but murder, arson, and burglary."

A ride down Griffin Avenue provided visitors an indelible impression of the little village. Smells, sounds, and sights assaulted the senses. The putrid odor from thousands of buffalo hides rotting in great stacks started many a horse to reeling. More pleasant was an impromptu concert that greeted a transient as he passed by York's store; there he saw a black man holding the reins for a mounted fiddler grinding out "Arkansas Traveler" to the delight of a crowd. Loitering cowboys occasionally passed around Jew's harps, and when stabler Pete Haverty got his organ, the music could be heard throughout the valley between the fort and the river. Rollie Burns described his first visit to Griffin in 1877, while on a cattle buying trip. On the main street were freighters, some unloading wagons, and others starting for Fort Worth with mountains of hides; trail outfits, too, were taking on supplies. "Alongside this busy element," he remembered, "was another, half drunk, boisterous, and bent on raising hell." One visitor recalled that the business district "was a Babel of boisterous talk, whoops, curses, laughter, songs and miserable music." The passing of time no doubt sweetened the memory. Cowboy Ken Cary more accurately declared that "Fort Griffin was more disgusting, after first glance, than alluringly picturesque."

Inside the dives lining Griffin Avenue the coarse scene of filthy transients enjoying a visit to the Flat was even more primitive. "I've seen men and women dancing there in the dance halls without a bit of clothing on," remarked one visitor. Another man affirmed that indeed "the women were scarcely dressed"; they also danced with the patrons, and when the music stopped, "you bellied up to the bar, took a drink and paid fifty cents for it." Animating the drab adobe and picket hovels were women known only by names such as Polly Turnover, Slewfoot Jane, and Monkey-face Mag.

Despite the wide-open conditions, not more than a handful of saloons ever opened their doors at the same time. Many tried to enter the lucrative trade, but the few proprietors lucky enough to gain a foothold connived with the legal community to limit competition. No one was above the law. Even Frank Conrad once had to climb out of a jury box to fight a charge of "selling spirituous liquors without a license." At the peak of the buffalo slaughter a Stribling and Kirkland circular advertised only five Griffin bars; Henry Herron later recalled that as many as five more operated for various periods. Among the lucky owners was Mike O'Brien, who came to hunt bison but quickly found serving drinks more profitable and infinitely more entertaining. Few of his former associates passed through town without stopping at the Hunters' Retreat; Charley Meyers's Cattle Exchange drew much of the drovers' trade. Under one sprawling roof "Uncle Billy" Wilson ran a beer and dance hall, variety show, restaurant, and lodge called the Frontier House. A frequent patron commented that "a blueprint would have been interesting."

None, however, was more popular than Donnely and Carroll's Bee Hive. The saloon gained notoriety as the scene of at least one fatal gunfight and one unprovoked murder. English drifter Jim Grahame, otherwise known as *Dallas Daily Herald* correspondent "Comanche Jim," claimed credit for naming the place. He also asserted that over the entrance he painted a "rough representation of a beehive" under which he scrawled a rhyme that had the drunken inhabitants beckoning visitors to "come in and try the flavor of our honey."

The seasonal nature of hunting and trailing also drew professional gamblers who made Fort Griffin an important stop on their "circuit." Reportedly, a game could be found in the back room of any saloon. The weakly regulated activity invited the use of marked decks, loaded dice, and other aids. "The ordinary fellow did not have the ghost of a show," commented Henry Herron. "I saw a buffalo hunter come to town one day and market his season's kill for $1,500.00," he continued. "The next morning he had to borrow money for his breakfast. The gamblers had gotten all of it."

Prostitutes also scrambled for the money of free-spending transients. In 1877 the *Dallas Daily Herald* reported that "Griffin, which has long been the roost of a large quantity of 'soiled doves,' can now boast of a larger flock than any other town on the frontier." According to Jet Kenan, "Fort Griffin would not have been Fort Griffin" without its "red light district." For about two blocks the brothels extended in a broken line down each side of the main street near the river. The women worked with the blessings of saloon keepers and merchants alike. During the day prostitutes "boldly and openly took their 'friends' around from bar to bar and store to store"; together with the shopkeepers, Kenan claimed, they would "bleed them of every possible dollar in every conceivable manner." At night women worked the saloons, "drinking, cursing, smoking, and contributing greatly to the loud hilarity."

The prostitutes, who added so much color to the stories that men told, led anything but glamorous lives. Low pay and high expenses kept them in poverty. Their fondness for gaudy clothes, material possessions, and alcohol and drugs further drained their earnings. The degrading conditions of prostitution, moreover, elicited the most wretched of human qualities, producing hardened, cynical, grasping women. Among themselves, any number of negative forces—competition, suspicion, jealousy, and petty incidents—checked the bonds that mutual privation might have formed. And because their profession rested outside the law, they were at the mercy of the legal system. The justice of the peace set the rules for the illicit trade, and the women normally observed them. The local court, they knew, provided their only protection against the abuses of an uncaring and often hostile society. For example, Griffin's justice of the peace, who usually ignored petty crimes in the black community, came to the defense of some African American prostitutes harassed by a group of drunken black cowboys. He promptly had the men arrested for brandishing their weapons "in a private house" and fined each of them. Rarely did the county and district courts become involved in the prostitutes' affairs.

The profiles and experiences of prostitutes along Griffin Avenue were neither flattering nor heartening. Although many were youthful, some stayed in the profession long after their looks had faded. Two of the nine women who listed their occupation as "courtesan" for the 1880 census were in their mid- to late thirties; others, who had been teenagers during the town's heyday, had reached their early twenties and looked forward to middle age with few prospects for improving their social condition. Some were married, such as Minnie Delno, who got the sobriquet "Hurricane Minnie" for her forced union with "Hurricane Bill" Martin. But marriage did not add stability to their lives; instead, it made them even more disreputable. A society that already frowned on the trade held a special contempt for a married prostitute. Their husbands, moreover, represented the dregs of society, assuring that the women would remain at the bottom of the social ladder. Bill Martin, for example, became legendary for his frequent brushes with the law. Few women escaped this miserable environment. Griffin resident George Newcomb claimed that a local man had once tried to marry a particularly striking young prostitute—"white and fair"—but authorities supposedly refused him a license because she "had some Negro blood." The sorry legacy of a broken life was often passed down to the children of prostitutes as well. In the same house that Sarah Dickinson operated, her twelve-year-old daughter also entered the profession.

Beyond Griffin Avenue was a more conservative society that frowned on the dissolute lifestyles of its neighbors. The occasional trial for adultery and the formation of a temperance union in 1875 demonstrated the rigid moral standards that governed the rest of the community. Only the economic force behind the vices of prostitution, gambling, and unbroken revelry kept the local dives in business. Early in 1876 the *Dallas Daily Herald* reported that some upset citizens chased several of the most disreputable prostitutes out of town, "this done on the principle that bad meat draws flies." In June, when several more arrived to take their places, townsmen threatened them, too. A prominently posted notice, signed "Vigilance," read: "Leave or you are doomed." Evidently merchants checked their zealous neighbors; in September, a docile Griffinite registered a complaint in the *Fort Worth Democrat*, feebly pleading with the sheriff to appoint a deputy to control the rampant vice. The "hard-visaged," part-Indian Kate Gamel was certainly not intimidated by hollow threats. At her cramped adobe brothel that Henry Herron called "a known rendezvous for criminals," officers laid an ambush one dark evening. The outlaws reportedly escaped by spurring their horses over the bluff and into the swollen Collins Creek.

In this pitiable environment Charlotte Tompkins briefly enjoyed part control of a boarding house, the Gus, as well as a saloon. But even though she transcended the normal sphere of her gender, Tompkins could not escape the degrading consequences that attended a woman's entry into this male-dominated environment. More widely known as "the poker queen" Lottie Deno, she gained a reputation for her ladylike dress and the cool manner in which she relieved her rough patrons of their money. Yet just as men mistakenly attributed the raucous gaiety of prostitutes' lives for insouciance, they also misinterpreted Tompkins's aloof demeanor. She certainly shared the desperation of other women who worked on Griffin Avenue. Whether by dint of business acumen or simply because she had accumulated some working capital, Tompkins managed outwardly to earn a more honorable living. But where other saloon owners such as Hank Smith, Owen Donnely, and Charley Meyers were accepted socially, Griffinites shunned Charlotte Tompkins. On one occasion she registered her defiance by staging a "masque ball" while other townspeople gathered at a nearby hotel for a dance. Several old-timers nevertheless asserted that such strength of character was only superficial.

The tragic and impenetrable life of Tompkins invited speculation. Former sheriff John Jacobs called her "unapproachable" and claimed that "she had nothing to do with the common prostitutes." Just before she arrived at the Flat, however, a Jacksboro court had fined her $100 and costs for running a brothel. Supposedly she had worked other "fort towns" on the Texas frontier as well. Her circumstances at Griffin began to sour about the same time as the apparent murder of a tawdry young drifter, Johnnie Golden. Henry Herron commented that Golden was a "nice looking boy, had a little money to spend, and spent it freely." And although little evidence supported his claim, Herron asserted that "Lottie fell for him." Equally dubious was a rumor that she was the unwilling paramour of saloon keeper Dick Shaughnessey. Old-timers nevertheless asserted that the whiskey peddler became jealous and paid Constable Bill Gilson and an accomplice, Dan Draper, $250 to kill his supposed rival. The circumstances of Golden's death certainly implicated them. The pair claimed that they had served him an arrest warrant and were taking him to the post guardhouse, even though the local "calaboose" was only twenty yards away. Gilson and Draper further maintained that Golden's death came at the hands of "rescuers" who fired on them from a ravine; the powder burns on the dead man's body, however, cast doubt on the alibi. In any event, the citizens of Shackelford County "ran Gilson off" after a brief inquest.

Shortly afterward, Tompkins's business situation also deteriorated, forcing her hasty departure from Fort Griffin. For a woman to obtain a mortgage on a bar or brothel was really not so unusual, and neither were the consequences when she could not meet her financial obligations. Typically, courts in tolerant frontier towns overlooked illegal activities as long as participants squared their own affairs discreetly. But in January 1878, shortly after George Matthews brought suit against Tompkins for a $290 debt, she found herself fighting a second charge of "keeping a disorderly house." At first she refused to acknowledge the local court. Her stubbornness cost Owen Donnely and Charley Meyers five hundred dollars—the price of her forfeited bail. An arrest warrant soon compelled her to appear for trial, where a jury found her guilty on both counts. Tompkins appealed the pandering charge, but mounting attorneys' fees and the considerable sum that she still owed to her former confederates prompted her to take expedient measures. Rather than wait for the outcome of the new trial—which, ironically, cleared her—she simply fled.

Stribling and Kirkland, representing George Matthews, later traced Tompkins to Bracketville, adjoining Fort Clark. Unknowing sympathizers believed that Tompkins, still grieving over Johnny Golden, had finally had enough of Fort Griffin. Although the sketchy details surrounding her life as Lottie Deno eventually grew to mythical proportions, her departure was no more mysterious than that of any number of men and women who left town owing money or evading the justice system.

Just as the so-called "lady gambler" inspired exaggerations and even outright fabrications, other dubious tales circulated that probably had just enough basis in fact to seed Griffin's reputation for unequaled violence. Gunman Jeff Milton claimed that as he tried to break up a bar fight between two buffalo hunters, one of them shot the other, splattering Milton with "blood and brains." Jeff, according to his biographer, "learned right there the importance of tending to his own business." On another occasion, an inebriated "tough" supposedly killed a Tonkawa Indian and was simply thrown in the calaboose "until he sobered up." Another time a drunken Lipan Apache was said to have stumbled into a Griffin hotel, where a woman killed him for his disruptive behavior. And when a partially deaf man refused to acknowledge a deputy's order to halt, the lawman reportedly emptied his pistol into the man and then offered to bet that he could cover the bullet holes with a silver dollar. Soldiers also contributed to the list of unprovoked and uncorroborated killings: a post guard murdered a buffalo hunter; a lieutenant, who had lost all his poker money to an enlisted man, shot him in the back; and a recently discharged "Scotty" killed a soldier even as the victim's wife fell to her knees, begging him not to shoot. In each case nobody seemed particularly interested in bringing the killers to justice, nor did anyone mention that any of them ever served a day in jail.

In contrast to these doubtful reports, the court strove assiduously—but seldom satisfactorily—to bring murderers to justice. Between 1875 and 1881 the 12th District Court, which included the counties administratively attached to Shackelford, issued eleven warrants for suspected killers. No case better illustrated the court's persistence than a bill against J. E. Kennedy, who was jailed at Fort Griffin for the 1877 killing of a man on the buffalo range. When he escaped, Texas Rangers recaptured him. After a mistrial, a new jury sentenced him to hang; upon appeal he won a new trial and a change of venue. Finally, after two years of legal maneuvering, he received a sentence of ninety-nine years.

Some other cases, although ending badly, still merited the earnest attention of the court. When a man fired a shot through a saloon window, killing Thorndale man Andrew Brownlee, a coroner's inquest swiftly rounded up witnesses and conducted a thorough interrogation. Narrowing their list of suspects to drifter James Oglesby, a posse combed the town and surrounding area for him. Soon the pitch blackness of night ended the search, and Oglesby escaped, leaving a fugitive warrant on the docket along with an underlined notation left by the court's transcriber—MURDER!

Three years later the court was again unsuccessful when it tried Henry Cruger for killing quartermaster clerk June Leach. The case dragged on for more than a year before jurors finally issued a verdict of not guilty. The slaying evolved out of an argument at a billiard table when Leach accidentally stepped on Cruger, who rebuffed an apology with the admonition that he would "whip him" if it happened again. To the good fortune of the accused murderer, testimony conflicted about what happened next, but witnesses—subpoenaed from as far away as Mason County—agreed that after a brief fight Leach fell dead from Cruger's gunshot.

Even after the Flat's heyday waned, the court still had trouble securing murder convictions. The shooting of Jewish merchant "Cheap John" Marks in 1879 nevertheless stirred the court to conduct a scrupulous investigation. The "pesky drummer," as editor Robson once called him, had left town for the Panhandle owing money to Griffinite Frank Schmidt. Special deputy William King, accompanied by the creditor, went after Marks, and upon apprehending him about fifty miles from town, camped for the night. Schmidt claimed that while King was hunting turkey for their dinner, Marks had somehow secured a gun. When Schmidt supposedly attempted to seize the weapon, it discharged, fatally wounding Cheap John in the back. Hearing the shot, King raced back to camp. Skeptical over Schmidt's story, he left him to care for the unconscious and dying man and then went on to Fort Griffin, where he notified Texas Rangers. After Marks died, four Griffin-bound waggoners happened upon the scene and helped bury him, then carried Schmidt with them. A jury—after hearing the testimony and cross-examination of both Schmidt and King, as well as the statements of the four travelers—returned the supposed murderer his $5,000 bail and set him free.

Contrary to the perception of the Northwest Texas frontier as a place where violent acts were accepted casually, gratuitous killings were rare and violence was never taken lightly. For example, Griffinites held a public meeting in January 1877 to express sympathy to the families of two bystanders who were killed in a senseless crossfire. Several months later, at isolated Rath City, hunter Tom Lumpkins shot an unarmed man who had taken exception to his constant carping. As another man tried to subdue Lumpkins, bartender "Limpy Jim" Smith ran up and jerked him aside and then shot Lumpkins point-blank. The surly hunter, still firing, stumbled backwards out of the saloon, followed by Smith, who reportedly kept a stream of bullets flying as he came. At the bartender's insistence a group of men accompanied him to Fort Griffin, where he surrendered himself to authorities. With the sympathetic testimony of the other hunters, a grand jury decided not to prosecute.

While assiduously attempting to bring "deserving" killers to justice, local courts did not overlook the petty crimes that plagued the unstable frontier society. Many were the reports of minor thefts and the records of prosecutions. During the hot summer of 1875, for example, traveler Billy Smith, overcome by heat, awoke to discover that someone had gone through his pockets, robbing him of a lottery ticket, some tobacco, and his keys. County Clerk J. N. Masterson recounted another typical incident, complaining that a thief had broken into his office and stolen $4 in change. Another time a man named Christianson was arrested for breaking into the home of Mrs. Mary Mitchell and taking $165 in greenbacks and some silver. The court at all levels—justice of the peace, county, and district—prosecuted such indignities zealously. Thieves seemed always to be sitting in jails at Griffin and Albany or working on roads between the two towns. County Judge W. H. Ledbetter normally assessed sixty days to nine months for petty thefts. Judge Fleming was even harsher. In 1876 he sentenced one George Robinson to two years at hard labor in the state penitentiary for taking clothing valued at $49. The next year he meted out the same punishment to a man for stealing almost $500 and a butcher knife. Fleming prosecuted cases of swindling, forgery, and other non-violent crimes as well.

Still, the legal community was sometimes frustrated. Hurricane Bill Martin, for example, was a one-man crime wave. He constantly sparred with the courts but was seldom held accountable for his many illicit activities. He reportedly loaded wagons with buffalo hides from stacks lining the river bottom, then rode into town and sold them to the very men whom he had "fleeced." He was also believed to have been the leader of a gang of horse thieves, and ironically he was the only one who survived a vigilante roundup. A deposition recorded that after Sam Stinson accused him of stealing a watch and chain, Martin pulled out his army Colt and "dropped it down on his [Stinson's] head saying, 'You can't give me any such game.'" Somehow Martin was again found innocent. Extenuating circumstances in another case forced the court to try him for "discharging a firearm" instead of attempted murder. In several other cases he was charged with assault, forfeiting bonds, and trying to enter the underworld of gambling, liquor, and prostitution.

While the resolute efforts of the court faded in the minds of former Griffinites, memories of killings and the tales of men such as Hurricane Bill seemed to grow. One-time sheriff John Jacobs related to fellow officer Henry Herron that "conditions got so bad . . . he could not feel easy sleeping in the same place two nights in succession." Fort Griffin was "a veritable robber's hole," according to rancher Emmett Roberts. "They would throw a blanket over your head and take your money in a flash." A surveyor, C. U. Connellee, recalled that "of all the places I have ever been, that was the worst." Long familiar with the frontier, he asserted that "men who had committed crimes, and fleeing from the law often went as far as they could from civilization, and that was the end."

Nothing did more to burn indelibly the image of Fort Griffin as a violent frontier town than a fatal gunfight at Donnely and Carroll's saloon. The "Shooting Bee," as the spontaneous incident came to be known, emanated from a poorly handled confrontation between Griffin authorities and local ranch hands Billy Bland and Charley Reed. Befitting the image of drunken cowboys, the pair raced their horses down Griffin Avenue, guns ablazing. Entering the Bee Hive, they interrupted dancers by trying to shoot out the lights. As Bland was taking aim on another fixture, Deputy Bill Cruger, accompanied by County Attorney Robert Jeffries, barged into the saloon and demanded that the revelers "put up their hands." The abrupt order provoked Bland into wheeling around and firing in the deputy's direction. When Cruger started shooting, both Jeffries and Reed joined the sharp firefight. The lawman and attorney sustained minor wounds; two bystanders were less fortunate. Newlywed Dan Barrow, shot through the forehead, died instantly. As a Lieutenant Myers tried to flee, he suffered a mortal wound in the back. As for the instigator, Billy Bland, a bullet passed completely through his body, leaving him writhing on the floor. Some men took him to the Occidental Hotel, where "Aunt Hank" Smith said "the poor fellow begged to be killed." According to Phin Reynolds, "Reed left the country that night."

For such a wide-open town, the legal system generally executed its duties in a credible manner. Few times did peace officers experience such mortal tumults as did Deputy Cruger. In fact, a former Griffinite recalled that "no man ever became so bad but that he might land in the 'calaboose' if the marshal so decided." Zeno Hemphill, a would-be badman, might have agreed. In 1878 he and some other cowboys had reportedly planned to kill special deputies Henry Herron and Dave Barker for nothing more than the notoriety. The two officers, appointed to help keep order during a meeting of the Northwest Cattle Raisers' Association, learned of the plot and waited in a crowded saloon for their supposed executioners. When Hemphill knocked a woman backward with the intention of starting a brawl, Herron grabbed the man's six-shooter and "whacked him over the head." Barker then pulled his own gun and covered the crowd while Herron hustled Hemphill off to jail.

Henry Herron, reflecting on his Griffin days, remarked that the calaboose was always occupied. "They were in there for every kind of offense, ranging from fighting to horse stealing and murder, but not many for murder." A jailer normally escorted prisoners to a blacksmith, who fit them for shackles; at night they were chained to the wall. If assaults were common, so were assault charges. The justice of the peace did not keep records, but the district court issued twenty-four warrants for such crimes between 1875 and 1880. Many of the accused simply fled town, and the legal community was probably satisfied to be rid of them. And while a few fought the charges and won, most lost and faced fifty-dollar to one-hundred-dollar fines. Still others earned jail time. Robert Brown, for example, was sentenced to two years' hard labor at the state penitentiary for "assault with intent to kill."

Despite a generally credible record, the law at times was ineffective. Vigilantes, composed of both court-appointed officials and respected citizens, ran amok during 1876, executing almost a score of suspected horse and cattle thieves. A succession of sheriffs, responsible for the entire county, did not often have the time nor the inclination to concentrate on controlling Griffin's transient revelers. Townspeople begged in vain for the court to appoint a deputy to control the gangs of raucous buffalo hunters and trail drivers, but finally had to hire a local officer at their own expense. Jet Kenan remarked that even then "a man had to act very, very badly to be molested by the 'marshal.'" Certainly the violent death of Johnny Golden undermined the reputation of the local legal community. His killers were never brought to trial. The elaborate story that Gilson and Draper told of a "lost" warrant and a three-o'clock-in-the-morning shootout kept the officers out of jail, but also made the court appear indifferent.

Where African Americans were concerned, the law also broke down, but only because it reflected the attitude of the Anglo-dominated society. Joe McCombs claimed that a drunk hunter once burst into the mess hall at the post and fired over the heads of some buffalo soldiers, prompting them to flee. When troops cornered the hunter, Sheriff John Larn convinced the commander to release the man into his custody and afterward let him go. Another time, when a black soldier full of "tarantula juice" shot his gun in the street and declared that he could "smash any 'white descendant of a female canine' in town," officers allowed some irate townsmen to take care of the matter. In buoyant prose a correspondent for the *Fort Worth Daily Democrat* wrote that "by careful maneuvering he at length succeeded in acquiring a 'head' of gigantic dimensions, and was forced to make a retrograde movement on the Fort." The dispatch ended with the comment: "No arrests."

Regarding violence that occurred entirely among African Americans, local authorities throughout Texas routinely turned their backs. Fort Griffin was no exception. For example, an exchange of gunfire between two black men at the Clear Fork crossing went unaddressed, even though one of them, Joe Brandt, was gravely wounded.

Another racial incident, although it occurred after Griffin's wildest days had passed, demonstrated both the court's insistence on following "proper legal procedure" and its attitude toward African Americans. In 1879, Captain S. H. Lincoln, on the eve of his transfer to another post, shot and killed black infantryman Charles McCafferty. The private had escaped the guardhouse, where he had been confined for habitual drunkenness, and headed for town. He promptly became inebriated again, and upon spotting the captain at Conrad and Rath's, he unleashed a verbal assault that ended when the army officer physically removed him from the store. The drunken soldier—in front of everybody in town—then knocked the officer off the sidewalk with a roundhouse punch to the jaw. The ignominious blow prompted Lincoln to draw his pistol and shoot the impudent McCafferty, who died the next day. Despite being released on a two-thousand-dollar bond, the captain left Fort Griffin for his new assignment, forcing Texas Rangers to bring him in. A preliminary hearing bound him over for the "felonious" murder of Charles McCafferty, but in the civil trial Judge Fleming reminded the jury that murder was distinguished from manslaughter by "malice aforethought." The lesser charge, he advised, could also be mitigated by "provocation." In his own defense, Lincoln reportedly declared that his action was "the only dignified course to pursue." Evidently, the jury agreed and found the captain "not guilty."

Certainly, violence and any number of petty crimes and vices underscored the instability of Fort Griffin's boomtown environment. Nevertheless, rough but otherwise unmenacing people and a lighter side of life also represented "wildness" in this frontier society. Buffalo hunters and cattle drivers, little concerned about manners and morals, descended in raucous packs upon Fort Griffin after long periods with little human contact. More frolicsome than reckless, they typically spent a few harmless days and nights of unbridled revelry before resuming their monotonous routines. Skinners and nonprofessionals among the hunters and a handful of "maverick" drovers caused most of the trouble that gave the two groups their undeserved reputation for violence. Rootless opportunists, itinerant pioneers, and people from the interior who ached for a little excitement and some quick money also contributed to occasional lawlessness. Yet even among these largely anonymous men and women, very few came West intending to launch a career outside of the law.

Typical of many buffalo hunters was "Charlie," who traveled to Griffin at the head of his crew when the season ended in 1875. After cashing a large check at Conrad's store, he paid his men, and they camped with about thirty other outfits under the big pecan trees lining the Clear Fork. "I never intended to get drunk," he said, "but what could a fellow do?" According to a friend, Charlie "had a glorious spree"—twenty-one days long, in fact. Once, after he had passed out, some of his men set a stuffed panther over him. When the hunter awoke and saw the beast staring down at him he lurched backward into the river and had to be "fished out."

Cowboys had their fun, too. Frontiersman Jim Gordon recounted that a pretentious Englishman once arrived at Griffin and hired two men to escort him to the ranch of a countryman. Word reached some herders farther up the trail, who prepared a reception as the "lord" and his guides made camp for the evening. With whoops and gunshots, the cowboys pulled the Englishman's well-appointed wagon into a creek. Boldly he emerged in cap and gown, brandishing a small pistol, only to face a dozen gun-wielding "desperadoes" trying hard to suppress an explosion of laughter. After reaching his destination, the Englishman endured further indignities such as affectedly rough language and manners and the sight of the cook dishing out supper in a pair of the visitor's own kneepants. "He was mad as a hornet," Gordon recalled fondly. "Many were the tricks we played on him but eventually he came to be naturalized and proved a jolly good fellow."

Such earthy amusements were typical in an environment where large numbers of unattached men did "manly" things together. Few places gained a greater reputation than Fort Griffin as an oasis where frontiersmen could enjoy themselves unencumbered by conventional social pressures. And not all the fun was just drinking, gambling, and prostitution. Jet Kenan recalled that "many times saloons sent for me to participate in boxing matches . . . or to preside over a 'Kangaroo Court.'"

Dancing and "varieties" were more common forms of entertainment. "Frank Smith & Co. have completed their music hall in Fort Griffin and have secured the services of ten or twelve well known *artistes*," the *Echo* reported in 1876. "They are performing nightly to crowded and delighted audiences."

Concerning a prominent local merchant, Captain Robson chided: "We noticed Caleb Cupp one day this week amusing himself by holding two Tom-cats up by their tails, while the cats amused themselves by picking fur from each other." Pitting animals against each other was always a crowd pleaser. Another time the editor noted that "next Saturday there will be a fight at this place, between a young black bear and Hemphill's two bull dogs, for $50 a side." He did not follow up the report, but presumably the dogs won. A few weeks later the *Echo* reported that Mr. Chifflet, the local tanner, "has a bear skin robe which is a beauty."

Another favorite diversion was horse racing. Stabler Pete Haverty often staged contests at a track across the river. Like many of his patrons, however, he was often in debt because of his losses. In the fall of 1876 the *Fort Worth Daily Democrat* reported that local tough John Selman and bootlegger Jack Greathouse had declared John Larn the winner in a close race—by precisely three inches. "Some dissatisfaction was manifested at the decision," reported the correspondent, adding that bettors were incredulous at the judges' "being endowed with vision of such mathematical nicety, as to be able to determine the exact number of inches the winning horse was ahead at the string."

Like the cowboys who found sport in the Englishman's misery, men who idled countless hours at Fort Griffin found that a ruse or practical joke could provide an amusement that demanded repeated tellings long after the event. "Uncle Billy" Wilson seemed always to be working on a scheme. Jet Kenan claimed that Wilson once concocted a "wonder cement" that he matched against all comers—"Old Hickory, Spauldings, and others." He appeared to patch up some broken dishes with the competing glues and then dropped them all into boiling water. Soon every dish had come apart—except those mended with Uncle Billy's secret compound. According to Kenan the trick was that a friend of Wilson, an accomplished engraver, had etched matching lines on the top and bottom of some china that looked remarkably like cracks. Since few people washed china in boiling water, his scheme worked.

On another occasion Edgar Rye, editor of the *Albany Tomahawk*, fell for a practical joke that Captain Robson could not resist reporting. Rye, upon learning that a woman from Fort Worth had just arrived in town searching for another woman's husband, wrote a few indignant lines, ending with the demand, "Explain!" A few days later the supposed out-of-towner confronted Rye, demanding that *he* explain. As the editor rose to offer an alibi, he looked up into the muzzle of a gun. Aghast, the floundering Rye lost his hat and glasses, then tripped over his stool. Rising to his knees, he begged her not to shoot. Suddenly the "woman" and a group of men standing at the window burst into laughter. His antagonist, it turned out, was a townsman "in drag."

As Rye could attest, Fort Griffin was not the only Texas frontier town to see bawdy action, and neither did it have a corner on lawlessness. Pranksters at the county seat exploded a barber pole with gunpowder, to which Captain Robson lamented: "the old striped sign is seen no more in the land." And, as Albany began to intercept some of the trailing business in the spring of 1879, it also reaped some of the unpleasantries. "Every day or two," the *Echo* reported, fist-fights had erupted. "Someone would appear on the streets with a black eye or banged up nose," but as in Fort Griffin the law swiftly put an end to it.

Ironically, Frank Conrad's daughter had left the county before she became a crime victim. Between Fort Worth and Weatherford stage robbers relieved her of one hundred dollars. Virtually every edition of the *Echo*, the *Fort Worth Daily Democrat*, and the *Dallas Daily Herald* carried stories from around the state that comprised a woeful record of crime. Robson complained that Northerners viewed Texas as a "community of murderers and robbers." Blaming frontier conditions and the ubiquitous carrying of weapons, he admitted that his fellow citizens were a law-breaking people "to a fearful extent." B. B. Paddock of the *Democrat* was more defensive, asserting that Texas was not alone in experiencing violent acts. Economic times, he declared, had "thrown upon the country hundreds and thousands of men who, having no families or homes, become reckless and careless, and are wandering over the country depredating upon the rights of others and committing acts of violence."

In the public perception, as in fact, Fort Griffin was nevertheless among the toughest spots on a tough frontier. To contemporaries, distance and unfamiliarity no doubt caused imaginations to magnify the image of lawlessness. The tunnel of memory likewise inflated the level of violence, the colorful descriptions, and fond reminiscences of an otherwise bleak and harsh environment. Fort Griffin in part earned its reputation; violence touched nearly every segment of society, and when trailers hit town, no one could avoid hearing hoots, hollers, and gunfire as they spurred their frenzied horses up and down Griffin Avenue. But revelers most often knew how far they could push local authorities, and more violent offenders knew that when they acted, consequences would surely follow.

Annie Black and the Soiled Doves of San Angelo

SUZANNE CAMPBELL

SUZANNE CAMPBELL IS HEAD ARCHIVIST OF THE WEST TEXAS COLLECTION AT ANGELO STATE UNIVERSITY IN SAN ANGELO.

IN THIS SELECTION, CAMPBELL DISCUSSES THE HISTORY OF PROSTITUTION IN SAN ANGELO. SHE DETAILS THE CAREERS OF SUCCESSFUL MOTHER AND DAUGHTER MADAMS ANNIE BLACK AND BIRDIE AYERS.

Conditions in early day San Angelo have been the subject of numerous stories. John A. Loomis, Concho County rancher, wrote one such account in his memoirs, a place he described this way: "As a natural (of being near the Fort) the saloons, gambling houses and houses of prostitution catered to the army . . . Killings were so common that they occasioned little comment."

Loomis also described early attempts at law enforcement and judicial practice. The first courts were crude at best. Some of the early elected officials were illiterate and without any knowledge of the law. Dr. Escal Duke, long time member of this organization, once related the story of the

"Annie Black and The Soiled Doves of San Angelo" by Suzanne Campbell from *The West Texas Historical Association Yearbook* Vol. LXXXIII, Oct. 2007, Volume 83, pp. 45–53.

first lawyer to hung up his shingle in San Angelo. Not smitten by the prospects of law and order, a group of cowboys and gamblers held a kangaroo court and decided the lawyer had fifteen minutes to leave town. When the attorney learned of the decision, he told the "jury" he would give them back five of the fifteen minutes.

The first sheriff of Tom Green County, Frank LaMott, was a popular gambler and "a gentlemanly fellow" according to Loomis. A few citizens of the county complained about his profession and suggested he should quit gambling or resign. LaMott resigned—gambling was much more profitable.

Loomis described J. G. Preusser, an early county judge, as intelligent saying his decisions were "just, if somewhat 'illegal' at times." Once when he made a decision that the officer of the court said was not in accordance with the law, Preusser allegedly answered, "Damn the law . . . It's justice we want."

Little wonder prostitution went unchecked in San Angelo for years. With the establishment of Fort Concho in 1867, the first of San Angelo's soiled doves arrived. They were the women who accompanied the military to the frontier—camp followers and laundresses.

Each troop at the post was allowed four laundresses who received government rations and were paid for washing men's clothing. Dr. W. F. Buchanan, post surgeon, reported problems with several of the black laundresses in the summer of 1875. He filed on three for what he considered their "utter worthlessness, Drunkness [sic], and Lewdness."

The women removed from the fort grounds frequently found their way across the river to San Angelo where they mixed with others who gathered to relieve soldiers of their pay. There was no effort in Tom Green County to control any of the previously mentioned vices until 1880, and that effort seemed to be based more on economies than morality.

In his book, *The Gentle Tamers*, Dee Brown described how the women of easy virtue filled a void on the frontier where women were scarce. The saloon and the ladies who frequented them were often the only home many of the men knew. They provided a modicum of civilization "whether the males were aware of it or not."

District Court Case No. 22 of Tom Green County, filed at Benficklin on 25 August 1880, is the first surviving case lodged against a group of females for vagrancy. Vagrancy was the legally accepted term for prostitution. In April 1892, the *San Angelo Standard* published City Ordinance No. 14 defining vagrancy. Among those considered vagrants were: a person who "strolls about to tell fortunes, exhibit tricks not licensed by law;" a common prostitute; a professional gambler; any person who goes about the streets begging alms but is not afflicted or disabled; and an habitual drunkard. Punishment for any of the above was a fine of not less than $2.50 or more than $10.00. The majority of the early charges of vagrancy can be traced back to one of two offenses—prostitution or gambling.

Court Case No. 22 listed the sixteen ladies who were picked up and charged. Of these, two were or had been married, at least one was black, and one was the well known "Rowdy Kate." The case charged that they were idle persons living without any visible means of support, and "being then and there common prostitutes against the peace and dignity of the state." From then until the turn of the century, the ladies of the evening, along with the owners of gaming tables, were routinely picked up twice a year and fined. Once they paid their fines, all returned to work. The fine was viewed in much the same manner as the occupation tax imposed on business men and women in the county.

To give an idea of the scope of taxable vices, in September 1885, the *Standard* reported on the Grand Jury indictments for Tom Green County. The list included twenty-five charged with unlawfully exhibiting a gaming table, twenty-nine for vagrancy, and thirteen for keeping a disorderly house, defined as a place where prostitutes or lewd women were allowed to enter. It was also reported that all vagrancy cases would be transferred to the Justice Court, and all gambling cases to the County Court.

Into this den of iniquity came a woman, a wife and mother, whose "working name" was Annie Black. Her legal name, according to family sources, was Rachel Angelyne Francis or Franca. She married John Ayers and had four children: Alfred, William, James, and Birdie. What happened to John Ayers is unknown, nor do we know why Rachel turned to prostitution. Rachel appeared in Tom Green County as Annie Black on July 29, 1891, when she was picked up and charged with vagrancy.

In a rather unusual action, Peter Crane was called as a witness for the State against Annie Black. He was asked by the county attorney whether or not in the past ten years he had had "carnal intercourse with the defendant Annie Black which question Peter Crane refused to answer and for which offense said Peter Crane is fined by the court for contempt of court and his punishment assessed at a fine of twenty-five dollars, and one days imprisonment." Interesting enough, no further mention was made of Annie Black or the charges against her!

Annie must have been a good business woman. On September 16, 1899, Annie Black bought, for $600, Lot 6 of Block 10 on West Concho Avenue in the town of San Angelo. She paid $50 cash and financed the remainder with eleven promissory notes of $50 each. The property was paid off by April 1902. This lot corresponds to the home where Annie and her girls lived on West Concho Avenue. Exactly one year later in 1900, Annie purchased the lot next door for $200.

Located directly behind this portion of West Concho was an alley known locally as "The Alley of Ill-Fame." For two blocks, lots were divided in half: those lots facing the street and those facing the alley. Obviously, the alley lots were much cheaper to buy. It was along the alley that transients and poorer prostitutes lived and worked. The majority of San Angelo's brothels at this time were located in these two blocks of West Concho. The soiled doves were "encouraged" to stay in this general area, and proper ladies never ventured in their space. Despite this unwritten law, there were sections of town where the two did mix. For instance, in the 1900 census, the enumerator listed Crickett Guess, a twenty year old white prostitute, living next door to J. W. Timmons, the district judge.

For Bennie Miskimmon, the ladies were an important source of revenue. In 1893 Bennie opened a millinery and dressmaking business when the family ranch was in jeopardy due to drought. She developed a system for taking orders from the ladies of Concho Avenue. She sent pictures and scraps of material, and the ladies chose what they wanted. A young African American boy took the orders and delivered the goods since it would have been improper for her to do so. According to Bennie, "Their money was as good as anyone else's and they had a lot of money."

The 1900 census listed Annie operating a boarding house at the West Concho location. Her two boarders, however, were listed as prostitutes. One was her daughter, Birdie, who went by the name Clarence Rose.

Annie Black was arrested and charged with vagrancy on numerous occasions despite the fact that she would have been considered a madam. Apparently, she was a "working madam" since most of the other ladies operating boarding houses in the same block were not picked up. After the turn of the century, the round ups of ladies and gamblers became quarterly. The fines remained the same, but the county doubled its revenue.

Other than her arrests, Annie Black remains unknown to history until 1906. On April 16, 1906, Annie Black sold her property on West Concho to her daughter, Birdie Ayers, a.k.a. Clarence Rose, and signed her will on the same day. The deed record states that Annie Black, "of Tom Green County for $6,000 paid in hand by Birdie Ayers (who is commonly known as Clarence Rose)" sold Lots 5 and 6 in Block 10 "together with the house and all improvements situated on said lots on either of them, and also all of the furniture, household furnishings and fixtures in said building, of every kind, character and nature what so ever, save and except the personal effects of said Annie Black."

Annie Black was arrested during the first three quarters of 1907. The next time Annie appeared in the records of Tom Green County was on January 28, 1909, when she died and was buried in Fairmount Cemetery in San Angelo. At the time of her death, Annie Black had real and personal property of $1,000. Wright and Wynn, San Angelo attorneys, indicated that she was "indebted to divers parties, for expenses of her last sickness and her funeral expenses." The exact amount of her debts were unknown at that time. Clarence Rose, not Birdie Ayers, filed application to probate the last will and testament of Annie Black on February 20, 1909. Clarence Rose was named executrix without bond.

By April 5, 1909, opposition had mounted to the will of Annie Black. The first to file was Mrs. Allie E. Cox and husband, Arthur. She produced documents in court showing that she was the daughter of Annie Black. In addition she had a will she claimed was written by Annie Black. Through her attorney, John J. Cox of Goldthwaite, she claimed that Annie Black had been induced to sign the will filed by Clarence Rose. The court rejected her claim.

A few weeks later on April 23, 1909, Alfred Moses Ayers, William Wallace Ayers, and James Madison Ayers, children and heirs of Annie Black, opposed the will. First they denied she had executed the will. Then, they claimed Birdie Ayers had coerced Annie to sign the document in question since their mother was not of sufficient mental capacity to understand.

The two men who witnessed the signing of Black's will, Clarence Smith and S. B. Runyon, both testified that indeed the mark on the paper, along with their signatures, were made when Annie, about age fifty-five, was of sound mind. Throughout the will Annie Black referred to

Birdie Ayers as her good and faithful friend. There was never any acknowledgment that Birdie was her daughter. In a statement given in June 1927, Birdie stated "That she was well acquainted with Annie Black from 1895 to long after April 16, 1906." She, too, gave no indication of their relationship.

Three men appointed by the court appraised the personal property of the deceased. Their inventory included a diamond ring valued at $125, a diamond broach for $100, and six suits of clothing valued at $100. The total value of the estate was $835, and her expenses were $557 leaving $278 for her daughter.

Annie Black's daughter, Birdie Ayers, followed in her mother's occupation. Birdie was born May 4, 1880, to John D. and Angelina Ayers. Her first arrest in San Angelo came in February 1900, under the name of Clarence Black. From that point on she was listed in court documents as Clarence Rose. Her last arrest in Tom Green County was in July 1907.

The social standing of the women on the frontier was basically divided into two classes: those who were soiled doves and those who were not. There was no mingling of the two. But from time to time in most communities across the West, a lady of the evening married a local man. Sometimes the marriage proved successful, but at times they were cut short by divorce or death. For example, the *Standard* on July 30, 1887 told of the suicide of one Henry Dierks who had married Mrs. Anna Pierce only days before. The new wife was described as "a nymph du pave." The day they married, the bride went to the fort to ply her trade. The groom went after her and took her home. The next day Dierks told her he would take poison if she went back. She did and he did.

Family stories say Birdie married a well-to-do store owner who died and left her some money with which she bought property. No records have been found to support this notion. After buying Annie's property, Birdie began acquiring other real estate in San Angelo. Her first purchase was three lots in the Park Heights Addition for $800. The only condition to the purchase was that any house erected on the property could not cost less than $1,500.

The next year Birdie purchased two additional lots and part of another on West Concho for $3,000. These lots were located on the south side of the avenue, ran to the bank of the Concho River, and faced the original property bought from Annie Black.

In July 1909, Birdie leased her property that included a two-story frame home with twelve rooms to Bobbie McGregor. McGregor, like Birdie, was a madam and operated the house as a brothel. The lease ran from July 12, 1909 to July 11, 1911, for a price of $1,800. McGregor paid $150 at the signing and $75 per month. At the time Birdie signed the lease she was a single woman. Apparently, she was thinking ahead because by September of 1909 she had married John Walter Reese of El Paso. Reese served as a Texas Ranger (Special Enlistment) and was also a police inspector in El Paso.

The marriage did not last long, and their divorce was granted on March 24, 1910, in El Paso. Their property was separated. Included in her property was a black mare named "Ruby" and her eight month old colt. These were to be delivered from the property at Columbus, Texas, owned by Reese, to Birdie's brother William at Clairmont, Texas.

Birdie returned to San Angelo and resumed her business. However, in October 1914, in Los Angeles, California, she married Joyce A. (Curley) Shield, the son of Tom Green County Sheriff, Gerome Shield. This was an abusive marriage, and they separated March 1, 1915. The couple had a four month old son, Champ B. Shield, born in Del Rio, Texas. The divorce was granted February 1, 1916, and she received custody of the child.

Sometime after the divorce, Curley Shield and Birdie Ayers had a daughter, Angelyne Shield, born in April 1917, in San Angelo. It is not known if they were married at the time. Though unsubstantiated, the family said that Champ, while a toddler, became ill and died. Birdie blamed Curley for his death, which caused the divorce. Angelyne continued to live with her mother, although she remembered as a child going to visit the Shield family who were not particularly cordial.

Prior to 1920, Birdie Ayers married Hubert Wolters of San Angelo. They had one daughter in 1920 and in 1925 were living in the house where Annie and Birdie had worked. In 1927 Birdie and H. E. Wolters, who were then living in Lomita, California, sold property in San Angelo. Birdie bought two lots in the Miles Addition of San Angelo in February 1928, but sold them in December of that same year.

During the Depression Birdie lost her remaining property in San Angelo, divorced Mr. Wolters, and moved in with her brother, William and his family, who then lived in Yuma, Arizona. He worked for the Bureau of Reclamation. Birdie spent her remaining years in California near her two daughters and her brothers. She spoke little of her early life in San Angelo. She died January 22, 1958, in Los Angeles.

San Angelo never dealt harshly with her soiled doves. In fact, in 1914 the newspaper reported that the court system had "difficulties in getting up juries on account of the unwillingness of men to serve with the prospect of having to decide in favor of the law in prostitution cases." The number of ladies fluctuated with the economy of the city. Boom periods such as the fort days, World War I and II, and the oil boom, all saw an increase in the number of soiled doves. Today, one of the city's favorite tourist attractions is Miss Hattie's Brothel Museum. It is a monument to a portion of history that is often overlooked. The red light districts and the ladies who inhabited them are just as much a part of the history of the frontier as the soldiers, buffalo hunters, cowboys, outlaws, and ordinary citizens who made San Angelo and West Texas what it is today.

"The Town Is Gone":

Indianola Hurricanes, 1875 and 1886

MIKE COX

FORMER COMMUNICATIONS MANAGER FOR THE TEXAS DEPARTMENT OF TRANSPORTATION, JOURNALIST, AND SCHOLAR, MIKE COX IS THE AUTHOR OF A NUMBER OF BOOKS, INCLUDING *THE TEXAS RANGERS: WEARING THE CINCO PESO, 1821–1900*, *TIME OF THE RANGERS: TEXAS RANGERS FROM 1900 TO THE PRESENT*, AND *TEXAS DISASTERS: TRUE STORIES OF TRAGEDY AND SURVIVAL*.

LOCATED ON MATAGORDA BAY, INDIANOLA PLAYED AN IMPORTANT ROLE IN LONE STAR HISTORY. THE SECOND BUSIEST PORT (AFTER GALVESTON) IN TEXAS, IT BOASTED A POPULATION OF 5,000 AND SERVED AS THE SEAT OF GOVERNMENT FOR CALHOUN COUNTY. BUT MISFORTUNE—IN THE FORM OF DEVASTATING HURRICANES—STRUCK TWICE IN JUST ELEVEN YEARS, CAUSING THE TOWN'S DEMISE. THE INDIANOLA TRAGEDY SHOULD HAVE SERVED AS A CAUTIONARY TALE FOR GALVESTONIANS, 150 MILES UP THE COAST, WHO WOULD FACE THEIR OWN DISASTER IN 1900.

★ ★

Sitting at their rolltop desks penning articles for the next edition, the staff of the *Galveston Daily News* had no shortage of local news on September 21, 1875. Less than a week before, their city had taken a glancing blow from a powerful hurricane. Caught in the storm, the steamship *City of Waco* had gone down in the bay with the loss of fifty-five souls. But Galveston had been on the fringe of the storm, which the U.S. Army Signal Service now believed had done its worst damage farther down the coast from the prosperous island port.

Suddenly, the tempo of city sounds coming through the *Daily News* building's open window changed. Looking outside the window to see what all the commotion was about, Editor-in-Chief D. C. Jenkins saw people hurrying toward the docks. He and others in the building quickly joined the crowd and soon heard the news: A ship flying her flag at half-staff had cleared the sandbar at the entrance to the bay.

Onlookers ranging from bankers to dray drivers stood anxiously on the pier as crew members of the *Harlan*, one of the Morgan Line's steamships, tossed their lines. They knew something tragic had happened. Then someone shouted stunning news. Indianola, 150 miles down coast from Galveston, had been devastated by the hurricane. Scores had been killed, and many others were reported missing.

The *Harlan*'s master hurried ashore and personally delivered a letter to the newspaper from W. H. (Jim) Crain, the district attorney in Indianola.

"We are destitute," the hastily written message began. "The town is gone. One-tenth of the population . . . gone. Dead bodies are strewn for twenty miles along the bay. Nine-tenths of the houses are destroyed. Send us help, for God's sake."

The *Harlan*'s arrival confirmed what had been a growing concern. With the telegraph connection to Indianola dead, Galvestonians had assumed that the worst of the storm must have been toward the middle of the coast. Nothing had been heard from Indianola since September 15, the day the storm had battered Galveston with gale-force winds, heavy rain, and high water.

Soon more grim news made its way to Galveston. "Many of our acquaintances and friends are drowned," Indianola businessman Henry Seeligson wrote. "The writer is thoroughly exhausted, having been out with a burying party all last night, but will have to go down the bay this evening again to bury others."

In 1875 an estimated 5,000 people lived in Indianola, a city on Matagorda Bay. As the state's second-busiest port, Indianola enjoyed a flourishing commerce. But proximity to the sea comes with a high price.

On Wednesday, September 15, Indianola had bustled with more than the normal level of activity. A spectacular murder trial was under way at the Calhoun County courthouse, with Bill Taylor facing a possible death sentence for the March 11, 1874, shooting in Indianola of William Sutton and his friend Gabriel Slaughter. The killing had been the most recent outbreak of violence in an ongoing grudgefest that came to be known as the Sutton-Taylor feud. With partisans of both factions in town for the trial, tension ran high.

But as lawyers prepared their opening arguments, trouble of another sort bore down on Indianola. Through telegraphic reports, the U.S. Army's Signal Service headquarters in Washington had been following the progress of a tropical cyclone that had blown past Haiti and Cuba and now churned somewhere in the Gulf of Mexico.

As testimony continued in the Taylor trial, a strong wind blew from the east. Atmospheric moisture created a halo around the sun before it disappeared. Under a gray sky, the barometric pressure began dropping. Clearly the coast was in for a blow, but no one in Indianola seemed particularly concerned.

That changed on Thursday morning, when heavy waves broke on a normally placid bay shore. The wind began to howl, and by noon water surged across Main Street "like a mill race." Using rowboats, people began relocating to the northern side of town as businessmen removed cash and assorted valuables from their safes. The barometer continued to fall.

Planks from what had been Indianola's wharves now battered against the sides of buildings in the ever-rising storm surge. Soon the buildings along Water Street began collapsing.

People needed to get to higher ground. But the storm surge had already cut off the roads. At the railroad station a passenger train sat on the tracks, unable to get out of town; its steam boiler had been drained and could not be refilled because salt water had washed into the depot's cistern.

Even with water covering the floor of the jail, Sheriff F. L. Busch refused to move the prisoners, including Taylor. District Attorney Crain, thinking Taylor more properly deserved hanging than drowning, took the keys from the sheriff's office and let Taylor and two other prisoners out on their promise that they would not try to escape.

A short time later, with deputies preoccupied by the worsening storm, Taylor broke his promise, fleeing town on stolen horses. After reaching higher ground, the accused murderer thoughtfully left the horse behind and proceeded on foot.

Though Taylor had only his own safety in mind, others did all they could to save their fellow townspeople. Jim Crain had fought Yankees during the Civil War as a soldier in Terry's Texas Rangers. Astride a big, black horse, he carried as many people as he could to higher ground. Struggling to hold onto his strong horse, people clutched Crain's saddle and stirrups. Some clung to the horse's tail as the veteran cavalryman half-swam his mount to safety.

Seeligson also rode his horse through the wind-blown rain, his face stinging like he had been slapped. Finally making it to his house, he jumped from the exhausted animal and put his family in a wagon, still hoping to make it to higher ground. After only a few blocks, he realized he could go no farther.

"The waters were . . . full six feet deep and running at a fearful rate," he later recalled. Somehow, he and his family made it to the courthouse, where they rode out the storm.

Elsewhere in town, many people were not as fortunate. From the sturdy, stone courthouse, Seeligson and others watched as the storm swept a building with more than thirty people inside out into the wild waters of Powderhorn Bayou. Two-thirds of them drowned.

Suddenly the water broke through the door of the courthouse, forcing the Seeligsons and everyone else inside to scurry upstairs to the second floor.

"The building, although constructed . . . of the stoutest masonry, with foundation six feet deep and five in diameter, rocked as though an earthquake was in progress," Seeligson remembered.

"The rushing of the waters through the lower doors and windows and the [wind] was so deafening that one could scarcely hear his own voice."

The most tragic news story of his career swirling around him, *Indianola Bulletin* editor C. A. Ogsbury had to think of his family first. With his wife and two children and his mother-in-law, he watched the devastation from the second-floor window of neighbor R. D. Martin's residence. "The situation was awful," Ogsbury later wrote. "Screams from women and children could be heard in every direction."

At 5 P.M. that day, Sergeant C. A. Smith recorded a barometric reading of 28.90 and a wind speed of 82 mph. Fifteen minutes later the cups of the anemometer blew away, the last reading showing 86 mph.

Early Friday morning the winds finally died down as the hurricane moved farther inland. When the storm surge receded, Indianola lay in ruins. Only eight buildings, one of them being the courthouse, had survived the wind and water. Bodies lay scattered as far as 20 miles from town, along with dead livestock and pets.

An estimated 270 persons died in the storm, but with Indianola cut off from the rest of the state, it took a while for news of the tragedy to spread. The first ship to reach the wrecked city, the *Harlan*, immediately made for Galveston with the district attorney's urgent plea for help.

After a twelve-hour ride, a reporter for the Victoria newspaper finally reached Indianola at 9 A.M. on Sunday, September 19. Based on the journalist's dispatches, the *Advocate* hit the streets with this stacked headline:

> ***Indianola!***
> ***Thursday's Storm!***
> ***A Day of Danger***
> ***And Night of Horror!***

"It is difficult even to identify where many of the buildings [had] stood," the article reported.

Indianola rebuilt, but it never fully recovered from the 1875 storm. And eleven years later another hurricane devastated the port city.

On August 18, 1886, Signal Service observed Isaac Reed received a wire from Washington: A hurricane had entered the Gulf of Mexico and likely would bring gale force winds to the eastern Gulf coast. Indianola being on the western side of the Gulf, the government did not order Reed to raise his station's storm flag.

That instruction did come the following day, but by then, it made no real difference. Although a minimal hurricane, the storm caused maximum damage to Indianola. "Buildings which stoutly withstood the great cyclone of 1875, went down as if made of pasteboard," the *Victoria Advocate* reported eight days later.

As had been the case eleven years before, Indianola had no shortage of heroes.

Captain Reed stayed in the Signal Service station all night, recording the rising wind and falling barometric pressure and telegraphing the numbers to Washington.

John S. Munn, an attorney from Victoria, had been in town that Thursday for a court case. The howling of a cat awakened him shortly after 1 A.M. on Friday. "A seething, foaming torrent passed through the streets," he recalled, "buildings tottered for a moment, trembled, groaned, and in a twinkling disappeared in the spray and darkness." Leaving his hotel, Munn made his way across town. "The spray cut the flesh like shot," he said.

"Boys, come up and help me close the back door," he heard Captain Reed shout from the building that housed his office. Inside, Munn found Reed still taking observations by the light of a lamp as telegraph operator L. H. Woodworth tapped out the numbers. Also riding out the storm in the frame government building were Dr. H. Rosencranz, T. D. Woodward of the U.S. Customs Service, and W. J. Morrison.

"Great goodness," Munn heard Captain Reed shout over the wind. "The barometer is still falling." The captain said he would screw down the anemograph, "so that if the office goes and I am lost it may be found and read."

When the building began to move, Munn and the others decided they needed to get out. Tony Lagus's nearby grocery seemed like a safer structure.

"The water is up to my waist at my house," Reed said. "My family may be lost but my post of duty is here." As Munn left, he and the others argued that Reed had better get out. The building continued to shake. The captain finally relented to their arguments and said he would be along shortly; the doctor decided to wait with him.

Just as the two men finally walked out of the building, it fell down, pinning them under heavy lumber.

Reed had been correct in that his house was full of salt water—7 feet deep, to be exact—but his wife and family survived. The captain did not.

"Your dear papa was drowned in a terrible cyclone at 6 o'clock on the morning of the 19th," Alice Reed wrote a son who had been away at the time. "The building falling forward, he was caught under it. When they came down out of the office they left a lamp burning; it upset, [and] caught fire."

Whipped by the fierce winds, the fire rapidly intensified.

"We stopped for a while," Munn recalled, "and gazed with horror on this unexpected danger. It was then that the ladies shed tears, every lip faltered, every cheek blanched, how were it then possible to escape death[?]"

At that point, Munn continued, one woman said, "Well, I guess we have our choice, to be drowned or roasted."

Quickly spreading from the Signal Service office, the fire raced through every building on its side of the street, including August Frank's warehouse, the Lagus grocery store, Steinbach's market, and a liquor store. Jumping across the street, the flames consumed a hotel, a bakery, a dry-goods store, a drug store, a private residence, and other buildings.

"The howling blast, the roaring sea, the crash of falling timbers, the explosion of [gun] powder in stores, the crackling of flames as they shot up from, and lapped over the doomed buildings which rapidly yielded to wind, wave and fire, tottered, quivered and shrieking, fell into ruins and disappeared," Munn wrote breathlessly.

This time no one wanted to rebuild in Indianola.

County residents voted 188 to 7 on November 2, 1886, to move the Calhoun County seat to Port Lavaca, located on a high bluff. The following April a fire destroyed the few buildings the hurricane had left standing. On May 7, 1887, the federal government announced that it intended to close Indianola's post office.

Galveston had been the first city to organize a relief party for Indianola after the 1875 storm, and its citizens contributed money again after the 1886 hurricane. No one in Galveston or anywhere else wished Indianola ill, but the island city certainly profited from its rival's demise.

Galveston could have profited in another, much more important way, had it chosen to. The tragedy at Indianola, the *Galveston Daily News* observed, "teaches us the importance of fortifying the beach against the assaults of the terrible Gulf breakers, which are dangerous at 35 miles per hour." The newspaper article went on to envision a system of 5-foot brick walls, high enough above sea level to keep a tidal surge from sweeping the city's streets as had twice been the case in Indianola. "As the city's [Galveston] permanent prosperity has been doubly assured by the late storm," the newspaper continued, "let the work be—first, durable, and next, speedy."

Such a project would cost Galveston $180,000 "for the most needy part of the city," the newspaper estimated. Unfortunately, nothing came of the proposal.

Fourteen years later a storm destroyed much of the town, forcing Galveston to adopt even more drastic measures of protecting itself from Indianola's fate.

The Great Storm

GARY CARTWRIGHT

NOTED WRITER AND REPORTER GARY CARTWRIGHT EARNED HIS JOURNALISM DEGREE FROM TEXAS CHRISTIAN UNIVERSITY IN FORT WORTH. HIS ARTICLES HAVE APPEARED IN SUCH PUBLICATIONS AS *LIFE*, *ESQUIRE*, AND *HARPER'S*. CARTWRIGHT WORKED FOR THE *FORT WORTH PRESS*, THE *DALLAS TIMES HERALD*, AND THE *DALLAS MORNING NEWS*. A STAFF MEMBER AT *TEXAS MONTHLY* SINCE 1982, HIS BOOKS INCLUDE *BLOOD WILL TELL: THE MURDER TRIALS OF T. CULLEN DAVIS*, *CONFESSIONS OF A WASHED-UP SPORTSWRITER: INCLUDING VARIOUS DIGRESSIONS ABOUT SEX, CRIME, AND OTHER HOBBIES*, *DIRTY DEALING: DRUG SMUGGLING ON THE MEXICAN BORDER AND THE ASSASSINATION OF A FEDERAL JUDGE—AN AMERICAN PARABLE*, *TURN OUT THE LIGHTS: CHRONICLES OF TEXAS DURING THE 80S AND 90S*, AND *GALVESTON: A HISTORY OF THE ISLAND*.

THE GREAT GALVESTON STORM OF 1900 STILL RANKS AS THE WORST NATURAL DISASTER IN AMERICAN HISTORY. THE DEVASTATING HURRICANE KILLED AT LEAST 6,000 ISLANDERS AND COUNTLESS HOMES, SCHOOLS, CHURCHES, AND BUSINESSES WERE DEMOLISHED. IN THIS SELECTION, CARTWRIGHT PROVIDES A COMPELLING ACCOUNT OF THE SAVAGE STORM AND ITS TERRIBLE AFTERMATH.

★ ★

Friday, September 7, 1900, started out oppressively hot, then turned into one of those seemingly perfect days when the wind swings around and blows out of the north and the heat of summer starts to retreat. Frayed strings of clouds stitched a satin blue sky, promising the relief of rain. Long swells broke on the beach, and young sports who should have been tending to business on the Strand took off early to frolic in the breakers. This was a day for getting out, for experiencing life.

Isaac Cline saw the surf, too, but wasn't amused. Cline, the chief of the U.S. Weather Bureau's Galveston Station, had been plotting a storm that had started days earlier in the Cape Verde Basin, off the western coast of Africa. Swept along by the easterly trades, the storm had blown just north of Cuba on Tuesday. By Thursday it had passed through the Straits of Florida and was traveling across the Gulf of Mexico in a northwesterly direction, headed toward the Texas coast. On its present course it would likely make landfall well to the east of Galveston, which would put the Island on the comparatively safe left side of the storm's vortex. Cline dutifully hoisted storm-warning flags on the pole above the Levy Building, where the Weather Bureau was located.

Later in the day Cline walked along East Beach, feeling uneasy and trying to put things into logical order. He was a practical man, a scientist, and a physician, and he had a low tolerance for inexactitude. Something didn't add up. The barometer was falling slowly, as one might expect, and the wind was blowing out of the north at a brisk fifteen to seventeen miles per hour. And yet the tide was four and a half feet above normal and rising; it had already inundated the Flats on the Island's east end. That was what worried Cline. The tide was rising even though the wind was blowing directly *against* it. Normally, a north or offshore wind meant a low tide—on such occasions, Islanders joked that you could walk halfway to Cuba. The phenomenon of high water with opposing winds was an uncommon occurrence, but Cline knew its name: it was called a storm tide.

Cline had been with the Weather Bureau for eighteen years, eleven of them in Galveston, and in all that time the only severe hurricane to hit the Gulf Coast was the one in 1893 that drowned 2,000 people on the Louisiana, Mississippi, and Alabama coasts. The 1886 hurricane that wiped out Indianola was a trifle by comparison. In 1900 there was little information available on the habits of tropical storms, but Cline knew that under the right conditions they were capable of devastation beyond belief. The sixteen-foot storm tide that swept over the Ganges delta and blasted Calcutta in 1864, for example, drowned 40,000 people. All that afternoon Isaac Cline and his brother Joseph, who was also a meteorologist with the Weather Bureau, distributed information about the storm's movement and warned people to move away from the beach.

Rain started just after midnight and fell steadily all night. At one in the morning Joseph Cline finished up at the bureau and went home to bed. Joseph lived four blocks from the beach, in Isaac's two-story frame house at 25th and Avenue Q. It was a sturdy house, constructed to withstand any storm in memory, and it was raised on pilings well above the high-water mark of the 1875 hurricane. Nevertheless, Joseph slept fitfully until four, when some "sense of impending disaster" awakened him. He went to the south window and looked out. In the few hours that he had slept, the backyard of the Cline home had become part of the Gulf of Mexico. "I shook my brother awake and told him that the worst had begun," Joseph Cline said.

Joseph hurried back to the Levy Building to file a report over the bureau's national circuit, and Isaac Cline harnessed his horse to a two-wheeled cart and drove along the beach from one end of town to the other, warning people of the approaching storm.

By nine o'clock rain was running calf-deep down the street in front of Louisa Rollfing's house, a few blocks from the beach. People in her neighborhood were enjoying the downpour. Children and even a few housewives removed their shoes and stockings and waded amid pieces of driftwood and clumps of seaweed. On the beach, waves crashing against the streetcar trestle shot into the air high as telephone poles. Everyone was having fun until someone came up from the beach and told them that the bathhouses were breaking to pieces. "Then it wasn't fun anymore," Louisa recalled. Her husband, August, was working with a paint crew downtown, and she sent her eldest son by streetcar to tell August to come home immediately. Her son reported back later with this message: "Papa says, 'You must be crazy,' he will come home for his dinner." Water was already coming in over the doorsill. Louisa began packing.

Two competing forces were tearing at the Island. Far out at sea the storm was piling up walls of water and pushing them toward shore, and on the mainland a north wind was pushing in the opposite direction. The tide had forced itself steadily into the harbor, raising bay waters six feet, and the north wind drove angry brown waves against and over the wharves and railroad tracks. By one in the afternoon the wagon bridge and the three railroad bridges across the bay were all submerged. If anyone had thoughts of escaping to the mainland, it was too late.

Rabbi Henry Cohen was returning from temple when he noticed a long exodus of people moving up Broadway from the east end, carrying odd pieces of household goods and armloads of clothing. Broadway was the Island's highest point, a sort of continental divide, 8.7 feet above sea level: from there the Island tapered down to the bay and the Gulf, where the distinction between sea and land was measured in inches. But there was no record of a flood tide seriously threatening Broadway. Though the rain was pounding down and the sky was dark as twilight, the rabbi observed among the refugees something resembling a holiday mood. Children ran ahead, sliding on the mud slicks. The rabbi found spare umbrellas and blankets and passed them out, and Mrs. Cohen gave apples to the children.

Mollie Cohen finally persuaded her husband to come inside and put on some dry clothes. The electricity was off, and they sat down to lunch by candlelight. "We had a storm like this in "86," she told the children as they ate. "My father's store on Market Street was flooded." At that moment a gust of wind shook the house, causing plaster to shower from the ceiling. "It's just a little blow," she tried to assure them. Presently, the rabbi went to the door and looked out. He couldn't see the boulevard through the dark curtain of rain, but he could see water lapping over the first step of his front porch. "It looks as if the water has reached Broadway this time," he said, gathering the children and steering them away from the door. "Come in the parlor, Mollie, and let's have some music."

August Rollfing had finally realized the seriousness of the situation and sent a wagon from Malloy's Livery Stable to fetch his family and take them to the home of his mother on the west end. "It was a terrible trip," Louisa Rollfing recalled. "There were electric wires down everywhere and we had to go slow. The rain was icy cold and hurt our faces like glass splinters, and little

'Lanta pressed her face hard against my breast and cried all along the way." By the time they reached 40th and Avenue H, their horse was up to his neck in water. They were only a block from their destination, but when they tried to turn down 40th, a man shouted for them to stop. "You can't get through," he said. "There's a deep hole ahead." Louisa made a desperate decision: their only hope was to try and reach her sister-in-law's home at 36th and Broadway.

The tower that Nicholas Clayton had built above St. Mary's Cathedral began to lurch and sway—and the statue of Mary, Star of the Sea, placed there to protect, now threatened to crash through the ceiling and crush the people who had taken refuge beneath. The lower apartments of the rectory had already flooded, forcing Father James Kirwin and other priests and members of the household staff to move to the second floor. The cathedral and the rectory seemed about to disintegrate. Windows exploded, shooting shards of glass across the room. Cornice work tore lose and rambled down the seashell pavement like concrete tumbleweeds. Father Kirwin observed, "Slates from roofs were flying more thickly than hail and more deadly than Mauser bullets." Ironically, slate shingles had been a safety precaution mandated by city ordinances after the great fire of 1885. Now they were cutting people in half.

Through broken windows priests witnessed the tableaux of death, conscious, perhaps, that there was something almost biblical in the strength and random cruelty of the storm. A family of four, desperately trying to reach the cathedral, appeared for an instant, then vanished in the darkness. A panicking horse galloped through the surging waters of 21st Street, on a rendezvous with death. At that exact moment the wind ripped an enormous beam from a building and launched it, end over end, as casually as an Olympian might toss a baton, killing the horse in his tracks. Above the fury they could hear shotgunlike explosions as the iron bands and clasps that anchored the two-ton tower bell began to break free. A second tower at the front of the cathedral groaned, then its iron crosses toppled and crashed through the roof. Moments later the tower itself gave way and pitched forward into the racing brown torrent that used to be 21st Street. The bishop touched Father Kirwin's arm and told him; "Prepare these priests for death."

A German servant girl working in the home of W. L. Moody, Jr., was sent outside on an errand, and returned to report that the water standing in the yard tasted salty. Salty? How could that be? Then Moody began to understand, and ordered his servants to evacuate his wife and children to the home of his father, a block west on 23rd Street. The unthinkable had happened—the entire Island was covered by water. The Gulf and the bay had converged, and for the time being, Galveston was no longer an island, but merely part of the ocean floor, its houses and buildings protruding like toys in a bathtub.

By three-thirty Isaac Cline had recognized the scale of the disaster and drafted a final message to the chief of the Weather Bureau in Washington, D.C., advising him that great loss of life was imminent and the need for relief was urgent. Joseph Cline waded through waist-deep water to deliver the message to Western Union, only to discover that all the telegraph wires were down. He was able to get a telephone message through to the Western Union office in Houston, but he had no sooner delivered his report than the line went dead. Now Galveston was completely cut off from the outside world, alone with the fury of the gale and the rage of the tide.

Having done his duty, Isaac Cline left the bureau in the hands of assistants and waded nearly two miles to his home, thinking of his pregnant wife and three young daughters. Because of complications with the pregnancy, he had been unable to move his wife to a more secure place in the center of town. The wind wasn't yet constant—Cline estimated the gusts at between sixty and a hundred miles per hour—and by waiting for the lulls between gusts he was able to make headway. He had never seen anything like this: nobody on the Island had. Entire roofs were sailing through the air like discarded pages of newspaper. Timber and pieces of brick rocketed out of nowhere, splitting the paling and weatherboarding of houses. Nothing was where it had been that morning. Homes were gone. Streets had disappeared. Waves had washed wreckage against the pilings of his own home, creating a dam and backing up water to a depth of twenty feet: Cline's house was now in the center of a small lake.

Issac Cline found his family and about fifty neighbors huddled together on the second floor, frightened but apparently well. Joe Cline, who had made one last attempt to warn people to seek shelter in the city's center, arrived a few minutes later, badly shaken. "I tried to tell them that the worst was yet to come," he said. "I saw a family trying to reach the Catholic Convent, but they never made it. I saw people killed by flying debris and people drowned." Isaac began to realize that they were witnessing a sort of cataclysmic chain reaction. As buildings nearest the beach were wrecked, the wreckage was collected by winds and waves and driven against other buildings, which in turn collapsed and joined the grinding, swelling, insatiable mass. The storm was creating a battering ram of debris, mowing down everything in its path, scraping the earth clean. Soon it would be their turn.

The storm was intensifying with each minute. At five the anemometer at the weather station recorded a two-minute gust at 102 miles per hour. Fifteen minutes later the wind carried the instrument away. By six the tide was swelling at an incredible rate of 2.5 feet an hour, and the wind was shifting around to the northeast. At about seven-thirty, in a single enormous swell, the tide rose four feet in four seconds. The center of the hurricane apparently passed west of the Island between 8 and 9 P.M. By then the velocity of the wind was estimated at 120 miles per hour. The tide on the side of the Island nearest the Gulf was at least 15 feet, and breakers 25 feet or higher crashed over the beachline.

Every church, hospital, business building, or home still standing became a shelter for the homeless. Sailors tied boats to the fence in front of the Sealy mansion at 24th and Broadway, and pulled people out of the storm surge and onto the porch: more than four hundred found shelter at Open Gates that night. In a frantic effort to do what they could, against a force nobody could comprehend, workmen braced walls with beams, and nailed shut doors and windows. Holes were drilled in floors, inviting floodwaters to enter, in hopes that the water would help anchor houses and keep them from floating off. From one end of the Island to the other—in their instinctive struggle to survive for even one more minute—people committed astonishing, desperate, heroic, and sometimes foolish acts.

A nurse on duty at a home near the beach wrapped the body of a stillborn infant in a blanket, administered a sleeping potion to the helpless, pain-racked mother, and then, as the house began to disintegrate, calmly made preparation for her own escape. She put on a man's bathing suit, cut off her hair with scissors, and plunged into the sea. From eight in the evening until two in the morning, she clung to a piece of driftwood, finally washing ashore on the mainland. Naked, bleeding, and shivering in the cold rain, she found a shaggy dog and snuggled up against him until daylight.

The highest structure on the Island, the 220-foot tower above St. Patrick's Church, crashed unceremoniously into the street. But the storm was so loud nobody heard it. By seven in the evening the church was rubble. More than a thousand refugees took shelter at the Ursuline Convent and Academy, including several hundred blacks. When the north wall collapsed, the blacks began to sing and pray. "They shouted and sang in true camp-meeting style," wrote Father Kirwin, "until the nerves of the other refugees were shattered and a panic seemed imminent. Mother Superioress Joseph rang the chapel bell and caused a hush of the pandemonium. When quiet had been restored the mother addressed the negroes and told them that this was no time nor place for such scenes."

On the beach three miles west of town, the sisters of St. Mary's Orphanage herded their ninety-three children from room to room as the storm worsened. Their final refuge was the second-floor girls' dormitory. A caretaker brought a coil of clothesline from a store room, and the sisters wrapped the ropes around their own waists and then around the children's. A short time later the roof caved in, and all the nuns and all of the children except three were crushed or washed to their deaths.

When the front section of YMCA secretary Judson Palmer's house on Avenue P½ washed away, Palmer, his family, and fourteen others crowded into an upstairs bedroom and began to pray. Palmer's young son, Lee, prayed for the safety of his dog, Youno, and asked Jesus to "give us a pleasant day tomorrow to play." One room after another collapsed and disappeared, until all that remained was a room at the north end, part of the roof and the bathroom. As water continued to rise, Palmer and his wife and child climbed onto the edge of the bathtub. When the water reached their chins, the boy put his arms around his father's neck and asked if everything was all right. Palmer never got a chance to reply. At that moment the final section of the house gave way, hurling everyone into the roiling current. For three hours Palmer drifted on a floating shed. Eventually, he was rescued, but he never saw his wife or little Lee again. Of the fourteen neighbors who had taken refuge in the Palmer home, only one survived.

Far down the west end of the Island, Henry R. Decie, his wife, and baby boy took shelter in the home of a neighbor. The Decies were resting on the end of a bed, the baby between them, when the water began to rise "four or five feet in one bound." At that same moment a wave slammed into the side of the house and took it off its blocks. "My wife threw her arms around my neck," Decie recalled, "and kissed me and said, 'Goodbye, we are gone.'" The house shook violently, dislodging a beam that came crashing down. Decie tried to scoop his son into his arms, but the heavy timber caught the child and killed him instantly. "Another wave came," Decie said, "and swept the overhanging house off my head. I looked around and my wife was gone. Catching a piece of scantling, I held on to it and was carried thirty miles across the bay, landing near the mouth of Cow Bayou."

Though the front and rear porches of Isaac Cline's home had been smashed to sticks, the fifty refugees inside told themselves that the house was secure. Joseph Cline remembered feeling strangely calm. He kept thinking of an uncle who, alone of all those aboard a sinking ship, saved himself by hanging onto a plank and riding it five miles to shore. Around him, people were singing or praying or crying—or wandering about aimlessly, looking for some place that might give them an advantage when the end came. "I knew the house was about to collapse," Joseph Cline said, "and I told my relatives and friends to get on top of the drift and float with it."

The storm had been pounding against a quarter-mile-long section of streetcar trestle, built out over the Gulf. Suddenly, the trestle pulled loose from its mooring—rails, ties, crosspieces, and all. The storm surge and the 120-mile-per-hour winds carried a 200-foot trestle section like a scythe out of hell directly toward Isaac Cline's home. A fraction of a second before the collision, Cline felt his house move off its foundation. Then it began to topple and break apart. Cline tried to wrap his arms around his wife and six-year-old daughter, but the impact threw them into a chimney and swept the three of them beneath the wreckage, to the bottom of the water. Cline lost sight of his daughter. A dresser pinned him against a mantel, and his wife was trapped nearby, her clothing tangled among the wreckage. It's over, Cline thought. Surrendering to the inevitable, he told himself: "I have done all that could have been done in this disaster, the world will know that I did my duty to the last, it is useless to fight for life, I will let the water enter my lungs and pass on. . . ." Then he lost consciousness.

Joseph Cline had been standing near a window on the windward side. When the house began to capsize, he grabbed the hands of Isaac's other two daughters, smashed the window glass and storm shutters with his back, and let the momentum carry the three of them through the window. The building settled on its side, rocked a bit, and then rose to the surface of the floodwaters. Joe Cline and his nieces were alone on the top side of a flotilla of wreckage, momentarily safe and drifting with the tide. Rain was driving down, and pieces of timber went by like swarms of giant insects. A dim moon shone through broken clouds, making it possible for Joseph to see a short distance. Heaving masses of debris, like the one that served as their rescue ship, stretched for blocks. Cline and the two youngsters were the only humans in sight.

In a night of catastrophic losses it was impossible to separate coincidence from miracles, but there was an abundance of each. Isaac Cline regained consciousness to find himself hanging between two timbers: the wave action against the timbers had apparently pressed the water out of his lungs. There was a flash of lightning and Cline saw his youngest girl, alive and floating on the wreckage a few feet away. A short time later another flash revealed his brother and his other two daughters, still riding their raft of debris. "I took my baby and swam toward them," Isaac Cline recalled. "Strange as it may seem these children displayed no sign of fear, as we in the shadow of death did not realize what fear meant. Our only thought was how to win in this disaster."

For four hours they drifted through endless darkness and despair. Over the downpour and the wail of wind, they heard houses being crushed, and the screams of the dying. Isaac and Joseph Cline turned their backs to the wind, placing the children in front to protect them from flying debris. To shield their own own backsides, they gathered planks from the floating wreckage and propped them up like chairbacks. "The wind-driven debris was showering us constantly," Isaac Cline wrote. "Sometimes the blows were so strong that we would be knocked into the surging waters, but we would fight our way back to the children and continue the struggle to survive."

Periodic flashes of lightning added to the surreal specter, and revealed the terrible carnage—and sometimes the approach of new danger. At one point they saw a weather-battered hulk that had once been a house, streaming in their direction, one side upreared at a forty-five-degree angle. The hulk towered six or eight feet above them, and was bearing down like a derelict freighter, crushing everything in its path. Joseph Cline retained sufficient presence of mind to leap just as the monster reached them, gaining a grip on the hulk's top edge. His weight was enough to drag it lower in the water, and with his brother's help he pulled the upper side down. They climbed on top with the children, just as the drift upon which they had been floating went to pieces under their feet.

For a time their new makeshift raft was swept out to sea, but then the wind became southerly, indicating that the storm's center was bending northward and heading inland. Gradually, they could see the lights of shore. They were drifting toward a steady point of light, and as they got closer, they realized that it was a house on solid ground. Battered and exhausted, they climbed through an upstairs window, into a room where a group of refugees were huddled. This house, they learned later, sat at the corner of 28th and Avenue P, only five blocks from where Isaac Cline's home once sat. Their journey through hell had delivered them close to the place where they started.

By midnight the storm had passed over the Island, and the tide was falling rapidly. In the back-yard of the Kempner home at 16th and Avenue I, the water dropped from more than eight feet to less than six feet in the time it took Ike Kempner to swim from his back porch to the stable and back. Kempner had gone in search of his coachman, who had been sent to release two carriage horses. When the coachman failed to return, Kempner tied a rope to his belt and went looking for him. As it turned out, the coachman and horses were safe: they had found a high, dry spot on the porch of a neighbor. "After that, I needed a stiff drink," Kempner recalled. Since the flood was obviously receding, Kempner and his friend Safford Wheeler started on foot to inform their neighbors. "In our dripping clothes and shoes, we were cordially received at four or five residences. In each, we were promptly tendered refreshments, and after imbibing several we found the 'spiritual courage' to continue spreading the good news."

In high fettle, Kempner and Wheeler began to wade in chest-deep water in the direction of the Tremont Hotel, their mission being to toast the renewal of life with whoever was there. Unfortunately, they found the hotel doors locked. They rang the bell but got no response. Undeterred, the two millionaires gathered paving blocks they found floating along Tremont Street, and used them to smash hotel windows. They were so engaged when a security officer from the hotel appeared and placed them under arrest.

August Rollfing was frantic. At the peak of the storm he had stood on the counter of a store with eighty strangers, holding a small boy he had never seen before on his shoulders and praying that his own family had somehow survived. When the water began to recede, Rollfing ran toward the west end neighborhood where his mother lived. He was relieved to see her house still standing—it was the only one on the block that was—but when he got inside and asked about Louisa and his children, his mother just shook her head. "They are not here, my boy," she told him. "I haven't seen them." She begged August to wait until daylight, but he bolted out the door and disappeared into the rain.

His throat dry and his chest burning, August raced along 23rd Street in the direction of Broadway, thinking that his family might have taken shelter at his sister Julia's house. A faint moon broke through the clouds, and August saw some sort of gigantic shadow stretching across Avenue N, blocking his path. It looked like a levee, or a small mountain range, and it stretched from east to west, as far as he could see. August was nearly to the base of the shadow when he realized that what he was looking at was a monstrous wall of wreckage. It was taller than a two-story building, and six to eight blocks wide. It started at the Flats on the far east end of the Island and ran all the way to 45th Street. In its relentless, grinding fashion the battering ram that Isaac Cline described had rumbled across 1,500 acres of the Island, finally playing itself out against a break-water of its own creation.

August Rollfing stood looking up at this grotesque monument to death, trying to comprehend. "It seemed endless," he said. "House upon house, all broken to pieces, furniture, sewing machines, pianos, cats, dogs . . . and what was underneath? How many people had gone down with their houses? And behind the wall of debris, nothing! Absolutely nothing! The ground was as clear as if it had been swept, not even a little stick of wood. For blocks and blocks, nothing, and then that terrible pile of debris . . . and what was in and under it."

By the time August Rollfing reached his sister's home, the rain had almost stopped and a fresh breeze was whipping straight out of the south. In a few hours it would be light. Julia's home was still standing, more or less. There was a twenty-foot hole in one wall where the kitchen had broken loose, and the house had been lifted off its brick pillars on two sides so that it leaned like a house in a child's drawing. When August saw that his wife and children were safe and well, he collapsed in a heap on the stairway.

Sunday morning was a scene out of hell, played against a brilliant blue sky and a drowsy sea. At low tide the Gulf seemed as peaceful as a sleeping teenager, spent and unaware of its night of murderous violence. Small groups of people began to appear in the streets, tentative at first, as though they didn't want to disturb anything. Bruised and stunned, wet and chilled to the bone, they stumbled about, trying to assimilate the scope of this tragedy.

Those who had stoves and chimneys standing did what they could to cook breakfast. Others looked for dry wood. The entire Island was water-logged and covered with an inch-thick layer of foul-smelling slime. Still others dared to survey the damage. It was worse than anyone imagined—far worse. In the blackest hour no one had conjured up a vision like the one that spread before the survivors this Sunday morning. One-third of the Island was scraped clean, and the other two-thirds battered almost beyond recognition. In the Sunday morning stillness people climbed on top of the debris and looked around. They heard faint cries from people buried alive. At first, their impulse was to attempt rescues, digging with their bare hands or whatever tool they could find, but it was hopeless. No human effort could alter the inevitable or limit the final suffering of those who were trapped and waiting to die.

A more urgent concern was aiding the injured and homeless. There wasn't a building on the Island that escaped damage. More than 3,600 houses were totally destroyed, as were hundreds of buildings and institutions. Like an avenging angel on a special mission, the storm had been coldly selective in its choice of targets. Sacred Heart Catholic Church was in ruins, while just across 14th Street the mansion of Walter Gresham had escaped with only damage from the high water. The fourth floor of the Moody Building was gone, sheared away as though by a giant knife. St. Mary's Cathedral was nearly destroyed, but miraculously the tower that Nicholas Clayton built survived, and Mary, Star of the Sea, continued to stand watch. The east wall of the Opera House had collapsed, and the interior was coated with slime the consistency of axle grease. Except for a few scattered bricks, there was no trace of St. Mary's Orphanage. Railroad tracks were buried or twisted into hideous forms, trees uprooted, telephone poles flattened, streets and sidewalks buckled or washed away, wires ripped loose, gas and electric lines ruptured, sewers plugged with vegetable, animal, and human remains. Huge oceangoing ships had torn loose from their ropes and cables and had been swept across the bay and deposited on the mainland. The British steamship *Taunton* was carried from its anchorage at the mouth of the ship channel to a thirty-foot bank at Cedar Point, twenty-two miles from deep water. Household items, clothing, trade goods, machinery, almost every material possession that wasn't stored higher than fifteen feet was saturated with salt water and scum, and either ruined or badly damaged. Weeks and even months later, bicycles that seemed no worse for the experience suddenly fell apart, rusted from the inside.

There were so many bodies that after a while the senses numbed, and the corpses seemed to be merely some sort of demented design. They were heaped together in the streets, strewn across vacant lots, sticking from mounds of wreckage, floating in shallow pools of water, scattered along the beach, bobbing in the filthy backwash of the bay. Most were naked, mutilated, and dashed beyond recognition. They hung like macabre ornaments from trees, trestles, and telephone poles. One observer counted forty-three bodies dangling from the framework of a partially demolished railroad bridge. The horror and the unspeakable suffering of the victims' final moments were often preserved in ghastly frescoes of death. The body of twelve-year-old Scott McCloskey, son of a sea captain, was found with his left arm shattered, his right arm still wrapped protectively around the body of his younger brother. A woman, her long blond hair entangled in barbed wire, reached back in death as though to disengage it. Miles down the beach from the orphans' home, the bodies of a nun and nine children, still tied together with clothesline, lay half-buried in sand and seaweed.

For days survivors continued to search among the ruins, hoping to find some trace of loved ones. Most of the dead were so badly battered they couldn't be identified. Father Kirwin, who had waited out the storm in St. Mary's Cathedral, told of seeing a man going from corpse to corpse, looking into their mouths, hoping to recognize his wife's bridgework. Twenty days after the storm Isaac Cline found the body of his wife, under the wreckage that had carried the rest of her family to safety. He knew it was she because of her diamond engagement ring.

Late Sunday morning Mayor Walter Jones called an emergency meeting at the Tremont Hotel. Most of the city's leading citizens were there—Ike Kempner, John Sealy, Rabbi Henry Cohen, members of the Deep Water Committee. Not a single department of city government was functioning, so the mayor appointed these men to an ad hoc Central Relief Committee, with the power to do whatever they believed necessary. Looters were already roaming the Island, stripping the dead and ransacking shops, banks, and warehouses. The mayor declared martial law, and local militiamen were ordered to shoot looters on sight. By one account as many as seventy-five "ghouls" were summarily gunned down.

The Central Relief Committee in effect assumed the monumental job of governing the Island for the duration of the emergency. There was no communication with the mainland, except by boat. The three railroad bridges and the wagon bridge had been destroyed. The only city-owned craft afloat that could navigate the shallow waters of the bay was a twenty-foot steam launch, and even that was badly battered. Nevertheless, a crew and messengers volunteered. After a perilous journey across the bay, they scrambled ashore at Texas City, ten miles to the north, and made their way overland, across a flooded prairie littered with debris and corpses. At a railroad they found a handcar and pumped along the tracks for fifteen miles until they met a train that took them to Houston. The journey took sixteen hours.

The committee decided that every able-bodied man would be required to work on cleanup squads. Everything had to be rationed—food, medicine, water, transportation. Commissaries were set up in each of Galveston's twelve wards, dispensing supplies to those with no money. Hotels and restaurants accommodated all who applied, with or without money, and shop owners handed out canned goods as long as their supplies lasted. Galveston got its water from artesian wells eighteen miles from the city, and though the thirty-six-inch main under the bay survived the storm, the pumping station did not. Most residences still retained cisterns from the old days, but only a few were positioned high enough to escape contamination. It was almost a week before the pumping station was repaired, and in the meantime supplies of water came from these few cisterns, and from water barrels shipped from the mainland.

The homeless took refuge anywhere they could—in the train station, at city hall, in commercial buildings, in warehouses, in hotels and private homes. Saloons, gambling halls, and whorehouses were either closed or turned into temporary shelters. Churches that were still standing welcomed worshipers from those that were not: four Protestant denominations worshiped in Rabbi Cohen's temple. Most Islanders willingly opened their homes and shared what they had. But when the relief committee asked W. L. Moody, Jr., to take in a group of orphans, he refused. "We had no place for them," his daughter Mary explained later. "We had no water, no food. We couldn't take care of orphans. It would have been impossible." Will Moody, Jr., and his family had waited out the worst of the storm in his father's mansion. The colonel and his wife were in New York at the time—it was Moody company policy that Will Junior and his father couldn't both be off the Island at the same time. Moody did permit the relief committee to use his father's yacht, but only after his wife and daughter had been ferried safely to the mainland.

At first, the number of dead was estimated to be no more than five hundred, and some members of the relief committee insisted on the legal formality of a coroner's inquest. By Monday morning, however, that suggestion was dismissed as ludicrous. The death count was running into the thousands. Funeral homes and improvised morgues were already overflowing with corpses uncomfortably close to putrefaction. Work crews attempting to load bodies on carts reported that the corpses were falling to pieces. The only solution, it became apparent, was immediate and wholesale burial at sea. All day Monday and Tuesday carts and wagons full of corpses plodded along the ravaged streets of Galveston, in the direction of the wharves, arms and legs protruding under tarpaulins. The job of loading the bodies onto barges and taking them to sea was so abhorrent that recruits had to be rounded up at bayonet point and plied with whiskey. "An armed guard brought fifty negroes to the barges and went on with them," wrote Father Kirwin, who had helped supply whiskey to the white volunteers. "The barges were taken out into the Gulf and remained there all night, until it was light enough for the negroes to fasten the weights and throw the bodies overboard. When the barges returned those negroes were ashen in color."

Two days later Father Kirwin's face was similarly ashen. A member of his congregation came to the cathedral and told the priest: "My mother-in-law is back." "That's impossible!" said Father Kirwin, reminding the man that they had dumped his mother-in-law's weighted body eighteen miles out to sea. But she *was* back, as were the bodies of hundreds of others: they had washed up on the beach overnight. The committee had to rethink its strategy. Since it was no longer possible to haul decaying bodies through the streets, the committee decided to burn corpses on the spot. The bodies, and the mountain of debris created by the storm's battering ram, were burned in sections. From one end of the Island to the other, funeral pyres burned night and day: at night you could see their glow from the mainland. No one alive during that terrible time would ever forget the sight, or the smell.

In her report to the Red Cross, a volunteer named Fanny B. Ward recorded a conversation with a custodian of one of the bonfires.

"This here fire's been going on more than a month," the fireman told Miss Ward. "To my knowledge, upwards of sixty bodies have been burned in it—to say nothing of dogs, cats, hens, and three cows."

"What is in there now?" she asked.

"Well, it takes a corpse several days to burn all up. I reckon there's a couple of dozen of them—just bones, you know—down near the bottom. Yesterday we put seven on top of this pile, and by now they are only what you might call baked. Today we have been working over there (pointing to other fires a quarter of a mile way) where we found a lot of them, eleven under one house. We have put only two in here today. Found them just now, right in that puddle."

"Could you tell me who they are?"

"Lord no," he said. "We don't look at them any more than we have to, else we'd been dead ourselves before today. One of these was a colored man. They are all pretty black now, but you can tell them by the kinky hair. He had on nothing but an undershirt and one shoe. The other was a woman; young, I reckon. At any rate, she was tall and slim and had lots of long brown hair. She wore a blue silk skirt and there was a rope tied around her waist, as if somebody had tried to save her."

With a long pole the fireman poked an air hole near the center of the smoulder heap, and Fanny Ward stepped back from the unearthly smell and took a new position windward. Sparks showered the ground, leaving bits of bone and singed hair. She stooped and picked up a curling yellow lock, tears in her eyes as she wondered what mother's hand had lately caressed it.

"That's nothing," remarked the fireman. "The other day we found part of a brass chandelier, and wound all around it was a perfect mop of long, silky hair—with a piece of skin, big as your two hands, at the end of it. Some woman got tangled up that way in the flood and just naturally scalped."

No one would ever know for certain how many Islanders died, but the most reliable estimate was somewhere between six and seven thousand. Since the population of the city in 1900 was 37,700, that meant that in the hours between Saturday afternoon and Sunday morning one out of every six citizens of Galveston perished. Thousands more were killed on the mainland. The storm was recorded as the worst disaster in the history of the United States. An article a month later in the *National Geographic* described Galveston as "a scene of suffering and devastation hardly paralleled in the history of the world."

One reason the death count was so inexact was the massive migration that followed the storm. In the immediate aftermath people were playing huge sums for boat passage to the mainland. Once rail service was restored, railroads gave victims free transportation anywhere in the United States, and hundreds of families took advantage of it. Many never returned. So great was their suffering and grief—so terrible the memory of that night—that they didn't even bother to go back for their possessions, or to look for or bury their dead.

Many predicted that the city would never be rebuilt, or if it was rebuilt, it would be relocated on the mainland. But Joseph Cline reminded skeptics that Galveston was the only city on the Gulf west of New Orleans. "Commerce always takes precedence over life," Cline said. He was right. Within eleven days one of the railroad bridges across the bay had been repaired, and rail service restored. There was talk of a new causeway, ten feet higher than before. Repairs and extensions to the wharves were pushed forward. Saloons, gambling joints, and whorehouses reopened. The streets hadn't yet been been cleared of the dead, but already the electric trolley was running again. Cotton arrived by rail and barge, was processed, and then loaded aboard oceangoing ships. On October 14, 30,300 bales cleared port.

When Will Moody, Jr., told the colonel that people were leaving the Island and that business was bound to suffer, the colonel uttered one of the best-known and most cynical remarks in Galveston lore. "Good," he declared. "Remember, we both love to hunt and fish. The fewer people on the Island, the better the hunting and fishing will be for us."

The colonel was speaking metaphorically. The Island would recover—there was no doubt about that—and in the meantime it was a buyer's market. Property values had dropped drastically. Indeed, prospects for hunting and fishing hadn't been this good since Samuel May Williams and other founders of the original Galveston City Company began dividing up the Island in 1838. The colonel returned from New York convinced that the eastern press had greatly exaggerated the damage done by the storm—he'd even brought a stack of newspapers to show his son—but when he saw with his own eyes that the devastation was even worse than reported, the Moody Family made plans accordingly. Two weeks after the hurricane, Will Moody, Jr., purchased a thirty-room mansion at 2618 Broadway, for ten cents on the dollar.

Reform, 1874–1900

IRVIN M. MAY, JR.

IRVIN M. MAY, JR. (1939–2000) TAUGHT FOR MANY YEARS AT BLINN COLLEGE IN BRYAN. A SPECIALIST IN THE HISTORY OF AGRICULTURE, DR. MAY AUTHORED *MARVIN JONES: THE PUBLIC LIFE OF AN AGRARIAN ADVOCATE* AND WAS COEDITOR OF *ENRICHING AMERICA'S PAST* AND *SOUTHWESTERN AGRICULTURE: PRE-COLUMBIAN TO MODERN*.

IN THIS SELECTION, DR. MAY PROVIDES AN OVERVIEW OF TEXAS FROM 1874 TO THE DAWN OF THE TWENTIETH CENTURY, A PERIOD OF SIGNIFICANT CHANGE. HE DISCUSSES THE TRANSFORMATION IN AGRICULTURE, INDUSTRY, TRANSPORTATION, EDUCATION, AND POLITICS IN THE LONE STAR STATE. MAY ALSO CONSIDERS THE REFORM EFFORTS OF ATTORNEY GENERAL AND GOVERNOR JAMES STEPHEN HOGG.

★ ★

"Each age is a dream that is dying or one that is coming to birth," observed Franklin D. Roosevelt, who was born in 1882 and became one of the greatest presidents of the twentieth century. In the culminating years of the nineteenth century, 1874–1900, Texas experienced an age that made a significant impact upon its future. This meant reform: to amend or improve by change

From *The Texas Heritage,* 3rd ed., edited by Ben Procter and Archie P. McDonald, "Reform, 1874–1900" by Irvin M. May, Jr. pp. 115–136.

of form or removal of faults or abuses; to put or change into an improved form or condition. When the dreams of that era produced reforms, the results became the immediate foundation of twentieth-century Texas.

What were some of the dreams of the Texan of 1874? Redeemers desired a change in government and a reform of Radical Republican rule. Pioneers wanted a better life and therefore pushed Anglo civilization westward throughout Texas. Entrepreneurs Henry J. Lutcher, G. Bedell Moore, and John Henry Kirby sought wealth in the tall yellow pine forests of East Texas. The railroad, sometimes called the iron horse, captured the spirit of the age, supplied needed transportation, and contributed to the accumulation of great amounts of wealth; but unwise use of the railroad's power and unethical business practices resulted in government regulation. There were dreams of better education for all, and blacks especially hoped that the Declaration of Independence would finally be fulfilled for them. The political scene witnessed various changes to encourage industrialism and to provide more democracy. Democrats, Republicans, Grangers, Greenbackers, and Populists had their own visions for Texas, and the era produced the last great Texas governor, James Stephen Hogg. As we will see, the years 1874–1900 were an era of change for Texas and the nation.

Statistically Texas experienced great change between 1874 and 1900. Population increased from 818,579 in 1870 (nineteenth in the United States) to 3,048,710 in 1900 (sixth in the nation). Accompanying this increase, the state's urban population rose from 6.7 percent to 17.1 percent. While this trend began to accelerate, Texas still remained a rural state. When the era began, nearly 60 percent of the state was a frontier, with Washington, Harris, and Rusk counties having the most people, and Galveston, San Antonio, and Houston being the largest cities. Thirty years later, the urban twentieth-century pattern had come clearly into focus, with Dallas, Bexar, and Harris being the largest counties and San Antonio, Houston, and Dallas the largest cities. Metropolitan Texas had emerged.

Accompanying the population trends, the economy also underwent substantial change. The state's railroad mileage increased from twenty-eighth in the nation in 1872 to first in 1904. The value of industrial products rose from $11,517,302 in 1870 to $119,414,982 in 1900, although the percentage of industrial workers only grew from 1 to 1.5 percent of the population. Agriculture supplied the foundation for Texas industry, and the leading industry in 1870 was flour and grist mill products. This industry fell to third in 1900, surpassed by lumber, first, then cottonseed oil and cake. During the twilight of the nineteenth century, Texas was not yet an industrial state, and its economy was not based upon oil. Although oil had been discovered in Nacogdoches County in 1866 and near Corsicana in the 1880s, the most valuable mineral produced in Texas was still coal, which increased in value from $1,000,000 in 1870 to $5,300,000 in 1900.

As expected, Texans were still agrarian. On the farms and ranches, Texans faced fluctuating cotton prices: from 11.1 cents per pound in 1874 to 5.7 cents per pound in 1898; cattle prices varied from $18.87 per head in 1870 to $24.97 per head in 1900. Rural neighbors talked about interest rates, crops, ticks, abuses by the railroads, and the weather.

As agricultural development moved westward, the Texas frontier continued to shrink. When the era began in 1874, the western border of organized counties included Clay, Jack, Young, Shackelford, Eastland, Brown, Coleman, San Saba, Menard, Mason, Gillespie, Kerr, Bandera, Uvalde, Kinney, and Maverick. East of that line, Stephens, Real, and Dimmitt counties would be organized later. When the era closed, only twenty-four Texas counties remained to be organized. The decimation of the native Indians, the railroad's expansion west, change in state land policy, and the lure of available land encouraged West Texas growth. Prominent in the development was the cattleman's expanding frontier.

The agricultural revolution, cotton, agricultural science, and lumber were significant to Texas during 1874–1900. However, the most important, with the greatest political results, was the agricultural revolution. Prior to 1870, subsistence agriculture had been the way of life on Texas farms, and little cultural difference existed between the farm and the city. The farmer did not have a sense of inferiority. That situation changed. With the emergence of industry after the Civil War, United States farmers believed that they had been reduced to second-class citizens. As agricultural historian Gilbert Fite explained, the agricultural revolution, building up in the 1870s and 1880s and reaching a climax in the 1890s, was a rebellion against the power of big business and in favor of the restoration of the farmers as the most influential group in the United States. Many Southern farmers, including Texans, were caught in a trap of poverty and low productivity. A surplus of produce and labor, and the inability to raise their standard of living by themselves spurred farmers to organize the Texas Farmers' Alliance and the Colored Farmers' Alliance in a desperate effort to solicit government action.

While this agricultural movement caused political reforms, changes occurred in the production of cotton, the state's principal cash crop. Cotton production moved from East Texas to the Blacklands and thereafter to the South Plains, where dryland farming required irrigation. There the prospects for profits overcame a prior anticotton bias, and cotton cultivation and processing became the major West Texas agricultural activity. Some astute cotton farmers knew that cotton production increased six times (from 516,000 to 3,438,000 bales), while the price declined by 50 percent.

Consistent with these hard-times developments, farm tenancy was the prevailing labor for cotton cultivation. From 1880 to 1900, the nation's tenancy increased from 25.6 percent to 35.3 percent; whereas, tenancy on Texas farms increased from 37.6 percent to 49.7 percent. While not as extensive as in many Southern states, Texas tenancy still trapped whites and blacks alike in poverty. Low interest rates, affordable land and machinery, and long-term credit were not available to those misfortunates who performed the needed service of cheap labor.

Encouragement to farmers to diversify came from prominent agricultural journals such as the *Texas Farm and Ranch* and progressive farmers and scientists such as Charles Bruce Richardson of Henderson. They wanted Texans to build upon the existing foundation of field crops, fruits, nuts, and vegetables as well as to adapt new crops to Texas. They hoped that soil conservation and a stable, independent farm culture would result. While the demand for corn and wheat increased during this era, the prices per bushel decreased. Wheat had a high of 94.4 cents per bushel and a low of 63.3 cents; corn, the state's staple crop, ranged from 40.9 cents to 29.7 cents per bushel. New varieties of soft winter wheat and the expansion of the wheat frontier to the Texas Blacklands increased production. Irrigated rice farming began near Beaumont in 1891. Other commercial crops included barley, rye, apples, peaches, and potatoes, but the extensive variety of commercial Texas agriculture seen in the twentieth century had yet to emerge.

Agricultural science enhanced the development of both private and public Texas lands during the era. Most of the time, private scientists took the lead in agricultural achievements. Thomas Volney Munson, a viticulturalist in Denison, established one of the most famous vineyards in the South. He received the French Legion of Honor for saving French vineyards from the dreaded disease phylloxera by grafting French vines onto phylloxera-resistant American grape rootstocks. Marcus Black made significant contributions to the peach industry and later to the Rio Grande Valley citrus industry. Emor Crew of Hempstead was an expert in the cultivation of celery, watermelons, and cantaloupes. John O. Meusebach experimented with developing new and better varieties of fruit as did Heford Halbert with pecans. The scientific investigations of Eduard Becker, William Falconer, and David and William Watson made Brenham an agricultural science center.

In 1887 the United States Congress passed the Hatch Act, which created the Texas Agricultural Experiment Station, in conjunction with Texas A&M. The public was still skeptical of book-learned agriculture. The state had inadequate facilities and funding for scientific investigations. Despite the prevailing anti-intellectualism, Mark Francis performed significant investigations of infectious and epidemic livestock diseases (such as Texas Tick Fever). Frank Gulley contributed cotton and silage studies, and Henry Harrington analyzed soils and fertilizers. Scientific agriculture increased the quality of agricultural instruction at both college and adult education levels. These results marked the beginning of public agricultural reforms in Texas.

Agriculture stimulated not only education but industry. In 1870 Texas industry consisted principally of local blacksmithing, wagon-making shops, flour mills, and perhaps brick kilns or cotton gins. Total Texas industrial production consisted of only 25 percent of the total value of agricultural products.

John Spratt observed in *The Road to Spindletop* that throughout the era Texas remained an industrially backward state with manufacturing concentrated in specific areas. The ten leading manufacturing counties of 1870, headed by Galveston, Marion, and Harris, produced 44 percent of all Texas manufactured goods. Thirty years later, Marion County did not make the list, and Galveston fell to fifth. The ten leading manufacturing counties were headed by Harris—dependent upon cotton, lumber and railroads—Dallas, and El Paso. These counties produced 35 percent of the state's manufactured goods.

During this era Galveston principally engaged in the mercantile and processing industries. Houston, however, experienced a great boom because progressive leaders there had developed the state's first and most extensive railroad system and had encouraged manufacturing and a diversified industrial economy. As expected, most manufacturing occurred east of Austin.

Sometimes entrepreneurs boomed; sometimes they busted. For example, the boom town of New Birmingham, a thriving Cherokee County community between 1888 and 1892 with its Tassie Bell iron furnace, ceased to exist after showing great potential.

Lumber proved to be the leading Texas industry on the eve of the twentieth century. As late as 1880, few people realized the economic significance of the great pine forests of East Texas. By the end of the 1880s, lumber surpassed cotton as the region's principal product. Texas's leading forestry historian, Robert Maxwell, noted the following developments in explaining East Texas's booming lumber industry: (1) the great white pine forests were being quickly reduced; (2) settlers migrating westward onto the Great Plains needed lumber; (3) the Panic of 1873 was ending, causing a revival in business optimism, and (4) a surge in railroad construction. These needs for lumber overcame a previous prejudice against yellow pine, and entrepreneurs quickly entered the tall forests.

Dreams of wealth attracted entrepreneurs from many places. Some were Texas-born such as the tall, robust John Henry Kirby, a poor country lawyer from Peachtree Village, Tyler County, who created the state's first million-dollar corporation, the Kirby Lumber Company. Pennsylvanians Henry Lutcher and G. Bedell Moore came to Texas in 1877 and developed the first large saw mills. Not only did they become financially successful, they contributed generously to civic projects in Orange, Texas. From Germany came Joseph Kurth, who migrated to Polk County and then moved to Lufkin. He created the Angelina County Lumber Company and became a leading Republican. His son Ernest, aided by Charles Herty, created the Southland Paper Mill in 1936 and produced newsprint from southern yellow pine in 1940. Thomas L. L. Temple arrived from Virginia, built a small saw mill at Diboll, and developed a diversified lumber and wood products company, the Southern Pine Lumber Company. These companies bought or leased vast tracts of land, created company towns, and opposed labor unions. While the lumber barons could be generous, civic-minded, and religious, they could also be tough, shrewd businessmen.

Production of lumber increased from 3 million board feet in 1880 to more than 2 billion in 1907 Texas became a leading timber state, but greedy, shortsighted people cut more trees down than could or would be planted to replace them. In 1900, 637 saw mills operated in Texas.

Fortunately, W. Goodrich Jones, a Galveston-born, Princeton-educated banker in Temple, was concerned for the future. The earliest prominent advocate of forest conservation, Jones actively encouraged conservation, management, and replantation of forest lands in 1889. Yet he failed to prevent the last leg of the timber boom which paralleled the rapid railroad development. With Kirby's support, Jones's efforts had laid the basis for the revival of the lumber industry in the twentieth century.

One of the state's greatest reforms was in transportation. When the era began, the principal form of travel consisted of expensive and slow wagons and stagecoaches. Galveston served the state as its major port, but some goods flowed down the Red River to the Mississippi, leaving Texas at Jefferson. In 1870, Texas had only 583 miles of railroad track, most of which radiated from Houston. The lack of adequate transportation had been a major factor in the state's lack of progress.

The next decade witnessed the growth of interstate railroads plus numerous feeder lines, the construction of which was funded by liberal government subsidies. In 1872 the Missouri, Kansas and Texas Railroad (Katy) crossed the Red River at Denison, and the next year the Houston and Texas Central Railroad was built northward from Houston through Hearne and Dallas to join the Katy, for the first time establishing major north-south rail transportation. Soon thereafter came the International and Great Northern Railroad, connecting Longview in East Texas with Hearne, Austin, San Antonio, and Laredo.

Part of the Atchison, Topeka and Santa Fe system, the Gulf, Colorado and Santa Fe Railroad linked Galveston with Fort Worth and Amarillo. That line crossed Collis Huntington's Southern Pacific Railroad, which ran from Beaumont to El Paso, at Richmond. Also proceeding west from Longview to Dallas, Fort Worth, and El Paso was Jay Gould's Texas and Pacific Railroad. To the north and west, the Fort Worth and Denver City Railroad went through Amarillo, and in 1893 it joined the Burlington system. Before the end of the era, Texas had an interlocking, interstate chain of railroads.

Numerous feeder lines supplemented the major companies to form the rail system. They ranged from short lines that tied county seats to interstate lines to lines that connected railroads to the lumber industry. Rusk Countians believed that a train should always come locomotive, or head-first, into the county seat. Thus the Henderson and Overton Railroad backed from Henderson, the county seat, the sixteen miles to a rendezvous with the International and Great Northern at Overton and then went cow-catcher ahead back to Henderson.

Three railroads penetrated the lumber country, which had not been served prior to 1870. The Houston East and West Texas Railroad went from Houston to Shreveport via Livingston and Lufkin. Known as "The Rabbit" or "Hell Either Way Taken," it became part of the Southern Pacific system. The Texas and New Orleans ran northwest from Beaumont along the route of many East Texas saw mills to Nacogdoches and then on to Dallas. The third major line became the Atchison, Topeka, and Santa Fe Railroad after the acquisition of John Henry Kirby's Gulf, Beaumont, and Kansas City. This railroad enabled Kirby and others to ship Texas longleaf pine timber to Great Plains cities and to Chicago.

The railroads had been aided by generous government land grants. Reflecting the wishes of businessmen and farmers, and following the examples of the United States Congress's Pacific Railway Acts of 1862 and 1864, the Texas legislature passed the Land Grant Act of 1876. This statute granted the railroads sixteen sections—a section is 640 acres—for every mile of track completed. Until 1882, forty railroads received 32,153,878 acres of land for 2,928 miles of track. Railroads had been promised 8 million more acres that were available. Small towns, dreaming of how much a local railroad would support their development, actively worked to attract a line. Towns provided tax exemptions, depots, and sometimes, although it was unconstitutional to do so, public bonds. As a result, Texas rose in railroad mileage to first in the nation with approximately 10,000 miles of track, some of which had been built with convict labor (much to the anger of citizens who wanted jobs). These railroads contributed significantly to the Texas population explosion of the era and provided new markets for agricultural products. On the other hand, the rail baron's price gouging, which made the farmers angry, intensified the state's agricultural revolution.

In concert with the lumber-railroad industrialization, labor unions developed in Texas. They were vigorously opposed by lumber barons and feared by Texas politicians who tried to industrialize Texas with New South appeals of cheap labor. Early Texas unions included the Screwmen's Benevolent Association and the Knights of Labor. The former were longshoremen, who, with screw jacks, packed cotton bales into ocean-going ships on the Galveston wharfs. As historian James Reese's article in the *Southwestern Historical Quarterly* (October, 1971) noted, the union had reached its peak by 1891. It was doomed because of the expansion of the cotton crop, the lack of skilled laborers, the competition from black longshoremen, and, above all, the introduction of high-density cotton compresses at the Galveston wharfs.

The Knights of Labor had existed nationally since 1866 and made their appearance in Texas in 1878. Reaching a membership of 30,000 members in 1885, the union appealed to most working classes. Welcoming women and blacks, the Knights worked to improve the livelihood of workers with better working conditions and regular pay days. They also supported political reforms such as direct election of United States senators.

In 1883 the Knights successfully struck against the Mallory Line at Galveston for discharging white union laborers and replacing them with black, nonunion workers. Other strikes were common, but the climax to the Knights' activity in Texas came when longstanding disputes between railroader Jay Gould and the union erupted in the Great Southwest Strike. Violence flared from March 10 to May 4, 1886. Governor John Ireland called out the Texas Rangers, and the union conceded defeat.

The reform labor spirit died, and during the remainder of the era the newly created American Federation of Labor (AFL) placed more emphasis on skilled labor while seeking less political action and direct confrontation. By 1900 the AFL, with 8,475 Texas members, had become the leading advocate of business unionism. While Texas was neither a prolabor or highly industrial state, the AFL had adjusted to reality with practicality.

Although not national leaders in industry or education, Texans had sustained life and conquered the frontier. Such actions left little time for sophisticated education and long-range planning. During the Radical Republican era, public education had been provided by a highly centralized state school system that was headed by a State Superintendent for Public Instruction. Reacting against the Radicals, in the Constitution of 1876, reformers wanted the focus of education to be like the 1840s model, making parents totally responsible for their children's education. Partially in order to have more hands during harvest time, partially as a reaction against black education, Texans abolished compulsory attendance. Schools became segregated. Blacks received the hand-me-down educational facilities of their local area. Community schools had no boundary lines and could not levy taxes. The dominant trend in education from 1874 to 1890, decentralization, had reached its peak.

Concerned about the impermanence of community schools and inadequate education, another reform movement's work led to the passage of the School Law of 1884. This statute returned control of the state's schools to an elected state superintendent, but the objectives of the law were infrequently met. For example, independent rural school districts rarely were created, few permanent buildings were constructed, and local taxes remained low.

The values of urban and rural educators often conflicted. Urban teachers viewed education as a necessary ingredient for adulthood in an urban America in which knowledge could be quantified, produced, and standardized. On the other hand, the little country schoolhouse remained a prominent fixture in Texas education until at least 1926. Here rural residents lavished great time and personal labor that went far beyond money. The country school served as a civic center. While urban educators wanted longer school terms, better education for teachers, professional supervision, and higher pay, rural Texans expected the teacher not only to distribute knowledge but to be an example for students to imitate. In rural areas, teachers "lived in glass houses." Admirably, rural parents drilled their students in their studies and quickly enforced school discipline.

This conflict of values continued throughout 1874–1900. Fortunately, few teachers were radical political reformers. Educational historian Jack Campbell concluded that the political conservatism of teachers in this era, plus their political connections, saved public education from the fate that befell the Radical Republicans. Despite hard work and good intentions, national educators hardly held Texas education in awe.

Higher education also underwent reform and change. Until the reform era, higher education in Texas had been ecclesiastical and primarily for whites. Existing in 1874 were Baylor, Texas Christian, Austin College, Southwestern University, Lon Morris College, St. Mary's, Trinity, Mary Hardin Baylor, and two black colleges, Paul Quinn (1872) and Wiley (1873). Rustic frontier Texans frequently referred to these institutions as "dude factories," implying that a real man could make better use of his time and talents than wasting years in college.

This attitude changed. As a result of the Morrill Act of 1862 and with the leadership of A. J. Rose, worthy master of the state Grange, Texas Agricultural and Mechanical College began in 1876. Seven years later, The University of Texas started and soon had begun schools of law and medicine. Aided by revenues from public lands, these two universities became the state's most prominent public institutions. Meanwhile, Sam Houston State Normal School opened its doors for teachers in 1879. Prairie View A&M, authorized in 1876 and begun in 1879, provided a similar service for black teachers. This institution later expanded as a black land-grant university under the Texas A&M University system.

Twenty other colleges founded during this era continue to operate. These colleges reflected church preferences or the desire of local citizens for a college. In 1883, Blinn College began as a Methodist academy and later became the first county-owned junior college in Texas. East Texas State University started as a private institution but later became public. Tarleton State and the University of North Texas were founded during this era as were Howard Payne (Baptist), St. Edward's (Catholic), Texas Lutheran, Southwestern Adventists, and Texas Wesleyan (Methodist). From 1874 to 1900 the state had greatly increased its number of college graduates.

If change and reform existed in education, the most significant change occurred in government. The Constitution of 1876 and the construction of the state capitol symbolized this reform. The new constitution signaled that the Redeemers had gained control of Texas politics. These Democrats wanted to reform Radical Reconstruction rule by trying to industrialize the South, reduce government, lower taxes, and oppose unions. In creating these reforms, they borrowed from the past as well as the present.

On September 6, 1875, ninety delegates came to Austin for the Constitutional Convention. This relatively undistinguished group included seventy-five Democrats and fifteen Republicans. Among them were twenty-nine lawyers, six blacks, and probably more than forty Grangers. Mediocre leadership prevailed except from famous Texas Ranger John "Rip" Ford and two rising political stars, John H. Reagan and Lawrence Sullivan "Sul" Ross.

When the constitutional convention ended on November 24, the resulting constitution reflected the dominant political spirit of the time. The new constitution reacted against the previous Radical constitution written in 1869 and favored a return to the ideals of Jefferson and Jackson, previously manifested in the Constitution of 1845. This meant frugal, limited government with greater democracy. The Constitution of 1876 reduced the governor's power and cut the office's annual salary by $1,000. In a strong demonstration of democracy, it provided for the popular election of the lieutenant governor, secretary of state, attorney general, comptroller, land commissioner, and treasurer. Judges were elected, and the terms of state senators reduced from six to four years. Grangers and Republicans helped defeat a poll tax that would have reduced voting rights for poor whites and blacks. But women remained without suffrage.

The conservative Constitution of 1876 borrowed from the past by returning the legislature to biennial sessions. The influence of the Constitution of 1845 can be seen in a debt ceiling of $200,000, a low tax rate, and the requirement that property be taxed in proportion to its value. In land policy, the framers borrowed from precedents such as the United States Homestead Act of 1862. This act and the Texas acceptance of it provided for 160 acres of land to each head of a family. While such land grants could sustain life in East Texas, this acreage was insufficient in West Texas. In passing this law, Texas revealed its Southern tradition.

When presented to the voters, neither the Democratic nor Republican parties officially endorsed it. Backed by Governor Richard Coke and the Grange, the voters approved the constitution by a margin of 136,606 to 56,562. This poorly organized document, with its more than 63,000 words, would be one of the nation's largest constitutions. By 1989, the voters had approved 326 amendments. The Constitution of 1876 placed too many restrictions on the governor and the legislature; yet attempts to write a new constitution in 1919 and 1975 both failed.

During the 1876 constitutional convention, the framers recognized the need for a new capitol. The expanding population, the closing of the frontier, immigration, and the people's increased desire for better civic services resulted in W. H. Stewart's resolution to set aside 3 million acres of public land to raise money for a capitol. In 1879, the Texas legislature appropriated 3,050,000 acres and created a Capitol Board to sell the land. It became the famous XIT Ranch. Two years later, a fire destroyed the old capitol, and in a sense of urgency, Elijah Meyers, a talented, hardworking but self-destructive hypochondriac, became the architect for the state capitol. Work began in 1882. On May 16, 1888, the state dedicated a dynamic Renaissance Revival capitol. It measured 556.5 feet from east to west, 288 feet north to south, and was crowned by a Goddess of Liberty, which was positioned 311 feet above the Texas soil.

Writing in the October 1988 issue of the *Southwestern Historical Quarterly*, architectural historian Willard Robinson noted the pride of "far sighted Texas forefathers who had a vision to build an edifice that, a century later, still reflects their pride in the state and its representative government, and that will continue to impress countless generations to come."

Politics experienced significant change during this age of reform. Texas reformers included not only the Redeemers but also the agrarian reformers who battled for agricultural concerns and the political manifestation of their way of life. As historian Randolph Campbell concluded in *A Southern Community in Crisis* (1983) these local politicians of the 1870s were similar and sometimes the same people who controlled Texas politics prior to secession. Change was painful. Somewhere in the process were those ordinary Texans such as Smith County farmer Martin Thompson from Screech Owl Bend, who planted his vegetables and cotton, acquired land, went to church, mourned the tragedy of the Civil War until his death, and joined his ancestors in Asbury Cemetery.

The Redeemers replaced Republican governor Edmund J. Davis with Richard Coke, a Virginia-born, former Confederate captain and Waco lawyer whose supporters included the Grange. In Texas two years later, Coke, a Democrat, had decisively defeated Republican gubernatorial nominee William Chambers, 150,681 to 47,719. Manifesting the same electoral pattern, Democratic United States presidential nominee, Samuel Tilden, received 108,383 votes in contrast to Republican Rutherford B. Hayes's 45,013 votes. Nonetheless, in the highly controversial Election of 1876, Hayes became president of the United States. As governor from 1874 to 1877, when he resigned to replace Republican Morgan Hamilton in the United States Senate, Coke quickly removed Radical Republicans from office and sought to reduce the public debt of $3,167,335. But Texas had not recovered from the Panic of 1873, and expenses for Texas A&M, frontier defense, veterans' pensions, and interest raised the debt to $5 million. The failure of Coke's successor, Richard Hubbard, to resolve the debt issue prevented him from winning the governorship himself.

The same year that Coke went to Washington, the Greenback Labor party came to Texas advocating inflation. Calling for taxation of national bonds, a federal income tax, restriction of working hours in industry, better schools, railroad regulation, lower state taxes, and economical government, the Greenbackers posed more of a threat to the Redeemers than did the Republicans. In their first gubernatorial campaign, they nominated prominent Robertson County railroad and land developer William Hamman.

In the election of 1878, the Democrats knew Hamman well, for he had been active in their party. Deadlocked between Hubbard and Congressman James Throckmorton, the Democrats turned to Chief Justice of the Texas Supreme Court Oran "The Old Alcalde" Roberts. A popular and lovable person, but a boring speaker who advocated small government, Roberts easily defeated Hamman by a vote of 158,933 to 55,002. Some Republicans followed E. J. Davis's support of Hamman; others cast 23,402 votes for Anthony Norton. Two years later, Roberts defeated Hamman again, 166,101 to 33,721, after Davis made his last Republican gubernatorial bid by getting 64,382 votes. That year Texans supported Democratic nominee Winfield Scott Hancock for president (155,963 votes) over Republican James Garfield (57,275) and Greenbacker James B. Weaver (27,471).

As expected, the voters approved of Roberts's Redeemer rule. A fiscal conservative, the tall, grey-bearded governor cut the debt by $1 million, reduced funds for frontier defense, cut *ad valorem* taxes by 40 percent, tried to improve the collection of taxes with the "bell punch" tax on liquor sales, cut funds for public education and offered public land for sale through the ridiculous Fifty Cent Law. Rampant land speculation resulted, and state government operated at a minimum level.

Republicans furnished little opposition to the Democrats during the period. In an effort to defeat the Democrats, Davis tried to fuse the Republicans with Greenbackers. With the approval of President Chester A. Arthur, Republicans supported the colorful orator and United States Congressman from Bastrop, George W. "Wash" Jones, a Greenbacker. Jones failed to attract a majority of farmers or laborers and lost the governor's race in 1882 to John "Oxcart John" Ireland by 150,809 to 102,501 votes.

After Davis died, in 1883, the Republicans continued to play a minor role in Texas politics. Leadership passed to Norris Wright Cuney, a shrewd customs inspector from Galveston, and, until his death in 1897, the most important black leader of his day. As head of the Republican party, he solicited black support until they became a party majority. Yet Cuney could neither unite all the anti-Democratic forces under Republican leadership nor resolve black-white disputes within Republican ranks. Consequently, gubernatorial candidates Anthony Norton in 1884, Archelaus Cochran in 1886, Webster Flanagan in 1890, and William Makemson in 1894 all failed, as did Prohibitionist candidates opposing the Democrats.

Reformers became the *status quo* in a short time, and the Redeemers were no exception. Ireland, a resident of Seguin, who previously had been defeated in a bid for governor and United States congressman, was a man of integrity. Climaxing his political career with victories over Jones in 1882 and again in 1884, Ireland changed Roberts's land policies by stopping the rapid land sales, in order to preserve land for future homesteaders. He advocated tougher law enforcement but retained Roberts's frugal financial program.

In the gubernatorial election of 1886, a slender, sensitive state senator with a camp-meeting drawl, Lawrence Sullivan Ross, easily received the Democratic nomination. Aided by an astute campaign manager, George Clark, Ross easily won by defeating Independent candidate Marion Martin. A Jeffersonian Democrat, Ross believed in limited government and conservative spending. During his administrations taxes fell and revenues rose. Another tough law-and-order man, Ross wanted prisons to be self-supporting and promoted the Gatesville State School for Boys. Realizing that the state should expand its charitable institutions, his administration created a state home for Confederate veterans, a deaf, dumb, and blind institute for black youths, and a state orphans' home. Although he desired to improve the Texas public school system, one of the nation's poorest, the legislature failed to endorse Ross's reforms for free text books and his desire that local taxes could support public schools. Ross had not been a reformer, but his administration included one of the era's greatest advocates for change, Attorney General James Stephen Hogg.

Leadership in Texas had not been limited to the governor. In the United States Senate were Samuel Bell Maxey (1874–1887), frequently supported by railroad and business interests, and Granger favorite Richard Coke (1877–1895). Congressmen Roger Mills of Waco fought for low tariffs, and John H. Reagan authored the Interstate Commerce Act and supported the Sherman Silver Purchase Act and Sherman Antitrust Act. Alexander W. Terrell later sponsored the Terrell Election Law, which provided for direct party primaries. While these were mature politicians, the era also saw the rise of congressmen Joseph Sayers, Joseph Bailey, and John Nance Garner. The core of the powerful Texas delegation during the New Deal—Sam Rayburn, Tom Connally, Marvin Jones, and Hatton Sumners—was born in this era.

The principal reform movement came from the agricultural revolution. Fearing the rise of the city, farmers turned to agricultural organizations. The first of these, the Patrons of Husbandry, better known as the Grange, made its appearance at Salado in 1873. The Grange, under the leadership of Redeemers William W. Lang and Archibald Ross, favored the Constitution of 1876, state support for education, and railroad regulation. They promoted crop diversification. They also advocated fellowship and cooperative marketing through the creation of the Texas Cooperative Association.

When the Grange and the Greenback movements declined, farmers, desiring direct political action, turned to the Texas Farmers Alliance or to the Populist party and voted for reform Democrats such as James Stephen Hogg or the Populist Jerome Kearby. The Texas Farmers Alliance had a precarious beginning. Low prices, the failure of the Texas Cooperative Association, and unfavorable weather made farmers responsive to the message of economic independence proclaimed by Alliance recruiter S. O. Dawes. By 1886 the Texas Farmers Alliance boasted of 100,000 members, and a white Baptist minister, Robert Humphrey of Lovelady, had organized the Colored Alliance in Houston County as a parallel group. Favoring railroad regulation and inflation while opposing high interest rates, the Texas Farmers Alliance met in Waco during January 1877. Charismatic Charles Macune announced the merger of the alliance with the Louisiana Farmers Union. Thus began a movement that resulted in the Southern Alliance (Farmers Alliance and Cooperative Union of America), the largest and most influential nineteenth-century farm organization. Spreading like wildfire, the Southern Alliance attracted over 1.5 million members, advocated Macune's subtreasury plan, and eventually became a significant element of the Populist party.

At that time the most powerful reformer in Texas politics was the 6'3", 300-pound James Stephen Hogg. A former East Texas journalist and an effective stump speaker who skillfully analyzed campaign audiences, Hogg made villains of fraudulent insurance companies and the railroads. Called a "reform leader, a progressive conservative," by his able biographer, Robert Cotner, Hogg favored business, but he wanted honorable business. He encouraged reputable insurance companies but succeeded in driving out many companies which had, by fraud and misrepresentation, swindled Texans. Believing in strict and fair law enforcement, Hogg incurred the wrath and political opposition of legendary rancher Charles Goodnight when, as the attorney general, he tried unsuccessfully to convict Judge Frank Willis for favoring large ranches. Operators of large ranches who leased public lands knew that Hogg favored schools and rural settlers when he obtained the return of over half a million acres to the state.

The Texas Constitution of 1845 had opposed monopolies, and now Texas farmers, led by the Grange and the Alliances, called for regulation of businesses that monopolized the processing of agricultural commodities such as beef and cotton. Influenced by the Sherman Antitrust

Act, Hogg assisted Representative Alvin Owsley and Commissioner of Insurance Statistics and History, Lafayette Foster, to write a Texas antitrust law. Hogg then successfully prosecuted the Texas Traffic Association, which was a railroad pool that fixed rates. Although unsuccessful in obtaining effective railroad regulation and lower rates for small rural communities, Hogg made railroad regulation and reform a major political issue in the election of 1890.

In 1890 voters considered a constitutional amendment for a railroad commission and the gubernatorial candidacy of Jim Hogg. Although suffering opposition from the railroads, led by their talented and ambitious lobbyist George Clark, Hogg still won the Democratic nomination and then a landslide victory over Webster Flanagan by 262,452 to 77,742 votes. Voters approved a proposal to create a railroad commission by 181,954 to 73,106 votes. Thus, reformers had little reason to join the Populists, and Hogg proceeded toward leading a moderate reform program.

The major item on Hogg's gubernatorial agenda was the railroad commission. Thomas J. Brown, Martin Crane, and Alexander Terrell led the Texas legislature in establishing it. Hogg then persuaded Reagan to resign as United States senator and become the first chairman of the Texas Railroad Commission. After 1891 the commission fixed schedules, reduced rates slightly, and reduced intrastate discrimination for over forty Texas railroads. The rails responded, again through Clark, who waged a vigorous gubernatorial campaign against Hogg in 1892. With support from most of the state's newspapers plus railroad, banking, and big-business interests, Clark posed a challenge to reform. Thus, the Democrats were split. More liberal than Hogg were the Populists, advocating the subtreasury plan and rallying behind the candidacy of Christian gentleman Judge Thomas Nugent. When the election ended, Hogg emerged with 190,846 votes, followed by Clark with 133,395 and Nugent with 108,483 votes. While Hogg had not received a majority, he remained governor. Considering that Hogg and Nugent were reformers, the Texas voters had rejected conservatism.

Hogg's second term (1893–1895) marked the passage of numerous reforms. Hogg promoted The University of Texas and Texas A&M, urged prison reform, and advocated the Perpetuities and Corporation Law, which gave land companies fifteen years to sell their land holdings, the Alien Land Act, which forced out-of-state landowners to sell their holdings, and the Stock and Bond Law, which gave the Railroad Commission power to regulate the sale of securities. On the negative side, the Hogg administration, acting within the spirit of the times, forced the railroads to provide separate facilities for blacks and whites.

After two terms Hogg tired of public life and desired financial security. He preferred business ventures to a seat as United States senator. Hogg wanted John H. Reagan to succeed him as governor, but Hogg's clever campaign manager, Edward House, had other ideas. House supported Attorney General Charles Culbertson, who received the Democratic nomination. Culbertson defeated Nugent, the Populist, by 216,373 to 159,676 votes.

Culbertson provided a moderate reform administration characterized by strict law enforcement. He preserved the Hogg reforms by giving the Railroad Commission greater authority, and he supported tougher antitrust regulations. Culbertson favored judicial reforms, rigid economy, and black education. To prohibit the Corbett-Fitzsimmons boxing match, he called the Texas legislature into special session. At the end of his governorship, Culbertson replaced Roger Mills in the United States Senate and was followed by another House-sponsored governor, the more conservative former lieutenant governor and United States congressman Joseph Sayers of Bastrop.

The Populist crusade culminated in the United States presidential election of 1896. During the final years of the agricultural revolution, Populist leaders actively solicited the black vote through the efforts of mulatto preacher John Ranger of Robertson County. In 1894 the Populists made gains in their gubernatorial vote and in black support, but far less than anticipated by their leaders. The nomination of William Jennings Bryan as the Democratic presidential nominee took the breeze out of the windmill, for the Texas Populists who then led the fight to prevent the national party from endorsing the great champion of free silver, Bryan, failed.

Texas Republicans joined with Populists in support of Jerome Kearby for governor. A famous criminal lawyer and former Greenbacker, Kearby waged an enthusiastic campaign. The Populist effort to form a biracial party failed as over 40,000 party members chose Culbertson over Kearby. It may be, as historians Cantrell and Barton suggest, that these white Populists could not accept the racial stigma associated with the Republicans. Nonetheless, Kearby lost to Culbertson by 298,568 to 238,688 votes, and Bryan on the Democratic ticket took the electoral vote by 290,526 to the Republican William Mckinley's 163,413 votes and the 79,572 votes the Populists could muster for Bryan's candidacy. McKinley won the election of 1896 and became president of the United States. While white supremacy was strengthened in Texas, the Populists had made an unsuccessful appeal to all reform Democrats. Nor had the Populists carried all the black vote. Black Republican William "Gooseneck Bill" McDonald had campaigned vigorously for Culbertson. Thereafter, the Texas Populists followed the national party with internal disputes, but with the rise of national prosperity, both died.

With the end of the Culbertson administration, the reform period ended. What was its meaning? Texas had assumed control of its own political destiny again. The economy had changed much for the better, and the agricultural revolution—a great dream itself—had come, made its impact, and died. The direction of education had changed, especially in the orientation of higher education but also in the conflict of educational values. The transportation revolution provided by railroads, albeit with abuses, encouraged the rise of industries with conservative government and helped lay a solid foundation for the dreams of entrepreneurs. Dreams for labor and blacks had not been fulfilled. Although adequately reflecting the will of the majority, the Constitution of 1876 was too short-sighted and restrictive of state government. Tougher law enforcement remained a political objective. Political reformers, once in power, were changed through the efforts of James Stephen Hogg. Finally, even though the intensity of Hogg's reform spirit failed to last, such has been the ebb and flow pattern of reform movements and dreams. But because of the reform movement, with its many well-intentioned leaders, Texas in 1900 was a better state than in 1874.

Yet Another Look at the Fergusons of Texas

JANE BOCK GUZMAN

JANE BOCK GUZMAN SERVES ON THE BOARD OF DIRECTORS OF THE DALLAS HISTORICAL SOCIETY AND THE DALLAS JEWISH HISTORICAL SOCIETY.

JIM AND MIRIAM FERGUSON, KNOWN BY TEXANS AS "PA" AND "MA," GOVERNED THE LONE STAR STATE IN THE EARLY DECADES OF THE TWENTIETH CENTURY. IN THIS SELECTION, DR. GUZMAN EXAMINES THE CAREERS OF THESE TWO COLORFUL AND CONTROVERSIAL POLITICIANS.

Texas politics and politicians have always been interesting, and James E. (Pa) and Miriam A. (Ma) Ferguson were among the most engaging characters in Texas political history. They both were elected governor, although most observers believed at the time that only one of them, Pa, actually performed the duties of the office. He was the only Texas governor ever to be impeached; she was the first woman elected to the highest office in the state.

James Edward Ferguson was born on August 31, 1871, near Salado in Bell County. His father died when he was four years old. After being expelled from school for disobedience, he left home at sixteen and wandered through the West, working as a miner and on a railroad gang.

"Yet Another Look at the Fergusons of Texas" by Jane Bock Guzman from *East Texas Historical Journal*, Vol. XLIV, No. 1, 2006, pp. 40–48. Reprinted by permission of East Texas Historical Association.

He returned home two years later to study law, and was admitted to the bar in 1897. His law practice was not lucrative enough, so he turned to real estate, insurance, and banking. He married Miriam Amanda Wallace on December 31, 1899.

Miriam and Jim had probably known each other all their lives. Her mother, Eliza Garrison Wallace, was a widow with two daughters when she married Joseph L. Wallace. Her first husband was Wesley G. Ferguson, the brother of James Edward Ferguson, Sr., and the uncle of James Jr. The two daughters from her first marriage were his first cousins, as well as Miriam's half-sisters; therefore, Miriam's mother was Jim Ferguson's aunt. Miriam was born on June 13, 1875, in Bell County, four years after Jim. Unlike her future husband, she had the benefit of higher education; she attended two colleges, Salado College and Baylor Female College at Belton, although she did not graduate from either.

The Fergusons held an interest in the Farmers State Bank of Belton for several years, and Jim, who managed the concern, was a member of the Texas State Bankers Association. In 1907 the Fergusons sold their share of the bank and moved to Temple, where Jim organized the Temple State Bank and became its president. He became involved in local politics, opposing prohibition even though he was a teetotaler. His position on this, one of the most pressing political issues of the era in Texas, put him in direct opposition to the Ku Klux Klan, a powerful force throughout the state that was promoting prohibition. Not only did Ferguson's stance distance him from other Texas politicians, it gained him the support and friendship of Texas brewers, who stood to lose their businesses if prohibition became law.

In 1914 Jim Ferguson decided to run for governor. Although never before holding elective office, he won the Democratic nomination when other "wets," or anti-prohibitionists, withdrew from the race to avoid dividing the vote. Ferguson found his calling in politics, employing a time-honored practice of appealing to the "common man." He wore a frock coat and deliberately used poor grammar, despite the fact that he was well read, to appeal to his "boys at the forks of the creek," as he called the tenant farmers. He frequently criticized "city slickers" and "educated fools who know nothing of the farmer's problems." Building on this populist theme, he usually added that he "warn't no college dude, and durned glad of it." This tactic—portraying himself as one of the people—was quite a leap, considering his presidency of a bank, his financial interest in ten others, and his ownership of 2,500 acres of black farmland—but it worked. Ferguson called for state regulation of rental fees landlords charged their sharecroppers and opposed bonus payments attached onto customary rent charges. He proposed laws limiting the amount of rent that landlords could demand from tenants, one-fourth for cotton and one third for grain crops. Ferguson insisted that by improving the lot of tenant farmers, the entire Texas economy would be strengthened. He also supported organized labor, which made him unpopular among business owners, and apologized for the fact that his mother had been educated by Ursuline nuns, explaining that she had been orphaned at an early age and that the nuns had taken her in. He added that she had married a Methodist minister and had never set foot inside a Catholic church. Fergusons appeal to tenant farmers succeeded; after capturing the Democratic nomination in the primary, he easily defeated his Republican opponent in the general election and took office.

Ferguson's apparent disdain for education was not universal, nor was it apparent in his early policy decisions. He often asserted his desire to improve the condition of rural schools in Texas, and during his first term in office textbooks were supplied free for the first time to children enrolled in Texas public schools. Despite his rhetoric to the contrary he also supported higher education, urging generous appropriations for colleges and making provisions for eight new ones. In fact, during his first term, the legislature authorized agricultural colleges at Stephenville and Arlington, appropriated funds for West Texas A&M, and established colleges that later became East Texas State University, Stephen F. Austin State University, and Sul Ross College.

Ferguson did, however, have personal issues with administrators at the University of Texas. Rumors abounded that the UT appropriations bill of 1915 had a number of items that would be vetoed. Ferguson, however, signed the bill without a veto after having discussed it with the University's acting president, W. J. Battle, and several members of the Board of Regents. But because of a recent change in administration at the state's flagship school, there had been no time to prepare a proper itemized budget. Therefore, what Ferguson and the legislature authorized was a proposed budget for the preceding biennium, with an addendum requesting that they be permitted to make such changes as might prove necessary. This was explained to Ferguson and to members of the legislature; the bill specifically stated that the regents might make necessary "changes and substitutions within the total"—in other words, shift money around—as long as they did not exceed the amount appropriated.

Changes were made, which the governor protested. He sent a letter to the regents asserting that Battle was not qualified to be president of the University. Although Battle was assured by the regents that he had their support, he withdrew his name for consideration after Ferguson challenged his ascension to the leadership position. Ferguson insisted that an auditor be appointed for the University, and the auditor found a few minor accounting errors. The governor used these as evidence of a widespread pattern of wrongdoing.

The Board of Regents elected R. E. Vinson to serve as president of the University in 1916. Ferguson, however, had his own candidate in mind, and was displeased with their decision. He believed that, as governor, he should have been consulted about the filling of such an important office, and he made his views plain to several of the regents. Shortly before Vinson's inauguration, he visited the governor along with Regent George W. Littlefield. During this meeting, Ferguson restated his opposition to Vinson and told the two men that he had inflammatory information about five faculty members. In September Vinson, now the President of the University, asked Ferguson to share this information so that he might submit it to the Board of Regents for evaluation, but the governor declined. He added that in the future, it "would be better for us to remain in our respective jurisdictions and no good purpose can be served by any further relation between us."

Ferguson decided that what he needed was a Board of Regents whose members would follow his wishes. He had already appointed Maurice Faber, a rabbi living in Tyler and the first clergyman to serve in such a capacity, to the board. Ferguson now demanded either Faber's complete support or his resignation. Faber refused to comply with either choice, so Ferguson wrote that he "did not care to bandy words with him, and that if Faber wanted Ferguson to remove him from office, he could rest assured that he (Ferguson), would not shrink for the task."

Apparently changing his mind about involving himself in university affairs, Ferguson attended a Board of Regents meeting in October 1916 to present his evidence against five faculty members and to show the extent of the graft he claimed infected the University. The governor's case was weak, but he insisted that Vinson and the board members should remove these faculty members. After investigating Ferguson's charges they refused to act. Their report was made public and led the governor to declare that the entire issue was "becoming more clearly defined as to whether the University shall run the people of Texas or the people of the state run their own University."

Ferguson must have been surprised at this turn of events; he had just removed three members of the San Antonio State Hospital and encountered only token resistance in replacing a member of the staff at Prairie View A&M College. As a result, he believed that he had more power than he actually did as governor. Ignoring the advice of his wife, who pleaded with him to drop the matter, he pressed onward with his vendetta. Meanwhile, during the legislative session of 1917, several legislators introduced resolutions asking that Ferguson be investigated, and several legislative committees censured the governor for misdeeds.

When the special session of the legislature adjourned in 1917, Governor Ferguson had to decide whether or not to sign the generous appropriations authorized for different state institutions, including the University of Texas. He asked the UT Regents to meet in his office on May 28. Rumors abounded that the governor would demand the removal of five faculty members and the expulsion of fraternities from the university. Fraternities were a favorite target of Ferguson, the populist; he declared that they drew a line between wealth and poverty at the university, and that their members lived in "stately mansions," while the poorer students lived in "crowded boardinghouses." He added that the university as a whole was an institution "of fads and fancies, grossly mismanaged."

The regents realized that if they followed the governor's wishes, the appropriations bill would be signed. The Ex-Students' Association issued a statement saying that it would be better to close the university rather that submit to the governor's demands. Ferguson vetoed the university appropriation on June 2, saying that he thought the bill was excessive. He made no mention of an injunction issued by a district court in Austin that had intended to prevent Dr. Fly of Houston, a new Ferguson appointee to the board of regents, from taking his seat. The district court also granted an injunction that enjoined the regents from removing any members of the faculty.

The regents met in Austin on June 5, hoping to compromise since the governor's veto had not been filed with the secretary of state. However, Ferguson then took an even stronger stand and demanded that nine members of the faculty, as well as all lawsuits and injunctions, be dismissed. No compromise was reached, the veto was filed, and the university was allowed the use of its available money and the salary of only one dean.

In July 1917 the injunctions were lifted, and six of the faculty members mentioned by the governor were removed. Ferguson believed he had won, and continued to ridicule the school in a speech he delivered at an Old Settlers' picnic at Valley Mills on July 13. He took a number of swipes at the university, ending his diatribe by declaring "I say that not only are too many people going hog wild over higher education, but that some people have become plain damn fools over the idea that we ought to have an army of educated fools to run the government."

This speech aroused the wrath of Will C. Hogg, secretary of the Ex-Students Association and the son of former governor James S. Hogg. The Ex-Students Association had been organizing opposition to the governor, encouraging former students to monitor the governor closely for any indication of misdeeds—which they soon discovered. Ferguson was indicted by a Travis County Grand Jury and later impeached by the Texas House of Representatives, meeting in a special session on August 1, 1917. The House impeached him on twenty-one charges of misconduct: these included findings that Ferguson juggled state accounts to serve his private financial interests; that he lied to the legislature earlier concerning the bad state of his personal finances; that he had secured a mysterious personal loan for $156,500, (rumored to have come from Kaiser Wilhelm of Germany—this was, after all, the early days of American involvement in WWI—but later found to have been made by San Antonio brewers); that he tried to become the dictator of the university; that he tried to bribe government officials; and finally, that he had intermingled his own and the state's accounts at the Temple State Bank to make money for himself. Ferguson excused himself on the last day of the trial before members of the Texas Senate and went to Fort Worth to attend a livestock show. The vote was twenty-five to three to convict Ferguson and remove him from office. William P. Hobby, the president of the senate, succeeded Ferguson as governor and called a special session of the legislature to appropriate new monies for the university, and things returned to normal. As a result of the conviction, Ferguson lost all his civil rights, including the right to hold office. He claimed that he was a martyr, put to death by the university clique and the newspapers.

Jim and Miriam Ferguson left Austin in disgrace and moved back to Temple, where the former governor started a weekly newspaper, *The Ferguson Forum*. He liked to call it "my little Christian weekly," and used it to communicate with his supporters, especially in East Texas, who waited eagerly for their papers every Friday. Ferguson used his paper to launch a diatribe against the Ku Klux Klan and the University of Texas, to lobby for repeal of the prohibition laws and elimination of the poll tax, and occasionally to slur Jews. He endorsed Henry Ford for president in 1924, saying, "He is the living personification and perfection of the principle of a dollar's worth of services for a dollar paid," and even sold subscriptions to the *Dearborn Independent* in his newspaper. Ferguson ran for governor again in 1918, against Hobby, despite being legally barred from doing so, and lost by a landslide. In 1920, he left the Democratic Party to run for president on the American Party ticket.

Ferguson's main political thrusts were against the Ku Klux Klan and prohibition. The Klan was founded after the Civil War by Confederate veterans, as a means of keeping former slaves "in their place." It collapsed early in the 1870s but was revived in 1915 by Dr. Hiram Evens, a Dallas dentist. In its early years the new Klan was an object of ridicule to some; invitations to a party honoring an engaged couple, Beatrice Wertheimer and Herbert Mallinson, asked guests to dress in Klan attire, which the society columnist of the local paper described as "grotesque." Despite such derision, the organization's membership grew in strength, especially in Dallas: October 24, 1923, was Ku Klux Klan Day at the State Fair of Texas. The Fergusons moved to Dallas briefly in 1923, but were unhappy there and soon moved back to Temple. One reason could be the fact that *The Ferguson Forum* did not flourish in Dallas. A lack of advertising from Dallas merchants led Ferguson to print his most infamous column in the March 15, 1923 issue. "The Cloven Foot of the Dallas Jew" was a diatribe listing the evils of the Jewish merchants of Dallas. This column was so extreme that Klan editors reprinted it in their paper one week later to expose Ferguson as an anti-Semite. The gist of his complaint was that the "Big Jews," i.e Alex Sanger, Herbert Marcus, etc., refused to advertise in *The Ferguson Forum*. The fact that these same individuals did not advertise in either the local Jewish paper or the Klan paper was a fact Ferguson either chose to ignore or deemed unimportant. Frustrated, and finally acknowledging that he was ineligible for state office himself, Ferguson decided to run his wife for governor in 1924. Miriam Ferguson was, by all accounts, a private person who was mainly interested in her home and family, but declared that she was running for office "for the vindication of our family name." When asked about her qualifications for office, she replied, "I know I can't talk about the Constitution and the making of laws and the science of government like some other candidates, and I believe they have talked too much, but I have a trusting and abiding faith 'that my Redeemer liveth,' and I am trusting to him to guide my footsteps in the path of righteousness for the good of our people and the good of our State."

The Ferguson campaign slogan was "Two governors for the price of one." Because Mrs. Ferguson had spent her first forty-nine years as a housewife and mother of two daughters, Dorrace and Ouida, and because her initials were M and A, she soon became known as Ma Ferguson. After finishing among the leaders in the Democratic primary, her campaign began to attract national attention. Reporters wanted human-interest stories, so Ouida Ferguson persuaded her mother to let the press photograph her peeling peaches in the kitchen of her birthplace, the Wallace family farm eleven miles outside of Temple. She was also photographed feeding a flock of white leghorn chickens, hoeing her garden, and standing beside a brace of mules. The caption of the picture showing her peeling peaches called her "Ma" Ferguson, and her husband automatically became "Pa." Pictures showing her wearing a bonnet were circulated widely, and led to her campaign song, sung to the tune of "Put on Your Old Grey Bonnet."

Get out your old time bonnet
And put Miriam Ferguson on it
And hitch your wagon to a star
So on election day
We each of us can say
Hurrah, governor Miriam, Hurrah.

Mrs. Ferguson won the Democratic run-off election in August of 1924, and easily defeated her Republican opponent in November. Posters and stickers appeared claiming "Me for Ma . . . and I ain't got a durned thing against Pa!"

Mrs. Ferguson was elected for several reasons. The Klan, though strong in membership, aroused fear in many due to the appearance of its hooded members. One of Mrs. Ferguson's first campaign promises was to see that an anti-mask law was enacted (which the State

Supreme Court soon found unconstitutional). Klansmen inspired terror by beating, whipping, and tar-and-feathering individuals they deemed immoral, including pimps, murderers, child-molesters, straying husbands and wives, abortionists, bootleggers, and gamblers, as well as African-Americans who did not "keep in their place." In addition, the Klan newspaper, *The Texas 100 Per Cent American*, was a continuous diatribe against the evils of Roman Catholicism. Many of Mrs. Ferguson's supporters were those who were weary of the constant fear the Klan inspired. Texas had a considerable Catholic population, as well as a number of those wishing an end to prohibition. They were among her voters, as were feminists who voted for her because she was a woman. Prominent business and political leaders around Texas endorsed her candidacy, including John Nance Garner, the vice-presidential candidate, who promised that a Democratic victory would mean a return to state and national prosperity. In an August 17, 1924 editorial, George Dealey, the editor of the *Dallas Morning News*, stated that Miriam Ferguson's election would "sound the death knell of the Klan as a political power base in the State." He was correct.

The Fergusons returned to Austin in the same 1917 Packard Twin-Six in which they had driven away in disgrace. Since Jim had never learned to drive, Miriam was at the wheel. When they had departed Austin several years earlier, Miriam had declared that a brighter day would dawn for them, and that they would return in the same Packard. It had been stored in a Temple garage until the governor-elect remembered her prediction and had it repaired, polished, and fitted with new tires for the triumphal return. As she pulled the car under the *porte cochere*, she exclaimed, "Well, we have arrived!" While walking around the old familiar grounds, she was aghast to discover that her name had been removed from a block of concrete at the threshold of the greenhouse she had built during her husband's administration. She immediately called a concrete worker to restore her name and date to the greenhouse.

Her administration operated smoothly at first. In addition to the anti-mask bill targeting the Ku Klux Klan, the chief legislation passed was a tick eradication bill crucial to the cattle industry of the state. However, controversies arose, usually centering around the governor's husband. For the most part, she governed in name only. Jim Ferguson's desk was next to hers (similar to those of Queen Victoria and Prince Albert), and everyone knew that he was the real power. He attended meetings of state boards, commissions, and agencies, with or without the governor, and received personal callers.

Jim's "little Christian weekly" was still going strong. There was no standard rate for advertising during this period, but those wishing for favorable attention from the Ferguson administration paid exorbitant prices for the privilege of promoting their concerns. For example, a special edition of the paper appeared on December 18, 1924, just before Miriam's inauguration. It contained more than twice as much advertising space as editorial copy—2,674 inches v 1,246 inches—and all but nineteen inches of advertising space were for firms wanting favors from the new administration. As a result, contracts were awarded for the building of highways to individuals or firms that had never built or maintained roads, including doctors, ranchers, politicians, and lawyers. The one thing they all had in common was that they either were loyal friends of the governor's husband or they had advertised in *The Ferguson Forum.*

The Ferguson's older daughter, Ouida Ferguson Nalle, had worked in the insurance business before her mother's inauguration. She then became an agent for the American Surety Company and wrote surety bonds for road and other contractors. Her clientele was strictly limited to those seeking business with the state. She was also a partner in a real-estate firm that promoted development at the Colorado River Dam near Austin. Her husband, George S. Nalle, promoted stock in a company that had a twenty-year lease on land containing lead ore. Nalle corresponded with friends of the administration, including several legislators, inviting them to buy stock and to send their checks to him in care of the governor's mansion in Austin.

Controversy also surrounded textbook contracts. Jim Ferguson was elected clerk of the Textbook Commission, and one of the pending state contracts was with the American Book Company. It called for the state to purchase thousands of copies of a spelling book at a price a nickel a copy more than it would have cost in Ohio, but the State Supreme Court found the contract valid. The biggest controversies, however, stemmed from the number of pardons criminals received during Mrs. Ferguson's administration. Rumors abounded, but no proof has ever surfaced that pardons were sold, although it seems unlikely that anyone who bought one would ever admit it.

During his wife's administration Jim Ferguson continued his law practice, and was counsel and advisor to several railroads. The newspaper prospered as well; a *Ferguson Forum* was launched in Austin, for which Jim solicited advertising on the governor's official stationery, and state employees were among the subscribers.

The proudest moment for the Ferguson family was the Amnesty Act for James E. Ferguson that Miriam signed into law with a gold pen on March 31, 1925. In the fall of the same year, however, several members of the House of Representatives began an abortive attempt to impeach Mrs. Ferguson, citing several irregularities in her administration. But the legislature was not sitting, and the governor would have had to call a special session, so nothing came of this.

Miriam Ferguson had declared she would only seek one term, but either she or her husband had changed their mind as her term neared its end. She lost to fellow Democrat Dan Moody in the primary, then completed her term. The Fergusons remained in Austin afterwards, living first in the Driskill Hotel, then a rented house, and finally settling into a home on Windsor Road they had built for them. While Miriam lived quietly, Jim kept up his opposition to Moody through his newspaper. In 1928, for the first time since 1914, no Ferguson name appeared on the ticket of any political party. However, with the coming of the Great Depression, the Fergusons saw an opportunity, and Miriam ran again in 1932, becoming the first Texas governor elected to two nonconsecutive terms. Miriam was not a candidate for re-election in 1934, but she ran, unsuccessfully, against W. Lee (Pappy) O'Daniel in 1940, an old enemy of her husband. She came in fourth in that race, her last.

On June 13, 1955, the Austin Junior Chamber of Commerce held a dinner in honor of Miriam Ferguson's eightieth birthday. Approximately 300 people attended the event at the Driskill Hotel, including former governor James V. Allred and Senate Majority Leader Lyndon B. Johnson. Governor Allen Shivers served as Master of Ceremonies. President Dwight D. Eisenhower sent his felicitations, and as a salute to her, the entire gathering sang her old campaign song, "Put on

Your Old Gray Bonnet." Jim had died more than a decade earlier, in 1944, and Miriam Ferguson passed away in 1961 and was buried next to her husband in the state cemetery in Austin. There is no doubt that their administrations were colorful. However, together they were responsible, more than any other politicians, for offering Texans a viable alternative to the Ku Klux Klan. While some of their actions may have benefited themselves or special interests more than the state or its residents, they never encouraged the violence and hatred that the Klan endorsed. Considering the climate of the day, Texas could have easily been governed by worse people.

Life in the Shadows of Oil Derricks

Ilta S. Hall

Lay historian Ilta S. Hall is a member of the East Texas Historical Association.

In this selection, Hall, using family reminiscences, discusses working class life in the East Texas oil fields during the 1920s and 1930s.

★ ★

Without a doubt, my grandmother was a colorful character. As a child, I can recall my Granny recounting stories from her childhood through the time she moved to Houston in 1946. These stories, filled with adventure, tragedy, and humor, astonished me as a young girl. On many occasions my mother would add her memories of the same incidents, tamed down, yet still exciting. Some of my favorites among Granny's recollections involved her early married years living in the East Texas oil fields. With much assistance from my mother, I have recorded these wonderful memories of life in the shadows of the oil derricks.

My Granny was born Elsie Lesteen Vest on July 28, 1906, in Dawson, Texas, which is located twenty-one miles southwest of Corsicana. She was the first child of her sharecropper parents,

"Life in the Shadows of Oil Derricks" by Ilta S. Hall from *East Texas Historical Journal;* XLVI, No 1, 2008, pp. 41–50.

Eula Florence Cagle and Thomas (Tom) Franklin Vest. She endured a childhood typical of most poor children; she worked long hours picking cotton, attended school sporadically, and helped her mother care for four younger siblings. Between growing up with a harsh father who demanded arduous work and often doing without basic necessities, Elsie emerged with a strong, survivalist personality and a desire for recognition and appreciation for her accomplishments.

Granny's family moved to Raleigh, Texas, when she was twelve years old. Her father worked as a blacksmith and on farms owned by others, hoping to save enough money to get into the cattle business. Tom went broke when his previous herd had to be destroyed due to blackleg disease. He could not get another loan at the bank to buy more cattle because he already owed too much, and the bank foreclosed on his land and his home. The only other occupation that Tom knew was farming, so he had to resort to sharecropping to provide for his family. As the oldest girl, Elsie was needed at home, making school attendance low on the list of priorities. When she was fourteen, Elsie played on the girls' basketball team and met a handsome twenty-year-old spectator named Robert Price. He was a cousin of her friend and he worked on his family's farm a few miles down the road from Raleigh.

Elsie and Robert (called Ott by his family) both attended the local Methodist church in Raleigh, and they soon fell in love. It was not unusual for teenaged girls of Elsie's age to get married because they were mature enough to handle a household on their own. Elsie was also anxious to get away from her father's harsh rules and the hard work on the farm. Elsie's parents agreed to the young couple's plan to marry because it meant one less mouth to feed. Family members and friends attended Ott and Elsie's wedding at the preacher's house on June 19, 1921. There were so many people in the house to witness their vows that the wooden floor fell in from the weight!

The newlyweds moved into a two-room wooden shack near Raleigh. Ott worked in the fields while Elsie stayed at home keeping house and canning. On June 18, 1924, the day before their third anniversary, Elsie and Ott became the parents of a baby girl. Elsie wanted the baby named after her, while Ott wanted to name the baby Pauline because he liked the name Paul. After much discussion, they named their daughter, my mother, Elsie Pauline, but Ott always called her Pauline.

The young family struggled to make ends meet and farming work for Ott was slow. Many north-east Texas folks were farmers and the competition triggered low agricultural prices. Also, many people had no money to buy food and grew their own crops. Elsie and Ott helped their families on their farms often, especially during cotton-picking time. Elsie grew tired of the laborious life and just scratching out a living. She wanted a better life for herself and her daughter, so she pressured Ott to get a better job, one that paid more money. A few of his unemployed friends were hired in the oil fields. Ott had grown up around Corsicana where oil was discovered in 1894 as contractor's drilled artesian wells to help the local farmers. He had seen oil derricks all over the town, as well as a refinery that produced kerosene and later gasoline for automobiles. To please Elsie, Ott began to look for a manual labor job in the oilfields.

When Pauline was three months old, Ott heard that drillers were hiring workers in the oilfield in Mexia. The discovery of oil in Mexia four years earlier had created a massive growth spurt for the little town in Limestone County. The population increased from near 3,500 to almost 35,000 in a few years, and the frenzy caused martial law to be established there for a short time.

Ott landed a job stacking pipe in the derricks. Drill pipe came in thirty-foot joints that were connected as the bit drilled deeper, pulled out and stacked when the cuttings needed to be removed from the hole, and then rejoined as drilling continued. The job was considered dangerous and most workers did not want to take such a risky position. Ott accepted the risks since it paid well. Elsie later boasted that it paid much more than what her brother Roy made working for the Works Progress Administration (WPA). With their few belongings. Ott brought Elsie and Pauline to the Wortham lease, where they lived in a tent house, a one-room structure with walls three-foot-high topped by a tent. They joined other former sharecroppers who set up tent cities or "rag towns" to call "home." Here, the family celebrated the baby's first Christmas.

Not satisfied with living in a tent, Elsie persuaded Ott to move to a small house located next to the railroad tracks in the middle of the Wortham Oilfield in February 1925. A big oil strike there the previous November led to the drilling of 300 wells in one year. Production and profits were high. Ott made enough money to purchase a used Buick touring car with a canvas top. Elsie learned to drive and visited her family in Raleigh to show off her new car and baby, let them see how well she was doing. She packed up and, in her ignorance, placed Pauline on the floorboard so that she would not fall off the seat. Upon their arrival at the Vest farm, Elsie's family reprimanded her for subjecting the baby to gas fumes. Undaunted, she paraded Elsie and the car in front of all her relatives before returning to Wortham.

Many oilfield workers, including Ott, found that when the oil drilling began to decline, they had to look for other work, any work. In August 1926, Ott took his family back to help with the harvest at the Price's family farm between Frost and Raleigh. They rented the old Vincent place and tried to make another go of sharecropping. After the harvest, the landowner kept most of the profit and refused to honor the deal he had made with the farmers. Unhappily, Ott and Elsie had to depend on help from their families to keep going.

Work in the oilfields picked up again in early 1929, but the closest employment that Ott found was near Luling. For a short while, the family lived in a two-room yellow house next to a house where Elsie's cousin and his wife were renting. Young Pauline received a little broom for Christmas. When she was sweeping the porch one day, the landlady's donkeys came up next to the house and frightened her. Instinctively, she poked her little broom at them; one of the donkeys grabbed it and ate it, causing Pauline to cry for hours.

There were only a few other children to play with Pauline. The landlords' children were occasional playmates but much of the time she played alone. When Pauline went with her mother to visit Ott on the derricks, her father would let her climb on the drill pipe and play in the "doghouse" where the workers changed clothes. The only place where she was not allowed to play was on the rig floor. Elsie boasted that Pauline spent more time in the oilfields than most workers.

When the stock market crashed in October 1929, the country's economy suffered. Many Texans became unemployed and families were hungry. The Great Depression had little effect on Elsie and Ott, who managed well enough since they had little money anyway. Many people were desperate after the stock market crash, but oilfield labor was about the most lucrative work to be found. Ten major oil companies operated in Texas in 1929, and many independent oil companies also employed oilfield workers. Also, there were important refineries in Port Arthur and Baytown. Ott continued to get steady work in the oil patch.

Elsie's talents and ingenuity helped her manage during the Depression. She made Pauline's clothes on a borrowed sewing machine. Outgrown clothing was sent to her brother Roy's daughter. There was no problem getting food on the lease because Ott had steady employment. He and Elsie bought coffee, flour, sugar, and other things that could not be grown on the farm to send back to their families along with some money.

When the wells were all completed, Elsie and Pauline stayed with the Vests a few weeks until Ott found another job in Van, twenty miles northeast of Tyler. The Pure Oil Company used seismograph soundings to direct their drilling and discover oil in Van in October 1929. This find attracted several oil companies that signed a joint agreement with Pure Oil for unitization to reduce competition and promote conservation. Ott took a position as a roustabout, tightening and loosening the joints of the drill string.

Shortly after the move to a boarding house, Elsie received a message that her mother was ill and in the hospital in Corsicana. Elsie took Pauline and drove to her mother's bedside. That day, Elsie's mother passed away at the age of forty-two from a ruptured appendix and gangrene. Her death was a blow to a family with two children still at home. Elsie tried even harder to send any extra funds home to her little sisters.

In the fall Pauline began attending kindergarten and gave Elsie the opportunity to seek her own job rather than spending her days at home canning fruit and vegetables. Elsie had never enjoyed staying at home. It was unusual for a wife to be employed and no other females in Elsie's family had ever worked outside the home, but she was bored there. A job gave her a chance to get out of the house, find adventure, and earn money of her own. She worked at Thompson Commercial Company in Van in the dry-goods department. She enjoyed meeting people and saved some of her money to buy her own car. She could buy fabric at a discount and sew for Pauline. The little girl was dressed well, with bloomers to match every dress. Having only one child, which was uncommon for most families, Elsie kept up her duties at home while enjoying her job. Most wives of oilfield workers stayed at home on the lease to raise their children and perform household chores. Many of the workers were young men who had not yet married. These single men found accommodations at "cot houses" or boarding houses.

Employment in Van began a period when the family moved wherever Ott could find work for independent contractors on another well. He heard about an Oklahoma promoter named "Dad" Joiner who spudded wells in Rusk County. Joiner, using only his intuition, had leased 10,000 acres in East Texas and began drilling, on his third attempt, the Daisy Bradford #3, he struck oil in October 1930. His discovery was followed by two tremendous strikes and the vast East Texas oilfield began production of over six billion barrels of oil in the next few years. Joiner attracted investors to the area and many independent drillers, called "wildcatters," began their own wells in search of a big strike. Ott worked as a roustabout whenever and wherever he could find work.

For the first two or three months, the Price family lived in a rooming house and ate meals with the owners and other boarders. The family had to move often because the rigs were drilled in a set number of days and when they were completed, the crews moved on. Wherever the next contract required them to drill was where they would live, sometimes in the same town, other times twenty or thirty miles away. A possessive woman, Elsie never wanted Ott out of her sight when he was not working. This attitude drove her to follow him to every oil lease. Elsie and Pauline would trail the group of roustabouts in their car, find a place to spend the night, and then locate a place to live. Because of the hard economic times, most people with a spare room would rent it, whether in a rooming house or a private home. Such frequent moves meant that Ott and Elsie had no furniture of their own. Nothing could be accumulated because they did not stay in one place long enough. Perhaps this was the reason that my Granny amassed so much "stuff" in her later years.

Every place the family lived, Ott planted a garden. They often had to move before anything was produced, but Ott enjoyed growing food. It gave him pleasure to give produce away and he enjoyed leaving the garden for the next renters. Between the garden and the lease store, food supplies were not a problem, although there may not have been a big variety. When Ott, Elsie, and Pauline visited the Vest farm, Grandpa Vest slaughtered hogs and sent them home with ham, bacon, and sausage from the smokehouse. On occasion, they bought chickens to add to the staples they purchased at the lease store.

Pauline went to school wherever they lived. During one four and one-half month period, she attended seven different schools, each one not long enough to learn the teacher's name or get a report card. Most of the schools were two rooms, one for first through third grades and the other for fourth through sixth grades. Teachers were available but some were not well educated. Children such as Pauline, who come from the oil leases, were put in the grade that their mothers thought they should attend. Pauline would find a chair and follow the other children's lead until it was time to move again. She learned to read, and Elsie listened to her read aloud and help her with the more difficult words if she knew them. The children were taught phonics and their books usually consisted of a reader, speller, and a math book.

Ott continued to work wherever he could. The East Texas oilfield was the largest oilfield in the United States, covering parts of Gregg, Rusk, Upshur, Smith, and Cherokee counties. Ott found employment on the Cook #2, owned by Mr. W. H. Cook, in December 1930; then for the Sun Oil Company at the J. W. Akin #1 site, and later on the T&P RR Company's Fee #1 site, among many others. He worked as a roustabout on several wells but because of his experience, he held the position of derrick man on a wildcat well near Troupe, Texas. He stood on crossed boards on the derrick where he grabbed a snap hook, pulled up a link of pipe, stacked it, and continued the process in and out of the hole. On one well between Gladewater and Longview, Ott assumed the position of driller. He always worked on rotary rigs, which were becoming more common than the traditional cable rigs. Rotary rigs required a minimum of five workers per shift. The "boss" of the rig was the tool pusher, followed by the driller, the derrickman, and two roughnecks.

The more Ott worked, the more Elsie hounded him to make more money, putting stress on their marriage. Occasionally, Ott went to local beer joints with co-workers at the end of the day, only to come home to Elsie's fury. Elsie gave up her job at Thompson's in Van to stay in closer proximity to Otto. They lived in several communities, including Troup, Arp, Overton, Henderson, Greggton, and Gladewater.

When the market became flooded with East Texas oil, prices fell from a dollar a barrel in 1930 to eight cents a barrel the following year. Also, because small producers controlled the East Texas oil-fields, the major oil companies called on the Texas Railroad Commission to limit oil production. The independent producers countered by marketing "hot oil" in defiance of the Railroad Commission's limitations. "Hot oil" was a term used to describe oil that was produced beyond the restrictions of the Railroad Commission or obtained illegally by siphoning from pipelines. A volatile situation existed in the East Texas fields, and jobs with independent producers were harder for Ott to find, so he took whatever positions were offered to him in order to provide for his family, even if they involved "hot oil."

When Pauline started the third grade, Ott got a job as a lease foreman for Stroube & Stroube, turning wells on and off as the Railroad Commission would allow. This independent company had made a tremendous strike in 1930 only 600 feet north of "Dad" Joiner's Daisy Bradford well, when oil prices were high and large profits common. Ott received top pay and he performed his duties independently of any crews. The family moved into a company house on a lease in White Oak, located east of Gladewater near Kilgore. This allowed them enough stability and purchased their first pieces of furniture. Elsie and Ott opened a charge account at the grocery store and could pay at the end of each month. Then Elsie could buy groceries without having cash and she allowed Pauline to buy ice cream or milk on their account, but never candy. The family never worried about what they did not have and they were relatively happy, except for incidents involving Ott's "drinking with the boys," which collided with Elsie's aspirations for a better life.

In 1933, Elsie's youngest sister Mackie came to live with the family and go to school because their father had remarried. She stayed until another sister, Evlin, got married and settled and Mackie went to live with them so that she could be closer to the rest of the family and her friends. With Pauline and Mackie attending school in White Oak, Elsie became involved with the Parent Teacher Association. The PTA put on plays and sold tickets to the community to raise funds for school projects. Elsie found her place in the limelight by acting in the plays and occasionally forcing a reluctant Pauline to take part. A highlight for Elsie occurred when Mackie won a trip through the 4-H Club to A & M College in College Station. Elsie accompanied Mackie as a representative from Gregg County.

On a visit to Grandpa Vest's farm, Pauline fell in love with a little brown goat. She begged to take it home, so Grandpa Vest put it in a gunny sack with its head sticking out and Pauline rode home sitting on the floorboard of the backseat, holding the goat she named Billy. Pauline played with the goat after school. They chased each other across the long front porch. One day, Elsie hung a pair of blue rayon pajamas she bought to wear on the College Station trip on the clothesline to dry and Billy ate one of the pajama legs. Elsie was so angry that she called a man to come and get Billy and barbecue him. When the man returned with a large pan of barbecue, the family, along with cousin David, who was staying with them, sat down to eat. Suddenly, David said "Baaaaa" and Pauline burst into tears. She felt betrayed by her mother, but Elsie felt no remorse. The meat was returned to the man and no one ate that night.

Ott and his family spent almost three years in White Oak. Other oilfield workers and their families continually moved on and off the lease, living wherever space was available. Oilfield boomtowns rarely had paved streets. The streets turned to mud whenever it rained and the big trucks transporting pipe kept the roads in a quagmire. In the leased company home, Ott, Elsie, and Pauline adjusted well. Many of the larger oil companies provided housing for their workers on their leases. These homes were rented to employees for a nominal costs and encouraged company loyalty and discouraged labor union support.

At the lease house, as usual Ott planted a garden. They had no running water, but there was a well on the end of the porch. There was an outhouse in the back and Pauline was assigned the job of scrubbing it with hot water and a broom every Saturday. Pauline despised the job, especially with the spiders.

At White Oak School, there was no electricity, and the children pumped their own water in the front yard into tin cups brought from home. One day, a boy who did not have a tin cup of his own tried to pump water into a snuff glass. In the process, the snuff glass broke so the boy threw the pieces and one hit Pauline in the arm, causing a surge of blood. The boy's father paid to get the wound stitched and Elsie sent Pauline back to school the next day.

Often guests or family members came to visit Ott and Elsie. Adults spent the evening playing dominoes or talking. The children were shielded from most "grownup talk." Most of the crime in the area was limited to petty thefts, but they never talked about crime, sex, or having babies around children. Elsie and Ott bought a radio, first with earphones and then later one without them to hear the latest broadcasts. Every Sunday the family attended church, returned home, and killed a chicken. They cleaned and fried it, accompanied by potatoes, and ate lunch around 2 P.M. They killed additional chickens when anyone else showed up for a visit.

As Pauline progressed in school, she enjoyed the traveling shows that performed at the schools once a month. Children could attend the shows for ten or fifteen cents admission, depending on the performance. Sometimes they would be entertained by bands or minstrel shows. Once, an expert archer demonstrated trick shots, including one where he shot objects out of a child's hand. The most memorable visits for Pauline were a performance of Shakespeare's "As You Like It" and an appearance by some members of Admiral Richard Byrd's expedition.

Elsie became more involved with social activities in White Oak. In addition to working with the school PTA, she joined the local Rebekah Lodge, which was the women's division of the Oddfellows. Because Elsie would not leave her daughter alone at the lease house, Pauline went along to all the meetings and sat in the anteroom with other members' children. Out of boredom during the two-hour meetings, they "hollered" at people who passed the window and Pauline stayed in constant trouble with Elsie.

Elsie did a great deal of community service work. She sewed dresses for neighbors and clothing for their children if they purchased the cloth, usually at a nickel a yard. She cut up worn men's shirts and made clothing for babies. She cooked meals and took them to those in the area who were in need. Elsie's humanitarian and social pursuits took up much of her time, so naturally, she could not handle all the duties of the household. A local black man told her that he had a daughter that needed to work and Elsie agreed to let Geneva do her housework and live with the family. She placed a cot in the comer of the garage for Geneva to sleep. Elsie treated Geneva well otherwise and enjoyed her cooking and cleaning abilities.

After Geneva arrived, one of Pauline's school friends showed her some white rabbits. Pauline asked Ott if she could have some rabbits since she was the only child on the lease and had no one to play with. He bought her two pairs and a double hutch. The rabbits multiplied so Ott bought another hutch. Elsie insisted that Pauline be in charge of their care since they were her pets and she did not want them to be eaten. When there were more rabbits than the hutches could hold, Ott built a pen on the ground for them. Elsie got angry with her daughter for trying to get Geneva to help her clean the pen, so she went out in the yard, lifted the side of the pen, and herded all the white rabbits, about seventy-five of them, into the nearby woods. Their descendents probably still live in the forests of East Texas. Pauline cried, but Ott was not concerned because the cost of feeding the rabbits was taking a toll. After this incident, Geneva's father discovered that his daughter was sleeping in a drafty garage, so he told Elsie that Geneva's mother needed her help and he took her home.

Working on the oil derricks had many dangers. Several times there were oil well fires on the leases. Ott and other workers took great risks in controlling the fires. Once while in White Oak, there was a heavy rain and the runoff flowed into a slush pit that contained oil from a well that had just come in. A bolt of lightning struck near the pit, igniting the oil. The water began to boil and the burning oil overflowed. Pauline followed her father as he and other workers heard the calls for help and tried to extinguish the flames by shoveling dirt over them. As the streams of overflowing oil and fire ran downhill, Ott called for Pauline to get back. The fire grew so fierce that it blocked her view of the men. Pauline watched with increasing uneasiness, then panic, fearing that the inferno had engulfed her father. Eventually, she could see Ott and the others through the flames that surrounded them as they continued shoveling dirt on the fire. Pauline believed that she saw angels in the sky above the flames and that God had sent them to save her father from harm. None of men suffered major injuries that night.

By 1934, the Great Depression had begun to have negative effects on the oil industry. Prices for petroleum continued to decline and oilfield jobs were scarce. Ott was temporarily promoted to a position reading gages for Stroube and Stroube Oil Company. He gauged oil in the tanks and turned valves on when required, running oil in the pipes to the refinery.

Disagreements between Ott and Elsie grew, and Ott's drinking increased. This brought the fragile marriage to the breaking point and Ott and Elsie separated. Ott had learned that he would lose his job, so he helped Elsie move into a rental house across the highway. Ott packed his duffle bag and joined some of his friends at a rooming house. Within six weeks, Elsie packed her car and moved their furniture to a four-room, yellow rent house on Eastview Street in Longview. Wasting no time, she went to work at K. Woolens in dry goods and enrolled Pauline in the fourth grade at the elementary school. Elsie's cousin, Dora Cagle, came to live with them for a short time and shared expenses.

Shortly after their divorce was final, Elsie began dating again. When a gentleman came to the house for dinner, Pauline was instructed to be on her best behavior. But, in the middle of the meal, Pauline got tickled at something that was said and strangled, spitting tea all over the table. The suitor never came back.

Elsie would not let Ott see Pauline often unless he brought money to help her. He went back to work on the derricks again, often as a driller, whenever he could find work, and he brought money to Elsie whenever he could. Elsie and Pauline lived in Longview for a year and a half until Elsie remarried. Her new husband, George, provided plenty of food for them because he owned an interest in a butcher shop at Greggton. The new family rented a house close to Pine Tree School, where Pauline attended the sixth grade. Unfortunately, George and his partner lost their lease on the butcher shop, so the family relocated to Overton for a short time, and then to Kilgore when George took a job at the Wickham Packing Company processing meat, including wild game.

George bought Pauline a horse because of their joint love of animals. The bay had been a bucking horse in the rodeo in Fort Worth that had lost his desire to buck, so he was a good deal. George and Pauline both enjoyed riding him while Elsie had a cow for milk. A few years later, Elsie had to have all her teeth pulled, so Pauline was allowed to drive her mother's car to school. Pauline attended Kilgore High School and was graduated in 1940, just before her sixteenth birthday. She sold her horse to help finance her first year at Kilgore Junior College. Then George accepted a job in Tyler at Rose City Packing Company, and the family moved into a nice brick house.

When Pauline completed her education at Tyler Junior College, she became a telephone operator for $15 a week. She lived at home until she moved to Georgia to accept a job making $50 a week and to experience freedom and adventure. After a while, Elsie joined her there. She and George had divorced, for which she offered Pauline no explanation.

With the beginning of World War II, Elsie and Pauline returned to East Texas. Elsie got a job at the Post Exchange at Camp Fannin and Pauline worked in a grocery store there. Elsie pretended that she and Pauline were sisters to meet soldiers at the camp at a dance featuring Ozzie and Harriet Nelson and their orchestra. One evening, Pauline went to the Post Exchange to have dinner with her mother. While waiting, Pauline met a wonderful young soldier from Louisiana. Pauline and John, the young soldier, fell in love. They married and moved to Houston after John's discharge in 1945.

Pauline and John are my mother and father. They raised four children who were entertained by Granny every day after she bought a house two doors away and married a soldier who grew up in Chicago. Granddaddy Ott and his new wife lived in East Texas, Midland, and Louisiana, where he continued to work for oil companies, lastly as a tool pusher, until his retirement in 1962. We grandchildren heard many stories about the oilfields whenever he visited, but none could compare with the tales with which Granny amused us. They have both passed away now, but their stories of life in the shadows of the East Texas oil derricks live on as we share their experiences with our children.

1920–1929: The Texas League During the Golden Age of Sports

Bill O' Neal

Bill O'Neal taught history for many years at Panola College in Carthage, Texas. He is the author of numerous books, including *The Johnson County War*, *Encyclopedia of Western Gunfighters*, *Tex Ritter: America's Most Beloved Cowboy*, and *The Texas League, 1888–1987: A Century of Baseball*.

Major League Baseball came to Texas in 1962 when the National League Houston Colt .45s (later renamed the Astros) played their inaugural season. The American League arrived in the Lone Star State ten years later with the relocation of the Washington Senators to Arlington, where they became the Texas Rangers. Prior to the arrival of the "Big Leagues," however, the Texas League had a long and illustrious history. In this selection, O'Neal discusses the League during the Roaring Twenties. Under the leadership of W. K. Stripling, Paul LaGrave, and Jake Atz, Fort Worth's Panthers dominated the period from 1920–1925. The Dallas Steers and Wichita Falls Spudders surpassed Fort Worth in the decade's latter years. Such legendary players as "Big Boy" Kraft, Joe Pate, Paul Wachtel, and Ike Boone thrilled Lone Star baseball fans, and from 1920–1929, the Texas League champion defeated their Southern Association rival eight times in the Dixie Series.

★ ★

"1920–1929: The Texas League During the Golden Age of Sports" from *The Texas League, 1888–1987: A Century of Baseball* by Bill O'Neal, 1987, pp. 51–66. Reprinted by permission of the author.

The decade of the 1920s is regarded by many as the Golden Age of Sports in America, and baseball enjoyed a heyday as the most popular professional game in the land. The ball was livelier now, and Babe Ruth led the sport into an exciting era of home run sluggers and high-scoring games. The day of tight pitchers' duels—contests which featured hit-and-run, stolen bases, and bunting to play for one run—faded rapidly under a barrage of home runs as batters swung from the heels. Fans responded eagerly to a more electric style of baseball that proved perfectly suited to the accelerated pulse rate of the Roaring Twenties.

Babe Ruth was a sensation in 1920 when he walloped an astounding 54 roundtrippers (he duplicated this total in 1928, but in 1921 he hit 59, and in 1927 he slugged 60 homers). Prior to the 1920s, the Texas League home run record was 22, set by San Antonio first baseman Frank Metz in 1911. The next season Metz hit 21 homers, but until the 1920s no other Texas Leaguer had ever hit more than 18 home runs.

The Texas League wasted little time in joining the power parade. Scores went up dramatically, as did batting averages and, of course, ERAs. The leading team batting averages during the previous decade had ranged from .240 to .270, but in seven of the ten seasons of the 1920s the team batting average leaders hit over .300, and in 1927 the Waco Navigators established a league record .316 team mark. A record 3,778 extra base hits were pounded out around the league in 1925, and 7,044 runs were scored that year. In 1926, 1,024 home runs were hit, and in 1929 Texas League batters rapped out a record 12,711 base hits. In 1921 "Hack" Eibel, a strong Shreveport first baseman who, like Babe Ruth, also was a lefthanded pitcher, blasted 35 home runs (and led the circuit in triples) to set a new Texas League record. But the mark did not last for long.

During the next three seasons, the home run leader was Fort Worth first sacker Clarence Otto "Big Boy" Kraft. The veteran slugger hit 32 homers in 1922 and 1923, then poled 55 in 1924—the highest total in organized baseball that season and a record which would stand for 32 years in the Texas League. Kraft retired after the 1924 season, but his place on the Fort Worth roster was capably filled by longtime major leaguer "Big Ed" Konetchy, who led the Texas League in 1925 with 41 roundtrippers and 166 RBIs. By this time every team in the circuit was on the prowl for sluggers, and hitting exploits continued through the decade. Indeed, in 1929 an all-time total of 17 players scored 100 or more runs during the season.

For the first six years of the 1920s, the Fort Worth Panthers dominated the Texas League with an awesome combination of power hitting and overwhelming pitching. The architects of the most sustained team success in league history was a management trio: two men who became part owners in 1916, W. K. Stripling (team president, 1917–1929) and Paul LaGrave (team secretary and business manager—equivalent to a modern general manager—in 1916–1929), and Jake Atz (field manager, 1914–1929). Stripling and LaGrave collected fine players and paid them so well that they stayed in Fort Worth, even after stellar performances brought offers to play in higher classifications. Of course, independent minor league owners were under no obligation to sell outstanding players, which is a major explanation for the Texas League dynasties of the period.

An infielder by trade, Jake Atz found himself in Fort Worth in 1914 as a 35-year-old player-manager. He did not manage a complete season until 1917, when he won 91 games for a second-place finish. He brought the Panthers (soon they were being called "Jake Atz's

Cats") in second again in 1918, and the next season won the most games — 94 — but lost in the playoffs to Shreveport. Then Atz's Cats hit their stride, winning six consecutive Texas League pennants. Atz's victory totals during his string of championships were: 1920 — 108; 1921 — 107; 1922 — 109; 1923 — 96; 1924 — 109; 1925 — 103. The 109 wins in 1922 and 1924 set an all-time Texas League record.

In each of the six years, Fort Worth far outdistanced the closest challengers. Although each season except 1923 was split (a ploy to create playoff competition), Fort Worth won both halves every year. The only playoff the Panthers had to face occurred in the second half of 1925, when Fort Worth tied with archrival Dallas. But Atz's Cats triumphed over Snipe Conley's Steers in three straight, and Fort Worth had won the second half as well as the first half, thus guaranteeing their sixth straight flag without a playoff series. In 1923, with no split season, Fort Worth finished thirteen and a half games ahead of second-place San Antonio.

Five players were on the Panther roster during all six championship seasons. Lefthander Joe Pate was a 20-game winner in each of the six flag years, and in 1921 and 1924 he won 30. Paul Wachtel, the righthanded spitballer, also was a six-time 20-game winner for the Panthers (he won 21 in 1919 and 19 in 1923). Pate and Wachtel won 26 apiece in 1920 to start the pennant run, and over the six years they made a combined contribution of 292-121 Ponderous Possum Moore caught for Fort Worth from 1919 through 1926; his best seasons were 1921 (.298) and 1924 (.311). Ziggy Sears, who spent 11 seasons in Texas League outfields, hit .304 in 1922, .323 in 1924, and .321 in 1925. Dugan Phelan, a five-year National League veteran, played 13 seasons in the Texas League; with Fort Worth he was a third baseman and pinch hitter who batted .300 in 1922.

Pate and Wachtel had impressive pitching support throughout the string. In 1920 and 1921 there were four 20-game winners on the staff: Pate and Wachtel won 26 each in 1920, while curveballing Buzzer Bill Whitaker was 24-6 and control artist Dick Robertson was 20-7: in 1921 Pate won 30, Wachtel 23, Whitaker 23, and southpaw Gus Johns won 20. There were three 20-game winners—Pate, Wachtel and Johns—in 1922, and in 1923, when Wachtel "slumped" to 19 victories and Pate won 23, Ulysses Simpson Grant "Lil" Stoner took up the slack with a 27-11 season (then he went directly to the major leagues). In 1925 Pate, Wachtel, and Johns won 20 or more, and southpaw Jim Walkup was 19-7. It was the greatest pitching staff in Texas League history.

The Panthers' leading slugger was Big Boy Kraft. He played seven seasons in Fort Worth (1918–1924), and in 980 Texas League games his batting average was .317. In 1921 he won the batting title with a .352 percentage, and he also led the league in at bats, runs, and hits. Kraft established the Texas League lifetime records for the most consecutive years scoring 100 or more runs, most years scoring 100 or more runs, making 200 or more base hits, making over 100 RBIs, leading in extra base hits and home runs. His finest season was 1924, when he hit .349 and belted 55 homers and an all-time record 196 RBIs.

The dominance of Fort Worth for the first six years of the decade overshadowed various heroics by players on other teams. Twenty-six-year-old Ike Boone, a six-foot, 200-pounder with three years' experience as a minor leaguer, signed on with San Antonio for 1923. It was to be his only year in the Texas League, but Boone had an unforgettable season, leading the league in batting average (.402), runs (134), hits (241), doubles (53), triples (26), RBIs (135) and total bases (391—the next year Big Boy Kraft established an all-time record 414 total bases). Boone also pounded 15 home runs and hit safely in 37 consecutive games—still the longest hitting streak in Texas League history. Boone finished the season with the Boston Braves, but he had enjoyed the most productive offensive year in modern Texas League play. Two seasons later San Antonio fans watched infielder Dan Clark flirt with .400 before finishing at .399. Wichita Falls Spudder fans cheered four batting champs during the decade: Red Josefson (.345 in 1920), Homer Summa (.362 in 1922), Arthur Weiss (.377 in 1924), and Tom Jenkins (.374 in 1926). Waco produced back-to-back batting champs: former major leaguer Del Pratt (.386 in 1927, plus a league-leading 32 home runs) and outfielder George Blackerby (.368 in 1928, plus a home run championship the next year).

A notable team exploit of the 1920s was Wichita Falls' impressive 1922 winning streak. On July 21 Victor Keen outdueled Snipe Conley and the Dallas Steers, 2-1 in 17 innings. Then the Spudders returned to Wichita Falls for a four-week home stand. During the streak Keen won seven games (he went 13-4, then finished the season with the Cubs), while Floyd "Rip" Wheeler also won seven (he was a 22-game winner in 1922 and again in 1923), including complete game victories in both halves of a doubleheader against San Antonio on August 3. On August 12 Keen squared off against Snipe Conley again. By the middle of the game spitballer Conley was complaining of burning lips, and soon his lips and tongue were so swollen that he could not talk. One of the Spudders—an aggregation notorious for their addiction to practical jokes—had applied colorless creosote to the game balls, and as Conley wet his fingers throughout the contest he severely burned his mouth. The Spudders won the game, 4-3, for their twenty-fifth consecutive victory. Spudder hopes of surpassing Corsicana's 27 straight in 1902 were thwarted the next day, when Roy Mitchell (who had beaten Wichita Falls the day before the streak started) pitched the Steers to a win. Dallas protested the Conley loss, however, and when the league upheld complaints over the "Creosote Incident," the official total stood at 24 consecutive victories—the second longest skein in Texas League history. But even after winning 24 in a row, the Spudders still trailed mighty Fort Worth by half a game. At season's end the Spudders were 94-61—good for second place to Fort Worth's 109-46 record.

A significant innovation of the 1920s was the Dixie Series, which became the most popular baseball event in the South for nearly four decades. As far back as the 1890s, Texas sportswriters had urged a post-season playoff series between the champions of the Texas League and the Southern League, forerunner of the twentieth-century Southern Association. But the Southern Association was more advanced in classification than the Texas League and had nothing to gain and a great deal of prestige to lose by such a series. In 1920, however, when Fort Worth and Little Rock clearly dominated their respective leagues, Paul LaGrave contacted R. G. Allen, president of the Little Rock club, and reached an agreement for a seven-game series after each team wrapped up its regular schedule. Little Rock, managed by Kid Elberfeld (who had played the 1896 season for Dallas en route to the major leagues), did not officially represent the Southern Association—which proved convenient for the association, since the powerful Panthers won the series. But the seven games had attracted 36,836 ticket-buyers and nearly $50,000 in gross receipts, and the opportunity for future profit was obvious.

In 1921 the Texas League was elevated to Class A status, and the two now-equal circuits made formal arrangements for the Dixie Series. Fort Worth prevailed again, this time over Southern Association winner Memphis, and the next year Panther fans chartered a "Dixie Special" and brought along a Dixieland band, cowbells, and raucous enthusiasm. Fort Worth lost to Mobile in 1922, but during the next three years Jake Atz's Cats beat New Orleans, Memphis, and Atlanta in succession. By this time the Dixie Series had attained the status of a "little World Series," and was avidly followed across the South and Texas.

In 1926 Fort Worth's long monopoly over the Texas League championship finally was ended by archrival Dallas. Panther ace Joe Pate at last went up to the major leagues, while Paul Wachtel, now 38, slipped to 16-19 (Wachtel could not advance to the majors during the 1920s because the spitball, his most effective pitch, had been outlawed). The league did not declare a split season, and the resulting 156-game pennant race proved to be the closest since before World War I. Galveston had dropped out of the Texas League in 1924, replaced by Waco, and the eight member cities in 1926 drew 1,159,906 paid admissions—an attendance record that stood for two decades.

Dallas attracted 286,806 of those fans. Snipe Conley had become a playing manager during the 1925 season, and in 1926 he pushed his team relentlessly toward a pennant. Snipe no longer pitched regularly, but 6'6" Slim Love (21-10) and southpaw Dick Schuman (17-5) led a solid mound corps, while R. L. Williams (.369), E. J. Woeber (.330 and 25 home runs), J. N. Riley (.329), and Charles Miller (.321, 30 homers and 118 RBIs) added lethal bats. Dallas battled for the lead throughout the year, but when Fort Worth dropped a late-season doubleheader, Conley's Steers took a stranglechold on first place. Then the Steers went on to beat New Orleans in six games for a Dixie Series triumph.

During league meetings preceding the 1923 season, circuit executives determined to follow the example of the rest of organized baseball and eliminate spitball pitching. Like the majors and other minor loops, the Texas League permitted current spitball practitioners to continue business as usual. Nine spitballers were sanctioned by the Texas League: Snipe Conley, Paul Wachtel, Slim Love, Ed Hovlik, Dana Fillingim, Hal Deviney, Larry Jacobus, Tom Estell, and Oscar Tuero. Most of these men were veterans nearing the end of the line; Estell and Tuero pitched until 1932, the last pitchers to *legally* throw a loaded baseball in the Texas League.

Edward Hock, who spent nine years in the Texas League, usually as a third baseman, was at shortstop for Houston when the Buffs lined up against Dallas on May 5, 1927. In the bottom of the third Dallas outfielder Rhino Williams walked. Fred Brainard dropped a sacrifice bunt, but both runners were safe when the ball was bobbled. Then Jodie Tate lashed a line drive up the middle. Moving to his left, Hock speared the ball, stepped on second for out number two, then chased down Brainard as he tried to scramble back toward third. It was the second unassisted triple play in Texas League history, following Roy Akin's unique effort from third base in 1912. Overall, there were six triple plays during the 1927 Texas League season.

Another remarkable fielding performance of the 1920s was turned in by Frankie Fuller, who played second base for San Antonio from 1920 through 1924 and for Houston in 1925. In each of the six seasons he led all pivot men in double plays, participating in a total of 531 double plays during the six years. Twice, Fuller took part in more than 100 double plays per season, and in 1922 he led the league in starting double plays—the only time a second baseman has surpassed all shortstops in that category.

The Wichita Falls Spudders proved to be the class of the league in 1927. The Spudders won their opener, and never relinquished the lead during the season. Third baseman Walter Swenson hit .300; second sacker Pete Turgeon, the Spudder leadoff man, hit .305, scored 115 runs, hit 31 doubles, 11 triples, 18 homers with 94 RBIs; center fielder Howard Chamney, an ex-University of Texas great who averaged .308 in 1,129 Texas League games from 1924 to 1932, hit .306; right fielder Lyman Lamb hit .314; even the utility man, Stanley "Rabbit" Benton, hit .322. But the offensive star of the team was left fielder "Tut" Jenkins, the defending champ (.374 in 1926) who hit .363 with 25 homers, 147 runs scored, and 129 RBIs.

Spudder pitching matched the explosive attack. At 23-9, old pro George Washington Payne led the league in victories; Frederick Fussell led the league in winning percentage (.724) at 21-8; Joe Kiefer was 20-9; spitballer Tom Estell was 16-7; and Milton Steengrafe was 15-6.

This powerful club overwhelmed the Texas League, finishing 102-54 (second-place Waco was 88-68), then swept New Orleans in four straight in the Dixie Series to complete a splendid season. It was the only time during the first 16 years of the classic that a team from either league took the Dixie Series in four games.

During the Texas League meeting in February 1928, it was decided to divide the season at mid-summer; 1928 would be the first time the league had ever determined beforehand to have a split season. Houston ran away with the first half, opening a lead of seven and a half games by June 29. Right fielder Red Worthington (.353 on the season) and catcher-manager Frank Snyder (.329) led the attack. "Pancho" Snyder had just finished a 16-year major league career, and he expertly handled a superb pitching staff that boasted no fewer than four 20-game winners: James Lindsey (25-10), Wild Bill Hallahan (23-12, with a league-leading 244 strikeouts and 2.25 ERA), Ken Penner (20-8), and Frank Barnes (20-9).

In the second half Wichita Falls aggressively defended their title. Although some of the big guns of 1927 had moved up, Tut Jenkins (.348 with a league-leading 27 homers, 121 runs scored, and 122 RBIs), Rabbit Benton (.324) and catcher Pete Lapan (.324) generated considerable offense, while Milt Steengrafe (22-8) and big league veteran Mike Cvengros (21-8) headed a pitching staff that was not up to the previous year's overall quality. But the Spudders dominated the second half, finishing with a margin of seven and a half games over second-place Houston. It seemed as though Wichita Falls would provide yet another dynasty for the 1920s.

In the best-of-five playoffs the Buffaloes won the first game in Wichita Falls, then dropped a decision to the Spudders. In the opening contest at Houston, Hallahan beat Cvengros, 1-0, on a two-hitter, and the Buffaloes wrapped up the series the next day. Having regained early-season form with their first flag since 1914, Houston downed Birmingham in the Dixie Series.

Competition was fierce throughout the Texas League in 1929. Fort Worth led in team batting (.303), but finished fourth; Waco led in home runs (188), but ended up fifth. During the year, Paul LaGrave died, and longtime Fort Worth president W. C. Stripling and the LaGrave estate sold their interests in the Panthers. Jake Atz, the brilliant field general who had served since 1914, including the past 13 consecutive years, left the team. The splendid management combination that had fashioned the Panther dynasty was dissolved before season's end.

Dallas, sparked by the explosive bats of outfielder Randy Moore (.369) and Simon Rosenthal (.339), took the first-half championship by merely a half game over Shreveport. Bridesmaid Shreveport finished second again in the last half, this time to Wichita Falls. The Spudders were led by George Washington Payne, who pitched in 55 games and finished at 28-12. As usual, Wichita Falls fans enjoyed a number of fine hitters: left fielder Fred Bennett (.368 and 145 RBIs); catcher Pete Lapan (.367); infielder Rabbit Benton (.327); and almost everybody else in the lineup.

The race for the batting title went down to the last day of the season. Randy Moore won by a single percentage point and established an all-time league record for base hits (245). Fort Worth center fielder Eddie Moore, a speedy ball hawk and baserunner, set the all-time mark for triples (30). Texas League fans enjoyed the aggressive baserunning of Houston outfielder Pepper Martin, who led the league in stolen bases both years (1927 and 1929) he played for the Buffs.

Wichita Falls ended 1929 with the best record in the league, but the Spudders lost out to Dallas in the playoffs. Although Payne pitched in three of the four games, the Spudder ace ironically could not gain a playoff win. The Dallas Steers, with their second title in four seasons, were defeated in the Dixie Series by Birmingham—snapping a six-year losing streak inflicted by the Texas League on their Southern Association opponents.

By the time the season closed, the New York stock market had begun to wobble toward its disastrous collapse. The 1920s had been a period of unparalleled fan interest and attendance. The decade had exhibited great teams, a number of admirable pitching performances, and, above all, unprecedented hitting. It was the most exciting, explosive baseball that had yet been played in the circuit. But the 1930s would bring the Great Depression to the cities and ball parks and club offices of the Texas League.

Red Burton and the Klan

Ben Procter

Ben Procter is Emeritus Professor of History at Texas Christian University in Fort Worth. His studies include the two volume biography *William Randolph Hearst*, *The Battle of the Alamo*, *Not Without Honor: The Life of John H. Reagan*, and *Just One Riot: Episodes of Texas Rangers in the 20th Century*.

The Ku Klux Klan was a formidable force in the Lone Star State during the 1920s. In this selection, Dr. Procter recounts the violent confrontation between a Klan mob and two intrepid Texas lawmen—Red Burton and Bob Buchanan—in McLennan County in 1921.

★ ★

A wave of fear swept across Texas in the summer and fall of 1921. Masked men in white robes paraded triumphantly; flaming crosses illuminated the sky, eerie and ominous in the darkness; and bands of nightriders, vigilante style, tortured or murdered their victims in the name of law and order. At crossroads and in Texas towns, billboards demanding "One Hundred Per Cent Americanism," "Booze Must and Shall Go," "Love Thy Neighbor as Thyself but Leave His Wife

"Red Burton and the Klan" from *Just One Riot: Episodes of Texas Rangers in the 20th Century* by Ben Procter, 1991, pp. 44–58. Published by Eakin Press. Reprinted by permission.

Alone," "Keep This a White Man's Country," apprised citizens that a new force, supposedly patriotic, most assuredly moralistic, definitely restrictive, was moving into their community. Preaching racism and religious bigotry, the Invisible Empire of Kleagles and Imperial Wizards and Grand Dragons called for a war against malevolent groups such as radicals, foreigners, and "niggers" to keep them from undermining "pure" American institutions. And how? The Ku Klux Klan had the answer. The best element of society must purge all "alien" forces, no matter how great the cost, no matter what the method.

For $10 "true" Americans could join the Klan; for $10 they could help save the United States. At last they had found an effective vehicle for alleviating the frustrations of a rapidly changing world, for fighting against conditions both disturbing and startling. To them it was shocking how much society was degenerating, how immoral people were becoming. The family, with its spiritual and moral base, was showing signs of fracturing, even of disintegrating. Some women were choosing a career instead of marriage; divorce in preference to self-sacrifice for their children; plunging necklines and rising skirts in defiance of modesty and decency. Yet political leaders on both the national and local levels, although staunch advocates of law and order, were apparently helpless to combat trends toward the disruption of society. Prostitution and gambling were increasing; "racketeer" and "speak-easy" and "booze" were becoming familiar terms in the English language; and that "Noble Experiment," the Eighteenth Amendment, was ineffective—and laughable.

To make matters worse, American institutions seemed to be under heavy attack. Since the Bolshevik Revolution of 1917, "true" Americans believed that Communists and radicals were trying to undermine the American system. United States Attorney General A. Mitchell Palmer had moved in the right direction by ferreting out those "traitors" in the government and bringing them to trial. But this "witch hunt," as the radical press called his actions, had definite limitations; in no way could he noticeably affect local situations. At the same time, the New Immigration, alien and Catholic, spouting strange political philosophies that were often critical of the American way of life, was also weakening this nation by its "mongrelizing taints." Those dark-skinned peoples, who lived in slums and tended toward vice and corruption, usually could not speak English, much less understand how democracy functioned. Equally alarming were attempts to paralyze the economy, to engulf the United States in depression. And who was to blame? Obviously, the "true" Americans agreed, it was the alien element, such as the "Uncle Shylock," the avaricious Jew who kept prices high and wages low.

So in October 1921, Klansmen were marching in Texas almost 100,000 strong, raising the fiery cross and the American flag in unison, denouncing the cancerous evils and corrupting vices in their midst, then enrolling "good solid middle-class citizens" in their ranks: lawyers, doctors, bankers, businessmen, even ministers and policemen. Already they had organized and paraded in Houston, Beaumont, Dallas, Fort Worth, Waco, Austin, and San Antonio. Now they were moving into rural communities. In East Texas and along the Gulf Coast their gospel spread like wildfire; on the Black Prairie in North Texas they were equally successful. The next region to "educate" lay in the center of the state, a land of rolling prairies dotted with small, fairly prosperous farming villages. But here the Invisible Empire hit a snag in the form of two law enforcement officers, Red Burton and Bob Buchanan.

Born on August 10, 1885, near Mart, Texas, Marvin "Red" Burton was the youngest son of John F. and Alice Cubley Burton. Originally from Montrose, Mississippi, his parents had migrated to Texas in the early 1880s and bought a farm between Mart and Waco. In that locale Red Burton grew to manhood, a typical product of his environment and of the era. Like most farm boys in Central Texas, he had specific family chores, helping his father in the fields and his mother around the house. Whenever possible he went to school, but scholastic endeavors did not prevent him from learning to fish, ride, and shoot well. Overall, life was not easy for Red; work hours were long and tasks often tedious. The span from childhood to maturity was brief.

Consequently, when only eighteen, Burton married a local girl and assumed the more difficult responsibilities of making a living. Starting without "a dollar in the world," he worked wherever possible, but essentially his life was without purpose or direction. In 1905 he landed a job on a ranch near Wortham, Texas. Then, in 1913, he returned to the Waco area and, with the savings of the last eight years, purchased a lot and built a house. Once again he was penniless and out of work, lacking even "money enough to buy . . . groceries."

But in 1914, after pouring concrete for stormsewers (and not too regularly), Burton informed his wife one morning: "I'm going to work at somethin'. I don't know what it does; I don't care what it pays. I'm going to work." Determined and almost desperate, he applied for a position with the Cleveland Construction Company. When the foreman sarcastically announced, "Sonny, we have work to do here but you wouldn't do it," Burton bristled, "You don't know me, man; I'll do anything honorable." And looking at the lean-muscled, 6'2 farm boy, almost skinny at 180 pounds, the foreman suddenly changed his mind. Perhaps something in Burton's voice, his clipped, terse comments, his firm, positive tone, carried conviction. Or possibly his appearance—light blue eyes, sandy red hair and ruddy complexion, a mask of defiance and resolution, huge hands, noticeably scarred and calloused, hanging like hamhocks from his shirtsleeves—made the foreman recognize a difference in this applicant. But whatever the reason, he found himself saying: "I'll tell you what, Sonny. You come over here tomorrow morning and . . . we'll run you off." That was one thing no one ever did. Burton stayed three years.

After that day, Red Burton never went hungry again; he was too much in demand. Within three weeks he was elevated to foreman, even though obviously inexperienced. When he expressed feelings of inadequacy, his boss explained the promotion this way: "I know you don't know a whole lot but you will work. I'll help you if you get in trouble." He never had to, however, for Burton learned his trade well. But even more importantly, he won the respect of the men under him. Those who met his standards could count on steady employment, while those who were "toughs" or troublemakers (and there were plenty of that sort in construction work) learned to steer clear of him or quit. He would—and could—back up his decisions.

In August 1917, Burton decided to change jobs, but not because he was unhappy. It was a matter of economics. The United States government, upon entering World War I, contracted the Grace Construction Company to build an airfield at Richfield, a few miles west of Waco. Since thousands of men were enlisting or being drafted into the armed forces, labor was hard to come by and even more difficult to keep. The Grace Company officials therefore offered Burton a job as foreman at double his present salary. They knew his reputation: that he was a tough taskmaster, that he inspired loyalty, that his men were ready to fight for him.

For two and a half weeks at Richfield, Burton measured up to all advance notices. Then, in an unexpected turn of events, the Waco Police Department drafted him into its ranks. Although the city council could in no way enforce such an act, Burton decided to serve for six months. He liked the idea of public service, of doing "things for other people." Besides, he was overworked, almost exhausted, and here was a chance, he reasoned, to "rest up" before returning to his old job.

How wrong he was! At nearby Camp MacArthur thousands of soldiers, mostly from the Midwest, had arrived and were inundating Waco, causing the usual problems between townspeople and the military. For the first few months, therefore, Burton had his hands full directing traffic as well as learning police procedures and gaining an understanding of the problems and techniques of law enforcement. Then he was assigned to night duty, patrolling residential and outlying districts on a motorcycle—and the orientation process began all over again. Gradually, as the months rolled by and as he became more involved, thoughts of returning to construction work faded away; each day he found "policing" more and more fascinating.

But in 1919, with the passage of the Eighteenth Amendment, Burton was caught in a situation which law officers have always dreaded. Besides having to enforce an unpopular law, he watched it corrupt some of his colleagues, thereby placing him in a difficult position. Because he was not "on the take," word went out to "get Red Burton lined up." After all, contraband liquor was bringing high prices and police salaries were low. Yet in spite of all inducements—promises of money, promotion, and favors—he steadfastly refused. So one morning in September his chief informed him that "for the good of the department" he was transferring him to a daytime schedule. Incensed over this roundabout way of curtailing his effectiveness (most of the contraband arrived at night), Burton replied: "Well, sir, if I thought it was better for the department, I wouldn't say a word"—and he quit.

Actually Burton only changed jobs, not professions. Because of his fine record, Bob Buchanan, the sheriff of McLennan County, offered him a deputy's commission. What a lucky break it was for both men. Besides seeing eye-to-eye concerning law enforcement, they became close friends. And on October 1, 1921, at Lorena, Texas, approximately thirteen miles south of Waco, they had need of each other. Together—and alone—they faced the Klan.

Robert "Bob" Buchanan was a rugged law-enforcement officer and a formidable opponent, cut from the same mold as frontier marshals and Texas Rangers. Although fifty years old, he looked much younger, possibly because of his smooth, tanned face and black, wavy hair. Physically he was an impressive man, carrying 225 pounds easily on a sturdy 6'1 build. A huge Colt .38 "thumbbuster" on a .45 frame strapped to his left hip made him even more imposing. Yet his eyes, coal-black, piercing, at times ominous and unfathomable, were his dominant feature. When someone challenged him, they were like gale warnings, prominent and threatening. No one was going to run over Bob Buchanan. He represented the law—and that meant fair, impartial enforcement. Never did he allow political pressure or expediency or friendship to interfere with duty. Of course, this strict adherence to the law, this tough application of justice, was also an Achilles' heel. But he knew no other way; to him any other conduct was unthinkable.

Even with law officers like Burton and Buchanan in McLennan County, the Klan leaders decided to act on October 1. Having already organized thoroughly in Waco, they planned a Saturday evening rally at Lorena, where they would march with fiery crosses through the black section of town and then convene, ironically enough, at the Baptist Church for an ice cream supper. Throughout Waco and the surrounding areas they tacked up notices, announcing in bold black type: "The Ku Klux Klan Will Parade Tonight at 8:30."

Surprisingly, neither Buchanan nor Burton was aware of these arrangements. Both were busy investigating a cotton theft in the nearby towns of Leroy and Mart. Yet while on the job they came to an understanding concerning the Klan. Each soon discovered that the other was not a member. In fact, they both voiced grave misgivings as to its purpose and activities, especially since a demonstration in Mart the previous Saturday had caused considerable damage. "If there is ever another parade in McLennan County while I am sheriff, I intend to find out who is responsible," Buchanan asserted emphatically, "and if I am out of the country, I want you to do it." Burton agreed. The matter was closed. Both sensed, however, that a "bad situation" might soon develop.

The two men had no idea that a confrontation was imminent. Upon their return to Waco that afternoon, however, several citizens from Lorena were waiting in Buchanan's office to inform him of a scheduled mass meeting and to appeal for help. Within a few minutes they had their answer. Turning to Burton, the sheriff asked, "Will you go down there with me?" And when Red replied he would, they were on their way.

It was a beautiful autumn afternoon as they rode to Lorena. The air was crisp, the sun bright, the countryside a greenish-brown, not quite ready to succumb to winter. With approximately 350 inhabitants, Lorena resembled many other Central Texas farm communities in the 1920s. Situated on a rolling black prairie, it rose into view easily, the spires from its several churches and the roofs of rambling two-story frame houses surrounded by large shade trees, obvious landmarks. Like so many small towns it had two principal avenues: Main Street, comprising most of the business district, and Highway 81, cutting through the best residential area. Where these two thoroughfares intersected, townspeople had built a funeral parlor, bank, Ford agency, and combination drug and general store, symbols of a permanent and growing community. Except for market day, Saturday mornings, and holidays, the atmosphere was always easygoing, relaxed, often phlegmatic.

But by the time the two lawmen arrived that evening, Lorena had changed dramatically. On the outskirts hundreds of cars, surreys, and wagons were parked haphazardly along the highway or in nearby fields. Along the streets vast throngs, estimated at 15,000 to 20,000 people, were milling about restlessly, though apparently in a festive mood. And as the sun quickly receded and the evening shadows lengthened, they eagerly anticipated the forthcoming events, for less than half a mile to the north hundreds of hooded, white-robed figures were assembling in a cotton field.

In order to maintain some semblance of authority and keep the peace, Buchanan promptly sought out the town leaders. Although known to be "pretty hotheaded" at times, he was extremely calm and "reasonable" that evening. Carefully, he explained his position. He had not come to stop their parade; on the contrary, as far as he was concerned they could march all night. But as sheriff of McLennan County, he announced, "I think I'm entitled to know who's responsible for it, so if anything happens I can know who to look for." For instance, he explained, whenever a circus came to town, the owners always made arrangements with him and the police regarding the parade. Consequently, if the leaders would identify themselves to him by raising their hoods when marching by, he would be satisfied.

Within thirty minutes, after much huddling and conferring, two McLennan County officials who were well-known to both Buchanan and Burton stepped forward to assume responsibility. Jovially the sheriff remarked that they need not lift their hoods because he would "know either of their hides in a tanning yard." So the matter was resolved—but not for long. A majority of the Klan leaders would not accept this agreement. Unhappy with the two officials for violating one of the basic rules of membership—that of secrecy—they rejected Buchanan's proposal, confident that their decision would cause no significant reverberations. After all, what could two law officers, alone and without public support, do? How could they prevent thousands from parading? The answers were obvious, the questions rhetorical. After taking precautionary steps, just in case the lawmen should react foolishly, the Klansmen quickly formed into lines of white-hooded figures, raised several American flags, lit huge crosses (one man, however, had wired one electrically), and began the march.

Meanwhile, Buchanan and Burton were chatting amicably and visiting with friends at the main intersection, unaware that the Klan was not going to cooperate. Then the situation changed dramatically. Out of the crowd the two county officials emerged in front of Burton, told him what had just happened, and rather fearfully asked if the sheriff would "think hard of them" if they did not participate. Rushing across the street, Red was repeating the conversation to Buchanan, who was listening silent and grim-faced, when a resounding roar announced the beginning of the parade. Out onto Highway 81 the Klansmen came, a sea of white-clothed figures outlined against the night. Without a word to anyone Buchanan, with jaw set, and wearing a mask of determination, began walking toward the marchers. Burton, remembering that the sheriff had earlier told him to "stay close" in case of trouble, followed some fifteen to twenty feet behind. Nearer and nearer they moved toward the mass of white, the crowd closing in behind them, both hostility and fear apparent in the expressions of the people.

Now the antagonists were face to face, just a few feet apart; yet Buchanan never hesitated or wavered. Whether unafraid of the consequences or feeling that he had no choice, he reacted bravely, even heroically. Confronting the first two leaders who were carrying a flaming cross, he reached out and slammed it to the ground, then raised up the hood of the nearest figure and resolutely declared: "I don't know you, but if I ever see your face again I will."

As Buchanan moved toward the second man, all hell broke loose. Stealthily, a robed form, later identified as a Waco policeman, crept up behind him and either with a blackjack or billyclub knocked him to the ground. Then, upon seizing the sheriff's pistol, the outraged Klansmen swarmed over him as he lay prostrate in the road, hitting and beating him repeatedly. At the same time Red Burton "was completely covered with men," two or three holding him while others pounded at his face and body. Physically powerful and doubly so because he was fighting for his life, he repeatedly broke away from one group only to be grabbed by another. Suddenly, two pistol shots rang out, startling the melee into silence. Buchanan, hurt and bleeding, yelled out: "Red, they've shot me."

Now the action became deadlier. Flicking out a pocketknife with a four-inch blade, the sheriff, even though badly wounded, slashed and stabbed two of his antagonists. Then Burton, like a man possessed, wild and uncontrollable after seeing his comrade fall, reacted almost unbelievably in the next few minutes. Never losing sight of the man who had shot Buchanan, he managed to pull a small .38 Colt automatic from his left pants pocket and fired two shots. The would-be killer dropped. Oblivious to the punishing blows from men who were still pommeling him, Burton fired the remaining seven bullets at Klansmen near the sheriff, definitely hitting one and possibly several others. For some reason the mob had failed to take his holstered single-action .41 Colt; but in his highly excited state of mind he had no time to ponder such an oversight, for he needed the weapon. Wrenching his pinned right arm free, he unsheathed the .41 Colt and stuck the barrel into the stomach of a prominent Lorena businessman, T. C. Westbrook, who was still trying to hold him. In a cold, deadly voice he said: "Mr. Westbrook, I love you like a daddy, but if I am not released I'm going to kill you." And for the first time since the fight began he was free of fists and arms and bodies.

Bruised and blood-smeared, Burton quickly assessed the situation as he stood in the highway exposed and unprotected—and it was not to his liking. In front of him, some ten yards away, the sheriff was staggering but on his feet, bleeding profusely from wounds in his right chest and leg. Approximately fifty feet to his left a robed Klansman was leveling a pistol at Buchanan, while at about the same distance on his right someone was also shooting at the sheriff.

Instinctively, Burton swung into action. With two shots he ended the threat to Buchanan, the man crumpling to the ground in a heap. Then he whirled to face his own assailant. In haste he fired several times, missing on each attempt but causing the man to flee. In fact, upon realizing that Burton could not be stopped and with bullets hitting indiscriminately in their midst, the crowd had dispersed, men and women scattering frantically in all directions.

Burton then turned to help Buchanan, but during the last exchange of gunfire someone had carried him to the drugstore at the intersection. So Red Burton hobbled and stumbled down the highway, unaware that he had been wounded in the right thigh. All about him was confusion. In a few short minutes Lorena had become a hate-filled disaster area. The town was a shambles, white robes and debris strewn everywhere, the streets spattered with blood, Klansmen confused and disorganized, their leaders striving to regroup. In the middle of the intersection a former Waco judge was damning and cursing the two lawmen at the top of his lungs, encouraging the apprehensive to more violence. For a fleeting moment Burton had "an evil thought," but with only one bullet left in his .41 Colt he decided not "to waste it on the old son-of-a-bitch."

After considerable physical exertion, Burton finally reached the front door of the drugstore, fearful that his comrade was mortally wounded because boastful Klansmen were shouting that they had killed Buchanan. Once inside he took command, threatening and cursing those who seemed to be more afraid of the Klan than of him. To Wiley Stem, a Waco policeman, he gave specific instructions to bolt the door and let no one in "unless someone had been injured." At the same instant he flipped back Stem's coat, grabbed his .45 Colt automatic, and grimly said, "Wiley, I need this and you have no use for it, so I'm taking it." Then he hurried over to Buchanan, who was sitting upright in a chair, obviously in pain and having difficulty breathing, blood flowing profusely from his chest. "Burton, they've killed me," the sheriff weakly exclaimed, to which Red replied: "No, Bob, those sons-of-bitches can't kill you; you just can't die."

But for the moment Burton could not be sure that anyone would not die. Outside the building Klansmen were milling about, venting their hate and frustration by angrily shouting: "Get a rope! Get a rope! Let's hang 'em." Inside, the foul stench of sweat and blood grew stronger, the moans of suffering men reverberating through the room as more and more wounded were brought in. Among them were Louis Crow, a prominent Waco businessman and ironically a close friend of the sheriff, with a deep stab wound in the chest; Ed Howard, a Waco policeman, knifed in the stomach; Carl West of Lorena, shot in the neck; and at least five others suffering from bullet or knife wounds. Already medical assistance was on the way, for Burton had summoned ambulances from Waco. But with the mob threatening to break in at any moment, and with an enraged Red Burton fingering a fully loaded gun and ready to kill anyone who threatened the wounded Buchanan, the chances of another bloodbath seemed definite.

Buchanan, however, realizing that trouble would continue as long as he and Burton were in town, repeatedly pleaded with his "friend" not to wait for the ambulance. Unsuccessful at first, he used the one argument which Burton could not resist. "I have always thought you were the best friend I had in the world," the sheriff declared, "and if you are, you will take me to the hospital." To that plea there could be only one answer. So Burton instructed Wiley Stem to "get a car" and bring it to the side entrance on Highway 81. Then he asked for someone to help him with the sheriff, but everyone shied away, fearful of what the Klan might do. He therefore draped Buchanan across his shoulder and back, holding him with his right hand, and dragged him across the room and out the side door through the crowd to the waiting car. Just in case the Klansmen intended to carry out their threats, he had Stem's .45 Colt automatic in his left hand, cocked and ready for action. But they had had enough of Burton for one night; they wanted no more. In silence they let the lawmen depart.

At breakneck speed Burton drove along the narrow winding highway to Waco, his thoughts a mass of mixed emotions. Worried and increasingly concerned, he kept checking on Buchanan, who was coughing spasmodically and sometimes gagging, watching him push a forefinger into the chest wound to stop the flow of blood. As ambulances passed by, clanging and screaming in the night, he bitterly reflected upon the events of the evening, the threats and violence, the unreasoning hatred of the mob, the feeling of loneliness when no one would help him. Suddenly, robed figures appeared on his right, running across a cotton field, and instinctively he reached for his .45 Colt automatic, feelings of vengeance and retribution welling up inside him. As if reading his mind, Buchanan spoke out almost pleadingly: "No, Burton, I think they whipped us; let's not have any more trouble."

So onward they raced toward Waco, Burton blaring the car horn to clear the way after reaching the city limits. Upon arrival at the Colgin Hospital, just across from the county jail (which was also the sheriff's home), they proceeded with the help of an attendant to the second-floor emergency room. Then events quite similar to the drugstore scene at Lorena happened all over again. With the Buchanan family and Burton standing guard at the door, doctors worked feverishly on the wounded and suffering men who streamed into the operating room. In the corridors, newspaper reporters and law officers, as well as county and district officials, were trying to piece together from the participants exactly what had happened, while outside in the street, thousands of people began gathering, surly and hostile, threatening to storm the hospital and lynch the two lawmen.

In all this frenzied commotion Burton remained calm and seemingly unmoved. Now painfully aware of both the multiple bruises on his body and the gunshot wound in his leg, he slumped into a chair to rest while listening without comment as I. Mac Wood, Buchanan's office deputy (and a Klansman), told what the mob was plotting. To pleas that he sneak out the back way and barricade himself in the county jail, Burton replied: "No, Mac, I have never had to be locked in jail yet." If, however, the Klansmen wanted trouble, he would accommodate them, Burton informed Wood, because he intended to come out soon.

At 4:00 Sunday morning Burton left the hospital. Although limping badly, he opened the front door, hobbled down the steps, and moved defiantly through the crowd, never speaking to or noticing anyone, yet expecting a confrontation each step of the way. After a few hushed, extremely tense minutes he had run the gauntlet and was safe within the county jail. For the moment he had faced the mob and had backed them down.

But the issue was by no means resolved, for the Klansmen were determined to win out. With Buchanan incapacitated, Burton was now in charge and therefore the key to the situation. Yet every attempt to outwit, pressure, or scare him failed miserably. When a fellow deputy, with whom he had worked closely, told him "to line up with the Klan" or "be a damn fool," Burton grabbed him by the back of the neck and the seat of the pants, unceremoniously dragged him into the county clerk's office, and ordered one of the secretaries to stamp "Canceled" across his commission as a deputy sheriff. Later the same day, two county commissioners tried still another approach, offering him a thirty-day paid vacation (to begin immediately) because they were afraid for his safety. Thanking them for their concern, he resolutely announced that he had "no intention of leaving." And if Klansmen wanted him, they would find him "in the sheriff's office," he asserted, "eighteen or twenty hours each day."

For over a week the pressure continued to mount, but Burton remained adamant. No matter that friends and prominent citizens asked him to submit to the Klan, no matter that public opinion was overwhelmingly against him and the sheriff, he would not back down, even after Crow died on October 4 and most of Waco turned out to mourn a "fallen hero." Scornful of hundreds of posters offering a "$5,000 Reward for Red Burton, Dead or Alive," he purposely appeared more prominently in public, challenging the Klan by his presence. Against a barrage of threats on his life, he countered with equally violent actions and statements. Whenever drivers happened to pull up beside him in a car, they found an automatic shotgun pointing out the window. During one difficult day after visiting Buchanan, who was still on the critical list, he bitterly and unwisely declared: "My greatest desire is that I may live to see . . . the streets of Lorena grow up in weeds."

Consequently, the Klansmen realized that only one course of action was left: Kill Red Burton! Throughout McLennan County and Central Texas word went out for Klansmen to assemble in Waco, whereupon they would march on the county jail and lynch Red Burton. On Wednesday afternoon, October 10, men began gathering on the city street corners, whispering their thoughts and plans. But as their numbers increased into the hundreds and then thousands, they boldly announced their intentions. Under the cover of darkness, with fiery crosses illuminating the sky, they were going to demonstrate what would happen to those who opposed the Klan.

By late afternoon Red Burton recognized the full extent of the danger. Yet he could do nothing. The Klansmen had the offensive; it was their move. That was the worst part—the feeling of helplessness, the loneliness, the waiting. To say the least, Burton was "considerably worried"; he knew that his opponents were deadly serious.

Darkness came quickly that October night in Waco. A light, cold mist was falling, the dampness bringing shivers to those in the streets. At approximately 8:00 P.M. three prominent citizens entered the county jail to see Burton, and to his surprise they wanted to help. "If you knew what all we know, you couldn't be in Waco, let alone sitting here in the sheriff's office alone," one of them began, because "[the Klan is] coming over here . . . to kill you." Under no circumstances could they condone such behavior; therefore, they were offering their services. They had already decided to hide him in one of their homes, to protect his family, and if necessary to stand with him against the mob; for, as one of them put it, "We need you, but we need you alive."

To accept their aid was definitely the sane choice, the human one; to reject it seemingly foolhardy. But Red Burton, even though deeply moved by their concern, would not run. After all, if the Klansmen really wanted to kill him, they would "finally do it," he explained, "so they had just as well get through with it tonight." He was not certain, however, that when actually facing him—and also the possibility of his retaliation—they could do murder. "But I am going to give them a chance," he told his startled friends. Presently he intended to make his usual nightly check around town.

As Burton recalled later, the next thirty minutes were a nightmare. Almost instinctively he reached for a sawed-off shotgun and placed it under his raincoat. Then over "strong protests" he opened the door and stepped out onto the street. With the sidewalks jammed with people, he had to push through the crowds, his ruddy face reflecting his grim determination. Up Austin Avenue to the Raleigh Hotel, then back to city hall and the police station he walked, catcalls and threats of violence all about him, a mob of people following and closing fast behind him. Crossing over to Sixth Street, he stopped at the Riddle Cafe for a cup of coffee. Sitting at a table near the back, he readied his shotgun as the angry crowd pressed against the large glass window panels. At that moment Mrs. Riddle hesitantly approached him, tears running down her cheeks, and whispered: "Mr. Burton, when you get ready to leave, my car is at the back door and . . . I am going to drive you away from here, because if you don't, those people are going to kill you." Burton again refused help. "Those men think they want to kill me but they don't," he replied, "because they realize that . . . some of them will be killed." Besides, he announced, while rising to pay his check, "I didn't come in your back door. I am going out . . . just as I came in." And he did, with no one challenging him or even attempting to slow him down en route to the sheriff's office.

Later, Burton readily admitted that he "really had no hopes of returning to the office alive." But now he felt safe. Perhaps his three friends, jubilantly returning to the jail, most accurately assessed what had just happened. As one of them put it: "Burton, you have done the smartest thing that a man ever did . . . we thought you were crazy but . . . if you had run as we advised you, this thing would have never ended; but now they have gone home with their tails tucked like a bunch of whipped puppies."

The violence was over; however, the evil effects, the cancerous suspicions, the hatreds and animosities, lingered. When Texas Governor Pat Neff ordered an immediate investigation, the Klansmen in Lorena and Waco withheld information and obstructed justice, threatening anyone who might think of testifying against them. Consequently, the McLennan County grand jury returned no indictments but issued "a sweeping rebuke" to Bob Buchanan for his actions. The citizens of Lorena acted in the same spirit; approximately 300 of them signed a petition, vindicating the Klan of its part in "the trouble" and damning the lawmen "for the blood that was spilled." So the bitterness would continue in the county, with people blaming one another for what had happened. And even though the Klan would continue to thrive in Central Texas for several years, the Lorena affair alarmed many thoughtful citizens and thereby aroused staunch opposition against the organization.

No one was a more outstanding opponent of the Klan than Bob Buchanan. A constant reminder of that terrible night, he continued to live for seven years, somewhat crippled by the bullet still in his right leg and physically unable to run for sheriff again. But he never apologized for his actions; instead he battled the Klan, whenever possible showing people what it really stood for. During the next few years he also fought several civil suits brought against him by those wounded at Lorena—and each time he won. In fact, so great was his reputation, so dominant his presence, that the Klan did not parade in Waco until after he retired from office on January 1, 1923.

As for Red Burton, Lorena was just the beginning of a long career in law enforcement. Because of Burton's dedication and valor as a chief deputy in McLennan County, Governor Neff appointed him a Texas Ranger in 1922; he was never disappointed. During the next eleven years Burton became almost a legend in the Ranger service, especially in cases concerning bootleggers, oil boomers, and Klansmen. Then, in 1933, he returned to Waco to serve as chief of detectives and later as chief of police. Upon retirement in 1951, despite all his many contributions to law enforcement over a thirty-five-year span, he would best be remembered for that night in Lorena—for the example that he and Bob Buchanan had set, where two peace officers, disregarding personal safety, faced the Klan and fought it to a standstill.

Whiskey and Blood

THAD SITTON

EMINENT ORAL HISTORIAN THAD SITTON IS THE AUTHOR OF SUCH STUDIES AS *FROM CAN SEE TO CAN'T: TEXAS COTTON FARMERS ON THE SOUTHERN PRAIRIES*, *BACKWOODSMEN: STOCKMEN AND HUNTERS ALONG A BIG THICKET RIVER VALLEY*, *HARDER THAN HARDSCRABBLE: ORAL RECOLLECTIONS OF THE FARMING LIFE FROM THE EDGE OF THE TEXAS HILL COUNTRY*, AND *THE TEXAS SHERIFF: LORD OF THE COUNTY LINE*.

IN THE FIRST HALF OF THE TWENTIETH CENTURY, FEDERAL AND STATE AUTHORITIES EXERCISED LESS CONTROL OVER LOCAL LAW ENFORCEMENT. TEXAS COUNTY SHERIFFS OFTEN RETAINED THE ABILITY TO BALANCE THEIR OWN INTERPRETATION OF THE LAW WITH THE VALUES AND EXPECTATIONS OF THE CITIZENS WHO ELECTED THEM. IN THIS SELECTION, DR. SITTON DISCUSSES THE EXPERIENCES OF LONE STAR SHERIFFS AS THEY CONFRONTED SUCH ISSUES AS GAMBLING, PROSTITUTION, AND MOONSHINING. SHERIFFS ALSO ENFORCED SEGREGATION IN TEXAS AND DEALT SWIFTLY WITH THOSE WHO CHALLENGED THE EXISTING SOCIAL ORDER.

★ ★

No sooner did a new sheriff like H. F. Fenton take office than he found himself in an ambiguous relationship with certain county traditions, extralegal and illegal—matters which, more than anything else, forced the sheriff to "interpret" the law or even ignore its violation. Many voters expected their sheriffs to respect these local traditions and became angry at them if they did not. Rather often, the underlying political dynamics of sheriffs' elections turned on such matters, with candidates friendly to extralegal or illegal local traditions opposed by candidates favoring their reform.

Most dry counties nonetheless had their customary wet spots at country clubs, Veterans of Foreign Wars (VFW) halls, and black "barrel houses." Public drunkenness was illegal but also traditional. Every Saturday night the sheriff had to pick and choose among his many candidates for arrest, and a strict interpretationist could jam his jail with angry intoxicated voters by 11 P.M. Drinkers often also were the fighters, participating in what H. F. Fenton called "just good old fistfights"—another outlaw tradition, fair combats between consenting males. Prostitution and gambling also were illegal, but discreet "red light districts" condoned by important citizens operated in many communities, and zealous gamblers from all echelons of county society wielded cards and dice. Should the sheriff so desire, he could ignore the Saturday night drunks and instead fill his jail with bank presidents, lawyers, sharecroppers, cowboys, pulpwood haulers, and other adherents of the sporting life.

If sheriffs strategically looked the other way at the violation of some state laws, they also enforced certain customary local rules not on the books. About 1950, "Jim Crow" laws still supported segregation, but in every multiracial community many extralegal customs elaborated on the formalities of apartheid to further separate the races, and people expected sheriffs to patrol the invisible lines and enforce the unwritten rules of local race relations. If a black man entered the wrong doorway to a place of business or sat on the wrong bench at the courthouse square, or if white youths prowled the black quarter after midnight, it was the sheriff's job to deal with these matters. Fearing racial troubles perhaps more than anything else, rural sheriffs of the 1950s and 1960s invariably sought to preserve racial harmony by more and better segregation.

Whether the traditional transgressors were drunks, gamblers, fighters, whoremongers, or whatever, a sheriff prided himself on enforcing the formal laws with discretion, common sense, and a degree of leeway, the better to "protect his people from abuse." "I don't think every man that messes up a little bit needs to go to jail," Truman Maddox explained:

> ***All rules are made to be distributed to the people as the person sees fit. Start with speeding. The law out here says fifty-five miles an hour. There's no one that would agree to give a man a ticket for fifty-six, but that is more than the law says he is allowed to do. There's a law against a man using abusive language, but a man can do that up to a certain point. He might raise a little cain and cuss and cut up a little bit, but go give that man a chance to go on home. If he's got too much to drink, give him a chance, let him go on home.***

As Maddox implied, sheriffs often did not operate in the same way as such mechanical enforcers of the law as municipal policemen, state troopers, or Texas Rangers. Sheriff Sonny Sessions affirmed: "A good sheriff is a buffer from other law enforcement. They're usually not very popular with the police departments. A good sheriff's gonna protect his people from abuse." In his study of the Texas sheriff, political scientist James Dickson noted how sheriffs often operated to buffer county citizens and county traditions from the full and immediate effects of enforced legal changes coming down from the state or federal levels of government. "His dual role, both as an agent of local government and state government, enables him to use his unusual brand of discretion in law enforcement to modify and adapt changes intruding from the upper reaches of the system. The sheriff provides the citizens of his county a cushion of time to decide how much of their old ways can be preserved within a facade of compliance with inevitable and unavoidable adjustments."

In truth, within this "facade of compliance" some sheriffs defended their counties' "old ways" with special vigor, and a few developed economic incentives for doing so. A sheriff was supposed "to defend his county against any of its enemies when they come into the land," legal scholar Walter Anderson noted. Sometimes these enemies of the county were outside criminals, and sometimes, a sheriff might conclude, they were Liquor Control Board (LCB) men, Texas Rangers, or FBI agents.

Sheriffs occasionally might set out to destroy local gambling and prostitution root and branch, but this was not the norm. Most accepted such petty criminal activity as unavoidable, made a show of catching and fining all the gamblers and whores they easily could, and went about their other business. Gambling traditions ran deep in Coleman County, as at other places. Just before World War I, "Coleman was a gambling town, the men of all ages gathering at one vacant house or another, the windows covered with blankets and the games going on by lantern or kerosene light." Sheriff Bannister had good informants to tell him where the gambling party of the night would take place, and on one occasion he caught twenty-four young Anglo males, representatives of most of Coleman's prominent families, shooting craps. All that long night, lights burned at the courthouse as families' lawyers met with the county attorney, attempting to keep the gambling arrests from besmirching their clients' permanent records. Sheriff Bannister also often pursued black crap shooters in the Coleman countryside, and by Sheriff H. F. Fenton's time after World War II, little had changed. About 1947, Fenton kicked in a door at a private residence on the "Hill," Coleman's black quarter, and caught twenty-one African American gamblers in the act. With far too many perpetrators to transport in his car, Fenton "just put 'em in a column of twos and marched 'em all the way from the Hill to the courthouse with a flashlight."

The zeal to gamble ran deep at the Texas grass roots and knew no racial boundaries. In 1947, Chief Deputy Jeff Guthrie heard "an ominous clicking sound emanating from a seldom used room" in the Gray County courthouse at Pampa and broke in to find several men shooting dice on the floor. In Wharton County, Sheriff Buck Lane kept a nickel slot machine as an office souvenir until the night he caught his two oldest sons, ages fourteen and twelve, playing the machine. At that point Lane recalled all the occasions that deputies had come into his office on one pretext or another and put coins into the gambling device. Reminiscing about the Peach Tree community in Tyler County, where he had grown up, lumberman John Henry Kirby noted that card playing and crap shooting were common male diversions, often practiced away from the house and the womenfolks, sometimes "down in a secluded thicket by firelight, rich pine knot constituting the fuel." In the Brazos River bottoms of Washington County, black men had gathered for the same outdoor diversions, as Ed Lathan described. "They would get out there by the wood pile in a great big ring, they'd have a big piece of quilting or cotton-sack duck, and that what they be dealing and shooting crap on. And guys used to take these soda bottles and fill em with kerosene, and get a rag and twist it plumb down in there, and light em, and that would give light to see while they gamble."

Some sheriffs felt the gambling urge as strongly as did the Washington County sharecroppers, and all sheriffs had decisions to make about their policies with regards to local gambling. No sooner was Henry Billingsley elected Angelina County sheriff in 1932 than a local businessmen offered to pay Billingsley two hundred dollars a month for the right to run a few slot machines. Billingsley declined the offer, as did Sheriff Buck Lane of Wharton County after a Corpus Christi man told him, "Just let me put in a few slot machines over here on the county line, and I'll give you a car and so much money." Noting that "you can't be on the take and be a good sheriff," Lane said that he kept his county "clean" of serious gambling and prostitution during his terms in office. As he explained to the public in a newspaper column, his position was "no public gambling allowed, that is to say, no slot machines, punch boards, numbers rackets, however, we are not bad about hunting up these little sporadic games that are had here and there by folks, for they are not what I would class as gambling, more or less a pastime for people at their barbecues and get togethers, and no one loses much or wins much."

Most sheriffs treated local gambling traditions much as did Buck Lane, although less tolerant citizens often lobbied for more stringent enforcement of the gambling laws. "Little sporadic games that are had here and there" were anathema to some—as were the traditional black gambling houses that came under grand jury attack during 1947. "From time immemorial in Wharton County," Lane wrote, "the negro has been allowed to openly run his gambling houses, that is, certain sections of the county, it was generally said, gambling or crap shooting was a religion with the negro." No more, however; Lane promised to follow the grand jury's request to shut these places down—or at least so he said. Week after week, year after year, Sheriff Lane's jail lists remain devoid of gamblers, black or white, amateur or professional.

Rather often, grand jury probes impelled sheriffs to take action against traditional gambling spots and red light zones the sheriffs previously had ignored. During 1949, for example, the Gregg County grand jury forced Sheriff Noble Crawford to raid Gladewater for marble tables, punchboards, and other penny-ante gambling devices. Minor gambling had flourished in the Conroe area until Sheriff Hershel Surratt died in office and the county commissioners appointed his wife to serve out his term. Working closely with other community churchwomen, Sheriff Fannie Pearl Surratt now launched her department on a vigorous antigambling purge of marble tables, pinball machines, and everything else. In Eastland County in 1951, with grand jury encouragement, Sheriff Frank Tucker shut down "cutthroat gambling gyps" at county fair booths run by the Eastland American Legion, and the veterans' group took out full-page newspaper ads in self-defense.

Grassroots gambling passions remained strong, however, and as soon as active suppression ceased, gambling devices and games of chance popped up like mushrooms in the sheriff's domain. A year after blocking the local businessman's slot machines, Sheriff Billingsley discovered that the man had introduced "racehorse machines" instead and had "paid the district judge at Fairfield $1,500 to enjoin me from bothering the machines." Perhaps serving as front man for local cotton growers (who always needed more pickers), a "colored citizen" approached Buck Lane during 1949 with the idea of "open gambling places" to draw additional workers to Wharton County during picking season. Gamblers were always knocking at the sheriff's front door with offers or sneaking around behind his back. A month before, a slot machine had shown up in a "black beer joint" in the Wharton County hinterland, peddled to the owner by a white salesman with the assurance that "he had it fixed with the law."

Prostitution and professional gambling often went on in closely related circumstances at red light districts as small as Coleman's "Rat Row" and Richmond's "Mud Alley" and as large as Galveston County. At the dawn of the twentieth century, most Texas courthouse towns and all larger cities had such districts, and some persisted into midcentury. At Brenham, seat of Washington County, the red light section was called "Tiperary," and at the state capital of Austin, "Guy Town." Prohibitionist sentiments closed Tiperary about World War I, and at the beginning of World War II, army commanders at Fort Crockett and Camp Wallace forced a temporary shutdown of Galveston's extensive red light district. Editors at the *Sheriffs' Association of Texas Magazine* accurately predicted that the banished Galveston prostitutes, now outside of regulation and medical supervision, soon would reestablish operations at nearby Houston, Beaumont, Port Arthur, and other war-industry boomtowns. An editorial of May 1942 argued that experienced law officers knew that "a well restricted and regulated district appears to be the only remedy. The red light district evil is as old as time, never having been successfully expunged from a community." Running the whores out of town accomplished little, the editors believed. "Long-nosed, gloom-spreading reformers have sought solution of the red light district since the days of Nero, but only to realize they were bucking nature, which has never been done successfully."

Sheriff Buck Lane told a historian that he had joined forces with other officers to drive the whores from Wharton County, and perhaps that was true, but the expulsion proved suspiciously effective. Like gamblers, prostitutes never showed up on the little sheriff's lists of jail prisoners, a fact suggesting that Lane believed he had better things to do. Even into the 1970s many sheriffs had the attitude towards red light districts and "victimless crimes" that "boys will be boys," a belief that sometimes put them at cross purposes with local reformers. During 1957, for example, a political war broke out in Fort Bend County between Sheriff R. Z. Cowart and Glymer Wright, editor of the *Fort Bend Reporter*. Wright claimed Sheriff Cowart had allowed vice to exist at Mud Alley, a gambling and prostitution area in the county seat of Richmond, and the sheriff replied that "the Alley is shut tight," a claim soon disputed by the editor. Over a decade later, Sheriff Aubrey Cole of Jasper County took public criticism for allowing black "barrel houses," mini–red light zones, to operate in rural precincts. Cole explained: "These rough, tough blacks, that Saturday night, done their thing, they kept it out there and didn't bring it down on the streets in town." Prominent people came to Sheriff Cole and encouraged him to leave the barrel houses alone "because they serve a purpose." Cole did so, and "after a while it got to where we didn't know what was going on and didn't want to know what was going on—let them have it [out] among themselves, and most of them licked their wounds and didn't report it."

In Bowie County, Fayette County, and a few other places, as late as 1970, certain traditional red light zones and houses of prostitution had attained the status of protected local institutions. For good political reasons, a succession of Bowie County sheriffs had allowed Texarkana's five historic whorehouses to go about their business. During the 1960s, politicians from outside Bowie County brought pressure to clean things up—pressure resisted by Homer Garrison, Jr., head of the Department of Public Safety until his death in 1967. After Garrison's death and the retirement of the district Texas Ranger, politicians forced Rangers and other state lawmen (but not the sheriff's department) into a sting operation at the Texarkana whorehouses, but local juries refused to convict prostitutes or madams. In Fayette County in 1972, bowing to outside political pressures, reluctant Texas Rangers forced Sheriff Jim Flournoy to close Edna's Fashionable Ranch Boarding House, a local institution fondly known as the "Chicken Ranch." Sheriff Flournoy glumly told a reporter: "It's been there all my life and all my daddy's life and never caused anybody any trouble. Every large city in Texas has things a thousand times worse. The girls started packing their things Tuesday night, I don't think anyone is out there." The petition to keep the Chicken Ranch open had "as many as several thousands of names. I don't think it will do any good, but I plan to go with several people to see Governor Briscoe." Newsman Lester Zapalac, publisher of the *La Grange Journal*, bitterly protested the demise of the Chicken Ranch. The institution was "beneficial to the community" and had contributed thousands of dollars to the new community hospital. "I've never seen anything bad come from it," the newsman told a reporter, "and I've lived here all my life. The girls buy all of their clothes here, their eats, it brings in business for the community. They pay taxes same as everyone else—city, county, federal income taxes. It's listed on the records as a rooming house. It keeps down rape, venereal disease. I think most of the people here are in favor of it. Sometimes, when there is a barbecue in town, the leftovers are sent out to the girls, and they always send back fifty or a hundred dollars to town."

Sometimes the local red light district took in virtually the whole county, as at the "Free State of Galveston" until 1957. Gambling, prostitution, and illegal alcohol rose to dominate the Galveston economy from the 1920s to the 1950s, a red-light heyday largely coincident with the political career of Galveston County's most famous sheriff, Frank L. Biaggne, who held office from 1933 to 1957. Sam and Rose Maceo, former barbers of Sicilian descent, controlled Galveston gambling, prostitution, and whiskey running from the 1920s, and by 1942 their empire centered on the Balinese Room pier, a two-hundred-yard, T-headed pier built into the breaking surf at the end of 21st Street. An elite restaurant with two bands occupied the land end of the pier, while a fully equipped gambling casino operated farther out in the Gulf. Texas Rangers and other state lawmen sometimes staged raids on the Balinese Club, but the staff often seemed to have been warned about their comings, and the long pier, with its guard stations and heavy glass doors, slowed the Rangers' assaults. No sooner did officers pass the front door than a guard pushed a button, warning casino staff to whisk cards and poker chips out of sight, fold slot machines into the walls like Murphy beds, and convert green-felted craps tables into backgammon and bridge tables. The Balinese pier was lengthy and the Texas Rangers not very fleet of foot, so time after time they found nothing illegal going on when they reached the pier's T-head. Sometimes casino staff added insult to injury along the way, as on the occasion when a band leader announced to restaurant customers, "And now the Balinese Room takes great pride in presenting, in person, the Texas Rangers!" then signaled his band to strike up "The Eyes of Texas" while a squad of Rangers thundered by in cowboy boots.

Sheriff Frank Biaggne once told a state investigative committee in Austin that he had never raided the Balinese Club because it was a private club and he was not a member. Furthermore, although Biaggne often might be seen knocking down free drinks and shooting dice at the Turf Club, another Galveston casino, the sheriff told the chairman of the state committee: "I don't gamble, your honor. I'm not a drinking man, and I don't know the taste of tobacco. Maybe I'm too good to be a peace officer."

For decades, Sheriff Biaggne's confidence was not misplaced. The Maceo brothers remained enormously powerful and friends to several governors, and the county attorney joined the sheriff in keeping Galveston running wide open. In 1951 the attorney noted that the last felony indictment for gambling in Galveston County had come twenty years back. Open gambling and prostitution had become a fact of life, and as long as there was no violence, officials did not bother with enforcement of the vice laws. Furthermore, this profitable "Little Havana" version of Galveston had friends in high places. Candidates for governor courted the Maceos Texas politicians often ate at the Balinese Room restaurant. When affable Sam Maceo staged a benefit for survivors of the Texas City explosion of 1947 and asked some of his friends from the entertainment world to come down, Frank Sinatra, Jack Benny, Gene Autry, Phil Silvers, Jane Russell, George Burns, and Gracie Allen showed up.

All good things had to come to an end, however, and by the mid-1950s the people that the Sheriffs' Association of Texas editor termed "long-nosed, gloom-spreading reformers" began to get the upper hand. Texas Ranger Clint Peoples assumed the identity of a Blanco County rancher, reached the Balinese Room casino, and held a dice table, twelve house men, and forty-eight gamblers at gunpoint while Rangers raced up the pier and Maceo employees hid all the other gambling equipment. Other successful "busts" followed this one, in 1954 fire destroyed the Maceo brothers' pleasure pier, and in 1957, State Attorney General Will Wilson and DPS head Homer Garrison launched an elite squad of Texas Rangers and LCB undercover men on wicked Galveston, closing bookie parlors, whorehouses, and gambling casinos. Rangers demolished thousands of gambling devices with sledgehammers and dumped them in the bay—so many that Galveston officials accused the state of creating a shipping hazard.

This outsider attack closely followed the one event most essential for its success, the defeat of Sheriff Frank Biaggne in the 1956 election. Sheriff-elect Paul Hopkins, a former DPS trooper, denied to reporters that he was a "reformer," but he planned "to enforce all the laws of the state of Texas as they are written on the statute book," and this included "waging an all out war on prostitution and its deadly partner, narcotics." Gamblers had come to Hopkins after the first primary and "offered me their help," but "I turned them down cold—I promised to uphold my oath of office if elected, and I intend to do just that." As Hopkins prepared to assume office (and Will Wilson and Homer Garrison at distant Austin readied their shock troops to attack Galveston vice), former sheriffs' association president Frank Biaggne planned his return to private life after twenty-four years in office.

Although every county might have its customary one-street or one-motel version of "Little Havana," policing problems caused by the traditional drug of alcohol took up far more of a sheriff's time. Moonshiners, bootleggers, and—above all—public drunks filled the sheriff's jail, and the sheriff's informal policies on enforcement of the liquor laws remained a hot political issue. By 1950 the Texas law enforcement map showed a checkerboard of wet and dry counties, each with its own peculiar problems. "Local option" on alcohol matters had ruled the day before the assertion of national prohibition from 1919 to 1933, and a more complicated form of local option returned after 1933. The Texas Liquor Control Act of 1937, and its subsequent elaborations and amendments, set the rules of the game. Counties could vote to prohibit alcohol totally; to allow alcohol, but only beer and wine; or to allow any and all alcohol. Political subdivisions (municipalities, commissioners' precincts) within wet counties could vote themselves dry, but subdivisions within dry counties could not vote themselves wet. Of Texas's 254 counties, 123 were entirely dry in 1941 and 142 entirely dry in 1951, and the political scuffle continued. No less than thirty-two local option elections were held in 1950.

Sheriff Leon Jones took office at Angelina County in 1951, and Jones found himself confronted with the typical problems of a dry county. "Dry" did not, of course, mean an absence of alcohol. Drinkers could have up to one-fifth gallon of hard liquor or a case of beer for personal use at any time—quantities quite sufficient to induce intoxication and bad behavior. Local people who despised "drug fiends" from the cities nonetheless drank themselves into fiendish states every weekend with traditional beer and whiskey, and after they crashed their cars on the highways or assaulted their families or neighbors, they became the sheriff's problem. Other people supplemented their incomes by saving such consumers the twelve-mile trip to the county-line bars of nearby Trinity County. A white-clad African American tamale vendor named Eddie pushed his cart around Lufkin's downtown. Sometimes Eddie cried "Hot!" to announce his product, and sometimes, when Eddie had more than tamales and circumstances seemed right, "Hot, and that ain't all!" Local bootleggers such as Eddie commonly waited until 10 P.M., when the Trinity County liquor stores closed, to begin to peddle their wares at the usual 100 percent markup over liquor store prices. "Hip-pocket" bootleggers walked the streets with a pint of whiskey in each hip pocket, constituting their legal fifth. After they sold one pocket "dry" to a customer, they slipped around to their stash, put another pint in their pocket, and went back to the street. Sheriff Jones could arrest a hip-pocket bootlegger only if he caught the person illegally selling liquor to someone or taking additional bottles from his illegal stash. One Lufkin taxi stand owner sold whiskey all the time, though the man was careful to keep only two pints in his desk. Sheriff Jones filed on him many times, but the owner always waited until he had five or so documents accumulated, then went to the county judge and offered to pay one fine if the judge dropped the other four. This happened over and over again, and the taxi man once informed the sheriff that he could do business like that at a greater profit margin than he could operate a legal liquor store in Trinity County.

Most dry-county sheriffs allowed a few discrete wet spots to operate as part of their compromise with local alcohol traditions, just as they often ignored well-behaved public drunks and prominent citizens with several cases of beer in their car trunk. Pat Riddell noted of his father, Sheriff Wallace Riddell, "He had a certain amount of tolerance, because if he didn't, a sheriff would drive himself crazy trying to look behind every car door and every trunk and under every hood." In truth, a sheriff could spend all of his time and his deputies' time on such minor enforcements of the liquor law, and to his ultimate political disadvantage. Sheriff Leon Jones, however, had been a Liquor Control Board officer, so he cracked down on informal black "joints," the Lufkin Country Club, the Elks, and the VFW, and he paid the political price. A lawyer at the country club asked him, "Do you think you can be Angelina County sheriff and do this?" Jones answered in the affirmative at the time, but he later admitted, "That may be why I'm not sheriff now."

Alcohol was rural Texans' recreational drug of choice during the 1950s, as it had been for many decades before, but problems associated with its traditional use shrank to irreducible, minimal levels during Sheriff Jones's tenure of office in Angelina County. With bonded whiskey available only twelve miles away, few moonshiners chose to operate, and bootleggers remained small-scale. Twenty years before, however, when Henry Billingsley first took office as Angelina County sheriff, things had been entirely different. By 1931, in the depths of the Great Depression, shut-down sawmills and five-cents-a-pound cotton had forced many desperate residents into the risky craft of whiskey making. Sober family men assumed the role of moonshiner and hid out along wooded creek and river bottoms, plying their outlaw trade. The sheriff before Billingsley had allowed his friends and neighbors considerable operating room, but not so Billingsley, elected by the dry majority on a reform platform promising more rigorous enforcement of national prohibition. As a result, Sheriff Billingsley soon found himself in an all-out war with the whiskey men and their customers and supporters, which, as the new sheriff soon discovered, included County Judge Butler Rolston.

The whiskey war in the dry county was an old story in rural Texas, and counties often passed through several cycles of outlawry and reform during the twentieth century. No sooner had the wave of prohibition sentiments caused many counties to reject legal alcohol during the years between 1900 and 1918 than moonshiners and bootleggers stepped in to service thirsty consumers. Every dry county created a market for local whiskey producers and for long-range bootleggers, who hauled in their product from the nearest legal purchase point. Beginning in 1919, national prohibition dried up all Texas counties at once, encouraging major cross-country bootlegging from the Republic of Mexico (at levels anticipating the 1990s drug trade) and stimulating whiskey production in any Texas county with readily available water, good places to hide stills, and less than zealous law enforcement. If a rural county had all these advantages and was close to a major market in an urban area or oil field, it became even more likely to experience a moonshine boom, and counties such as Harrison, Somervell, Falls, Trinity, and a few others became major regional whiskey producers during Prohibition years. As in the case of Angelina County, where several major sawmills suffered quick shutdowns after 1929, the Great Depression overlapped Prohibition and impelled into the trade a new wave of moonshiners, most of whom continued to operate after liquor became legal during 1933. Many counties swiftly voted themselves dry after that year, thus perpetuating both local prohibition and the outlaws who serviced citizens who did not agree with it. Local industries and cotton prices did not revive until World War II, and thousands of Texas whiskey makers began operations during the late 1930s, even though moonshine prices fell drastically after 1933.

Illegal whiskey making did not disappear following the repeal of national prohibition or the return of prosperity after 1941, but it waxed and waned during the 1930s, 1940s, and 1950s with the rise and fall of federal taxes on legal liquor. World War II saw a resurgence in the illegal whiskey trade, especially in counties near major new military bases such as Fort Hood. Sold for as low as two to three dollars a gallon, moonshine was still the "poor man's drunk," and many people had developed a liking for its raw, fiery taste. In Jasper County during World War II, as elsewhere, moonshiners and moonshine seemed to be everywhere. C. W. Gandy recalled: "You used to go to dances around here, and when you'd drive up it'd look like headlights. Every tree top around that place had a gallon of whiskey under it. Well, if you didn't drink with everybody it'd make 'em mad and you'd have to fight with 'em. And we'd generally get so drunk to keep from fighting 'em we'd end up sleeping on the porch at night all night long."

Gandy described local consumption, but a lot of Jasper County moonshine was destined for nearby Beaumont. In every county there were small operators, large operators, and sometimes a relationship between the two. Former sheriff Aubrey Cole explained the situation in Jasper County:

> ***There were three people in Jasper County that was the big whiskey men. They had the big rigs. They set up more or less like a small sawmill operation, worked a lot of people, ordered their grain, rye, and corn and sugar shipped in on the train. They went in wagons and unloaded it at the depot and hauled it out in the woods to their rig. Now, there were lots of people, topwater whiskey makers, that had a little old rig, little old thirty-gallon rig, ten-gallon thumping kegs, and they just might make a run or two of whiskey after the crop was laid by, mostly to get the baby a new pair of shoes with and to drink themselves. Most of them would sell their whiskey to these three big whiskey men, and they'd carry this raw-made whiskey to Beaumont.***

Sheriff Henry Billingsley's predecessor at Angelina County had ignored the "Strain Farm," a moonshining enterprise near the county line that was also "more or less like a small sawmill operation," as Aubrey Cole described Jasper County's three "big rigs." Without doubt the Jasper County sheriff did the same, since truckloads of corn chops and sugar rolling from the railroad into the county backwoods could hardly have been missed. Sheriffs varied greatly in attitudes and policies regarding their traditional whiskey outlaws. Some, such as Henry Billingsley, Frank Brunt, J. R. Sessions, and others, fought them tooth and nail. Many sheriffs went into action only after formal complaints had been filed, captured some moonshiners and bootleggers to seem diligent, and made a show of ruptured stills on the courthouse lawn, but otherwise they looked the other way. Sheriffs often personally disagreed with prohibition, as did, in various formal editorials, the Sheriffs' Association of Texas—the same association that elected Frank Biaggne as president. Especially during the 1930s a sheriff well knew that many locals made whiskey out of acute financial need and that some of them had voted for him in the last election. In fact, some of them were probably his own friends and family. Beyond this, some degree of collusion and "going on the take" probably was not that uncommon, especially during the impoverished Depression years. As an extreme case, in Jasper County, Beaver Bishop operated as a major moonshiner at the same time that, as the county sheriff, he suppressed his outlaw competitors. Convicted in federal district court in 1940 on a charge of "conspiracy to traffic in untaxed liquor," Bishop resigned as Jasper County sheriff and escaped with a suspended sentence and sixty days' confinement at New Orleans. However, in 1941 officers once again caught Bishop making whiskey.

The story of the reform sheriff, elected to clean up his county and going to war with entrenched moonshiners and bootleggers, repeated itself many times over. More often than not, lawman and local outlaws knew each other. The sheriff commonly viewed native whiskey men as wayward voters just trying to support their families, and many perpetrators recognized that the sheriff was just doing his job. These attitudes often resulted in a strange kind of friendly rivalry. The moonshiner did everything to avoid capture, but if caught, he usually interacted in a friendly way with the sheriff and gave him no trouble. For his part, the sheriff usually treated the whiskey maker with respect and courtesy, often taking his word that he would come into the courthouse to post bond the next day. In Angelina County, moonshiner George Carpenter said of his long-term adversary Sheriff Henry Billingsley, "He was a good sheriff, he never did mistreat nobody that he caught running whiskey." Honest sheriffs who played the game this way were even admired. The operator of the Strain Farm distillery told another man: "Henry Billingsley would not sell out. We ain't got enough money to buy him. He won't sell."

While quail hunting one day, Sheriff Roy Herrington of Anderson County noticed an old house in an open field with smoke coming through its rotted roof. Curious, he walked over, looked inside, and found a local man named Howard Barrett tending a whiskey still and fourteen barrels of mash. "I said, 'Howard, you doing any good?' He looked around and saw me. He said, 'Mr. Roy, I didn't know you was anywhere around this world.' I said, 'I'll tell you what, Howard, you take my car and go on in to town and tell this filling station man to bring his truck out here to get the still.'"

Reform sheriffs sometimes enjoyed the cat-and-mouse games they played with local moonshiners. Local outlaws often had detailed knowledge of many square miles of landscape and made full use of this knowledge to hide their stills. Sheriffs, on the other hand, prided themselves on how well they knew their counties and hired deputies from the same woods-wise communities the whiskey makers came from. The moonshiners' determination to hide was matched by the sheriff's determination to catch them making whiskey "on their still."

Whiskey makers used various strategies to escape detection. Often they set up operations in the most inaccessible place they could get into. They might crawl into the densest thicket or briar patch they could find and cut out a place in the middle to set up their still, or they might wait until the river rose in the fall and then wade or paddle out to one of islands in the maze of backwaters to set up there. Others dug their operations into cut banks on the bends of creeks, placed them under brush heaps, located them in the shattered forests just behind logging "fronts," or buried them completely in the ground.

Some major stills operated in remote locations behind large buffers of private property, and if the whiskey makers kept their mouths shut and sold only outside the county, they might escape detection for a long time. In Montgomery County in 1929, someone finally informed on a major distillery that had been running without the sheriff's knowledge for over three years. The vats, coils, and storage containers for this operation covered an acre. Gasoline pumps brought up water from the creek to fill mash tanks, and finished product rolled out by the truckload after dark to Houston and San Antonio. The still site was in a river bottom one mile from Deputy Clint Peoples's father's filling station and café, but no one had detected a hint of its presence until the informer turned it in.

Moonshiners operating in the deep woods guarded against the signs that might give them away—wood smoke, the sound of metal on metal, or the traces of corn chops left along a trail. Meanwhile, the sheriff and his deputies watched for just these things. They staked out remote roads, sniffed the wind, listened for careless sounds, walked the banks of remote creeks, and checked rural stores for excessive sugar purchases. Outlaws and lawmen played a game of strategy and counterstrategy. Whiskey makers had to have a good source of water, preferably from a spring or clear-water creek, and the sheriff and his men often searched these places for stills. Knowing that they did, the moonshiners sometimes piped in water from some distance away or drilled shallow wells so they could locate somewhere else. Moonshiners commonly walked to their stills down one trail, then walked out by another, as a precaution, so officers checked trails for one-way tracks—the telltale sign of outlaw foot traffic. When a moonshiner walked into the woods to his still from a county road, he usually took care to leave the road from a different point every time, only after some distance joining his main trail. Knowing this, sheriffs and deputies often walked parallel courses to a county road about a hundred yards out, trying to pick up the whiskey maker's primary trail after all his little subtrails had come together. Finding a still without the moonshiner present did the officer little good, especially since many whiskey men took care to operate on other people's property. Officers often found the still, looked it over, then put it under surveillance. Knowing this, moonshiners sometimes strung black threads around the underbrush at knee level so they could tell from the broken threads if their still had been located. After finding broken threads, the whiskey man might move his still. A few old hands operated at several locations scattered through the woods. If they got the idea that the law watched one location, they moved a few miles away to another.

Back-of-beyond still sites had their disadvantages, however. Such locations forced whiskey makers to haul heavy loads of corn chops, sugar, and finished product for long distances, painful foot travel that left many revealing traces, and in time many moonshiners chose a different strategy to avoid capture. As one veteran explained: "How in the hell you gonna hide from the people when you're selling whiskey? If you went in the woods twenty miles you just had the pleasure of toting your damn liquor and all your damn supplies in the woods and toting it out. So, you might as well go in the damn smokehouse." Some men set up near their own homes and vented still smoke from house chimneys and smokehouses. Increasingly, however, moonshiners who operated around their homes in smokehouses, barns, crawl spaces, and house lofts used smokeless homemade gasoline stoves to fire their stills. As one moonshiner described it, a man could rig up an excellent gasoline stove from a twenty-gallon drum with a valve welded on it, a bicycle pump, and the burner from a water heater. With such a rig a whiskey maker could, indeed, "go in the smokehouse."

Whiskey men showed remarkable ingenuity in attempts to hide stills under officers' noses. In Limestone County, one distillery operated in a large room hidden under a smokehouse and vented from beneath a nearby black yard pot, where someone kept a wood fire constantly burning. In Wichita County, officers discovered a still hidden under counters at the back of a popular café in the community of Bradley's Corner, and near Ranger, a massive, coal-fired steam tractor had been turned into a mobile whiskey operation. The tractor pulled a large trailer, which concealed a huge mash tank and accompanying still. Steam to heat the still and "cook off" the mash was piped in from the tractor's boiler. Operators moved the tractor moonshine rig around from time to time, but after a while an officer noticed that nobody ever plowed with it.

Moonshiners' ingenuity at hiding their stills almost was equaled by bootleggers' cleverness at concealing their stashes. In Leon County, officers caught one man hiding bottled product in a grave in a country churchyard. All one evening in Parker County, Dallas reporters hid behind tombstones in a cemetery to watch a lady bootlegger give curb service to driver after driver from a station beside her deceased husband's grave vault. After a while, according to the reporters, the sheriff drove into the cemetery, met briefly with the lady, then walked over to the newsmen and said, "I want you bastards out of my county by sunup." In Coleman County, Sheriff H. F. Fenton never found where some of his bootleggers hid their stashes, but he discovered that one man usually buried his in soft dirt at various places beside the road. After this pocket bootlegger had sold his two pints, he would drive up beside the buried liquor, crack his door, and reach down to get it, never leaving his car. Another Coleman County outlaw stashed his pints, fifty or so at a time, under the blankets of his baby's crib, and another man hid his beneath the board-sided sandbox by his back door, a play area for his children.

Moonshiners often sold to bootleggers, thus insulating themselves from direct sales of their product to strangers, who might turn out to be LCB agents or undercover men in the pay of sheriffs. Such strangers rather commonly got the goods on bootleggers. Sheriff Frank Brunt found his moonshiners hard to catch, but not so the hip-pocket bootleggers operating around Jacksonville. Brunt got LCB undercover men to buy from many of these, then he picked them up. "We started around there one Saturday," the sheriff said, "and we liked to fill the jail up with bootleggers. And with a few licks like that, well, I had 'em on the run."

H. F. Fenton's sandbox bootlegger had been turned in by the same snitch who revealed his other stash, a fifty-gallon barrel cleverly buried between the tire tracks of his dirt driveway. Informants, many of them whiskey outlaws themselves, told sheriffs where to find most stills and stashes. Henry Billingsley often encouraged whiskey makers to snitch on each other for personal revenge, small sums of money, or the satisfaction of putting a rival out of business. As Billingsley recognized, this often put the snitch out of the whiskey business as well, since he feared retaliation. In Henderson County, Jess Sweeten paid twenty-five dollars for every still revealed, and in Cherokee County, Frank Brunt paid fifteen dollars. Brunt also "put pressure" on captured moonshiners, before taking them in to jail, to encourage them to reveal other men's still sites, and some of them accommodated him. Corbett Akins and Henry Billingsley were woodsmen sheriffs, and they often found stills by sniffing for smoke, reading trail sign, and watching for bits of landscape that looked suspiciously rearranged. Billingsley, in particular, proved an uncanny stalker of men. Once, he crept up to one end of a river island to watch a whiskey man on his still. Suddenly suspicious, the moonshiner walked the length of the island, looking and listening, finally stopping close to the concealed sheriff. Then he shrugged his shoulders and walked back to his still, now, however, with Billingsley walking in step just behind him, the sound of his feet in the leaves covered by the sound of the moonshiner's. At the still, Billingsley said, "Hello, Barney!" and the man nearly fainted. On several occasions, Corbett Akins used bloodhounds to trail whiskey makers from their stills to their homes or from their homes to their stills. Once, Nathan Tindall released a whiskey man's mule and followed it on its familiar path to a creek-bottom still, where the sheriff found the mule's owner busily running product.

Not all the outlaws caught operating stills in the woods or freighting bootleg whiskey down county highways were childhood acquaintances of the sheriff and out-of-work family men. Some were outside professionals or hardened local thugs and the sort that Jess Sweeten called "born criminals." If Howard Billingsley found a moonshiner carrying a weapon, his cordial manner disappeared, and the man went immediately to jail in handcuffs. Once, Billingsley and a constable approached a still near Broadus, each from a different direction, and the sheriff narrowly averted two young moonshiners' shotgun ambush of the constable. The boys asked to say goodbye to their mother, but Billingsley wrote in his memoir. "No. They had come down there to kill an officer for destroying their still, and they wasn't entitled to any courtesy. We carried them to jail." Later, the boy's father showed up at the jail, started a fight with a deputy, and had his knife taken away. In Cherokee County, Frank Brunt's whiskey men tried to kill him more than once, and they had killed his sheriff brother. In 1923, Dallas County deputy John Wesley Massey surprised a group of moonshiners working their still on a river island, and the outlaws went for their guns. "I never pulled on another man who didn't have his gun out of his scabbard first," Massey told a reporter, but on this occasion two moonshiners died.

Long-range bootleggers, outside professionals running big loads to major markets, were the most dangerous whiskey outlaws, many sheriffs believed. Such men were a far cry from their local hip-pocket brethren working football crowds on Friday nights. Long-range bootleggers helped to explain why sheriffs showed so much interest in the hood-mounted Stockholm machine gun. Sheriffs went after long-range bootleggers by setting up highway traffic stops at places where firefights would not injure noncombatants. In Collin County in 1943, for example, Sheriff W. E. Button tired of bootleggers' running booze across his dry county to military bases and seized $15,656 worth of liquor and twenty-seven automobiles, some of them very expensive. In 1951, major bootlegging routes ran from wet Louisiana to what sheriffs' association magazine editors called "prohibition-ridden Oklahoma," and Panola County sheriff Corbett Akins waylaid one such Louisiana-to-Oklahoma truck carrying $9,000 worth of liquor. By spring of 1952, Cass County sheriff John W. Thompson announced the capture of thirty-one long-range "bootleggers and whiskey smugglers" and that liquor had been found "in every conceivable contraption—coffee trucks, undertakers' wagons, loads of hay, etc."

Sheriff-bootlegger confrontations of the 1940s and 1950s were nothing like the bloody days of liquor smuggling across the Rio Grande during national prohibition. In truth, border sheriffs seemed to have played only a limited role in the whiskey wars of the 1920s, a period when many federal men believed that some of the sheriffs were on the take. Before 1924, only a few Immigration River Guards impeded the flow of illegal alcohol across the 1,932-mile border between the Republic of Mexico and a thirsty United States. Trampled paths through canebrakes on both sides of traditional river crossings indicated the huge volume of the trade. Liquor smuggling went on at every level. Poor farmers made a little mescal and waded across the Rio Grande with tow sacks of their product to peddle in Texas border towns, and major pack trains guarded by groups of armed men carried large quantities of bonded liquor north. Top-level Chicago hoodlums bankrolled some of the latter operations. Sporadic battles broke out between the pack train smugglers and the agents of the U.S. Border Patrol, a branch of the U.S. Immigration and Naturalization Service created in 1924. Young E. A. "Dogie" Wright joined the Border Patrol at the height of the combat during 1927, and Wright believed that period to be "one of the most vicious times in the history of the Border. Those smugglers had been in a revolution since 1910. They were gunmen, they knew how to handle a gun. They were good horsemen, and they knew their brush country just like the palms of their hands. You weren't dealing with a greenhorn, you were dealing with a man equivalent to you. We lay on that river at night, and we were fighting all the time."

Nor did Wright exaggerate; the so-called "Volstead Wild West Show" peaked along the Texas border. During February 1927, according to official logs of the El Paso District, no single twenty-four-hour period passed without an armed skirmish between Border Patrolmen and smugglers. During 1927, thirty-two pitched battles took place, and 3,287 persons were arrested. As Dogie Wright tersely summed things up: "They fought over that liquor. When something's worth money, they'll fight over it, and a $1.50 bottle of whiskey was worth $25 in Kansas City. We lost a lot of men, but we killed a lot of smugglers." Not all border sheriffs hung back from these confrontations, and Sheriff Ron Hall of Dimmit County recalled many dark nights staking out river crossings, including one or two nights that he could not remember without a chill coming over him. In later years Hall told his wife that these experiences had left him deeply afraid of two things: "sitting before a lightened window with the shades up and a knife, I'm deadly afraid of a knife."

Sheriffs such as Ron Hall worked out many delicate adjustments between their enforcement of state laws and their defense of local traditions, some of them illegal or extralegal, but when drillers struck oil, "boomtown" traditions usually overwhelmed local sheriffs, setting the stage for intervention by Texas Rangers. For decades, oil-field workers and parasitic outlaws moved from strike to strike, reestablishing boomtown conditions wherever they went. Some of the outlaw "boomers" passed themselves off as experienced oil-field deputies to the beleaguered sheriffs on the scene, who were eager for help in dealing with the onslaught of humanity. Once hired, enforcing the law proved the least of the deputies' concerns. Trying to explain what had happened to him in Freestone County, adjacent to the Mexia oil boom, where martial law had been declared in 1922, Sheriff Jim Wasson told a committee of the Texas legislature: "Well, we just woke up one morning and found the crowd here; that is to say, the oil boom came all at once. We were officers without any experience and hardly knew what to do. The crooks were smart and experienced and saw the situation and took advantage of it." Winkler County's oil boom came in 1926, and the underworked sheriff, just elected by the county's "thirteen voting citizens," found himself swamped with twenty thousand wild strangers who arrived almost overnight. Boom culture swiftly seized Winkler County, as Texas Ranger Carl Busch recalled:

> ***There were twenty thousand people there, all in tents and shacks. They had muddy streets and board sidewalks. I was in the Ranger company then that was headed by Captain Bill Wright, an old-time Ranger that had a big old kind of a handle-bar mustache, and he had boots that went way up to his knees. He was a tough old codger! We would make raids on Saturdays and sometimes arrest 150 [people] and lay 'em on a mattress under a shed. Looked like a trotline, had 'em strapped to the ankles. They paid their fines to the justice of peace, and then the next week it'd be just the same story. The sheriff left in six months. He was a local man.***

Early and late in the history of Texas oil, the story of the sheriff who "left in six months" repeated itself at other booms. In Lee County in 1976, Joe Goodson ran to succeed his father but lost to his father's chief deputy. However, as Goodson said, "We had the oil boom in the Austin Chalk and things went crazy." The former deputy endured this for a while, but daily combats with tool pushers in beer joints was not what he had bargained for. He resigned at the end of 1978, and the county commissioners appointed Joe Goodson as sheriff. An oil-field man himself, Goodson noted, "I was tough, I'd been handling heavy steel all my life." Sheriff Goodson usually just walked up to fighters, crooked his finger for them to follow him outside, then stated his policy: "You know, I don't care how much you fight, but it's gonna cost you."

Lee County's 1970s boom was a pale shadow of what happened in earlier times at Mexia, Ranger, Borger, and other places, however, and these instant boomtowns soon generated their own corrupt version of local officials, including sheriffs. Young William Sterling moved to the boomtown of Breckenridge, Stephens County, after World War I and soon found himself appointed chairman of a grand jury investigating local corruption. "The news of easy money had filled the town with a milling throng, and crime was rampant," Sterling recalled, in words that well described any boomtown. He quickly determined that the sheriff and deputies "were taking bribes by the wholesale. They had placed their graft on a business basis. In exchange for official protection, the local 'laws' maintained a fixed scale of prices. The degree and form of each underworld activity governed the amount demanded." Rather quickly, the "best citizens" asked Sterling to run for sheriff, and he reluctantly agreed. Campaigning on platform promises of a "clean oil field" and that "the first man who offers me a bribe will land in the hospital," Sterling nonetheless lost the election in a runoff against the incumbent. Many flourishing businessmen and the most popular minister—their bread well buttered by the status quo—feared reform and supported the corrupt sheriff, Sterling claimed. However, William Sterling got some satisfaction later on, since "my opponent was sent to jail for bootlegging about the time as I was sworn in as adjutant general of Texas."

Sheriffs did not play prominent roles in the cleanups of Mexia, Limestone County, in 1922, or of Borger, Hutchinson County, in 1928. In fact, lawmen often ended up chained to the Texas Rangers' "trotlines" or thrown into their own jails. Senior Captain Frank Hamer of the Rangers presided over the reformation of Mexia, with some help from Governor Pat Neff's declaration of martial law on February 2, 1922, and the Texas National Guard. After martial law, Rangers freely rounded up gamblers, dope peddlers, moonshiners, and other outlaws. One of their rough-shod techniques was to examine suspects' hands; calloused hands indicated an honest oil-field worker, but smooth, well-kept hands marked an outlaw. Rangers ran over 3,000 individuals out of town, arrested 602 persons, captured twenty-seven stills, recovered fifty-three stolen automobiles, and destroyed 9,085 quarts of bootleg whisky. According to Hamer, Rangers learned that local officials were taking payoffs of up to $250 a day and that out-of-state crime syndicates were behind most of the illegal activities.

After the Borger boom began in 1926, local officials also quickly became overwhelmed and coopted. Forty-five thousand "oilmen, prospectors, roughnecks, panhandlers, fortune seekers, card sharks, bootleggers, whores and dope peddlers descended on Borger," and "in a few months the town was firmly in the hands of an organized crime syndicate." Citizens asked Governor Dan Moody to declare martial law, and he dispatched Ranger Frank Hamer to investigate. After a few days at Borger, Hamer reported that this boomtown had "the worst crime ring I have seen in my twenty-three years as an officer." Hamer found that city and county officials were not just on the take and looking the other way, but also were actively directing the Borger crime scene. Borger ran wide open, eighteen hours a day. Deep mud underfoot and black smoke drifting across from oil-field fires failed to deter pleasure seekers, who jammed the streets until midnight. At wide-open Borger, thugs stalked drunks after dark; gamblers, whores, and drug dealers hung out in the red-light district of Dixon Creek; and legal and illegal businesses alike paid protection to "The Line," Borger's criminal syndicate.

Governor Moody sent in the Texas Rangers in 1926, and officers soon found they had all they could handle with outlaw Borger. Governor Moody ordered Borger's mayor to place all city police officials directly under Frank Hamer, and the Rangers began to make some progress, but soon the honest county attorney was assassinated. In September 1926, Governor Moody finally declared martial law, because "there exists an organized and entrenched criminal ring in the city of Borger and in Hutchison county."

Now, the 56th Cavalry of the Texas National Guard joined the Rangers, and Borger began its second, and more stringent, reform. Nearly all city and county officials were suspended from office, and most were jailed. Rangers disarmed Sheriff Joe Ownbey and his deputy. Captain Lone Wolf Gonzaullas recalled: "Some of them tried to get smart with us, but we just smacked em around and hitched a few to the snorting pole at the jail. That took the wind out of em. You just can't imagine the pile of guns that stacked up as we took them off the Borger officers. And you should have seen how those fellows squirmed when the good people of the town came down to the jail to see em with the rings on em and chained to the snorting pole."

First, Rangers jammed Borger's jail full to overflowing, then they secured hundreds of additional outlaws to a heavy chain running down Borger's main street. Outside lawmen now began to visit Borger to "shop" for their wanted outlaws. Meanwhile, thousands of boomtown residents fled Borger by any means possible, even riding truckloads of drill pipe and the roofs of jam-packed passenger trains. Rufe Jordan of Pampa, age fourteen, came over to view the chastisement of Borger, though his deputy father had explicitly forbidden him to do so. Borger presented a cautionary example for the future sheriff of Gray County. "The soldiers and few Rangers had a huge pile of slot machines that were being bursted with sledge hammers. The Salvation Army was standing back out here, it was my understanding that the coins from the machines were to go to the Salvation Army, and they were beating the drums and singing rather loud, 'Blessed Be the Tie That Binds.'"

The East Texas boom began with Dan Joiner's well, near Henderson, which struck oil on September 5, 1930, and the field turned out to be huge, extending over twenty miles further north, but by that time the Texas government had learned its lesson. Rangers moved into Kilgore in force early in 1931 and worked closely with the Gregg County Sheriff's Department and the municipal police. Lone Wolf Gonzaullas immediately set up his "trotline" chain in plain sight in the Kilgore street, this by way of intimidation, and Rangers went about banishing known outlaws. Around the edges of the giant East Texas oil field, honest sheriffs held their ground against temptation and vice, though they took some casualties. On March 10, 1937, as the *Sheriffs' Association of Texas Magazine* noted, "shortly after midnight a cowardly and slimy assassin fired a charge of buckshot from the outside into his bedroom, immediately killing [Marion County] Sheriff Brown, who was ready to retire for the night. He was a vigorous enemy of all gambling, vice, and bootlegging, and it is known that the underworld had sworn bloody vengeance on their relentless foe."

Racial boundaries remained somewhat indeterminate during the social chaos of the first weeks and months of the existence of oil boomtowns such as Kilgore, Borger, and Ranger, but things soon sorted themselves out. Drillers customarily hired African Americans as mule skinners and for a few other jobs in the fields, but not for all, and the disorderly tent cities soon segregated themselves along racial lines. Likewise, the characteristic boomtown institutions of "cot houses," "hobo towns," and "taxi dancehalls" developed their Anglo and minority versions.

During a century of existence, however, established towns in Texas counties with large minority populations had evolved far more elaborate systems of racial apartheid, and citizens expected sheriffs to enforce the customary boundaries between the races, maintain the status quo, and keep the peace. Incumbent sheriffs running for reelection might not stand up at political gatherings to brag about how well they had kept local minorities "down" and under control, but—without a doubt—this issue dominated many elections. No sheriff wanted racial trouble, and to virtually all officers racial harmony was best maintained by more and better segregation. At Stanton, county seat of Martin County, Sheriff Dan Saunders told a reporter: "We have not had any racial troubles and don't contemplate any. Neither race fools around in the other's section of town." Most sheriffs and most Anglo voters believed that an officer needed to intimidate minority citizens as his most important contribution to preserving racial order. Sheriffs sometimes chose big hats, big guns, man-hound packs, and selective rough treatment of perpetrators to help overawe the underclasses and prevent trouble. To illustrate the social functioning of this old-time intimidation, Sheriff Tom Brown of Caldwell County recounted an incident described to him by an elderly black man who became nervous at the attitude of younger men listening to a successful Joe Lewis fight on the radio. "There ain't nobody in the world can whip that Joe Lewis!" one man cried, after Lewis knocked his opponent out, but the old man cautioned, "Sheriff Brown can get him down on Plum Creek."

By 1950 some of this system of racial apartheid had embodied itself in formal Jim Crow laws, but that portion was only the tip of the iceberg. Established towns had many unstated rules and invisible lines of racial segregation that minorities—and sheriffs—needed to know about. Tradition strongly enforced minority neighborhoods and labeled them with informal names often supplied by the dominant race—"Cocklebur" at Lockhart in Caldwell County, "Oxblood" at Wharton in Wharton County, "Fly Blow" at Kountze in Hardin County, and at many places just "the quarter." Minorities lived in their neighborhood, or neighborhoods, often set apart from the rest of town by a physical boundary of railroad, creek, or highway, and a good many places had informal curfews restricting minorities to their part of town after a certain hour of the night.

Certain customs were universal—for example, that of a minority person's giving way to an Anglo on a sidewalk—but local traditions of segregation were complicated, the rules unstated, and the boundaries often unmarked; minority persons unfamiliar with the customs of a town needed to be very careful. Tradition might invisibly mark certain benches around the courthouse square as "whites only" benches, and it would not do for a black stranger to sit on one of them. Stores had doors for whites and doors for minorities, and, once inside, custom dictated that minority customers wait politely until all Anglo customers had been served. It would not do to pass through the wrong door or to insist on "first come, first served." Nor could the minority customer dare to try on his or her article of clothing before purchase; this was commonly forbidden, according to customs of racial pollution, which worked only one way. Whites could not use houses, books, utensils, or clothing after blacks had used them, although the opposite was perfectly permissible. A black purchaser had better know his hat size.

Usually, the transgressor against these informal customs of aparthied escaped with an explicit correction and a rude word, but not always, and in these cases the sheriff often came to cast oil on the troubled waters (though perhaps not to arrest the Anglo perpetrators). Very occasionally, the built-in social trap went off with a vicious thud. Willie Massey recalled riding into Apple Springs, Trinity County, and being told by his father at some point, "Boys, pull off your hats, we're getting into town now." African Americans could not wear their hats in Apple Springs; a black man had been shot dead a few years before for entering an Apple Springs store with his hat on. During the 1970s, African Americans at Lockhart told historians of a deranged or suicidal black man who had repeatedly attempted to enter the wrong door of a local barbecue place at high noon on Saturday until outraged Anglos finally beat him to death.

Sheriffs tried their best to keep this sort of thing from happening; they disliked trouble in general and racial trouble most of all. Violent racial attacks by Anglos on minorities often proved unpunishable in local circumstances, since grand juries refused to indict or trial juries to convict, and racial attacks by minorities on Anglos threatened to trigger something even more embarrassing to the sheriff, the ferocious mob response of lynching.

Sheriffs hated and feared racial "incidents." Consequently, had the sheriff been summoned in time at Lockhart, he probably would have taken the black man into custody and saved his life. Likewise, should black "field hands" have dared to show up at Navasota with fine white Stetson hats or silk shirts on, the sheriff or his deputy might have sent them home to reattire themselves in racially appropriate overalls and straw hats, thus preventing trouble. By long-standing tradition, black males wearing upscale clothing on the streets of Navasota invited swift and violent attack. One man recalled: "You go there with a silk shirt on, they'd tear it off and spit on it—tear that shirt off you! You couldn't wear a silk shirt to Navasota, and you couldn't wear nothing during the week but blue duckings or khakis and straw hat. You get out with a white Stetson on and you'd come back with it all flopped down round your head."

As every sheriff knew, white Stetsons and other trivial violations of racial norms might cause drastic violence. African American servicemen returning to their home towns often got in trouble when they proved reluctant to reassume customary subservience. For example, in Wharton County during 1946, an Anglo customer at a filling station became irritated with the loud conversation of two blacks, one a serviceman and one a returned veteran. He walked over and told one of the black men to tuck in his shirt-tail, but the man refused, noting that "he was wearing the shirt." At that point the white armed himself with a length of pipe and called the sheriff's office. Two deputies arrived to talk to the black men, who had moved across the street to avoid trouble. An argument ensued, then a fight, and then a deputy shot the black veteran to death.

Clothing made a statement, especially on the back of a minority person, and a sheriff might fear the social consequences of this. Zoot-suit-clad Hispanics, with long-tailed coats and pegged pants, sometimes arrived at bus stops at Wharton, Carthage, and elsewhere during the late 1940s and early 1950s, and sheriffs Buck Lane and Corbett Akins gave them their attention and soon had them back on the buses and departing to somewhere else. Sheriffs personally disapproved of the zoot-suiters, but they also ran them out of town for their own protection. To a rural sheriff in a conservative county seat, a zoot-suiter looked like a racial incident about to happen. At Carthage, Sheriff Corbett Akins's preparation for banishment of a zoot-suiter itself approached the level of a racial atrocity. Akins jerked out the young man's "Hitler moustache and goatee" with pliers and sent him off to the bus stop in his underwear.

Zoot-suiters (and town blacks in silk shirts) obviously failed to contribute to the cotton harvest—one of the things sheriffs held against them. About 1950, sheriffs in cotton-growing counties still played an informal role in motivating black and Hispanic labor. Especially during the harvest season, editors of weekly papers commonly wrote about the need for more cotton pickers and the disgusting lethargy of "town blacks" and "Meskins" who refused to get out into the fields and work. Pressure mounted on sheriffs to do something about this, and many of them acquiesced. At more than a few places sheriffs arrested black men on the streets for vagrancy and forced them to pick cotton. Citizens often complained to Sheriff Buck Lane about idle blacks and Hispanics loitering about the Wharton streets, and Lane evoked the vagrancy law to harass them into agricultural labor. For example, in February 1945, Lane rousted a "pool hall full" of young Hispanics into employment, and in July 1945 he forced six young black women to go to work. As cotton-harvest season neared during 1945, Lane wrote in his column: "Beginning immediately, we, the officers, are going to encourage the local idlers and street-setters to begin helping out with the harvest of the large cotton and rice crops in the county, and we hope that those that are not working will realize these crops must be gathered, and will do their part to help feed America and clothe the world."

Periodically during the year, Anglo landowners called sheriffs like Buck Lane and asked them to help collect debts owed by blacks. Civil suits and writs of sequestration offered a formal route for accomplishing this, but landowners often had no documentary proof for their loans and hoped to use the intimidating sheriff to force blacks to "work it out" on their farms. This might have been the old way of doing things, but Texas's antipeonage laws made it illegal, and Lane repeatedly informed readers of his column that his office was not a debt collection agency. After discussing the matter at length with Sheriff Lane, journalist Wesley Stout explained: "There is more here than meets the eye; it is an old Southern custom for a Negro to borrow from a white in an emergency, promising to chop cotton or otherwise work the debt off. In former days, if the negro failed to pay off, the white man complained to the sheriff, who impounded the debtor. The peonage law made this a crime, though a lot of the old-timers haven't heard the news yet."

Blacks and Hispanics had their own perspective on the county sheriff, for whom they might or might not have been able to vote. They evaluated him in terms of how fairly he enforced the law across racial boundaries and—above all—by how effectively he protected them from the social, economic, and sexual aggressions of the dominant race. In rural Texas during the first four decades of the twentieth century, minority persons remained almost helpless in the face of Anglo exploitation. To physically fight back invited lynching, local courts refused to decide in their favor, and a minority person could not dispute an Anglo's word. Only certain informal rules of apartheid protected them from Anglo aggressions, and then only if the Anglos involved voluntarily recognized the rules or the sheriff intervened in their behalf.

Before the return of the minority vote, political realities did not encourage such interventions, but some sheriffs patrolled the boundaries between races in a more even-handed way and insisted on at least minimal racial justice. When Henderson county landowners hired blacks as sharecroppers, allowed them to bring crops to near harvest, then accused them of "half working" their fields and evicted them, the blacks appealed to Sheriff Jess Sweeten. After checking the fields and finding "good clean tomatoes and watermelons and peas and corn and cotton," Sweeten told the landowner, "'You're not gonna run him off. If you run him off, you're gonna pay him for his crop.' Now, believe you me, you talk about politics, that was darn bad politics! That nigger couldn't even go to the polls and vote, and he was getting a raw deal, and I just wasn't gonna stand for it." Likewise, Sheriff Buck Lane for years forced sexually adventurous Anglos to stay out of the Wharton "quarter" of Oxblood, a policy that Lane also freely admitted was bad politics. Lane wrote in his newspaper column: "It is no place to play around, that section of Wharton belongs to the colored people, it is their section of town, and they don't like it when the white man comes there and makes advances at the colored women."

In Caldwell County, Sheriff Walter Ellison served from 1915 to 1940, and some local black people called Ellison "Limpin' Jesus," though not to his face. In truth, Sheriff Ellison had one leg shorter than the other, and, after twenty years in office, the comparison to the Lord did not seem entirely inappropriate. Ellison was nearly colorblind as far as enforcing the law was concerned. He once jailed his father for public drunkenness, forcing his own brother to bail him out. African American Nelson Jones worked for Sheriff Ellison for years and knew him well, and Nelson—outspoken in later life about local whites—had little ill to say of the old sheriff.

"He was a good sheriff," Jones told an interviewer. "He'd pull a white man's leg as quick as he would a colored, just a pretty straight man. He just gonna do what he need do. The white, oh, he'd just eat him up, do him worse than he would a nigger."

With an appreciation for small favors, Caldwell County blacks approved a sheriff who approached race relations in this way. As Nelson Jones recalled from personal experience, the county had a history of racial harassments, and worse. When Jones was growing up, Anglos commonly shot into black houses at night, blocked their doors with wagons, and threw black people into the ice house swimming pool to sink or swim. "They'd do most anything to a colored man," Jones admitted, "and you had to treat them with a spoon, just like if they had feathers on them and the wind was high." In this context, Sheriff Ellison did the best he could to insist on safety and respect for minority citizens. Once, after a black minister complained of harassment by white troublemakers during Sunday morning services, the sheriff stationed himself on the church steps with a .30-30 carbine and touched off a few warning shots when the Anglo youths showed up. When Ellison approached retirement during the late 1930s, minority citizens probably felt something like "Old Henry Butler, age 84," who told Sheriff Dan Saunders of Martin County in 1964, "Mr. Dan, I just don't know what the colored people will do if you ever decide to leave Stanton."

Sheriffs' interventions in minority disputes often had a high-handed, paternalistic quality about them, even if well-intentioned, and so did sheriffs' enforcement of the law in minority communities. Buck Lane and Jess Sweeten both told of stepping in to settle bitter disputes in black church congregations. Sheriff Sweeten visited a Henderson County church where the war between minister and deacons had escalated until worshipers brought ice picks and straight razors with them to church services. A black minister from Athens accompanied Sweeten, and the minister instructed warring factions about proper Baptist procedures and compelled a vote to settle their dispute. Then Sweeten played the role of enforcer, telling the congregation: "This decision is going to stick. If anyone of you cause any trouble, I'll knock the back end of the jail out with you!"

"High-sheriff" behaviors dominated some officers' dealings with minority perpetrators—behaviors they probably would never have used with Anglos. After a woman complained to Sheriff Roy Herrington about her husband's "jumping on her and beating her up," Herrington visited the couple in their home and presided, pistol on hip, while the woman administered just retribution to the husband with a bed slat until she broke the slat. After that, Herrington warned the man not to retaliate or "I'm gonna be back and lock you up." On another occasion, Sheriff Herrington allowed two hostile female jail prisoners to work out their mutual hostility in a minimally supervised, hand-to-hand combat at the jail, then turned them loose. "I told 'em, I said, 'Y'all got it out of your system, both of you get gone.'"

Sheriff Corbett Akins sometimes felt himself too busy to intervene in black disputes, and on other occasions he intervened in a drastic manner. After being informed by a man that another black man was stealing his pulp wood, Akins told him to "go shoot the son-of-a-bitch," and the man did just that. According to Akins, another such "license to kill" came over a one-dollar debt and resulted in a death by butcher knife. Lane recalled: "The grand jury called me and asked me did I tell that nigger to kill that nigger. I said, 'I did, but I was just joking with him.' Well, they didn't indict him." Sheriffs like Akins sometimes seemed to find it too much trouble to apply full bureaucratic procedures of law enforcement to solve black problems or arrest black outlaws. Only slightly less high-handed than Akins's licenses to kill was Buck Lane's resolution of a stabbing incident between a black man and his former girlfriend. After a jealous argument over the woman's riding her new boyfriends around in the car, once communal property, the woman turned to flee, and "George accidentally stabbed her in the back when she turned to run and he reached to grab her." Lane explained to Wharton County citizens in his newspaper column: "I talked fairness to George that we had an agreement, if I'd let him off this time, he would not stab Josephine any more. I believe George, and I did not make George pay a fine."

Sheriffs' arrests of minority perpetrators more commonly were accompanied by informal punishments administered in the field, and the subsequent interrogations of minority persons more commonly involved threats, tricks, and physical coercions than did the cases of Anglos. Sheriff Tom Brown of Caldwell County once solved a case of a dead baby by checking the breasts of all the Hispanic women on a cotton farm until he found the guilty lactating mother, and (as noted previously) he frightened a jailed black man into confessing by imitating the voice of his murdered wife. Angry after repeated failed attempts to catch a black deserter, Sheriff Corbett Akins waded through muddy fields at night to apprehend the culprit at his farmhouse, then mounted the black man's back and forced him to crawl on all fours several hundred yards to Akins's patrol car—this by way of informal punishment. On one occasion, Sheriff Lester Gunn invited a TDC dog captain and his pack to help him catch a black car thief, and after the man became trapped under a concrete bridge, the officers "turned old Blue loose" to chew on him a little and break him from stealing cars. "Old Blue did a very good job on this nigger," the sheriff recalled, "We like to let him chew too long."

The failures, trials, and tribulations of minority citizens of Wharton County played a major role in Sheriff Buck Lane's newspaper columns of the 1940s and early 1950s. The sheriff depicted local blacks and Hispanics as childlike, emotionally unstable, prone to violence, stupid, and often ridiculous. For example, Lane's column of July 5, 1946, told of a black couple visited by a Hispanic man who soon evicted them from their own house. Asked why they let him do it, the black man replied, "Mr. Buck, you know a Mexican is sho-nuff fast with them knives." Lane also noted in his column that a black woman had called to tell the sheriff that a dog had bitten her little boy, asking, "Do he need to take them teethrumus shots?"

Even deadly violence lent itself to amusing interpretations in the sheriff's column. On July 12, 1946, Lane noted that three black men and one woman, "negroes of El Campo, got into a big fight. Nearly every one of them had to go to the doctor to be sewed up." The fight had broken out over a debt of fifty-five cents, "That is what you call not self control." Furthermore, a black barber at Wharton reading a newspaper in his barber chair, had been set upon by an irate husband. "Out of the blue sky, another negro steps in and starts to whittle on him. He did some fancy whittling too, before the barber could get untangled from his paper. The whittler said nothing, just did his whittling and left as he came." Later, this man turned himself in to the sheriff, telling him, "I cut up on so-and-so, it was about my wife." However, Sheriff Lane's tone turned suddenly serious for one minority-related news item reported on July 12, 1946. A drunken black former soldier tried to get into the same seat as an Anglo lady on the bus, prompting two white men to attack him. Lane reported that he had been jailed, and: "It is a pity that some of our Wharton County better negroes were not on that bus so they could have knocked him in the head and stopped him in the beginning. Just such business as this is no good for either race."

Although black-on-black violence lent itself to amusing stories, interracial violence—and any social changes that seemed to make it more likely—deeply troubled Sheriff Lane. On October 11, 1946, he wrote very seriously of "a good and respected old negro citizen" who had come to show him an NAACP brochure and to ask Lane's opinion about the black community's organizing a local chapter. Lane thought it a very bad idea and that such an attempt might start trouble.

> ***Why the negro people of Wharton County need this I cannot say, for I can name to you many negro people of this county who have advanced not by the efforts of any association, but simply by merit. They used their heads, and they worked, and they earned their advancement. I can say that if there is an association for the advancement of the white man, I have never heard of it. Believe you me, any man regardless of color or creed in Wharton County has the same chance to advance. I will discourage any such organization, for I think it would not be good for the people.***

Two years later, in his column of March 5, 1948, Lane again turned deadly serious about interracial matters. After pointing out how he had defended the black community by discouraging "the promiscuous prowling of white men in the negro section of Wharton," he discussed the current problem, blacks walking ten blocks through the white neighborhood to attend black basketball games scheduled in the white high school gym. "The negroes are coming into the white section at night after the basketball games are over," and white citizens have complained. The sheriff told his readers that he feared that "ambitious or drunk" young black men "might use the blind of attending the basketball game in the white section of Wharton to attack some white lady, or some white man may resent the negroes being in his neighborhood and start something." Nothing had happened yet, but it was time for Wharton to build a black gym. Sheriff Lane feared mob actions, "lynchings, race riots," and whites going on the rampage in the black community.

Few sheriffs besides the irrepressible Buck Lane would have dared to discuss sexual line crossers, lynchings, and race riots in their local newspaper, but the little sheriff's fears were not unreasonable. In 1948, many minority and Anglo citizens of Wharton County had seen, or had heard eyewitness accounts of, violent racial assaults of almost unbelievable horror. Nobody, and least of all Sheriff Buck Lane, thought that such things could not happen again. For example, thirteen years before, on November 12, 1935, just across the county line in Colorado County, a lynch mob of several hundred men and women had seized two teenaged blacks from the county jail and had hung them from a tree. The Colorado County sheriff either assisted the mob or got out of its way while it indulged itself in this ultimate "county tradition." After the deed was done, County Attorney O. P. Moore of Colorado County defended this traditional violence, stating that "I do not call the citizens who executed the negroes a mob, I consider their action an expression of the will of the people." Likewise, the Colorado County judge noted: "I am strongly opposed to mob violence and favor orderly process of the law. The fact that the negroes that brutally murdered Miss Kolman could not be adequately punished by the law because of their ages prevents me from condemning those citizens who meted out justice to the ravishing murderers last night."

By 1935, Texas lynch mobs such as the one in Colorado County had withdrawn into the cover of darkness to do their work, but earlier mobs had tortured, mutilated, burned, and hanged black men before large crowds in the broad light of day, with sheriffs often failing to prevent these atrocities. Such full-blown expressions of "the lynching ritual" had ended by World War II, although rural sheriffs certainly did not know that. Fearing this last and most horrific "county tradition" above all other local traditions of violence, sheriffs such as Buck Lane promoted racial harmony and the status quo by stringent enforcement of the laws and customs of racial segregation.

Newspapers and the 1936 Texas Centennial

PATRICK COX

PATRICK COX IS ASSOCIATE DIRECTOR AT THE DOLPH BRISCOE CENTER FOR AMERICAN HISTORY AT THE UNIVERSITY OF TEXAS IN AUSTIN. HIS BOOKS INCLUDE *RALPH W. YARBOROUGH: THE PEOPLE'S SENATOR* AND *THE FIRST TEXAS NEWS BARONS*. DR. COX IS ALSO COEDITOR OF *PROFILES IN POWER: TWENTIETH-CENTURY TEXANS IN WASHINGTON* (NEW EDITION).

IN 1936, TEXAS COMMEMORATED ITS ONE HUNDREDTH YEAR OF INDEPENDENCE. ACROSS THE STATE, PROUD TEXANS THREW FESTIVE CELEBRATIONS. WHILE DALLAS HOSTED THE OFFICIAL EXPOSITION, FORT WORTH OFFERED THE COMPETING TEXAS FRONTIER CENTENNIAL. DALLAS BUSINESSMAN STANLEY MARCUS ASSERTED THAT "MODERN TEXAS HISTORY STARTED WITH THE CELEBRATION OF THE TEXAS CENTENNIAL, BECAUSE IT WAS IN 1936 . . . THAT THE REST OF AMERICA DISCOVERED TEXAS." THE 1930S ALSO WITNESSED A CHANGE IN THE LONE STAR IMAGE. TEXAS MOVED AWAY FROM ITS SOUTHERN CONFEDERATE IDENTITY AND EMBRACED, INSTEAD, ITS FRONTIER HERITAGE. IN THIS SELECTION, COX ANALYZES THE IMPORTANT ROLE NEWSPAPER PUBLISHERS, SUCH AS GEORGE B. DEALEY OF THE *DALLAS MORNING NEWS* AND AMON G. CARTER, SR., OF THE *FORT WORTH STAR-TELEGRAM*, PLAYED IN THE GREAT CENTENNIAL CELEBRATION.

★ ★

The 1936 Texas Centennial joined the ranks of four other major expositions in the nation during the years of the Great Depression. Preceded by Chicago's Century of Progress Exposition (1933) and San Diego's Panama California International Exposition (1935), and followed by the Golden Gate International Exposition in San Francisco (1937) and the New York World's Fair (1939), the Texas Centennial Exposition was a celebration of U.S. history, knowledge, and commercial enterprise. As *Business Week* magazine described the Texas centennial celebrations of 1936, the festivities blended "patriotism and business." Promoters intended to attract outside capital and visitors and provide them with exposure to the Lone Star State. The exposition spread far beyond the fairgrounds in Dallas to become an exercise in redefining the state's character and its institutional memory. The state's newspaper publishers served as a driving force in the creation and promotion of centennial events. As they debated the course between tradition and modernization, the publishers also cemented the new western image of Texans, a legacy that was carried forward for the rest of the twentieth century.

The new Texan mythology—the western, cowboy mystique—owes much to the newspapers and publicists of this era. Myths are not entirely fiction. They represent historical events and people that are re-created and turned into legends. These mythic events and figures illustrate the central feature of the romanticized past. In the Depression of the 1930s, western images came to represent "individualism, self reliance, and integrity in the face of a corrupt world." The image of cowboys and outlaws was well defined by the 1930s. Dime novels, films, magazines, music, and newspapers utilized western figures as heroic characters. Billy the Kid, Buffalo Bill Cody, Frederick Russell, Owen Wister, and Theodore Roosevelt came to represent distinct figures in popular memory of the idealized West. Outlaws, cowboys, artists, writers, and politicians provided a grand tapestry upon which popular memory of the Texas past arose. Popular media helped define the image of the western cowboy and played the significant role in vitalizing Texas of the past.

Texans also continued to glorify their southern background. As Paul Gaston stated in *The New South Creed*, myths "are not polite euphemisms for falsehoods, but are combinations of images and symbols that reflect a people's way of perceiving truth . . . they fuse the real and the imaginary into a blend that becomes a reality itself, a force in history." Glorification of the antebellum South and the Confederacy in the six decades following the Civil War served as the central theme for public memory in the region. The entire fabric of southern history became woven into what became known as the Lost Cause interpretation. The motivation for the Lost Cause mythology came from the desire of southerners to cope with the seemingly un-American experience of defeat and at the same time to rationalize slavery, secession, and the failures of the Confederacy. Advocates successfully introduced a "correct" version of history that allowed for a southern bias in interpretation. Many historians now agree that "[i]n terms of how Americans have assessed and understood the Civil War, Lost Cause warriors succeeded to a remarkable degree."

Through the 1920s, Texans interpreted their history as viewed through the southern lens. From the 1870s through the early twentieth century, former Confederate leaders rose to dominant positions in the state's business, political, and educational centers. This legacy helped southerners justify their clouded past as they prepared for the future in a nation dominated by northern capital and enterprise. Newspapers recounted stories of Confederate veterans and eulogized their deaths. Associations of former Confederates gained widespread coverage and support for philanthropic efforts. Supporters downplayed slavery or the South's long record of racial violence, characterizing both issues—and African Americans themselves—as irrelevant. Reunions, meetings, commemorative events, statues, and buildings were a tribute to the Lost Cause and the southern interpretation of history. Little of past suffering, deprivation, death, and destruction made its way into print.

The Lost Cause provided more than a patriotic reinterpretation of the past. In the view of some historians, at its fruition, allegiance to the Lost Cause "elevated it above the realm of common, patriotic impulse" and made it the equivalent of a state religion in the South. Southern adherents created a mythological past that raised individuals to saintly positions who lived a godlike existence. "Lee and Davis emerged as Christ figures, the common soldier attained sainthood, and southern women became Marys who guarded the tomb of the Confederacy and heralded its resurrection." The Civil War became a sacred event with inviolate doctrines: the war occurred for the right to self-government, not slavery; and Confederates were not traitors but acted against a corrupt northern society bent on imposing its will on the South.

As the last generation of Confederate veterans died out and the grand reunions held their final parades in the 1920s, a successor movement made its way into Texas in the 1930s. The seeds of the Texas creation myth fell on well-prepared ground. Just as the Lost Cause found its impetus in the tumultuous decades after the Civil War, the rise of the new Texan mythology occurred during the nation's worst economic depression. The Texas myth followed the same pattern as the earlier New South construction. The unpleasant realities of the past were obliterated, while the pictures of pride and progress were displayed for all the world to see and read.

Since the 1930s had no revitalized economy or boom like the 1920s, urban promoters sought to provide the public with a past that they would feel proud of, one in which they had faced challenges fearlessly, so they would look beyond their existing problems and focus on the future. By utilizing traditional values associated with nineteenth-century rural principles, business and the media reassured people that they acknowledged and respected their honored past. As situations arose in the Great Depression that questioned the foundations of U.S. capitalism, its value was reaffirmed by recognition of a heroic past and its challenges, recalled through a history where individuals were able to overcome great odds and adversity. The promoters of this new heroic Texan image recalled earlier generations who seemingly made clear-cut decisions when confronting a common enemy. The pioneer Anglo Texans and creators of the Republic of Texas appeared as ready-made historical actors to replace the Confederates enshrined by the Lost Cause mythology.

Texas declared its independence from Mexico in 1836. After a series of disasters at the Alamo and Goliad and during a long retreat, a force led by Sam Houston defeated Santa Anna, the president of Mexico and leader of its army, at San Jacinto on April 21, 1836. The Republic of Texas existed for nearly a decade prior to its annexation into the United States. The infant republic endured and awaited admission to the United States as the nation debated over the extension of slavery and the admission of slave and free states. The state's revolutionary heritage, along with its colonial and Native American history, suddenly ascended in the 1930s as a rival to the celebration of the Confederate past.

How this spirited image of Texas' past became part of the collective memory of the state and the nation derived from the centennial celebrations of the 1930s. As John Bodnar explains concerning public memory in the United States, collective ideas originate from "a political discussion that involves not so much specific economic or moral problems but rather fundamental issues about the entire existence of society: its organization, structure of power, and the very meaning of its past and present." The Texas Centennial certainly occurred during one of the most economically trying times in the nation's history. Many civic leaders joined with the newspaper publishers to extol the financial benefits of these large-scale celebrations. "Texanism," the rise of a Texas heritage and associations, assumed a new mantle of importance. The beliefs, symbols, stories, language, images, and physical structures that encompassed this new public memory originated in this centennial era. Furthermore, the image of Texas as a distinct region apart from the Old South gained its impetus in the public sphere during this period. Much of this improvised cultural heritage (which maintains a presence to this day) originated with the ideas and promotions of the Texas daily newspaper publishers.

In 1936 Texas celebrated the one-hundredth anniversary of its independence with centennial activities across the state. The state and federal governments each provided $3 million to kick off the events. Local communities also sold bonds to finance construction of new projects. To prime the pump, Washington provided money for many of the buildings and Centennial projects, which provided thousands of jobs for Texans.

For more than a decade, Lowry Martin, advertising manager of the *Corsicana Daily Sun*, served as the workhorse of the centennial movement. A central part of Martin's strategy was to obtain massive support from the Texas newspaper industry and the endorsement by the state's political establishment. Themes focused on the individuality and frontier spirit of nineteenth-century Anglo Texans. During the years of planning, Jesse Jones served on the statewide coordinating committee, but his tenure was marked by uncertainty as to the scope of the centennial celebration. Competing business and political activities also distracted Jones from the task. Jones maintained reservations about the feasibility of having only one primary exposition site modeled after world fair expositions of the early twentieth century. The onset of the Depression and his appointment to the RFC brought an end to his leadership on the Centennial Commission, but Jones eventually played a role in obtaining federal government financing for many centennial-related projects during the 1930s.

Lowry Martin and the Texas Press Association kept the centennial celebration effort alive after Jones' departure from the board in 1930. Martin provided an ongoing stream of information, surveys, and promotions to newspapers. As economic conditions worsened throughout the state, the concept of a statewide commemoration of its birthday began to gain momentum. Many civic and political leaders viewed a centennial celebration as a potential stimulus to revive the flagging economy. The campaign resulted in a constitutional amendment passed by the state legislature and submitted to the voters during the November 1932 general election. The amendment, which called for a celebration combined with an unspecified commitment for funding by the state, passed during the same election in which Texans overwhelmingly voted for Franklin Roosevelt and John Nance Garner.

Houston's civic and political leaders believed the competition for the main exposition came down to a battle between Houston and Dallas. If the selection involved only historic considerations, Houston would have been a natural choice because of its role in Texas independence and the early republic. "But that equation is entirely eliminated by the centennial law," the *Houston Post* editors wrote. "It is now simply a matter of which city makes the highest bid."

A state commission selected Dallas as the location for the official exposition. Not to be outdone, Houston, San Antonio, and Fort Worth scheduled their own celebrations. Neighboring Fort Worth created the Texas Frontier Centennial and a "Winning of the West" celebration. San Antonio and Houston hosted events to commemorate battles of the Texas Revolution. The newly completed San Jacinto Monument and Historical Museum opened on the anniversary of Sam Houston's victory over Santa Anna's army in April 1836. Numerous events throughout the state extended the celebration to nearly every county. Huntsville, Sam Houston's hometown, featured the initial sale of the Texas Centennial postage stamp. Stamford held a cowboy reunion and roundup. Crystal City hosted a spinach festival and proclaimed the cartoon character Popeye as honorary mayor. Every major daily in the state published a special centennial edition, sometimes totaling more than 100 pages, stocked with history, anecdotes, and ads.

Centennial editions, similar to anniversary and other special commemorative publications, served newspapers and the larger community. These highly publicized newspapers validated the publication as the official collector and interpreter of historical memory. Centennial publications enhanced the role of cultural authority and opened the door for other businesses and individuals to enlist in the narrative effort. Editorial content and the selection of historical articles remained the prerogative of the editorial staff. The presentation was nearly as important as the content of these commemorative issues. Large, eye-catching print and artwork such as photos and other illustrations formed an essential part of the grand exposition that unfolded throughout the edition.

In 1934, on the *Houston Post*'s fiftieth anniversary, the newspaper featured a front-page reproduction of a congratulatory letter from President Roosevelt. Vice President John Nance Garner and other Texas political leaders sent messages commending the *Post* on its anniversary and civic leadership. *Fort Worth Star-Telegram* publisher Amon Carter proclaimed the *Post* to be a newspaper whose influence in Texas politics "at all times has been statewide." *Dallas Morning News* editor Ted Dealey noted the *Post* "grew with the city" and won for itself "respect and honor."

As a premier example of the commemorative editions of this era, the *Dallas Morning News* celebrated its 1935 golden anniversary in grand style. Alongside stories of the dedication of Boulder Dam and the discovery of a lost manuscript of Sam Houston's account of the Battle of San Jacinto, the *News* published congratulatory letters from President Roosevelt, Vice President Garner, and many other state and national leaders. Congratulatory messages from officials and other newspapers occupied several pages. The majority of the paper featured local histories and stories that accentuated the growth of Dallas and Texas—accounts of organizations, construction, industrial expansion, and the 1936 State Centennial—and photos from the previous fifty years. *News* president G. B. Dealey highlighted and recounted important stories of the previous fifty years of national and local importance. One story featured W. D. Austin, an original subscriber, who had read "every copy" of the newspaper since its initial publication in 1885.

Dealey's page one editorial on the fiftieth anniversary of the *News* amplified his philosophy and expounded on the role the newspaper had played in Dallas' development and growth. The *News* began when Dallas was "an overgrown, Topsy-like town, unkempt, with little paving." In working with civic leaders, the *News* "exerted all its power to lead and to co-operate with the thousands of men and women who are responsible for the Dallas of today." Dealey stated he intended to have the influence in promoting civic development expand statewide. "Always it has spent time, thought, money and effort in printing matter to inculcate a desire for attractiveness and beauty of every kind in its urban centers and countryside. It has desired to be the champion of all kinds of wholesome education and to develop the finer things of life." He also attributed the paper's success to "the efficient, ever-faithful and loyal interest of and work" of the *News* employees. Dealey planned to pursue the same course in the following years—striving to make the daily a respected and influential regional publication. The golden anniversary edition served as a prelude to even loftier plans for the *News* in the upcoming centennial year. The commemorative issues of that year provided the standard for other newspapers, from the hectic daily publications to the smallest weekly tabloids.

John Bodnar states in his analysis of collective memory that civic leaders select commemorative events for a number of reasons. These include events that calm anxiety and evoke change, and efforts to solicit support from the general citizenry and to promote exemplary behavior. The special editions of newspapers and centennial promotions in 1936 clearly supported each of these criteria. Anxiety over the ongoing economic depression maintained its hold over the population, and one of the stated goals of centennial proponents was to have a celebration that would improve the collective outlook of the citizenry. As evidenced by the intense competition among the large cities for the coveted centennial headquarters, widespread support from the major urban communities existed. In the promotions for all the celebrations, proponents urged citizens to participate and extol the virtues of a past built on traditional American ideas—independence, liberty, freedom of expression, and the desire to establish a better society.

As the leading proponents of the centennial, the state's major newspaper publishers reaffirmed their position at the center of cultural and political leadership. They recognized that their individual positions as community leaders, along with their role as newspaper publishers, depended on the success of the centennial-related activities. In addition, growth and financial success depended on the continuation of the daily newspaper as the focal point of communication in the community. As the centennial events gained acceptance and achieved regional and national recognition, the newspapers and their publishers reached the apex of approval by the citizenry.

Publishers also contributed to what may be termed the origin myth, which took firm root in the collective memory of Texans. *Fort Worth Star-Telegram* editor J. M. North described these sentiments in a 1935 letter to *Dallas Morning News* editor Ted Dealey. "The history of Texas began 100 years ago," North stated, which conveniently ignored the entire history and role of Native Americans, Spain, Mexico, France, and the United States prior to 1835. The historical interpretation promoted and distributed during the centennial provided an explanation that accommodated the racial and economic views of the state's hierarchy. Briefly, Texas fought for its freedom because of Spanish and Mexican misrule and oppression. These hardy Anglo-Saxon pioneers created a land of opportunity after the conquest of the native populations and the government in Mexico City. The state's business and political leaders combined forces to forge a new frontier and began promoting new communities where life would peacefully progress and where conflict would be downplayed and avoided. These themes accommodated the prevailing racial stereotypes, class distinctions, and cultural prejudices of the era. Mexican Americans were associated with barbarism and hostility. African Americans were viewed as inferior and uncivilized. This interpretation ignored cooperative efforts and public/private cooperation in favor of private initiative. The Populists, Socialists, and other political movements outside of the mainstream were conveniently ignored.

Once it was chosen as the main site for the state celebration, Dallas acted as a magnet for the state's celebration. Planning and promotion for the main event took place in Dallas. News of the event was disseminated from Dallas through special publications and the pages of the *Morning News* and the *Times Herald*. Newspapers throughout the state received *Centennial News*, a weekly publication with information on the progress of the event, and *Texas Centennial Review*, a newsletter with ideas and information on local events. From the largest cities to the smallest communities in the state, the centennial emerged as the leading issue of the day. Its patriotic message moved into diverse areas and populations, with its unifying themes of Texas history and view of Texas as a state that stood separate from the others in the nation. As the *Dallas Morning News* reported on April 1, 1935, "every progressive community in the state, it would seem, is busy" with a centennial program.

The selection of Dallas embarrassed and frustrated major daily newspaper publishers in Fort Worth, Houston, and San Antonio. Amon Carter, the *Star-Telegram*, and Fort Worth civic leaders moved to close the gap after learning that Dallas had the winning bid for the state centennial. As they worked to secure state funds for their own celebration, the *Star-Telegram* moved to quench some of the fire that burned in the competition for the centennial competition. The two newspaper enterprises, which often threw barbs at one another through their editorial pages, realized the centennial offered a potential economic boom in the midst of the Depression. "We can't conceive of people coming to see the Livestock Centennial and not seeing the main Centennial at Dallas," *Star-Telegram* editor J. M. North wrote to Ted Dealey of the *Morning News*. "We believe that two attractions will supplement and benefit each other and that neither can possibly be hurt by the other."

A number of precedents of cooperation between the Fort Worth and Dallas publishers existed before the centennial projects. The newspapers and civic leaders had cooperated to form the Trinity River Canal Association in 1930. The Trinity River flowed through both cities and several hundred miles later emptied into the Gulf of Mexico. Community and business leaders had sought millions of dollars in federal funding to dredge the Trinity River and open the waterway for commercial shipping and barge traffic. In support of the joint project, the *Morning News* stated, "[T]here need be no uneasiness about Fort Worth in the matter." For the first time, the *News* acknowledged Carter's motto for his newspaper and community. The *News* also acknowledged Carter's vision and political prowess. " 'Where the West Begins' looms now and aims to loom considerably more," the editorial stated. Carter's friend and Trinity River Canal booster Silliman Evans wrote, "[T]here can be no further doubt but that the Dallas Morning News has officially accepted Fort Worth as 'Where the West Begins.' "

Editor and Publisher magazine noted the centennial promotions were a boon to newspaper businesses in the state. While the promotions yielded increased employment, more advertising, and a jump in the tourist trade immediately, the benefits of these "farsighted newspapermen" would also accumulate in subsequent years. "The more people who visit Texas and see its wonders and get acquainted with its citizens, the more people will invest their capital and their lives in Texas, according to the shrewd judgment of Texas publishers," the article stated. George Dealey immodestly predicted that the exposition would create "more development and greater posterity in the state of Texas than have the last 25 years." Amon Carter, *Fort Worth Star-Telegram* publisher, Tom Gooch, editor of the *Dallas Times Herald*, James Pollock, business manager of the *Fort Worth Press*, and John Payne. *Houston Press* business manager, joined in the rosy predictions. For emphasis, the article included a cartoon of a cowboy wearing a large western hat with "Texas" on the brim and a basket over a candle that proclaimed "Texas Billion Power Candle Light."

With their rival expositions, Dallas and Fort Worth gained national headlines as evidence of a "major outbreak of exposition fever." In June 1936, *Business Week* magazine described the festivities as "an amiable blend of patriotism and business." The competing shows may have appeared to be a tribute to the rivalry between the two cities, but the magazine reasoned both communities would enjoy the "chime of cash registers" from crowds, anticipated to number in the millions, making their way to the two Texas cities. The article noted the substantial contribution from the federal government and the local and state contributions. It also lauded the two expositions' success in attracting large corporations such as the large automakers, for which each city constructed its own multimillion structures at the Dallas fairgrounds. The *Dallas Morning News* attempted to downplay the rivalry. In a July 15, 1936, editorial, the *News* stated, "In the Frontier Centennial our neighbor to the West preserves the tradition of the Old West in the spirit of the jazz age." The "highly publicized notion" of the competition between the Dallas and Fort Worth exhibitions was a "press agent's dream. It has no real bearing on the success of either the Centennial Central Exposition in Dallas or the Frontier Centennial in Fort Worth."

Centennial funds provided construction and landscaping for Fair Park in Dallas. Construction provided much-needed jobs, but labor strikes by Dallas building trades union members slowed down construction. The state contributed over $1 million, while the federal government contributed $1.5 million and funded more than fifty Dallas mural projects as part of the Public Works of Art Project. The Texas Hall of State, a million-dollar building to honor Texas heroes, became the center of the permanent buildings. The park site included museums and exhibition buildings for petroleum, industry, communications, agriculture, and transportation. Centennial visitors enjoyed rides and entertainment on the Midway, as well as a re-creation of Judge Roy Bean's courtroom in the Jersey Lily Saloon and Admiral Richard Bird's Little America camp in Antarctica. President Roosevelt, hosted at a dinner by R. L. Thornton and other Dallas bankers, appeared in Dallas amid great fanfare. The Dallas newspapers carried many positive promotional stories for the event. Few stories appeared that involved labor strife during the construction appeared in the dailies. The special centennial editions of the Dallas newspapers completely omitted any news of labor problems.

The main exposition also contained the Hall of Negro Life, the first time that African Americans were recognized at a national exposition. African American business and community leaders worked with centennial promoters for this landmark appearance. The *Dallas Express*, which had a history of attacking lynching, voting restrictions, and segregation, advocated inclusion of the hall in the centennial fairgrounds. The newspaper and local black leaders obtained entrance to the state fair in Dallas on a single day, designated "Negro Day." African American business leaders saw a greater opportunity for themselves through the Centennial. Once Dallas won the selection for the main centennial celebration, the *Express* told its readers that the Negro Chambers of Commerce was working with the Dallas business community to participate in the events and gain a share of the anticipated business. The *Express* stated that the "Dallas Negro Chamber of Commerce has sought to assure for the Negroes of Dallas suitable accommodations and participation in all of the departments of this celebration."

After agreeing to support the Dallas exposition and participate in the bond campaign, the Hall of Negro Life received $100,000 as part of the $3 million federal appropriation. The centennial exposition received support from African Americans in Texas despite the fact that unemployment and poverty ran much higher in black communities than white communities in both rural and urban areas. In Dallas, African Americans represented half the city's unemployed in the mid-1930s. Only one major African American business, the Excelsior Mutual Insurance Company, managed to survive to 1937. Thus the Hall of Negro Life represented a symbol of hope and accomplishment for the black community. Included in the hall were murals of African Americans providing contributions of music, art, and religion to the nation. The exhibit also represented a small achievement in opposition to the segregated life of the 1930s. A. Maceo Smith, an African American insurance executive, led a concerted effort to have the Hall of Negro Life included at the exposition. Smith's early work with the Dallas NAACP and white business leaders established a pattern that was expanded in the coming decades as the African American community began to increase its efforts to combat segregation.

At the dedication of the centennial exposition on June 7, a host of dignitaries and thousands of visitors attended. As Sam Acheson of the *Dallas Morning News* wrote, the festivities opened "before the largest crowd ever gathered in the Southwest." An estimated 250,000 people attended, "making it the greatest occasion in the history of Dallas and the most notable event in Texas since Sam Houston and his men changed the course of the New World at San Jacinto." Extensive coverage over radio stations and the state's newspapers heightened the enthusiasm for the great event. Texas governor James Allred introduced Secretary of Commerce Daniel Roper. As he inserted a gold key and unlocked the ceremonial gate, Roper proclaimed, "Texas welcomes the world."

Secretary Roper escorted a delegation of officials, some of whom were descendants of Stephen F. Austin, and other state and local leaders. Later that day, Roper dedicated the Federal Building and visited the Hall of Negro Life. In his speech that evening, entitled "Texas and the Nation," Roper surprised many by praising the progress of African Americans. "No people in all history can show greater progress in their achievement in seventy-three years than the American Negro," the Commerce secretary said. "This is traceable to their patient, loyal, patriotic attitude toward their country and to their gifts of soul and song." The Dallas newspapers carried the remarks as part of the coverage of the opening ceremony. But later, the *Dallas Morning News* carried more critical stories that depicted African Americans in a less flattering light. "History of Negroes from Jungles to Now" and "black faces deep into slices of watermelon" were among the racist, condescending phrases used in coverage of the Hall of Negro Life. The statements undoubtedly provided some comfort to fair organizers who acquiesced to the demands of African Americans. But to make sure that no one would overlook the state's Confederate heritage, a statue representative of the Confederacy stood in the center portico of the Centennial Building. Confederate leaders appeared prominently in murals in the Great Hall of State. President Franklin Roosevelt dedicated a statue of Robert E. Lee on his horse Traveler as one of the centennial highlights. Allegiance to the Old South and Confederacy remained strong, even as civic leaders elevated the Texas Lone Star alongside the Stars and Bars.

As mentioned earlier, Amon Carter pushed for a separate centennial site for Fort Worth. Following the untimely death of Will Rogers in 1935, Carter urged a memorial coliseum in honor of his friend. Rejected by the PWA, the plan was reborn in the form of a Frontier Centennial Exhibition. A 135-acre tract west of downtown Fort Worth, formerly occupied by the military, became the chosen site. The Fort Worth Frontier Centennial Exposition emerged as Amon Carter's cause célèbre. Carter united the Fort Worth business community behind the promotion as the western alternative to the Dallas celebration. The venue would offer the entertainment and lavish productions that Carter believed that the Dallas venue omitted. The *Fort Worth Star-Telegram* declared that Fort Worth would become the beneficiary of increased jobs and would receive favorable publicity for the city's businesses. Carter's newspaper and WBAP radio carried daily stories and promotions of the event. A series of front-page editorials in 1935 boasted of the benefits. "Fort Worth can stage a show that in appeal to visitors will equal that of any other city or the main Centennial itself at Dallas," Carter wrote. The benefits would bring "large and immediate cash-drawer returns to every businessman, professional man and property owner in Fort Worth."

Carter lobbied his friends in Washington to assist with the funding. After obtaining a loan and grant from the PWA along with privately funded bonds for the multimillion dollar project, Carter learned in early June 1936 that funds were insufficient to complete construction. He wrote Vice President John Nance Garner, only days prior to the dedication, that the Fort Worth production needed more money. "Costs have exceeded estimates thirty to forty percent." He claimed that the project provided jobs for more than 3,000 people. "Can you not see your way clear to giving us some relief immediately," Carter said. "I assure you that it would be a Godsend to us." Carter wrote RFC Chairman Jesse Jones soliciting loans up to $500,000. "There would not be a Chinaman's chance for you to lose a penny on this note," Carter stated. If Jones faced any legal problems, Carter observed, "[Y]ou would be fully justified in waiving them, as no doubt you have found necessary in many cases where you have rendered emergency financial assistance." Carter concluded that everyone would be protected in the investment and would be amazed at the "magnificent" production. "Nothing like it ever has been shown in America." Eventually, another $50,000 in federal money found its way to the Fort Worth promoters.

When Carter obtained funding for the Fort Worth exposition, he and fair organizers raced to open before their Dallas neighbors, but delays forced the Fort Worth exposition to open a month after the one in Dallas. Carter utilized the staff of the *Star-Telegram* and WBAP for publicity, planning, and accounting for the Fort Worth production. Prior to the official launch, Carter invited hundreds of newspaper publishers and editors to attend a preview. WBAP radio provided an hour-long show that fed to network radio around the nation. At the July opening, news reports stated the production was "a startling blending of Texas longhorns, cowpunchers, chuck-wagons, six-pistols and naked Indians, with show girls, Billy Roseian scenic effects, Paul Whiteman's music and Sally Rand's bubbles." President Roosevelt telegraphed congratulations to Carter from the schooner yacht *Sewanna* off the coast of Nova Scotia, "Best of luck to you all," the president wrote.

Governor Allred and other state political and business leaders officially launched the opening. New York director Billy Rose featured a highly anticipated floor show, the "Frontier Follies," at the Casa Mañana. One of the attractions of the show was a "chorus of some 500 beautiful girls." Rose also brought his acclaimed *Jumbo*, a one-ring-circus musical production, to the theatre. "The atmosphere of a Texas town of 1849 will be perfectly re-created," one account stated. "There will be soldiers, Indians, Mexicans, cowboys, wagon trains, stage coaches, buffalo, all the frontier business enterprises, such as trading posts, saloons and dance halls—all open for business." The floor shows and the liquor attracted the crowds. According to Carter's biographer, "[I]llegal liquor was served everywhere" because Amon had made a deal with the state's Liquor Control Board. The summer heat often made the Fort Worth exposition unbearable, but throngs of people continued to appear. Critics and visitors praised the productions for months.

The Texas Centennial Exposition in Dallas closed in November 1936. The Fort Worth Frontier Centennial suspended most operations by Thanksgiving. More than 6 million people attended the six-month-long celebration in Dallas and an estimated 1 million visited the Fort Worth show. Visitors included President Franklin Roosevelt and his wife, Eleanor Roosevelt, Vice President Garner, and a host of national and federal officials. Over 350,000 schoolchildren from Texas and other states attended the centennial celebrations. The Dallas and Fort Worth events, especially when combined with others around the state, expanded the national awareness of Texas. The festivities laid the foundations for a growing tourist trade. The centennial events also provided economic relief in the form of thousands of jobs and substantial improvements in many communities around the state. Finally, the celebrations offset some of the concerns about the ongoing economic depression and lifted the spirits of many of the state's citizens. For newspaper publishers, the increased revenues, circulation, and recognition provided welcome relief in the difficult years of the Great Depression. Publishers whose proclamations appeared extravagant in 1935 actually achieved many of their goals.

In Dallas, the closing of the fair led to a monumental decision: to create the Dallas Citizens Council, chartered in 1937 to plot the city's future. Charter members in the elite group included independent Dallas publishers G. B. Dealey and Edwin J. Kiest. The group embraced businessmen, insurance and utility executives, and bankers drawn from the city's civic leadership. No reporters, educators, attorneys, women, minorities, or members of the clergy were included in the original council. The organization sought to influence the course of business, civic projects, local politics, and major organizations such as the chamber of commerce. The group's membership changed, but the Council successfully controlled Dallas for the next fifty years. The Council accepted the premise that Dealey in particular had advanced for many years: Dallas, as represented by the business community, should speak with one voice and offer a business-oriented agenda for the people of Dallas. The insecurity created by the Depression, the success of the centennial celebration, and the near unanimous conviction that the city's business leadership provided the best direction created the glue that held this group together for years to come. The insular, self-perpetuating, confident organization best resembled the *Dallas Morning News*, which, under Dealey's leadership and with its consistent policy of promoting business, survived the economic challenges of the Depression and remained a closely held family operation with a secure base of longtime loyal managers and employees.

In another sense, the centennial events and their promotion by the state press illustrated the desire to accept Washington's expanded presence, especially in the form of federal dollars. As long as the social and political order remained in place in the state, Texans maintained their allegiance to the traditional one-party Democratic system. Projects such as those represented by the centennial allowed Texans to boast of their individuality which, on the surface, set them apart from the rest of the South and the nation. The New Deal projects and the expanding role of the federal government sometimes produced criticism and divisions within the business and political leadership of the state. Although some grew increasingly nervous about President Roosevelt's policies and the direction of the Democratic Party, Texas editors took solace in the knowledge that friendly Texans still commanded major positions in the legislative and executive branches. Even with their power and influence in Washington, newspaper publishers and Texans from all walks of life realized the Depression retained its grip over the region and the nation.

Kenneth Ragsdale, author of a history of the centennial, reports that many out-of-state visitors "expressed their praise for the 'new Texas'; they found not the 'countrified folks' they had expected, but an 'ultramodern' culture. This changing attitude among non-Texans ultimately created a great cultural impact on the state, negating the 'pride with shame' syndrome and instilling a new sense of state pride in Texas." Regional self-consciousness was, after all, not a congenital deformity. Dallas retailer and civic stalwart Stanley Marcus reflected on the impact of the centennial on his city and the state. "I've frequently said that modern Texas history started with the celebration of the Texas Centennial, because it was in 1936 . . . that the rest of America discovered Texas. The spotlight was thrown on Texas and people from all over the United States came here."

Labor strife also became a concern during the centennial celebration, and Texas newspaper publishers became more critical of organized labor by 1937. The sit-down strikes that closed many coalfields and manufacturing plants in 1936 garnered headlines and criticism from southern politicians and newspapers. Many believed that the strikes violated property rights, and that President Roosevelt and his administration provided tacit support to the unions. Sentiment against organized labor in Dallas among the business community discouraged union organizing, especially after the closing of the centennial expositions. But violence and death erupted during an especially bitter strike at the Dallas Ford Motor Company plant in 1937. Ford, long known as a bastion of antiunion sentiment, retaliated against organizers and workers in the summer and fall of 1937. The victims of Ford's hired thugs included plant workers, CIO organizers, and Dallas residents who expressed sentiments in favor of the employees. The enforcers attacked over fifty individuals and killed one man. In scenes reminiscent of the Klan activities of the early 1920s, targeted Ford employees were "taken for a ride" to an isolated area away from town, where they were beaten. The Ford gang seized Barto Hill, a labor organizer from Tennessee, and administered a beating, then stripped and tarred and feathered their victim, much as the Klan had done a decade earlier. They dumped Hill in front of the *Dallas Morning News* office. A photo of the victim appeared the following day in the newspaper. Governor Allred called in the Texas Rangers, and the National Labor Relations Board (NLRB) eventually conducted hearings on Ford's activities in Dallas.

Labor organizers claimed Ford's violent acts would end only when the business establishment and the daily press criticized the automaker's tactics. Unlike their reporting of the earlier Klan-orchestrated violence, the Dallas dailies downplayed the incidents and provided little coverage of the NLRB hearings and investigation. The dailies' concern over labor strife mirrored that of the Texas congressional delegation of this period. The national press, which included the *New York Times*, reported Ford's antiunion activities and the labor board's actions; it also noted the city's growing reputation for hostility to groups that opposed large businesses. After World War II began, Ford workers nationwide became members of the United Auto Workers as a result of federal court action and a national agreement between Ford and the unions.

Texas newspapers aligned with most Texas businesses in the 1930s in expanding their opposition to organized labor. In this case, the probusiness bias of the publishers clearly outweighed their editorial assessment of community living standards and working conditions. As in other southern cities, the dominant leadership accepted federal assistance to provide unemployment wages and other relief efforts. But they resisted any challenges to the prevailing wage schedules or large-scale efforts at unionization. Many business and political leaders also feared unionism, especially the CIO, as an open door to racial integration. The Dallas Open Shop Association, organized in 1919, opposed union activities in the city and subjected members who knowingly hired union workers to a $3,000 fine. The members represented the city's chamber of commerce, which worked closely with the Dallas newspaper establishment. The local AFL leadership cooperated with businesses that resisted CIO organizers, and the labor leaders refused to publicly condemn violence and atrocities. In 1937 the *Nation* called attention to the city's antilabor positions in the critical story "Dallas Tries Terror." Based on the resistance in the South to CIO organizing attempts in cities like Dallas, historian George B. Tindall concluded that the "South remained predominantly nonunion and largely antiunion."

Daily newspapers showed evidence of prosperity as a result of the 1936 centennial celebration. But the recession of 1937 hit Texas and the nation with a vengeance. The *Morning News* closed its long-running *Semi-Weekly Farm News* and merged it with the daily. Dealey complained in his annual report that with the exception of radio station WFAA, all of the Belo Corporation publications lost money in 1938. Dealey sold the afternoon *Dallas Journal* to Houston businessman James West. Commenting on the sale, Dealey reported that the corporation received only twenty cents on the dollar, "but we were perhaps lucky to receive anything."

Even after World War II began in Europe, publishers still faced difficulties in maintaining their newspapers as a profitable enterprise. George B. Dealey turned over the presidency of the *News* to Ted Dealey, his son. The Belo Corporation annual report disclosed that advertising rates still fell short of supporting the newspaper operation. The report stated that both "leading newspapers" in the city, the *News* and the *Times Herald*, lost money. However, the Dallas corporations survived, as they were "supported largely by radio revenues." Belo owned WFAA, while the rival Times Herald Corporation owned KRLD. Ted Dealey stated, "We have the modest conviction that the *Dallas News* is being managed more sanely and more wisely than is the business of our nearest rival" and that the "competitive situation will adjust itself." With this disclosure, he asserted, "[W]e confidently anticipate that, in the long haul, we will come out 'at the top of the heap.' "

Historian Dewey Grantham surmises that by the end of the 1930s, the New South formula won the debate over the character of the southern economy. The New Deal provided a source of new capital with few strings attached in the form of the federal government. Along with regulations for industry, finance, agriculture, and labor, some of the old walls of resistance and blame that Texans and other southerners hurled at the rest of the nation came tumbling down. The metropolitan newspapers of the state took the lead alongside Texas politicians who formulated these fresh ideas. Differences continued to exist and lead to conflict and criticism, especially when issues involved a challenge to the status quo, that is, when they related to segregation and the region's labor system. While displeasure with the Democratic Party increased in the years prior to World War II, the disputes failed to completely dampen loyalties to the national Democratic leadership. Publishers retained their close connections to the federal leadership and relied on the entrenched Texas congressional delegation and their allies in the government to offset any serious challenges to the dominant coalition back home.

While historians agree that the federal presence expanded in the South during the 1930s, disagreement exists on the extent of its impact on the region and its meaning for this generation of Americans. For many, especially the rural poor, African Americans, and Mexican Americans, their suffering continued and conditions sometimes deteriorated during the 1930s. Yet life for many rural and urban dwellers, including some minorities, showed some degree of improvement. Texas and the South were not entirely agrarian. Urban communities expanded and their workforce increased, due in part to widespread urban support for federal initiatives. These programs, aided and abetted by the urban daily press, provided an alternative to the poor tenant farmers of the region. Although they criticized many federal programs and only offered lukewarm support for others, Texas daily newspaper publishers acknowledged this shift in alignment and advocated the establishment of federal programs in the region. Public power, minimum wage, work standards, relief programs, federal loans to business, improvement of public education, and other New Deal programs found fertile ground and editorial support from the state's leading newspapers.

The Texas publishers adhered to their consensus philosophy that had carried them forward from the early years of the twentieth century. This approach continued in the difficult years of the 1930s when debate finally moved from disagreements over Prohibition to substantive issues that involved business expansion, labor and race relations, support for public education, and improved health services. The publishers also helped set a tone of race accommodation and tolerance, albeit within a segregated system. The newspapers remained opposed to federal antilynching legislation and affirmed their support of the poll tax. They steadfastly refused to carry news of accomplishments by African Americans and Mexican Americans. They tolerated the discrimination exercised in most of the New Deal programs in Texas and the rest of the South. Yet by the 1930s, the major dailies in the state refused to enter into the vile, race-baiting tirades to which many southern politicians and newspaper publishers subscribed. They endorsed the very programs that were to provide a seedbed of expanded opportunity to all people, regardless of their skin color or background. The differences in the racial communities remained wide, but some bridges were established through the support of the New Deal and its promise of a better life. The era marked the beginning of a period when the southern press would have to recognize a need for reshaping the region's economic and social structure.

Reviewing the accomplishments of the centennial year, the editors of the *Texas Almanac* believed the events signaled a "return of prosperity" and "served the purpose of bringing full realization that the old Texas had passed—that the centennial event meant more than the passing of a mere historic milestone." The soil and natural resources still held great wealth for the state's citizens and businesses. After 1936, proponents believed that expanded opportunities in the form of manufacturing would supersede agriculture and extractive industries that relied on natural resources. In the midst of the Great Depression, Texas had finally passed "into cultural and economic adulthood."

Disney Meets Davy

MARK DERR

WRITER AND HISTORIAN MARK DERR IS THE AUTHOR OF *SOME KIND OF PARADISE: A CHRONICLE OF MAN AND THE LAND IN FLORIDA*, *A DOG'S HISTORY OF AMERICA: HOW OUR BEST FRIEND EXPLORED, CONQUERED, AND SETTLED A CONTINENT*, AND *THE FRONTIERSMAN: THE REAL LIFE AND MANY LEGENDS OF DAVY CROCKETT*.

IN THIS SELECTION, DERR, A DISTANT RELATIVE OF THE TENNESSEE POLITICIAN AND ALAMO DEFENDER, DISCUSSES WALT DISNEY'S DAVY AND EXAMINES THE CROCKETT MANIA OF THE 1950S. HE ALSO CONSIDERS THE VARIOUS WAYS CROCKETT HAS BEEN PORTRAYED, FROM BOLD BACKWOODSMAN TO DRUNKEN BRAGGART TO NEW AGE PALADIN.

★ ★

On the evening of December 15, 1954, the ABC television network, fighting to establish itself opposite CBS and NBC, broadcast Walt Disney's "Davy Crockett, Indian Fighter" and created a cultural phenomenon that transfixed the nation for nearly a year. By February the final two episodes of the trilogy—"Davy Crockett Goes to Congress" and "Davy Crockett at the Alamo"—had aired before an estimated sixty million viewers. In May, Disney released the three as a motion picture called *Davy Crockett, King of the Wild Frontier*, having shrewdly filmed the programs, which were broadcast in black and white, in color for that purpose. School halls and back yards echoed with "The Ballad of Davy Crockett."[1] By the million, children daily died and rose again from the carnage of their Indian wars, the ruins of their private Alamos. Most of those enthralled viewers—and a large number of people who never saw the programs—can today chant a verse or two of Davy's twenty-stanza ballad, and more than a few remember their first coonskin cap. Even today their children are learning the ballad in school.

Fess Parker, the six-and-a-half-foot tall, thirty-year-old Davy, overnight went from being an obscure character actor, whose sole credit was as a victim of rampaging ants in *Them*, a grade-B science-fiction thriller set in New Mexico, to an international star. In 1955, he toured forty-two cities and thirteen foreign countries, promoting the programs, the film, and an array of "Walt Disney's Davy Crockett" paraphernalia. By a contractual arrangement with Disney that was a rarity at the time, Parker received a 10 percent royalty on the sale of official clothes and toys, which totaled in the tens of millions of dollars and made him a wealthy man.[2] Huge crowds of children greeted him wherever he appeared, often creating dangerous situations. "Crowds would push out windows in store fronts," Parker said. "In Holland I had to escape in a cab because I feared for the kids' lives."[3] Parker became so thoroughly typecast that even in his starring role as Daniel Boone in the long-running television series by that title, which aired several years later, he looked and acted like Davy Crockett.

Watching Disney's Davy on videotape thirty-seven years after its debut, I was struck more by the primitive production values and stunts than by the inaccuracies in the story line, which at least serve dramatic purposes. In the wake of such recent action-adventure extravaganzas as *Star Wars, Indiana Jones*, the two *Terminators*, even the antics of *Baron Münchausen*, the $750,000 Crockett film—not exactly low-budget for the time—resembles a home movie. Punches are clearly pulled, falls padded. The dialogue, like the action, is wooden. The Indians—white men in greasepaint—have their origins in Hollywood studios, not in life. Although the script initially parallels Crockett's biography and more or less serious legends, it departs in significant details—giving him a sidekick named Georgie Russel (Buddy Ebsen, who became more famous in *The Beverly Hillbillies*), leaving him a widower, and finally dropping his family completely. Absent altogether is Crockett the farmer, mill owner, and speculator scrambling to stay ahead of debt, the remarried man with a cabin full of children and a wife who can run the family enterprises better than he. In the third episode, Russel at last reveals that he has been writing pamphlets featuring his friend as a backwoods epic hero, and that the pamphlets have become increasingly popular. It is a clever explanation for Davy's fame, a poetic conflation of the historical process by which he became a legend.

Disney's Davy was the all-American manchild, the buckskin-clad paragon of the values that had won the West and was keeping the world safe for democracy—honesty, courage, and natural nobility. Able to read and write his name only with great difficulty, he was fluent in the ways of the wild, a superb tracker and hunter. The frontier, not civilization, was his true home, yet when duty summoned him to Washington to serve the people of West Tennessee, he willingly obliged. He lived for truth, justice, and liberty. He fought and killed Indians like a good scout when his country called, and then, when Justice demanded, he rode hell-bent-for-leather from Philadelphia to Washington and stalked into the House of Representatives to deliver a ringing denunciation of President Andrew Jackson's plan to force the southern Indians—the Creek, Cherokee, Seminole, Chickasaw, and Choctaw—to move west of the Mississippi.

In addition to creating the stalwart man, Disney's screenwriters paid homage to the Crockett legend, which had proved so popular over more than a century, by investing their Davy with preternatural power. Throughout the three programs, he practices grinning man and beast into submission, subjugating them by his will alone and good humor. He subdues a bear and later tries to pacify an Indian. Unfazed, his foe attacks, tomahawk raised, and Davy bests him in a bare-knuckle brawl. He wins every fight until the last one at the Alamo, where, swinging his empty gun through the final dissolve, he ascends into the pantheon of great warrior-heroes. He is a nineteenth-century Horatius, guarding the road into Texas, not the bridge to Rome.

Disney's timing was impeccable. Playing before tens of millions of viewers—nearly everyone with a television set—Davy turned ABC into the third nationwide network and did even more for Walt Disney. Davy was the star of Frontierland, one of four theme areas—the others being Fantasyland, Adventureland, and Tomorrowland—in Disneyland, the grandiose amusement park scheduled to open in July 1955 in Southern California. Featuring Crockett, Mickey Mouse, and a host of supporting characters, along with rides and displays, the park captivated the American public and established Walt Disney as the greatest showman of the age. His genius lay in his ability to blend a faith in human progress through technology with an idealized image of nineteenth-century small-town America as an idyllic place of wholesome good times, of families and friends. New machines would make the old home more real and perfect, more harmonious, as they did in Disneyland. The Disney vision offered progress without disruption or pain. His heroes might have difficulty reading and writing, but they were without major character defects that might cause one to question their motives or goodness.

Walt Disney's creations reflected and helped shape the mood of guarded optimism and self-congratulation that pervaded the nation in the mid-1950s. Having come through the Depression and emerged victorious from World War II, only to stumble into a stalemate in Korea, Americans appeared intent on pursuing prosperity and advancement. The popular press, radio, cinematic newsreels, and the fast-growing medium of television, which would collectively become the media, exuded sufficient optimism to take the edge off persistent reports of conflict, famine, a sluggish economy, and epidemics, even to make surviving a nuclear attack seem little more difficult than escaping a tornado—"duck and cover," the Civil Defense planners advised, when you hear the air-raid siren. Along with their advertisers, the media conveyed the message that business and industry would create a world richer in goods—from houses to cars to appliances—and more abundant in leisure than any imagined before. Judicious management of the national economy and control of wages, although the unions disagreed, would ensure the good life. Medical breakthroughs, like the new polio vaccine that would wipe out that scourge, promised to conquer a score of life-threatening diseases.

Political leaders in both parties and national publications like *Time* propounded the view that America's continued greatness was dependent on vigilant men, who would stand firm against Communism abroad and at home, men who not only had the capacity to harness the awesome power of the atom but also the wisdom to decide when and where to unloose it. Only with its defenses up, they argued, its institutions freed from the corrupting influence of subversives—anyone who questioned the existing system and policies—could America enjoy the fruits of its labor. Mainstream politicians who spoke out against the abuses of this red baiting were marked for defeat. In 1955, alienation was not a condition that applied to "decent" young people or professionals. What clouds there were, Davy and his fellow superheroes—strong, courageous, righteous men—could pocket and cart away.

In the first nine months of 1955, neither man nor beast escaped Davy Crockett. He was everywhere, a sudden infestation—the first of a series of "crazes" or fads that would mark the baby-boom generation, leading a number of marketing specialists, journalists, and demographers to conceive of that group of postwar children as a single monolithic entity that could be inspired to act en masse. No one had imagined that these children not only would immediately demand an object associated with the celluloid image but also could persuade their parents to go along. By some accounts, the magnitude of the response surprised even Walt Disney, who had planned the release for years and was a recognized master of the medium of television. "The Ballad of Davy Crockett," which jazz trombonist George Bruns and scriptwriter Tom Blackburn penned in twenty minutes as filler for the already completed programs—relying on rhyme, not sense—defined Davy as solidly as the film. Selling 18 million copies and recorded by no fewer than twenty crooners, including Parker himself, it was the number-one song of 1955, going away. A shelf of Crockett books—ranging from juvenile to adult fiction, biography, and autobiography—hit 14 million in sales. *The Story of Davy Crockett*, an indifferent biography by Enid La Monte Meadowcroft containing more fiction than fact—this Davy killed him a "b'ar" when he was all of ten—skyrocketed from a steady 10,000 a year in sales since its publication in 1952 to 300,000. A Crockett comic strip was syndicated in 200 newspapers. Disney distributed, under the title "Davy Crockett Says," newspaper columns featuring a picture of Fess Parker as Davy and homilies regarding honesty, trust, justice, duty, and even frugality. As the demand for coonskin caps outstripped supply, the price of pelts soared from $0.25 to $6.00 a pound. After decimating populations of raccoons, trappers turned to wolves, foxes, skunks, and opossums. Manufacturers sold the substitutes as the genuine item and also bought and recycled old fur coats.

Every child needed at minimum a coonskin cap and some semblance of a flintlock, and parents, with memories of their own Depression deprivations still fresh—many a child in the 1930s missed out on Buck Rogers toys, for example—were eager to oblige. For this Baltimore boy, aged five, a nine-iron made an enduring Old Betsy, a more sturdy long rifle than those bought for hard dollars—and it was more accurate. Parents routinely bribed their children to engage in desired behavior with a sampling of the 3,000 Crockett items—everything from the ubiquitous cap and toy gun to towels, sheets, books, records, lunch boxes, fringed shirts and pants, pajamas, moccasins, soap, balloons, and wading pools—that filled the stores.[4] Adults were not exempt: Offering a free "Davy Crockett" tent—actually a renamed pup tent—to each purchaser of a Norge appliance, Borg-Warner Corporation gave away a total of 35,000 by May.

By then, Crockett paraphernalia had reached $100 million in sales and prognosticators confidently predicted the total would soar to $300 million during the Christmas rush. In some department stores, Crockett accounted for as much as 10 percent of sales.[5] Sensing windfall profits, manufacturers and retailers began mislabeling unsold products with "Davy Crockett" and turning out vast quantities of poorly made goods. In Boston, a shoe store unloaded 3,000 moccasins after placing a "Davy Crockett" sign in front of them. Elsewhere old Daniel Boone caps, assigned a new identity, found buyers. In Albany and Rochester, New York, fake-fur hats proved easily inflammable.[6] F.A.O. Schwarz executive Philip Kirkham sounded a cautionary note, predicting that authentic Crockett toys would last on the market, because Davy was universal, but the rest of the junk would fade away.[7] No one listened.

As abruptly as it had begun, the craze went into free fall. In Washington, D.C., Crockett T-shirts that once sold by the thousand at $1.29 each gathered dust on the shelves when marked down to $0.39. From around the country came equally grim reports. In December, a number of disappointed retailers grumpily declared "kids more fickle than women."[8] *Variety* announced, "Davy was the biggest thing since Marilyn Monroe and Liberace, but he pancaked. He laid a bomb."[9]

ABC's *Disneyland* aired two new episodes—"Davy Crockett's Keelboat Race" and "Davy Crockett and the River Pirates," featuring Big Mike Fink (The King of the River), the Mississippi, and a catchy tune—in November and December. The slapdash programs cleverly played on the legends of the big river, allowing Davy, the masterful Everyman, to best the conniving, unsportsmanlike Fink—a man so locked in legend that his reality has all but vanished—in an epic keelboat race and then to destroy a den of evil thieves. The beaten Mike Fink did not tip his hat to the victor; he ate it, honoring a bet and spreading the fun. Crockett's one attempt at navigating the Mississippi in 1826 had nearly cost him his life, when his boat sank, but that accident was of no interest to Walt Disney, who presented the new programs—released to cinemas early in 1956 as *The Legends of Davy Crockett*—as nothing more than fiction. Eager to cash in on the phenomenal success of the first three episodes, he had turned fully to the tales, even having his screenwriters invent their own. But the King of the Wild Frontier and the King of the River together could not win over an audience that had lost interest. Davy had become ordinary, another program to watch or ignore. *The Wonderful World of Disney* on NBC repeated all five programs (now available on videotape) every three years into the 1970s without fanfare.

Explanations for the collapse were as diverse as those for the beginning of the fad. Some observers blamed the bad publicity attendant to problems with the production and sale of Crockett memorabilia. Others attributed the demise to critics who charged that Disney had made a hero of a reprehensible lout, a besotted liar and clown. While a number of retailers and journalists suggested that the children had grown bored or fickle and turned their short, collective attention span elsewhere, other commentators posited that they had become disaffected after learning that their hero was a fraud. Although some of the hypotheses appear somewhat silly in retrospect, the debate itself was born of genuine interest in the nature of the craze, which was the first with its origins in television. Advertisers, sociologists, marketing experts, and politicians were impressed by the power of television to influence not only public opinion but also mass behavior.

Even as hazardous merchandise drove consumers to other products, a rancorous trademark fight between Disney and a Baltimore garment maker sowed uncertainty and fear among businesses that they might be liable in a lawsuit. The dispute also prevented Disney from exercising the kind of quality control it generally enforced to protect its reputation.

On May 6, 1955, when business was booming, Walt Disney Productions went into U.S. District Court in Baltimore to file suit against Morey Schwartz, his wife Hannah, and their companies—Schwartz Manufacturing Company and Davy Crockett Enterprises, Inc., asking that their trademark, "David Crockett, Frontiersman," be declared null and void and that Disney be granted exclusive rights to its own "Walt Disney's Davy Crockett" and any permutation thereon.[10] Disney stated that its *Davy Crockett* was a fiction, conceived in 1950 "to describe the exploits of the early American pioneer and politican named David Crockett." Over the next five years, it had employed as many as 400 actors, writers, cartoonists, artists, and marketers to develop the films, the promotional material—including books and cartoons—and the merchandise. Disney considered marketing central to the financial success of the project, and so arranged for 125 licensees to produce 1,000 articles under its imprint. For all its obsession with detail, however, Disney failed to register its trademark or even have its lawyers check on other claimants to Crockett.

On the face of it, there was little reason to worry. Since the 1830s, the Crockett name had been used to sell everything from citrus to chewing tobacco and liquor. A legend of enormous proportion, Davy Crockett was fully in the public domain. A clipper ship, *David Crockett*, plied the seas from San Francisco to Wall Street during the 1850s and '60s, promising the most comfortable, fastest delivery under sail. She could make the passage in 115 days, Wm. T. Coleman and Company boasted in its advertisements, which featured a bearded Crockett riding a pair of alligators and a version of the famous Crockett motto: "Be sure you're right, then go ahead." In 1889, Betterton and Company took out a trademark on Davey Crockett Wisky, and in 1906 Union Distilling Company registered Davy Crocket Pure Copper Whiskey.[11] Both companies were playing on Crockett's notoriously poor spelling and his love for alcohol, "arden spirits," as he called it, in which he indulged much of his adult life. The registrations on both trademarks lapsed.

Then, in 1946, Morey and Hannah Schwartz registered the trademark "Davy Crockett, Frontiersman" with the U.S. Patent Office under No. 434,317. A manufacturer of military uniforms, Schwartz was inspired by his frequent visits to San Antonio, home of the Alamo, to shift production to western wear at the end of the war. But as textile mills completed the transition from military production, they began shipping their full runs of "hard-finish worsteds' to large apparel makers, leaving small companies like the Schwartzes' without access to the quality cloth they needed to compete. Their business failing, Morey and Hannah Schwartz transferred their Davy Crockett patent to Henry Kay, who produced western wear through his advance Tailoring Company of Baltimore. When the Disney-inspired craze began, Kay, unable to raise capital to expand his business, sold the trademark back to the Schwartzes, who established Davy Crockett Enterprises, Inc., in their hometown. They began sending letters and telegrams to producers of Crockett goods demanding 5 percent of their net sales as royalties and threatening legal action if they failed to comply.

The manufacturers complained to Disney, to their associations, to each other, and to the press that they feared retaliation if they ignored the Schwartzes' demand. It was then that Walt Disney

Productions sued, seeking to appease its licensees and protect itself from charges of trademark infringement. Disney alleged that Morey and Hannah Schwartz were interfering with the production and marketing of "Walt Disney's Davy Crockett." In a countersuit, the Schwartzes portrayed themselves as small merchants victimized by a huge and powerful company from California named Disney. The press treated the whole affair with a dash of humor. "Old Davy Crockett and his winning ways have a pack of lawyers fussing and feuding and businessmen befuddled," said William E. Giles in *The Wall Street Journal* on May 11. "Hitching up his buckskins, and with his big butcher [knife] in his belt, Disney charged into Baltimore's Federal Court and brought suit against Davy Crockett Enterprises, run by an oldtime Baltimore garment maker . . . ," said *Time*.[12] For the sake of business, if not justice, the two parties settled the suit on July 12, agreeing to split the fast-growing profits through cross licensing.

After news of the settlement broke, a covey of Crockett's direct descendants filed a motion to intervene, claiming that neither Disney nor Schwartz had a right to profit from their forebear's name. Seeking royalties for themselves, the Crockett descendants had organized two groups in Illinois: the David Crockett Descendants' Fund, an educational and charitable trust; and Crockett Kids, Inc., to market the Crockett name. Lawyers for the Schwartzes and Disney united to argue that allowing the fund's trustees—Bourke C. Crockett, Margie Flowers, Pauline Flowers Tillery, Oscar Doetsch, and Albert J. Watts—to break their uneasy truce would be tantamount to bringing mass confusion and ruin on the world of Crockett merchandising. Bloodlines, they said, did not carry a right to monopolize an ancestor's name. The motion to intervene was dismissed on October 6, 1955, with the heirs unrewarded. By then, the buying frenzy was slowing, consumers having received the message that greed mattered more than quality or the safety of their children.

The great success of Disney's Davy set off an intellectual debate as intense in its way as the frenzy for Crockett products. No sooner had the "craze" begun than a number of social critics, journalists, educators, and even politicians began to proclaim that Davy represented values ranging from anti-intellectualism to unbridled individualism that, if followed, would subvert their programs and institutions. Teachers around the country complained that their pupils were uncontrollable, spending more time singing "The Ballad of Davy Crockett" than reciting their ABCs. Invoking their fictional counterparts in a song, Fess Parker and Buddy Ebsen appealed to the kids to "do the right thing" and behave, without visible effect. Educators and journalists also engaged in a running debate over whether Davy subsumed all other frontier heroes—like Daniel Boone and Kit Carson, himself a somewhat overrated figure—thereby impoverishing the imaginations of their students, or inspired them to explore American history, thereby enriching them.

In Washington, D.C., late in the spring of 1955, a group of schoolchildren touring the Capitol asked to see the statue of their idol Davy, which they believed must be prominently displayed. Their teacher pointed to a figure dressed in buckskins, with a cap on his head and rifle in his hand, and called him Crockett. But it was Dr. Marcus Whitman, the Protestant missionary who traveled extensively through the West in the 1830s and early 1840s and helped open the Oregon country to settlement.[13] Crockett does not stand in bronze or marble in the Capitol, where he was a controversial, if colorful figure.

Teachers and students were not alone in their confusion. Texas Congressman Martin Dies asked his colleagues in the House to follow Davy's famous maxim and vote only for what was right, rather than what was expedient.[14] Other congressmen joined the fray and soon found themselves divided along party and sectional lines, with various Democrats from Tennessee and North Carolina seeking a piece of the glory by declaring Crockett a native of their states—although raised in Tennessee, he was born in the independent State of Franklin, which North Carolina considered part of its domain.

Liberal Democrats worried that the Republicans would adopt Davy and his coonskin as their campaign symbol. They over-looked the fact that Tennessee Senator Estes Kefauver, a Democrat, had been campaigning in the famous headgear since 1948, choosing instead to recall that in 1840 the Whigs, the party of the rich and privileged, had successfully, if cynically, employed the cap, the log cabin, and hard cider as symbols in order to prove themselves champions of the "common man" and place their candidate, William Henry Harrison, in the White House. If the victor at Tippecanoe could do it, the Democrats reasoned, why not the allied commander of Europe? Eisenhower hardly needed such help in 1956, but that did little to assuage the Democrats' concerns. In the pages of magazines and newspapers, on radio and television, they launched an ad hominem attack on the fictional Davy Crockett that, while sometimes farcical, had a major, negative impact on the way Crockett came to be perceived and portrayed.

Brendan Sexton, education director for the United Auto Workers in Detroit, opened the campaign soon after the Disney programs appeared. Sexton feared that Republican and anti-unionists, embracing the celluloid Crockett, would use his uncompromising individualism and martyrdom at the Alamo as a club against organized labor. He thought they would say that real Americans, like Davy, had no need or desire for a union because its emphasis on collective action and a strict seniority system for determining promotions and layoffs—the traditional "last hired, first fired" rule—was antithetical to individual opportunity. With the nation's economy in a slump and the campaign against Communism—and by extension, socialism and labor—at a fever pitch, many workers were beginning to believe that they could better serve their interests by dealing directly with management. Deciding to discredit the perceived messenger, rather than address the concerns of workers, Sexton gave a radio talk and interviews charging that Crockett was "a drunk and brawler, a wife deserter, hireling of big business, and shiftless no-account."[15]

Columnist Murray Kempton, who wrote on labor issues for the *New York Post*, picked up the refrain and charged that Crockett could be bought for the price of a drink. His diatribe inspired outraged children to demonstrate in front of his newspaper's office. John Fischer, editor of *Harper's*, one of the nation's most venerable liberal periodicals, was more caustic in his comments. After repeating Sexton's claims, he added that Crockett was "a poor farmer, indolent and shiftless. . . . He was never king of anything, except maybe the Tennessee Tall Tales and Bourbon Samplers' Association."[16] Attempting to turn anti-Communist, red-baiting sentiment against Crockett, Fischer also stated that the myth making associated with Davy most resembled that which created the benevolent image of Papa Joe Stalin.

Conservative commentator William F. Buckley, Jr., tweaked the liberals for their discomfort, announcing on his radio program that "the assault on Davy is one part traditional debunking campaign and one part resentment by liberal publicists of Davy's free approach to life. He'll survive the carpers." The liberals also found themselves criticized by the emasculated American Communist Party for attacking the nation's democratic traditions, an interesting argument grounded to some degree in Karl Marx's conception of the radical way people along the frontier organized their political and judicial institutions.[17]

Underlying the criticism of Crockett was the growing belief that the myths of America and its heroes were at variance with its history, that westward expansion was more the story of destruction of the Indians and nature for profit than of valiant white settlers struggling to survive against the elements, that slavery was a cruel and dehumanizing institution, that democracy and opportunity were not extended equally to all people. As this necessary corrective took hold, the extreme negative views of Crockett gained ascendancy over Disney's Davy. Presenting a rogues' gallery of the "Braggarts of the Backwoods," on April 11, 1960, *Life* declared Crockett "an epic boaster." *People* on January 12, 1987, ran a photo of Fess Parker with the comment that Crockett "was a flamboyant frontiersman who owed his reputation to his ability to tell tall tales. But there were a few facts that even his prodigious fibbing couldn't hide—that the king of the Wild Frontier was a drunk, a carouser, a less-than-honest politician and Army scout who'd hired someone else to finish his term of enlistment."[18] Popular histories began to follow suit, as did film characterizations. In the 1987 NBC television film *The Alamo: Thirteen Days to Glory*, for example, Brian Keith portrayed Crockett as a kindhearted, boastful, ultimately courageous drunkard.

The Disney Company engaged in revisionism of a different sort when, in the late 1980s, it created a new five-part Davy Crockett series, featuring a sensitive, New Age hero in tune with nature, brave, peace-loving, and humorous in a sincere way. One expected the backwoods stalwart to consult crystals. The audience and critics generally nodded through the episodes, which aired on NBC's *Magical World of Disney* and now periodically appear on the Disney Channel on cable television.

The polar images of the fictional Crockett are the negative and positive of a freeze-frame portrait of a four-dimensional man—fixed and predictable, the way Americans too often demand their heroes, and antiheroes, to be. Crockett the legend is plastic enough to adjust to changing fashion and accommodate himself to those who would make him a guardian of the environment or a wild man weaned on whiskey, a braggart, a "screamer," or "ring-tailed roarer," in the language of the nineteenth-century comic fictions. But Crockett the man hangs trapped between those poles, lost in the nation's ambivalence about its past. He is a victim of a collective inability to determine any longer how to define a brave man, by what actions or standards—those of war and exploitation or of peace and caring. Is it necessary that a hero—or public official—be a saint, free of earthly flaws? The only man or woman who can meet that standard is a one-dimensional character in a poor fiction, boring precisely because he or she is perfect. But how many and what kind of failings are acceptable? Where is the line between human frailty and venality? The answer to those questions can only become clear once the individual is freed from the constraints of ideology and viewed in the context of his or her life, aspirations, and accomplishments.

"Latin Americans" in the Postwar Era, 1945–1960

ARNOLDO DE LEÓN

ARNOLDO DE LEÓN IS C. J. "RED" DAVIDSON PROFESSOR OF HISTORY AT ANGELO STATE UNIVERSITY IN SAN ANGELO. HIS BOOKS INCLUDE *THE TEJANO COMMUNITY, 1836–1900, THEY CALLED THEM GREASERS: ANGLO ATTITUDES TOWARD MEXICANS IN TEXAS, 1821–1900, ETHNICITY IN THE SUNBELT: MEXICAN AMERICANS IN HOUSTON*, AND *MEXICAN AMERICANS IN TEXAS: A BRIEF HISTORY*. DR. DE LEÓN IS ALSO COAUTHOR OF *THE HISTORY OF TEXAS*.

IN THIS SELECTION, DE LEÓN PROVIDES AN OVERVIEW OF TEJANO LIFE AT MIDCENTURY. HE EXAMINES SUCH TOPICS AS POLITICS, SCHOOL DESEGREGATION, LABOR UNIONS, INTELLECTUAL PRODUCTIVITY, AND TEXAS-MEXICAN SOCIETY. MOREOVER, DR. DE LEÓN CONSIDERS THE IMPORTANCE OF TRAILBLAZERS LIKE HENRY B. GONZÁLEZ, RAYMOND TELLES, HECTOR P. GARCÍA, CARLOS E. CASTAÑEDA, AND J. T. CANALES. WHILE TEJANOS MADE IMPORTANT GAINS DURING THIS PERIOD, HE ASSERTS THAT "MUCH REMAINED TO BE ACCOMPLISHED IN THE STRUGGLE FOR EQUALITY."

★ ★

World War II exerted profound influences on the state of Texas. In its wake, the war for democracy produced several years of prosperity as returning veterans and civilian defense workers hastened to spend incomes accumulated during the conflict. Industrialization rode a new wave as oil refining, chemical and petrochemical production, and defense industry plants surged in the 1950s. Cities burgeoned, moreover, as people from rural areas and small communities gravitated toward urban centers. As of 1960, 63.4 percent of the Texas's 9.6 million people made the state's metropolitan counties their place of residence.

On the other hand, some features of the Texas landscape did not change much, at least not until the late 1950s. Politics, for one, retained its conservative bent. On the one hand, many Texas Democrats preferred disassociation with the national party's support for unionism and civil rights, while on the other, Texas Republicans refused to relax their opposition to constitutional liberties and welfare assistance. In race relations, the strength of Jim Crow sentiments led to the passage of several segregationist laws in 1956–1957, and while their purpose was to prop up long-standing discrimination against African Americans, by implication they extended to those of Mexican descent. Meantime, right-wing extremism prevailed as Wisconsin Senator Joseph McCarthy's campaign against Communists at the national level found supporters throughout Texas. Reactionaries demanded the removal of controversial books from libraries, the dismissal of teachers considered too liberal for local standards, and the suppression of left-wing ideas.

Nonetheless, Texas began to take new directions in the postwar era (especially towards the late 1950s) that opened up fresh possibilities for Texas Mexicans. In that period, the old agrarian order long committed to the subordination of Tejanos lost the political advantage to urban commercial interests, farm ownerships made a transformation from individually owned concerns into mechanized corporate entities, and many who had been field hands moved to the cities where industry offered better wages. By the mid–1950s, furthermore, McCarthyism was on the wane, and no longer a political issue handicapping "foreigners" from pursuing the American dream.

TEXAS-MEXICAN SOCIETY AT MIDCENTURY

The interruption in population growth that occurred during the 1930s ended during World War II and the 1950s; the number of Tejanos now increased from about 1,000,000 in 1950 to 1,400,000 in 1960. According to the census of 1960, 86 percent of white persons of Spanish surname in Texas were native born.

Like the rest of the state's population, the Texas-Mexicans in the post–World War II years became more urbanized. During the war, a rural area–to city migration had occurred due to rising occupational prospects and demand for laborers in the new urban industrial sectors, and improved wages in the 1950s persuaded others to relocate. Farm hands were also pushed out of bucolic work by the transformation then underway: new mechanization and improved techniques permitted farmers to produce more without the previous reliance on manual labor. Whereas 57 percent of Texas Mexicans resided in urban areas in 1940, 78 percent of Texas Mexicans did so by the 1950s, and the pattern accelerated thereafter. By 1960, some 30,000 Mexican Americans lived in Dallas, 75,000 in Houston, and 243,000 in San Antonio (by then, only Los Angeles, California, had more Mexicans than the Alamo City). In the 1950s, Texas Mexicans made up 50 percent of El Paso's population.

In their socioeconomic standing, close to 75 percent of Texas-Mexican males remained members of the proletariat. According to the 1950 U.S. census, Tejanos lived on a yearly median income of about $1,000. Anglo Americans at that time made twice that much.

Many Tejano city dwellers faced the same conditions that had vexed their parents and grandparents. These included neglect from city government concerning squalid living conditions, high infant death-rates, and rampant scourges such as tuberculosis, diarrhea, and typhus. The 1950 U.S. census identified 33 percent of urban homes owned or rented by Tejanos in the state as being substandard.

In the rural areas, living conditions for Tejanos were even more bleak. Seasonal work in the cotton fields for which farmers paid around $1.25 per hundredweight (that is, per hundred pounds picked) remained an option for survival, though families participating in the migrant cycle made less than $400 per year during the 1950s. In face of the lean wage rates and competition from Mexican illegals (called "wetbacks" during the era, or *mojados* in Spanish), whose numbers mounted during World War II because of alleged labor shortages in state agriculture, Tejanos took off for the Midwest in hordes. There, lodging in the sugar beet and tomato fields was as primitive as in Texas, though wage rates exceeded those in the home quarters.

Others joined the intrastate migration, either in family units or with troqueros. They responded to the beckonings of farmers for whom they had previously worked, then followed the well-traveled route from South Texas, through the Coastal Bend area, into Central Texas, and then to West Texas. Along the way, they encountered all too familiar problems: having to improvise to find shelter (usually in the fields but more likely beneath the protection of bridges or deserted sheds or chicken coops), entering towns that lacked parking areas for trucks as well as bathing facilities and toilets, and facing inadequate means to battle disease, especially dysentery, due to the poor sanitary measures afforded them. Those who returned to their hometowns (many did not, augmenting Tejano communities along the migrant trail) awaited the new planting and picking seasons by working in whatever jobs became available. The migrant workers' children meantime, tried to obtain schooling for a few months in the spring.

On the other hand, the resilient Tejano middle class continued to be augmented, primarily in the urban sites. The 1940s and 1950s constituted watershed years for Mexicans in terms of opportunities for socioeconomic advancement. In 1950, middle-class categories (professionals, managers, proprietors, clerical, sales, and craftsmen) for men rose to 25 percent, up from the 15 percent reported for 1930.

LABOR MOVEMENTS IN A CONSERVATIVE AGE

Texas-Mexican labor organization declined somewhat in the postwar era. As noted, labor historians consider the era of the 1930s to have been one of acute union activity; that intensity lessened between 1945 and 1960 because of the probusiness sentiments that seemed endemic to the state, apprehension among activists of being branded Communist agitators or labor racketeers and being incarcerated for un-American activities, the many options available to employers to suppress walkouts, and because unions discouraged Tejano workers from membership. In the case of the ILGWU, for instance, the national office showed reluctance to invest money in Texas to organize and train union leaders. The result was more workers in the state's garment factories during the 1950s but a decline in union numbers.

Overall, it appears that the postwar era became one of setbacks in the face of self-organization. In El Paso, the Amalgamated Clothing Workers struck for higher wages that same year, but the company imported Mexican nationals to break the walk-out. In 1948, workers at the Rio Grande Valley Gas Company in Harlingen, Texas, sought to organize a union, but management hired illegal aliens to replace the organizers and their supporters. Then, in 1951, Mexican-American women garment workers belonging to the ILGWU staged a walkout of a Houston plant, but the factory went out of business shortly after. In early 1959, Mexican Americans struck against the Tex-Son Company of San Antonio, which specialized in the making of young men's wear. Beating of strikers ensued, but workers and sympathizers picketed merchants carrying Tex-Son products and appealed to religious groups and fellow unions in San Antonio for assistance. Ultimately replacements and antilabor legislation weakened the job action, and by 1962 the strike had foundered.

POSTWAR POLITICS

Though World War II was very much a watershed in opening up new opportunities for Texas Mexicans, civil rights between 1945 and the late 1950s did not come to Tejanos automatically. With the war's end, white society once again regressed toward old attitudes. One West Texan veteran, for instance, groaned that he and fellow G.I.'s had not fought Hitler to have "ill-smelling Mexicans" now clamor for integration. Public establishments still refused to serve Tejanos, even recently discharged soldiers, among them Medal of Honor winners. White neighborhoods, eating places, picture shows, tonsorial shops, swimming pools, and even hospitals were considered off-limits to Mexican Americans. Throughout the state, police authorities and other law enforcement agencies such as the Border Patrol—an agency of the Immigration and Naturalization Service responsible for keeping immigrants from entering the U.S. illegally—regularly reminded Tejanos of their second-class citizenship through disparagement or intimidation. On the job, a similar retreat from the racial tolerance exhibited during the war years occurred. Employment opportunities for Tejanos diminished quickly. Those who had occupied skilled positions during the war now faced demotion, or even dismissal, while new employees found little available beside unskilled tasks. In South Texas, the press, influential businessmen, and farmers no longer preoccupied themselves with fair-play for Texas Mexicans, and although Governor Coke Stevenson in 1943 created the Good Neighbor Commission to better relations between Texas and both Mexico and Mexican Americans, the agency was staffed by personnel with little commitment to alleviating discrimination.

Politically, Texas Mexicans in the immediate postwar years still had to pay the poll tax and cope with other voting and office-holding restrictions. They were handicapped by the lack of necessary funds to field candidates from their own neighborhoods and had to campaign against Anglos who felt politics to be their exclusive domain. Moreover, bossism still survived at midcentury. In South Texas, businessmen and farmers possessed enough economic power to control the votes. The political condition of Texas Mexicans thus remained at a level only slightly improved since the 1920s, when the Anglo-American domination of the border towns from South Texas to Far West Texas dealt a crushing blow to the Mexican-American presence in public offices.

But a resurgence of Tejanos in politics occurred by the 1950s, as "progressive" Anglo business leaders in the cities stood up to the power of the old guard that dominated the machines. The challengers tried to incorporate middle-class Mexican Americans into local government so as to establish a climate conducive to business expansion. In San Antonio, especially, power brokers by the early 1950s sought to enlist blacks and Mexican Americans for progressive slates, though Tejanos who did win by tacit agreement of these movers and shakers often found it difficult once in office to work effectively for Tejano causes because of their ties to Anglo sponsors. However, in 1956, an independent grass-roots campaign produced the election of Henry B. González to the Texas legislature, making him the first Tejano to serve in the state senate in the twentieth century. Voter registration and a get-out-the-vote campaign in El Paso led to the election in 1957 of Raymond Telles, the city's first Mexican-American mayor. He won reelection two years later without opposition.

Compared to the other sections of the state, South Texas and Far West Texas had produced more prominent civic leaders, been the primary centers of activism in the Tejano community, and generally held an edge on the number of Tejanos in office. Indeed, of the six Tejanos in the state house in 1960, two were from San Antonio, one from El Paso, and the other three from the South Texas border area. At midcentury, therefore, it was still difficult to organize Mexican Americans in the rural counties of West and Northwest Texas due to their physical isolation.

RENEWED STRUGGLES FOR A BETTER LIFE

Out of World War II and the Korean War emerged politically minded Mexican-American veterans who set out on a concentrated course to erase the inequalities that their people faced. The military experience had defined for them the meaning of citizenship and exposed them to the inconsistencies of a country that espoused equality but did not practice it. In San Antonio, therefore, civic leaders took activist stances through organizations such as the Loyal American Democrats, the West Side Voters League, and the Alamo Democrats. Eleuterio Escobar revitalized La Liga Pro-Defensa Escolar in 1947 to again press for equal and adequate educational facilities and more educational opportunities for Mexican-American children.

Also organized in San Antonio that year by business and professional men was the Pan American Progressive Association (PAPA). As a nonpartisan entity, it sought ways in which to improve the lives of the Mexican-descent population of the city, including the integration of residential areas in San Antonio. But PAPA's life appears not to have extended beyond the early 1950s.

In Corpus Christi, World War II veteran Dr. Hector P. García in 1948 founded what evolved into the most vigorous advocacy organization of the postwar, the American G.I. Forum. Originally established in an effort to expedite federal benefits for Mexican-American ex-servicemen, the G.I. Forum attained a new standing in 1949 with the famous Félix Longoria affair at Three Rivers, Texas. When the local funeral home refused to hold services for Longoria, a slain World War II soldier, Dr. García publicized the incident—which gained nationwide attention—as one more example of entrenched racial intolerance in the rural regions of South Texas. Through the intervention of Senator Lyndon B. Johnson of Texas, Longoria's remains were interred at Arlington National Cemetery.

The courageous stand that the G.I. Forum took on the incident vaulted the group into the role of spokesperson for disadvantaged Mexican Americans. G.I. Forum chapters from across the state now united with LULAC councils to press for sociopolitical advances. Involved in these struggles were leaders from the 1930s and World War II years, among them Alonso Perales, M. C. Gonzales, J. T. Canales, James Tafolla, George I. Sánchez, and Carlos E. Castañeda. But joining them in the era between 1945 and 1960 (and after for that matter), were Gus García, Ed Idar, Cristobal Alderete, John J. Herrera, and of course, Dr. García.

Also part of this activist cadre were women from the two organizations. Representatives of Ladies G.I. Forum Auxiliaries and Ladies LULAC Councils engaged in programs established to: buy milk tickets for children whose parents suffered from tuberculosis; purchase glasses for needy students; distribute toys to the poor at Christmas time; raise funds to provide clothing for children in hospitals; and donate money to the March of Dimes and the Polio Drive. Alongside men, women helped back Little League baseball clubs to aid adolescents in acquiring a positive attitude for themselves; they worked in poll-tax-raising drives and rallies and were often the prime figures in the establishment of new councils throughout the country by spearheading efforts to integrate public accommodations and voice the concerns of Mexican-American women. Many gained recognition within their respective organizations as exemplary models of commitment to the cause of Mexican-American rights.

SCHOOL DESEGREGATION EFFORTS

For years, activists had noted the lack of education for Tejanos as the major stumbling block towards the people's progress. The presence of inferior "Mexican schools," especially, stigmatized children as being less than full-fledged citizens, hindered their ability to learn the English language, and impeded their participation in matters relevant to the community. Because middle-class leaders understood schooling to be a gateway to social betterment, they sponsored efforts to educate Tejano children by means that included back-to-school drives, public service announcements over radio, community rallies, teenage hops, and king and queen balls.

The middle-class leaders also undertook legal measures, according to historian Guadalupe San Miguel's study of the Texas-Mexican campaign for educational equality. Following World War II (before the founding of the G.I. Forum), LULAC took the lead in seeking legal reversals to educational wrongs. In California, the League contested the pattern of segregation in *Méndez* v. *Westminster School District* (1945), and the subsequent ruling by the Ninth Federal District Court in Los Angeles—that segregation of Mexican-American children indeed infringed on guarantees made by the Fourteenth Amendment—had inspired the drive to desegregate schools in the Lone Star State. Therefore, in January 1948, Minerva Delgado and several parents in Central Texas, counseled by LULAC, alleged that school segregation in the region was in breach of the Constitution. Soon after, the G.I. Forum closed ranks behind LULAC with moral support and financial contributions garnered from across the state. In *Delgado* v. *Bastrop ISD* (1948), a district court agreed with the aggrieved plaintiffs, declaring that separating students in different buildings violated the law.

Despite this legal pronouncement and supportive regulations issued by the state superintendent of public instruction to integrate, most school districts generally overlooked the *Delgado* decision. Undaunted, Mexican-American leaders took other segregation cases to court, including the significant *Hernández* v. *Driscoll Consolidated Independent School District* (1957). In their complaint, LULAC and the G.I. Forum argued that the segregation of Mexican-American children in the first two grades and their subsequent detention at that level for a total of four years was an unreasonable practice predicated on notions about race or ancestry. In January 1957, a federal district court agreed with the charge. Despite such significant victories, school districts devised ways of evading court orders. These included gerrymandering districts (dividing districts unfairly to insure segregation), building schools for specific neighborhoods, and offering freedom-of-choice plans that allowed Anglos to select the school they preferred to have their children attend.

The commitment to educational matters produced, in 1957, what came to be known as the "Little Schools of the 400." The brainchild of National LULAC President Félix Tijerina, the program, first implemented in Ganado, Texas, by seventeen-year-old Isabel Verver, sought to have preschool Tejanos learn four hundred English key words and phrases that would allow them to succeed in their first year in school. Implemented initially in Jackson County, the project proved so popular by 1958 that the Houston entrepreneur enacted similar programs in other parts of the state and gained the endorsement of Price Daniel, the governor of Texas. The next year, the state legislature funded Tijerina-type schools to the tune of $1,300,000. The concept of the "Little Schools of the 400" survived into the 1960s, though budget cutting undermined it by the middle of that decade. The federal government, however, later modeled its Head Start program on Tijerina's creation.

Hernández v. Texas

LULAC and the G.I. Forum also joined forces to have Mexican Americans recognized as a *class* whose rights Texans transgressed. To this end, Gus García took the case (with the assistance of attorneys John J. Hererra and James de Anda) of Pete Hernández, who had been accused of murdering Joe Espinosa in Edna, Texas, in 1950. In his motion against the state, García contended that the omission of Mexican Americans from jury service in Jackson County violated their right as a *class* to equal protection under the law. Hernández was tried nonetheless, and the jury rendered a guilty verdict and condemned him to life imprisonment.

The United States Supreme Court agreed to hear *Hernández* v. *State of Texas* and LULAC and the G.I. Forum members supplied the needed funds for the attorneys' Washington stay. In May 1954, the high court agreed unanimously that Texas laws that discriminated ostensibly on the basis of *class* (or against "other whites," such as Mexicans) did in fact defy the rights and assurance granted by the Constitution. Hernández was retried and again found guilty (though given a lesser sentence), but the Supreme Court's decision was far-reaching as it acknowledged that Tejanos (to whom Jim Crow laws did not ostensibly apply) had long been the victim of discriminatory treatment. The verdict did not change race relations in Texas immediately, but future generations of Tejanos would profit from its implications.

The ACSSP

In the background of such efforts to protect the legal rights of Mexican Americans in the United States existed an organization recently rediscovered by the historian Ricardo Romo called the American Council of Spanish-Speaking People (ACSSP). Founded in 1951 by the educator George I. Sánchez, ACSSP pursued litigation in the area of civil rights and assisted sister civic action groups in other parts of the United States. With monies received from the American Civil Liberties Union, it financed several civil rights cases during its brief period of existence, among them *Hernández* v. *State of Texas* (1954) and *Hernández* v. *Driscoll Consolidated Independent School District* (1957). By the late 1950s, however, the ACSSP faced decline as Sánchez and other members of the Council found less time to dedicate to the organization and funds became more difficult to acquire. In 1959, the ACSSP passed into history, having set an example as a courageous attempt to utilize the legal system as a recourse for redress on behalf of Spanish-speaking Americans.

Los Del Otro Lado

In seeking to improve the lives of Mexican Americans after World War II, both LULAC and the G.I. Forum resisted what Tejanos of the era referred to as the "Wetback Problem." In the eyes of these organizations, the presence of *braceros* (day laborers from Mexico brought to the U.S. on contract) and "wetbacks" cheapened wages for Texas-Mexican residents, supplanted them from agricultural jobs, intensified health problems in the colonias, and generally gave "Latin Americans" (the preferred self-referent used by Mexican-American leaders circa the 1930s to the 1950s to combat the image held by Anglos that Tejanos were not "Americans") a bad name. The braceros were part of an official labor agreement negotiated between the United States and Mexico during the war years to provide field hands for United States farm estates facing labor shortages. Although Mexico had banned the movement of braceros into Texas because of the state's well-known racism, it relented in 1947 and removed Texas from the "blacklist." Illegal entrants ("wetbacks"), on the other hand, had arrived in Texas after 1942 in response to the state's great demand for farm workers and continued to be preferred by growers as they could be hired without bureaucratic interference and could be easily exploited by avaricious farm managers.

To combat the "Wetback Problem," the G.I. Forum and LULAC lobbied to extradite illegals, to terminate the bracero program, and to have the border better patrolled in order to halt unauthorized crossings into Texas. In 1953, the G.I. Forum published an investigative report titled *What Price Wetbacks?* as part of its ongoing efforts to combat the presence of undocumented workers. The pamphlet illuminated the exploitation of wetback labor and explained the effects these laborers had upon health standards in border communities. The survey further faulted law authorities for a lax enforcement of the immigration statutes.

Politicians seemed indifferent to the Forum's concerns (preferring to ignore the issue because it helped the nation's growers maintain a supply of cheap labor), but the public ultimately became alarmed over the "wetback menace." With popular support, therefore, the Immigration and Naturalization Service in July 1954, ventured upon a widesweeping campaign called "Operation Wetback." In corroboration with local and federal authorities, the Border Patrol mounted raids into the rural areas of Texas to arrest illegals and evict them to Mexico. The drives affected many American citizens of Mexican descent who witnessed close relatives forcibly repatriated. The American G.I. Forum and LULAC both countenanced the project, though they did make attempts to insure that the rights of the Texas-Mexican citizens were respected. But their stand caused friction within the ranks of the Tejano community, leading many to question the sensitivity of the Forumeers, LULACers, and other supporters of the xenophobic campaigns.

ACADEMICIANS AND WRITERS

Previous generations of Texas Mexicans had contributed to a literary past, some in English, some in Spanish. Juan Seguín and José Antonio Navarro had both left memoirs, and a small number of Tejanos had also penned autobiographies. Lay historians had put together informal histories to note the role Tejanos played in the Texas saga. Other writers had dealt with ongoing concerns of importance to the Tejano community. Spanish-language newspapers regularly printed creative literature, and Tejano authors of fiction had published through other outlets.

In the postwar era, academicians, intellectuals, and others with a talent for composition added to that literary record. Noteworthy writers include historians, the most renowned being Dr. Carlos E. Castañeda. A professor of history at the University of Texas until his death in 1957, Castañeda wrote numerous works during the period between the Great Depression and the 1950s that sought to explain the Spanish/Mexican contribution to Texas history, among them the now classic, seven volume study, *Our Catholic Heritage* (7 vols; Austin: Von Boeckmann-Jones, Co., 1936–1958). His lifetime bibliography of twelve books and seventy-eight articles contributed to Texas and borderlands scholarship by identifying the debt American history owed to Spain and Mexico.

Dr. Américo Paredes, a University of Texas folklore teacher, writer, and poet educated in the Brownsville schools, in 1958 published *"With His Pistol in His Hand": A Border Ballad and Its Hero* (Austin: University of Texas, 1958), a book studying the kinship between the corrido and the real historical events surrounding the episode of Gregorio Cortéz. The lay historian Mercurio Martínez coauthored *The Kingdom of Zapata* (San Antonio: The Naylor Co., 1953), and Cleofas Calleros in numerous pieces preserved the history of Spaniards and Mexicans in the El Paso Valley.

New Mexico-born-and-educated George I. Sánchez, who taught in the Department of History and Philosophy of Education at the University of Texas from 1940 to 1972 (when he passed away), authored or edited some fifty books, monographs, and special reports as well as some eighty articles, many of which dealt with his deep concern with the quality of education for Mexican-American students. As a graduate school professor at the University of Texas, Sánchez directed in excess of sixty-five Master's theses and twenty-eight doctoral dissertations, and he taught as a visiting professor in universities both in the United States and overseas.

In the early 1930s, Jovita González became one of the first Mexican Americans to publish English-language translations of traditional Tejano storytelling, submitting articles to various scholarly outlets, including the yearly publications of the prestigious Texas Folklore Society. She continued to write sketches, short stories, and poems during the 1950s.

Activists also contributed to the literature issued during the period. J. T. Canales, the former legislator from Brownsville, authored several essays between 1930 and 1945 on behalf of civil rights causes, then in 1945 reminisced in "Personal Recollections of J. T. Canales." He produced other historical pieces after 1945, among them *Bits of Texas History in the Melting Pot of America* (2 vols; Brownsville: privately printed, 1950, 1957) as well as titles on his kin Juan Cortina, among them *Juan N. Cortina Presents His Motion for a New Trial* (San Antonio: Artes Gráficas, 1951). Alonso Perales, the LULAC activist, published *El méxico americano y la politica de sur de Tejas* (San Antonio: Artes Gráficas, 1931) and *En defensa de mi raza* (San Antonio: Artes Gráficas, 1936 and 1937) to highlight the political disadvantages of Tejanos in South Texas. In 1948, he compiled a volume of statements on discrimination and published them in *Are We Good Neighbors?* (San Antonio: Artes Gráficas, 1948).

THE END OF AN ERA

From 1945 to 1960, Texas Mexicans continued to experience oppression and exploitation, most severely in the rural regions in which racial attitudes relegated Tejanos to a second-class status. But circumstances in the late 1950s for Texas Mexicans no longer resembled those of the 1940s. Within the community, for one, improved familiarity with American mainstream life offered more promise. While Tejano society had command of the Spanish language, observed Mexico's national holidays, and enjoyed Mexican music and other traditions of the motherland, a number of factors strengthened their attachment to United States institutions: World War II had acquainted Tejano veterans with an Anglo-American world they had previously known only vicariously; the G.I. Bill of Rights had proved instrumental in the education of many ex-servicemen, compulsory-school attendance laws came to be more strictly enforced, and the consumer culture of the era seduced the multitudes, many of whom had been United States born and knew no other than American life. Continued cultural syncretization improved Tejanos' chances to capitalize on the age's new opportunities.

Meanwhile, de facto Jim Crow traditions for Texas Mexicans in the urban areas faced new threats due to the increasing influence of Mexican-American leaders and their sympathizers in the NAACP and labor unions as well as to initiatives undertaken by government and the courts to integrate public education and juries. By the late 1950s, political circumstances themselves conspired to weaken racism against Tejanos. The liberal wing of the Democratic party experienced a resurgence, and members of the Congress such as Lyndon Baines Johnson and Ralph Yarborough did not look upon Jim Crow as an appropriate system for the modern age. In Austin, legislators such as Henry B. González and Abraham Kazen initiated campaigns to overturn segregation. As the decade closed, however, much remained to be accomplished in the struggle for equality. The 1960s and 1970s would see newer approaches in the campaign to achieve those ends.

Buddy Holly and the Fifties: The Birth of Texas Rock

RICK KOSTER

JOURNALIST AND SCHOLAR RICK KOSTER IS THE AUTHOR OF *LOUISIANA MUSIC* AND *TEXAS MUSIC*.

IN THIS SELECTION, KOSTER DISCUSSES THE HIGHLY INFLUENTIAL, BUT TRAGICALLY BRIEF, CAREER OF LUBBOCK DENIZEN AND ROCK 'N' ROLL PIONEER BUDDY HOLLY. KILLED IN A 1959 PLANE CRASH, HOLLY RECORDED A NUMBER OF CLASSICS, INCLUDING "THAT'LL BE THE DAY," "PEGGY SUE," AND "RAVE ON." KOSTER ALSO CONSIDERS SUCH LONE STAR "ROCK FRONTIERSMEN" AS THE BIG BOPPER (WHO LOST HIS LIFE WITH HOLLY), ROY ORBISON, BOBBY DAY, JESSE BELVIN, MAC CURTIS, AND GENE SUMMERS.

★ ★

A cynic might say that rock 'n' roll is what happened when a white guy decided he would play black rhythm and blues—which was in fact the case when Bill Haley and the Saddlemen covered Jackie Brenston's "Rocket 88" in 1951.

Though the phrase "rock 'n' roll" had long been utilized in blues songs as a euphemism for protracted bouts of "the nasty," and references to "rockin' " had cropped up in precisely those

R&B recordings Haley sought to emulate (Roy Brown's 1948 tune "Good Rockin' Tonight," for example), it wasn't until Haley and the Saddlemen sold 75,000 copies of "Rock This Joint" that a fevered thirst for rock 'n' roll began to grow in white America. And when the Saddlemen recorded "Crazy Man Crazy" in 1953, and it became the first rock song to make the *Billboard* charts, the whole concept was about to become a phenomenon.

The Saddlemen would change their name to the Comets and score several rapid-fire hits, including, of course, "Rock Around the Clock," but fate decreed that Elvis Presley would become the first real rock star. Haley, despite his record sales, was a dumpy, balding guy relegated to metaphorical mop-up duties; if Elvis was the king of rock 'n' roll, Haley was, perhaps, the janitor. It was a situation that would haunt Haley throughout his ever-dwindling career. He relocated to Harlingen, Texas, and though he continued to sell records and perform on nostalgia tours and has-been packages, he eventually grew bitter and drank heavily. Toward the end of his life he was diagnosed with a brain tumor, his behavior became erratic and delusional, and he finally succumbed to a heart attack in 1981 at the age of fifty-five.

Back at the dawn of rock, however, between Elvis's penthouse and Haley's boiler room, there was plenty of opportunity for would-be rock stars, and Lubbock's Buddy Holly would soon fit the bill in a shimmering way. Born Charles Hardin Holley in 1938, he studied violin and piano at an early age, but switched at seven to guitar, inspired by the sounds of Jimmie Rodgers, Hank Williams, and a variety of country and gospel radio.

He formed a high school band, the Western and Bop Band (with Bob Montgomery and Larry Welborn), which nabbed a half-hour Sunday afternoon radio show on local station KDAV, on which they were Richie Buddy and Bob. Welborn was replaced with Don Guess, and in 1956, they signed the band, now called the Three Tunes, as a country act (a misspelling in the contract resulted in Buddy's more familiar "Holly" surname).

A few singles were released, including an early version of "That'll Be the Day," but country radio yawned. It was just as well; the C&W concept became an afterthought in Holly's mind after the Three Tunes opened a show for Elvis at the Lubbock Youth Center.

Holly immediately wanted to rock. He formed the Crickets with drummer Larry Allison, guitarist Niki Sullivan, and bassist Joe Maudlin, and with that alliance two major rock precedents were established: The now-accepted two guitars/bass/drums format came into being, and Holly began to write his own material.

Decca wasn't impressed with Holly's new visions, though, and after fruitless sessions in Nashville with noted producer Owen Bradley, the band returned to Lubbock. In early 1957, Buddy Holly and the Crickets drove to nearby Clovis, New Mexico, to the studios of producer/songwriter Norman Petty, where they cut a rock arrangement of "That'll Be the Day" and several other tunes.

Petty signed on as Holly's manager, and the new tracks convinced Decca that Holly had more possibilities as a rock artist. A subsequent meeting with all concerned resulted in a unique and complicated marketing strategy: Holly would record as a solo artist for Decca's Coral subsidiary and as the front man for the Crickets on another Decca label, Brunswick.

The blueprint worked. "That'll Be the Day" was a number 3 hit for Holly, while the follow-up, "Peggy Sue," credited to the Crickets, sold over a million units and necessitated the band's first national tour. By 1958, they'd charted "Oh, Boy!," "Maybe Baby," "Think It Over," "Early in the Morning," "Rave On," and "Fool's Paradise," and had toured England to the appreciation of fans like John Lennon, Paul McCartney, and Eric Clapton—all of whom would go on to own several houses as a result of their Holly-inspired attempts at songcraft.

There was a reason for Holly's appeal. Think of him as a savory, multilayered musical lasagna, served up in magnificent, two-minute explosions of hum-along genius. In every tune was the charm of Holly's TV weatherman appearance, the life-is-a-perennial-sock-hop theme, a gentle confidence that attracted rather than repelled, and the buoyant image of his genuine performance enthusiasm.

In fact, it is probable that Holly would have curried favor indefinitely with the burgeoning rock audience. But in October 1958, upset at discovering Norman Petty's name listed as cowriter on several of his songs, Holly split from Petty and the Crickets and moved to Greenwich Village, where he married Maria Elena Santiago. Holly did some recording in New York, but, in financial limbo over the managerial imbroglio, Holly agreed to go out on a Winter Dance Party Tour of the Midwest in early 1959.

Performing with Holly on the tour were ex-Cricket guitarist Tommy Allsup and Waylon Jennings. Weary of bus travel, Holly and some of the other featured performers in the show, Richie Valens and J. P. "The Big Bopper" Richardson, chartered a plane after the Clear Lake, Iowa, concert. In an event immortalized years later in Don McClean's "American Pie" as "the day the music died," the plane crashed a few minutes after takeoff, killing all aboard.

As with any popular musician who dies prematurely, Holly's legacy of demo tapes, unfinished studio tracks, and former bandmates all popped up for commercial consumption in a variety of cobweb configurations. At the time of his death, "It Doesn't Matter Anymore" was released, and *The Complete Buddy Holly Story*, a nine-record set, and the 1978 film *The Buddy Holly Story* pretty much covered the territory.

The Crickets, with a variety of personnel changes, played on into the sixties, and two, Larry Allison and Sonny Curtis (who joined up after Holly's death), had moderate solo success.

One of the victims in the crash that killed Holly was J. P. Richardson, another Texan, who was born in Sabine Pass in 1932. A career disc jockey who started as "The Big Bopper" at Beaumont's KTRM just out of high school, Richardson became one of the region's most popular radio personalities.

Weaned in the mid-fifties from his early C&W predilections to the rockabilly of Elvis and Jerry Lee Lewis, Richardson's secret ambition was to be a pop hero. He began assimilating demos of songs he'd started writing during a brief stint in the army and, by 1957, had enough interesting material that he attracted the attention of Mercury's Shelby Singleton, who signed Richardson along with fellow Texans Johnny Preston and Bruce Channel.

Richardson cut two straight country singles under his own name, then, as the Big Bopper, released a novelty record he'd written called "The Purple People Eater Meets the Witch Doctor." It was the B-side of the disc, though, a rockabilly original called "Chantilly Lace," that became an international hit.

In 1957–58, the Big Bopper had other hits with his own compositions, including "Running Bear," "Little Red Riding Hood," and "Big Bopper's Wedding," though he wouldn't live long enough to see Johnny Preston score a number 1 hit with "Running Bear" in 1960.

Richardson, meanwhile, developed a stage show based on the Bopper persona, and became a popular attraction on a number of traveling rock packages. It was on one such tour that, feeling ill and not up to a long bus ride, the Big Bopper begged a seat on the plane carrying Holly and Richie Valens.

* * *

If the Big Bopper's potential as a writer was never sufficiently developed to have indicated precisely what his future held another Texan emerged in the fifties with incredible writing potential, and the transcendent voice of a playful angel: Roy Orbison.

Born in Vernon, Texas, in 1936, Orbison received a guitar for his sixth birthday. By eight, he had secured a regular Saturday morning slot on KVWC's *Amateur Hour* and, within two years, was hosting the program.

After his family moved to the West Texas oasis of Wink, Orbison played in a high school band called the Wink Westerners, a self-described western swing outfit that in fact played everything from Webb Pierce to "Moonlight in Vermont."

The Westerners metamorphosed into the Teen Kings, an outfit that attained the lofty status of local television celebrities. In 1955, Orbison utilized that fame to get backstage at Fort Worth's Panther Hall to meet Elvis Presley. But it wasn't until he became pals with Pat Boone, while they were both students at North Texas State University, in Denton, that Orbison started to make the musical transformations that would lead to massive success.

Boone, already a pop star on the Dot label, encouraged Orbison to experiment more with the rock and rockabilly sounds emanating from Sam Phillips's Sun Studios in Memphis, home to Elvis, Carl Perkins, Jerry Lee Lewis, and Johnny Cash. This wasn't the first time Sun had been mentioned to Orbison. Cash had already recommended Orbison to Sam Phillips after the two singers appeared on a regional TV show together. Though Phillips didn't act at the time, Orbison's name stayed with him.

After backing Boone as a rhythm guitarist on a studio date, Orbison himself received a chance to record with Norman Petty at the very same Clovis, New Mexico studio that had launched Buddy Holly.

Now billed as Roy Orbison and the Teen Kings, they recorded "Ooby Dooby," a quasi-rockabilly tune from their repertoire written by a duo of NTSU upperclassmen named Dick Penner and

Wade Moore. A friend of Orbison's, an Odessa record store owner named Cecil Hollerfield, knew Sam Phillips from the early days of Sun, and entreated him to give "Ooby Dooby" a listen.

This time Phillips was impressed, and "Ooby Dooby" sold three hundred thousand copies when released in 1956. Orbison relocated to Nashville, became pals with Elvis (who talked him into buying a Cadillac with his first Sun royalty check), and, in addition to his Sun contract, signed to write songs for Acuff-Rose publishing. One of his first attempts, a tune he wrote for his wife called "Claudette" (which was appropriate since that was her name), became a big seller for the Everly Brothers. But while his reputation as a writer grew, his recording relationship with Sun proved less than fruitful, and in 1959 Orbison moved over to Monument Records. His career as a rockabilly artist was effectively over, but that was okay; he was about to become a spectacularly successful pop star.

* * *

There were, naturally, other Texans active in the blossoming rock 'n' roll scene. The Champs, a group of West Coast session men recording on the Challenge label, included Rankin's Chuck Rio on sax, Sidney's Jim Seals on guitar, and Cisco's Dash Crofts on guitar and mandolin. Their 1958 instrumental, "Tequila," hit number 1, sold over six million copies, and won a Grammy award. The band charted several more songs into the early sixties, but none matched the success of "Tequila." Seals and Crofts went on to form the Dawnbreakers and, of course, in the seventies, had terrific success as the cash-generating soft-rock duo.

Fort Worth's Robert Byrd achieved brief success working under the nom de rock Bobby Day. Though he worked with Johnny Otis, Day is most famous for his 1958 song "Rockin' Robin," which he recorded for Class Records and which went to number 2 on the charts. Day also released "Little Bitty Pretty One" for Class, and as lead singer with the Hollywood Flames, a top twenty hit with "Buzz Buzz Buzz." Day's "Over and Over" would be a number 1 seller for Brits the Dave Clark Five in 1965.

Ray Peterson, who was from Denton, had an Orbison-like four-and-a-half-octave vocal range and a similar affection for ballads. After singing to amuse fellow polio patients in the Warm Springs Foundation Hospital, Peterson started working in clubs and eventually relocated to the West Coast. RCA signed him in 1958 and released "Let's Try Romance." A few similarly indifferent singles followed, but Peterson scored big with a 1959 version of Baker Knight's "The Wonder of It All." A string of hits followed, including "Tell Laura I Love Her" (1960) and "Corinna, Corinna" (1961).

Two other panhandle musicians followed in Buddy Holly's golden footsteps. Buddy Knox and Jimmy Bowen (from Canyon and Dumas, respectively) formed Buddy Knox and the Rhythm Orchids and, in 1956, entered Norman Petty's Clovis studio. In a session memorable for Petty's use of a cardboard box instead of a drum kit (the better to deal with the infernal noise of an actual kit), they cut Knox's "Party Doll" and Bowen's "I'm Stickin' with You." Originally issued back-to-back on the same local single, both tunes were released separately on New York's Roulette—and sold over a million copies each.

Jesse Belvin, from San Antonio, was a singer/songwriter who had a studio Jones that considerably predated Brian Wilson. He cowrote "Earth Angel," which was a 1955 hit for the Penguins, and in 1956 recorded four separate vocal tracks to create the illusion of a band. He called his "group" the Cliques, and the song, "Girl of My Dreams," sold respectably. He also scored with "Good Night, My Love," but his incredible potential was snuffed out in an auto accident which also killed his wife.

Rockabilly, the potent cocktail mixing country and blues that started it all had its proponents long after the defections of Holly and Orbison. Most notable were Ronnie Dawson and Sid King and the Five Strings. Dawson, born in Dallas in 1939, was a teen star who released his first single in his early teens, "Action Packed" backed with "I Make the Love" on the regional Backbeat label. Known as the Blond Bomber, the youngster had a bigger hit with "Rockin' Bones," on Rockin' Records. Both singles sold well enough to attract the attention of Dick Clark. Clark called to offer a contract with his Swan Records as well as an appearance on *American Bandstand*, but the payola scandals rocked the record industry and stalled Dawson's career—temporarily.

Sid King was born Sidney Erwin in Denton in 1936. His early musical years were steeped in country, and he led a band called the Western Melodymakers. But as rockabilly became a force, King changed the name of his band to the Five Strings and moved into the new territory.

A 1954 single for Starday, "Who Put the Turtle in Myrtle's Girdle," drew the attention of Columbia Records, and the Five Strings signed a contract. Though they released several sides for the next half-decade, it was as live performers in Europe that the Five Strings really held court. Rockabilly was huge overseas, and King and company toured for years on the strength of their driving rhythms. Sid's brother, Billy, the band's lead guitarist, was a terrific influence on rockabilly guitarists, and in his own home state made a huge impression on no less than Ronnie Dawson and the Reverend Horton Heat.

Both brothers continue to tour Europe periodically, and there are plans for a CD of old and new material, but, they pay the bills cutting hair in their Cutting Shop in the Dallas suburb of Richardson—which is also a virtual museum of rockabilly. Plus, you can get one of those really cool fifties haircuts from the guys who actually pioneered the look.

Two other north Texas rock frontiersmen still crank it out: Fort Worth's Mac Curtis and Dallas's Gene Summers. Curtis was a wee sixteen when he signed a rockabilly contract with King Records, for whom he released three singles. He also appeared on Alan Freed's *Rock 'n' Roll Revue* at the Paramount Theater in New York before halting his career with a three-year military stint. Post-army, Curtis worked as a broadcaster before relocating to L.A, in 1971, where he jump-started his career by signing with the Rollin' Rock label. As with many of these performers, Curtis's records continued to do brisk business in rockabilly-happy Europe, and he's continued to play overseas regularly. Recently, Hightone Records has released *Rockabilly Uprising: The Best of Mac Curtis*, a more-than-worthy CD documenting Curtis's ever-youthful spirit.

Summers, who was also infected with the new virus called rock 'n' roll, formed bands out of high school and was soon appearing in a variety of North Texas clubs in support of Chuck Berry, Gene Vincent, Connie Francis, and several other burgeoning stars. He also recorded numerous local sides, including 1963's "Big Blue Diamonds," which hit the national charts. Continually active throughout the sixties and seventies, Summers also became the subject of an intense revival in Europe, where he continues to perform systematically. He's released dozens of albums for dozens of domestic and foreign labels, including a new compilation scheduled for release by Dallas's Crystal Clear Sound.

In any case, as the decade drew to a close, Roy Orbison was about to become an international voice to be reckoned with. And in the shadow of Buddy Holly's death, it was not yet possible to see the gathering tide that would betoken the very British invasion he helped inspire.

Sam Rayburn

D. CLAYTON BROWN

D. CLAYTON BROWN IS PROFESSOR OF HISTORY AT TEXAS CHRISTIAN UNIVERSITY IN FORT WORTH. HE IS THE AUTHOR OF *ELECTRICITY FOR RURAL AMERICA: THE FIGHT FOR THE REA* AND *GLOBALIZATION AND AMERICA SINCE 1945*.

TEXAN SAM RAYBURN (1882–1961) STANDS AS ONE OF THE NATION'S EMINENT LEGISLATIVE LEADERS. KNOWN POPULARLY AS "MR. SAM," HE SERVED AS SPEAKER OF THE U.S. HOUSE LONGER THAN ANY OTHER INDIVIDUAL. HARRY TRUMAN PRAISED RAYBURN AS "ONE OF THE GREATEST AND MOST RESPECTED STATESMEN WHO EVER LIVED." IN THIS SELECTION, DR. BROWN EXAMINES THE LIFE AND CAREER OF THIS DISTINGUISHED DEMOCRATIC POLITICIAN.

★ ★

When Sam Rayburn died on November 16, 1961, the world knew it had lost a great leader. "Sam Rayburn . . . was the greatest of the great Speakers of the House of Representatives," wrote Harry Truman. "He was the second most powerful person in the United States Government. It is my opinion that Sam Rayburn was one of the greatest and most respected Statesmen who ever lived." Eleanor Roosevelt wrote: "He was one of the finest Speakers and Representatives. My husband at all times had great respect and affection for him." These statements of eloquence refer

"Sam Rayburn" by D. Clayton Brown from *Profiles in Power: Twentieth Century Texans in Washington* edited by Kenneth E. Hendrickson, Jr. and Michael Collins, 1993. Reprinted by permission of D. Clayton Brown, Professor of History, Texas Christian University.

to the political side of Mr. Sam's life, a life that began in the Texas House of Representatives when he was twenty-five and continued until his death at age seventy-nine. Other statements made at the time of his death had a more personal tone. Montana Senator Mike Mansfield wrote: "I feel that I have lost both a father and a brother, but I know that the nation's loss is greater still. He is the last of the old frontiersmen." And from former President Dwight Eisenhower came this short and poignant phrase: "As his friend of many years, I mourn his passing." Journalist Eric Sevareid combined the political and personal nature of Rayburn when he said: "He was the salt, soil and substance of our political system and inheritance. We shall not see his like again in the Speaker's chair, for the old ways, the old image of America are going as the old men go."

This last statement referred to the value system that was so much a part of Rayburn's personality. The longest serving Speaker of the House came from common stock, the class of American yeomen synonymous with self-sufficient farmers whose lifeblood was the soil. The Rayburn class, like generations of pioneer stock preceding them, lived close to nature and the earth, and as was the case of an America of bygone days, they depended on one another and developed a sense of fair play. These people believed in trust and honesty, explaining the pioneer belief that a man was only as "good as his word."

Rayburn, born in 1882 in Tennessee, moved with his family to the high-yield cotton growing area of Northeast Texas in 1887 and settled near the town of Flag Springs. Sam was one of eleven children. Though the family scraped for every dollar, it should not be assumed that the Rayburns were poor. In the agrarian environment in which they lived cash was scarce for nearly all. "We were short of money," Rayburn once recalled, "but we had a comfortable home, plenty to eat. My father couldn't put us all through college, but most of us went anyway." As a boy Sam learned to be resourceful, not to settle for less, and to be ready to make the sacrifices required to achieve a goal. His long days spent working the cotton rows alongside his father and brothers, his observance of the rotation of the year's seasons, and seeing new life come forth each spring gave him patience and taught him that hard labor would, over time, bear fruit. But in this environment of hardship, an environment in which baptisms were conducted in a pond or creek, the young Rayburn learned that money and material wealth were not always labor's reward. Instead one's compensation might be a modest life filled with contentment and satisfaction, or one of public service, as long as it was a life filled with respect for one's self and others. Around the rural town squares of Rayburn's youth, men and women who held this southern agrarian value system were plentiful.

Rayburn's personality at all stages of his career reflected this background. His friends always described him as hard-working, patient, and steadfast to his word. His personal life and business conduct were said to be simple, but he ran the House of Representatives, by everyone's assessment, out of his hip pocket. His refusal to keep notes was famous, and he always explained that when a man was honest he didn't need to worry about what he said. The "Rayburnisms," short quips of personal philosophy, were part of his mode of operation. They included: "Any fellow who will cheat for you will cheat against you;" "Any jackass can kick a barn down, but it takes a carpenter to build it," and his most repeated Rayburnism, "If a man has good common sense, he has about all the sense there is." Such views of life were once heard throughout rural America, and they endeared Rayburn to his friends and won him respect around the world. At the peak of his power, when he was regarded as second in power only to the president of the United States, he was admiringly and simply called "Mr. Sam."

Rayburn's adult life prior to becoming a member of Congress had both common and uncommon features. In 1900, when he was eighteen years old, he left home in order to attend Mayo Normal College at Commerce, Texas, where he worked as a janitor, dairy-hand and at other odd jobs to pay his tuition. Financial strains forced him to leave Mayo and to teach school for awhile, but he finished the curriculum at Mayo in time to graduate with his class. He returned to teaching in small country schools, but in 1906 he left teaching in order to enter politics. The Texas House of Representatives was his first political goal, and that year he was elected to represent Fannin County.

Only twenty-four years old when he took the oath of office as a Texas legislator, Rayburn kept a low profile during his first year. He entered the University of Texas law school in Austin to take a special three-month review class which proved to be sufficient preparation for Rayburn to pass the state bar exam. During his second term Rayburn chaired two committees and served on four others. Well liked and highly respected, Rayburn was elected Speaker of the Texas House during his third term, an amazing feat for such a young man. His one term as the Texas Speaker was not particularly eventful, but he was remembered as a party loyalist who still managed to be fair and impartial. Rayburn himself said that he had enjoyed being Texas Speaker more than he had enjoyed holding any other public office.

The young Texan's move to Washington, D.C., occurred in 1912 when he was elected to represent Texas's Fourth Congressional District. In a race of eight candidates, Rayburn won by 493 votes over his closest rival. During his campaign he pointed to his clean record in the Texas House and freedom from special interests. He championed lower tariffs, the need for inheritance and income taxes, electoral reform, and the right of workingmen to organize. These issues were popular in 1912, as evidenced by their presence in the platform of the Progressive party, led by Theodore Roosevelt. Rayburn's goal to reach Washington was well known by his friends in Austin, and his decision to run came as no surprise.

Thus at the age of thirty-one, unmarried and free of family responsibilities, Rayburn settled down to a career in the U.S. House that went uninterrupted until his death. He was a strong supporter of President Woodrow Wilson and received an assignment to the Committee on Interstate and Foreign Commerce. He fought for regulation of the railroads and supported the American role in World War I. Rayburn, however, "realized there would be a long, long period of hard work, careful planning, and continual friend-making," wrote one biographer, "before he would be eligible for the final goal: to serve as Speaker of the U.S. House of Representatives." Indeed that was the case. Rayburn entered into a period of quiet and routine work until events turned to his favor in 1931 when he became chairman of the Committee on Interstate and Foreign Commerce.

This period of calm, however, should not be overlooked or relegated to a minor place in Rayburn's career. To begin with, he maintained his personal ethics, which meant punctual attendance at meetings, acceptance of extra work, and a spirit of cooperation. His willingness to accept tasks of drudgery gained favor with senior Democrats who in turn promoted his career. Later, when he was Speaker of the House, Rayburn gave the following advice to freshmen legislators: "Get to know your committee chairman, let him know you want to work and help him do a good job of running the committee so it can make a record, and he'll help you with your problems." Particularly helpful to young Rayburn were John Nance Garner of Texas, who acted as House Democratic whip, William C. Adamson, chairman of the Committee on Interstate and Foreign Commerce, and Tennessee Congressman Cordell Hull.

Democrats were, of course, out of favor during the Republican-party dominated 1920s. Young Democrats were therefore relegated to strengthening the party in their home districts, maintaining ties with House leaders, and gaining seniority. Rayburn was unhappy during these years. His party was in the minority, and he had little chance to promote his constituents' interests or his career. He started reading during his spare time and nearly always kept one book in his office and another in his Washington apartment. It was during this Republican era that his parents died and his attempt at marriage to Metze Jones failed. The marriage ended in divorce after about three months, and Rayburn never talked about it, neither to family members nor political friends. It was always a matter that both he and Metze kept to themselves. Rayburn was greatly disappointed with this failure because he had always wanted a large family and frequently said that he regretted "not having a little towheaded boy to teach how to fish." Therein lay his devotion to the House. A long day for Rayburn was standard; he commonly went into his office on Saturdays and always seemed bored on weekends, restlessly awaiting the arrival of a new week of business. The enthusiasm and love that would have gone to a family went instead to the House and his constituents. His single attempt to marry and have children was opened and closed during the quiet Republican years. Any damage that his divorce might have caused with the voters of the Fourth District did not materialize.

Until the national public sentiment changed, bringing the election of a Democratic Congress, Rayburn had little to do. Like other Democrats, his best friend during these years was time, and hence seniority, and while he kept his seat on the Interstate and Foreign Commerce Committee and continued to work alongside Garner and the Democratic leadership, these quiet years offered little opportunity for legislative activity. He fended off challengers in the Fourth District and solidified his position at home. Until things changed, Rayburn simply had to endure. Nonetheless, during these years Rayburn had managed to become well known in the House and well liked by the Democratic elders and the ranking Democrat on his committee.

The Republican era ended dramatically with the Wall Street crash of 1929: the Democrats won control of both houses in 1930. For Rayburn things started moving quickly. He took over as chairman of the Interstate and Foreign Commerce Committee in 1931, and he played an important role in the nomination of Franklin D. Roosevelt for president in 1932.

The 1932 Democratic convention could have been disastrous for Rayburn. He was indebted to Garner, who had guided him as far back as 1913, and felt that he must remain loyal to a fellow Texan with a chance, albeit slight, to receive the party's nomination. But on the other hand Roosevelt was quite popular, and, given President Herbert Hoover's vast unpopularity, the Democratic nominee was expected to become the next president. Therefore had Rayburn offended Roosevelt, or had Garner fought hard for the nomination, Rayburn might have endangered his career. Garner showed statesmanship; he did not want the convention to deadlock as it had in 1924 and therefore released his delegation after the third ballot. Rayburn had hoped this would happen, and as soon as Garner made the decision, Rayburn swung the Texas vote over to Roosevelt, even though some members of the Lone Star delegation wanted to keep fighting for Garner.

When the New Dealers, with a flurry of activity, descended upon Washington after Roosevelt's victory, Rayburn was in a position full of power and opportunity. As chairman of his committee, Rayburn played a major role in the preparation of several pieces of reform legislation, some of them with far-reaching impact. In these particular battles, as well as in others, he used his middle-of-the-road, or compromise, philosophy in order to strike a bargain that was fair to all.

In 1933, after the Wall Street crash and the resulting revelations of considerable fraud in the brokerage industry, "the reputation of Wall Street for financial wisdom, care of other people's money, and common honesty," wrote one historian, "was never lower." Wall Street investors considered themselves to be responsible members of a private elite, but the general public and the Roosevelt administration had a different opinion of them. The original draft of the Securities Act of 1933, put together by the Roosevelt brain trust, went to Rayburn's committee, but Rayburn felt that the original bill would put too much authority into the hands of the Federal Trade Commission (FTC). The Commission "would become the Czar of American business," wrote one observer, "because it required all companies to get FTC permission before issuing stock."

Rayburn therefore persuaded the brain trust to write a less authoritarian bill and held hearings on it with his committee. Representatives of Wall Street met with Rayburn and tried to kill the bill. He listened to their objections but left the meeting convinced that the bill was fair and operable. He took it to the House floor, where he answered all objections and explained the details of the legislation. It passed. The Senate version was not as well written, so ultimately the House bill became law as the Truth-in-Securities Act. A Rayburn characteristic vital to understanding his success was apparent in this episode. He had refused to hold all brokerage firms accountable for the wrong-doing of some and had refused to go along with the New Dealers' attempt to concentrate complete authority in a government body. On the other hand, he did not yield to the objectionable demands of the industry. His sense of fair play had shone through, and while the press and the general public had not noticed it, his practice of even-handedness had been duly noted by insiders.

The ease with which Rayburn had guided the passing of the Truth-in-Securities bill, however, was not an omen of things to come. Roosevelt wanted to regulate the stock exchanges so as to protect the public interest. Among other provisions of his proposal, he wanted to establish more realistic conditions for buying stocks "on the margin," a practice widely abused and partly responsible for the crash in 1929. Again the measure went to Rayburn's committee, and again it authorized the FTC to regulate the industry. In this instance Wall Street was ready for a fight and "some of the mightiest names of high finance," wrote one observer, "flanked by their legal and financial experts, came swarming into Washington for public hearings before Rayburn's committee." Rayburn faced an array of belligerent witnesses and after several weeks of testimony asked Roosevelt's experts to draft a revision incorporating some of the objections presented to the committee.

Rayburn took it to the floor where critics described the measure as a communistic idea. The industry had rallied considerable opposition, and Rayburn faced tough opponents. Fortunately, senior Republican Carl Mapes of Michigan agreed with Rayburn and provided some help. Support for the bill proved to be stronger than it first appeared. It passed 281 to 84. A similar measure passed the Senate, and in the conference committee Rayburn conceded that a special Securities Exchange Commission should be created to carry out the new law. Rayburn had become identified with one of the most important examples of New Deal legislation, the Securities Exchange Act.

The major battle of Rayburn's career, however, still waited—in the Public Utility Holding Company Act of 1935. It dealt with the pyramiding of stocks, or the creation of holding companies. By the 1930s the practice of stock pyramiding had become a political issue, and the Roosevelt administration sought to stop it. Rayburn had a particular interest in this subject and served as the House sponsor of the regulatory bill. The bill contained one provision that was particularly offensive to the utility companies—the "death sentence," which called for abolition rather than regulation of holding companies. Wendell Willkie, the 1940 Republican candidate for president, led the fight against the bill and exerted considerable pressure against Congress. Rayburn's committee conducted the House hearings on the bill; so great was the pressure that his committee broke rank and voted to remove the death sentence clause despite Rayburn's efforts to keep the measure intact.

Being floor leader of the bill, Rayburn had to fight hard to defend it, but despite his best efforts, he could not persuade the House to reinstate the death sentence provision that had been removed by his own committee. The House vote marked a severe loss for Roosevelt—and for Rayburn. In the Senate the death sentence had remained intact, but the House conference committee refused to budge, forcing Roosevelt to accept a compromise that killed the death sentence proviso.

Despite Rayburn's loss in fighting for the death sentence provision, his role in the passage of the Public Utility Holding Company Act oddly enough brought important developments for him. To begin with, he had accepted the responsibility to defend a piece of legislation that was particularly technical and difficult to understand. (He had, of course, relied on White House assistance in this respect.) Nearly everyone was impressed with his knowledge of detail and ability to counter the charges made by opponents who could be quite adept at exposing flaws in the proposal. At the same time Rayburn had resolutely stood firm. He had refused to back down on the death sentence, even to the extent of being overturned by his committee. This was unusual behavior for Rayburn, who liked to avoid punitive legislation. But his unflinching position in the struggle had endeared him to the president, "a powerful asset," wrote a biographer "when the time came to make his bid for a House leadership position."

Rayburn's legislative style and personal way of dealing with people was best illustrated in the creation of the Rural Electrification Administration (REA) in 1936. By that time most urban residents had electrical service, but only 10 percent of the farms had service, and in many areas the percentage was far lower. Morris Cooke, the "father of the REA," had persuaded Roosevelt to create the agency by executive order in 1935, but its temporary status and lack of dependable funding had thwarted its progress. In 1936, Senator George Norris, "father of the TVA," and Rayburn jointly introduced legislation for a permanent REA. Rayburn's committee held hearings on the measure and Rayburn led the floor fight for its passage.

In this case Rayburn followed his usual practice of taking the middle position. Norris wanted to exclude power companies from receiving REA funds, but Rayburn disagreed, saying that they could be of some help. The goal was to extend service to farmers, he would say, not to punish the electrical industry. Rayburn's provision remained intact in the House bill, but Norris had kept the companies out of the Senate bill. Now the two highly respected members of Congress, anxious to see their people in the countryside enjoy modern conveniences, reached an impasse at the conference committee. "We quarreled for a long time," Norris recalled, "but neither side would yield an inch."

Norris left the room, determined to keep the power industry out of the program. Rayburn immediately followed and, catching up to Norris, said: "Now Senator, don't be discouraged . . . just let it rest awhile. Within a few days we will notify you we are ready to have another meeting."

By the next meeting, the House conferees had developed a compromise. Why not let rural electric cooperatives, or public bodies, have first preference in qualifying for REA loans but still keep the door open to any power companies that applied to the REA? Norris conceded. In 1936 the Rural Electrification Administration, with its new statute of authority, embarked on a program to organize cooperatives and extend electrical service throughout rural America. Rayburn was, of course, the cosponsor of the bill, and the REA was one of his proudest achievements. It proved to be one of the most successful and lasting contributions of the New Deal and remains today a fixture in American rural life.

By 1936 Rayburn had developed into a legislator who clearly disliked punitive laws and preferred compromise whenever possible; he was well known as a man of conviction willing to fight to the end when a fight was necessary. The Texas lawmaker was also well-positioned from a tactical point of view in the House. Roosevelt liked him and regarded him as a firm believer in New Deal reforms. His career was poised for another jump which came in 1936.

That year, while Roosevelt ran for reelection, House Speaker Joseph W. Byrnes died. Rayburn at the time was in Texas and went to Byrnes's funeral in Nashville, Tennessee. The vacancy of the Speakership brought an opportunity for Rayburn to climb higher in the House leadership. Majority Leader William Bankhead quickly replaced Byrnes, leaving open the position of Majority Leader, the position normally presumed to be next in line to that of Speaker. Rayburn committed himself to run for that position against John J. O'Connor of New York, a Tammany Hall Democrat. O'Connor had already announced his candidacy for Majority Leader and had obtained pledges of support soon after Byrnes's funeral.

Rayburn let it be known that he was a candidate but took a slower approach, and while O'Connor appeared to be the front-runner, the president had not indicated his choice. Vice-President Garner stepped into the race and effectively damaged O'Connor by exploiting his reputation as a mouthpiece for Tammany Hall. Roosevelt indicated his preference for Rayburn, and two state delegations, Louisiana and Pennsylvania, announced their support for the Texan. Rayburn was gathering momentum, and when Massachusetts representative

John McCormack came out for him, big-city bosses moved their support to him as well. More joined the Rayburn camp, and he wound up winning the job of Majority Leader easily by a vote of 184 to 127 when Congress convened in January 1937. He could now expect to reach the Speaker's chair in a reasonable time unless something went dreadfully wrong. Garner's contribution to Rayburn's success should not be overlooked. As vice-president and as an experienced Democratic politician, his anti-O'Connor campaign obviously had an impact on the race.

Compared with his experience during the early years of the New Deal, Rayburn's stint as Majority Leader was uneventful. However, Speaker Bankhead suffered poor health, requiring Rayburn to preside frequently over the House in the Speaker's chair. This had the effect of conditioning him and his fellow representatives for Rayburn's election to the speakership in 1940. That year Bankhead died, and with no nominee from the Republicans, the House elected Rayburn Speaker. He reached his life's goal, but would always say: "I came within a gnat's heel of remaining a tenant farmer."

As in the case of his ascending to the chair of the Commerce Committee, Rayburn's achievement of the speakership came at a time when events seemed to heighten the responsibility of his new job. Soon after he took over as presiding officer, the House was embroiled in one of its most dramatic debates, one with serious consequences: the extension of the military draft in September 1941. In the previous year the government had established a peacetime draft as a measure of military preparedness, but the conscripts, according to law, were limited to one year's service. As war raged in Europe, however, Roosevelt wanted the period of service extended on grounds that the United States could not afford to be without enlarged armed services as Britain stood alone against Nazi Germany.

The real fight over this request came in the House, where isolationist sentiment was strong. Rayburn took the position that foreign policy should remain largely the prerogative of the president and argued for the extension. Rayburn's biographer stated that the Texan exerted unusual effort to persuade those House colleagues not adamantly opposed to the bill. "I need your vote," he would say. "I wish you would stand by me because it means a lot to me." Members of the Congress faced a heart-wrenching decision: a vote against the bill might imperil the country, but a supporting vote would bring the United States closer to war. American sentiment at that point was leaning toward noninvolvement in the European conflict.

When House debate began, it was emotional. As Speaker, Rayburn had to be fair and could not threaten or pressure anyone opposing him. During the vote, however, he used the weapons of his position to encourage passage. As the clerk called the roll, the count went back and forth, and it was impossible to predict the final tally. As the clerk counted, one member changed his yea to a nay, narrowing the vote to 203 to 202 in favor of passage. At this point Rayburn froze the vote and announced passage of the bill. Some confusion appeared on the floor, as opponents wanted to make a move to recast the vote, but Rayburn informed them that only a person from the winning side could make such a motion. Opponents still objected and wanted to reconsider the vote. Twice Rayburn refused, and he carried the day. His tactics could be interpreted as "strong-arming" the isolationists, but the bill nonetheless became law.

When the Japanese attacked Pearl Harbor and Germany subsequently declared war on the United States, Rayburn's tactics were seen as life-saving measures, and his prestige grew. He was seen as a leader and not a strong-armed politician. "He had pushed the Speaker's powers to the limit," wrote one observer, "and had triumphed, not only for himself but, as later events proved, for the nation as well."

Once the United States entered the war, a strong sense of unity and purpose swept across the country, and that sense of togetherness was reflected in the House. Indeed, a striking example occurred in 1944 when Rayburn became involved with the project to develop the atomic bomb. The Manhattan Project, code-name for the U.S. nuclear weapons development project, had been underway since the nation's entry into World War II, but in 1944 it needed more funding. Until this point the administration had managed to take funds from various agencies in such a way as to avoid a special appropriation. Now, in a dramatic visit to Rayburn's office, Secretary of War Henry Stimson and Army Chief of Staff George Marshall asked him to obtain a $2 billion appropriation for the project without letting the House know the purpose of the money. In other words, to approve the appropriation without revealing the project to members of Congress. In both chambers the congressional leadership managed to get the money without disclosing the secret. Rayburn simply asked, and since the House respected him so much, the members agreed. Not until the bomb was used against Japan did Congress realize what had happened.

As Rayburn settled down in the spring of 1945 with a sense of relief after the hectic events of 1944, President Roosevelt died. Although insiders in Washington knew of his growing weakness, Roosevelt's death still came as a surprise. Rayburn and Vice-President Harry Truman had already become close friends, sharing drinks together in late afternoon sessions at the Speaker's "Board of Education." Like many Americans, Rayburn was shaken by Roosevelt's death. He had felt a sense of closeness to the man who had brought relief directly to his constituents with rural electrification, farm-to-market roads, educational projects in soil conservation, public power, and other sorely needed projects. His grief, however, did not let him slow down because the war was winding down. The United States now had a long agenda of needs, both domestic and international, and Rayburn was close to the new president. He and Truman had a first-name friendship: Harry and Sam.

The 1946 midterm elections gave the Republicans control of both chambers of Congress, and Rayburn had to step back in the line of ascension to Minority Leader. He talked about retiring, but the Democratic leaders persuaded him to accept the lesser post, arguing that no one else in the House could handle it. He detested having to step aside for a party that he considered unsympathetic to the needs of the common man, but for Rayburn a satisfying victory for his party came in 1948 when Truman ran for reelection; the Republican presidential candidate, Thomas Dewey, was favored to win, but Truman's "whistle stop" campaign overpowered him. Democrats regained control of Congress, and Rayburn returned to the Speaker's chair.

In 1952 the Republicans nominated Dwight Eisenhower for president while the Democrats nominated Adlai Stevenson. Eisenhower was so popular in Texas that many Democrats there endorsed him, refusing to campaign for Stevenson. They were known as "Shivercrats" since Texas Governor Allan Shivers led them. Rayburn remained loyal to his party, which meant an open break for him with the Shivers camp. Eisenhower endorsed state ownership of the Texas tidelands, a dispute involving jurisdiction over offshore oil resources, and his victory in 1952 ended the dispute. Congress passed a bill giving Texas its jurisdiction, and Eisenhower happily signed it. Rayburn opposed the measure but was outgunned, particularly in view of the fact that in 1952 Republicans again captured the House, relegating him to Minority Leader for the second time. In the Fourth District the question over the tidelands never became an issue for Rayburn, and his fight with some Texas Democrats had no impact on his constituents. His enormous power and prestige in the House were not tarnished, and when in 1954 the Democrats regained control of Congress, he returned to the Speaker's chair.

Here he stayed, becoming the longest-serving Speaker in American history. Free of serious challengers at home and recognized worldwide as a statesman, Mr. Sam was becoming well known around the country, due in part to the television coverage of the 1952 Democratic convention and also to his reputation as a fair leader of the House. Rayburn had always treated his opponents with respect and avoided exercising his power excessively. "It is a wise man," he would say, "who realizes that the church is bigger than its pastor."

By the mid 1950s Rayburn had become untouchable. His personality and history of leadership, which stretched back to 1931 when he chaired the Interstate and Foreign Commerce Committee, were well known, and among young members of Congress he was an awesome figure, almost a living legend. For the rest of his career, "the golden years," as described by one biographer, he relied to a considerable extent on his persuasiveness to wield power. A combination of circumstances also strengthened his hand. For one thing, he and Eisenhower had similar personalities and philosophies in spite of some obvious differences that each was always quick to point out. Each had a middle-of-the-road philosophy and "a strict sense of national duty. Both understood the necessity of compromise. Both were men of good-will, abhorring venomous personal attacks." And even though they disagreed on specific matters, they created an environment of mutual trust and respect between the House of Representatives and the White House. In this period of "consensus politics," the emphasis should be placed on Rayburn's and Ike's sameness, their similar approach to duty, and their emphasis on good-will. To be sure, partisan politics never disappeared, and each on occasion had sharp criticisms of the other. But they were still much alike. The general public recognized the similarity, extending their trust and dependence to them to work out the daily business of governing. As a consequence, the consensus of the 1950s, at least between Congress and the White House, originated in part from the relationship of the president and the Speaker.

To some extent Rayburn's influence at this point extended to the Senate, where Lyndon Johnson, a fellow Texan and Rayburn protege, was Majority Leader. The Rayburn-Johnson relationship has been the object of several writers, and in some ways it is a perplexing subject. Johnson had come to the House in 1937 as a staunch supporter of Roosevelt, and he worked hard to please Rayburn, who was Majority Leader at the time. Rayburn liked Johnson and through the years had a father-son relationship with him. When Johnson rose to Senate Majority Leader, he and Speaker Rayburn maintained their closeness and worked to achieve harmony. Since both branches of the Congress were led by Texans with similar ideologies who shared a close friendship, the daily business of government flowed smoothly.

Certainly these were Rayburn's best years. His history of service and devotion to civic duty, plus his behind-the-scenes manner of conducting business, explained why *Look* magazine wrote of him: "he is more valuable to have on your side than any other man in Washington, if its pending legislation you have in mind.

In 1957 Rayburn accomplished a goal that originated in the latter years of his life: he opened the Sam Rayburn Library at Bonham, Texas. It was built by the Rayburn Foundation solely with private funding that began with the $10,000 Collier Award which he received in 1949 for outstanding legislative service. He wanted the building to serve as a research center for congressional affairs and named one of his staff members, H. G. Dulaney, as director. Rayburn used the building as his office when he was in Bonham, but he encouraged the facility's use by students, including school children, as a resource center. The library, under the leadership of Mr. Dulaney, has retained the Rayburn personality and style. It is a beautiful marble building that houses Rayburn's papers and other documents and includes a replica of Rayburn's House office. But, most important, the library has an open-arms attitude toward the public and maintains a friendly atmosphere.

Rayburn's library seemed to be the final tribute to a distinguished career, the ending point of his political life. But Rayburn still had energy. In 1960 he backed Lyndon Johnson's bid for the Democratic nomination for president. During the early months of the campaigning, Massachusetts Senator John F. Kennedy worked hard in the state primaries and surged forward after winning the West Virginia primary, while Johnson remained at work in the Senate. Rayburn had originally thought Kennedy was too young and inexperienced to be president, a thought shared by many prominent Democrats such as Eleanor Roosevelt. Kennedy, nonetheless, outmaneuvered Johnson and won the nomination on the first ballot.

Probably the most intriguing part of the 1960 race was Johnson's acceptance of the vice-presidency. Rayburn and Johnson were solidly opposed to it, but Kennedy wanted Johnson, realizing that he needed southern support to win the election. Johnson agreed, but warned Kennedy that Rayburn first had to be convinced. Rayburn remained opposed, but after Kennedy personally pleaded his case and Mr. Sam's own advisors worked on him, the Speaker agreed. Rayburn quickly swung behind Kennedy, frequently saying, "That boy grows on you." Kennedy showed the highest respect for Rayburn and agreed with the *New York Times* when it asserted that Rayburn was "Mr. Everything."

Rayburn now approached the final episode of his career: the fight over the House Rules Committee, one of the "worst fights of my life," he said. At the age of seventy-nine, Rayburn, whose only health problem was failing eyesight, wanted to amend the powers of the Rules Committee, which could keep legislation off the floor. By 1960 the committee was controlled by conservatives who were opposed to the proposals of the Kennedy administration, and Rayburn wanted to keep the Rules Committee from ruining the new president's domestic programs.

He personally took over the battle against Howard Smith, the committee chairman. The Speaker proposed that the committee be enlarged so as to allow the appointment of more liberals to it. In some respects it was a fight over ideology. In an emotional struggle reminiscent of the New Deal battles, Rayburn won by five votes. It was a particularly sweet victory for him, one that put to rest the rumors that he was losing his grip on the House. Again, Rayburn had made the right move. His prestige and command of respect were at that point not exceeded by any public figure. As Rayburn himself put it, "It's easy to be an obstructionist; its hard to be a constructionist."

Time was running out for Rayburn. At home in July 1961, he complained of back pain and went to his local doctor who found nothing wrong. Back in Washington he started losing weight and strength, but still there was no correct diagnosis of his condition. Convinced that he could overcome the mysterious illness, he went home in September for a prolonged rest. Further tests at Baylor Medical Center in Dallas revealed what Rayburn had dreaded: cancer. The disease had already spread and doctors gave him about two weeks to live. He lasted for six weeks before dying at the Risser Clinic in Bonham, on November 16, 1961.

There followed one of the greatest outpourings of public grief ever associated with a legislative leader in American history. His funeral service, conducted at the First Baptist Church of Bonham, was attended by President Kennedy, former Presidents Truman and Eisenhower, and future President Johnson. A crowd of twenty thousand stood outside the church. His biographers, D. B. Hardeman and Don Bacon, concluded that Rayburn's pastor at the Primitive Baptist Church at Tioga best described the Speaker at his funeral: "He has fought a good fight. He has been a fair and loyal man . . . He has kept faith with the democracy of our country." Thirty years later, H. G. Dulaney, when asked to compare other political leaders with Rayburn said, "It can't be done. Rayburn is incomparable."

Racial Politics in Dallas in the Twentieth Century

THEODORE M. LAWE

THEODORE M. LAWE SERVES AS HISTORIAN AND CURATOR FOR THE A.C. MCMILLAN AFRICAN AMERICAN MUSEUM IN EMORY, TEXAS.

IN THIS ESSAY, LAWE PROVIDES AN OVERVIEW OF AFRICAN AMERICAN POLITICAL HISTORY IN TWENTIETH CENTURY DALLAS. BECAUSE OF THE EFFORTS OF ITS STALWART BLACK RESIDENTS, AIDED BY FEDERAL JUDGES, DALLAS HAS ESCAPED "ITS ONCE RIGIDLY SEGREGATED PAST." LAWE CONTENDS THAT DALLAS, AT THE END OF THE TWENTIETH CENTURY, "WAS AN AFRICAN AMERICAN POLITICAL SUCCESS STORY."

★ ★

At the end of the twentieth century, Dallas was viewed as a progressive city that had made a complete departure from its once rigidly segregated past. The most visible indicator was the election of an African American mayor, Ron Kirk, who claimed victory over an influential white opponent. During Mayor Kirk's two-term administration, he was credited with successful bond elections to build the American Airlines Center, and successfully organized voters and city business leaders in a project to approve the initial planning and construction of the

"Racial Politics in Dallas in the Twentieth Century" by Theodore M. Lawe from *East Texas Historical Journal*, Vol. 46, Issue 2, 2008, pp. 27–39. Reprinted by permission of East Texas Historical Association.

Trinity River Project, a key component for future growth in the city. Several prior attempts to get this project supported had been defeated, which proved Kirk's ability to bridge former divides within the city's structure.

In addition to Kirk's election, at the closing of the twentieth century, four African Americans and three Latinos sat on the fifteen-member Dallas City Council. The nine-member local board of education included three elected African Americans and three Latinos, and the five-person Dallas County Commissioners Court had an elected African American commissioner on that body for over twenty years. The county treasurer, elected at large, was an African American female. Five African Americans served in the state legislature at the end of the century from Dallas County, including one state senator African Americans were also elected judges in Dallas County District Courts, justices of the peace, and constables, along with appointed judges in Municipal Courts and the first African American from Dallas was in the United States African Americans were finally well represented in the local city administration, legislative bodies, the judiciary, county commissioners court, and the board of education. Dallas was an African American political success story; political pluralism had seemingly arrived.

Such political accomplishments were the results of population growth in the African American community and the community's development of sophisticated political skills, which resulted from direct community intervention tactics, federal legislation, Supreme Court decisions, over 100 years of community struggles and demands, and other external influences. But more specifically, African American accomplishments came at a high cost from a long and painful history—they were active actors in their own success, not passive observers depending on external forces. According to the Dallas Black Chamber of Commerce (formerly the Dallas Negro Chamber of Commerce), this success came "from long, patient hours of planning and negotiating by dedicated persons associated with the Black Chamber."

To understand the significance of these accomplishments requires an understanding of the incremental changes in the African American Community that were socially, economically, and politically driven. These changes extended for a hundred years and involved thousands of people and the creation of many committees and organizations.

A look back shows that the early part of the twentieth century found African Americans in Dallas County struggling to survive. Most worked in menial jobs such as maids, busboys, waiters, porters, and in agriculture. The best job available to African Americans was a Pullman porter that required constant travel but at least provided a clean uniform. To help alleviate the lack of economic opportunity, the community organized several self-help groups to promote social and economic progress. The largest African American owned business, organized in 1901, was the New Century Cotton Mill Company, which survived until around 1908. Investors in both Dallas and New England raised $400,000 to finance New Century. Its owner was J. E. Wiley, a transplant from Chicago and the second African American lawyer to organize a practice in Dallas.

African Americans, out of necessity and institutional segregation, also organized their own cultural pursuits. The major annual recreational affair was the Colored Fair and Tri-Centennial Exposition, which began in 1901. Annual Emancipation Day celebrations drew large crowds.

The Dallas Black Giants were active in the Texas Colored Baseball League. *The Dallas Express*, a newspaper founded in 1892 by Mississippian W. E. King, was the recorder and voice for the African American community. *The Southwestern Baptist Newspaper* published by Reverend E. W. D. Isaac, the Senior Pastor at New Hope Baptist Church, was the primary religious organ for Dallas' African American community.

From 1900 to 1910, the African American population in Dallas increased from 13,646 to 20,828—over a fifty percent increase. During this period, several African American professionals moved to Dallas, led by Dr. Benjamin R. Bluitt, who built the city's first "Negro-owned" and operated sanitarium. William M. Sanford and Sandy Jones operated the Black Elephant varieties theater. Dock Rowen founded a successful insurance company, grocery store, and money-lending business. Dr. M. C. Cooper became Dallas' first African American dentist. In 1905, Ollie Bryan became Dallas' first African American woman to practice dentistry. The presence of such prominent professionals was a boon for the community since they provided leadership and served as role models for uplift and economic advancement.

In 1916, the Knights of Pythias built the first commercial building in Dallas for African Americans, designed by architect William Sidney Pittman, the son-in-law of Booker T. Washington. The building, located at 2551 Elm Street, provided office space for doctors, dentists, lawyers, and other professionals. It was designated as a City of Dallas Landmark in the 1980s.

Dallas' African Americans did not passively accept Texas' southern system of institutional segregation. In 1911, J. A. Gilmore refused to give up his seat in the "white-only" section of a streetcar and was ousted from the train by the conductor. The Court of Civil Appeals later ruled that the conductor was lawful in enforcing the "Jim Crow" law, but he used undue force. Gilmore was thus awarded $100.

In 1918, a group of socially sensitive men organized the Cotillion Idlewild Club for the purpose of providing social recognition and presenting young ladies to society. Because of the uniqueness of the club, *LIFE* magazine sent a photographer to Dallas to attend the annual affair. A favorable article appeared in a subsequent issue of the magazine.

The third decade of the twentieth century saw several events that demonstrated growth and maturity on the part of African Americans in Dallas. In 1921, St. James A.M.E. Temple opened a new state-of-the-art church designed by architect William Sidney Pitts. In the same year, Thad Else opened the first hotel in Freeman's Town, an establishment designed and built by African Americans that provided a vital place for a community subject to Jim Crow segregation. In 1928, the African American community raised $50,000 to help fund the proposed $175,000 community based Y.M.C.A. The first two African American Boy Scout troops were organized at El Bethel Church in Oak Cliff and St. Paul A.M.E. Church in North Dallas. In 1934, Father Max Murphy, a graduate of St. Peter's School in Dallas, became the first African American priest to perform a mass in the Dallas diocese.

From a political perspective African Americans more actively participated in the political processes after the 1950s when African Americans in Dallas were no longer willing to ask for a change and wait patiently to see what happened, but to organize for change for themselves.

Until the 1960s, social inequality was mandated by Jim Crow etiquette. Historically, the African American church provided a venue for self-expression and served as an erected shelter against a hostile white community. The political and social issues in Dallas involved both whites and African Americans on the issues of housing, jobs, law enforcement, enfranchisement, and public accommodations. Indeed, no area of life for African Americans in Dallas was exempt from racial discord.

At the beginning of the twentieth century, Dallas was a violent place for African Americans. According to W. Marvin Dulaney, a Dallas historian, in March 1910, Allen Brooks an elderly black man, was accused of abusing a white child. After his arrest (but before he could receive a trial), he was taken from the jail by a mob of approximately 5,000 people and lynched. He was later dragged through the streets of downtown Dallas and pieces of his clothing and parts of his mangled body were handed out as souvenirs. A second case came in 1921 when members of the Dallas Ku Klux Klan kidnapped Alexander Johnson, a bellhop at a local downtown hotel, whose only "crime" was to have supposedly bragged about having sex with white female hotel guests. For such an offense, he was branded with the KKK symbol and killed. In both cases, no one was ever prosecuted. Rumors swirled that Dallas police officers that were KKK members took part in both incidents. The two episodes were emblematic of how violent life was for African Americans in Dallas at the beginning of the twentieth century as well as how racially charged the political environment was. Too often, such lynchings and violence had the intended effect of intimidating African Americans. Approximately 340 African Americans were lynched in Texas from 1885 to 1942. Northeast Texas was one of the most lawless and lynching-prone areas in the state.

Dallas' history is well documented with examples of segregationist and apartheid measures that denied African Americans their constitutional rights. For example early local ordinances barred African Americans access to housing, law enforcement, voting, public facilities, health care, and employment. The Texas Poll Tax passed in 1902 and the Democratic White Primary Law passed in 1903 were major instruments used to disenfranchise African Americans in Dallas and throughout the state of Texas. In 1907, the Dallas City Council revised its Charter to codify rigid segregation of all races in all aspects of city life: public schools, housing, amusements, and churches. The City of Dallas further restricted where African Americans could live by adopting additional Charter amendments in 1916. In the 1930s, the Dallas City Charter was amended to require all candidates for city government offices to run at-large and on a non-partisan basis, which effectively prevented African Americans from holding public offices. Reverend Alexander Stephens Jackson and Attorney Ammon S. Wells voiced African Americans protests to these circumstances through local Republican politics in Dallas County, but given that Texas was a one-party state dominated by Democrats, such actions had very little effect.

During the war years and the out migration of African Americans from the South, African Americans in Dallas, as throughout the South, started to increase their demands for full citizenship by organizing civic and protest groups, community based organizations, and social clubs. In 1918, African Americans formed a Dallas chapter of the NAACP under the leadership of George F. Porter, a schoolteacher, and attorney Ammon S. Wells. Porter was one of the first teachers in Dallas to protest the unequal pay for African American teachers employed in the same job as white teachers. During this time, the KKK-dominated police department intimidated the NAACP by requiring that they have oversight at NAACP meetings. The Dallas Negro Chamber of Commerce (an offspring of the Negro Business League) was formed in 1926 to promote minority owned businesses and to generally improve African Americans' living conditions. The Chamber later hired A. Maceo Smith, a graduate of Fisk and New York Universities, as its Executive Secretary. In addition to re-organizing the Negro Chamber of Commerce in 1933, he became the publisher of the *Dallas Express Newspaper* in 1935. The African American Museum at Fair Park celebrates his contributions to the community with an annual community service awards brunch held in his honor.

In 1935, Ammon S. Wells unsuccessfully ran for state representative for the seat vacated by Sarah T. Hughes, who resigned to become a Dallas County District Judge. In a field of sixty candidates, Wells received 1,001 votes, an impressive showing considering the winner polled 1,844 votes. Well's candidacy signaled to the African American leadership that they could have success in electing their own in Dallas with more attention given to voter registration and voter turnout.

In 1936, a cross-section of the African American community organized the Progressive Voters League under the leadership of the Reverend Maynard Jackson and A. Maceo Smith with the charge to represent the community's interests and recommend candidates for political support. In 1937, the League's agenda centered on hiring African American police officers, low-cost public housing, additional public schools, and municipal job opportunities. Under the direction of the League, the African American community cast deciding votes in the city council election of 1937. Such a show of political strength encouraged the city council to vote to integrate the Dallas Police Department and to encourage building a second African American high school to supplement the existing Booker T. Washington High—Lincoln High School. The City of Dallas Park Board also released plans for a new recreation center in the African American community and, in 1941, construction began on the first housing project in Dallas for African Americans—Roseland Homes. According to Dallas Historical Society's "Portrait of an Educator," Principal John Leslie Patton encouraged the teaching of racial pride through innovative approaches to African American history as early as the 1930s. J. Mason Brewer, a noted African American folklorist, was a part of the school's faculty at the time.

Also, in 1936, the African American community, through the Negro Chamber of Commerce, secured $100,000 in federal funds to build "The Hall of Negro Life" at the Centennial State Fair. Raising the funds proved difficult. A. Maceo Smith, orginator of the idea, was initially turned down for funding by a joint state legislative committee and the City of Dallas. Through the help of John Nance Garner, vice president of the United States, funds were eventually obtained. The money arrived just three months before the exposition opened and on June 19, 1936, The Hall of Negro Life opened in Fair Park. Over 400,000 people visited the exhibit, with an estimated sixty percent being white. Harlem Renaissance painter, Aaron Douglas, painted four large murals in the main lobby; one of the murals is currently in the Corcoran Museum in Washington, D.C. and the Fine Arts Museum of San Francisco owns another. The famous Cab Calloway and his Cotton Club Orchestra, along with the Duke Ellington Orchestra, performed at the celebration. The building was immediately demolished after the Fair; perhaps signifying the white establishment's indifference to African American racial pride, it was the only exhibit hall not a part of the Pan American Celebration a year later in 1937. Sixty years later, the site received its proper reverence when it became the home of the African American Museum at Fair Park, the largest of its kind in the Southwest with 25,000 square feet of exhibit space.

During the 1930s, African Americans symbolically elected a "bronze mayor" to represent their interests. Dr. Edgar E. Ward and A. A. Braswell held this position in the late 1930s. Because no public hotels were available to African Americans, many special guests stayed in the homes of the "bronze mayors."

In 1945, Maynard H. Jackson, one of the leaders in the Progressive Voters League, became the first African American to run for the Dallas School Board, and although he was unsuccessful, its symbolic importance cannot be understated. In 1959, Attorney C. B. Bunkley, another African American, ran for the School Board; he also was overwhelmingly defeated by Nevelle E. McKinney—34,330 to 13,411 votes. By the 1940's, the African American leadership in Dallas realized that real progress would only come from making progressive plans. They set three priorities: to organize campaigns to overturn the Democratic White Primary; to equalize salaries of African American teachers; and to integrate the University of Texas Law School. In 1942, African Americans in Dallas organized the Dallas Council of Negro Organizations. This group retained Attorney W. J. Durham to represent Thelma Paige and to file a lawsuit, *Page v Board of Education, City of Dallas*. In 1943, African American educators finally received a victory when the court held that the Dallas Independent School District had to equalize teachers' pay. This was the first action of its kind in the state of Texas and it forced other Texas cities to follow suit.

Public school access was important, but movements needed leaders and leaders were trained within the world of higher education. African Americans in Texas were banned on the basis of race from most of the state-supported institutions; Prairie View Normal Institute (now Prairie View A & M) was the only state funded school for African Americans, although African Texans did have access to a number of all-black private colleges, including Wiley College in Marshall. But there were no professional or graduate schools or programs for African Americans, which greatly hindered economic and social advancement for the state's minority citizens.

The issue of lack of educational equality due to the "separate but equal" clause was not limited to African Texans—it affected African Americans throughout the nation. In fact, the NAACP had endeavored to overturn this egregious injustice for years. Led by its brilliant legal counsel, Thurgood Marshall, Texas presented the national organization with an opportunity. Heman M. Sweatt, a graduate of Wiley College, applied for admission to the University of Texas Law School in 1946. Although he was qualified in every area, the university rejected his application solely on the basis of race. Sweatt, supported by the NAACP and with Marshall as lead attorney, filed suit and challenged the rejection. The suit was first argued in state court and the trial judge immediately recognized the potential of the case to overturn "separate but equal." Marshall argued that the state was required to admit Sweatt since Texas had no "black" law school and thus did not satisfy "separate but equal."

The presiding judge delayed the case and Texas' officials scrambled to find a solution. State elected officials decided that the only way out of their dilemma was to fund and open a separate school and in February 1947 a temporary law school, The School of Law of the Texas State University for Negroes, opened in Austin. Satisfied with the Texas' response, the state court subsequently rejected Sweatt's suit.

Marshall appealed the decision and in 1950 the United States Supreme Court held that the University of Texas had to admit Sweatt to its law school, ruling that the temporary law school was not an equal facility. The court ruled very narrowly and the decision did not overturn the "separate but equal" clause, but most observers recognized that the end was near for basis of southern institutional segregation. Sweatt enrolled at the law school for the 1950–1951 academic year, along with a few other African Americans. Marshall would use the *Sweatt* decision as a foundation for his monumental argument in the landmark *Brown v. Board of Education, Topeka* decision in 1954.

During the 1940s another milestone in Dallas took place when the first African American, John King, was allowed to serve on a Dallas jury. African Americans had been barred from serving on juries for over fifty years. Political progress also began to pay bigger dividends in the 1940s when an African American became a precinct chair in the Democratic Party and participated in the Democratic County Convention for the first time. During this time, the Dallas City Council also authorized the hiring of fourteen African American police officers with limited authority to patrol the streets in African American communities. The first two officers hired were Lee Gilbert Bilal and Benjamin Thomas, the first hired in Dallas in over fifty years. The city council also authorized the building of several segregated public housing projects in West Dallas for African Americans and a middle-class housing subdivision to maintain racial residential segregation in an area that became known as Hamilton Park, named for Dr. R. T. Hamilton, an influential African American physician. Donald Payton, a Dallas historian, remembers the Hamilton Park community in which he was raised to be one of pride and influence.

In the decade of the 1950s, the African American community was under constant threat of bombings that started as early as 1941 with the bombings of eighteen houses bought by African Americans in then "all white" South Dallas. The Reverend Donald Parish of True Lee Baptist Church vividly remembers his father, who was a member of the special grand jury that investigated the bombings, grabbing shotguns and gathering his entire family on the front porch every time there was a rumor of bombings. Marilyn Mask, a retired school administrator, revealed to a reporter of the *Dallas Morning News* how her employer tried to coerce her into moving from the then all-white Park Row/South Dallas area. The Texas Rangers and the Dallas Police Department investigated the bombing incidents and although they made several arrests, only one man was ever tried and he was found not guilty. Two of the men arrested said that they had been paid by white community organizations to toss bombs at African American homes. The local white religious community was also implicated. Although African Americans had taken the initiative to improve their political, social, and economic conditions prior to the decade of the 1950s, it took the U.S. Supreme Court decision in *Brown v. Board of Education in 1954* to give more muscle and direction to these grassroots efforts. After the *Brown* decision, the political game changed. Racial politics became more confrontational.

Dallas hosted the NAACP National Convention in 1954, and 7,500 conventioneers celebrated the *Brown* victory. Nobel Laureate Ralph Bunche gave the closing address and he forcefully called for full rights for African Americans. During the convention, St. Paul Hospital announced that it was for the first time allowing five African American doctors permission to serve patients at its hospital.

In 1955, in an attempt to implement *Brown v Board of Education*, twenty-eight African American students attempted to integrate all-white schools, but Dallas' school authorities denied them entry. The White establishment continually challenged desegregation within the city. The Reverend C. W. Criswell, the most powerful minister in Dallas and the pastor of the largest Baptist church in America, spoke as a demagogue against school desegregation in 1955. His position was balanced by speeches from Rabbi Levi Olan of the Temple Emanuel, who confronted Dallas and his congregation on the moral demands to end poverty and improve education. Olan was a member of the delegation that greeted Dr. Martin Luther King, Jr. at Love Field in 1963, when he came to speak at a voter registration drive. White city officials successfully dodged segregation for the remainder of the 1950s and through the 1960s. It was not until Sam Tasby, a taxi driver and father of six children, filed a federal lawsuit in 1970 did the school district earnestly begin to desegregate in 1971, under a federal court order with busing as the chosen mechanism. The school district would remain under court order for more than thirty years.

In retaliation for the NAACP's school desegregation suits, in 1956 the attorney general for the State of Texas, John Ben Shepherd (with the acquiescence of Governor Allan Shivers), organized a campaign to outlaw the NAACP and to intimidate its leaders. As in other parts of the state, the Dallas NAACP's records were confiscated, which crippled the effectiveness of the organization. A. Maceo Smith, a local leader who worked for the Federal Housing Authority, was thus forced to resign as state executive secretary of the NAACP and to terminate ties with the local chapter. The NAACP did not come back to its original strength for several years until Minnie Flanagan became president in 1959 and linked the civil rights organization to the local sit-ins movement.

In 1960, the Dallas School Board held an "integration referendum." Dallas' voters rejected integration by a four-to-one margin. The Dallas School Board adopted a plan in 1961 to desegregate the district one grade a year, starting with the first grade in the 1961–1962 school year. Dallas' defiance of the Brown Decision was consistent with other approaches in Texas and throughout the South.

Also, during this time, the State Fair of Texas was under attack from the African American community for only allowing African American entrance to the fair during "Negro Achievement Day." In an attempt to segregate the Fair, in the 1930s fair officials set aside the day as the lone day African Americans could attend the State Fair. After many years of protests, in 1953, African Americans were allowed to attend the full run of the State Fair of Texas with the exception of certain rides and restaurants. Dating back to 1901, African Americans had organized and promoted their own "colored fair." In a *Dallas Morning News* article, Bessie Slider Moody details her involvement at age sixteen with the NAACP Youth Council and their efforts to desegregate the State Fair of Texas and the Dallas Public Library.

On the suggestion of Roy Wilkins, the National Executive Secretary of the NAACP, the Dallas community formed the Committee of 14 (later called the Bi-racial Committee) in 1960 to negotiate and "manage desegregation" in Dallas. The Dallas Citizens Council appointed the seven whites; the African Americans came from the Negro Chamber of Commerce and the NAACP. At the first meeting, A. Maceo Smith (an African American) charged the committee with six objectives:

1. provide integrated food services;
2. provide integrated public accommodations;
3. provide equal employment opportunities for Negroes at City Hall
4. removal of racial designation signs from all public places;
5. provide integrated seating accommodations at sporting events and at other public places; and
6. open accommodations in hotels and motels.

The Committee of 14 was challenged in its approach to "managed desegregation" from various sectors of the African American community that believed in more direct action. Among those who supported sit-ins and more direct action were such leaders as Reverend T. D. R. Thompson, Reverend Aston Jones, Reverend Rhett James, Reverend Earl E. Allen, Dr. Dudley Powell, and such organizations as the Student Non-Violent Coordinating Committee (SNCC) and the Dallas Coordinating Committee on Civil Rights (composed of the NAACP and SNCC). The biggest public demonstration occurred in March of 1965 when an estimated 3,000 people marched and rallied in downtown Dallas. Evidence shows that Black Dallas was divided on strategy for achieving racial integration, but united behind the objective of integration.

Two prominent African American ministers who affiliated with the Committee of 14 harshly criticized those who advocated direct action and called for a "moratorium on picketing" in Dallas. The Reverend E. C. Estelle of the St. John Baptist Church said that "direct action had diminishing returns and public opinion had turned against civil rights demonstrations." The Reverend B. L. McCormick stated, "There was no need for a city ordinance prohibiting discrimination because none existed." It should be noted that Reverend E. C. Estelle was a strong supporter of the Reverend J. H. Jackson, the leader of the National Baptist Convention USA, Inc., who was opposed to the strategy of Martin Luther King, Jr. and promoted "gradualism" to desegregation and knocking down the doors of Jim Crow.

In 1964, African Americans began to receive appointments to civic boards and commissions. Dr. William Flowers was appointed to the Advisory Health Board and John H. Glenn and the Reverend Caesar Clark to the City Planning Commission. Conditions changed drastically when the United States Supreme Court declared the Texas Poll Tax unconstitutional in 1966. Soon after, Attorney Joseph Lockridge was elected the first African American to the

Texas legislature from Dallas. The Reverend Zan Holmes later succeeded Lockridge and he remembers being told by the rest of the Dallas delegation never to vote in favor of single-member districts. Holmes disobeyed, and was cursed and called a "nigger" on the floor of the house by the chairman of the Dallas delegation. In 1966, Attorney L. A. Bedford, who had earlier run for the state legislature, was appointed the first African American judge in the Municipal Courts. Judge Bedford remembers those days as being exciting times. He said that he always strived to be a "hard-working judge and fair in my rulings."

A chapter of the National Urban League was organized in Dallas in 1967, with the goal of helping African Americans identify employment opportunities. Also in 1967, Dr. Emmett Conrad was elected the first African American school board member. Latino Trini Garza, was appointed as well. Dr. Conrad's election to the Dallas School Board was in a citywide election and he gained white as well as African American votes. When he was elected in 1967, the school district had failed to follow through on the federal court order to integrate its junior high schools by 1965 and its senior high schools by 1967. Dr. Conrad won his seat on the school board with the support of the League for Educational Advancement. He succeeded in beating the Citizens for Good Schools' candidate, Albert Roberson, by 4,000 votes, even though the Citizens for Good Schools had won every seat on the school board since its inception in 1950. After serving on the school board from 1967 until 1977, Dr. Conrad eventually served on the Ross Perot Committee studying education in Texas and later served on the Texas State Board of Education.

The following year, C. A. Galloway became the first African American to serve an unexpired term on the Dallas City Council when he was appointed to the position. More concrete political progress came in 1968 when George Allen, a former member of the City Planning Commission, was elected to the Dallas City Council in a citywide election with white community support. Lucy Patterson, a social worker and granddaughter of pioneer school principal, Norman W. Harlee, later joined him in 1973.

The killing of nine African American men and the wounding of eleven others by the Dallas police over the course of several months in 1972 brought the two factions of the African American community together. In that same year, A. Maceo Smith led a coalition before the Dallas City Council representing approximately thirty community organizations. He called for establishing a community relations commission and improvements in investigating complaints against the police department relating to the failure to appoint an African American deputy police chief as well as the assignment of more African American officers to African American neighborhoods. Smith's appearance received results. Dallas received an African American deputy police chief in 1973 and an assistant city manager in 1974. As a further indicator of political and social change in 1975, the Dallas Negro Chamber of Commerce changed its name to the Dallas Black Chamber of Commerce and broadened its membership to include African American political leaders.

At the same time, a new generation of grassroots activists such as Peter Johnson, Al Lipscomb, Elsie Faye Heggins, and J. B. Jackson began to take on leadership roles along with Diane Ragsdale, Marvin Crenshaw, and Roy Williams, and others, some of them in prominent positions. All of these people were introduced to politics through participation in the Fair Park homeowners' protests involving eminent domain. The new grassroots leadership approach was to file federal lawsuits aimed at creating more district elections for maximizing grassroots political participation. In essence, their efforts were directed at institutional and systemic changes rather than individual concessions. In the 1970's, the federal lawsuit of *Lipscomb et al v. Wise* (Dallas Mayor Wes Wise) began the process that eventually led to single-member district elections for the Dallas City Council and the Dallas School Board, a key component of increasing African American representation. After several years in federal court and multiple rulings, district elections were finally mandated. In 1991, Dallas instituted a 14-1 political configuration, following earlier attempts to implement an 8-3 Council and a 10-4-1 Council. What this meant was the end of the at-large system, which was the centerpiece of the Dallas Citizens Council political machine. The new council make-up greatly curtailed the business community's control of city affairs and public education issues, another long-time centerpiece of the white establishment's control. Lipscomb, Heggins, and Ragsdale were later elected to the Dallas City Council; J. B. Jackson became active in mass transportation issues through DART and continued his role as a political strategist.

Marvin Crenshaw made several unsuccessful attempts for mayor. Roy Williams' book on Dallas politics, *Time Change*, explains how, because of single-member districts, more than twelve African Americans became members of the Dallas City Council in the last decades of the twentieth century, a numbers serving multiple terms, which indicated growing African American political strength. Among the unsung heroes that worked tirelessly for institutional change were Kathleen Gilliam, then president of the Board of Education, and Yvonne Ewell, who led the East Oak Cliff Sub-District of the Dallas Independent School District. Ewell was also active in bringing about change in the employment practices of the Dallas based major television network affiliates. Iola Johnson was hired as the first African American female news anchor in the Southwest in 1973. According to Al Lipscomb, the dean of African American politicians, "Dallas has great potential to show other cities how the concept of inclusion works.

According to Alwyn Barr in *The African Texas*, African American office-holders in Texas increased from twenty-nine in 1970 to over three hundred in 1990. Within the private-sector, in 1977, a local group known as the Committee of 100, which was comprised of young African American white-color workers in non-traditional jobs, hosted a dinner for seventeen whites and seventeen African Americans to discuss the need for improvements in local corporate hiring and the image of the African American community in the press. The initiative demonstrated new leadership and, in a change from earlier activism, involved no one from the African American religious community. In another radical change, several white bankers and industrial leaders occupied roles, indicating that Dallas' white citizens had finally realized that working with African Americans was the best direction for the future of Dallas. Although no noticeable results came from this pioneering meeting, at least African American and white leaders initiated and began to form a base from which future cooperation could develop.

The decades of the 1980s and 1990s saw the Dallas City Council appoint two African Americans as city manager and the selection of the first African American and Latino as Dallas

Superintendent of Schools. African Americans Sam Lindsey and Shirley Acy also occupied the positions of city attorney and city secretary, respectively. Al Lipscomb fondly remembers the backroom arguments that led to these appointments. President Bill Clinton later appointed Sam Lindsey the first African American federal judge in North Texas. As the twentieth century came to a close, African Americans served in the appointed positions of chairmen and directors of the board of the DFW International Airport, which aided in more construction and concessions contracts awarded to African Americans and Latinos. John Wiley Price was elected also County Commissioner in 1984 and he became one of the most powerful politicians in the city of any race.

Seven African Americans sued the Dallas Housing Authority in federal court in 1975 on the grounds of racial segregation and unequal conditions. The case eventually resulted in improved public housing conditions; a final settlement known as the "Walker Decree" was reached in 2004.

In 1995, Ron Kirk, an attorney, former lobbyist, and Texas Secretary of State, became Dallas' first African American mayor. His election was monumental in more ways than one since it brought together a working coalition between the white business establishment and the African American community. Kirk made a historic appointment when he selected the first African American as the city's police chief. His administration ended in 2002 not because of electoral defeat (he remained popular with all constituents throughout his tenure), but because of term limitations.

As a powerful reminder of the "Old Dallas" that was run as an white business oligarchy, there is a picture prominently hung in Dallas City Hall that includes all of the Dallas decision makers from that era, including the mayor, federal judge, and the business community. There is not an African American face in the photograph.

Clear relationships can be drawn between African American grassroots organizations and political concessions in Dallas. Black Dallas leadership prior to 1950 was vastly different from post 1950 leadership. Before the 1950s, and immediately after the *Brown v. Board of Education* decision, the NAACP dominated African American politics. The NAACP strategy of filing federal lawsuits challenging Jim Crow practices within the context of Constitutional rights, played a pivotal role in implementing court-ordered school desegregation mandates. A. Maceo Smith, Juanita J. Craft, and W. J. Durham led the campaigns and were the key players for the NAACP efforts. Juanita J. Craft, after serving on the Dallas City Council, died in 1985 at the age of eighty-three and left her house to the City of Dallas to be used as a landmark designated Civil Rights House. The house was the historic gathering place for civil rights lawyers such as Thurgood Marshall, who led so many NAACP efforts to end institutional segregation. W. J. Durham, a lawyer who moved to Dallas after the bombings in Sherman, Texas in the 1930s, provided the NAACP with strong analytical legal support. He was reputed to be one of the finest trial lawyers in Texas. Durham, assisted by C. B. Bunkley, Jr., was legal counsel in the historic cases of *Sweatt v. Painter* and *State of Texas v. NAACP.*

Beginning in the 1960s, the federally funded North Texas Legal Services organization assisted African American grassroots organizations in preparing their challenges to unequal political representation on the Dallas City Council, the Dallas School Board, and conditions in public housing. They replaced the NAACP as the legal entity challenging the system for a level playing field.

The progression of African Americans in Dallas does not mean that racism has necessarily ended. The white backlash to the "new politics" was white flight from the city and the school system. A prime example of the phenomenon is statistics from the early 1970s, which show that at least fifty-four percent of the students in the Dallas Independent School District were white. By the end of the twentieth century, white enrollment hovered around ten percent. According to the *Dallas Morning News*' commissioned report prepared by Booz/Allen/Hamilton, "Dallas residents are migrating from the city to the suburbs at a faster rate than anywhere else in the nation." The in-migration to the city is coming from South Texas, Mexico, and other countries in Latin America." In fact, new arrivals in Dallas from 1990–2000 numbered approximately 174,000 people; seventy-five percent of those were Latinos.

Given current trends, the next twenty years will witness more meaningful participation of minorities in the Dallas political process. As the Latino voting base becomes larger and more sophisticated, more Latinos will be elected to public office. Coalition politics in Dallas is the wave of the future.

In summary, the demise of Jim Crow policies and practices in Dallas can be attributed to the efforts of African American plaintiffs and local federal judges in the persons of Judge Jerry Buchmeyer and Judge Barefoot Sanders. These two federal judges made rulings that desegregated housing, schools, and changed the political structure of the local governing bodies; namely, the Dallas City Council, Dallas Independent School District, Dallas County Community College District, and the Dallas County Commissioners Court.

Lyndon, We Hardly Remember Ye: LBJ in the Memory of Modern Texas

RICKY FLOYD DOBBS

RICKY FLOYD DOBBS IS ASSOCIATE PROFESSOR OF HISTORY AT TEXAS A&M UNIVERSITY—COMMERCE. HE IS THE AUTHOR OF *YELLOW DOGS AND REPUBLICANS: ALLAN SHIVERS AND TEXAS TWO-PARTY POLITICS*.

LYNDON BAINES JOHNSON (1908–1973) TOWERED OVER TEXAS AND THE COUNTRY DURING THE MIDDLE PART OF THE TWENTIETH CENTURY. SERVING IN THE HOUSE, THE SENATE, THE VICE PRESIDENCY, AND THE OVAL OFFICE, LBJ IS BEST REMEMBERED FOR CIVIL RIGHTS, THE WAR ON POVERTY, THE GREAT SOCIETY, AND VIETNAM. TODAY, ALMOST 40 YEARS AFTER HIS DEATH, HE "REMAINS A HOT PROPERTY FOR" HISTORIANS AND POLITICAL SCIENTISTS. THE "GENERAL PUBLIC'S MEMORY" OF JOHNSON, HOWEVER, IS RECEDING. INDEED, TO MANY MODERN TEXANS, LBJ "NO LONGER SEEMS RELEVANT." IN THIS SELECTION, DR. DOBBS DISCUSSES OUR FADING MEMORY OF THIS COLOSSAL FIGURE.

★ ★

My only memory of Lyndon Johnson just happens to be his last public event. I remember his funeral. The whole first grade sat (so-called "Indian-style") on the floor of our open classroom. We watched the televised goings-on in Washington; I watched the Hill Country burial

"Lyndon, We Hardly Remember Ye: LBJ in the Memory of Modern Texas" by Ricky Floyd Dobbs reprinted from *Lone Star Pasts: Memory and History in Texas* editors Gregg Cantrell and Elizabeth Hayes Turner by permission of the Texas A&M University Press.

at home with my mother. There wasn't much else on television back in those days. All three networks were all Lyndon, all day.

In retrospect, Johnson's obsequies seem muted, especially in comparison to the Reagan funeral extravaganza that consumed a whole week in June 2004. The most Texan of "Texan" presidents died on January 22, 1973. By afternoon on the twenty-fourth, the former president's body lay in state at the LBJ Library in Austin. An estimated thirty-two thousand persons paid their respects before its departure for Washington and the Capitol rotunda. Forty thousand more viewed the casket there, and a "Service of Tribute" celebrated LBJ's life of public service at National City Christian Church. The next afternoon, Johnson's body returned to Texas for interment on the former president's Gillespie County ranch.

Johnson died only four years after leaving the White House. He had deceived the nation repeatedly about a far-off war. He had escalated American involvement in Southeast Asia, ignored advice to alter course, and saw the whole gamble come crashing down around him as America's cities burned and its youth rebelled. In 1973, not many were in the mood to forgive and remember. Johnson had died before his friends could properly build a memory of his accomplishments.

Even before his death, some suggested his legacy would be bigger than Vietnam. His personality alone, some claimed, would secure him a prominent place in American history and Texas memory. In 1969, journalist Marshall Frady described him as "an awesome phenomenon simply as a human being, with an epic ego, exuberances, glooms, ambitions, paranoias, generosities, will: a kind of ill-starred, left-handed Prometheus." Three years after his death, *Texas Monthly* remembered him as "a great original, a man whose energy and personality knew few bounds, the polar opposite both of Richard Nixon's rootless ambition and Gerald Ford's midwestern blandness." Eventually, time and his acolytes' advocacy restored Johnson's historical reputation. Paul Burka described 2000 as "a very good year" for Lyndon Johnson, "his best one since 1964." Historians reexamined Johnson's accomplishments, and the ongoing release of taped White House phone conversations strengthened his image. Johnson remains a hot property for students of the past.

Unfortunately, the general public's memory of Lyndon Johnson has begun to fade. The scholarly attention LBJ has received over a twenty-year period cannot fully correct collective memory. Though historical sites and museums do a fine job of presenting the real Johnson, their ability to mold public perceptions is limited by the public's willingness to come through the door. Public school social studies curricula and textbooks might transmit scholarly understanding of the past, including insight into LBJ. But that is hardly their sole purpose, let alone their chief goal. The current generation's level of awareness of Johnson confirms this view. Lyndon Johnson no longer seems relevant to modern Texas, and he is best remembered for irrelevancies and failings rather than his contributions to the life of the state and nation.

A pleasure trip to the Hill Country in late July might be thought mad. During spring and fall, the Hill Country charms, but it is still Texas in the summer. Summer 2004 defied usual weather patterns, however. When I arrived for a tour and visit with National Park Service staff at the LBJ Ranch, it was overcast, mild, drizzling, and green. Even today, Johnson still looms over his particular patch of earth. It is the best place in Texas to get to know him and one of the few where his memory has yet to fade.

The LBJ ranch is a hybrid site. The National Park Service (NPS) administers the ranch complex and lands; the Texas Parks and Wildlife Department runs a state park across the Pedernales River from the Johnson place. Together, they share a visitor center on state land. NPS staffers describe the ranch as a "natural park" rather than merely a presidential historical site. Wildlife roams freely about. It is also a "working ranch," and descendants of its original Hereford stock lumber through the brushy country. Though LBJ is everywhere, interpretive exhibits in the visitor center might surprise those waiting for the NPS tour bus. These exhibits emphasize the cultural diversity of the Hill Country, making plain that Lyndon Johnson emerged from the region rather than the other way around. Indians, Tejanos, southern whites, African Americans, and Germans all made an impression on the place that molded a president.

Thematically, the influence of "place" on Johnson, as well as his "complexity," drives the NPS interpretation of the LBJ Ranch. Throughout the nine-mile bus tour ranger comments and voiceovers reinforce these themes. Passing the river, a mention of the Hill Country's flash floods gives way to James Califano's disembodied voice describing the president's idea of a joke: driving a carload of visitors full-tilt into the river in his amphibious car. Luxury autos Johnson used to hunt deer and to fly down ranch roads sit on display, even as visitors come to terms with his boyhood experience of poverty and isolation. A one-room school Johnson attended later hosted the signing of the Elementary and Secondary Education Act (1965). Here rangers discuss his "mythic belief" in education as social leveler and cure-all. NPS interpreters consistently link Johnson's personality traits and beliefs directly to a place, building, or object. At the ranch's highest point, the bus stops and allows visitors to take in a wide vista. The voiceover is by LBJ himself, and the topic is the Hill Country's effect upon him.

Park rangers know that many visitors don't care much for Lyndon Johnson. Even thirty years after his death, he remains controversial. Tour narrators point out a "duality" to LBJ's personality and ambition, making him at once "selfish" and "compassionate." No secret is made of his outsized ego or of his other failings. Concluding that Johnson "had many sides both positive and negative," Ranger David Shaffer bids visitors farewell and hopes they have gained new insight into a multifaceted leader. Throughout, the NPS rangers demonstrate professionalism and tact, but they also know their stuff. They converse easily not only about flora and fauna but also about arcane information on the Gulf of Tonkin incident and scholarly debate over Johnson's presidency.

In Austin, official memory of Lyndon Johnson finds its zenith at the Lyndon Baines Johnson Library and Museum at the University of Texas. The university has grown spectacularly since the library opened in 1972. Still, the white stone edifice looms over the campus's eastern edge. Out here the university's trademark Spanish colonial architecture gives way to late-twentieth-century box. Former library director James Middleton and countless scholars have used the library's holdings to rescue Johnson's reputation. Its exhibits sanitize the truth now and then, but the museum usually remains true to the former president's "warts and all" dictum. For example, his eighty-seven-vote 1948 U.S. Senate victory over Coke Stevenson receives truthful, if not exhaustive, attention. For many people, the 1948 "landslide" represents LBJ's original sin, an indicator of innate depravity. Some leap from here to the Kennedy assassination to Vietnam, seeing emerging evil with facile clarity. Examined alongside his 1941 Senate defeat examined earlier in the museum, the 1948 vote typifies garden-variety Texas election theft, if only more historically significant. Context is the mortal enemy of memory.

Later museum exhibits depict "Two Americas" as having existed before LBJ entered the White House. A comfortable, well-fed, prosperous America lived alongside a poor, marginalized one. Race separated still two other Americas. Fate thrust Lyndon Johnson into this circumstance. After experiencing the John F. Kennedy assassination in a darkened twenty-foot hallway, tourists walk out into exhibit space detailing efforts to right these wrongs. A wall adorned with the legend "The Thousand Laws of the Great Society" lists the Johnson administration's legislative victories in its war against racism and poverty. A few of these measures merit special attention with video terminals offering greater depth about Head Start, Medicare, and "A Broadened Concept of Freedom."

Johnson tried to bridge two Americas, but he helped create another division almost as huge as those he tried to heal: the rift over Vietnam. The museum captions offer factual information, but sometimes they are a little too generous. For example: "Only after he is given firm assurance that the attack occurred" did LBJ act after the 1964 Gulf of Tonkin incident. The truth is more complicated. The exhibit demonstrates Johnson's anguish over Vietnam and how he worked himself still harder in response to his inability to control the situation. The huge Texan's frustration with a small country leaps from White House photos of Johnson as commander-in-chief. In the modern context of another far-off war, a look back at a president plainly in over his head brings into question whether the will to forget can overwhelm both history and memory.

It is hard to peg either the ranch or the LBJ Library's impact upon collective memory. Measurement might seem a simple matter of statistics. Visitation at Lyndon B. Johnson National Historical Park has steadily declined since 1973, its best year. The year Johnson died, 579,200 visited, but a year later 200,000 fewer turned out. Attendance declined erratically until 1987 and then fell off sharply after 1989. The NPS reported its worst year ever at the park in 2003 when only 85,339 showed up. Anecdotal evidence suggests that traveling retirees make up a significant portion of tourists. Located some seventy miles west of Austin, the ranch is off the beaten path. One must go there deliberately. National Archives and Records Administration (NARA) figures for the Lyndon Baines Johnson Library and Museum in Austin also show decreasing visitation. In 1976, 701,472 persons visited, the most ever; 1973 came in second with 683,505 patrons. Since 1994, fewer than 300,000 have walked through yearly. After three particularly bad years, 2000–2002, when attendance fell below 200,000, numbers have rebounded, with 228,682 visiting in 2004.

Can one construct a causal link between the LBJ ranch, the LBJ Library, and Texas collective memory? It would take a lot more imagination and facility with a graphing calculator than is present here. What's more, a hazard exists in looking too hard at numbers. If collective memory is partially chosen, not many have chosen the scholarly rendering offered by NPS and NARA. If collective memory might be imposed or absorbed, better places exist to find Texans' collective picture of LBJ. Peter Seixas, Peter Stearns, and Sam Wineburg suggested in 1999 that historians who study collective memory in "museums and through monuments" miss a more significant institutional contributor to society's understanding of the past—the schools. The LBJ Library claims 12,764,000 visitors since 1972. But, as Seixas, Stearns, and Wineburg point out, "the entire population" encounter and process "school accounts of the past during formative impressionable years."

Multiple processes and actors produce the schools' influence upon collective memory. Authority over Texas textbook content inheres in elected officials and functionaries of the state bureaucracy. Locally elected school boards and their appointed administrators have some say in how that content is disseminated. In individual schools, other factors come into play: the principal's willingness to give teachers free rein, or not; a teacher's competence in the subject area; principals,' teachers,' and students' personal views about the relevance of history. Tracing out these local differences would be damnably difficult. The state education bureaucracy's influence upon collective memory is the most easily traced because it begins the process of shaping memory. That bureaucratic influence and the assumptions behind it merit attention. Lyndon Johnson's textbook persona offers some insight into that influence and those assumptions.

In 1916, the National Education Association (NEA) announced "the cultivation of good citizenship" as the "conscious and constant" justification of teaching "social studies." The NEA incorporated history into a group of disciplines individually unworthy of study and declared the past important only so far as it related to "the present life interests of the pupil." Such a utilitarian approach meant that texts and curricula would determine what memories were worth preserving and transmitting. That preservation and transmission had to serve present interests; learning about the past, like any other form of knowledge, had no value in and of itself. Texas schools have never adjusted well to modern ideas such as female linebackers, mandatory attendance, or proper funding. So it took time for this rationale for social studies to meld with or even overwhelm Texans' unnatural affection for their own past. However, a "culture war" now rages in the state's schools, and the utilitarian basis for teaching history predominates regardless of political orientation.

Today's textbooks, for all grades and all subjects, must "align" with the state curriculum, which is called Texas Essential Knowledge and Skills (TEKS). TEKS is a lengthy, jargon-laden document crafted by bureaucrats to humor politicians who promised better schools to please constituents. Properly "aligned" texts prepare students for the state assessment of student progress, the Texas Assessment of Knowledge and Skills (TAKS). Checking this "alignment" is a power of the elected State Board of Education (SBOE). In 2000, the SBOE stipulated that new texts to be adopted in 2002 must promote "appreciation of democratic values and patriotism." Board members even drafted definitions of "patriotism," "free enterprise," and what it meant to properly "appreciate" them. The board's attempt to apply these definitions has drawn national attention to Texas' textbook adoption process.

Appreciation of these concepts required students "to think well of; to understand and enjoy; to recognize and to be grateful for" them. Texas' primary and secondary schools' textbooks focus less upon history than operant conditioning. These books deliver approved information to enhance performance upon an arbitrarily created examination designed for "educational progress." In this, they differ little from other states' texts. However, given Texas' recent atypical presence on the cutting edge of "education reform," they carry greater weight. An examination of the texts, then, might also illuminate current collective memory of LBJ and also offer insight into its future.

Factually, the textbooks tend to get it right. With respect to Johnson there are surprisingly few factual errors, though at times one can still find some half-truths or the occasional fabrication. Omission and overstatement appear frequently. Some things seem to happen for no apparent reason. The adoption process and utilitarian rationale of social studies instills a deadly factuality. But history is more than facts: It is context, interpretation, analysis, and connectedness. It is *life.*

So what of Johnson? How do the textbooks treat him? What memories of him are worthy of preservation? What follows is a composite summary of LBJ's life to 1960 patched together from the approved texts:

> ***LBJ grew up "in the dry Texas Hill Country." He was not poor, but he was not rich either. But, the Hill Country was a poor region and he saw poverty first-hand. After college he taught school briefly in Cotulla. He then headed the National Youth Administration in Texas and "made sure the agency provided jobs fairly." After leaving the NYA, he won a seat in the House and later, the Senate. Once in the Senate, he helped pass the Civil Rights Act (1957), and in his spare time, he got Felix Longoria buried at Arlington National Cemetery. LBJ was a colorful fellow, "a stereotypical Texas politician—loud and slightly crude." By employing the "Treatment" he became an effective Senate leader. In 1960, John Kennedy "shocked" his supporters by taking LBJ as his running mate as a "strategic choice." He helped the ticket "where Kennedy was not particularly popular."***

As is often the case throughout the textbooks, what is omitted is probably more damning of the process than what remains. Several books are coy about the type of school Johnson worked in at Cotulla. Those that offer descriptors tend to use the term "poor." But, there's more there. Johnson worked at the "Mexican" school in Cotulla and pressed white teachers there to take themselves and their charges seriously. None of the texts that mention LBJ's stint with the National Youth Administration bothers to explain how anyone could doubt the fairness of New Deal relief employment. In fact, Johnson's fair hiring and pay policies for blacks and Tejanos ran counter to New Deal employment relief throughout the South. The controversial 1948 Senate race gets only a cursory mention, perhaps because space does not allow greater detail. Some of the texts acknowledge that the liability of JFK's Catholicism was offset by Johnson's presence on the 1960 Democratic ticket. Most avoid or shade this issue and LBJ's significance to Kennedy's narrow victory.

Once Johnson becomes president, textbook coverage becomes much more extensive, though not always more illuminating. The critical event in the Johnson narrative always happens in Dallas. Seventh-grade texts glide through the assassination quickly. It happened. Johnson became president. Most high school American history texts hint at conspiracy. *The Americans* is the worst; a whole paragraph entitled "Unanswered Questions" describes investigations since the Warren Commission, implying that the case is still open. A feature blurb tells readers that "newly declassified information has added some weight to a body of evidence that JFK was shot from the front," though it cautions that "no information has yet . . . conclusively disprove[d]" the Warren Commission's findings. *America: Pathway to the Present* explains that "some investigations support the theory" of Oswald's involvement "in a larger conspiracy." "Many Americans continued to believe" in a conspiracy despite the Warren Commission's report, says *American Nation*.

The assassination dramatizes why collective memory is not history and should not be allowed to become history. "Many Americans" believe a lot of things that are not verifiable, true, or based on sound evidence. The Warren Commission's findings have not been "conclusively" repudiated because they probably represent the soundest account of events. It is a mistake to devote too much space to a single moment in time, no matter how tragic, and opening the door to that moment's most darkly dubious interpretations compounds that mistake. For Americans of a certain age, Kennedy's death represents a watershed event, a loss of innocence, or so they say. However, will it matter as much at the fiftieth anniversary in 2013? History must offer perspective here and now. The Kennedy assassination began the Johnson presidency. Any poetic uncertainty hovering over November 22 brings into question everything Lyndon Johnson did afterward.

All the texts correctly acknowledge that LBJ seized the moment to drive existing antipoverty and civil rights initiatives through Congress. But the books often reduce the Texan to a functionary—only a signer of the Civil Rights (CRA) and Voting Rights (VRA) Acts. Johnson had developed a real revulsion to the injustices of segregation and disfranchisement. His discomfort emerged as early as his teaching career. Neither John nor Robert Kennedy saw civil rights as America's great moral challenge from 1961 to 1963. They discouraged protests, bargained with segregationists, and authorized a program of FBI surveillance and harassment of the movement. Johnson certainly was not perfect. He periodically used the word "nigger," and he had not quite defeated his own ingrained racial attitudes. LBJ was a recovering southerner. He acknowledged that the South and the nation had a problem, and he fought it. He never quite beat it within himself, but he struggled on because it was the right thing to do. But the ambiguity and complexity of Johnson the Civil Rights Crusader is not present in these texts—only a man sitting behind a big desk signing bills.

In pushing, signing, and believing in civil rights legislation Johnson performed a redemptive service for his region and state. This essentially thankless task is also missing from the textbooks. Some seventh-grade Texas history students learn that "some members of Congress" opposed the CRA and VRA but do not learn why. Others learn even less from their texts.

One might think the reasons for opposition to these landmarks of legislation would be self-evident, but modern students labor to chronologically sort segregation and the stegosaurus. Dealing fully with civil rights issues means acknowledging that something now considered to be basically good and just could once have engendered serious opposition. As Yvonne Frear's essay in this volume demonstrates, many students already dispute the relevance of the past. When student skepticism combines with a bureaucracy's determination to inculcate patriotism through instructional materials, the mix kills history, renders it irrelevant, and creates collective memory, or forgetfulness, in its place.

Now much maligned as a facilitator of poverty rather than its sworn enemy, Lyndon Johnson's own preferred legacy also suffers in the textbooks. Usually, both the War on Poverty and Great Society (and they are distinct, though often conflated in textbooks) appear with key components detailed in short descriptive paragraphs. These descriptions offer limited evaluation of effectiveness but bandy about dollar amounts as though mid-1960s costs have any relevance to today's students. Several explain that Johnson antipoverty programs nearly halved the nation's poverty rate, from 21 to 11 percent between 1962 and 1973. Specific real-life examples of how these programs changed lives are few. Instead, LBJ emerges as a free-spending liberal driving the nation into debt. No wonder opposition arose so quickly to this largesse. High taxes, the belief that government aid created dependency, and fear that LBJ's program strengthened federal government at the expense of the states drove the criticism. Race apparently had nothing to do with it, according to textbooks. True, principled conservatives did fret over these issues, but the conservative backlash did not arise simply from anger at taxation. Taxes had been higher under Kennedy and Eisenhower. Civil rights and antipoverty efforts blended easily in many minds. None of the texts ventures that possibility.

The Great Society was "a vast program of social welfare laws," intones a seventh-grade text. No, there's more to it than that. Visit an octogenarian relative and wonder at what might account for her longevity. Drive a country road and notice the hawks perched from time to time on telephone poles. Go see a play with your kids at a children's theater. Watch *Sesame Street* and learn the alphabet. Marvel at how a seatbelt keeps heads a comfortable distance from the windshield during fender benders. Send in a monthly payment on a government-insured loan that got you through college. All have ties to the Great Society. Sociologist James W. Loewen criticized texts for nearly always portraying the government in a favorable light, crediting it with progress forced by outside activism. When dealing with the federal government since 1933, Texas' modern textbooks often do the opposite: minimizing or overlooking the good done by government.

Perhaps as a byproduct, the textbook Johnson lacks a political identity. Based upon his record against poverty and segregation, LBJ as president governed as a liberal. Students rarely get the news that bluntly, however. In *The American Nation in the Modern Era* we get a hint. "If you look at my record, you would know that I am a Roosevelt New Dealer," it has Johnson proclaiming, along with, "As a matter of fact, John F. Kennedy was a little too conservative to suit my taste." One Texas history text muddles the matter, claiming that by 1968 conservatives supported more aggressive measures in Vietnam, but "liberals wanted to withdraw entirely." Was Lyndon Johnson not a liberal? Here modern conceptions about the political ideology most willing to use force intrude upon a much more ambiguous past. What is not ambiguous, however, is Vietnam's influence upon LBJ's place in public memory.

Like the assassination, but for better reasons, Vietnam won't go away either. Seventh-grade textbooks focus on Texas, so the narrative only touches upon the conflict. LBJ is passive throughout. High school American history books offer greater depth. Some play "what if." What if Kennedy had not been killed? "Shortly before his death, Kennedy had announced his intent to withdraw" from Vietnam, claims *The Americans*. On the contrary, JFK merely authorized advisors in private to plan for a withdrawal after the 1964 elections. Publicly, he made cryptic statements about the conflict being South Vietnam's to "win or lose." The tricky question of what Kennedy might have done weighs heavily upon Johnson's reputation. Kennedy's skepticism about Vietnam grew through 1963. Lyndon Johnson came into office skeptical as well but listened too much to holdover advisors, mistrusted his own instincts, and tried to score political points with toughness. The result proved disastrous for him and for the nation.

Lyndon Johnson unquestionably misled the public about the Gulf of Tonkin incident in August 1964, paving the way for escalation in the years following. It is a truly blameworthy moment, and Texas high schoolers get the truth from their textbooks. That is, if they ever get to that point in history class. In 2002, as the SBOE scrutinized new texts, *Dallas Morning News* education reporter Joshua Benton interviewed some Dallas area teachers and discovered that the recent past got short shrift in most classrooms. Teachers explained their difficulties in getting past World War II. Benton predicted the social studies segment of the eleventh-grade TAKS would change all that. The TAKS would "force" more recent history into the classroom, "including the Vietnam war." Unlike previous years, a Texas Education Agency social studies official pointed out, "administrators are paying a lot of attention to social studies now." Indeed, administrators started preparing much earlier. Some lamented this changing emphasis. An associate dean of Texas A&M University's education school admitted, "Folks sure don't make it to the end of the book, but they don't make it because they're doing some very good things." Benton himself complained that things that "get kids fired up" about history "could be lost" in an attempt to cover the whole curriculum.

Benton's prediction might not ring true three years later. After all, as a Carrollton–Farmers Branch Independent School District administrator told the reporter, "What gets monitored, gets done." Students first encountered the eleventh-grade social studies TAKS in 2003. In principle, the examination follows the TEKS curriculum. Therefore, exposure to the entire curriculum alone will produce satisfactory scores or actual knowledge, if that's what the state had in mind. The 2003 exam posed fifty-five questions that should have covered all twenty-six TEKS competencies for U.S. history since 1877. Of those twenty-six, only seven involve history, and only two dealt with American history since 1933. One specifically addressed the civil rights movement; the other is a catchall for everything else. Given these parameters, one could guess that 1963–69 might largely escape notice. On a sample test provided by TEA, ten of fifty-five questions dealt with either pre-1877 U.S. history or world topics ranging from the Black Death to the Aswan Dam. While preparation would have been uneven across Texas' thousand-plus school districts early on, TAKS results ought to allow some measurement of success in imparting the TEKS. We will know soon enough. Those earliest test takers enter colleges and universities in 2004 and afterward.

I remember hearing almost nothing about LBJ in either seventh-grade Texas history or high school American history. Our junior high class stopped at 1845, drew the Alamo for fifty points on an exam, and did a lot of "definitions." That is, we defined chapter vocabulary terms in writing after scanning the textbook for the "definition" of Mirabeau Lamar or *Adelsverein*. Our teacher focused mainly on his playbooks and periodically bellowed "shut up" when we hormone-addled youths got out of hand. In high school, my teacher knew her stuff and worked to present it well and relatively truthfully. Still, we never got to LBJ. Perhaps we didn't have time. In the early 1980s, the Vietnam misadventure and the death throes of Jim Crow remained painfully recent. The era of Lyndon Johnson may have simply been too controversial. But, I also grew up in a benighted time: before Ross Perot and House Bill 72, George W. Bush and TEKS.

If controversy once kept LBJ out of classrooms, chronological distance should have allowed his return, and students should know more about him, particularly given modern "standards." So I polled more than 100 students in university U.S. history survey classes. All seemed to know that Johnson was president once, but beyond that most claimed to know nothing. The survey was not scientific, but impressionistic. Of 159 students aged seventeen to sixty-five, 72 claimed to know nothing of his accomplishments, to have heard nothing of him that made an impression. A slender majority had some idea of the man, some impression of him, or knew of some event in his presidency.

Most who had a mental image of LBJ viewed him negatively. Based on photographs, one student decided that he "didn't appear friendly" and looked "stern and strict." Others echoed this sense; he did not look likable. Modern politicians joke with David Letterman, appear on *Saturday Night Live*, and answer questions about their underwear to become more likable. Johnson came from a political tradition that felt the nation's business was above that sort of thing, and consequently, he never adjusted well to television. Some students know about the "Treatment," with one describing a leader who "would eat really bad smelling food then get right in your face in order to intimidate." Another had heard that he liked to urinate on Secret Service agents. Other negative impressions came back describing LBJ as a "good old boy," "wishy-washy," or a stereotypical politician. One student remarked that his dad thought Johnson a "crook," and still another claimed his family knew one of the president's mistresses.

Some had better, yet more vague, impressions of Johnson. He was a "good man," a "concerned" leader, or "someone the people loved." Occasionally, someone indicated LBJ's support for civil rights as the basis for their positive view. Only seven of eight-seven offering detailed responses mentioned this portion of Johnson's legacy, arguably his most redeeming achievement. Plenty of students had mistaken impressions, such as believing that Johnson had resigned to avoid impeachment and removal from office. Several thought him a Republican; still others believed him "conservative." One even described him as a "mild mannered" sort. Three associations dominated these students' knowledge of LBJ: November 22, 1963, Vietnam, and Dallas's LBJ Freeway.

The assassination happened in Texas, in a political climate so charged that Dallas's leaders urged citizens to behave themselves prior to Kennedy's visit. Conspiracy theories abound, and people still go for them. These theories often ensnare Vice President Johnson as instigator, accomplice, or dupe. In 2003, just before the fortieth anniversary of the assassination, an ABC News Poll showed that 65 percent of Americans believed that questions remained unanswered regarding the crime, and 70 percent believed in a conspiracy beyond Lee Harvey Oswald. A media ruckus ensued when the History Channel trotted out eleven hours of documentaries collectively styled "The Men Who Killed Kennedy." History Channel promotions of one episode, "The Guilty Men," tantalized with the hook, "The roots of the crime lie buried deep in the heart of Texas and revolve around Lyndon Baines Johnson and high powered supporters of the assassination who felt their fortunes threatened by JFK's presidency."

Blood, Money & Power: How LBJ Killed JFK, a book by former Austin lawyer Barr McClellan, spawned the History Channel documentary. McClellan claimed that Dallas football entrepreneur Clint Murchison, former vice president Richard Nixon, FBI director J. Edgar Hoover, and Johnson met at Murchison's Dallas residence the night before the assassination to finalize plans to kill President Kennedy. Former Johnson aides Bill Moyers and Jack Valenti, among others, brought sufficient pressure to force the network to air a panel discussion of professional historians who then eviscerated McClellan's yarn. *Blood, Money & Power* is only the latest attempt by a Texan to link Johnson to practically every evil imaginable. Its refutation is cold comfort for those who want collective memory to resemble history. ABC's poll showed that Americans aged eighteen to thirty-four are even more likely than their elders to believe a conspiracy was behind JFK's assassination.

Twenty-six of eighty-seven detailed responses in the student survey mentioned the assassination and/or LBJ's succeeding Kennedy. More students knew this fact than any policy initiative or personality trait. Antipoverty efforts, Medicare, and Job Corps received no mention at all. Instead, the assassination overshadows all else. A handful mentioned Johnson as a possible conspirator. Had the survey directly brought up the assassination, more students likely would have gone this direction. It disheartens one that they know so little else, a single moment in a decade of change and upheaval. Perhaps, with time, the circumstances of Lyndon Johnson's move to the White House will fade in relation to his own accomplishments, as with Theodore Roosevelt. But, frankly, William McKinley was no Jack Kennedy.

American history survey students at least appear keenly interested in Vietnam. It is always late in the semester when class attendance counter-intuitively tapers off before finals. Advance notice that there will be two days of lecture on Vietnam fills the classroom. It was their parents' (sometimes grandparents') war, and it frequently pops up online, in movies, television, books, and periodicals. Reminders of America's involvement in Southeast Asia abound in modern Texas. Dat Nguyen, once a Texas Aggie standout, recently retired from the Dallas Cowboys. Vietnamese and Cambodian immigrants have thriving communities within the state's major cities, and the Fox television network's *King of the Hill* features an upwardly mobile Laotian family as Hank Hill's next-door neighbors. Interestingly, the war's presence in our lives does not mean its deeper lessons register with today's college students. Vietnam helped ensure the insulation of most from the ongoing war in Iraq, a topic one almost never hears in students' hallway conversations. This protective insulation was Lyndon Johnson's (inadvertent) doing because his handling of the war helped doom the draft. Still, few students seem to have thought it out that far.

However, ask what LBJ did or what his greatest failure was, and Vietnam leaps easily to mind for many. Twenty students elaborated on their survey forms about America's longest war. Their responses ran the gamut from incorrect, to speculatively incorrect, to insightful or ambivalent. One student counted Johnson's ending Vietnam as his greatest achievement; still another cited simply "Vietnam" as an achievement. (One encounters students unaware that the United States lost the war.) One guessed that he might have made some good decisions with respect to Vietnam, but that student did not elaborate. While blaming LBJ for the Indochina morass, a student judged him poorly equipped to deal with the situation. Vietnam, for another, was part of fixing "Kennedy's mess." None blamed Johnson or any other politicians for America's defeat, an otherwise perennial complaint. Instead, a number criticized his determination to stay when the U.S. should have left. Winning and losing mattered less than having wasted the nation's resources.

Tied with Vietnam in students' minds is the Lyndon B. Johnson Freeway (1-635). The proximity of my own teaching institution, Texas A&M University–Commerce, to Dallas certainly accounts for this response. At first glance, one could dismiss these twenty responses as having a bit of fun with the professor. However, they came evenly distributed across seven survey sections with four different instructors in three different academic sessions. Reference to a freeway might be the testing reflex kicking in—desperation to put something remotely true in a blank space. Some insisted, in the absence of any other evidence, that Johnson could not have been "that bad" with such a large stretch of road named after him. For Dallas area residents younger than fifty, this notion likely makes perfect sense, viz President George Bush Turnpike.

Surprisingly, Dallas did not wait until Johnson died to name 1-635 after him. In October 1961 a unanimous city council decision honored the vice president. Considering that a well-heeled right-wing mob attacked LBJ and Lady Bird at the Adolphus Hotel barely a year earlier, the timing is surprising. Bickering broke out in early 1962 about whether the naming was appropriate or even legal. Was it a federal or city responsibility? No bids had been made on right-of-way acquisition for the project. *Dallas Morning News* writer Mike Quinn remarked, "This is conservative territory and how they will like seeing LBJ's name at 8 A.M on the way to work is anybody's guess." When the first $100 million length opened from Stemmons Freeway (1-35E) to Marsh Lane in March 1967, Johnson was president and American combat forces were bogged down in Vietnam. The opening attracted protestors. A northwest Dallas mothers' group came to demand the pedestrian walkway at Marsh Lane be covered completely to prevent accidents or childish tomfoolery. The event is now long forgotten, certainly for modern students, rather like everything else Lyndon Johnson did. It is the way of all flesh for politicians. You rise, have things named for you, and then you are forgotten except as an address. Lyndon B. Johnson, meet Marvin D. Love.

Why is there such a gap between the Lyndon Johnson of history and the Lyndon Johnson of Texans' collective memory? Two answers offer themselves. First, modern Texans associate Lyndon Johnson with unpleasant aspects of state identity. Second, he does not fit well with the modern political climate.

"What is the ape to men?" Nietzsche's Zarathustra asked. "A laughing stock or a painful embarrassment" was the answer. Embarrassment over LBJ started early for some Texans. Larry McMurtry bemoaned Johnson in *In a Narrow Grave*. In that collection of essays on Texas published in 1968, McMurtry ridiculed Johnson's ranch, his boorishness, even his ears. Thirty years later, while writing a biography of Lady Bird, native Texan Jan Jarboe Russell listened to him on newly released tapes. The voice brought back memories of childhood. "Everything about him—his body, his ranch, his Lincolns, his bear hugs, but most of all his voice—seemed ridiculously out of proportion," she wrote. "Johnson was the last of the really big hicks." Texans respond the forty-third president's accent with a wink and a nod. We know the truth. Crawford ranch aside, George W. Bush is no agrarian. He's a city boy. Just like most of the rest of us.

Modern Texas is urban and predominantly middle class. Johnson's style, his accent, and the things he cared about emerged from a very different Texas. His Texas was rural, backward, segregated, and poor. Many present-day Texans would rather not think on such things, even if they know about them. Modern automobile license plates feature the space shuttle, a cowboy, a cactus, and an oil rig. Where's the cotton? The lynching tree? The soup line? Before World War II, most Texans lived in a netherworld of barely getting by. Hope for better times and opportunities for getting out were few. From suburban living rooms it might all seem bucolic, like the ubiquitous Hill Country landscape over the sofa. But it was hell. Past poverty and past realities might be too big an embarrassment, and perhaps Johnson himself, his style and his accent, represents too painful a reminder. These might explain many modern Texans' ambivalence toward Johnson.

And, of course, Texas has changed politically as well. The change first emerged in the last two decades of LBJ's career. In 1952 and 1956, Texas went for Republican Dwight Eisenhower despite Senator Johnson's best efforts. A Republican, John Tower, replaced him in the U.S. Senate in 1961. In 1971, former Texas governor John Connally joined the Nixon administration as treasury secretary and a few months after LBJ died in 1973, his former protégé switched parties. Today, Texas state government, its congressional delegation, and its electorate are solidly Republican. Lyndon Johnson doesn't fit Texas anymore. He was a Democrat: he had liberal inclinations throughout his career. He believed government could do good for citizens. He tried to expand economic opportunity so more Americans could enjoy life within the Great American Middle Class. He spoke of social justice and racial equality. And he acted upon his words. Many twenty-first century Texans often complacently see poverty and racism as things of the past or of overactive imaginations. They don't want to hear Lyndon's voice anymore.

Some will question this essay's focus upon a single man. After all, haven't historians finished with the Great Man as the center of history? This essay is a project in collective memory—the residue that remains in the public mind after historical truth has either been forgotten or rejected. For such a project, the Great Man is a particularly apt figure of study. He provides a benchmark from which to examine the overall durability of historical truth. If that is true, then history had better watch out. Texans increasingly have trouble remembering so obvious a figure as Lyndon Baines Johnson.

Women in Texas

Cary D. Wintz

Cary D. Wintz is Professor of History at Texas Southern University in Houston. A specialist in African American and Texas history, his studies include *Black Culture and the Harlem Renaissance* and *Harlem Speaks: A Living History of the Harlem Renaissance*. Dr. Wintz coauthored *Texas: The Lone Star State* and coedited *Major Problems in Texas History* and *Black Dixie: Afro-Texan History and Culture in Houston*.

Women have played an important role in shaping Texas. From Caddo leader Santa Adiva to Spanish rancher Maria Hinojosa de Balli, from Anglo pioneers Jane Long and Mary Austin Holley to suffragists Rebecca Henry Hayes and Annette Finnigan, from civil rights advocates Maria Hernandez and Lulu B. White to Governors Miriam Ferguson and Ann Richards, Congresswoman Barbara Jordan, and Senator Kay Bailey Hutchison, Dr. Wintz surveys the challenges faced by, and contributions made by, women in Lone Star history.

★ ★

A cold wind blew across the narrow bay from onshore signaling the arrival of the season's first winter storm. The north winds would bring with them the opportunity to scavenge for oysters in the low tides. The sky was gray, almost the same steel-gray of the gulf waters. Two women and a young child left a crude half-tent shelter that they had rigged at the abandoned stockade and trudged across the dunes to the narrow beach carrying sacks, which they hoped to fill with crabs or oysters for their evening dinner. The younger woman, a black in her early teens, led the way, looking carefully up and down the beach for any signs of Indians as she hurried toward the shore. The other, a white woman, barely twenty and visibly pregnant, followed, her progress slowed by her young daughter who was almost hidden by the tall grasses that stretched halfway up the dunes. As she approached the beach, her eyes scanned the bleak horizon looking for a sail that might signal the return of her husband, or at least bring news of him.

Jane Long, accompanied by her young daughter Ann and a young slave woman known as Kian, spent the winter of 1820–1821 on Bolivar peninsula, while her husband, Dr. James Long of Louisiana, conducted his ill-fated military mission against Spanish forces in Texas. Jane Long and Kian contended with hunger, cold, isolation, and the threat of attacks by hostile Indians. Kian successfully nursed Long through illness and childbirth in mid-December; at one point the women went three days without food before Kian managed to find an oyster reef in the shallows of Galveston Bay. On another occasion the women dressed in military uniforms, hoisted a red flannel petticoat up the flagpole of the abandoned fort, and fired off the fort's old cannon in order to convince a passing band of Karankawa Indians that the post was still manned by soldiers. The two women and two children survived the harsh winter through a combination of courage, ingenuity, and luck. Their ordeal came to an end when a Mexican rider appeared on the deserted beach with the message that the Spanish had captured and executed Dr. Long. Unwilling to let matters rest, Jane Long and her entourage traveled by horseback, first to San Antonio de Béxar and then to Monterrey, seeking to have her husband's "murderers" brought to justice. Although her determination impressed Mexican officials, she received no satisfaction, only polite expressions of sympathy. Finally Long gave up and returned to her home in Mississippi. A year later, however, she would return to Texas, along with Kian and her two daughters, as one of Stephen F. Austin's original "old three hundred" colonists.

Jane Long's courage and determination, as well as the fact that she was perhaps the first Anglo-American woman to come to Texas—and the first to give birth there—have earned her a place in Texas mythology as the "Mother of Texas." Kian, who shared all of the original adventures, returned to Texas with Long (as her servant and life-long companion), and raised her own family in and around the lower Brazos River town of Richmond, can claim with equal justice the title "Mother of Black Texas." However, women's history in Texas predates Jane Long and Kian. Spanish women, Indian women, and the women ancestors of the American Indians influenced the history and development of the area that we know as Texas long before the arrival of Jane Long and Kian. Indeed, Texas history may be viewed as a series of migrations that brought people into the region. Women, of course, participated in each of these successive waves of immigration and influenced the culture established by each set of newcomers.

While archaeologists continue to search for the clues that will settle the debate over when humans first arrived in North America and subsequently in Texas, there is no debate over the fact that women played a significant role in Texas's earliest cultures. Whether these first inhabitants came 12,000 years ago or 25,000 years ago, the role that women played in early cultures is fairly well known. (Our knowledge of these first inhabitants of Texas comes from the work of archaeologists and anthropologists who have examined the artifacts of early cultures, and from anthropologists who have studied nineteenth- and twentieth-century cultures with economic, social, and technological practices similar to those of earlier cultures.)

Paleo Americans, as the predecessors of the American Indians are generally termed, lived by hunting and gathering. In the more distant past their livelihoods centered around hunting large game, such as the mammoths, mastodons, and prehistoric bison that once were plentiful in North America; around ten thousand years ago, as these ice-age animals became extinct, the peoples' methods of getting food shifted, first to hunting small game and gathering wild plant food, and then, in most areas, to agriculture or a combination of agriculture, hunting, and gathering. Women performed essential tasks in these early cultures. Generally labor was divided along sexual lines. Among the nomadic hunters of large game, women cared for the children, prepared food, processed meat and hides, prepared clothing, sometimes erected shelter, often made tools, and saw to it that all household possessions were properly packed for transport during seasonal migrations. Meanwhile, men primarily were responsible for hunting. As big-game hunting gave way to hunting and gathering, women generally assumed more responsibility for acquiring food—especially the gathering of wild plant food—and processing and storing food. In these early cultures, women played important and occasionally dominant roles in the ceremonial and religious lives of their people. The transition to agriculture tended to make the division of labor along sexual lines more rigid. For those cultures that remained seminomadic, or combined agriculture with a continued reliance on hunting and gathering, women generally added production of the crops to their other labors, while men continued to hunt (and make war). In those societies that settled down in permanent or semipermanent agricultural villages, women acquired additional duties associated with maintaining the home, food preparation, the manufacture of clothing, and caring for the young. They also helped tend the crops, but by this time men began to assume more of the responsibility for farming and home construction.

By the time that Europeans first arrived in the region that became Texas the various Paleo-American cultures had given way to four major Native-American cultures, plus several other minor cultures. The role of women varied considerably from culture to culture. Among the groups that shared the Western Gulf cultures, along the coastal prairies and in the arid lands of South Texas and northern Mexico, there was little division of labor along sexual lines. Life was so harsh and the environment so unproductive for these hunter-gatherers that all members of the community spent virtually all of their time in the search for food. In contrast, among the Lipan Apaches, who occupied the plains of West and Southwest Texas, the roles of men and women were clearly delineated. While men were buffalo hunters and warriors, women cultivated the fields, butchered the buffalo, dressed the buffalo hides and turned them into the leather used to cover tepees and make clothing. Women also built the teepees, made the clothing, and fashioned tools out of buffalo bone. After the acquisition of horses made buffalo hunting and warfare rich and rewarding professions, the importance of agriculture, and consequently the position of women in the Apache economy, declined, and Apache men frequently made the women abandon their unharvested fields and pack up the village to follow the buffalo herds, or to engage in military activity.

Among the Caddos of East and Northeast Texas, women attained position and influence unmatched in early Texas. Two Caddo confederacies existed in Texas in historic times, the Kadohadacho and Hasinai, as well as related cultures to their south and north. By most standards the Caddo had developed the most impressive civilization in Texas. They were highly skilled farmers, lived in permanent agricultural villages, and participated in an extensive trading network with Indians to the east and west of Texas. The Caddo also maintained a very elaborate political and social system. In addition, Caddo culture, as well as that of related groups such as the Wichitas and Tonkawas, was matriarchal. At the beginning of the world, according to Hasinai mythology, there was one woman, and this woman had two daughters; from these two the human race descended. In historical times the oldest competent woman, the "mother of the house," was the dominant figure in the family; typically the family consisted of a woman, her sisters, her husband, unmarried children, and married daughters and their families.

Caddo women also could hold great political and economic power. Fray Gaspar Jose de Solis, who traveled among the Caddo late in the 1760s, described his encounter with a woman of great wealth and power known as Santa Adiva. Her house, he wrote, "is very large and has many rooms. The rest of the Nations bring presents and gifts to her. She has many Indian men and women in her service called *tamas comas*, and these are like priests and captains among them. She is married to five Indian men." Another early European explorer described a "queen" among the Kadohadacho—a term that probably referred to the mother of the heir apparent, or the sister of the current ruler, but who was herself a person of great power. In other respects the role of women in Caddo life reflected the more structured, hierarchal nature of Caddo society. Labor was divided along sexual lines, with men performing the heavy work of clearing and plowing the fields, building the houses, and hunting, while women tended the fields and harvested the crops, prepared the food, tended house, and gathered wild herbs, fruits, berries, and nuts. Both men and women held positions in the political and religious hierarchy.

The first Europeans in Texas arrived as part of a series of Spanish expeditions in the sixteenth century, and a French expedition in the seventeenth century. These were exploratory undertakings that did not involve European women. However, women were involved in the Spanish settlement of Texas, which began late in the seventeenth century. While the mission, the principal institution for spreading the Spanish Empire north into Texas, was male dominated, the soldiers who manned the presidios that supported the missions frequently brought their families with them, so nearly half of the population of the initial civil settlements at San Antonio and Nacogdoches were women. Even the missions, founded by priests to convert the Indians and transform them into law-abiding Spanish subjects, actually resembled walled villages with a population of Indian, Mexican, and Spanish men, women, and children. A census of the population of the missions in Spanish Texas in 1783 indicated that the population of the five San Antonio missions consisted of 207 adult men, 149 adult women, 123 male and 75 female children. The population was more balanced in the towns of Spanish Texas; in 1783 San Antonio counted 331 adult men and 311 adult women, while Nacogdoches numbered 129 adult men and 104 adult women.

Women also played an active role in Spanish Texas. Although Spanish custom and law, as well as the rules of the Catholic Church, severely restricted women's rights, on the fringes of the Spanish empire women were able to assert themselves fully. Whether the opportunity they enjoyed was due to the "democratic" nature of the frontier, the fact that the strength of traditional restrictions against women was diluted by distance and the necessities of frontier life, or the high mortality rate which often forced widows to take over responsibilities generally fulfilled by men, women in Spanish Texas ran businesses and ranches, received land grants, and occasionally even helped lead settlers into Texas, while still performing their traditional duties as wives, mothers, companions, and helpmates. Though women assumed these many roles and tasks, on the official level Spanish Texas remained a male-dominated society, as evidenced by census reports that listed women separately only if they were widows, and, indeed, that treated widowhood as the principal female occupation.

Nonetheless, the degree to which women found room to assert themselves in Spanish Texas is surprising. Fate—often in the form of the death of a spouse—left many women in charge of property and the heads of households, even if adult sons were present. Other women achieved prominence through their economic achievements or their political skills. María Josefa Granados owned the largest general store in San Antonio in the 1780s, while Doña María Hinojosa de Ballí expanded the landholdings that she inherited from her husband until she owned about one-third of the lower Rio Grande Valley, including Padre Island, and truly merited the designation as Texas's first cattle queen. Doña María del Carmen Calvillo not only presided over the ranch that she inherited from her father in 1814, but she expanded its livestock holdings and built a sugar mill, granary, and large irrigation system. María Betancour earned her fame as one of the early pioneers in San Antonio. In 1731, as a twenty-eight-year-old widow and mother of five, she helped lead thirty-one Canary Islanders to San Antonio, became a fixture in the city's life, and named the main plaza there the Plaza de las Islas in honor of the Islanders' origins. Early in the nineteenth century Maria Cassiano, another descendant of María Betancour, was the wife of the Spanish Governor of Texas who assumed the responsibilities of office whenever her husband was absent.

Of course, for most women in Spanish Texas life entailed neither glamour, wealth, nor power; most worked hard as wives and mothers, farmers or ranchers, or seamstresses, cooks, peddlers, or laundresses. Even on the ranches life was spartan—houses were poorly built and usually consisted of only one room—and women worked from dawn to dusk tending the garden, caring for children, cooking, making household necessities such as soap and candles, spinning, weaving, and fashioning clothing and shoes. The women of Spanish Texas were restricted by Spanish law, which prevented them from voting, as well as by religion, both of which bound them to marriage. On the other hand, Spanish law did give women rights in court, allowed them to sue and be sued, and to enter into legally-binding contracts. Spanish law also protected the property rights of women: it allowed them to maintain property separate from that of their husbands; it protected wives by preventing creditors from seizing their home to satisfy their husband's debts; and it guaranteed women legal right to half-interest in all profits a married couple earned. These latter two rights would persist after the collapse of Spanish rule and provide the basis for the homestead exemption and community-property rights.

The early nineteenth century brought dramatic changes to Texas. First, in 1821, following a ten-year struggle, Mexico received its independence from Spain. As important as this event was, it was overshadowed by an even more momentous development—the Anglo migration to Texas and the demographic revolution that followed. Mexican independence had little direct impact on women in Texas. The legal rights and restrictions women experienced under Spanish jurisdiction did not change substantially. However, some women who lost their husbands to the long struggle for independence successfully sued the Mexican government for survivor's benefits. A few used this income, together with the profits they made from shrewd land dealings, to amass substantial wealth. On the other hand, the revolution did not add to women's political and legal rights or to their social status. The arrival of Anglo-American immigrants, together with African Americans and German immigrants, had a much more profound impact on Texas. By the middle of the 1830s Hispanics were the majority ethnic group only south of the Nueces River and in the Rio Grande Valley, and Hispanic cultural influences, while far from gone, no longer dominated Texas north and east of San Antonio.

Women played a major role in the Anglo migration to Texas. The first Anglo woman known to enter Texas was Jane Long. Almost two years before her adventures on Bolivar Peninsula, she made her first trip to Texas to join her husband, who was attempting to establish a republic for land-hungry Anglos in Spanish Texas. Following the collapse of this expedition and the Bolivar adventure, Jane Long returned to Texas and joined the Austin colony as one of the Old Three Hundred. In 1834 Long and Kian, who would be her lifelong companion, opened an inn at Brazoria; in 1837 they opened another inn, and then a plantation near Richmond. The Long establishments, first in Brazoria, then in Richmond, hosted the most prominent Texans, including Stephen F. Austin and Mirabeau B. Lamar. The latter used the Long inn in Richmond as his campaign headquarters when he ran for president of Texas in 1838. By 1850 Jane Long was one of the sixteen wealthiest people in Texas.

Other women also achieved prominence in early Texas. Mary Austin Holley, a widow who came to Texas from Connecticut, achieved fame by publishing in 1833 a very popular guide for prospective immigrants to Texas entitled *Texas, Observations Historical, Geographical, Descriptive in a Series of Letters*, which provided settlers with detailed and practical advice about what household equipment to bring to Texas and what type of life they could expect to have there. Holley, an avid promoter of Texas colonization and a speculator in Texas land, never achieved the economic security (either from her writing or investments) that she suggested awaited all who moved to Texas and returned to Louisiana, where she worked as a governess. Other women were more successful. Many widows received land grants from Austin and other empresarios in their own right; others, whose husbands died in Texas, managed the lands they inherited and added to their estates.

Most women who immigrated to Texas came with husbands and families. Lucky ones like Mary Crownover Rabb, an eighteen-year-old bride from Arkansas who settled near La Grange in 1823 with her husband and a large group of her husband's relatives, arrived with a ready-made community; other women came only with husband and children; and still others came without husbands, such as Abigail Fokes, a widow with six children who settled on the San Gabriel River in 1835. Stephen F. Austin's 1830 "Register of Families" listed twenty widows, most with children, in his colony. The experiences of these Anglo women on the Texas frontier differed little from those of the Spanish and Mexican women who preceded them. Their life was difficult and the living conditions were primitive. They worked alongside their husbands and older children, clearing the land and planting crops. Like Hispanic women, Anglos found that the social and legal restrictions that limited the rights of women in the early nineteenth century often weakened as one moved west. In the Anglo colonies men outnumbered women in the early years, sometimes as much as two-to-one—a situation which added to the value and influence of women, but one which also could place them under the social and economic subjugation, albeit the loving subjugation, of a male relative. In addition, the social mores of the early nineteenth century still placed married women in a subservient position and expected them to behave in ways that seem strange today. For example, it was not unusual for women in early nineteenth-century Texas to serve meals to their husbands and then retire to the kitchen to eat separately from them.

In spite of the primitive living conditions and the restrictions forced upon their gender, women contributed significantly to colonial Texas. Some successfully managed land or businesses and achieved economic success; others played important roles as community builders. The establishment of schools and churches in early Texas owed much to the work of women. Mary Rabb, Lydia McHenry, and others were instrumental in bringing the Methodist Church to Texas early in the 1830s, while Mary McKinzie Bell was central in the history of the Presbyterian church in Texas. Mexican women worked to overcome the lack of resources that limited the strength of the Catholic Church in Texas during the early nineteenth century. For example, women in San Antonio and Nacogdoches raised funds to repair church buildings in their communities, while Doña Patricia de la Garza de León provided much of the support for the parish Church at Victoria. Most of the work done by Anglo women to bring protestant churches to Texas was done out of public view, because gender restrictions prevented women from assuming formal positions of leadership. On the other hand, women assumed a highly visible role in the early efforts to establish educational institutions, for teaching was one of the few acceptable occupations for women in colonial Texas. Women not only worked as teachers, but they established or helped to establish schools in Independence, Houston, Matagorda, and Washington County. Most of these institutions were private academies or boarding schools that did not survive more than a year or two; efforts to establish public school systems in Texas did not succeed until after the Civil War.

During the turbulent decade of the Texas Revolution and republic, the position of women in Texas underwent a subtle transformation as Anglo culture supplanted Hispanic culture. These changes affected both Anglo and Hispanic women, as well as the growing population of black women. In the second quarter of the nineteenth century, Anglo culture generally placed greater restrictions on the property rights of women than had Hispanic culture; on the other hand, the initial stirrings of feminism and women's suffrage would make their way into Texas from north rather than from south of the Rio Grande.

The mythology of the Texas Revolution, which produced larger-than-life male heroes and tales of heroic encounters between Texans and Mexicans, also encompassed women—most notably Emily Morgan, who reportedly joined Santa Anna's entourage as his army pursued Texas refugees during the Runaway Scrape, sent word to Sam Houston about Santa Anna's position, and then kept the Mexican general "occupied" as the Texans launched their attack at San Jacinto. Morgan, a mulatto and most likely a slave who was rewarded with freedom for her heroism, was immortalized in the song *The Yellow Rose of Texas*. Less well known are the activities of those women left at home while their husbands fought the Mexicans at the Alamo, Goliad, and San Jacinto. They ran the farms and plantations in their husband's absence and organized the evacuation of their families as Mexican armies approached. Others were more directly involved in the war, including several who survived the siege of the Alamo. One of these, Suzanna Dickinson went to the Alamo with her husband and served as a cook and nurse throughout the battle; another, Andrea Candaleria, served as a nurse for James Bowie during the siege (and was one of the few Tejano women at the Alamo).

In spite of the fact that a number of Tejano men and women supported the Texas struggle against Santa Anna, Texas independence generally had a negative impact on them. Many Anglos were bitter over the atrocities committed at Goliad and the Alamo, some were reluctant to accept Tejanos as equals, and others were determined to eliminate the Mexican influence, if not their very presence, in South Texas. The Anglos' attitudes generated racial conflict that resulted in prejudice against Mexicans in Texas that occasionally erupted in violent acts. Mexican women found themselves victims of both gender and racial prejudice. For example, Doña Patricia de León, who had helped build the Catholic church in Victoria and who had supported the Texas Revolution, was forced to leave Texas and lost control over the extensive property that she had inherited from her husband, empresario Martin de León.

The role of Hispanics in Texas was further diminished by the demographic changes that followed the Texian victory at San Jacinto. Texas independence and then statehood triggered a massive immigration to Texas, the population of which soared: from approximately 50,000 in 1836 to 212,592 in 1850 and to 604,215 by 1860. While a sizeable portion of these immigrants came from Germany, the vast majority came from the United States, especially the southern states, and they helped bind Texas to the United States in general and to the South in particular. The sexual imbalance continued, especially on the frontier, but not to the degree that it had among Anglos in colonial Texas. In 1860 men outnumbered women in Texas by approximately 36,000.

Women's rights during this period included those based on American (and English) law as well as those derived from Hispanic practices. More dramatic, however, were the restrictions Texas society now placed on women's rights. Women could not vote or hold public office, sue or testify in court, or gain entry into most professions; married women did not have full control over their earnings or full guardianship of their children. Women were not permitted to present public lectures or sermons and were shackled by a double standard in morality. The mid-nineteenth century also witnessed the emergence of the "cult of true womanhood," which honored women as the guardians of home and hearth, entrusted them with nurturing the children and with safeguarding the moral values of the community; at the same time it did not view them as mental or physical equals of men. The first half of the nineteenth century, then, confronted American (and Texas) women with severe social, political, and economic restrictions; however, this same period also witnessed the emergence of the first organized women's rights movement. Women, especially in the northern and northwestern states, defied restrictions on public political expression by becoming actively involved in and even spokespersons for a number of social reform programs. Furthermore, at this time women began to gain entry into a number of professions, achieved greater economic rights and greater control over property, and launched their struggle for suffrage. These reforms, however, made few inroads into Texas in the first half of the nineteenth century.

The influx of Anglo women was not the only demographic change Texas experienced early in the nineteenth century—many migrants from the United States brought their slaves with them. While the Spanish were the first to bring African slaves into Texas, blacks did not comprise a major element in the population until the 1820s, when Anglos began importing slaves as labor for the production of cotton and later sugar cane in the fertile river bottoms of the state. As a result, the black population soared from approximately 450 late in the eighteenth century to about 5,000 in 1836 and to over 182,000 in 1860.

The vast majority of black women in early-nineteenth-century Texas were slaves. While sharing some experiences with Anglo and Hispanic women (such as harsh working conditions and primitive living conditions), black women had their rights restricted far more by slavery than by gender discrimination. Slave codes restricted the legal rights of all blacks, and the lack of legally recognized marriage contracts left slave women with even less legal and social protection than their nonslave counterparts. Slave women, of course, had virtually no voice in the decision to migrate to Texas. While the trip to Texas could be arduous for Anglo women, and while many came to Texas as the result of decisions made by their husbands, fathers, or other male relatives, their immigration could not compare with that of Silvia King, who reported that she was marched in chains from the slave market in New Orleans to a plantation near LaGrange: "it was a horrible time because we were all chained up . . . when one got tired or sick, the rest had to drag and carry him." Once in Texas slave women experienced an equality of sorts in the cotton fields. They did the same work as men, usually six days a week from sunrise to sundown, or, as some put it, from "can see to can't see." Sarah Ashley recalled, "I used to have to pick cotton and sometimes I picked 300 pounds and toted it a mile to the cotton house . . . I never got whipped because I always got my 300 pounds." On some plantations women with young children received less demanding work assignments. In any event, not all black women submitted to slavery without resistance. A number ran away, protesting the violence of the system or the destruction of slave families; some committed acts of violence against their masters or overseers.

In spite of the difficulties that enslaved black women faced and the severe restrictions placed on free blacks in antebellum Texas, some black women achieved a measure of success. A slave woman named Minerva often served as overseer on a Brazoria plantation in the slaveowner's absence. Fanny McFarland, a free black woman, lived in Houston for years, even though she had no legal right to reside in Texas; she worked as a laundress and engaged with some success in real estate speculation. Harriett Reynolds owned and operated a fairly successful ranch in Jackson County.

The Civil War influenced dramatically the lives of all women in Texas, but most especially those of black and Anglo women. Wars consume men, and in the process thrust new responsibilities onto women. The Civil War, by precipitating the abolition of slavery, also bestowed freedom on black women.

As the conflicts over the expansion of slavery, abolitionism, and sectionalism deepened in the 1850s, Texas women were drawn into the political arena. Just as abolitionism drew women into political activity in the North, women's participation in the debates of the day in Texas, first over slavery, then over secession, eroded traditional restrictions on women's involvement in public issues. While most women in the Lone Star State supported slavery, states' rights, and later the Confederacy, some were outspoken unionists, a few were even abolitionists. Melinda Rankin, a Presbyterian missionary who came to Texas in the 1850s, lost her job because of her advocacy of abolitionism and her outspoken unionism. Elise Waerenskjold, an immigrant who settled in North Texas late in the 1840s and became a leader in the Norwegian community, advocated women's rights, education, and abolitionism. Her critique of slavery centered on her conviction that all humans were equal and that slavery was "contrary to the will of God."

Once the war began, Texas women generally supported the conflict in the same manner as did others in the South and those in the North—by filling jobs that men vacated when they marched off to battle. In Texas, women ran the farms, plantations, and businesses. They also wove cloth for uniforms, made bandages, ran hospitals, and attempted to bolster morale among the civilian population and, through their letters, the men on the front lines. In Austin the Ladies Needle Battalion sewed uniforms for soldiers, while in East Texas Harriet Perry reported that the women and the slaves kept busy by making cloth for the army "up to 90 yards of cloth a week" in some households. Some Texas women played an even more active role. Sally Scull ran the Union blockade by shipping cotton overland to Mexico and exchanging it for munitions for the Confederate military. Sophia Porter, the "Texas Paul Revere," rode her mule across the icy Red River to notify Confederate forces of the location of Union soldiers who had quartered at her trading post. Chipita Rodriguez, who ran an inn in San Patricion was as spy for the Union; she was hanged in 1863 after being framed for murder.

While isolation from the major theaters of war spared Texas much of the devastation experienced by other Confederate states, Texans did face hardship. Over 100,000 Texans fought in the Civil War. Women separated from their husbands or widowed by the war not only experienced loneliness but were forced to assume many of the roles that men traditionally served. In addition, although escaping the more direct ravages of battle, they endured shortages that were sometimes extreme. Paper, medicine, and some foodstuffs were in short supply, as was salt, which was essential to food preservation in the prerefrigeration era. In Galveston, when a group of women organized a protest against shortages and the high price of basic commodities, Confederate military leaders arrested them and removed them from the island.

Black women also shared in the hardships of war. Not only did they spin thread to make cloth for Confederate uniforms, but, like Anglo women, many had to endure the absence of their loved ones: some black men were forced to attend their masters on the battlefield, others had run away to join the Union forces. After the slaves were emancipated, black women assumed an even more active role in Texas society. Like Anglo pioneer women, they participated in organizing their communities and played a major role in establishing schools and churches. They also moved quickly into the workforce. Some labored alongside their husbands; single women, including widows, became working single head of households. Black women toiled as agricultural workers, sharecroppers, farmers, laundresses, and domestics. They adjusted quickly to the wage-labor market. Some negotiated their own sharecropping contracts, while others became active in the state's fledgling labor movement. In 1877, under the slogan "we will starve no longer," black laundresses in Galveston organized a strike for higher wage. This labor strike was the first by the women of Texas, and it reflected the growing involvement of women in social and political reform movements in decade following the Civil War.

In these years, Texas again experienced a large influx of settlers. The expansion of agriculture, the spread of the open-range cattle industry, the construction of railroads, and the first stirrings of industrial development attracted hundreds of thousands of new residents to Texas and transformed the state demographically, economically, and politically. The population of Texas increased from about 600,000 in 1860 to over 3,000,000 in 1900, with most of the new residents settling on farms as the Texas frontier moved west. The population of Texas also remained predominantly male (about 110 men for every 100 women) through the end of the century.

Women participated in all aspects of the post–Civil War expansion of Texas. During the heyday of the Texas cattle industry, a number of women, following in the footsteps of successful Hispanic women of the colonial period, achieved success as cattle ranchers. Lizzie Johnson made a fortune by investing in cattle in the 1870s; she was also one of the first women to participate in a cattle drive along the Chisholm Trail. Following the death of her husband, Captain Richard King, Henrietta King ran the famed King Ranch for forty years, from 1885 to 1925. With the help of her son-in-law, she eliminated the ranch's debt and doubled its land holdings to over 1 million acres. She also promoted the development of South Texas by donating land for Kingsville and other townsites and by contributing funds to aid the development of the First Presbyterian Church of Kingsville, Texas A&I University, and other community institutions. Some Mexican women remained active in the ranching industry in the late nineteenth century. Margarita Villareal and several others operated ranches in far South Texas after the Civil War.

Far more women were involved in farming than in ranching. As late as 1940 half of the women (and men) in Texas worked at farming—either on family farms or as tenant farmers or sharecroppers. On the frontier farm there was little differentiation in the work regimen of men and women. Women, in addition to their duties as wives and mothers, participated in planting and harvesting crops, caring for livestock, and even clearing land. On more prosperous farms in settled areas, women's work usually was confined to "household duties," which included planting, tending, and harvesting gardens, canning and preserving foods, assisting in the slaughter of livestock, salting or smoking fresh meat, spinning thread and weaving cloth, making clothes, washing clothes, cleaning house, and raising children. For these post–Civil War pioneers, life on the frontier could be as primitive as it had been for their predecessors fifty or even one hundred years earlier. Generally, new arrivals on the Texas High Plains set up housekeeping in a tent or covered wagon before moving into a frame house of one or two rooms; some spent an extended period of time in dugouts or in sod houses.

Women also continued to be involved in organizing and working with the basic community institutions—home, school, and church. Some, such as Margaret Adams McCollum Mooar, became active in women's clubs. Mooar, determined to inform the women of West Texas about the national issues that affected their lives, helped found the "Up-to-Date History Club" in Colorado City in 1892. For the most part, though, women on the frontier concentrated on recreating whatever life and culture they had left behind. For some this meant organizing schools and churches, working as school teachers or music teachers, and bringing "culture" to the West; others, perhaps those with less formal educations, focused on transplanting their eastern cultural values and basic domestic skills.

The most notable change in the role of women in late-nineteenth-century Texas was that increasingly it expanded to include involvement in political and social reform. As Texas women became more politically active, a second theme would emerge in the history of Texas women—their struggle for equal rights. Women were active in the various organizations that made up the agrarian movement, they played a major role in the prohibition movement, and they voiced concern about other social and political issues. While Texas was not a center of feminism in the late nineteenth century, Texas women increasingly interpreted their responsibilities as the guardians of the home and public virtue under the "cult of true womanhood" as necessitating their active involvement in politics and in social reform organizations.

Since the majority of women lived on farms or in farming communities, it is not surprising that they became involved in agrarian protest movements. Texas farmers did not fare well in the thirty years that followed the Civil War. Continually declining agricultural prices and deflation were especially debilitating to the debt-ridden agrarian class. The shift from subsistence to commercial agriculture left farmers at the mercy of transportation systems, banking institutions, and marketing processes with which they had little experience or understanding, and over which they had virtually no control. And as government fell increasingly under the control of business and industrial interests, farmers became frustrated over their lack of political influence. They responded to the crisis with the formation of the Grange and Greenback parties in the 1870s, the Farmer's Alliance in the 1880s, and the People's party in the 1890s. Texas women participated in several phases of this agrarian protest.

In 1873, when the Grange first appeared in Dallas, it was the first farmer's organization in which women were engaged to any significant degree. The Grange accepted women as members but it generally restricted them to involvement in women's auxiliaries or Grange youth groups. Nevertheless, for the first time Texas women participated openly and in large numbers in a political organization, and although their role was limited they acquired a political consciousness and leadership skills that would be valuable to them in future political efforts. The experience that women gained in the Grange enabled them to assume a far more active role in the Farmer's Alliance. The Alliance, which had been founded in Lampassas in 1875, did not become a significant instrument of agrarian protest until the mid-1880s. More than any other political organization in nineteenth-century Texas, the Farmer's Alliance accepted (indeed, it actively sought) the involvement of women on an equal footing with men. As a result of the opportunity afforded to them, women such as Fannie Moss, Dr. Helen Lawson Dabbs, and Bettie Gay played active roles by writing numerous articles and essays about the Alliance (and about the rights of women) and serving as delegates to Alliance conventions. Fannie Moss served as secretary-treasurer of the Texas Farmer's Alliance from 1892 to 1894; her successor in this position was Dr. Francis Elizabeth Daniel Leak. Bettie Gay, who wrote extensively on the relationship between women and the Alliance, argued that the Alliance would redeem women from the unnatural position of inferiority in which society had placed them and restore them to their proper sphere of equality; she insisted that women could be active in the politics of the Alliance without neglecting their responsibilities in the "home sphere."

The Texas women who were active in the Farmer's Alliance also tended to be active in other reform organizations. A number participated in the St. Louis convention that resulted in the founding of the People's party in 1892, although many Texas women had their enthusiasm for the new party dampened by its failure to endorse women's suffrage. The most popular reform movement among Texas women of the period was prohibition. Many Texans (and Americans) in the late nineteenth and early twentieth centuries believed that alcohol abuse was linked to an array of social and moral problems from crime to poverty, to prostitution, divorce, and delinquency. Furthermore, most advocates of prohibition approached the issue as a moral crusade; they refused to consider compromise, and they branded their opponents as sinners. The debate in Texas over this issue generated excited and heated political conflict, which in the words of former governor Oran M. Roberts "stirred up society to its very foundations with a greater manifestation of universal feeling and interest than had ever occurred before in Texas."

Women emerged as an active force in the debate over prohibition with the establishment of Texas's first chapter of the Women's Christian Temperance Union (WCTU) in Paris in 1882, following a speech there by Frances Willard, president of the national body. The WCTU recruited the wives of a number of prominent Texas political leaders, including Matilda Cassa Denton Maxey, wife of Senator Samuel Bell Maxey. However, its most important Texas recruit was Helen Stoddard, a Fort Worth mathematics professor who joined the organization in 1887. Stoddard served first as the legislative chair of the Texas WCTU, during which time she successfully lobbied for the passage of a series of reform laws, including an act that mandated the inclusion of curriculum material on alcohol and drug abuse in the state's public schools. Beginning in 1891, Stoddard served sixteen years as president of the WCTU.

Women were attracted to the WCTU and the prohibition issue for a variety of reasons. The definition of the campaign against alcohol as a moral struggle fit well with the popular image of the role of women as defenders of the home and of community morality. Also, many women believed that the misuse of alcohol induced men to wife battering and child abuse—issues of great concern to women. Finally, the WCTU was the first organized political association of Texas women; consequently it provided the first political forum for women's issues, including ones that ranged far beyond the scope of prohibition. It was, for example, the first organization in the state to endorse women's suffrage, and its legislative program included the enactment of anti-tobacco legislation as well as a state child-labor and pure-food-and-drug act; the WCTU also championed the creation of a state college for women. In 1903, after a ten-year political struggle, the WCTU saw the establishment of the Texas Industrial Institute for the Education of the White Girls of the State of Texas in Arts and Sciences (now Texas Woman's University); Stoddard, who had directed the campaign for the college, was one of three women named to the institution's first board of regents—the first women to hold such a position in the state.

In spite of their increased activity in politics and social reform, Texas women did not see their overall status change significantly in the latter part of the nineteenth century. Women remained politically disfranchised; they could not serve as lawyers, sit on juries, or hold elected public office, and, except for on the farm and in the home, their presence in the workplace still was rare. The census of 1870 listed only 5 percent of women over the age of ten as employed; by 1900 this figure had risen only to 13 percent. Of those who did work outside of the home (aside from agricultural labor), most found employment as domestics. Other women worked as seamstresses, laundresses, hotel employees, milliners, tailors, and laborers. Only a handful of women managed to gain entry to the professions at this time; the 1880 census listed a few women bankers, lawyers, doctors, and ministers. Even the traditional women's professions, nursing and teaching, still were dominated by males as late as 1880.

The political experience gained by Texas women through their involvement in the Grange, the Farmer's Alliance, and the prohibition movement provided the foundation for their increased political activity and for their greater political success in the progressive movement of the twentieth century. Additionally, Texas women entered the progressive movement through their involvement in women's clubs, which increasingly became centers of social reform, and the women's suffrage movement. Each of these approaches had its roots in the nineteenth century but achieved real success during the Progressive era. The prohibition movement, especially the WCTU, continued to build on the base it had laid in the late nineteenth century. After failing to win referendums on prohibition in 1887 and 1911, the movement successfully lobbied for statewide prohibition and the approval of the national prohibition amendment in 1918. Women's clubs, often dismissed merely as social organizations, in reality became the principle vehicle for the political activism of Texas women. Indeed, women's clubs and prohibition groups were fundamental components of the alliance that comprised Texas progressivism. The clubs channeled women's political energies into community development activities, which left their mark on Texas, and committed themselves to a broad agenda of social reform. For example, following the passage of a resolution supporting public libraries at the first statewide meeting of the Texas Federation of Women's Clubs, in Tyler in 1898, Texas women's clubs began an active campaign to establish public libraries across the state. Over 85 percent of the public libraries in Texas trace their origins to this movement. Prison reform was another issue that women's clubs championed. Many Texas women believed that through their influence the state's prisons could accomplish what they had failed to achieve under male leadership—the social rehabilitation of inmates. As early as 1906 the Texas Federation of Women's Clubs endorsed prison reform, but they did not focus their energies on this issue until after 1918. In that year an investigation of prisons prompted the Women's Clubs to put forth their plan for reform, which included placing a woman on the three-person Texas Prison Board, placing women on the staff of all prisons, and placing the women's prison under the full control of women. Women would not have as much luck with prisons as they did with libraries. They enjoyed limited but short-lived success in prison reform in the 1920s during the administration of Governor Dan Moody (1927–1931), but most of their gains were reversed by his successor, Ross Sterling.

Women's clubs in Texas pursued a broad-based agenda that encompassed self-improvement, community action, social reform, and political reform. The program of the Current Topics Club of El Paso, which included a study of Ibsen's plays and Roman history as well as an examination of the issues of household economy, cooperative living, and the rehabilitation of convicts, illustrates well this scope of interests. The Texas Federation of Women's Clubs, organized in 1897 as the Texas Federation of Women's Literary Clubs, dropped the "literary" from its name in 1899 as it broadened its agenda to include such things as compulsory school attendance, pure food and drugs, and issues protecting children and women. By 1907 they could claim credit for state laws that established a juvenile court system, regulated adoption, and provided for compulsory blood tests for marriage licenses. In 1908 the *Dallas Clubwoman* published a list of the projects that should attract the energies of Texas women. The list included: the improvement of parks, public health, and sanitation; pure-food legislation; civil service reform; laws controlling child labor and improving the status of women workers; and expansion of libraries and public education. These issues were not only important to women's clubs; they also represented the basic elements of the progressive agenda. In no sense were the interests of Texas club women confined to local issues. Under the leadership of Anna Pennybacker, who served as president of the Texas Federation of Women's Clubs from 1901 to 1903 before assuming the leadership of the national body (General Federation of Women's Clubs) from 1912 to 1916, the Texas organization endorsed world peace and U.S. participation in the League of Nations.

In addition to the Texas Federation of Women's Clubs, other women's organizations with more specific interests helped promote social and political reform. Ella Caruthers Porter helped establish the Texas Congress of Mothers (which later became the Parent-Teacher Association—or PTA) in 1909. Local mother's clubs, which first appeared in Texas in the mid-1890s, worked primarily to improve schools and the services they provided. Porter, who had first become interested in issues affecting women and children through her work in the WCTU, used the state organization to lobby for a number of social reforms, including a state child-welfare commission, which was established in 1918 under the direction of Ms. Claude De Van Watts. Black women also established a number of women's clubs during the first quarter of the century that were committed to self-improvement and community service.

Since the Texas Association of Women's Clubs was segregated, in 1905 Ms. M.E.Y. Moore founded the Texas Association of Colored Women, and in 1911 Jovita Idar established The League of Mexican Women (*La Liga Femenil Mexicanista*), which advocated education for women and opposed racial discrimination.

In spite of the broad range of concerns of the various women's clubs, the major political goal of Texas women during the progressive movement was women's suffrage. The roots of the Texas suffrage movement reach back to the immediate post–Civil War years when women petitioned unsuccessfully to get women's suffrage included in the Constitution of 1869 and then in the Constitution of 1875. In 1887, following their defeat in the state prohibition referendum, the WCTU endorsed women's suffrage. The first organizations in Texas created specifically to promote women's suffrage appeared in the late nineteenth and early twentieth centuries. In 1893, Rebecca Henry Hayes of Galveston, an associate of Susan B. Anthony and vice-president of the National American Woman Suffrage Association, organized the Texas Equal Rights Association to promote the "industrial, educational, and legal rights of women and to secure suffrage to them;" ten years later Annette Finnigan of Houston, an associate of Carrie Chapman Catt, founded the Texas Woman Suffrage Association. Neither of these organizations survived long. However, a third organization, the Texas Equal Suffrage Association, founded in 1915 under the leadership of Minnie Fisher Cunningham, spearheaded the successful drive for women's suffrage. With effective grass-roots organization, skillful lobbying efforts, and the ability to take advantage of the patriotism generated by World War I and the support of both President Woodrow Wilson and Governor William P. Hobby, suffragettes achieved victory in their long struggle for the vote. Black women, such as Christia Adair, joined in the campaign for women's suffrage, even though the Texas Equal Suffrage Association was segregated and most black men in Texas had been effectively disfranchised by 1915. In 1917 the Texas Federation of Colored Women's Clubs endorsed suffrage, and in 1918 Ms. E. P. Simpson of El Paso unsuccessfully attempted to affiliate the El Paso colored Women's Club with the National American Women's Suffrage Association. In a special session in 1918 the legislature granted women the right to vote in primary elections; at the request of Governor Hobby in 1919, the legislature submitted a state constitutional amendment enfranchising women—an amendment that the voters rejected. Finally, in that same year, the Texas legislature's favorable vote made Texas the ninth state and the first southern state to ratify the Nineteenth Amendment to the U.S. Constitution. One year later, with ratification by the necessary three-fourths of the states, white women had gained the right to vote in Texas and throughout the United States.

The enfranchisement of Texas women removed the final legal barrier to their participation in all aspects of the political process. A few women had held public office prior to 1918, usually on local school boards or in appointed positions, and for several decades they had worked diligently in reform movements and in lobbying efforts. But the acquisition of the right to vote in primary elections in 1918 and in all elections in 1920 allowed women to take an even more active role in state politics. After gaining the right to vote in primaries in 1918, over 385,000 women registered to vote and then immediately elected the first woman to statewide office in Texas when they selected Dr. Annie Webb Blanton as the state superintendent of public instruction.

During the decade following suffrage, hundreds of Texas women followed Blanton's example and ran for local or state office. Many were successful. By the end of the 1920s, 109 of the state's 254 counties had women treasurers; two women, Edith Wilmans (in 1922) and Helen Moore (in 1928), won election to the Texas House of Representatives, and in 1926 Margie Neal was elected to the Texas Senate and became the first woman to serve on the Texas State Democratic Executive Committee. In 1928 Minnie Fisher Cunningham became the first woman in the country to run for a seat in the U.S. Senate; and, in 1924, Texas elected a woman as governor.

In addition to their success at the polls, Texas women also utilized the political skills they had gained through their experiences in reform movements and the suffrage campaign to structure a sophisticated political machine in the early 1920s. Soon after the enactment of the Nineteenth Amendment, the Texas Equal Suffrage Association was reorganized as the Texas League of Women Voters under the leadership of Jessie Daniel Ames. By 1922 the League had allied with the Texas Federation of Women's Clubs, the Congress of Mothers, the PTA, the WCTU, the Texas Federation of Business and Professional Women's Clubs, and the Texas Graduate Nurses Association to form the Joint Legislative Council. This "petticoat lobby," as its detractors labeled it, proved to be an effective force in the legislature in the early 1920s. During the four years of its existence, it saw its entire legislative package enacted into law, including improved funding for public education, public health programs, and new labor laws; it also advocated prison reform and stricter enforcement of prohibition laws.

The most dramatic evidence of the new role of women in Texas politics was the election of Miriam A. Ferguson as governor of Texas in 1924 and again in 1932. "Ma" Ferguson was a controversial political figure. Many Texas women opposed her candidacy on the grounds that she was only a stand-in for her husband, James "Pa" Ferguson, who was ineligible to run for governor following his impeachment in 1917, and because James had been one of the state's most adamant opponents of women's suffrage. On the other hand, Jessie Daniel Ames, former suffragist and first president of the Texas League of Women Voters, campaigned for Miriam Ferguson because of her anti—Ku Klux Klan stance. As Governor, Miriam Ferguson clearly allowed her husband to influence her administration. On the other hand, she supported aid to education and prison reform, issues that the petticoat lobby had endorsed, and she appointed Emma Meharg as Texas's first woman secretary of state.

Whether Miriam Ferguson truly was governor or just a figurehead, her campaign and presence in the governor's mansion reflected the changes that women's suffrage had brought to Texas politics. Recognizing the new power women exercised at the polls, some campaign literature early in the 1920s began to focus its appeal directly to women voters. Women's groups opposed Tom Connally's bid for a Senate seat in 1922, castigating him for opposing the Federated Women's Clubs' legislative agenda in Congress and for failing to support the woman's suffrage amendment. Furthermore, Miriam Ferguson's campaign directly confronted the issue of a woman campaigning for office, as well as her principal opponent's link to the Klan. In a Spanish-language appeal to the Hispanic voter she assured her supporters that "*Yo sere el Gobernador y no Jim*" (I will be the governor and not Jim); another broadside read, "We will vote for a woman with a bonnet and a dress before we will vote for a man with a pillow case and sheet on."

Women continued to be active in Texas politics in the 1930s and 1940s. The victory in the suffrage campaign and occasional victories at the polls did not end the quest for equal rights, for women continued to face discrimination in many areas. Texas women did not gain the right to serve on juries until the 1950s, and they did not gain complete equality in property and contract rights until the 1970s. Efforts to secure the passage of an equal rights amendment in the 1920s were unsuccessful. Although only about one-third of the women had entered the workforce (including a growing number of married women by 1930) and women had found increased employment opportunity as clerical workers and in retail sales, women professionals continued to be confined primarily to occupations that had become stereotyped as "women's work." In 1930 women comprised over 80 percent of the teachers and 90 percent of the nurses and librarians, but less than 2 percent of the lawyers and doctors. During the Great Depression, Texas women experienced discrimination in employment and in New Deal agencies. New Deal agencies that found work or provided job training for the unemployed generally restricted women to "traditional" jobs (sewing, food processing, health care, and domestic service), and some officials did not approve of jobs for married women. In San Antonio, New Deal officials channeled most black women into training programs for domestic service, or into segregated programs. World War II, like other major wars, brought more women into the workforce, and into jobs traditionally held by men.

One political gain that Texas women made in the mid-twentieth century was the increasingly prominent role that they played in national affairs. No Texas woman was more visible during this period than Oveta Culp Hobby. Her career in politics began in 1926 when, at the age of twenty-one, she served as parliamentarian to the Texas House of Representatives. In the 1930s she worked for the Texas State Banking Commission and married former governor William P. Hobby. During World War II she became the first commander of the newly organized Women's Army Corps; then, during the Eisenhower administration, she headed the Department of Health, Education and Welfare, becoming the second woman ever to serve in the cabinet. Following her retirement from politics, she became the publisher of the *Houston Post*.

The political agenda of Texas women had changed somewhat by the middle of the twentieth century from the strong commitment to social reform that had typified their activities in the first quarter of the century. Organizations such as the League of Women Voters focused more on international issues, voter registration and education, and expanding the political rights of women by abolishing the poll tax and overturning the laws that prevented women from serving on juries. The political activities of women became more diversified in the postwar period. Women served as volunteers and held leadership positions in both the Democratic and Republican parties and were especially instrumental in establishing the latter as a viable political force in the state. They also were active in some of the political fringe groups that were common in the state and the nation during the era of political excess that grew out of McCarthyism. In Houston, the Minute Women became a powerful force in local politics, especially school-board politics, as they campaigned to "save" Texas from communism in the early 1950s. In the late 1950s professional atheist Madalyn Murray O'Hair made Austin the home of her campaign to take prayer out of the public schools and to purge religion and religious symbols from all government activities.

But even as Texas approached the mid-twentieth century, African American and Hispanic women were still struggling for their basic political and civil rights. This struggle was initiated largely by women in the second quarter of the century. Black women played a central role in the founding of chapters of the National Association for the Advancement of Colored People (NAACP) in Houston in 1912 and in Dallas in 1918. Lulu B. White, a school teacher born in Elmo, Texas, in 1898, became active in the Houston branch of the NAACP in the mid-1920s. In 1939 she became president of the Houston branch, and in 1943 she became its executive secretary. An uncompromising foe of segregation, she led the challenge for the integration of The University of Texas that resulted in the landmark Supreme Court decision, *Sweatt* v. *Painter*. Christia Adair, the former black suffragette, also became active in civil rights and in the Houston chapter of the NAACP, campaigning to end restrictions on black suffrage, integrate public facilities, and end racially motivated violence. Juanita Craft did similar work in Dallas; as an NAACP organizer she was credited with establishing 182 chapters of the organization in Texas. In addition she spearheaded voter registration drives, fought discrimination, and organized youth clubs. Following the *Smith* v. *Allwright* decision by the Supreme Court in 1944, which made possible black participation in Texas politics in significant numbers for the first time since the 1890s, voter registration drives and get-out the-vote campaigns became the focus of the political activity of black women. Hattie Mae White was the first to benefit from these developments. In 1958 she became the first black elected to political office in Texas since the early twentieth century when she won a seat on the Houston school board. A few years later Juanita Craft became the first black woman elected to the Dallas city council.

The most significant change that Mexican-American women confronted in the twentieth century was the migration of hundreds of thousands of persons from Mexico to Texas. By 1988, Hispanics were the largest minority in the state, numbering almost 4 million and comprising 23 percent of the population. During the first half of the century, reform efforts in the Mexican-American community were centered in labor organizations. Mexican-American women played a major role in these activities. For example, in 1938 the twenty-year-old Emma Tenayuca organized a strike of 10,000 largely Mexican-American pecan shellers; this was the largest labor action Texas had seen to that time. As the strike dragged on, and as the strikers endured abuse and violence, the action was transformed into a broad-based struggle for jobs, equal rights, and protection against deportation. Tenayuca became a local folk heroine for her fiery leadership and courage. Other Mexican-American women were instrumental in improving the working conditions and wages of garment workers in Dallas and San Antonio.

Women also played a major role in the political organization of the Mexican-American community. In 1929 Maria Hernandez helped found one of the first organizations in the state dedicated to protecting the civil rights of Mexican Americans. After World War II, political energies in the Mexican-American community shifted from labor struggles to civil rights. Women became involved in LULAC and the GI Forum, where they worked to end discrimination and gain equal rights. Mexican-American women frequently faced the same kind of prejudice from men within their community as Anglo women had faced when they had first became politically active in the mid-nineteenth century. Frequently Mexican-American women were forced to limit their political involvement to women's auxiliaries of LULAC and other organizations. Nevertheless, Mexican-American women made political gains. In 1974 Irma Rangel became the first Mexican-American woman elected to the Texas legislature.

The person who symbolized the success of minority women in Texas politics in the second half of the twentieth century was Barbara Jordan. Like Oveta Culp Hobby, Jordan's first political success came in the state legislature in Austin, before she moved on to Washington and the national spotlight. Jordan grew up in Houston's Fifth Ward and attended Texas Southern University prior to earning a law degree at Howard. In 1966 she became the first black elected to the Texas Senate in the twentieth century; six years later she became the first woman from Texas elected to Congress. During the televised Watergate impeachment hearings, Jordan entered the national spotlight as perhaps the most articulate, certainly the most compelling, orator on the House Judiciary Committee. Before ill health forced her to retire from Congress in 1979, some political observers suggested that she had the potential to become the first black and the first woman president.

In the late 1960s and 1970s, inspired by the civil rights movement and the antiwar movement, feminism enjoyed a resurgence in Texas. The new feminist agenda centered on: ending job discrimination for women; eliminating sexism in the media and in education; increasing the number of women in elected political positions; assuring equal status for women under the law; addressing social problems confronting women such as wife battering, rape, and child abuse; and guaranteeing women access to legal abortion. The issue that became the focus of the women's movement in the 1970s was the effort to secure ratification of the equal rights amendment to the U.S. Constitution; in the 1980s the abortion issue dominated the women's movement. Both of these issues (but especially the abortion issue) divided women as had no others. Although the Texas legislature approved ratification of the equal rights amendment, the measure failed to gain the approval of the necessary three-fourths of the states and was not ratified. As of 1997 the right of women to legal abortion had not been restricted in Texas.

Women succeeded in attaining many of their political objectives in Texas. Women's groups set up shelters for battered women and rape crisis centers in most of the state's major communities. In 1972, by an overwhelming majority, Texas voters added an equal rights amendment to the state constitution that eliminated virtually all of the legal discrimination against women. In 1973, a Texas attorney, Sarah Weddington, successfully argued the case for legalized abortion before the Supreme Court. Even though job discrimination did not vanish in Texas, by the 1990s women had gained access to management positions and entry into the professions in unprecedented numbers.

Women's success in politics also was impressive. On the local level, women became a major political force. Beginning with the election of Carole Keeton Rylander as mayor of Austin in 1977, and the election of Kathy Whitmire as mayor of Houston in 1981, women mayoral candidates have had remarkable success in Texas's major cities; in the late 1970s and 1980s Houston, Dallas, San Antonio, Austin, El Paso, Galveston, and Nacogdoches have all had women mayors, and Whitmire of Houston had held the post longer than any other person in the city's history. Indeed, in 1990 the state's largest city had a woman mayor, a woman school superintendent, a woman police chief, an African-American woman as president of its largest university, and a woman as president of its chamber of commerce. Minority women have shared in this political success. In Houston, for example, the mid-1990s saw African-American, Mexican-American, and Asian-American women serving on the city council, and Sheila Jackson Lee, an African-American woman, representing the city in the U.S. Congress.

Women's influence in state politics also increased. Between 1922 and 1985, forty-six women served in the state legislature; in 1985, nineteen women (seventeen in the House, two in the Senate) served there. However, even though women have comprised the majority of the state's population ever since 1960, they still make up less that 14 percent of the legislature. Furthermore, since Miriam Ferguson was elected for her second term as governor in 1932, no woman won election to statewide office for fifty years. In 1972 Frances Farenthold, a two-term veteran of the Texas House of Representatives, made a credible run for the governor's office. She finished second in a field of seven in the Democratic primary before losing to Dolph Briscoe in the run off. Ten years later Ann Richards became only the third woman to win a statewide race when she was elected state treasurer. However, 1990 was the banner year for women politicians in Texas. That fall 21 women were elected to the legislature (as late as 1970 there were only two, Farenthold and Jordan). Kay Bailey Hutchison, a Republican, defeated another woman, Nikki Van Hightower, for state treasurer. And Ann Richards was elected Governor of Texas, the second woman to hold that office and the first to be elected in her own right. Two years later Kay Bailey Hutchison became the first woman from Texas elected to the U.S. Senate.

As Texas approaches the twenty-first century, no one can seriously question the fact that women play a major role in the state. The 1990s not only have witnessed a woman in the governor's mansion and a woman representing Texas in the U.S. Senate, but women administering the government of several of the state's major cities, holding positions of responsibility in corporations, medical institutions, colleges and universities, and the media. Texas women work as physicians, attorneys, accountants, and engineers, as well as in the "traditional" professions of nurse and teacher. As they have done since they first arrived in Texas, women continue to contribute to the task of creating the community in which they live, organizing its principal institutions, and working to ameliorate the social problems that exist there. As new waves of migration bring new groups of residents into Texas, women will continue to participate in the building of new communities. And Texas women will continue to assert their right to an equal partnership in the state that they have helped to build.

"We Want Aggies, Not Maggies": James Earl Rudder and the Coeducation of Texas A&M University

Christopher Bean

Christopher Bean is a doctoral student in history at the University of North Texas in Denton. He has written on the Freedmen's Bureau in Texas.

World War II hero James Earl Rudder served as president of Texas A&M from 1959 until his untimely death in 1970. Under his leadership, significant changes occurred at the institution, including the admission of women and minorities and the abrogation of mandatory military training. According to LBJ, Rudder's "heroism on the Normandy beaches in a time of war was only a prelude to his contribution in peace as an educator, public official and concerned citizen." In this selection, Bean discusses President Rudder's tenure at Texas A&M, a period of major transformation.

★ ★

"We Want Aggies, Not Maggies": James Earl Rudder and the Coeducation of Texas A&M University by Christopher Bean from *East Texas Historical Journal*, Vol. XLIV, No. 2, 2006, pp. 17–27. Reprinted by permission of East Texas Historical Association.

In 1930, when twenty-year old James Earl Rudder enrolled at A&M College of Texas, two Texas institutions converged for the first time—one already established, the other yet to be. For the next four decades, through depression, a world conflagration, and post war uncertainty, an unbreakable bond remained. Late in the 1950s Rudder returned to the school as its president, a second convergence that proved a blessing to the college, because just on the horizon awaited one of the most trying times in the long history of A&MC—the 1960s. With leadership, discipline, and vision, Rudder guided the school through this most turbulent of times. Prior to Rudder's tenure, A&M was an all-male, segregated, provincial military school. Afterward, it became one of the Southwest's premier educational institutions. Although aided and assisted by other administrators and faculty, Rudder remains the seminal figure in this transition.

The Agricultural and Mechanical College of Texas opened its doors in 1876 with a class of 106 students. The school began as an all-male military institution with compulsory participation in the Corps of Cadets, an organization that became the most visible symbol of the school and one that played an integral role in its initial growth. The school consequently developed a strong military character. It regularly commissioned more officers than any of the service academies, including West Point. Former students achieved outstanding records in all of the country's wars from the Spanish-American War to the present. More than 20,000 former students served during World War II, twenty-nine of them at the rank of general.

After the First World War, the A&MC experienced rapid growth and became recognized for its programs in agriculture, engineering, and veterinary and military sciences. The college even branched out, establishing complexes throughout the state. These changes resulted in the organization of limited graduate degree programs by 1936. Driving this growth was the discovery of oil on state lands during the 1920s. Beginning in 1931, A&M received one-third of the income derived from the state's Permanent University Fund. These oil revenues kept costs and tuition down and spurred enrollment growth even during the Great Depression. By the 1950s, A&M College confronted many new challenges: changing population dynamics; decreasing enrollment; and developing fissures between the student body and faculty. "[At this time] Texas A&M confronted change without really changing," wrote historian Henry C. Dethlof, while another historian argued that this was a time of "turmoil, unrest, and lack of progress; indeed, the institution appeared to be in retrogression, with loss of student members, and agitation among the faculty and the student body."

Despite this situation, no leader pushed for change. Various issues loomed ahead for not only the school, but also for the nation as a whole. Coeducation, racial integration, curricular and administrative changes, elective military training, and the admission of civilian students were topics that the college would have to address soon. Furthermore, with explosive growth in the state's population, concerns about a broader university complex and a focus on research and academics surfaced. The future of the college depended on how the administration approached these matters.

This was the situation that faced James Earl Rudder when he arrived as vice-president of the college early in 1958. Born on May 6, 1910, in Eden (Concho County), Rudder was one of thirteen children. From his father he received an indelible work ethic and from his mother a moral compass. After excelling at football for two years at John Tarleton Agricultural College, Rudder transferred to A&MC in 1930, where for the next two years he helped anchor the offensive line for the Aggie football team. After a brief stint coaching at Brady High School, where he met his future wife, Margaret Williamson, and at Tarleton College, Rudder was called to active military duty in the summer of 1941. For the next year or so, he moved from one assignment to another, advancing to company commander at Fort Sam Houston, Texas, and executive officer and Army component operations staff officer (G-3) for the 83rd Infantry Division. In the summer of 1943, Rudder received orders giving him command of the 2nd Ranger Battalion.

During the D-Day landings on June 6, 1944, "Rudder's Rangers" scaled the one-hundred-foot Pointe-du-Hoc cliffs and destroyed a German battery that threatened the landing. After the war, General Omar Bradley remarked "No soldier in my command has ever been wished a more difficult task than that which befell James Earl Rudder." In November 1944, Rudder received orders reassigning him to the 109th Infantry Regiment, 29th Infantry Division. Army brass wanted Rudder to transform the 109th as he had the Rangers. Eight days after he took command, the Germans launched what would become the Battle of the Bulge. In spite of the suddenness of the attack, Rudder led the 109th through the battle admirably. By war's end, Rudder had received every military decoration except the Congressional Medal of Honor. After the war, he served as vice president of labor relations for the Brady Aviation Company and three terms as mayor of Brady. While mayor, Rudder befriended several powerful men, including future president Lyndon B. Johnson and Governor Allan Shivers. In 1955 Governor Shivers appointed Rudder Texas Land Commissioner in order to clean up the corrupt mess left by Bascom Giles. With the land commissioner's office restored to its proper place, Rudder, realizing that his work was completed, decided to accept the position of vice president of A&MC.

The title of vice-president made Rudder the principal administrator of the college. Marion Thomas Harrington held the joint title of president of the college and of the college system, but Rudder was, in effect, the real "president." Harrington's position was more like that of chancellor at a modern university system. Regardless of his impressive accomplishments in public service, Rudder appeared to be a questionable choice for the position. "[M]ost academic people counted him at best an 'unlikely' candidate to head a major university," wrote one historian of the school. "Rudder gave every appearance of being an Aggie of the old school, with old-school ties, loyalties, traditions, and basic conservatism. A university in the throes of change, many anticipated, would not be helped along the way by such a man as Earl Rudder." He had reservations about taking the job for this reason. According to his wife, Rudder believed that the "academics" would resent him because he was not one of them.

Prior to Rudder's arrival, the first salvos on several major issues that he would face had already been fired. An internecine conflict had erupted over compulsory military training. In 1957 President David W. Williams, at the request of the board of directors, distributed a questionnaire among the faculty seeking opinions on a variety of policy questions, one of which pertained to compulsory military training. In spite of the faculty's vote (forty-nine to one in favor of optional military training) school officials retained compulsory military training for freshmen and sophomores. The conflict soon became public. What made this quarrel significant was that it involved nearly every constituent body of the university—the president, chancellor, board of directors, and the faculty—plus outside forces such as state officials and local merchants.

The question of coeducation crept into the discussion, and soon the two issues became one. This inevitably brought the student body, which generally held views completely opposite those of administrators, into campus politics. Joe Tindel, editor of the school newspaper *Battalion*, advocated the admission of women to the college. The *Bryan Daily Eagle*, concurring with Tindel, editorialized, "The world changes and A&M must change with it." The student senate, however, voted eleven to five in favor of a resolution calling for Tindel's resignation. The dispute became violent when William Boyd Metts, creator of the Aggie Association for the Advancement of Coeducation, was hospitalized after inhaling fumes from a bomb thrown into his room. The controversy expanded when several women filed suit against the college in 1958 and 1959, asking to be admitted into the school. The cases reached the state supreme court and, in one instance, the United States Supreme Court. Both courts, however, refused to hear the case. With each new chapter in the saga, one newspaper noticed that the school appeared to be "redividing like a swirling amoeba."

In an interview with the *College Station Battalion*, Rudder described his position on the issue. "[T]he decision is in keeping with the Board of Directors' desire—it is my job to run A&M as the Board wants it to run," he replied. When the interviewer asked Rudder about the future, he retorted, "I don't have a crystal ball." As a result, Rudder was labeled as wanting to retain the "old school" in spite of changing times. In reality, his authority was limited by the board of directors; rather than dictating policy, he was implementing that of the board.

In a sense Rudder was "*old school*." He was sympathetic to the college that he remembered—all male and military. Now he was an administrator, partly responsible for the day-to-day activities and future policy of the school, and like any good leader, he did what was best, even if that contradicted his personal prejudices and attitudes.

Almost unnoticed and with little fanfare, Rudder was named president of Texas A&M on July 1, 1959, when Harrington advanced to the position of chancellor. With this promotion, Rudder gained authority and a proximity to the board that he had lacked as vice-president. Now he was "at the helm" with the power and influence to take the school in the direction he desired. Rudder could "batten down the hatches" against the coeducation advocates or accept that the time for coeducation at the college had come. But with the position came sole responsibility for those policy decisions. With the spotlight on him, Rudder was in his element.

On March 26, 1960, when he was inaugurated, Rudder did not directly address the coeducational issue, although he did mention how the school was to provide the young *men* of Texas the greatest of benefits. Instead, he stressed the role of A&M College in the history and future development of Texas and the nation. Rudder also addressed the need for the school to lead the charge in a nation relying ever more heavily on technology, one in which an increasingly higher percentage of people attended college. "This is now the responsibility of our nation," he declared. "It soon will pass to our children. Their ability to assume the task is in no small measure dependent upon the availability to them of higher education, and its quality." He added that the United States needed to redirect its priorities, considering that it spent more on cigarettes, recreation, liquor, and legalized gambling than on education. "The crucial question is whether we will or not," he said. "It will be expensive. Modern education facilities come high; research is especially costly. Our nation can afford it; to survive, we must afford it. We can spend our money for no finer, more fruitful or more deserving endeavor."

Rudder then began the task of mending the wounds of the prior years while trying to pilot the school in its academic development. Many on the faculty and staff believed that Rudder would fail. These individuals underestimated him. If they had known Rudder, they would have realized that in all previous assignments he had succeeded in tense and complex situations. "James Earl Rudder was a fighter who never quit anything until it was finished," remarked one observer. "As many have said since, he turned out to be the right man in the right place at the right time."

Rudder began to quiet the tumultuous situation. In a measure "to define challenges and opportunities anticipated in the future," he and the board of directors authorized a long-range planning study of the college. "This is an event which is an important milestone in the history of A&M College," declared Rudder. The project began in 1961 under the title "Century Study." It called for the participation of practically everyone involved with the university. Rudder asked participants to keep four questions in mind: What kind of graduate and citizen should this college seek to produce? What should be the mission of A&M College during the next fifteen years? To what degree of academic excellence shall they aspire? What should be the scope and size of the school by 1976? Members were told not to "reflect in your report existing traditions or policy." We must, concluded Rudder, let "success fully plan the future of this great institution and effectively project these plans to the citizens we serve."

As he had done on previous occasions, Rudder looked to those who knew more about the situation than he did. Rather than believing that he had all the answers, he sought everyone's opinion and assessment of a problem before he implemented a solution. This was one of the reasons that he was such an effective leader. Rudder entered into a situation knowing that in order to solve problems he had to have the cooperation of the "frontline troops"—those who had been there from the beginning. To obtain this cooperation, Rudder needed his subordinates' confidence and respect. Rudder made them understand that their opinions mattered.

The college evaluation initiated by Rudder resulted in four independent studies. The Century Council, comprising one hundred outstanding citizens from more than 1,200 applicants (some alumni, others not), produced the *Report of the Century Council.* The report sought "to determine those structural and program modifications which would enable the [college] to achieve a position of state, national, international prominence among universities of higher learning and make recommendations." Many of the council's findings were vague, however—the council recommended a "greater emphasis on excellence," for example. The group also recommended that the ROTC program "currently in effect at the college be continued," noting that leaders "produced under this program are of inestimable value to our state and nation." Because the average A&M College student scored slightly below the national average on the college entrance exam, the study advocated a "continuous study of selective admissions policy." The group referred the matter of coeducation to the board. Remarking on its "divided opinion," the council members believed that "the Board will make a wise and effective disposition of this matter."

In another self-study, administrators and faculty produced the *Report to Commission on Colleges, Southern Association of Colleges and Schools*. This report was for the school's major accrediting association. While the other reports issued recommendations pertaining to the student body, curriculum, and school administrators and faculty, this study focused on improving the college's physical facilities. The report proposed a $55 million construction program to build or improve facilities for engineering, biochemistry, oceanography, and meteorology programs, as well as a student center, improved library facilities, a data processing center, and a TV closed-circuit studio.

A committee of faculty and staff also produced a study entitled *Faculty-Staff-Student Study on Aspirations*. "The recommendations of the general report," remarked one historian, "are important in view of what came to be." In addition to suggesting a tenure policy for faculty that conformed to those used at other schools, higher salaries for higher professional ranks, and annual salary increments, the report also recommended merit raises. It recommended other moves to attract and retain faculty, including improved physical facilities, the development of a graduate school, higher admissions standards, endowed faculty chairs, and changing the name of the institution "to foster and maintain a university image." The study further proposed an "end to compulsory military training and all-male admissions policy." According to the report, the Corps of Cadets took precedence over all other aspects of student life, "determining habits, attitudes and ambitions." Furthermore, the school's military emphasis "limited the true pursuit of scholarship and the development of an environment which will contribute to this scholarship." The emphasis on military training caused potential students to select other schools. The group recommended that military training be voluntary for all students, that the Corps no longer exist as a residential organization, and that an adult director reside in each unit.

Treading on the very foundations of A&M College traditions, this report came as a surprise to some, particularly Rudder. But, as he himself had stated, he wanted honest and candid answers. According to rumors his first reaction to the *Faculty-Staff-Student Study on Aspirations* "was a loud exclamation followed by tossing the report into the garbage can." Rudder personally supported the traditions of A&M College, including the all-male admission policy and compulsory military training. What really matters, however, was not his reaction to the study or his personal biases about coeducation or compulsory military service, but rather his ability to set aside such beliefs and "do what needed to be done." He took action when others had resisted or hesitated.

"It [the report] helped to define Rudder's job," said one historian. "Rudder meant to finish the job." He and the board accepted almost all of the findings of the various studies and published them in a summary report entitled *Blueprint for Success*. Despite being broad in its context, "the meaning, purposes, and importance [of the report] . . . cannot be overestimated in its significance" to the development of the university. They "charged all members of the faculty and staff of the Agricultural and Mechanical College of Texas, in whatever capacity they may serve, that their watchword and goal shall be *excellence* [emphasis in original]." In spite of the enormous expenditures, most of the building projects proposed were completed before the centennial and faculty salaries were increased without raising tuition. Enrollment doubled, exceeding 16,000 by 1972.

In conjunction with these changes, two other notable transitions also occurred under Rudder's tenure at the college—the school became coeducational and its name was changed to Texas A&M University. On April 28, 1963, with support from Rudder, the board unanimously voted that eligible women "would be admitted into graduate programs and veterinary medicines as day students," effective June 1, 1963. The admission of women was on a limited basis for undergraduate courses, however. In addition to the normal requirements for admission, the woman had to be a wife or daughter of an enrolled student, faculty, or staff member. Numerous individuals and organizations favored the move. Some openly displayed their approval of the decision, but others expressed their support covertly—afraid of ostracism and retaliation. "The [decision] proves that the college fathers are willing to act in an objective manner not motivated by tradition for tradition's sake," applauded an editorial in the local paper. "With the board operating in a flexible manner attuned to the changing world we live in Texas A&M is well on its way to the excellence sought by school officials." Another proponent appealed to the proper sensibilities of the men of the school and the state. "It's about time they had some coeds there and started having a little fun," he said. "It might help out football recruiting!" Nevertheless, for many, including members of the Corps, this fight was not over.

In the fall of 1963, fifteen women enrolled. They had to sign a contract stating that they would withdraw if the new policy was reversed. By spring 1964, 183 women had enrolled, and Stella Haupt, the first woman to enroll under the new policy, earned an M.A. degree that fall. A year later, the number of women enrolled had nearly doubled to 321. At long last, the college was coeducational. But for critics of coeducation, Rudder was in their "cross-hairs as the prime culprit."

Rudder and his associates in the college's administration expected the firestorm of criticism and the fears about what the admission meant to the Corps, perhaps even its continued existence. Some feared the abolition of the football team. Rudder realized that his decision would be unpopular among some groups, and that admitting women was a policy that he would have to sell to the students and alumni. The president of the board of directors, Sterling C. Evans, wrote to the Association of Former Students explaining the decision. Evans stated that the board had no intention of making the college an "all-out coed institution." Evans noted, "The admission of women will not bring sudden or drastic change to the school." Nor did he foresee any changes to the Corps, which was the real issue to many of the critics.

To address this concern, Rudder called a meeting of the entire Corps at G. Rollie White Coliseum in April 1963. He informed the crowd of more than 4,000 that the board had absolute authority on this and other matters. Greeted with chants of "We don't want to integrate" accompanied by boos and hisses, Rudder nevertheless explained his position: "If we had not voted to admit women to our school of veterinarian medicine, many students would go to Texas Tech." When asked about effects of the policy on the Corps of Cadets, Rudder replied, "If the Corps of Cadets does what it stands for, its future is bright."

Some in the audience grudgingly accepted the argument, but many of the cadets did not. For had those who booed and hissed really thought about it, they would have remembered that James Earl Rudder was a former member of the *Corps of Cadets* and *old soldier*. He was solidly in favor of the Corps, but he realized that many students who wanted to study at Texas A&M simply did not want to join the Corps. Rudder would never allow a decision or policy to undermine one of the most cherished and storied traditions of the school, especially one so dear to his heart. Despite the justifiable arguments and concerns, he realized the Corps benefited from coeducation.

Those opposed to the decision engaged in the loudest and most obstreperous behavior. "I'm 54 years old and I still like girls," opined one graduate, "but not at A&M." "Big mistake," remarked another critic. Another found a Biblical precedent for not admitting women. "We men know how to appreciate, love and honor our women," he declared, "but we know also what a fix Eve got us in the Garden of Eden. Let us not let that happen at A&M." Several opposition groups formed in response to the decision, including the Committee for an All-Male Military Texas A&M and the Senior Committee for the Preservation of Texas A&M. The Committee for an All-Male Military Texas A&M "marched" on the state capital to oppose coeducation. Chanting "We want Aggies, not Maggies," and claiming women would halt the program of excellence at the school, over 300 members of the Corps, along with several representatives of the A&M Mothers' Club and Aggie-Exes, gathered in the rotunda as State Representative Will L. Smith submitted an anti-coeducation resolution. In addition, one senator submitted a resolution that threatened to cut off state funds if the school admitted women. Despite overwhelming passage in the House of Representatives of a resolution requiring the state to maintain one major university for men and one for women, a senate filibuster killed the resolutions.

The Senior Committee for the Preservation of Texas A&M initiated an intense letter writing campaign to enlist support for their cause. One editor who was solicited for his support noted the futility of it all. He stated that this was

> ***a cause every bit as worthy as impeaching Earl Warren or repealing the income tax—and with about the same chance of success, which is a big fat zero. Still, the fool-hardy valor of its adherents . . . commands the same sort of admiration which generations have felt for Giacomo Casablanca, the boy who 'stood on the burning deck, whence all but he had fled; the flame that lit the battle's wreck, shone 'round him o'er the dead.' Giacomo wound up fricasseed, and so, I fear, will the 'no coeds in Aggieland' alumni. You can't fight city hall or the board of directors. Besides, I'm a subscriber to the theory that there is nothing like a dame.***

In 1965, A&M's board of directors authorized President Rudder to use his discretion in the admission of women. This had the "overall effect of completely ending the prohibition on coeducation." The full admittance of women, however, happened with little of the bitterness and emotion present a few years earlier—in part because many of the fears never materialized, in part because the country had changed.

Rudder's prediction that admitting women would be a positive change also contributed to the lack of animosity. He repeatedly told students and alumni that the admission of women would strengthen, rather then undermine, the foundations and traditions of the school. Much of the student population believed coeducation beneficial rather than detrimental. In a student poll in 1965, sixty-three percent favored unlimited coeducation over a return to the all-male policy. As a result of Rudder's "discretionary powers," more applications were approved, and by the fall of 1969, applicants "who could meet the same academic qualifications as men were being admitted." By 1971, the administration admitted women on an equal basis with men. In 1971, 1,700 women attended the school. By 1980 that number had increased to more than 12,000. By 2006, women made up half of the student body at the school and held many positions in the university believed out of reach for women only a few decades ago.

Even the Corps, the most cherished of the school's institutions, was not immune to change. In 1965 compulsory enrollment in the Corps was abolished in favor of a volunteer system. By 1970 only a quarter of the student body remained in the Corps. Four years later, it was opened to women. About fifty women were organized into an all-female unit. The members were called "Waggies." The change made the Corps stronger, but its exuberance and discipline were undiminished. The group had become an "even more elite and selective organization by virtue of its volunteer status." In the end, none of the fears associated with the admission of women came to fruition. The traditions, except female exclusion, remained. "The old school, and the old fraternity, did not die," wrote one historian, "instead they merely changed their complexion." Many of the school's traditions—reveille, Silver Taps, Aggie Muster, and others—remained part of the vibrant spirit of the school.

With little fanfare or turmoil, Rudder also presided over racial integration at Texas A&M in the fall of 1964. The lack of resistance to integration was atypical of other Southern universities, but A&M was an atypical Southern university. Although located in the "more Southern" part of the state, the university differed from other institutions because of its focus on the military. Blacks did not threaten nor offend the social sensibilities at Texas A&M—women represented the *real* threat. The military traditions and structure of the school epitomized masculinity. The admission of minority men never threatened to change the fabric of the school.

By the end of the 1960s the old college had become a new, vibrant, energetic institution with a bright future. With each passing year, women and minorities became more important to the university. Enrollment increases shattered all projections and to accommodate that growth numerous construction projects were completed. And Rudder led the university throughout this remarkable transformation. "[H]e was constantly in the middle of it," wrote one historian. "He never spared himself. He was tough, but fair. Usually congenial, he could be abrasive if he thought it would help. He held an open mind, and would act on advice contrary to his own preconceived ideas when it appeared that such advice was better informed. He was a forthright, vigorous man, whose integrity, personal honor, and dedication were unquestioned."

In January 1970, while at his home, Rudder suffered a partial stroke and was rushed to a local hospital. In his absence, three vice-presidents shared the responsibilities of administering the Texas A&M University system. Doctors transferred Rudder to a hospital in Houston when it appeared at first to be a heart ailment turned out to be a cerebral hemorrhage. To stop the bleeding, physicians operated to remove a blood clot. After improving briefly, Rudder took a turn for the worse. The stress of the operation and the hemorrhage caused a stomach ulcer. More operations were conducted to stop the intestinal bleeding, but his condition worsened, and Rudder passed away on March 23, 1970, at the age of fifty-nine.

Rudder's body lay in state in the rotunda of the administration building on the campus of A&M. A public memorial service attended by such dignitaries as Governor Preston Smith, former governor Allan Shivers, numerous local, state, and national politicians, and many military comrades, including former Rangers, was held at White Coliseum. Those such as Generals Norman D. Cota and Troy Middleton, who commanded the 28th Infantry Division and the VIII Corps, respectively, during the Battle of the Bulge; Senator John G. Tower, and former governor John Connally could not attend, but expressed their condolences via telegrams. Also in attendance was former president and friend Lyndon B. Johnson. "His heroism on the Normandy beaches in a time of war was only a prelude to his contribution in peace as an educator, public official and concerned citizen," Johnson remarked. "Earl Rudder brought Texas A&M University to new heights of achievement, excellence and prestige," said Senator Ralph Yarborough. "He was the best," quoted Representative Olin L. Teague. With military honors, Rudder was buried near the campus.

In some ways Rudder was the most unlikely of candidates to bring about many of the changes at Texas A&M. He was from the South, imbued with military traditions and values, and was, for all intents and purposes, a product of the nineteenth century. But Rudder was the person most responsible for the admission of women and minorities and ending compulsory military training at the school. Not necessarily because of his ideological beliefs as a crusader, but because he knew it to be the right and necessary step to attain particular goals.